THE PAPERS OF
WOODROW WILSON

Volume 39: Contents and Index
Volumes 27-38, 1913-1916

Arthur S. Link, Editor

David W. Hirst,
Senior Associate Editor

John E. Little and Fredrick Aandahl,
Associate Editors

The Papers of Woodrow Wilson
Volumes Published since 1975

Volume 22: 1910-1911
696 pages.   1976.

Volume 23: 1911-1912
705 pages.   1977.

Volume 24: 1912
672 pages.   1978.

Volume 25: 1912
700 pages.   1978.

Volume 26:   (Index)
326 pages.   1979.

Volume 27: 1913
631 pages.   1978.

Volume 28: 1913
630 pages.   1978.

Volume 29: 1913-1914
592 pages.   1979.

Volume 30: 1914
552 pages.   1979.

Volume 31: 1914
592 pages.   1979.

Volume 32: 1915
600 pages.   1979.

Volume 33: 1915
640 pages.   1980.

Volume 34: 1915
640 pages.   1980.

(continued on back flap)

THE PAPERS OF

WOODROW WILSON

VOLUME 39

SPONSORED BY THE WOODROW WILSON
FOUNDATION
AND PRINCETON UNIVERSITY

THE PAPERS OF
WOODROW
WILSON

CONTENTS AND INDEX, VOLUMES 27–38

Volume 39 · 1913–1916

PRINCETON UNIVERSITY PRESS
PRINCETON, NEW JERSEY
1985

Note to scholars: Princeton University Press subscribes to the Resolution on Permissions of the Association of American University Presses, defining what we regard as "fair use" of copyrighted works. This Resolution, intended to encourage scholarly use of university press publications and to avoid unnecessary applications for permission, is obtainable from the Press or from the A.A.U.P. central office. Note, however, that the scholarly apparatus, transcripts of shorthand, and the texts of Wilson documents as they appear in this volume are copyrighted, and the usual rules about the use of the copyrighted materials apply.

Publication of this book has been aided by a grant from the National Historical Publications and Records Commission.

Printed in the United States of America
by Princeton University Press
Princeton, New Jersey

CONTENTS

Explanatory Note, ix

Contents

  Wilson Materials

    Addresses, messages, statements, and press releases, 3
    Political correspondence, reports, and memoranda
      From Wilson, 12
      To Wilson, 25
    Diplomatic notes, messages, memoranda, and aide-mémoire
      By Wilson and from Wilson, 38
      To Wilson, 40
    Correspondence, reports, memoranda, and aide-mémoire about
      general diplomatic affairs
      By Wilson and from Wilson, 40
      To Wilson, 49
    Personal correspondence
      From Wilson, 62
      To Wilson, 72
    Telephonic messages, 78
    Interviews, conferences, and dialogues, 79
    Press Conferences, 80
    News Reports, 81
    Writings, 81

  Collateral Materials

    Political correspondence, reports, memoranda, and aide-mé-
      moire, 82
    Diplomatic correspondence, reports, memoranda, and aide-
      mémoire, 86
    Personal correspondence, 102
    Diaries and reminiscences, 103

Illustrations, 105

Indexes by volume, 109

Index, 111

  Edith Bolling Galt Wilson, 272
  Ellen Axson Wilson, 272
  Woodrow Wilson, 275

EXPLANATORY NOTE

THE Table of Contents is divided into two main sections: Wilson Materials and Collateral Materials. Together, they include under special editorial headings and in alphabetical or chronological order all the items printed in Volumes 27-38. Correspondence, reports, memoranda or aide-mémoire by Wilson and to Wilson are arranged alphabetically under separate categories depending on whether the subject matter is primarily political, diplomatic or personal. Wilson's public addresses, statements, press releases, press conferences, interviews with him or news reports about him are arranged chronologically under the relevant heading. Collateral correspondence, reports, memoranda or aide-mémoire follow the same arrangement as that described for the Wilson Materials. Illustrations are listed separately.

The index includes all persons, places, and subjects mentioned in the text and footnotes. All books, articles, pamphlets, and poems are indexed by author and title. Book titles and plays appear in italics; quotation marks are omitted for articles, editorials, and poems. Page references to footnotes which carry a comma between the page number and the "n" cite both text and footnote, thus: "162,n1." Absence of the comma indicates reference to the footnote only, thus: "286n3." The page number refers to the page on which the textual reference occurs. In larger entries initials are provided for individuals at the first mention only.

All entries consisting of page numbers only and which refer to concepts, issues, and opinions (such as democracy, the tariff, the money trust, leadership, and labor problems), are references to Wilson's speeches and writings. Page references that follow the symbol Δ in such entries refer to the opinions and comments of others who are identified. The present index supersedes the individual indexes of Volumes 27-38 in that it corrects errors and omissions discovered since their publication. *Subjects* are indexed selectively, not exhaustively; this is not intended to be a concordance to Wilson's writings.

Phyllis L. Marchand indexed volumes 27-38. The consolidation and initial arrangement of the Table of Contents was done by Manfred Boemeke. It was typed by Denise Thompson. Anne C. Venzon consolidated the individual volume indexes and prepared the typescript. The Table of Contents and major entries in the Index were checked against the volumes by Edward Bever and Sarah Bever.

David W. Hirst oversaw the preparation of the volume and reviewed, edited, and compacted all entries. All the aforementioned persons worked with consummate care, skill, and devotion.

THE EDITOR

Princeton, New Jersey
November 1, 1983

THE PAPERS OF

WOODROW WILSON

VOLUME 39

CONTENTS
FOR VOLUMES 27–38

WILSON MATERIALS

Addresses, messages, statements, and press releases

Address to the Commercial Club of Chicago, Jan. 11, 1913, **27:** 29

Remarks in Trenton to the New Jersey electors, Jan. 13, 1913, **27:** 40

Annual Message to the legislature of New Jersey, Jan. 14, 1913, **27:** 46

After-dinner talk in Atlantic City to the New Jersey senators, Jan. 28, 1913, **27:** 85

Statement on signing seven bills regulating New Jersey corporations, Feb. 20, 1913, **27:** 120

Message to the legislature of New Jersey, Feb. 25, 1913, **27:** 133

Farewell remarks to the New Jersey legislature, March 1, 1913, **27:** 141

Remarks to neighbors in Princeton, March 1, 1913, **27:** 142

Remarks at a Princeton smoker in Washington, March 3, 1913, **27:** 147

Inaugural address, March 4, 1913, **27:** 148

Warning to office seekers, March 5, 1913, **27:** 153

Statement on relations with Latin America, March 12, 1913, **27:** 172

Statement on the pending Chinese loan, March 18, 1913, **27:** 192

Statement on the declination by William F. McCombs to serve as Ambassador to France, March 23, 1913, **27:** 217

Appeal for aid to flood victims in Ohio and Indiana, March 26, 1913, **27:** 229

Address to a joint session of Congress on tariff reform, April 8, 1913, **27:** 269

Remarks in Washington to the Gridiron Club, April 12, 1913, **27:** 294

Welcome to the Daughters of the American Revolution in Washington, April 14, 1913, **27:** 306

Address in Newark on jury reform, May 1, 1913, **27:** 373

Address in Jersey City on jury reform, May 2, 1913, **27:** 386

Welcome to the new British Ambassador at the White House, May 3, 1913, **27:** 395

Message to American Indians, May 24, 1913, **27:** 469

Statement on tariff lobbyists, May 26, 1913, **27:** 473

Statement on signing the sundry civil bill, June 23, 1913, **27**: 558

Address on banking and currency reform to a joint session of Congress, June 23, 1913, **27**: 570

Address at the Gettysburg battlefield, July 4, 1913, **28**: 23

Remarks at the White House to a delegation of southern bankers, Aug. 7, 1913, **28**: 127

Statement on rural credits, Aug. 13, 1913, **28**: 146

Remarks at the White House to western bankers, Aug. 14, 1913, **28**: 156

Address to a joint session of Congress on Mexican affairs, Aug. 27, 1913, **28**: 227

Statement upon passage of the tariff bill, Sept. 9, 1913, **28**: 267

Remarks at the White House upon signing the tariff bill, Oct. 3, 1913, **28**: 351

Thanksgiving Proclamation, Oct. 23, 1913, **28**: 424

Statement on the Vanderlip plan, Oct. 24, 1913, **28**: 429

Address at Congress Hall in Philadelphia, Oct. 25, 1913, **28**: 435

Talk at Swarthmore College, Oct. 25, 1913, **28**: 439

Address in Mobile on Latin American policy, Oct. 27, 1913, **28**: 448

Draft of an address to Congress on Mexico, Oct. 31, 1913, **28**: 479

Annual Message to Congress, Dec. 2, 1913, **29**: 3

Remarks at the White House to a delegation from the National Woman Suffrage Convention, Dec. 8, 1913, **29**: 21

Remarks upon laying the cornerstone of the Central Presbyterian Church of Washington, Dec. 19, 1913, **29**: 44

Remarks at the White House upon signing the federal reserve bill, Dec. 23, 1913, **29**: 63

Statement on consent decrees, Jan. 19, 1914, **29**: 141

Address on antitrust legislation to a joint session of Congress, Jan. 20, 1914, **29**: 153

Draft of a statement on the repeal of the Mexican arms embargo, Jan. 31, 1914, **29**: 207

Remarks at the White House to a committee of working women, Feb. 2, 1913, **29**: 215

Statement on the repeal of the Mexican arms embargo, Feb. 3, 1914, **29**: 216

Statement on the death of Senator Bacon, Feb. 14, 1914, **29**: 248

Remarks at the White House to the commissioners to the International Conference on Safety of Life at Sea, Feb. 23, 1914, **29**: 280

Remarks in Washington at a dinner honoring George Washington Goethals, March 3, 1914, **29**: 306

Statement on the resignation of John Bassett Moore, March 4, 1914, **29**: 309

Address to Congress on Panama Canal tolls, March 5, 1914, **29**: 312

Remarks at the White House upon signing the Alaska railroad bill, March 12, 1914, **29**: 332

Remarks in Washington to the National Press Club, March 20, 1914, **29**: 361

CONTENTS 5

Statement on the Mexican situation, April 14, 1914, **29:** 433

An ultimatum to General Huerta, April 18, 1914, **29:** 460

Address to Congress on the Mexican crisis, April 20, 1914, **29:** 471

Statement of United States policy toward Mexico, April 23, 1914, **29:** 488

Memorial address at the Brooklyn Navy Yard, May 11, 1914, **30:** 13

Memorial address on Commodore John Barry in Washington, May 16, 1914, **30:** 34

Address at the opening of The American University, May 27, 1914, **30:** 89

Remarks to the Princeton Alumni Association of the District of Columbia, May 29, 1914, **30:** 103

Memorial address to the Grand Army of the Republic at Arlington National Cemetery, May 30, 1914, **30:** 110

Memorial address to the Daughters of the Confederacy at Arlington National Cemetery, June 4, 1914, **30:** 141

Commencement address at the United States Naval Academy, June 5, 1914, **30:** 145

Remarks to the Class of 1879 at Princeton, June 13, 1914, **30:** 176

Flag Day address in Washington, June 15, 1914, **30:** 184

Remarks on the business outlook to the Virginia Press Association at the White House, June 25, 1914, **30:** 210

Remarks at the White House to a woman suffrage delegation, June 30, 1914, **30:** 226

Fourth of July address in Philadelphia, **30:** 248

Statement on the Warburg and Jones nominations, July 8, 1914, **30:** 263

Special message to Congress, Aug. 3, 1914, **30:** 337

Press release about a message to the European leaders, Aug. 4, 1914, **30:** 342

Remarks at the White House to the Federal Reserve Board, Aug. 13, 1914, **30:** 376

Remarks at the White House to a delegation of businessmen, Aug. 14, 1914, **30:** 378

Appeal to the American people for neutrality, Aug. 18, 1914, **30:** 393

Remarks in Washington to delegations representing the cotton interests, Aug. 24, 1914, **30:** 441; Sept. 24, 1914, **31:** 79.

Address to a joint session of Congress, Sept. 4, 1914, **30:** 473

Proclamation for a day of prayer for peace, Sept. 8, 1914, **31:** 10

Remarks at the White House to the Belgian commissioners, Sept. 16, 1914, **31:** 33

Outline of an address to the American Bar Association, Oct. 20, 1914, **31:** 183

Remarks in Washington to the American Bar Association, Oct. 20, 1914, **31:** 184

Remarks at the White House upon the inauguration of the Federal Reserve System, Oct. 21, 1914, **31:** 196

Address to the Pittsburgh Y.M.C.A., Oct. 24, 1914, **31:** 220

Thanksgiving Proclamation, Oct. 28, 1914, **31:** 241

Statement on the Colorado coal strike, Nov. 29, 1914, **31:** 367

Statement opposing a defense inquiry, Dec. 7, 1914, **31:** 409

Annual Message to Congress, 1914, Dec. 8, 1914, **31:** 414

Remarks in Washington to the American Red Cross Society, Dec. 9, 1914, **31:** 430

Remarks at the White House to the Ohio Valley Improvement Association, Dec. 10, 1914, **31:** 446

Remarks at the White House on the race question, Dec. 15, 1914, **31:** 464

Appeal for Belgian relief, Nov. 14, 1914, **31:** 559

Speech at Arlington National Cemetery accepting statue of Philip Kearny, Nov. 11, 1914, **31:** 561

Remarks at the White House to a delegation of Democratic women, Jan. 6, 1915, **32:** 22

Remarks from a rear platform in Richmond, Ind., Jan. 8, 1915, **32:** 28

Jackson Day address in Indianapolis, Jan. 8, 1915, **32:** 29

Talk to the Washington Y.M.C.A., Jan. 26, 1915, **32:** 125

Address in Washington to the American Electric Railway Association, Jan. 29, 1915, **32:** 149

Address in Washington to the United States Chamber of Commerce, Feb. 3, 1915, **32:** 178

Remarks at the White House to the National Council of the Boy Scouts of America, Feb. 11, 1915, **32:** 215

Address in Washington on behalf of Berea College, Feb. 24, 1915, **32:** 282

Unpublished statement on the ship-purchase bill, March 4, 1915, **32:** 313

Statement on the achievements of the Sixty-third Congress, March 4, 1915, **32:** 316

Address in Washington to the Annual Conference of the Methodist Episcopal Church, South, March 25, 1915, **32:** 429

Address on board *Moreno*, March 29, 1915, **32:** 451

Remarks in Washington to the Maryland Annual Conference of the Methodist Protestant Church, April 8, 1915, **32:** 494

Welcome to the Daughters of the American Revolution in Washington, April 19, 1915, **33:** 14

Remarks to the Associated Press in New York, April 20, 1915, **33:** 37; April 21, 1915

Remarks to Potomac Presbytery, April 21, 1915, **33:** 49

Address in Philadelphia to newly naturalized citizens, May 10, 1915, **33:** 147

News release about the first *Lusitania* note, May 13, 1915, **33:** 181

Remarks at a luncheon in New York, May 17, 1915, **33:** 209

Statement on the condition of the Atlantic Fleet, May 18, 1915, **33:** 216

Welcome to the Pan American Financial Conference in Washington, May 24, 1915, **33:** 245

Appeal for funds for Mexican relief, May 28, 1915, **33:** 275

Reflections on Memorial Day, May 31, 1915, **33:** 287

Statement on the Mexican situation, June 2, 1915, **33:** 303

Flag Day Address in Washington, June 14, 1915, **33:** 391

Proclamation concerning the National Negro Exposition, July 2, 1915, **33:** 464

Press release on the program for preparedness, July 21, 1915, **34:** 3

Outline of a statement on his relationship with Mary Allen Hulbert, Sept. 20, 1915, **34:** 496

Draft of a first statement on his relationship with Mary Allen Hulbert, Sept. 20, 1915, **34:** 496

Draft of a second statement on his relationship with Mary Allen Hulbert, c. Sept. 20, 1915, **34:** 497

Address in Washington to the Grand Army of the Republic, Sept. 28, 1915, **34:** 534

Statement on voting for woman suffrage in New Jersey, Oct. 6, 1915, **35:** 28

Remarks at the White House to the Naval Consulting Board, Oct. 6, 1915, **35:** 29

Announcement of his engagement to Edith Bolling Galt, Oct. 6, 1915, **35:** 32

Address in Washington to the Daughters of the American Revolution, Oct. 11, 1915, **35:** 47

Thanksgiving Proclamation, Oct. 21, 1915, **35:** 89

Draft of an address to the Manhattan Club, Oct. 28, 1915, **35:** 121

Address on preparedness to the Manhattan Club, Nov. 24, 1915, **35:** 167

Appeal for support of the Red Cross war relief fund, Nov. 24, 1915, **35:** 243

Remarks at the White House to delegates from woman suffrage groups, Dec. 6, 1915, **35:** 292

Annual Message on the State of the Union, Dec. 7, 1915, **35:** 293

Talk to members of the Democratic National Committee at the White House, Dec. 8, 1915, **35:** 312

Remarks in Washington to the American Red Cross, Dec. 8, 1915, **35:** 316

Address to the Chamber of Commerce of Columbus, Ohio, Dec. 10, 1915, **35:** 321

Address to the Federal Council of Churches in Columbus, Ohio, Dec. 10, 1915, **35:** 329

Remarks in Washington to the Gridiron Club, Dec. 11, 1915, **35:** 339

Draft of a press release, Dec. 17, 1915, **35:** 363

Proclamation concerning Polish relief, Dec. 18, 1915, **35:** 367

Announcement of marriage to Edith Bolling Galt, Dec. 18, 1915, **35:** 371

Outline of an address to the Pan American Scientific Congress, Jan. 6, 1916, **35**: 439

Address in Washington to the Pan American Scientific Congress, Jan. 6, 1916, **35**: 441

Remarks in New York to a suffrage delegation, Jan. 27, 1916, **36**: 3

Remarks in New York to the Clerical Conference of the New York Federation of Churches, Jan. 27, 1916, **36**: 4

Address in New York on Preparedness, Jan. 27, 1916, **36**: 7

After-dinner remarks in New York to the Motion Picture Board of Trade, Jan. 27, 1916, **36**: 16

Address in Pittsburgh on preparedness, Jan. 29, 1916, **36**: 26

Address in Pittsburgh to an overflow meeting, Jan. 29, 1916, **36**: 35

Address in Cleveland on preparedness, Jan. 29, 1916, **36**: 41

Remarks from a rear platform in Waukegan, Ill., Jan. 31, 1916, **36**: 52

Remarks from a rear platform in Kenosha, Wis., Jan. 31, 1916, **36**: 53

Remarks from a rear platform in Racine, Wis., Jan. 31, 1916, **36**: 54

Address in Milwaukee on preparedness, Jan. 31, 1916, **36**: 55

Address in Chicago on preparedness, Jan. 31, 1916, **36**: 63

Remarks from a rear platform in Davenport, Iowa, Feb. 1, 1916, **36**: 75

Remarks from a rear platform in Iowa City, Feb. 1, 1916, **36**: 76

Remarks from a rear platform in Grinnell, Iowa, Feb. 1, 1916, **36**: 76

Address in Des Moines on preparedness, Feb. 1, 1916, **36**: 77

Address in Topeka on preparedness, Feb. 2, 1916, **36**: 87

Address to an overflow meeting in Topeka, Feb. 2, 1916, **36**: 96

Address in Kansas City on preparedness, Feb. 2, 1916, **36**: 100

Address to the Business Men's League of St. Louis, Feb. 3, 1916, **36**: 110

Address in St. Louis on preparedness, Feb. 3, 1916, **36**: 114

Remarks from a rear platform in East St. Louis, Feb. 3, 1916, **36**: 121

Address in Washington to the Chamber of Commerce of the United States, Feb. 10, 1916, **36**: 152

After-dinner remarks in Washington to members of the Grand Army of the Republic, Feb. 10, 1916, **36**: 160

Remarks at the White House to a group of Hungarian Americans, Feb. 23, 1916, **36**: 205

Talk to the Gridiron Club in Washington, Feb. 26, 1916, **36**: 218

Statement about Senator Gore's speech on possible war with Germany, March 2, 1916, **36**: 238

Draft of a resolution affirming the rights of American citizens on

the high seas, March 2, 1916, **36:** 239

Statement explaining the purpose of the expeditionary force to Mexico, March 10, 1916, **36:** 284

Press release announcing the dispatch of a force to pursue Villa, March 10, 1916, **36:** 287

Statement reaffirming the limited objectives of the expeditionary force in Mexico, March 13, 1916, **36:** 298

Draft of a notice to press associations about coverage of the Punitive Expedition, March 17, 1916, **36:** 332

Notice to press associations about coverage of the Punitive Expedition, March 21, 1916, **36:** 351

Statement and warning about misinterpreting the purpose of the Punitive Expedition, March 25, 1916, **36:** 364

Tribute to Thomas Jones Pence, March 27, 1916, **36:** 371

Memorial address on Francis Asbury in Washington, March 31, 1916, **36:** 391

Address in Washington celebrating the centennial of the United States Coast and Geodetic Survey, April 6, 1916, **36:** 417

Jefferson Day address in Washington, April 13, 1916, **36:** 472

Welcome to the Daughters of the American Revolution in Washington, April 17, 1916, **36:** 489

Address to a Joint Session of Congress, April 19, 1916, **36:** 506

Draft of after-dinner remarks to the American Newspaper Publishers' Association, April 27, 1916, **36:** 560

Remarks at the National Service School for Women in Chevy Chase, Maryland, May 1, 1916, **36:** 572

Press statement on the Scott-Obregón conference, May 4, 1916, **36:** 604

Draft of a statement on the Scott-Obregón agreement, May 5, 1916, **36:** 607

Remarks in Washington celebrating the centennial of the American Bible Society, May 7, 1916, **36:** 629

Remarks in Washington to the National Press Club, May 15, 1916, **37:** 46

Remarks from a rear platform at Salisbury, N. C., May 20, 1916, **37:** 78

Address in Charlotte, N. C., May 20, 1916, **37:** 79

Address in Washington to the League to Enforce Peace, May 27, 1916, **37:** 113

Declaration designating June 14 as national Flag Day, May 30, 1916, **37:** 122

Memorial Day Address at Arlington National Cemetery, May 30, 1916, **37:** 123

Remarks in Annapolis to the graduating class of the Naval Academy, June 2, 1916, **37:** 147

After-dinner remarks in Washington in honor of Bishop Earl Cranston, June 2, 1916, **37:** 148

Commencement address at the United States Military Academy at West Point, June 13, 1916, **37:** 212

Flag Day address in Washington, June 14, 1916, **37:** 221

Remarks at the White House to Virginia Democratic leaders, June 15, 1916, **37:** 228

Draft of an address to Congress on the Mexican crisis, June 26, 1916, **37:** 298

Remarks in Philadelphia to the Associated Advertising Clubs, June 29, 1916, **37:** 324

Remarks to the New York Press Club, June 30, 1916, **37:** 332

Address at the dedication of the American Federation of Labor Building in Washington, July 4, 1916, **37:** 353

Address in Detroit to businessmen, July 10, 1916, **37:** 383

Luncheon address in Detroit, July 10, 1916, **37:** 387

Remarks in Detroit to the employees of the Ford Motor Company, July 10, 1916, **37:** 395

Remarks at Union Station in Toledo, Ohio, July 10, 1916, **37:** 395

Address in Washington on the American spirit, July 13, 1916, **37:** 414

Remarks at the White House upon signing the rural-credits bill, July 17, 1916, **37:** 427

After-dinner remarks to postmasters in Washington, July 20, 1916, **37:** 442

Declaration regarding Greenland, July 27, 1916, **37:** 485

Press release on the formation of the Council of National Defense and the National Research Council, July 28, 1916, **37:** 491

Statement on Belgian Relief Commission, Nov. 3, 1915, **37:** 542

Statement on the impending nationwide railroad strike, Aug. 14, 1916, **38:** 32

Plan for the settlement of the impending railroad strike, Aug. 16, 1916, **38:** 38

Veto of the army appropriations bill, Aug. 17, 1916, **38:** 40

Statement on the proposals for the settlement of the railroad crisis, Aug. 19, 1916, **38:** 49

Address to a joint session of Congress on the threatened railroad strike, Aug. 29, 1916, **38:** 96

Remarks at the White House upon signing various bills, Aug. 29, 1916, **38:** 101

Remarks at the White House upon signing the child-labor bill, Sept. 1, 1916, **38:** 123

Speech in Long Branch, N. J., accepting the presidential nomination, Sept. 2, 1916, **38:** 126

Address on Abraham Lincoln near Hodgenville, Ky., Sept. 4, 1916, **38:** 142

Address in Atlantic City to the National American Woman Suffrage Association, Sept. 8, 1916, **38:** 161

Remarks upon the adjournment of Congress, Sept. 8, 1916, **38:** 164

Campaign speech at Shadow Lawn, Sept. 23, 1916, **38:** 212

Address in Baltimore to the Grain Dealers' National Association, Sept. 25, 1916, **38**: 261

Campaign speech to young Democrats at Shadow Lawn, Sept. 30, 1916, **38**: 301

Address to the Commercial Club of Omaha, Oct. 5, 1916, **38**: 336

Remarks in Omaha to the Historical Society of Nebraska, Oct. 5, 1916, **38**: 342

Address in Omaha on the melting pot, Oct. 5, 1916, **38**: 343

Campaign address at Shadow Lawn, Oct. 7, 1916, **38**: 362

Statement on the *U-53* incident, Oct. 9, 1916, **38**: 374

Press release on the purpose and functions of the Council of National Defense, Oct. 10, 1916, **38**: 387

Remarks at a luncheon in Indianapolis, Oct. 12, 1916, **38**: 411

Address in Indianapolis on good roads, Oct. 12, 1916, **38**: 412

Address in Indianapolis to farmers, Oct. 12, 1916, **38**: 419

Campaign address at Shadow Lawn, Oct. 14, 1916, **38**: 430

Address at Shadow Lawn to Wilson volunteers, Oct. 16, 1916, **38**: 445

Statement on the replies of the European heads of state about Polish relief, Oct. 17, 1916, **38**: 458

"Wilson Day" letter, Oct. 15, 1916, **38**: 461

Luncheon address to the Chicago Press Club, Oct. 19, 1916, **38**: 475

Address in Chicago to nonpartisan women, Oct. 19, 1916, **38**: 481

Address in Chicago to new citizens, Oct. 19, 1916, **38**: 489

Campaign address to farmers at Shadow Lawn, Oct. 21, 1916, **38**: 500

Remarks at a reception in Cincinnati, Oct. 26, 1916, **38**: 524

Luncheon address to women in Cincinnati, Oct. 26, 1916, **38**: 526

After-dinner remarks to the City Club of Cincinnati, Oct. 26, 1916, **38**: 534

Nonpartisan address in Cincinnati, Oct. 26, 1916, **38**: 537

Campaign address to New Yorkers at Shadow Lawn, Oct. 28, 1916, **38**: 549

Unpublished statement on the *Marina* incident, Oct. 31, 1916, **38**: 570

Remarks to workers at Johnson City, N.Y., Nov. 1, 1916, **38**: 571

Luncheon address in Buffalo, Nov. 1, 1916, **38**: 572

Campaign address in Buffalo, Nov. 1, 1916, **38**: 580

Luncheon talk in New York, Nov. 2, 1916, **38**: 591

Campaign address in Madison Square Garden, Nov. 2, 1916, **38**: 597

Talk to young people in Cooper Union, Nov. 2, 1916, **38**: 602

Remarks to an overflow audience outside Cooper Union, Nov. 2, 1916, **38**: 606

Final campaign address at Shadow Lawn, Nov. 4, 1916, **38**: 608

Remarks in Washington to the National Grange, Nov. 14, 1916, **38**: 637

Thanksgiving Proclamation, Nov. 17, 1916, **38**: 667

Reply to Samuel Gompers at the White House, Nov. 18, 1916, **38:** 673

Political correspondence, reports, and memoranda

From Wilson to
Charles Francis Adams, Nov. 2, 1914, **31:** 258
William Charles Adamson, Jan. 20, 1914, **29:** 152; Jan. 26, 1914, **29:** 173; Feb. 18, 1914, **29:** 269; Feb. 25, 1914, **29:** 288; March 30, 1914, **29:** 383; May 4, 1914, **29:** 542; Aug. 5, 1914, **30:** 348; Feb. 17, 1915, **32:** 241; March 16, 1916, **36:** 322; April 7, 1916, **36:** 428; May 23, 1916, **37:** 96
Jane Addams, Nov. 2, 1915, **35:** 158; Oct. 17, 1916, **38:** 460
Joshua Willis Alexander, Feb. 17, 1915, **32:** 242; May 1, 1916, **36:** 575; July 21, 1916, **37:** 451
Elias Milton Ammons, April 25, 1914, **29:** 503; April 28, 1914, **29:** 528; May 16, 1914, **30:** 37; May 20, 1914, **30:** 48; Aug. 21, 1914, **30:** 422; Nov. 12, 1914, **31:** 309; Dec. 10, 1914, **31:** 449
George Weston Anderson, June 19, 1916, **37:** 267

Augustus Octavius Bacon, July 24, 1913, **28:** 68; Nov. 6, 1913, **28:** 500; Feb. 2, 1914, **29:** 213
Newton Diehl Baker, July 24, 1913, **28:** 69; March 5, 1915, **32:** 324; Nov. 12, 1915, **35:** 193; Feb. 28, 1916, **36:** 227; March 5, 1916, **36:** 251; March 6, 1916, **36:** 259; May 5, 1916, **36:** 612; May 23, 1916, **37:** 96; June 9, 1916, **37:** 175; July 24, 1916, **37:** 469; Aug. 7, 1916, **37:** 537; Sept. 7, 1916, **38:** 155; Sept. 30, 1916, **38:** 312; Oct. 10, 1916, **38:** 386; Nov. 16, 1916, **38:** 663
Warren Worth Bailey, July 3, 1916, **37:** 346
Ray Stannard Baker, June 23, 1916, **37:** 286
John Hollis Bankhead, June 28, 1916, **37:** 316
Wharton Barker, Aug. 31, 1916, **38:** 122
Henry A. Barnhart, Feb. 17, 1916, **36:** 187
Daniel Moreau Barringer, Feb. 4, 1915, **32:** 190
James Levi Barton, July 25, 1913, **28:** 82
Bernard Mannes Baruch, May 5, 1916, **36:** 611; Aug. 19, 1916, **38:** 50
Elsworth Raymond Bathrick, Dec. 14, 1914, **31:** 462
Sylvester Woodbridge Beach, June 26, 1916, **37:** 305
Herman Bernstein, June 9, 1914, **30:** 162; Sept. 20, 1916, **38:** 188
Samuel Reading Bertron, Feb. 6, 1914, **29:** 226
Harvey Bittner, Aug. 30, 1916, **38:** 117
Frederick Leonard Blackmon, Feb. 17, 1915, **32:** 241
Ewing Charles Bland, March 5, 1915, **32:** 325
Maurice B. Blumenthal, Oct. 30, 1916, **38:** 562
Edward William Bok, Aug. 1, 1916, **37:** 508; Aug. 11, 1916, **38:** 27
LaMont Montgomery Bowers, Nov. 18, 1913, **28:** 563; Dec. 19, 1913, **29:** 46

Louis Dembitz Brandeis, April 24, 1913, **27:** 353; May 22, 1913, **27:** 465; May 29, 1913, **27:** 487

Desha Breckinridge, March 10, 1914, **29:** 326

Henry Skillman Breckinridge, Feb. 10, 1916, **36:** 165

Howard Allen Bridgman, Sept. 8, 1913, **28:** 265

Nathan Philemon Bryan, May 12, 1913, **27:** 418

William Jennings Bryan, Jan. 22, 1913, **27:** 67; Feb. 23, 1913, **27:** 128; Feb. 27, 1913, **27:** 138; May 21, 1913, **27:** 462; May 26, 1913, **27:** 474; April 2, 1914, **29:** 395; Dec. 10, 1914, **31:** 447; Dec. 29, 1914, **31:** 547; Feb. 19, 1915 (3), **32:** 258-59; June 9, 1915 (2), **33:** 375, 376; Sept. 27, 1916, **38:** 280; Nov. 17, 1916, **38:** 668

James Viscount Bryce, March 14, 1914, **29:** 345; July 6, 1914, **30:** 260

Albert Sidney Burleson, Jan. 6, 1913, **27:** 15; Feb. 23, 1913, **27:** 127; Feb. 26, 1913, **27:** 136; March 30, 1913 (3), **27:** 238, 239; April 4, 1913, **27:** 260; May 29, 1913, **27:** 487; June 2, 1913, **27:** 491; Nov. 25, 1913, **28:** 589; Feb. 15, 1916, **36:** 178; April 2, 1916, **36:** 400; April 20, 1916, **36:** 513; Nov. 16, 1916, **38:** 664

William Tobias Butler, March 9, 1916, **36:** 276

Charles Pope Caldwell, July 17, 1916, **37:** 428

Carrie Clinton Lane Chapman Catt, June 19, 1916, **37:** 266; Aug. 10, 1916, **38:** 19

William Lea Chambers, Aug. 9, 1916, **38:** 12; Aug. 14, 1916, **38:** 32

Mary M. Childs, Nov. 18, 1914, **31:** 329

William Edwin Chilton, April 7, 1914, **29:** 410

Champ Clark, March 6, 1913, **27:** 157; May 4, 1914, **29:** 543; Dec. 10, 1914, **31:** 448; Feb. 16, 1915, **32:** 240; Oct. 27, 1915, **35:** 114; March 15, 1916, **36:** 315

Genevieve Bennett Clark, Feb. 15, 1916, **36:** 179

James Paul Clarke, Dec. 27, 1915, **35:** 396; Jan. 13, 1916, **35:** 471; May 11, 1916, **37:** 15; May 15, 1915, **37:** 54

John Hessin Clarke, July 18, 1916, **37:** 431

Henry De Lamar Clayton, Oct. 10, 1913, **28:** 385; Oct. 20, 1913, **28:** 420; May 18, 1914, **30:** 44

Bainbridge Colby, Aug. 31, 1916, **38:** 123

John Rogers Commons, Feb. 4, 1915, **32:** 189

Edwin Grant Conklin, Sept. 6, 1916, **38:** 147

James Harry Covington, Aug. 27, 1914 (2), **30:** 454, 455

James McMahon Cox, March 26, 1913, **27:** 230; July 17, 1916, **37:** 428

James McMahon Cox and Samuel Moffett Ralston, March 26, 1913, **27:** 230; March 27, 1913, **27:** 232

Kenyon Cox, Sept. 13, 1913, **28:** 276

Charles Richard Crane, May 15, 1914, **30:** 31; Feb. 16, 1916, **36:** 185; Feb. 21, 1916, **36:** 202; March 21, 1916, **36:** 348

Charles Robert Crisp, March 31, 1914, **29:** 387
Charles Allen Culberson, June 19, 1914, **30:** 194; July 30, 1914, **30:** 320; Aug. 21, 1914 (2), **30:** 423; Sept. 10, 1914, **31:** 21; May 5, 1916, **36:** 609
Homer Stillé Cummings, June 15, 1916, **37:** 229; Oct. 24, 1916, **38:** 517; Nov. 9, 1916, **38:** 624

Josephus Daniels, Feb. 23, 1913, **27:** 128; Aug. 22, 1914, **30:** 435; Oct. 7, 1914, **31:** 131; Nov. 6, 1914, **31:** 270; July 21, 1915, **34:** 4; Aug. 2, 1915, **34:** 56; Dec. 8, 1915, **35:** 316; July 18, 1916, **37:** 431; Aug. 3, 1916, **37:** 518; Aug. 16, 1916, **38:** 38; Oct. 16, 1916, **38:** 450
Winthrop More Daniels, Jan. 16, 1913, **27:** 58; Jan. 21, 1913, **27:** 66; Oct. 29, 1914, **31:** 247
Joseph Edward Davies, April 22, 1913, **27:** 345; Dec. 30, 1913, **29:** 88; March 8, 1916, **36:** 274; March 15, 1916, **36:** 315; April 2, 1916, **36:** 401; April 14, 1916, **36:** 482; April 19, 1916, **36:** 510
Ellen Duane Davis, Aug. 5, 1916, **37:** 529
John Warren Davis, March 17, 1913, **27:** 190
Frederic Adrian Delano, July 24, 1916, **37:** 467; July 26, 1916, **37:** 479
Thomas Dixon, Jr., July 29, 1913, **28:** 94; Sept. 7, 1915, **34:** 426
Frank Ellsworth Doremus, Sept. 4, 1914, **30:** 475
Edward Olin Downes, Aug. 7, 1916, **37:** 538
John Steele Duncan, Oct. 24, 1916, **38:** 517

Joe Henry Eagle, Aug. 7, 1913, **28:** 128
John Coates Eastman, March 30, 1913, **27:** 241
Editor of the *American Federationist*, July 9, 1914, **30:** 264
Editor of the *Washington Post*, Oct. 8, 1913, **28:** 373
Eighth grade school children of New Jersey, April 4, 1913, **27:** 260
Charles William Eliot, March 14, 1914, **29:** 345; July 27, 1914, **30:** 309; Aug. 14, 1914, **30:** 379; Aug. 22, 1914, **30:** 432; Jan. 22, 1915, **32:** 105; Oct. 2, 1916, **38:** 319
Henry Bradford Endicott and George Francis Johnson, Oct. 17, 1916, **38:** 461
Matthias Cowell Ely, March 27, 1913, **27:** 480; June 4, 1913, **27:** 494
William Corcoran Eustis, Jan. 17, 1913, **27:** 59
Powell Evans, Oct. 20, 1914, **31:** 187

John Villiers Farwell, Aug. 1, 1916, **37:** 512
Scott Ferris, May 13, 1914, **30:** 27
Sara Bard Field, June 16, 1916, **37:** 237

James Fairman Fielder, March 27, 1913, **27**: 233; March 30, 1913, **27**: 240; Oct. 8, 1913, **28**: 373

Irving Fisher, Aug. 8, 1916, **38**: 9; Oct. 21, 1916, **38**: 510

John Joseph Fitzgerald, May 9, 1913, **27**: 410; Aug. 3, 1914, **30**: 337

Duncan Upshaw Fletcher, March 21, 1913, **27**: 201; Jan. 9, 1914, **29**: 114; Jan. 19, 1914, **29**: 141; Oct. 25, 1915, **35**: 106; Aug. 23, 1916, **38**: 77

Henry De La Warr Flood, July 29, 1913, **28**: 95; Dec. 10, 1914, **31**: 448

Henry Ford, Sept. 6, 1916, **38**: 147; Sept. 20, 1916, **38**: 187

Henry Jones Ford, Aug. 28, 1913, **28**: 242

Raymond Blaine Fosdick, March 10, 1914, **29**: 327

Martin David Foster, July 3, 1916, **37**: 347

Robert Thomas Frazier, Jr., Aug. 31, 1916, **38**: 122

Andrew Furuseth, June 30, 1913, **28**: 15; March 2, 1915, **32**: 309; March 10, 1915, **32**: 357

Augustus Peabody Gardner, Nov. 26, 1914, **31**: 357

Obadiah Gardner, Aug. 19, 1916, **38**: 51; Sept. 20, 1916, **38**: 189

Harry Augustus Garfield, May 23, 1916, **37**: 97; Sept. 22, 1916, **38**: 201

Lindley Miller Garrison, April, 10, 1913, **27**: 282; June 16, 1913, **27**: 526; Aug. 19, 1913, **28**: 192; Sept. 26, 1913, **28**: 329; Oct. 11, 1913, **28**: 390; Feb. 24, 1914, **29**: 284; May 20, 1914, **30**: 49; Aug. 6, 1914, **30**: 352; Dec. 21, 1914, **31**: 502; Dec. 29, 1914, **31**: 547; July 21, 1915, **34**: 4; Aug. 16, 1915, **34**: 216; Aug. 18, 1915, **34**: 235; Aug. 19, 1915, **34**: 248; Jan. 15, 1916, **35**: 481; Feb. 9, 1916 (2), **36**: 144, 146; Feb. 10, 1916 (2), **36**: 162, 164

Lindley Miller Garrison and Josephus Daniels, Dec. 22, 1914, **29**: 54

Henry George, Jr., April 21, 1913, **27**: 342

James Watson Gerard, Oct. 16, 1914, **31**: 167

Joseph Gilman, Oct. 3, 1916, **38**: 334

Washington Gladden, Dec. 14, 1915, **35**: 353; Oct. 24, 1916, **38**: 517

Carter Glass, Jan. 1, 1913, **27**: 4; Jan. 9, 1913, **27**: 24; Jan. 28, 1913, **27**: 84; May 8, 1913, **27**: 409; Dec. 23, 1913, **29**: 62; May 12, 1914, **30**: 24; Jan. 18, 1916, **35**: 501; June 15, 1916, **37**: 229

Franklin Potts Glass, Feb. 20, 1914, **29**: 274

Martin Henry Glynn, Oct. 15, 1914, **31**: 156; March 7, 1916, **36**: 263; April 17, 1916, **36**: 497; June 1, 1916, **37**: 133; June 22, 1916, **37**: 282

Samuel Gompers, March 17, 1913, **27**: 191; May 6, 1913, **27**: 403; Sept. 23, 1913, **28**: 319; July 9, 1914, **30**: 264; July 29, 1914, **30**: 313; Nov. 20, 1914, **31**: 340; Jan. 10, 1916, **35**: 458; Jan. 11, 1916, **35**: 462; Feb. 7, 1916, **36**: 137; June 8, 1916, **37**: 170

William Gordon, March 2, 1916, **36:** 240

Samuel Jordan Graham, Jan. 8, 1914, **29:** 111

Charles Henry Grasty, March 17, 1913, **27:** 192; March 5, 1914, **29:** 311

Alexander White Gregg, Feb. 14, 1916, **36:** 175

Thomas Watt Gregory, Sept. 14, 1914, **31:** 29; Nov. 7, 1914, **31:** 275; Dec. 16, 1914, **31:** 467; July 12, 1915, **33:** 493; Aug. 18, 1915, **34:** 235; Jan. 19, 1916, **35:** 502; March 2, 1916, **36:** 240

Solomon Bulkley Griffin, Oct. 10, 1916, **38:** 389

William Birch Haldeman, May 14, 1915, **33:** 196

George Ellery Hale, July 28, 1916, **37:** 494

William Bayard Hale, Jan. 15, 1914, **29:** 133

Alice Morrell Hallett, Oct. 23, 1916, **38:** 511

James Alphonsus Hamill, March 7, 1914, **29:** 323

Charles Sumner Hamlin, Feb. 14, 1916, **36:** 177; July 29, 1916, **37:** 498; Oct. 23, 1916, **38:** 512

Ole Hanson, July 18, 1916, **37:** 432

Norman Hapgood, April 22, 1914, **29:** 483; June 9, 1914, **30:** 162; June 15, 1916, **37:** 230; July 7, 1916, **37:** 374; July 20, 1916, **37:** 446; Aug. 5, 1916, **37:** 528; Aug. 9, 1916, **38:** 12; Aug. 11, 1916, **38:** 27; Aug. 12, 1916, **38:** 29; Aug. 17, 1916, **38:** 42; Aug. 23, 1916, **38:** 78; Aug. 30, 1916, **38:** 117; Sept. 20, 1916 (2), **38:** 189; Sept. 27, 1916, **38:** 281

William Procter Gould Harding, May 4, 1914, **29:** 543; Aug. 23, 1915, **34:** 295

Thomas William Hardwick, March 15, 1915, **32:** 375

Florence Jaffray Hurst Harriman, Aug. 16, 1915, **34:** 216

Francis Burton Harrison, Sept. 25, 1913, **28:** 323; Jan. 12, 1915, **32:** 536; Oct. 11, 1915, **35:** 52; Oct. 16, 1915, **35:** 72; Oct. 14, 1915, **38:** 438; Nov. 15, 1916, **38:** 648

Samuel Miles Hastings, July 28, 1916, **37:** 492

James Hay, Aug. 2, 1915, **34:** 58; Nov. 6, 1915, **35:** 180; Jan. 18, 1915, **35:** 499; Jan. 24, 1916, **35:** 512; Feb. 15, 1916, **36:** 178; March 21, 1916, **36:** 348; March 24, 1916, **36:** 360

Frank J. Hayes, Oct. 5, 1914, **31:** 124; Oct. 23, 1914, **31:** 215; Dec. 10, 1914, **31:** 449

William Heinecke, Oct. 13, 1916, **38:** 427

Francis Joseph Heney, July 4, 1916, **37:** 358

Robert Lee Henry, Aug. 27, 1914, **30:** 454; Oct. 22, 1914, **31:** 205

Alonzo Barton Hepburn, June 24, 1913, **28:** 3

Henry Lee Higginson, July 24, 1914, **30:** 302; Aug. 3, 1914, **30:** 338; Aug. 22, 1914, **30:** 432; Oct. 23, 1914, **31:** 215; Oct. 29, 1914, **31:** 247; Nov. 16, 1914, **31:** 320; Feb. 1, 1915, **32:** 167; Nov. 22, 1915, **35:** 235; March 7, 1916, **36:** 265

Gilbert Monell Hitchcock, Aug. 28, 1913, **28:** 241

Henry French Hollis, Oct. 20, 1913, **28:** 418; June 2, 1914, **30:**

134; June 16, 1914, **30:** 187; May 30, 1916, **37:** 128; June 7, 1916, **37:** 166; Aug. 12, 1916, **38:** 29

John Appleton Haven Hopkins, Nov. 16, 1916, **38:** 663

William Edward Horton, Dec. 17, 1913, **29:** 36

Hester Eloise Hosford, Jan. 21, 1915, **32:** 95

Edward Mandell House, Feb. 5, 1913, **27:** 101; Feb. 7, 1913, **27:** 102; May 17, 1913, **27:** 445; Sept. 18, 1913, **28:** 288; Nov. 5, 1913, **28:** 490; Jan. 3, 1914, **29:** 99; Jan. 6, 1914, **29:** 102; Feb. 18, 1914, **29:** 270; Feb. 25, 1914, **29:** 288; March 7, 1914, **29:** 322; March 30, 1914, **29:** 383; May 15, 1914, **30:** 30; Oct. 10, 1914, **31:** 140; Oct. 16, 1914, **31:** 167; Dec. 1, 1914, **31:** 377; Dec. 2, 1914, **31:** 379; Dec. 7, 1914, **31:** 410; Dec. 9, 1914, **31:** 427; Dec. 26, 1914 (3), **31:** 530, 531; July 12, 1915, **33:** 492; Oct. 4, 1915 (2), **35:** 18, 19; March 9, 1916, **36:** 276; April 13, 1916, **36:** 477; April 15, 1916, **36:** 485; April 21, 1916 (2), **36:** 520; April 22, 1916, **36:** 525; May 17, 1916 (2), **37:** 61; May 29, 1916, **37:** 118; June 6, 1916, **37:** 163; June 11, 1916, **37:** 206; June 22, 1916, **37:** 280; July 2, 1916, **37:** 345; Sept. 29, 1916, **38:** 296; Oct. 24, 1916, **38:** 516; Oct. 30, 1916, **38:** 561; Nov. 6, 1916, **38:** 618

House of Representatives, Jan. 28, 1915, **32:** 142

Houston Chronicle, Sept. 8, 1914, **31:** 12

David Franklin Houston, Jan. 1, 1914, **29:** 91; March 21, 1916, **36:** 348

Edward Percy Howard, July 24, 1916, **37:** 468

Frederic Clemson Howe, June 15, 1916, **37:** 230; Aug. 22, 1916, **38:** 63; Aug. 23, 1916, **38:** 78

Charles Evans Hughes, June 10, 1916, **37:** 186

William Hughes, Aug. 22, 1913, **28:** 204; Aug. 29, 1913, **28:** 246; Jan. 21, 1915, **32:** 94

Cordell Hull, Aug. 5, 1916, **37:** 528

Edward Nash Hurley, May 12, 1916, **37:** 25

Paul Oscar Husting, Jan. 12, 1915, **32:** 58; May 1, 1916, **36:** 576

William Huttig, Sept. 20, 1916, **38:** 187

Charles Samuel Jackson, July 24, 1916, **37:** 469

Giles B. Jackson, July 23, 1915, **34:** 16; Sept. 7, 1916, **38:** 156

Ollie Murray James, Oct. 20, 1915, **35:** 88; June 22, 1916, **37:** 282

John Franklin Jameson, Nov. 16, 1916, **38:** 664

The Jane Jefferson Club of Colorado, Aug. 7, 1916, **37:** 536

George Sibley Johns, Jan. 19, 1915, **32:** 90

Alice Johnson, March 5, 1914, **29:** 311

Edwin Stockton Johnson, May 18, 1916, **37:** 70

Harry Leonard Johnson, Oct. 21, 1916, **38:** 510

Robert Underwood Johnson, May 10, 1913, **27:** 412; Dec. 14, 1914, **31:** 461

David Benton Jones, Dec. 31, 1913, **29:** 90

Thomas Davies Jones, April 22, 1914, **29:** 483; June 5, 1914, **30:** 149; June 12, 1914, **30:** 173; July 23, 1914 (2), **30:** 298, 300; Aug. 6, 1914, **30:** 353; Aug. 9, 1916, **38:** 13; Aug. 11, 1916, **38:** 28; Aug. 17, 1916, **38:** 43
William Atkinson Jones, April 26, 1916, **36:** 555

Francis Fisher Kane, Sept. 26, 1913, **28:** 329
Walter Winston Kenilworth, Feb. 25, 1914, **29:** 288
William Kent, June 29, 1914, **30:** 224; Feb. 7, 1916, **36:** 136; Feb. 28, 1916, **36:** 227; March 9, 1916, **36:** 277; July 18, 1916, **37:** 432
William Squire Kenyon, Feb. 4, 1915, **32:** 190
John Worth Kern, May 15, 1914, **30:** 31; June 23, 1914, **30:** 202; Aug. 20, 1914, **30:** 405; Oct. 12, 1914, **31:** 145; Dec. 10, 1914, **31:** 450; Sept 27, 1915, **34:** 527; April 12, 1916, **36:** 464; April 21, 1916, **36:** 521; May 4, 1916, **36:** 603; Aug. 21, 1916, **38:** 58
James Kerney, May 12, 1913, **27:** 418; Oct. 3, 1914, **31:** 123
Claude Kitchin, Oct. 27, 1915, **35:** 114; Nov. 2, 1915, **35:** 157; Dec. 18, 1915, **35:** 370; Jan. 24, 1916, **35:** 510; Jan. 26, 1916, **35:** 526; March 27, 1916, **36:** 370
Martin Augustine Knapp, Aug. 2, 1914, **30:** 329
Martin Augustine Knapp and others, July 29, 1914, **30:** 314

Robert Marion La Follette, July 25, 1913, **28:** 82
George Mason La Monte, July 29, 1913, **28:** 93
Franklin Knight Lane, March 27, 1913, **27:** 232; June 12, 1913, **27:** 511; July 10, 1914, **30:** 276; Nov. 20, 1914, **31:** 341; Sept. 10, 1915, **34:** 442; March 9, 1916, **36:** 277; March 13, 1916 (2), **36:** 299; April 21, 1916; **36:** 521; May 26, 1916, **37:** 111; June 29, 1916, **37:** 328; Aug. 31, 1916, **38:** 121
Robert Lansing, June 9, 1916, **37:** 176; July 12, 1916, **37:** 408; Aug. 26, 1916, **38:** 84; Oct. 2, 1916 (2), **38:** 319; Nov. 5, 1916, **38:** 617
Leona Laura Larrabee, Sept. 27, 1916, **38:** 281
Elisha Lee, Aug. 13, 1916, **38:** 31
Asbury Francis Lever, May 8, 1914, **30:** 8; Aug. 11, 1916, **38:** 24
James Hamilton Lewis, July 15, 1914, **30:** 284; May 4, 1916, **36:** 602
William Libbey, April 18, 1916, **36:** 504
Henry Dickinson Lindsley, Feb. 10, 1916, **36:** 165
Walter Lippmann, Sept. 29, 1916, **38:** 295; Oct. 30, 1916, **38:** 559
Henry Cabot Lodge, Feb. 19, 1914, **29:** 271
Robert Scott Lovett, Oct. 10, 1916, **38:** 389
Seth Low, Dec. 1, 1914, **31:** 376; Dec. 21, 1914, **31:** 503; Jan. 5, 1915, **32:** 18; April 19, 1915, **33:** 26; Nov. 8, 1915, **35:** 180; Dec. 13, 1915, **35:** 348; Jan. 17, 1916, **35:** 492; March 3, 1916, **36:** 245; March 13, 1916, **36:** 299

Seth Low and others, Dec. 21, 1914, **31:** 503
Frederick Bicknell Lynch, Dec. 16, 1915, **35:** 361

William Gibbs McAdoo, June 27, 1913, **28:** 10; Oct. 6, 1913, **28:** 366; Oct. 11, 1913, **28:** 390; Nov. 7, 1913, **28:** 505; Oct. 3, 1914, **31:** 123; Nov. 8, 1914, **31:** 279; Nov. 17, 1914, **31:** 324; March 8, 1915, **32:** 336; Aug. 19, 1915, **34:** 248; Aug. 23, 1915, **34:** 294; Sept. 17, 1915, **34:** 481; Sept. 24, 1915, **34:** 512; Jan. 14, 1916, **35:** 475; Jan. 19, 1916, **35:** 502; May 29, 1916, **37:** 119; Oct. 6, 1916, **38:** 350; Oct. 9, 1916, **38:** 374
William Gibbs McAdoo and Albert Sidney Burleson, March 2, 1916, **36:** 239
William Frank McCombs, April 7, 1914, **29:** 409; April 22, 1916, **36:** 525; June 3, 1916, **37:** 156; Sept. 20, 1916, **38:** 189
Cyrus McCormick, July 23, 1914, **30:** 301
Vance Criswell McCormick, July 12, 1916, **37:** 408; Aug. 4, 1916, **37:** 523; Aug. 31, 1916, **38:** 122; Sept. 15, 1916, **38:** 172; Sept. 26, 1916, **38:** 280; Sept. 29, 1916, **38:** 296; Oct. 17, 1916, **38:** 461; Oct. 25, 1916, **38:** 522; Nov. 13, 1916, **38:** 636
Porter James McCumber, April 7, 1914, **29:** 409
John Avery McIlhenny, March 4, 1914, **29:** 309
Frank McIntyre, Nov. 15, 1916, **38:** 648
Alexander Jeffrey McKelway, May 18, 1916, **37:** 69; July 19, 1916, **37:** 436; July 25, 1916, **37:** 471; Sept. 29, 1916, **38:** 296
John Lowndes McLaurin, Aug. 7, 1915, **34:** 121
James Clark McReynolds, April 17, 1913, **27:** 321; April 19, 1913, **27:** 334; Dec. 19, 1913, **29:** 45; June 12, 1914, **30:** 172; July 21, 1914, **30:** 293
Dudley Field Malone, Sept. 8, 1914, **31:** 11; Feb. 5, 1915, **32:** 192; June 9, 1916, **37:** 176; June 12, 1916, **37:** 207; Aug. 3, 1916, **37:** 517; Aug. 8, 1916, **38:** 8
James Robert Mann, Nov. 18, 1915, **35:** 213
Theodore Marburg, Feb. 3, 1915, **32:** 188
William Luke Marbury, Oct. 11, 1913, **28:** 390; Feb. 5, 1914, **29:** 220
Thomas Riley Marshall, April 18, 1914, **29:** 461; Sept. 11, 1914, **31:** 23; Aug. 3, 1916, **37:** 517; Sept. 27, 1916, **38:** 282
Thomas Staples Martin, July 16, 1915, **33:** 512; March 17, 1916, **36:** 330
Thomas Staples Martin and John Joseph Fitzgerald, March 26, 1913, **27:** 229
George Thomas Marye, Feb. 17, 1916, **36:** 188
Royal Meeker, March 26, 1913, **27:** 230; Nov. 16, 1916, **35:** 205
John Purroy Mitchel, May 5, 1913, **27:** 401; May 6, 1913, **27:** 402; May 8, 1913, **27:** 409; Oct. 20, 1913, **28:** 419; Jan. 20, 1916, **35:** 505

John Bassett Moore, March 17, 1913, **27**: 191; April 12, 1913, **27**: 297; April 16, 1913, **27**: 314; April 21, 1913, **27**: 341; Oct. 20, 1913, **28**: 420

John Pierpont Morgan, Jr., Sept. 17, 1914, **31**: 39

Henry Morgenthau, April 21, 1916, **36**: 522; May 19, 1916, **37**: 73; May 23, 1916, **37**: 96; June 5, 1916, **37**: 163

Robert Russa Moton, Nov. 6, 1914, **31**: 270; Nov. 18, 1914, **31**: 329

Alfred Henry Mulliken, July 22, 1914, **30**: 294

Hugo Münsterberg, Nov. 10, 1914, **31**: 293

Henry Lee Myers, July 28, 1916, **37**: 494

Francis Griffith Newlands, June 6, 1913, **27**: 502; Dec. 23, 1913, **29**: 63; Feb. 4, 1914, **29**: 219; Feb. 9, 1914, **29**: 243; Feb. 23, 1914, **29**: 281; June 15, 1914, **30**: 181; June 29, 1914, **30**: 224; July 23, 1914, **30**: 300; Aug. 21, 1914, **30**: 424; Aug. 24, 1914, **30**: 442; July 7, 1914, **30**: 494

Oliver Peck Newman, Nov. 14, 1913, **28**: 540; Oct. 13, 1914, **31**: 147

Lucius William Nieman, Nov. 23, 1914, **31**: 346; Jan. 29, 1915, **32**: 160; Feb. 11, 1915, **32**: 219; Oct. 16, 1916, **38**: 450

James Richard Nugent, Nov. 14, 1910, **35**: 536; Dec. 9, 1910, **35**: 536

Adolph Simon Ochs, Oct. 10, 1916, **38**: 388

James Aloysius O'Gorman, April 20, 1913, **27**: 336; May 5, 1913, **27**: 399; Oct. 21, 1913, **28**: 421; April 21, 1916, **36**: 520

Jeremiah A. O'Leary, Sept. 29, 1916, **38**: 286

Richard Olney, April 30, 1914, **29**: 536; May 6, 1914, **30**: 3; Aug. 13, 1916, **38**: 31; Sept. 29, 1916, **38**: 295

William Church Osborn, March 31, 1914, **29**: 387; April 6, 1914, **29**: 408

Sergio Osmeña, Sept. 7, 1916, **38**: 155

Robert Latham Owen, Dec. 23, 1913, **29**: 62; April 20, 1914, **29**: 471; June 18, 1914, **30**: 191; June 22, 1914, **30**: 201; June 23, 1914, **30**: 203; Nov. 9, 1915, **35**: 183; Nov. 15, 1915, **35**: 205; Jan. 14, 1916, **35**: 474; Feb. 7, 1916, **36**: 137; June 5, 1916, **37**: 162; June 12, 1916, **37**: 207

Lemuel Phillips Padgett, June 8, 1916, **37**: 170

Robert Newton Page, Feb. 23, 1915, **32**: 275

Walter Hines Page, Jan. 2, 1913, **27**: 6

Alexander Mitchell Palmer, Feb. 5, 1913 (2), **27**: 97, 98; Feb. 25, 1913, **27**: 134; May 7, 1913, **27**: 406

John Milliken Parker, Nov. 15, 1916, **38**: 650

William Robinson Pattangall, Aug. 13, 1913, **28**: 149

Adam Edward Patterson, Aug. 5, 1913, **28**: 115

George Foster Peabody, Oct. 30, 1916, **38**: 562

Bliss Perry, Oct. 30, 1916, **38**: 563
James Duval Phelan, Jan. 11, 1915, **35**: 462; June 8, 1916, **37**: 172
William Phillips, Sept. 24, 1915, **34**: 511; Nov. 4, 1916, **38**: 616
Amos Richards Eno Pinchot, Aug. 19, 1916, **38**: 52; Sept. 20, 1916, **38**: 190
Henry Means Pindell, May 21, 1913, **27**: 462
Key Pittman, March 23, 1914, **29**: 373
Policy Committee of the Colorado Mine Workers, Sept. 17, 1914, **31**: 40
Atlee Pomerene, Sept. 29, 1915, **34**: 538; May 12, 1916, **37**: 25; Sept. 27, 1916, **38**: 281
George Pope, Aug. 20, 1916, **38**: 55
Louis Freeland Post, Nov. 14, 1913, **28**: 540
Edward William Pou, Feb. 11, 1915, **32**: 219; Feb. 29, 1916 (2), **36**: 231; March 15, 1916, **36**: 314; June 12, 1916, **37**: 207; June 15, 1916, **37**: 230
Ralph Pulitzer, Oct. 9, 1913, **28**: 381; Nov. 11, 1914, **31**: 295

Henry Thomas Rainey, May 10, 1916, **37**: 10; Oct. 23, 1916, **38**: 512
Sam Taliaferro Rayburn, June 9, 1914, **30**: 162
Samuel Rea, April 22, 1913, **27**: 346
William Cox Redfield, Feb. 26, 1913, **27**: 138; Aug. 12, 1913, **28**: 144; Dec. 20, 1913, **29**: 48; April 14, 1914, **29**: 435; April 21, 1914, **29**: 478; May 7, 1914, **30**: 4; Oct. 3, 1914, **31**: 122; July 31, 1915, **34**: 48; Aug. 4, 1915, **34**: 81; March 27, 1916, **36**: 369; April 4, 1916, **36**: 410; June 7, 1916, **37**: 166
Eugene Elliott Reed, March 7, 1913, **27**: 158; March 14, 1914, **27**: 178
James Alexander Reed, June 13, 1913, **27**: 515; Oct. 23, 1913, **28**: 425
Paul Samuel Reinsch, June 30, 1913, **28**: 15
Robert Goodwyn Rhett, Aug. 23, 1916, **38**: 77
Joseph Taylor Robinson, May 20, 1913, **27**: 457; April 21, 1914, **29**: 479
John Davison Rockefeller, April 25, 1914, **29**: 503; April 26, 1914, **29**: 512
John Davison Rockefeller, Jr., April 29, 1914, **29**: 533
Alfred Thomas Rogers, Feb. 8, 1916, **36**: 140
Franklin Delano Roosevelt, April 1, 1914, **29**: 392
Benjamin Jefferson Rosenthal, Aug. 23, 1916, **38**: 78
George Rublee, Aug. 3, 1916, **37**: 517
Juliet Barrett Rublee, June 2, 1914, **30**: 135

Wilbur Fisk Sadler, Jr., Oct. 26, 1915, **35**: 110; March 13, 1916, **36**: 300; May 19, 1916, **37**: 74

Willard Saulsbury, Jan. 9, 1913, **27:** 25; Aug. 15, 1914, **30:** 384; Feb. 14, 1916, **36:** 175

Jacob Henry Schiff, Jan. 16, 1915, **32:** 82; Aug. 31, 1916, **38:** 123

Hugh Lenox Scott, Dec. 16, 1913, **29:** 36; Feb. 14, 1916, **36:** 176

Samuel Seabury, Sept. 20, 1916, **38:** 190

Louis Seibold, Sept. 21, 1916, **38:** 194

Donald Douglas Sells, Oct. 24, 1916, **38:** 518

John Franklin Shafroth, July 6, 1916, **37:** 369

The Shakespeare Tercentenary Committee, April 30, 1916, **36:** 570

Albert Shaw, March 17, 1914, **29:** 350

Morris Sheppard, Jan. 21, 1916, **35:** 506

Joseph Swagar Sherley, July 6, 1914, **30:** 260; May 19, 1916, **37:** 74

John Knight Shields, March 3, 1914, **29:** 304; March 7, 1914, **29:** 322; March 12, 1914, **29:** 332; May 18, 1916, **37:** 69

Benjamin Franklin Shively, Oct. 20, 1913, **28:** 418; March 3, 1914, **29:** 305

Furnifold McLendel Simmons, Sept. 4, 1913, **28:** 254

Thetus Willrette Sims, March 3, 1914, **29:** 304

Joel Byron Slocum, Feb. 8, 1916, **36:** 140

John Humphrey Small, Aug. 4, 1916, **37:** 524

Ellison DuRant Smith, March 5, 1914, **29:** 310; July 20, 1915, **33:** 535; Sept. 24, 1915, **34:** 512

Hoke Smith, June 8, 1916, **37:** 173

Marcus Aurelius Smith, March 30, 1914, **29:** 384; April 6, 1914, **29:** 408

Rudolph Spreckels, March 15, 1913, **27:** 188; Aug. 30, 1916, **38:** 118

William Spry, Sept. 30, 1915, **34:** 539

Charles Manly Stedman, April 18, 1916, **36:** 503

Dan Vorhees Stephens, Oct. 3, 1913, **28:** 352

Joseph H. Stewart, March 22, 1913, **27:** 214

Frank Parker Stockbridge, Nov. 1, 1915, **35:** 146

Horace Edward Stockbridge, Oct. 23, 1916, **38:** 511

William Joel Stone, Dec. 23, 1913, **29:** 63; Aug. 13, 1914, **30:** 378; Dec. 14, 1914, **31:** 461; Jan. 27, 1915, **32:** 134; Feb. 25, 1915, **32:** 288; Feb. 22, 1916, **36:** 204; Feb. 24, 1916, **36:** 213; Feb. 28, 1916, **36:** 226; March 24, 1916, **36:** 360; April 19, 1916, **36:** 511; April 21, 1916, **36:** 520; May 16, 1916, **37:** 58; June 8, 1916, **37:** 173; July 12, 1916, **37:** 408; Nov. 15, 1916, **38:** 650

Moorfield Storey, Aug. 10, 1916, **38:** 19

Daisy Allen Story, July 27, 1916, **37:** 482

Oscar Solomon Straus, Sept. 22, 1913, **28:** 316

Jerry Bartholomew Sullivan, Sept. 20, 1916, **38:** 190

William Sulzer, July 17, 1913, **28:** 37; July 29, 1913, **28:** 94

Hatton William Sumners, Aug. 2, 1915, **34:** 58

Claude Augustus Swanson, July 27, 1916, **37:** 481

Edwin Forrest Sweet, July 14, 1915, **33:** 506
Herbert Bayard Swope, July 6, 1916, **37:** 369

William Howard Taft, April 25, 1916, **36:** 545; May 18, 1916, **37:**
     69; Nov. 16, 1916, **38:** 662
Ida Minerva Tarbell, Sept. 14, 1916, **38:** 170; Sept. 26, 1916, **38:**
     280; Oct. 3, 1916, **38:** 322
George Canada Taylor, June 2, 1914, **30:** 135
Arthur W. Tedcastle, Sept. 14, 1914, **31:** 30
Charles Spalding Thomas, June 10, 1913, **27:** 507; Aug. 8, 1916,
     38: 9
Henry Burling Thompson, May 27, 1913, **27:** 480
Mary Wilson Thompson, Aug. 3, 1916, **37:** 518
William Howard Thompson, June 25, 1913, **28:** 6
Samuel Huston Thompson, Jr., Sept. 21, 1916, **38:** 194
John Randolph Thornton, July 15, 1913, **28:** 35; Feb. 23, 1914,
     29: 281; Feb. 27, 1914, **29:** 297; March 5, 1914, **29:** 310; July 1,
     1914, **30:** 240; Feb. 15, 1915, **32:** 235
Benjamin Ryan Tillman, Dec. 15, 1914, **31:** 466; Jan. 13, 1915,
     32: 62; Jan. 6, 1916, **35:** 446; Feb. 14, 1916, **36:** 174; March 10,
     1916, **36:** 279; March 31, 1916 (2), **36:** 396; April 25, 1916, **36:**
     545; May 22, 1916, **37:** 94; June 27, 1916, **37:** 308; July 27,
     1916, **37:** 481
Nancy Saunders Toy, Jan 31, 1915, **32:** 165; Feb. 4, 1915, **32:** 190
Arthur W. Trenholm, Aug. 2, 1914, **30:** 328
Frank Trumbull, Sept. 10, 1914, **31:** 20; Jan. 30, 1915, **32:** 163
Henry St. George Tucker, Jan. 3, 1913, **27:** 7
Joseph Patrick Tumulty, Sept. 2, 1913 (2), **28:** 248; Jan. 4, 1914,
     29: 100; Jan. 6, 1914, **29:** 101; Jan. 24, 1914, **29:** 170; Feb. 19,
     1914, **29:** 271; March 14, 1914, **29:** 344; May 25, 1914, **30:** 73;
     June 12, 1914, **30:** 173; Dec. 8, 1914, **31:** 424; Feb. 19, 1915, **32:**
     258; April 24, 1915, **33:** 68; April 28, 1915, **33:** 86; June 8, 1915,
     33: 370; July 26, 1915, **34:** 27; July 30, 1915, **34:** 45; Aug. 3,
     1915 (2), **34:** 64, 65; Aug. 7, 1915, **34:** 120; Nov. 1, 1915, **35:**
     150; Jan. 3, 1916, **35:** 423; Jan. 12, 1916, **35:** 467; Jan. 15, 1916,
     35: 481; Jan. 22, 1916, **35:** 508; Jan. 23, 1916, **35:** 509; Feb. 9,
     1916, **36:** 144; March 23, 1916, **36:** 356; April 27, 1916 (2), **36:**
     562; April 30, 1916, **36:** 569; May 17, 1916 (2), **37:** 62; July 27,
     1916, **37:** 491; Nov. 3, 1915, **37:** 541; Aug. 11, 1916, **38:** 24; Aug.
     18, 1916, **38:** 45; Aug. 25, 1916, **38:** 84; Sept. 18, 1916, **38:** 181;
     Sept. 21, 1916, **38:** 193; Oct. 17, 1916, **38:** 459; Oct. 24, 1916,
     38: 516

Edwin Stuart Underhill, April 3, 1914, **29:** 401
Frederick Douglass Underwood, Oct. 17, 1916, **38:** 466
Oscar Wilder Underwood, Feb. 24, 1913, **27:** 131; March 14, 1913,
     27: 177; April 10, 1913, **27:** 282; April 16, 1913, **27:** 314; April
     18, 1913, **27:** 327; April 19, 1913, **27:** 334; Oct. 20, 1913, **28:**

419; Jan. 23, 1914, **29**: 163; April 7, 1914, **29**: 410; Oct. 17, 1914, **31**: 168; Dec. 15, 1914, **31**: 465; Jan. 16, 1915, **32**: 82; May 5, 1916, **36**: 612

La Vanguardia, Nov. 15, 1916, **38**: 649
Charles Richard Van Hise, March 10, 1914, **29**: 326; July 13, 1914, **30**: 281
Frank Arthur Vanderlip, Oct. 24, 1913, **28**: 430
Jaime Carlos de Veyra, Nov. 15, 1916, **38**: 648
Walker Whiting Vick, Dec. 7, 1914, **31**: 411; Dec. 15, 1914, **31**: 467
Oswald Garrison Villard, July 23, 1913, **28**: 65; Aug. 19, 1913, **28**: 191; Aug. 21, 1913, **28**: 202; Aug. 29, 1913, **28**: 245; Sept. 22, 1913, **28**: 316; Oct. 3, 1913, **28**: 352; Oct. 17, 1913, **28**: 413; Aug. 24, 1914, **30**: 443; Sept. 4, 1914, **30**: 479; Dec. 21, 1914, **31**: 502; Sept. 7, 1915, **34**: 428; Oct. 28, 1915, **35**: 120; Nov. 2, 1915, **35**: 157

Robert Ferdinand Wagner, April 23, 1916, **36**: 529; April 27, 1916, **36**: 562
David Ignatius Walsh, May 28, 1914, **30**: 96; June 9, 1914, **30**: 163
Francis Patrick Walsh, June 20, 1913, **27**: 552
Thomas James Walsh, March 15, 1916, **36**: 316; June 26, 1916, **37**: 304; Aug. 22, 1916, **38**: 63; Nov. 16, 1916, **38**: 662
Paul Moritz Warburg, April 30, 1914, **29**: 536; July 25, 1914, **30**: 304; Aug. 16, 1916, **38**: 39
Robert Lewis Waring, June 1, 1914, **30**: 493
Booker Taliaferro Washington, March 2, 1914, **29**: 302
S. Townsend Weaver, Sept. 7, 1916, **38**: 157
Edwin Yates Webb, April 8, 1914, **29**: 413; Aug. 23, 1916, **38**: 78
Jesse Floyd Welborn, Oct. 30, 1913, **28**: 475
William Henry Welch, July 24, 1916, **37**: 468
John Wesley Wescott, Jan. 30, 1913, **27**: 92; May 2, 1916, **36**: 580; June 23, 1916, **37**: 286
John Philip White, Sept. 24, 1914, **31**: 81
John Philip White and others, Sept. 5, 1914, **30**: 485: Sept. 17, 1914, **31**: 40
William Allen White, May 15, 1914, **30**: 32
Brand Whitlock, April 4, 1916, **36**: 409
William Royal Wilder, Oct. 24, 1916, **38**: 518
Louis Wiley, May 11, 1916, **37**: 14; June 22, 1916, **37**: 282
Daniel Willard, Aug. 16, 1916, **38**: 38
Charles Richard Williams, Nov. 16, 1916, **38**: 664
John Sharp Williams, Oct. 11, 1913, **28**: 389; Oct. 23, 1913, **28**: 425; Jan. 27, 1914, **29**: 184; April 2, 1914, **29**: 394; April 22, 1914, **29**: 482; Jan. 7, 1915, **32**: 26; Feb. 23, 1915, **32**: 274; Aug. 6, 1915, **34**: 107; Aug. 17, 1915, **34**: 226; Aug. 21, 1915, **34**: 273;

Nov. 8, 1915, **35:** 181; Feb. 7, 1916, **36:** 137; March 7, 1916, **36:** 264

James Franklin Williamson, Sept. 30, 1916, **38:** 312

John Adams Wilson, Aug. 22, 1916, **38:** 63

William Bauchop Wilson, Dec. 1, 1913, **28:** 601; May 13, 1914, **30:** 29; July 14, 1914, **30:** 283; Sept. 30, 1914, **31:** 101; April 20, 1916, **36:** 515; May 1, 1916, **36:** 576; July 31, 1916, **37:** 504; Aug. 9, 1916, **38:** 12; Oct. 23, 1916, **38:** 513

Stephen Samuel Wise, June 4, 1914, **30:** 144; Nov. 18, 1915, **35:** 212

Henry Otto Wittpenn, July 23, 1913, **28:** 65

Leonard Wood, Jan. 9, 1913, **27:** 25; July 1, 1914, **30:** 240

Charles Albert Woods, April 19, 1913, **27:** 335; April 25, 1913, **27:** 359

Lawrence Crane Woods, March 3, 1914, **29:** 305; Oct. 17, 1916, **38:** 466

Robert Wickliffe Woolley, March 7, 1916, **36:** 263

John Downey Works, April 9, 1913, **27:** 277

Louis J. Wortham, Feb. 16, 1916, **36:** 186

Theodore Wright, Oct. 10, 1916, **38:** 389

Arthur Yager, Nov. 15, 1916, **38:** 649

Florenz Ziegfeld, Jr., April 17, **36:** 498

To Wilson from

Charles Francis Adams, Nov. 5, 1914, **31:** 267

William Charles Adamson, Jan. 18, 1914, **29:** 139; Feb. 16, 1914, **29:** 265; Feb. 23, 1914, **29:** 282; Feb. 27, 1914, **29:** 297; April 1, 1914, **29:** 394; April 23, 1914, **29:** 496; Aug. 5, 1914, **30:** 351; Feb. 18, 1915, **32:** 252; March 13, 1916, **36:** 304; April 4, 1916, **36:** 415; May 21, 1916, **37:** 92; June 30,1916, **37:** 337; Nov. 16, 1916, **38:** 666

Jane Addams, Jan. 29, 1915, **32:** 162

Jane Addams and others, Oct. 29, 1915, **35:** 134

Jesse Corcoran Adkins, June 6, 1916, **37:** 176

American Union Against Militarism, May 8, 1916, **36:** 632

Elias Milton Ammons, April 25, 1914 (2), **29:** 501, 503; April 28, 1914, **29:** 529; May 16, 1914, **30:** 37; May 18, 1914, **30:** 45; Aug. 25, 1914, **30:** 452; Nov. 6, 1914, **31:** 272; Nov. 19, 1914, **31:** 334; Dec. 10, 1914, **31:** 452; Sept. 28, 1914, **31:** 557

George Weston Anderson, June 2, 1916, **37:** 152

Augustus Octavius Bacon, July 25, 1913, **28:** 82; Nov. 4, 1913, **28:** 488

Warren Worth Bailey, July 1, 1916, **37:** 342

Newton Diehl Baker, Feb. 24, 1916, **36:** 214; March 6, 1916 (2), **36:** 259; April 7, 1916, **36:** 431; May 9, 1916, **37:** 9; May 20,

1916, **37:** 84; June 3, 1916, **37:** 156; June 21, 1916, **37:** 278; July 8, 1916, **37:** 380; July 10, 1916, **37:** 397; July 21, 1916, **37:** 455; Aug. 4, 1916, **37:** 524; Sept. 16, 1916, **38:** 177; Sept. 18, 1916, **38:** 181; Sept. 23, 1916 (2), **38:** 238; Sept. 25, 1916, **38:** 272; Oct. 14, 1916 (2), **38:** 438, 439; Nov. 12, 1916, **38:** 636

John Hollis Bankhead, June 29, 1916, **37:** 330

Wharton Barker, Aug. 29, 1916, **38:** 103

Bernard Mannes Baruch, Aug. 17, 1916, **38:** 43

Elsworth Raymond Bathrick, April 18, 1913, **27:** 327

Sylvester Woodbridge Beach, June 20, 1916, **37:** 270

Herman Bernstein, Jan. 28, 1915, **32:** 148; March 22, 1916, **36:** 356

Samuel Reading Bertron, Feb. 4, 1914, **29:** 219

Frederick Leonard Blackmon, Feb. 13, 1915, **32:** 231

Edward William Bok, Aug. 5, 1916, **37:** 534

LaMont Montgomery Bowers, Nov. 8, 1913, **28:** 507; Nov. 25, 1913, **28:** 589; Dec. 29, 1913, **29:** 87

Louis Dembitz Brandeis, April 29, 1913, **27:** 365; May 19, 1913, **27:** 456; May 26, 1913, **27:** 476; May 27, 1913, **27:** 481; June 14, 1913, **27:** 520; Aug. 14, 1916, **38:** 33

Henry Skillman Breckinridge, Feb. 10, 1916, **36:** 165

Howard Allen Bridgman, Sept. 4, 1913, **28:** 256; Sept. 16, 1913, **28:** 277

David W. Brown and others, May 5, 1914, **29:** 546

William Jennings Bryan, June 25, 1913, **28:** 6; Aug. 6, 1913, **28:** 121; Sept. 4, 1913, **28:** 255; Oct. 7, 1913, **28:** 369; April 2, 1914, **29:** 395; April 10, 1914, **29:** 421; Dec. 19, 1914, **31:** 490; Feb. 17, 1915, **32:** 242; May 19, 1915, **33:** 218; June 8, 1915, **33:** 370; June 9, 1915, **33:** 375; Oct. 8, 1916, **38:** 372; Nov. 10, 1916, **38:** 629

James Viscount Bryce, March 6, 1914, **29:** 320; Nov. 16, 1916, **38:** 665

Albert Sidney Burleson, Feb. 25, 1913, **27:** 135; July 28, 1915, **34:** 38; March 4, 1916, **36:** 249; June 7, 1916, **37:** 169; Sept. 1, 1916, **38:** 124

Charles Creighton Carlin, Sept. 17, 1914, **31:** 43

Carrie Clinton Lane Chapman Catt, Oct. 6, 1915, **35:** 30; June 16, 1916, **37:** 237; Aug. 7, 1916, **37:** 539; Aug. 12, 1916, **38:** 30

William Lea Chambers, July 26, 1914, **30:** 305; Aug. 4, 1914, **30:** 343; Aug. 17, 1915, **34:** 249; July 19, 1916, **37:** 438; Aug. 4, 1916, **37:** 525; Aug. 13, 1916, **38:** 30; Aug. 18, 1916, **38:** 48; Sept. 21, 1916, **38:** 199

William Eaton Chandler, March 14, 1913, **27:** 178

Champ Clark, Feb. 11, 1915, **32:** 221; March 10, 1916, **36:** 287; March 13, 1916, **36:** 306; Sept. 1, 1916, **38:** 125

James Paul Clarke, May 12, 1916, **37:** 27

Henry De Lamar Clayton, Oct. 11, 1913, **28:** 391

Bainbridge Colby, Aug. 30, 1916, **38:** 121

John Rogers Commons, Feb. 8, 1915, **32:** 199

William Adams Copeland, Aug. 18, 1914, **30:** 400

Edward Samuel Corwin, April 13, 1913, **27:** 299

James McMahon Cox, March 26, 1913, **27:** 230; March 28, 1913, **27:** 234

Charles Richard Crane, Feb. 10, 1913, **27:** 107; Jan. 10, 1915, **32:** 52; Jan. 27, 1916, **35:** 535; Feb. 14, 1916, **36:** 177; Feb. 17, 1916, **36:** 191; June 11, 1916, **37:** 206; June 14, 1916, **37:** 288

Charles Robert Crisp, March 27, 1914, **29:** 381

Charles Allen Culberson, Aug. 22, 1914, **30:** 433

Josephus Daniels, Oct. 6, 1914, **31:** 126; Nov. 7, 1914, **31:** 276; Dec. 7, 1914, **31:** 411; April 10, 1915, **32:** 501; July 23, 1915, **34:** 17; Aug. 12, 1915, **34:** 173; Aug. 20, 1915, **34:** 267; May 13, 1916, **37:** 39; May 17, 1916, **37:** 65; June 1, 1916, **37:** 143; June 19, 1916, **37:** 267; July 17, 1916, **37:** 428; Aug. 2, 1916, **37:** 515; Aug. 15, 1916, **38:** 35; Oct. 14, 1916, **38:** 441; Oct. 26, 1916, **38:** 545

Joseph Edward Davies, Dec. 27, 1913, **29:** 78; July 30, 1914, **30:** 320; Aug. 21, 1914, **30:** 427; Feb. 22, 1915, **32:** 271; April 17, 1916, **36:** 500; June 10, 1916, **37:** 204

Ellen Duane Davis, Aug. 3, 1916, **37:** 522

Frederic Adrian Delano, Aug. 5, 1914, **30:** 350; July 21, 1916, **37:** 463; July 25, 1916, **37:** 472

Thomas Dixon, Jr., July 27, 1913, **28:** 88

Cleveland Hoadley Dodge, April 1, 1913, **27:** 247; April 8, 1913, **27:** 274

Josephine Marshall Jewell Dodge, July 4, 1914, **30:** 257

William Lewis Douglas, Oct. 17, 1916, **38:** 468

Edward Olin Downes, Aug. 4, 1916, **37:** 526

Ed L. Doyle, April 21, 1914, **29:** 479

Garrett Droppers, March 23, 1916, **36:** 358; Oct. 25, 1916, **38:** 523

William Edward Burghardt Du Bois, Oct. 10, 1916, **38:** 459

Charles William Eliot, Feb. 12, 1914, **29:** 246; March 12, 1914, **29:** 338; July 25, 1914, **30:** 305; Jan. 19, 1915, **32:** 93; Feb. 15, 1915, **32:** 238; Oct. 6, 1916, **38:** 352

Matthias Cowell Ely, May 19, 1913, **27:** 456; May 28, 1913, **27:** 482

Joseph I. Essig and others, Oct. 19, 1914, **31:** 183

William Corcoran Eustis, Jan. 17, 1913, **27:** 61

Elizabeth Gardiner Evans, May 9, 1916, **37:** 9

John Henry Fahey, Feb. 10, 1916, **36:** 168

Henry Pratt Fairchild, March 17, 1914, **29:** 352

John Villiers Farwell, July 29, 1916, **37:** 499

Scott Ferris, May 11, 1914, **30:** 20

Sara Bard Field, June 12, 1916, **37**: 208; July 7, 1916, **37**: 375

James Fairman Fielder, March 28, 1913, **27**: 235

Irving Fisher, Aug. 5, 1916, **37**: 531

John Francis Fitzgerald, Sept. 10, 1913, **28**: 270

Duncan Upshaw Fletcher, Jan. 14, 1914, **29**: 132; Oct. 21, 1915, **35**: 96

John Charles Floyd, Sept. 17, 1914, **31**: 41

Henry Ford, Sept. 1, 1916, **38**: 125

Henry Jones Ford, Aug. 26, 1913, **28**: 227

James Berwick Forgan and others, Sept. 21, 1914, **31**: 75

Martin David Foster, April 27, 1914, **29**: 513; July 4, 1916, **37**: 359

John Fox, April 13, 1916, **36**: 481

Robert Thomas Frazier, Jr., Aug. 30, 1916, **38**: 119

Hollis Burke Frissell, Nov. 3, 1914, **31**: 261

Andrew Furuseth, Oct. 29, 1913, **28**: 469; March 1, 1915, **32**: 304; March 6, 1915, **32**: 333

James Ambrose Gallivan, Nov. 11, 1914, **31**: 297

Obadiah Gardner, July 29, 1916, **37**: 498; Sept. 15, 1916, **38**: 173

Harry Augustus Garfield, May 16, 1916, **37**: 60; Sept. 5, 1916, **38**: 145

Austin Bruce Garretson and others, Aug. 29, 1916 (2), **38**: 93, 94

Lindley Miller Garrison, April 8, 1913, **27**: 274; Aug. 19, 1913, **28**: 192; Sept. 19, 1913, **28**: 300; Oct. 6, 1913, **28**: 366; Feb. 19, 1914, **29**: 273; Feb. 25, 1914, **29**: 289; April 28, 1914, **29**: 525; May 2, 1914, **29**: 541; May 8, 1914, **30**: 7; May 21, 1914, **30**: 60; Oct. 22, 1914, **31**: 210; Dec. 21, 1914, **31**: 506; Dec. 23, 1914, **31**: 517; Feb. 1, 1915, **32**: 168; Feb. 14, 1915, **32**: 234; Feb. 26, 1915 (2), **32**: 291, 293; Aug. 12, 1915, **34**: 173; Aug. 17, 1915, **34**: 227; Aug. 19, 1915, **34**: 250; Jan. 12, 1916, **35**: 468; Jan. 14, 1916, **35**: 480; Feb. 9, 1916, **36**: 143; Feb. 10, 1916, **36**: 164

Lindley Miller Garrison and Josephus Daniels, Dec. 18, 1914, **29**: 37

Joseph Gilman, Oct. 2, 1916, **38**: 321

Washington Gladden, Dec. 11, 1915, **35**: 344

Carter Glass, Jan. 3, 1913, **27**: 11; Jan. 27, 1913, **27**: 79; June 18, 1913, **27**: 535; May 9, 1914, **30**: 10; June 15, 1916, **37**: 231

Martin Henry Glynn, April 12, 1916, **36**: 471

Edward Field Goltra, Dec. 20, 1913, **29**: 50

Samuel Gompers, March 14, 1913, **27**: 180; April 30, 1913, **27**: 366; Sept. 22, 1913, **28**: 317; July 27, 1914, **30**: 309; Oct. 16, 1914, **31**: 168; Nov. 18, 1914, **31**: 330; Jan. 15, 1915, **32**: 78; Nov. 16, 1915, **35**: 206; Dec. 10, 1915, **35**: 338; Jan. 28, 1916, **36**: 23; April 29, 1916, **36**: 567; Oct. 17, 1916, **38**: 468; Tribute to Wilson, **38**: 671

Elliot Hersey Goodwin, June 16, 1913, **27**: 530

Elgin Ralston Lovell Gould, Dec. 24, 1913, **29**: 75

Samuel Jordan Graham, Jan. 6, 1914, **29:** 105; Oct. 20, 1916, **38:** 499

James Richard Gray, Sept. 10, 1913, **28:** 271

Alexander White Gregg, Feb. 9, 1916, **36:** 151

Thomas Watt Gregory, Sept. 4, 1914, **30:** 480, Sept. 11, 1914 (2), **31:** 24; July 10, 1915, **33:** 491; Aug. 20, 1915, **34:** 266; Dec. 10, 1915, **35:** 336; Feb. 17, 1916, **36:** 188; Feb. 18, 1916, **36:** 195; Feb. 25, 1916, **36:** 217

Sidney Lewis Gulick, Feb. 9, 1914, **29:** 243

George Ellery Hale, July 25, 1916, **37:** 472

William Bayard Hale, Jan. 13, 1914, **29:** 130

James Alphonsus Hamill, March 5, 1914, **29:** 318

Peter Joseph Hamilton, Nov. 11, 1916, **38:** 633

Charles Sumner Hamlin, June 16, 1914, **30:** 188; Feb. 11, 1916, **36:** 171; July 27, 1916, **37:** 489; Aug. 15, 1916, **38:** 35; Oct. 20, 1916, **38:** 497

Norman Hapgood, April 21, 1914, **29:** 481; June 8, 1914, **30:** 161; June 11, 1916, **37:** 206; June 12, 1916, **37:** 210; June 18, 1916, **37:** 264; June 28, 1916, **37:** 321; June 29, 1916, **37:** 328; July 5, 1916, **37:** 362; July 6, 1916, **37:** 372; Aug. 3, 1916, **37:** 522; Aug. 7, 1916, **38:** 3; Aug. 9, 1916, **38:** 14; Aug. 10, 1916, **38:** 23; Aug. 14, 1916, **38:** 34; Aug. 28, 1916, **38:** 86; Sept. 15, 1916, **38:** 175; Sept. 16, 1916, **38:** 178; Sept. 25, 1916, **38:** 273; Oct. 30, 1916, **38:** 564

William Procter Gould Harding, Aug. 30, 1915, **34:** 373; Aug. 10, 1916, **38:** 22

Thomas William Hardwick, March 11, 1915, **32:** 366

Florence Jaffray Hurst Harriman, Aug. 8, 1915, **34:** 135

Francis Burton Harrison, Aug. 30, 1916, **38:** 119; Oct. 14, 1916; **38:** 438; Nov. 11, 1916, **38:** 632; Nov. 15, 1916, **38:** 656

James Hay, Nov. 4, 1915, **35:** 173; Jan. 9, 1916, **35:** 502; Feb. 5, 1916, **36:** 134; Feb. 8, 1916, **36:** 141; Feb. 11, 1916, **36:** 170; March 22, 1916, **36:** 354; April 19, 1916, **36:** 514; May 5, 1916, **36:** 619

A memorandum by James Hay on the House and Senate versions of the army bill, April 19, 1916, **36:** 514

Frank J. Hayes, Dec. 8, 1913, **29:** 25; Sept. 30, 1914, **31:** 106; Dec. 9, 1914, **31:** 446; Dec. 18, 1914, **31:** 488

Frank J. Hayes and others, Sept. 16, 1914, **31:** 37

James Marshall Head, Jan. 22, 1913, **27:** 67

Francis Joseph Heney, July 1, 1916, **37:** 338

Robert Lee Henry, Oct. 2, 1914, **31:** 119

Henry Lee Higginson, March 21, 1914, **29:** 367; July 22, 1914 (2), **30:** 294; Aug. 20, 1914, **30:** 420; Oct. 22, 1914, **31:** 212; Oct. 26, 1914, **31:** 238; Jan. 27, 1915, **32:** 140; Feb. 2, 1915, **32:** 176; Nov. 18, 1915, **35:** 216; Feb. 25, 1916, **36:** 218; March 4, 1916, **36:** 250

Henry French Hollis, Oct. 17, 1913 (2), **28:** 414; May 29, 1914, **30:** 110; June 13, 1914, **30:** 181; May 24, 1916, **37:** 101; Aug. 10, 1916, **38:** 22

John Appleton Haven Hopkins, Nov. 14, 1916, **38:** 642

Edward Mandell House, Jan. 3, 1913, **27:** 11; Jan. 9, 1913, **27:** 26; Jan. 27, 1913, **27:** 80; May 4, 1913, **27:** 396; May 6, 1913, **27:** 404; May 15, 1913, **27:** 436; May 20, 1913, **27:** 458; May 26, 1913, **27:** 476; Sept. 11, 1913, **28:** 275; Dec. 20, 1913, **29:** 49; Jan. 6, 1914, **29:** 103; Feb. 13, 1914, **29:** 247; Feb. 21, 1914 (2), **29:** 277; March 3, 1914, **29:** 308; March 26, 1914, **29:** 380; March 31, 1914, **29:** 390; April 3, 1914, **29:** 401; May 1, 1914, **29:** 541; May 12, 1914, **30:** 27; May 14, 1914, **30:** 30; May 15, 1914, **30:** 33; July 1, 1914, **30:** 242; July 15, 1914, **30:** 285; Aug. 4, 1914, **30:** 345; Oct. 9, 1914, **31:** 139; Oct. 14, 1914, **31:** 148; Oct. 15, 1914, **31:** 161; Nov. 9, 1914, **31:** 291; Nov. 23, 1914, **31:** 349; Nov. 24, 1914, **31:** 353; Nov. 28, 1914 (2), **31:** 363; Dec. 5, 1914, **31:** 403; Dec. 11, 1914, **31:** 452; Dec. 14, 1914, **31:** 462; Dec. 25, 1914 (2), **31:** 523, 524; Jan. 2, 1915, **32:** 6; Jan. 5, 1915, **32:** 19; Jan. 9, 1915, **32:** 43; Jan. 18, 1915, **32:** 84; Feb. 26, 1915, **32:** 294; June 16, 1915, **33:** 409; July 31, 1915, **34:** 53; Aug. 8, 1915, **34:** 133; Nov. 8, 1915, **35:** 183; Nov. 20, 1915, **35:** 231; Nov. 21, 1915, **35:** 234; Dec. 1, 1915, **35:** 279; Dec. 4, 1915, **35:** 285; Dec. 27, 1915 (2), **35:** 398; March 10, 1916, **36:** 291; April 13, 1916, **36:** 479; April 15, 1916, **36:** 485; April 16, 1916, **36:** 488; April 20, 1916, **36:** 518; April 21, 1916 (2), **36:** 523; April 23, 1916, **36:** 530; April 24, 1916 (2), **36:** 542, 543; May 5, 1916, **36:** 616; May 10, 1916, **37:** 11; May 14, 1916, **37:** 45; May 15, 1916, **37:** 56; May 18, 1916, **37:** 71; May 19, 1916, **37:** 76; May 28, 1916, **37:** 117; May 29, 1916, **37:** 121; May 30, 1916 (2), **37:** 128, 129; May 31, 1916, **37:** 133; June 2, 1916, **37:** 151; June 9, 1916, **37:** 177; June 10, 1916, **37:** 203; June 12, 1916, **37:** 211; June 15, 1916, **37:** 236; June 19, 1916, **37:** 268; June 20, 1916, **37:** 269; June 23, 1916 (2), **37:** 290, 291; July 1, 1916, **37:** 337; July 5, 1916, **37:** 364; July 6, 1916, **37:** 374; July 11, 1916, **37:** 402; July 13, 1916, **37:** 420; July 25, 1916, **37:** 474; Aug. 3, 1916 (2), **37:** 518, 521; Aug. 6, 1916, **37:** 535; Aug. 8, 1916, **38:** 11; Sept. 3, 1916, **38:** 139; Sept. 29, 1916, **38:** 297; Sept. 30, 1916, **38:** 317; Oct. 1, 1916, **38:** 317; Oct. 5, 1916, **38:** 349; Oct. 13, 1916, **38:** 429; Oct. 16, 1916, **38:** 453; Oct. 23, 1916, **38:** 515; Oct. 27, 1916, **38:** 545; Oct. 30, 1916, **38:** 560; Nov. 4, 1916, **38:** 616; Nov. 6, 1916, **38:** 619

A proposed amendment by the House on the army reorganizational bill, May 5, 1916, **36:** 619

David Franklin Houston, Dec. 23, 1913, **29:** 69; Dec. 29, 1914, **29:** 86; March 20, 1916, **36:** 344; July 7, 1916, **37:** 376

Edward Percy Howard, July 7, 1916, **37:** 377

Frederic Clemson Howe, Nov. 21, 1914, **31:** 342; June 9, 1916, **37:** 180; Aug. 21, 1916 (2), **38:** 58, 61

A suggested Democratic party platform declaration regarding democracy and imperialism by Frederic Clemson Howe, June 9, 1916, **37:** 181
Robert Stephen Hudspeth, Sept. 21, 1916, **38:** 197
Charles Evans Hughes, June 10, 1916, **37:** 186
William Hughes, Aug. 28, 1913, **28:** 245
Paul Oscar Husting, Jan. 5, 1915, **32:** 19; May 5, 1916, **36:** 617

Andrew Clerk Imbrie, March 6, 1916, **36:** 261

Charles Samuel Jackson, July 21, 1916, **37:** 463
John Franklin Jameson, Nov. 15, 1916, **38:** 654
Anna Johnson, Oct. 24, 1916, **38:** 520
Edwin Stockton Johnson, May 11, 1916, **37:** 20
Robert Underwood Johnson, May 9, 1913, **27:** 411
Warren Forman Johnson, March 29, 1915, **32:** 454
David Benton Jones, Dec. 23, 1913, **29:** 67; Sept. 24, 1914, **31:** 81; June 15, 1915, **33:** 401
Thomas Davies Jones, April 24, 1914, **29:** 500; June 9, 1914, **30:** 164; July 20, 1914 (2), **30:** 291, 292; Aug. 4, 1914, **30:** 344; Aug. 10, 1916, **38:** 22
Wesley Livsey Jones, Sept. 29, 1913, **28:** 344
David Starr Jordan, Dec. 20, 1915, **35:** 373

Edward Keating, Sept. 19, 1914, **31:** 556
William Williams Keen, Jan. 25, 1915, **32:** 119
Helen Adams Keller, Nov. 16, 1915, **35:** 206
Paul Underwood Kellogg and others, March 31, 1913, **27:** 242
William Kent, June 27, 1914, **30:** 217; Jan. 27, 1916, **36:** 19; Feb. 23, 1916, **36:** 206; Feb. 24, 1916, **36:** 215; March 7, 1916, **36:** 265
William Squire Kenyon, Feb. 3, 1915, **32:** 188
John Worth Kern, April 30, 1916, **36:** 570
James Kerney, May 6, 1913, **27:** 402; May 8, 1913; **27:** 409; Oct. 1, 1914, **31:** 116; Feb. 22, 1915, **32:** 272
Claude Kitchin, Oct. 29, 1915, **35:** 132; Dec. 20, 1915, **35:** 373
Martin Augustine Knapp and others, July 29, 1914, **30:** 313

Robert Marion La Follette, March 3, 1915, **32:** 312
George Mason La Monte, July 25, 1913, **28:** 83; July 30, 1913, **28:** 96; Oct. 6, 1915, **35:** 30
Franklin Knight Lane, Feb. 28, 1913, **27:** 139; May 6, 1914, **30:** 3; July 10, 1914, **30:** 274; Nov. 18, 1914 (2), **31:** 331; Jan. 9, 1915, **32:** 43; Sept. 9, 1915, **34:** 437; March 2, 1916, **36:** 241; March 10, 1916, **36:** 290; March 13, 1916, **36:** 300; April 20, 1916, **36:** 518; June 1, 1916, **37:** 139; June 27, 1916, **37:** 313; Aug. 28, 1916, **38:** 88
Walter Lanfersiek, Jan. 15, 1916, **35:** 487

Robert Lansing, Aug. 18, 1915, **34:** 237; Nov. 17, 1915, **35:** 210; Nov. 20, 1915 (3), **35:** 227, 228, 230; Dec. 3, 1915, **35:** 283; Dec. 21, 1915, **35:** 374; Jan. 6, 1916, **35:** 446; Feb. 25, 1916, **36:** 216; Aug. 24, 1916, **38:** 83; Sept. 29, 1916, **38:** 297; Oct. 16, 1916, **38:** 452; Oct. 24, 1916, **38:** 521

Leona Laura Larrabee, Sept. 18, 1916, **38:** 185

Asbury Francis Lever and others, July 12, 1915, **33:** 495

James Hamilton Lewis, July 16, 1914, **30:** 286; May 1, 1916, **36:** 576

Michael Liebel, Jr., March 18, 1916, **36:** 336

Benjamin Barr Lindsey, Aug. 9, 1916, **38:** 14

Jonas Lippmann, Oct. 30, 1916, **38:** 559

Henry Cabot Lodge, Feb. 20, 1914, **29:** 275

Thomas Bell Love, Dec. 20, 1913, **29:** 48; Jan. 29, 1916, **36:** 51

Seth Low, Dec. 4, 1914 (2), **31:** 389; Dec. 16, 1914, **31:** 474; Dec. 22, 1914, **31:** 513; Dec. 29, 1914, **31:** 548; April 16, 1915, **32:** 532; April 20, 1915, **33:** 49; Sept. 8, 1915, **34:** 433; Nov. 5, 1915, **35:** 177; Dec. 8, 1915, **35:** 317; March 1, 1916, **36:** 237; March 10, 1916, **36:** 291

Seth Low and others, Feb. 22, 1915, **32:** 272; March 5, 1915, **35:** 537

Edward George Lowry, March 21, 1914, **29:** 366

Frederick Bicknell Lynch, Dec. 11, 1915, **35:** 346

Frederick Henry Lynch, Sept. 25, 1916, **38:** 276

William Gibbs McAdoo, April 10, 1913, **27:** 283; May 7, 1913, **27:** 406; June 18, 1913, **27:** 536; July 1, 1913, **28:** 20; July 18, 1913, **28:** 40; Sept. 10, 1913, **28:** 271; Sept. 30, 1913, **28:** 346; Oct. 7, 1913, **28:** 371; Oct. 24, 1913, **28:** 434; Nov. 6, 1913, **28:** 501; Nov. 10, 1913, **28:** 524; Nov. 22, 1913, **28:** 579; Dec. 20, 1913, **29:** 49; Dec. 23, 1913, **29:** 66; May 20, 1914, **30:** 50; May 26, 1914 (2), **30:** 84; Sept. 2, 1914, **30:** 467; Sept. 3, 1914, **30:** 471; Oct. 29, 1914 (2), **31:** 249, 252; Nov. 6, 1914 (2), **31:** 271, 272; Nov. 7, 1914, **31:** 276; Nov. 16, 1914, **31:** 321; Nov. 17, 1914, **31:** 328; Nov. 28, 1914, **31:** 360; Feb. 12, 1915, **32:** 226; Aug. 21, 1915 (2), **34:** 274, 275; Aug. 23, 1915, **34:** 294; Sept. 22, 1915, **34:** 503; Oct. 6, 1915, **35:** 31; Dec. 9, 1915, **35:** 318; Dec. 10, 1915, **35:** 338; Dec. 11, 1915, **35:** 345; Jan. 10, 1916, **35:** 459; Jan. 14, 1916 (2), **35:** 475; June 10, 1916, **37:** 186; Sept. 7, 1916, **38:** 158; Sept. 21, 1916, **38:** 195; Sept. 24, 1916, **38:** 260; Oct. 4, 1916, **38:** 335; Oct. 6, 1916, **38:** 354; Oct. 11, 1916 (2), **38:** 393, 394; Oct. 13, 1916, **38:** 428; Oct. 16, 1916, **38:** 454

Charles Williston McAlpin, Oct. 24, 1916, **38:** 521

William Frank McCombs, March 13, 1914, **29:** 342; April 4, 1914, **29:** 404; April 11, 1914, **29:** 422; April 13, 1916, **36:** 480; April 20, 1916, **36:** 543; Sept. 21, 1916, **38:** 201

Cyrus McCormick, Jr., July 12, 1914, **30:** 278

Vance Criswell McCormick, Aug. 2, 1916, **37:** 513; Sept. 12, 1916, **38:** 170; Sept. 28, 1916, **38:** 283

Charles Stedman Macfarland, Nov. 6, 1916, **38:** 619

Alexander Jeffrey McKelway, Feb. 11, 1913, **27:** 108; May 17, 1916, **37:** 65; July 17, 1916, **37:** 429; July 20, 1916, **37:** 447; Sept. 28, 1916, **38:** 284

John Lowndes McLaurin, Aug. 5, 1915, **34:** 99; Sept. 1, 1915, **34:** 400

Benton McMillin, Nov. 15, 1916, **38:** 653

James Clark McReynolds, Feb. 25, 1913, **27:** 136; Sept. 2, 1914, **30:** 469

Dudley Field Malone, Jan. 18, 1915, **32:** 86; Dec. 16, 1915, **35:** 363; Jan. 10, 1916, **35:** 460; June 1, 1916, **37:** 143; June 2, 1916, **37:** 155; June 7, 1916, **37:** 167; July 25, 1916, **37:** 475; Aug. 2, 1916, **37:** 513; Aug. 5, 1916, **37:** 533

Theodeore Marburg, Feb. 8, 1915, **32:** 198

Wilbur W. Marsh, July 31, 1916, **37:** 508

Thomas Riley Marshall, Aug. 2, 1916, **37:** 516; Sept. 22, 1916, **38:** 212; Nov. 9, 1916, **38:** 625

Anne Martin and Mabel Vernon, Aug. 11, 1916, **38:** 28

Royal Meeker, Jan. 1, 1913, **27:** 4; March 21, 1913, **27:** 204; March 3, 1916, **36:** 247

Charles W. Mills, Dec. 5, 1914, **31:** 406

John Purroy Mitchel, May 8, 1913, **27:** 409; Oct. 8, 1913, **28:** 374; Jan. 19, 1916, **35:** 503

John Knox Montgomery, Dec. 18, 1913, **29:** 44

John Bassett Moore, Oct. 16, 1913, **28:** 412; Feb. 2, 1914, **29:** 215

John Pierpont Morgan, Jr., Sept. 24, 1914, **31:** 82

Henry Morgenthau, March 23, 1916, **36:** 356; May 18, 1916, **37:** 72; June 2, 1916, **37:** 151

Robert Russa Moton, Nov. 16, 1914, **31:** 321

John R. Mott, Nov. 10, 1916, **38:** 631

Alfred Henry Mulliken, July 14, 1914, **30:** 283

Alfred Henry Mulliken and Elliot Hersey Goodwin, June 23, 1914, **30:** 205

Hugo Münsterberg, Nov. 7, 1914, **31:** 276; Nov. 19, 1914, **31:** 336

Henry Lee Myers, July 26, 1916, **37:** 480

Suggested planks by the National American Woman Suffrage Association for the Democratic platform, April 14, 1916, **36:** 484

Francis Griffith Newlands, Feb. 6, 1914, **29:** 227; March 5, 1914, **29:** 317; April 29, 1914, **29:** 535; June 27, 1914, **30:** 219; July 1, 1914, **30:** 242; July 6, 1914, **30:** 261; July 22, 1914, **30:** 295; Aug. 22, 1914, **30:** 433; Aug. 29, 1916, **38:** 102

Lucius William Nieman, Dec. 5, 1914, **31:** 406; Jan. 26, 1915, **32:** 133

Georgia Nugent, Aug. 9, 1916, **38:** 15

James Aloysius O'Gorman, April 1, 1913, **27:** 245
Jeremiah A. O'Leary, Sept. 29, 1916, **38:** 285
Richard Olney, May 4, 1914, **29:** 543; May 26, 1914, **30:** 85
William Church Osborn, March 29, 1914, **29:** 382; April 3, 1914,
    29: 402; April 10, 1916, **36:** 458
Sergio Osmeña, Aug. 30, 1916, **38:** 119
Robert Latham Owen, Sept. 9, 1913, **28:** 269; July 28, 1914, **30:**
    312; Nov. 1, 1915, **35:** 151; Nov. 13, 1915, **35:** 201; Jan. 5, 1916
    (2), **35:** 433; Jan. 7, 1916 (2), **35:** 447; Jan. 8, 1916, **35:** 456;
    Jan. 26, 1916, **35:** 530; Jan. 29, 1916, **36:** 51; June 2, 1916, **37:**
    151; June 3, 1916 (2), **37:** 161, 162; June 8, 1916, **37:** 174
Suggested plank for the Democratic platform by Robert Latham
    Owen, June 8, 1916, **37:** 174

Walter Hines Page, June 12, 1915, **33:** 387
Alexander Mitchell Palmer, Feb. 3, 1913, **27:** 97; Feb. 7, 1913,
    27: 103; Feb. 24, 1913, **27:** 132; June 14, 1916, **37:** 227
Adam Edward Patterson, July 30, 1913, **28:** 97
George Foster Peabody, Oct. 27, 1916, **38:** 549
Thomas Jones Pence, Jan. 23, 1915, **32:** 115; Sept. 15, 1915, **34:**
    471
William Phillips, Sept. 22, 1915, **34:** 504; Sept. 22, 1916, **38:** 209
Amos Richards Eno Pinchot, Jan. 27, 1916, **36:** 22
Gifford Pinchot, Jan. 29, 1916, **36:** 48
Frank Lyon Polk, June 17, 1916, **37:** 245; Aug. 9, 1916, **38:** 13
George Pope, Aug. 18, 1916, **38:** 46
Louis Freeland Post, Nov. 16, 1916, **38:** 665; Nov. 7, 1916, **38:**
    666
Edward William Pou, Feb. 9, 1915, **32:** 207; March 13, 1916, **36:**
    300; June 9, 1916, **37:** 181; June 12, 1916, **37:** 209
William Frank Powell, Aug. 25, 1913, **28:** 221
Ralph Pulitzer, May 29, 1913, **27:** 487; Oct. 10, 1913, **28:** 385;
    Nov. 13, 1914, **31:** 314

Manuel Luis Quezon, Nov. 18, 1916, **38:** 675

James Willard Ragsdale, Aug. 6, 1913, **28:** 123
Samuel Moffett Ralston, March 27, 1913, **27:** 233
Samuel Rea, April 17, 1913, **27:** 322
William Cox Redfield, Feb. 28, 1913, **27:** 139; Dec. 18, 1913, **29:**
    40, April 15, 1914, **29:** 443; April 18, 1914, **29:** 461; May 5,
    1914, **29:** 544; Sept. 18, 1914, **31:** 45; Oct. 3, 1914, **31:** 124; July
    12, 1915, **33:** 497; Aug. 3, 1915, **34:** 71; Dec. 22, 1915, **35:** 383;
    Jan. 4, 1916, **35:** 427; Feb. 3, 1916, **36:** 127; March 23, 1916,
    36: 357; April 3, 1916, **36:** 406; June 3, 1916, **37:** 160; June 12,
    1916, **37:** 211; Aug. 29, 1916, **38:** 105

A memorandum by William Cox Redfield on a foreign trade plank for the Democratic platform, June 3, 1916, **37**: 160

James Alexander Reed, June 11, 1913, **27**: 508; Sept. 4, 1913, **28**: 253

Paul Samuel Reinsch, Nov. 11, 1916, **38**: 631

Robert Goodwyn Rhett, Aug. 22, 1916, **38**: 75

Joseph Taylor Robinson, April 17, 1914, **29**: 457; April 22, 1914, **29**: 486

John Davison Rockefeller, April 25, 1914, **29**: 504; April 26, 1914, **29**: 512

John Davison Rockefeller, Jr., April 27, 1914, **29**: 513; Sept. 22, 1914, **31**: 77

Jennie Bradley Roessing, April 14, 1916, **36**: 484

Franklin Delano Roosevelt, March 31, 1914, **29**: 390

Alfred Thomas Rogers, Feb. 6, 1916, **36**: 136

Benjamin Jefferson Rosenthal, Aug. 21, 1916, **38**: 60

Julius Rosenwald, Nov. 13, 1914, **31**: 314

George Rublee, Aug. 1, 1916, **37**: 512; Aug. 7, 1916, **38**: 4

Juliet Barrett Rublee, May 27, 1914, **30**: 93

Wilber Fisk Sadler, Jr., Oct. 30, 1915, **35**: 138; March 11, 1916, **36**: 292

Willard Saulsbury, Aug. 14, 1914, **30**: 380; Sept. 14, 1914, **31**: 32; Feb. 17, 1916, **36**: 191; Sept. 8, 1916, **38**: 164

Jacob Henry Schiff, Jan. 15, 1915, **32**: 77; Aug. 29, 1916, **38**: 104

Hugh Lenox Scott, Feb. 11, 1916, **36**: 171; Feb. 18, 1916, **36**: 197

Henry Rogers Seager and others, Nov. 9, 1915, **35**: 184

Anna Howard Shaw, Oct. 6, 1915, **35**: 30

Morris Sheppard, Sept. 6, 1913, **28**: 259; Oct. 29, 1914, **31**: 248

John Knight Shields, March 5, 1914, **29**: 317; May 10, 1916, **37**: 12

Benjamin Franklin Shively, Oct. 18, 1913, **28**: 415

Furnifold McLendel Simmons, Sept. 2, 1913, **28**: 247; Sept 4, 1913, **28**: 253; Sept. 5, 1913, **28**: 258

Joel Byron Slocum and Charles Matthias Reed, Feb. 7-8, 1916, **36**: 139

Thetus Willrette Sims, Feb. 27, 1914, **29**: 298

John Humphrey Small, Aug. 2, 1916, **37**: 513

Marcus Aurelius Smith, April 1, 1914, **29**: 392

Rudolph Spreckles, Aug. 21, 1916, **38**: 61

William Spry, Nov. 18, 1915, **35**: 213

Augustus Owsley Stanley, Dec. 9, 1913, **29**: 25

Dan Voorhees Stephens, Sept. 30, 1913, **28**: 346

Warren Sanford Stone and others, Aug. 18, 1916, **38**: 47

William Joel Stone, Oct. 8, 1913, **28**: 374; Dec. 20, 1913, **29**: 48; Dec. 23, 1913, **29**: 66; Dec. 12, 1914, **31**: 457; Dec. 18, 1914, **31**: 487; Jan. 27, 1915, **32**: 139; Feb. 24, 1915, **32**: 286; Feb. 25, 1915, **32**: 289; Dec. 13, 1915, **35**: 352; Feb. 24, 1916, **36**: 209;

Feb. 28, 1916, **36:** 225; March 6, 1916, **36:** 258; March 15, 1916, **36:** 319; March 22, 1916, **36:** 355; April 17, 1916, **36:** 500; April 20, 1916, **36:** 517; May 15, 1916, **37:** 56; July 8, 1916, **37:** 382; July 10, 1916, **37:** 397; Oct. 28, 1916, **38:** 559

Moorfield Storey, Aug. 21, 1913, **28:** 203

Moorfield Storey and others, Aug. 15, 1913, **28:** 163; Jan. 6, 1914, **29:** 105

Jerry Bartholomew Sullivan, Sept. 15, 1916, **38:** 174

William Sulzer, July 15, 1913, **28:** 35; July 22, 1913, **28:** 64

Hatton William Sumners, July 31, 1915, **34:** 53

Edwin Forrest Sweet, July 26, 1915, **34:** 27

Herbert Bayard Swope, July 3, 1916, **37:** 352

William Howard Taft, Nov. 14, 1916, **38:** 644

Ida Minerva Tarbell, Oct. 2, 1916, **38:** 322

Robert Herberton Terrell, Oct. 20, 1914, **31:** 192

A memorandum for the President on woman suffrage by Charles Spalding Thomas, Aug. 7, 1916, **38:** 4

Henry Burling Thompson, May 26, 1913, **27:** 475

Mary Wilson Thompson, July 30, 1916, **37:** 502

Samuel Huston Thompson, Jr., Sept. 20, 1916, **38:** 192

John Randolph Thornton, Feb. 21, 1914, **29:** 275; Feb. 25, 1914, **29:** 288; June 29, 1914, **30:** 225; Feb. 12, 1915, **32:** 227

Benjamin Ryan Tillman, Jan. 5, 1916, **35:** 434; Jan. 8, 1916, **35:** 456; Feb. 14, 1916, **36:** 173; March 9, 1916, **36:** 278; March 29, 1916, **36:** 376; May 17, 1916, **37:** 66; June 23, 1916, **37:** 288

Martin Travieso, Jr., Nov. 11, 1916, **38:** 633

Address to the President by William Monroe Trotter, Nov. 6, 1913, **28:** 491

Address to the President by William Monroe Trotter, Nov. 12, 1914, **31:** 298

Joseph Patrick Tumulty, July 28, 1913, **28:** 90; Sept. 2, 1913, **28:** 247; Nov. 6, 1913, **28:** 501; Jan. 6, 1914, **29:** 101; Jan. 24, 1914, **29:** 170; April 26, 1914, **29:** 511; June 12, 1914, **30:** 174; June 22, 1914, **30:** 202; Oct. 9, 1914, **31:** 138; Nov. 12, 1914, **31:** 310; Dec. 4, 1914, **31:** 388; Jan. 15, 1915, **32:** 78; Jan. 21, 1915, **32:** 95; Feb. 20, 1915, **32:** 265; Feb. 26, 1915, **32:** 293; April 24, 1915, **33:** 68; July 31, 1915, **34:** 52; Aug. 6, 1915, **34:** 116; Oct. 25, 1915, **35:** 107; Oct. 29, 1915, **35:** 135; Nov. 1, 1915, **35:** 149; Nov. 19, 1915, **35:** 221; Nov. 25, 1915, **35:** 253; Nov. 29, 1915, **35:** 265; Jan. 15, 1916, **35:** 478; Jan. 17, 1916, **35:** 492; Jan. 25, 1916, **35:** 524; Feb. 9, 1916, **36:** 145; Feb. 24, 1916, **36:** 211; March 17, 1916, **36:** 333; April 30, 1916, **36:** 569; May 12, 1916, **37:** 27; May 17, 1916, **37:** 67; June 13, 1916, **37:** 217; July 7, 1916, **37:** 375; July 18, 1916, **37:** 434; July 27, 1916 (2), **37:** 490, 491; Aug. 10, 1916, **38:** 20; Aug. 22, 1916, **38:** 66; Aug. 25, 1916, **38:** 83; Oct. 23, 1916, **38:** 513; Nov. 18, 1916, **38:** 674

A memorandum by Joseph Patrick Tumulty on a speech by Elihu

Root to New York Republicans, Feb. 16, 1916, **36:** 186
Frank Trumbull, Sept. 11, 1914, **31:** 26; Jan. 29, 1915, **32:** 162

Oscar Wilder Underwood, Jan. 13, 1913, **27:** 44; Feb. 20, 1913, **27:** 123; March 17, 1913, **27:** 192; April 17, 1913, **27:** 322; April 22, 1913, **27:** 347; Jan. 24, 1914, **29:** 170; Dec. 16, 1914, **31:** 473; Jan. 18, 1915, **32:** 85; Feb. 8, 1915, **32:** 197

Frank Arthur Vanderlip, Oct. 23, 1913, **28:** 428
Henry van Dyke, Sept. 6, 1916, **38:** 210
La Vanguardia, Nov. 11, 1916, **38:** 632
Charles Richard Van Hise, July 9, 1914, **30:** 272
Wilhelmina Caroline Ginger Van Winkle, July 16, 1916, **37:** 426
Jaime Carlos de Veyra, Nov. 11, 1916, **38:** 632
Walker Whiting Vick, Dec. 11, 1914, **31:** 453
Oswald Garrison Villard, July 21, 1913, **28:** 60; Aug. 18, 1913, **28:** 185; Aug. 27, 1913, **28:** 239; Sept 18, 1913, **28:** 289; Sept. 29, 1913, **28:** 342; Oct. 14, 1913, **28:** 401; March 5, 1914, **29:** 319; Dec. 16, 1914, **31:** 475; Oct. 30, 1915, **35:** 141

Festus John Wade, Oct. 25, 1913, **28:** 444
Robert Ferdinand Wagner, April 23, 1916, **36:** 530
Lillian D. Wald, April 21, 1916, **36:** 524
David Ignatius Walsh, Oct. 26, 1914, **31:** 237
Francis Patrick Walsh, June 20, 1913, **27:** 553
Thomas James Walsh, March 14, 1916, **36:** 311; March 16, 1916, **36:** 324; June 20, 1916, **37:** 269; Aug. 18, 1916, **38:** 46; Oct. 9, 1916, **38:** 376
Alexander Walters, Jan. 8, 1913, **27:** 19; Jan. 10, 1916, **35:** 461
Paul Moritz Warburg, Aug. 14, 1916, **38:** 32
Robert Lewis Waring, May 26, 1914, **30:** 491; April 12, 1915, **32:** 515
Booker Taliaferro Washington, Feb. 25, 1914, **29:** 290
Jesse Floyd Welborn, Nov. 10, 1913, **28:** 518; Sept. 18, 1914 (2), **31:** 48; Sept. 23, 1914, **31:** 78
Harry Andrew Wheeler, July 29, 1916, **37:** 504
John Philip White, April 21, 1914, **29:** 479; May 18, 1914, **30:** 46
John Philip White and others, Sept. 14, 1914, **31:** 31; Sept. 29, 1914, **31:** 99
White House staff, May 1, 1914, **29:** 540; June 10, 1914, **30:** 166; Jan. 5, 1915, **32:** 20; Feb. 27, 1915, **32:** 294; Aug. 20, 1915, **34:** 267; Aug. 19, 1916, **38:** 52
Brand Whitlock, Feb. 28, 1916, **36:** 230
Charles Richard Williams, Nov. 10, 1916, **38:** 629
John Sharp Williams, Nov. 17, 1913, **28:** 560; March 31, 1914, **29:** 387; April 23, 1914, **29:** 495; April 24, 1914, **29:** 500; Jan. 27, 1916, **36:** 20; March 2, 1916, **36:** 240
Wayne Cullen Williams, Oct. 24, 1916, **38:** 520

James Franklin Williamson, Sept. 23, 1916, **38:** 239
William Bauchop Wilson, Oct. 23, 1913, **28:** 426; Nov. 30, 1913, **28:** 599; Dec. 4, 1913, **29:** 14; Dec. 10, 1913, **29:** 31; May 11, 1914, **30:** 16; July 13, 1914, **30:** 282; Oct. 7, 1914, **31:** 131; April 25, 1916, **36:** 549; Aug. 5, 1916, **37:** 530; Oct. 16, 1916, **38:** 457
Stephen Samuel Wise, Nov. 12, 1915, **35:** 194
Robert N. Wood, Aug. 5, 1913, **28:** 115
Samuel Baker Woods, Jan. 16, 1913, **27:** 73

Arthur Yager, Dec. 12, 1914, **31:** 465

Diplomatic notes, messages, memoranda, and aide-mémoire

By Wilson and from Wilson to
Circular notes to the powers, April 1, 1913, **27:** 250; Aug. 8, 1913, **28:** 130; Nov. 7, 1913, **28:** 504; drafts, Oct. 24, 1913, **28:** 431; Nov. 7, 1913, **28:** 502; outline, Oct. 24, 1913, **28:** 434
Draft of a statement to the government of Colombia, Sept. 29, 1913, **28:** 342
Message to the British government concerning events in Mexico City, May 9, 1914, **30:** 9
Special commissioners, May 21, 1914 (2), **30:** 56, 58; May 24, 1914 (2), **30:** 69 (draft), 70; May 26, 1914, **30:** 83; May 27, 1914, **30:** 91; May 29, 1914 (2) **30:** 99, 100; May 31, 1914, **30:** 120; June 2, 1914, **30:** 135; June 3, 1914, **30:** 137; June 30, 1914, **30:** 228
Francis Joseph I, June 28, 1914, **30:** 222
Presidents of Argentina, Brazil, and Chile, July 7, 1914, **30:** 262
Message for the Constitutionalists, July 16, 1914, **30:** 285
Francisco Villa, July 20, 1914, **30:** 290
Venustiano Carranza, July 20, 1914, **30:** 290
José Manuel Cardoso de Oliveira representing American interests in Mexico, July 20, 1914, **30:** 291; March 6, 1915, **32:** 331
Venustiano Carranza and Francisco Villa, July 23, 1914, **30:** 297
Various Dominican leaders, July 27, 1914, **30:** 307
Venustiano Carranza, July 31, 1914, **30:** 321; March 11, 1915, **32:** 363; March 13, 1915, **32:** 369
Francisco Villa, Aug. 25, 1914, **30:** 450; Aug. 9, 1914, **30:** 494
Paul Fuller, Aug. 26, 1914, **30:** 494
Venustiano Carranza, Aug. 26, 1914, **30:** 495
William II, Sept. 15, 1914, **31:** 32 (draft)
Reply to the German government's note regarding control of customs in Haiti, Sept. 16, 1914, **31:** 34
Raymond Poincaré, Sept. 19, 1914, **31:** 54; Dec. 7, 1914, **31:** 410
James Watson Gerard, Oct. 19, 1914, **31:** 181; Feb. 10, 1915, **32:** 207; Feb. 19, 1915, **32:** 260
Message for the Russian government, Oct. 19, 1914, **31:** 187
Message to the British government regarding the Declaration of London and proposed Order in Council, Oct. 16, 1914, **31:** 163; Oct. 21, 1914, **31:** 198

Venustiano Carranza and Eulalio Gutiérrez, Nov. 13, 1914, **31:** 313

Draft of a Pan-American pact, Dec. 16, 1914, **31:** 471; Jan. 29, 1915, **32:** 159; May 3, 1916, **36:** 595

Drafts of messages to the British government protesting interference with neutral commerce, Dec. 16, 1914, **31:** 477; Dec. 24, 1914, **31:** 525; March 19, 1915, **32:** 399; March 28, 1915, **32:** 443

Message to the British government regarding the purchase and use of German ships in neutral trade, Jan. 20, 1915, **32:** 101

Draft of a note to the German government, Feb. 6, 1915, **32:** 194

Note to British and German governments concerning the war zone declaration and the use of neutral flags on merchant ships, Feb. 19, 1915, **32:** 260

Message to the British government regarding interference with neutral trade with Germany, March 2, 1915, **32:** 317

Nicholas II, March 18, 1915, **32:** 396

Draft of a reply to the German note on the exportation of arms to the Allies, April 19, 1915, **33:** 20

Draft of a note to Germany on the *Falaba* case, April 24, 1915, **33:** 73

Drafts of the first *Lusitania* note, May 11, 1915, **33:** 155; May 12, 1915, **33:** 174

Drafts of the second *Lusitania* note, June 3, 1915, **33:** 328; June 7, 1915, **33:** 355

Drafts of the third *Lusitania* note, July 19, 1915, **33:** 530; July 21, 1915, **33:** 545

Drafts of a reply to the Austro-Hungarian note regarding the exportation of arms to the Allies, Aug. 5, 1915, **34:** 92; Aug. 6, 1915, **34:** 115

Draft of a note to the Austro-Hungarian government on the recall of Constantin Theodor Dumba, Sept. 22, 1915, **34:** 503

Draft of a note verbale to the German government on the inauguration of submarine warfare against armed merchantmen, March 2, 1916, **36:** 245

Drafts of the first *Sussex* note to Germany, April 10, 1916, **36:** 452; April 12, 1916, **36:** 467, 491

Drafts of the second *Sussex* note to Germany, May 7, 1916, **36:** 649; May 8, 1916, **36:** 650

Benedict XV, May 15, 1916, **37:** 55

Note to the Mexican government justifying the presence of American troops in Mexico, June 18, 1916, **37:** 248

Note to the Mexican government on the Carrizal incident, June 25, 1916, **37:** 293

Note to the Mexican government on the settlement of the Mexican-American crisis, July 6, 1916, **37:** 368

Draft of a message to various heads of state, c. July 20, 1916, **37:** 445

Note to the British government protesting the blacklist, July 26, 1916, **37**: 476

Draft of a reply to the Mexican note proposing a conference to settle the Mexican-American crisis, July 27, 1916, **37**: 483

To Wilson from

The Japanese government on the desire for amicable relations, June 3, 1913, **27**: 493

Paul Fuller, Aug. 20, 1914, **30**: 408

Francisco Villa, Aug. 18, 1914 (2), **30**: 444

William II, Sept. 7, 1914, **31**: 17

Raymond Poincaré, Sept. 10, 1914, **31**: 38; translation, 38

Sir Cecil Arthur Spring Rice, Sept. 19, 1914, **31**: 58

Venustiano Carranza, Sept. 7, 1914, **31**: 74; translation, 74; March 9, 1915, **32**: 346

Nicholas II, April 15, 1915, **32**: 525; Aug. 7, 1916, **37**: 538

The Austrian government on the *Ancona* incident, Dec. 15, 1915, **35**: 365

The Mexican government on the crossing of American troops into Mexico, March 19, 1916, **36**: 339

Benedict XV, May 15, 1916, **37**: 54

The Mexican government on the Carrizal incident, June 24, 1916, **37**: 292

The Mexican government on mediation of the Mexican-American crisis, July 4, 1916, **37**: 360; July 12, 1916, **37**: 410; July 19, 1916, **37**: 437; July 19, 1916, **37**: 438

Correspondence, reports, memoranda, and aide-mémoire about general diplomatic affairs

By Wilson and from Wilson to

William Charles Adamson, Feb. 18, 1914, **29**: 269; July 20, 1914, **30**: 289

Jane Addams, June 28, 1916, **37**: 316; Aug. 5, 1916, **37**: 527

List of American plotters and liars in Mexico, c. March 25, 1916, **36**: 364

Diplomatic representatives of Argentina, Brazil, and Chile, April 25, 1914, **29**: 507

Julean Herbert Arnold, May 23, 1913, **27**: 465

Newton Diehl Baker, March 31, 1916, **36**: 395; April 12, 1916, **36**: 463; July 4, 1916, **37**: 359; Oct. 25, 1916, **38**: 523; Oct. 30, 1916, **38**: 560

Warren Worth Bailey, July 14, 1915, **33**: 506

Emily Greene Balch, Aug. 2, 1915, **34**: 58; Aug. 28, 1915, **34**: 350

John Barrett, July 29, 1913, **28**: 95; Dec. 27, 1915, **35**: 395

Benjamin Franklin Battin, April 14, 1916, **36**: 482

William Jennings Bryan

1913

Jan. 16, 1913, **27**: 57; Feb. 14, 1913, **27**: 111; Feb. 21, 1913,

27: 124; March 20, 1913, **27:** 197; April 8, 1913, **27:** 272; April 29, 1913 (3), **27:** 362, 363; May 1, 1913, **27:** 372; May 2, 1913, **27:** 382; May 3, 1913, **27:** 395; May 28, 1913, **27:** 482; June 13, 1913, **27:** 515; June 17, 1913, **27:** 531; June 19, 1913, **27:** 552; June 21, 1913, **27:** 555; June 23, 1913, **27:** 557; June 25, 1913, **28:** 4; June 27, 1913, **28:** 10; July 1, 1913, **28:** 17; July 3, 1913 (2), **28:** 21, 22; Aug. 18, 1913, **28:** 184; Aug. 20, 1913, **28:** 197; Aug. 25, 1913, **28:** 220; Aug. 27, 1913, **28:** 232; Sept. 5, 1913, **28:** 257; Sept. 11, 1913, **28:** 274; Sept. 24, 1913, **28:** 320; Sept. 29, 1913 (2), **28:** 339, 342; Oct. 1, 1913, **28:** 347; Oct. 3, 1913, **28:** 354; Oct. 6, 1913, **28:** 365; Oct. 14, 1913, **28:** 401; Oct. 24, 1913, **28:** 433; Nov. 7, 1913 (2), **28:** 505, 506; Nov. 23, 1913, **28:** 585; Dec. 17, 1913, **29:** 36

1914

Jan. 15, 1914, **29:** 133; Jan. 19, 1914, **29:** 143; Jan. 19, 1914 (2), **29:** 146; Jan. 20, 1914, **29:** 152; Jan. 26, 1914, **29:** 171: Jan. 31, 1914, **29:** 206; Feb. 1, 1914, **29:** 210; Feb. 5, 1914, **29:** 221; Feb. 20, 1914, **29:** 274; March 12, 1914, **29:** 331; March 20, 1914, **29:** 360; March 30, 1914, **29:** 384; April 10, 1914, **29:** 421; April 13, 1914, **29:** 430; April 19, 1914, **29:** 466; May 12, 1914, **30:** 25; May 19, 1914, **30:** 47; June 5, 1914, **30:** 148; June 10, 1914, **30:** 164; June 11, 1914, **30:** 171; June 13, 1914, **30:** 175; June 16, 1914, **30:** 188; June 22, 1914, **30:** 200; June 25, 1914, **30:** 213; July 1, 1914, **30:** 241; July 7, 1914, **30:** 262; July 10, 1914, **30:** 273; July 13, 1914, **30:** 280; July 14, 1914, **30:** 283; July 23, 1914, **30:** 301; July 24, 1914, **30:** 303; Aug. 4, 1914, **30:** 342; Aug. 5, 1914, **30:** 346; Aug. 19, 1914, **30:** 402; Aug. 20, 1914, **30:** 404; Sept. 4, 1914, **30:** 478; Sept. 10, 1914, **31:** 19; Sept. 18, 1914, **31:** 43; Oct. 1, 1914 (3), **31:** 114; Oct. 2, 1914, **36:** 657; Nov. 13, 1914, **31:** 313; Dec. 3, 1914, **31:** 382; Dec. 26, 1914, **31:** 524; Dec. 26, 1914, **31:** 530; Dec. 29, 1914 (2), **31:** 545, 546

1915

Jan. 7, 1915, **32:** 25; Jan. 12, 1915, **32:** 60; Jan. 13, 1915, **32:** 62; Jan. 14, 1915 (2), **32:** 67, 68; Jan. 16, 1915, **32:** 80; Jan. 22, 1915, **32:** 100; Jan. 27, 1915 (2), **32:** 139; Jan. 28, 1915 (2), **32:** 146; Jan. 29, 1915, **32:** 159; Feb. 19, 1915 (3), **32:** 258, 259; Feb. 25, 1915, **32:** 287; Feb. 26, 1915, **32:** 291; March 4, 1915 (2), **32:** 316, 319; March 6, 1915, **32:** 331; March 8, 1915, **32:** 339; March 10, 1915 (3), **32:** 352, 353, 356; March 11, 1915 (2), **32:** 364, 365; March 12, 1915 (3), **32:** 367, 368; March 16, 1915 (4), **32:** 382, 391, 392; March 17, 1915, **32:** 393; March 18, 1915 (2), **32:** 395, 398; March 19, 1915, **32:** 399; March 21, 1915, **32:** 408; March 22, 1915, **32:** 414; March 24, 1915 (5), **32:** 424, 426, 427; March 25, 1915 (4), **32:** 431, 432, 433, 438; March 28, 1915, **32:** 451; March 29, 1915, **32:** 451; March 30, 1915, **32:** 457; March 31, 1915 (2), **32:** 458, 461; April 3, 1915 (4), **32:** 468, 469; April 5, 1915 (4), **32:** 477, 478, 479; April 6, 1915 (2), **32:** 487; April 8, 1915, **32:** 497; April 12, 1915 (2), **32:** 508; April

14, 1915, **32**: 520; April 16, 1915 (5), **32**: 527, 528, 529, 531; Feb. 8, 1915, **32**: 541; April 18, 1915, **33**: 12; April 19, 1915 (3), **33**: 20, 23, 28; April 21, 1915 (2), **33**: 51, 52; April 22, 1915 (2), **33**: 61, 62; April 26, 1915 (2), **33**: 68, 69; April 27, 1915 (4), **33**: 71, 80, 81; April 28, 1915 (2), **33**: 85; May 5, 1915 (2), **33**: 105, 108; May 6, 1915, **33**: 115; May 10, 1915 (3), **33**: 139, 140; May 11, 1915 (2), **33**: 154, 155; May 12, 1915 (2), **33**: 164, 174; May 13, 1915 (6), **33**: 181, 183, 185, 187; May 14, 1915 (5), **33**: 191, 194, 195; May 20, 1915 (4), **33**: 223, 224; May 23, 1915 (2), **33**: 237, 239; May 27, 1915 (2), **33**: 264, 266; May 28, 1915, **33**: 278; June 2, 1915 (7), **33**: 302, 306, 308, 309, 314; June 4, 1915, **33**: 335; June 5, 1915, **33**: 343; June 7, 1915 (2), **33**: 349

James Viscount Bryce, March 22, 1913, **27**: 213; Nov. 21, 1913, **28**: 571

Albert Sidney Burleson, Jan. 5, 1916, **35**: 431

Charles Pope Caldwell, July 13, 1916, **37**: 413

George C. Carothers, April 21, 1914, **29**: 480; April 24, 1914, **29**: 498

Venustiano Carranza, Jan. 19, 1914, **29**: 143

Memorandum urging Carranza to accept mediation, April 28, 1914, **29**: 525

Philip H. Chadbourn, Jan. 24, 1916, **35**: 520

Frank Irving Cobb, June 3, 1915, **33**: 320

Charles Richard Crane, Oct. 3, 1913, **28**: 353; May 21, 1914, **30**: 58; Aug. 4, 1914, **30**: 343

Charles Robert Crisp, March 31, 1914, **29**: 387

Baron Sutemi Chinda, May 14, 1913, **27**: 428; May 19, 1913, **27**: 453

Josephus Daniels, Aug. 11, 1913, **28**: 142; May 12, 1914, **30**: 27; Aug. 4, 1915, **34**: 81; Oct. 10, 1916, **38**: 386

Adolfo Díaz, Feb. 20, 1914, **29**: 275

Memorandum on the safeguarding of diplomatic correspondence, Feb. 8, 1915, **32**: 541

Cleveland Hoadley Dodge, March 10, 1913, **27**: 167; April 5, 1913, **27**: 263

Frank Ellsworth Doremus, April 1, 1913, **27**: 244

Draft of a joint resolution on Mexico, Oct. 31, 1913, **28**: 478

Maurice Francis Egan, June 10, 1913, **27**: 507

Wilhelm August Ferdinand Ekengren, Oct. 16, 1915, **35**: 73

Charles William Eliot, Jan. 20, 1913, **27**: 65; Jan. 30, 1913, **27**: 92; March 19, 1913, **27**: 194; May 4, 1914, **29**: 544; May 25, 1914, **30**: 73; Aug. 19, 1914, **30**: 403; Aug. 22, 1914, **30**: 432; Feb. 18, 1915, **32**: 244; Feb. 23, 1915, **32**: 275; May 20, 1915, **33**: 226; July 22, 1915, **34**: 11; July 30, 1915, **34**: 45; Jan. 18, 1916, **35**: 500; June 30, 1916, **37**: 336

Henry Burchard Fine, March 10, 1913, **27:** 167; March 11, 1913, **27:** 169; March 13, 1913, **27:** 175; April 11, 1913, **27:** 290
Henry Jones Ford, Jan. 23, 1914, **29:** 164
Rudolph Forster, July 21, 1913, **28:** 59; June 28, 1915, **33:** 456
John Fox, April 12, 1916, **36:** 465; April 16, 1916, **36:** 488
Harry Freidenwald, Dec. 31, 1915, **35:** 412

Domicio da Gama, Dec. 27, 1915, **35:** 396
Domicio da Gama and others, April 25, 1914, **29:** 506
Harry Augustus Garfield, April 24, 1914, **29:** 499; April 27, 1914, **29:** 512; March 7, 1916, **36:** 264; April 27, 1916, **36:** 562
Lindley Miller Garrison, Feb. 18, 1914, **29:** 269; Feb. 24, 1914, **29:** 284; May 13, 1914, **30:** 28; June 4, 1914, **30:** 144; June 29, 1914, **30:** 225; July 2, 1914, **30:** 245; Aug. 8, 1914, **30:** 362; Sept. 15, 1914, **31:** 33; Dec. 1, 1914, **31:** 375; Feb. 24, 1915, **32:** 285
James Watson Gerard, May 23, 1915, **33:** 238
James Cardinal Gibbons, Aug. 21, 1914, **30:** 424; May 15, 1916, **37:** 56
Franklin Potts Glass, May 13, 1914, **30:** 28
Samuel Gompers, Aug. 11, 1915, **34:** 164; Sept. 24, 1915, **34:** 512; July 6, 1916, **37:** 369; July 19, 1916, **37:** 436; July 25, 1916, **37:** 470; July 28, 1916, **37:** 494
William Elliott Gonzales, June 17, 1913, **27:** 531
Charles Henry Grasty, March 5, 1914, **29:** 311; Jan. 5, 1916, **35:** 432
Sir Edward Grey, April 6, 1916, **36:** 421; May 24, 1916, **37:** 102
Benjamin Howell Griswold, June 7, 1915, **33:** 350
George Wilkins Guthrie, April 29, 1913, **27:** 364; March 25, 1915, **32:** 435

Matthew Hale, Sept. 14, 1916, **38:** 171
William Bayard Hale, April 19, 1913, **27:** 335; Oct. 24, 1913, **28:** 431; Nov. 11, 1913, **28:** 525; Nov. 16, 1913, **28:** 557; Dec. 19, 1914, **31:** 496
Thomas William Hardwick, May 9, 1915, **33:** 134
Francis Burton Harrison, March 6, 1915, **32:** 330
Albert Bushnell Hart, May 21, 1915, **33:** 229
Jacob Henry Hollander, March 24, 1913, **27:** 219; April 8, 1913, **27:** 272
Hamilton Holt, June 7, 1916, **37:** 166
Edward Mandell House
1914
June 22, 1914, **30:** 201; June 26, 1914, **30:** 214; Aug. 4, 1914, **30:** 342; Aug. 5, 1914, **30:** 345; Aug. 6, 1914, **30:** 352; Aug. 25, 1914, **30:** 450; Sept. 8, 1914, **31:** 10; Sept. 19, 1914, **31:** 55; Oct. 23, 1914, **31:** 214; Oct. 29, 1914, **31:** 246
1915
Jan. 5, 1915, **32:** 17; Jan. 16, 1915, **32:** 81; Jan. 17, 1915,

32: 83; Jan. 18, 1915, **32**: 84; Jan. 28, 1915, **32**: 144; Jan. 29, 1915, **32**: 157; Feb. 13, 1915, **32**: 230; Feb. 15, 1915, **32**: 234; Feb. 20, 1915, **32**: 265; Feb. 22, 1915, **32**: 268; Feb. 25, 1915, **32**: 287; March 1, 1915, **32**: 300; March 12, 1915, **32**: 366; March 18, 1915, **32**: 396; March 22, 1915, **32**: 409; April 1, 1915, **32**: 462; April 15, 1915, **32**: 523; April 19, 1915, **33**: 16; April 22, 1915, **33**: 62; May 3, 1915, **33**: 93; May 5, 1915, **33**: 105; May 16, 1915, **33**: 205; May 18, 1915, **33**: 217; May 20, 1915, **33**: 223; May 23, 1915, **33**: 239; May 26, 1915, **33**: 257; July 3, 1915 (2), **33**: 469, 470; July 7, 1915, **33**: 479; July 14, 1915 (2), **33**: 505, 506; July 19, 1915, **33**: 526; July 21, 1915, **34**: 5; July 27, 1915, **34**: 31; July 27, 1915, **34**: 32; July 30, 1915, **34**: 44; Aug. 4, 1915, **34**: 79; Aug. 4, 1915, **34**: 80; Aug. 5, 1915, **34**: 98; Aug. 7, 1915, **34**: 121; Aug. 21, 1915, **34**: 271; Aug. 25, 1915, **34**: 315; Aug. 31, 1915, **34**: 381; Sept. 7, 1915, **34**: 425; Sept. 20, 1915, **34**: 493; Sept. 27, 1915, **34**: 527; Sept. 29, 1915, **34**: 537; Oct. 18, 1915, **35**: 80; Oct. 18, 1915 (2), **35**: 82; Nov. 11, 1915, **35**: 187; Nov. 12, 1915, **35**: 192; Dec. 17, 1915, **35**: 364; Dec. 24, 1915, **35**: 387
1916
Jan. 9, 1916, **35**: 457; Jan. 11, 1916, **35**: 462; Feb. 12, 1916, **36**: 173; Feb. 16, 1916, **36**: 185; Feb. 23, 1916, **36**: 205; March 20, 1916, **36**: 340; April 21, 1916, **36**: 520; April 29, 1916, **36**: 567; May 5, 1916, **36**: 608; May 8, 1916, **36**: 652; May 9, 1916, **37**: 3; May 12, 1916, **37**: 24; May 16, 1916, **37**: 57; May 18, 1916 (2), **37**: 68; May 22, 1916, **37**: 92; June 22, 1916, **37**: 280; July 23, 1916, **37**: 466; July 27, 1916, **37**: 480; Oct. 10, 1916, **38**: 388

Frederic Clemson Howe, June 30, 1916, **37**: 336; Aug. 7, 1916, **37**: 537

Victoriano Huerta, March 7, 1913, **27**: 158

Paul Oscar Husting, March 2, 1916, **36**: 239

Edward Corbin Jenkins, March 17, 1913, **27**: 190

Hiram Warren Johnson, April 10, 1913, **27**: 282; April 18, 1913, **27**: 326; April 22, 1913, **27**: 343; April 23, 1913, **27**: 351; April 30, 1913, **27**: 366; May 6, 1913, **27**: 404; May 11, 1913, **27**: 412

Memorandum regarding the policy of the American members of the Joint Commission, c. Oct. 8, 1916, **38**: 373

Thomas Davies Jones, March 22, 1913, **27**: 214; March 24, 1913, **27**: 219

William Atkinson Jones, June 8, 1914, **30**: 160; June 11, 1914, **30**: 172; June 25, 1914, **30**: 213

David Starr Jordan, April 21, 1913, **27**: 342

Francis Clement Kelley, March 17, 1915 (draft), **32**: 393; March 18, 1915, **32**: 398

William Kent, April 10, 1913, **27:** 283; April 27, 1914, **29:** 512; June 30, 1914, **30:** 230; March 15, 1916, **36:** 317; April 25, 1916, **36:** 546

Joseph Rucker Lamar and Frederick William Lehmann, May 15, 1914, **30:** 32
Franklin Knight Lane, Aug. 3, 1914, **30:** 336; Sept. 7, 1915, **34:** 427; Sept. 17, 1915, **34:** 481; July 7, 1916, **37:** 375
Franklin Knight Lane and others, Sept. 7, 1916, **38:** 155
Robert Lansing
1914
Aug. 22, 1914, **30:** 431; Aug. 25, 1914, **30:** 451; Sept. 17, 1914 (2), **31:** 38, 39; Sept. 26, 1914, **31:** 84; Sept. 28, 1914, **31:** 89; Oct. 15, 1914, **31:** 154; Oct. 20, 1914, **31:** 187; Oct. 21, 1914, **31:** 198; Oct. 22, 1914, **31:** 209; Nov. 23, 1914, **31:** 345; Nov. 30, 1914, **31:** 369; Dec. 1, 1914, **31:** 376; Dec. 10, 1914, **31:** 447; Dec. 14, 1914, **31:** 460
Jan.–June 1915
Jan. 29, 1915, **32:** 161; Feb. 11, 1915 (2), **32:** 216; March 28, 1915, **32:** 443; May 20, 1915, **33:** 224; June 7, 1915, **33:** 349; June 14, 1915, **33:** 394; June 15, 1915, **33:** 400; June 16, 1915, **33:** 405; June 17, 1915 (2), **33:** 414; June 18, 1915, **33:** 419; June 22, 1915, **33:** 437
July–Dec. 1915
July 2, 1915 (5), **33:** 465, 466, 467; July 5, 1915, **33:** 474; July 7, 1915 (2), **33:** 479, 481; July 8, 1915, **33:** 487; July 9, 1915, **33:** 490; July 13, 1915, **33:** 499; July 14, 1915, **33:** 505; July 21, 1915, **33:** 545; July 23, 1915, **34:** 15; July 27, 1915 (2), **34:** 30; July 29, 1915 (2), **34:** 41, 43; July 31, 1915, **34:** 46; Aug. 1, 1915, **34:** 54; Aug. 2, 1915 (3), **34:** 55, 56; Aug. 4, 1915, **34:** 78; Aug. 5, 1915, **34:** 92; Aug. 6, 1915, **34:** 105; Aug. 8, 1915, **34:** 132; Aug. 9, 1915 (3), **34:** 142, 144; Aug. 11, 1915, **34:** 164; Aug. 13, 1915, **34:** 183; Aug. 16, 1915, **34:** 216; Aug. 19, 1915, **34:** 247; Aug. 21, 1915, **34:** 271; Aug. 26, 1915 (2), **34:** 329; Aug. 27, 1915 (2), **34:** 340, 341; Aug. 31, 1915 (3), **34:** 382, 385, 388; Sept. 1, 1915, **34:** 399; Sept. 3, 1915, **34:** 408; Sept. 7, 1915 (2), **34:** 425, 427; Sept. 8, 1915 (2), **34:** 432; Sept 10, 1915 (2), **34:** 438; Sept. 11, 1915 (2), **34:** 447, 448; Sept. 13, 1915 (2), **34:** 460; Sept. 15, 1915, **34:** 471; Sept 22, 1915, **34:** 503; Sept. 27, 1915, **34:** 527; Sept. 30, 1915, **34:** 539; Oct. 21, 1915, **35:** 91; Oct. 25, 1915, **35:** 107; Oct. 27, 1915, **35:** 113; Oct. 31, 1915 (2), **35:** 143, 144; Nov. 1, 1915, **35:** 149; Nov. 13, 1915, **35:** 201; Nov. 17, 1915 (2), **35:** 207, 208; Nov. 21, 1915, **35:** 233; Nov. 24, 1915 (2), **35:** 244; Nov. 29, 1915; **35:** 265; Dec. 2, 1915, **35:** 281; Dec. 5, 1915 (6), **35:** 286, 289, 290, 291; Dec. 18, 1915 (3), **35:** 368, 369; Dec. 24, 1915 (2), **35:** 388, 389; Dec. 26, 1915, **35:** 391; Dec. 27, 1915, **35:** 394; Dec. 29, 1915 (3), **35:** 406, 407; Dec. 31, 1915 (2), **35:** 411

1916

Jan. 2, 1916, **35:** 420; Jan. 7, 1916, **35:** 447; Jan. 10, 1916 (2), **35:** 457; Jan. 17, 1916 (2), **35:** 491, 498; Jan. 19, 1916, **35:** 501; Jan. 24, 1916 (2), **35:** 516, 519; Jan. 25, 1916, **35:** 523; Feb. 2, 1916, **36:** 110; Feb. 3, 1916, **36:** 122; Feb. 4, 1916, **36:** 129; Feb. 16, 1916, **36:** 184; March 1, 1916 (2), **36:** 233, 237; March 2, 1916, **36:** 239; March 8, 1916 (2), **36:** 273; March 13, 1916, **36:** 298; March 30, 1916 (3), **36:** 381, 382, 384; April 3, 1916, **36:** 402; April 7, 1916 (3), **36:** 427, 428; April 12, 1916, **36:** 464; April 17, 1916 (4), **36:** 490, 496, 497; April 23, 1916, **36:** 529; April 24, 1916, **36:** 534; May 8, 1916, **36:** 650; May 12, 1916, **37:** 24; May 15, 1916, **37:** 54; May 17, 1916, **37:** 61; May 22, 1916, **37:** 94; May 25, 1916, **37:** 108; June 18, 1916, **37:** 248; June 21, 1916 (5), **37:** 271, 273, 275, 277; July 6, 1916, **37:** 367; Sept. 29, 1916 (2), **38:** 294; Oct. 2, 1916, **38:** 319; Oct. 6, 1916, **38:** 352; Oct. 23, 1916, **38:** 512; Oct. 26, 1916, **38:** 544; Oct. 30, 1916, **38:** 560; Nov. 14, 1916, **38:** 640; Nov. 16, 1916, **38:** 661

Memorandum on various points to be included in the address to the League to Enforce Peace, May 24, 1916, **37:** 102

Marion Letcher, April 24, 1914, **29:** 497

Charles Herbert Levermore, March 28, 1916, **36:** 374

Li Yüan-Hung, June 7, 1916, **37:** 167

John Lind, June 11, 1913, **27:** 508; June 17, 1913, **27:** 531; Aug. 4, 1913, **28:** 110; Aug. 12, 1913, **28:** 145; Aug. 13, 1913, **28:** 148; Aug. 19, 1913, **28:** 191; Aug. 22, 1913, **28:** 207; Aug. 24, 1913, **28:** 219; Aug. 27, 1913, **28:** 239; Aug. 28, 1913 (2), **28:** 241; Oct. 1, 1913, **28:** 347; Oct. 9, 1913, **28:** 381; Oct. 10, 1913, **28:** 384; Oct. 10, 1913, **28:** 602; Jan. 28, 1914, **29:** 186

Henry Cabot Lodge, Feb. 19, 1914, **29:** 271

Boaz Walton Long, April 3, 1915, **32:** 470

Abbott Lawrence Lowell, July 5, 1915, **33:** 476

William Gibbs McAdoo, Nov. 3, 1914, **31:** 258; Nov. 9, 1914, **31:** 283; June 22, 1915, **33:** 438; Aug. 21, 1915, **34:** 272

Porter James McCumber, Jan. 29, 1914, **29:** 197; April 7, 1914, **29:** 409

William Calhoun McDonald, May 8, 1916, **36:** 653; May 17, 1916, **37:** 62; June 8, 1916, **37:** 170

Charles Stedman Macfarland, March 26, 1913, **27:** 231

Dudley Field Malone, Nov. 23, 1914, **31:** 345

William Luke Marbury, Feb. 5, 1914, **29:** 220

Draft of a resolution on the Mexican crisis, June 26, 1916, **37:** 304

Plan of action in the Mexican crisis, June 25, 1916, **37:** 293

Memorandum about a conversation with John Lind on Mexico, Jan. 8, 1914, **29:** 110

John Bassett Moore, Oct. 9, 1913, **28:** 381; Oct. 24, 1913, **28:** 433; Oct. 30, 1913, **28:** 474; Nov. 21, 1913, **28:** 571; Dec. 29, 1914, **29:** 86

John Pierpont Morgan, Jr., Aug. 22, 1914, **30**: 431; Sept. 4, 1914, **30**: 483
John R. Mott, Feb. 24, 1913, **27**: 131; March 13, 1913, **27**: 175; March 21, 1913, **27**: 202
James Mudge, April 21, 1914, **29**: 475

Byron Rufus Newton, June 9, 1916, **37**: 177

Richard Olney, March 8, 1913, **27**: 162; March 10, 1913, **27**: 167; March 11, 1913: **27**: 168; March 14, 1913, **27**: 177
Nelson O'Shaughnessy, Oct. 13, 1913, **28**: 399; Nov. 1, 1913, **28**: 482; Nov. 14, 1913, **28**: 539; April 14, 1914, **29**: 434; April 16, 1914, **29**: 449; April 17, 1914, **29**: 456; April 18, 1914, **29**: 460
Robert Latham Owen, April 20, 1914, **29**: 471; July 21, 1915, **34**: 6

Thomas Nelson Page, Jan. 28, 1915, **32**: 146; Sept. 10, 1915, **34**: 442; March 31, 1916, **36**: 395; April 3, 1916, **36**: 403
Walter Hines Page, Jan. 2, 1913, **27**: 6; March 28, 1913, **27**: 234; April 2, 1913, **27**: 254; Oct. 11, 1913 (2), **28**: 388; Oct. 29, 1913, **28**: 470; Nov. 9, 1913, **28**: 516; Nov. 12, 1913, **28**: 529; Nov. 13, 1913, **28**: 537; Nov. 19, 1913, **28**: 566; Dec. 6, 1913, **29**: 19; Jan. 6, 1914, **29**: 103; Jan. 29, 1914, **29**: 196; Feb. 24, 1914, **29**: 283; March 7, 1914, **29**: 321; March 25, 1914, **29**: 376; April 2, 1914, **29**: 396; May 18, 1914, **30**: 42; June 1, 1914, **30**: 130; June 4, 1914, **30**: 143; June 19, 1914, **30**: 195; July 28, 1914, **30**: 311; July 30, 1914, **30**: 320; Sept. 14, 1914, **31**: 29; Oct. 16, 1914 (2), **31**: 161, 166; Oct. 28, 1914, **31**: 242; Nov. 10, 1914, **31**: 294
John Clinton Parker, July 3, 1916, **37**: 347
James Duval Phelan, April 9, 1913, **27**: 277
William Phillips, Oct. 21, 1914, **31**: 197; Oct. 18, 1915, **35**: 83; Oct. 29, 1915, **35**: 127; Dec. 27, 1915, **35**: 397
Amos Richards Eno Pinchot, June 30, 1916, **37**: 336
Frank Lyon Polk, Sept. 22, 1915, **34**: 503; March 14, 1916, **36**: 307; March 21, 1916, **36**: 351; June 5, 1916, **37**: 162; July 13, 1916, **37**: 414; July 21, 1916, **37**: 453; July 27, 1916, **37**: 482; Aug. 10, 1916, **38**: 19

Manuel Castro Quesada, July 4, 1916, **37**: 358
Manuel Luis Quezon, March 12, 1915, **32**: 369

George Lawrence Record, June 1, 1914, **30**: 131
John Reed, June 17, 1914, **30**: 189
Paul Samuel Reinsch, Nov. 9, 1914, **31**: 289; Feb. 8, 1915, **32**: 196; July 31, 1915, **34**: 49
Junius Benjamin Remensnyder and others, April 21, 1914, **29**: 476

James Linn Rodgers, March 20, 1916, **36:** 343; June 25, 1916, **37:** 293
Juliet Barrett Rublee, June 2, 1915, **33:** 314

Louis de Sadeleer, Oct. 7, 1914, **31:** 131
Jacob Henry Schiff, Dec. 8, 1914, **31:** 425
Charles Ernest Scott, Jan. 10, 1914, **29:** 118
Hugh Lenox Scott, April 16, 1914, **29:** 450; April 26, 1916, **36:** 553; April 30, 1916, **36:** 571
Notes for a meeting with the Senate Foreign Relations Committee, Jan. 25, 1914, **29:** 170
Senate of the United States, Aug. 8, 1916, **38:** 10
Anne Ledell Seward, July 5, 1915, **33:** 473
Albert Shaw, March 17, 1914, **29:** 350
Morris Sheppard, July 28, 1915, **34:** 34
Furnifold McLendel Simmons, June 13, 1914, **30:** 176; July 8, 1915, **33:** 489
Thetus Willrette Sims, March 3, 1914, **29:** 304; June 17, 1914, **30:** 188
Marcus Aurelius Smith, March 30, 1914, **29:** 384
Sir Cecil Arthur Spring Rice, May 22, 1914, **30:** 82; Sept. 21, 1914, **31:** 64; Oct. 1, 1914, **31:** 115; Oct. 9, 1914, **31:** 138; Oct. 16, 1914, **31:** 166; Oct. 23, 1914, **31:** 214; Oct. 26, 1914, **31:** 235; Oct. 28, 1914, **31:** 243; Dec. 21, 1914, **31:** 502; Dec. 23, 1914, **31:** 514; May 2, 1916, **36:** 580
William Spry, Oct. 1, 1915, **35:** 3; Nov. 17, 1915, **35:** 210
William Joel Stone, Sept. 21, 1914, **31:** 64; Oct. 1, 1914, **31:** 115; Jan. 7, 1915, **32:** 26; March 28, 1916, **36:** 374
Pleasant Alexander Stovall, April 3, 1916, **36:** 403
Oscar Solomon Straus, May 5, 1915, **33:** 106
James Mark Sullivan, Dec. 6, 1914, **29:** 21

William Howard Taft, May 13, 1915, **33:** 184; April 14, 1916, **36:** 481
Thaddeus Austin Thomson, Feb. 18, 1915, **32:** 245
John Randolph Thornton, Feb. 23, 1914, **29:** 281; Feb. 27, 1914, **29:** 297
Benjamin Ryan Tillman, March 31, 1916, **36:** 396
Haigazann Hohannes Topakyan, Oct. 28, 1915, **35:** 119
Joseph Patrick Tumulty, Feb. 19, 1914, **29:** 271; June 29, 1914, **30:** 223; July 10, 1915, **33:** 490; July 11, 1915, **33:** 492; July 13, 1915, **33:** 498; Sept. 9, 1915, **34:** 434; March 25, 1916, **36:** 364; c. April 3, 1916, **36:** 409; May 2, 1916, **36:** 580; May 17, 1916, **37:** 62; c. May 19, 1916, **37:** 76; c. June 27, 1916, **37:** 314
Sir William Tyrrell, Nov. 22, 1913, **28:** 574

Henry van Dyke, June 5, 1913, **27:** 498; June 13, 1913, **27:** 515
Ambrose White Vernon, April 14, 1916, **36:** 483

Oswald Garrison Villard, April 24, 1914, **29:** 499; May 26, 1915, **33:** 257

Lillian D. Wald, July 3, 1915, **33:** 472
Duval West, Feb. 9, 1915, **32:** 203; Feb. 10, 1915, **32:** 210; April 12, 1915, **32:** 508
Henry White, Dec. 8, 1914, **31:** 425
White House Staff, Aug. 15, 1914, **30:** 383
Whom it may concern, Aug. 4, 1913, **28:** 109
William II, June 15, 1913, **27:** 521
John Sharp Williams, April 22, 1914, **29:** 482; Aug. 21, 1914, **30:** 424; July 8, 1915, **33:** 556
Henry Lane Wilson, May 15, 1913, **27:** 435; June 14, 1913, **27:** 518
Huntington Wilson, March 20, 1913, **27:** 198
William Bauchop Wilson, July 5, 1915, **33:** 473; June 19, 1916, **37:** 266; July 3, 1916, **37:** 346
Simon Wolf, April 7, 1916, **37:** 110; May 29, 1916, **37:** 119

Yoshihito, Nov. 15, 1916, **38:** 648

To Wilson from
William Charles Adamson, Feb. 16, 1914, **29:** 265; July 16, 1914, **30:** 286
Jane Addams, Aug. 2, 1916, **37:** 515
Jane Addams and others, June 27, 1916, **37:** 308
Alvey Augustus Adee, March 25, 1913, **27:** 224
Emilio Aguinaldo, May 23, 1913, **27:** 468
Eliseo Arredondo, June 2, 1915, **33:** 307

Warren Worth Bailey, July 12, 1915, **33:** 494
Newton Diehl Baker, March 10, 1916 (3), **36:** 280, 282, 284; March 12, 1916, **36:** 295; March 15, 1916, **36:** 313; March 16, 1916, **36:** 322; March 31, 1916, **36:** 397; April 4, 1916, **36:** 414; April 5, 1916 (2), **36:** 416; April 10, 1916, **36:** 456; April 20, 1916, **36:** 519; May 3, 1916 (2), **36:** 583, 584; May 4, 1916, **36:** 603; May 5, 1916, **36:** 618; May 13, 1916, **37:** 38; May 23, 1916, **37:** 97; May 29, 1916, **37:** 121; June 3, 1916, **37:** 156; June 18, 1916, **36:** 263; June 24, 1916, **37:** 291; June 26, 1916 (2), **37:** 296, 305; June 28, 1916, **37:** 316; July 1, 1916, **37:** 337; Aug. 30, 1916 (2), **38:** 119; Sept. 23, 1916, **38:** 219; Sept. 25, 1916, **38:** 271; Oct. 27, 1916, **38:** 546; Nov. 19, 1916, **38:** 675
Memorandum by Newton Diehl Baker on the objectives of the expeditionary force in Mexico, March 10, 1916, **36:** 286
Suggestions by Newton Diehl Baker for an address to Congress on the Mexican crisis, June 26, 1916, **37:** 297
James Whitford Bashford, Jan. 10, 1913, **27:** 27; March 12, 1915, **33:** 23

Benjamin Franklin Battin, Aug. 29, 1916, **38:** 104; Sept. 22, 1916, **38:** 207

Herman Bernstein, May 20, 1916, **37:** 84

Most Reverend Giovanni Bonzano, May 22, 1916, **37:** 95

Henry Skillman Breckinridge, Aug. 8, 1913, **28:** 130; Feb. 7, 1916, **36:** 139

William Jennings Bryan

January–June 1913

Jan. 3, 1913, **27:** 8; Jan. 5, 1913, **27:** 14; March 21, 1913, **27:** 202; March 23, 1913, **27:** 218; March 24, 1913, **27:** 220; April 15, 1913, **27:** 311; April 28, 1913 (2), **27:** 361; April 29, 1913 (2), **27:** 362, 364; April 30, 1913, **27:** 365; May 1, 1913, **27:** 372; May 2, 1913, **27:** 382; May 3, 1913, **27:** 396; May 18, 1913, **27:** 448; May 24, 1913, **27:** 470; May 26, 1913, **27:** 477; May 27, 1913, **27:** 481; June 2, 1913, **27:** 492; June 4, 1913, **27:** 494; June 12, 1913, **27:** 512; June 14, 1913, **27:** 518; June 16, 1913, **27:** 526; June 20, 1913, **27:** 553; June 21, 1913, **27:** 554; June 25, 1913, **28:** 4; June 30, 1913, **28:** 16

July–December 1913

July 1, 1913, **28:** 18; July 8, 1913, **28:** 26; July 20, 1913 (4), **28:** 47, 48, 49; July 26, 1913, **28:** 83; July 31, 1913, **28:** 100; Aug. 10, 1913, **28:** 136; Aug. 15, 1913, **28:** 162; Aug. 16, 1913 (2), **28:** 175; Aug. 18, 1913, **28:** 184; Aug. 19, 1913 (2), **28:** 192, 193; Aug. 20, 1913, **28:** 197; Aug. 22, 1913 (2), **28:** 205, 206; Aug. 23, 1913 (2), **28:** 216; Aug. 24, 1913, **28:** 218; Aug. 26, 1913 (2), **28:** 223, 224; Aug. 27, 1913, **28:** 231; Sept. 1, 1913, **28:** 246; Sept. 3, 1913, **28:** 250; Sept. 9, 1913, **28:** 268; Sept. 17, 1913 (2) **28:** 281, 282; Sept 19, 1913, **28:** 292; Sept. 25, 1913 (3), **28:** 324, 325, 326; Sept. 26, 1913, **28:** 329; Oct. 3, 1913 (2), **28:** 353, 354; Oct. 4, 1913 (2), **28:** 357, 358; Oct. 22, 1913, **28:** 422; Oct. 28, 1913, **28:** 455; Nov. 5, 1913 (2), **28:** 490, 491; Nov. 7, 1913, **28:** 505; Nov. 13, 1913, **28:** 533; Nov. 21, 1913, **28:** 572; Dec. 6, 1913, **29:** 20; Dec. 18, 1913, **29:** 39

January–June 1914

Jan. 14, 1914, **29:** 131; Jan. 15, 1914, **29:** 134; Jan. 17, 1914, **29:** 136; Jan. 19, 1914 (2), **29:** 142, 144; Jan. 23, 1914, **29:** 172; Jan. 29, 1914, **29:** 204; Feb. 11, 1914 (2), **29:** 244, 245; March 28, 1914, 381; April 10, 1914, **29:** 420; April 13, 1914 (2), **29:** 426, 429; April 19, 1914, **29:** 465; April 21, 1914, **29:** 476; May 14, 1914, **30:** 29; May 18, 1914, **30:** 45; May 19, 1914, **30:** 47; May 20, 1914, **30:** 49; May 30, 1914, **30:** 113; May 30, 1914, **30:** 118; May 31, 1914, **30:** 121; June 10, 1914 (2), **30:** 166, 170; June 12, 1914, **30:** 174; June 13, 1914, **30:** 180; June 23, 1914, **30:** 203

July–December 1914

Aug. 3, 1914 (2), **30:** 339, 340; Aug. 8, 1914, **30:** 362; Aug. 10, 1914, **30:** 372; Aug. 17, 1914, **30:** 390; Aug. 18, 1914, **30:** 396; Aug. 24, 1914, **30:** 443; Aug. 28, 1914 (2), **30:** 456, 457; Aug. 29, 1914 (2), **30:** 459; Sept. 3, 1914, **30:** 471; June 24, 1914, **30:**

493; Sept. 9, 1914 (2), **31:** 16, 18; Sept. 11, 1914, **31:** 23; Sept. 16, 1914, **31:** 37; Sept. 19, 1914, **31:** 56; Sept. 30, 1914 (3), **31:** 102, 103; Nov. 12, 1914, **31:** 310; Dec. 1, 1914, **31:** 378; Dec. 2, 1914, **31:** 380; Dec. 3, 1914, **31:** 382; Dec. 7, 1914, **31:** 411; Dec. 9, 1914, **31:** 431; Dec. 12, 1914, **31:** 456; Dec. 16, 1914, **31:** 473; Dec. 17, 1914 (2), **31:** 476, 480; Dec. 18, 1914, **31:** 482; Dec. 24, 1914 (2), **31:** 521; Dec. 26, 1914, **31:** 533; Dec. 26, 1914, **31:** 546
January–March 1915
Jan. 6, 1915, **32:** 24; Jan. 7, 1915, **32:** 27; Jan. 9, 1915, **32:** 42; Jan. 12, 1915 (3), **32:** 58, 59, 60; Jan. 15, 1915, **32:** 75; Jan. 19, 1915, **32:** 91; Jan. 22, 1915, **32:** 105; Jan. 23, 1915 (2), **32:** 113, 114; Feb. 9, 1915, **32:** 202; Feb. 12, 1915, **32:** 222; Feb. 15, 1915 (2), **32:** 235, 237; Feb. 18, 1915 (3), **32:** 245, 248, 249; Feb. 19, 1915, **32:** 259; Feb. 22, 1915, **32:** 269; Feb. 25, 1915, **32:** 288; March 1, 1915 (2), **32:** 301, 302; March 2, 1915, **32:** 309; March 3, 1915, **32:** 311; March 5, 1915, **32:** 326; March 6, 1915, **32:** 333; March 8, 1915, **32:** 338; March 10, 1915 (2), **32:** 353, 355; March 11, 1915 (2), **32:** 364, 365; March 13, 1915, **32:** 369; March 16, 1915, **32:** 392; March 20, 1915, **32:** 404; March 22, 1915 (3), **32:** 409, 412, 414; March 23, 1915, **32:** 421; March 24, 1915, **32:** 427; March 25, 1915 (4), **32:** 432, 434, 436, 437; March 27, 1915, **32:** 439; March 29, 1915 (2), **32:** 451, 453; March 31, 1915, **32:** 458

April 1915
April 2, 1915 (4), **32:** 464, 466, 468; April 3, 1915 (3), **32:** 469, 471, 474; April 5, 1915, **32:** 477; April 6, 1915, **32:** 487; April 7, 1915 (2), **32:** 488, 490; April 8, 1915, **32:** 497; April 9, 1915, **32:** 499; April 12, 1915 (2), **32:** 507, 509; April 14, 1915, **32:** 519; April 15, 1915, **32:** 524; April 16, 1915 (4), **32:** 526, 527, 529; Feb. 12, 1915, **32:** 541; April 17, 1915, **33:** 3; April 19, 1915 (5), **33:** 26, 28, 29, 30, 31; April 20, 1915 (2), **33:** 41, 43; April 21, 1915, **33:** 52; April 26, 1915, **33:** 69; April 27, 1915 (3), **33:** 71, 77, 80; April 28, 1915, **33:** 82; April 30, 1915, **33:** 88
May–June 1915
May 1, 1915, **33:** 91; May 3, 1915 (3), **33:** 93, 95, 99; May 4, 1915, **33:** 101; May 5, 1915, **33:** 106; May 6, 1915 (2), **33:** 113, 115; May 7, 1915, **33:** 120; May 8, 1915, **33:** 131; May 9, 1915, **33:** 134; May 10, 1915 (2), **33:** 141, 142; May 12, 1915 (3), **33:** 165, 167, 173; May 13, 1915 (7), **33:** 180, 182, 183, 185, 186, 187; May 14, 1915, **33:** 192; May 16, 1915, **33:** 205; May 17, 1915, **33:** 212; May 18, 1915, **33:** 217; May 19, 1915, **33:** 220; May 26, 1915, **33:** 258; May 28, 1915 (2), **33:** 275, 276; June 2, 1915 (4), **33:** 304, 305, 308, 310; June 3, 1915 (4), **33:** 321, 326, 331, 333; June 4, 1915, **33:** 337; June 5, 1915 (2), **33:** 342, 343; June 7, 1915, **33:** 351
James Viscount Bryce, March 21, 1913, **27:** 203; April 2, 1913, **27:** 254; Nov. 7, 1913, **28:** 506; Dec. 19, 1914, **29:** 47; March 6, 1914, **29:** 320; June 19, 1914, **30:** 195
Albert Sidney Burleson, Jan. 4, 1916, **35:** 429

Charles Pope Caldwell, July 11, 1916, **37**: 404
William Banks Caperton, Aug. 11, 1915, **34**: 164
Andrew Carnegie, May 21, 1914, **30**: 61; Jan. 31, 1915, **32**: 167
Venustiano Carranza, April 22, 1914, **29**: 483
Frank Irving Cobb, May 21, 1915, **33**: 233
Charles Richard Crane, March 21, 1913, **27**: 203; May 18, 1914, **30**: 46; Jan. 15, 1916, **35**: 483
Charles Robert Crisp, March 27, 1914, **29**: 381

Josephus Daniels, Aug. 8, 1913, **28**: 130; April 16, 1914, **29**: 453; May 12, 1914, **30**: 26; July 30, 1915, **34**: 45; Aug. 2, 1915, **34**: 61; Aug. 3, 1915, **34**: 70; Aug. 14, 1915, **34**: 197; Sept. 3, 1915, **34**: 410; Oct. 9, 1915, **35**: 45
Robert Beale Davis, Jr., Aug. 28, 1915, **34**: 367; Sept. 7, 1915, **34**: 437
Adolfo Díaz, Feb. 3, 1914, **29**: 222
Cleveland Hoadley Dodge, March 10, 1913, **27**: 168; April 1, 1913, **27**: 247; April 8, 1913, **27**: 274
Frank Ellsworth Doremus, March 25, 1913, **27**: 225
Michael Francis Doyle, April 28, 1916, **36**: 566

Maurice Francis Egan, June 13, 1913, **27**: 517
Wilhelm August Ferdinand Ekengren, Oct. 13, 1915, **35**: 58
Charles William Eliot, Jan. 27, 1913, **27**: 80; March 20, 1913, **27**: 198; April 29, 1914, **29**: 533; May 7, 1914, **30**: 5; Aug. 6, 1914, **30**: 353; Aug. 20, 1914, **30**: 418; Aug. 22, 1914, **30**: 434; Feb. 19, 1915, **32**: 263; July 16, 1915, **33**: 513; July 26, 1915, **34**: 29; Jan. 15, 1916, **35**: 486; Jan. 21, 1916, **35**: 506; June 28, 1916, **37**: 322
Francisco Escudero, July 24, 1913, **28**: 70; Oct. 7, 1913, **28**: 370

John Cardinal Farley and others, July 14, 1916, **37**: 421
Henry Burchard Fine, March 11, 1913, **27**: 169; March 12, 1913, **27**: 173; March 15, 1913, **27**: 188; March 25, 1913, **27**: 225
Henry Jones Ford, March 15, 1913, **27**: 188; April 30, 1913, **27**: 370; Jan. 17, 1914, **29**: 137
Francis Joseph, Aug. 21, 1916, **38**: 62 (translation)
Paul Fuller, Aug. 28, 1914, **30**: 459; Sept. 21, 1914, **31**: 65
Report by Paul Fuller on his mission to Mexico, Sept. 21, 1914, **31**: 65
Paul Fuller and others, Dec. 8, 1914, **31**: 426

Domicio da Gama, Dec. 20, 1915, **35**: 372
Harry Augustus Garfield, April 23, 1914, **29**: 496; March 3, 1916, **36**: 247; April 24, 1916, **36**: 544
Lindley Miller Garrison, Feb. 25, 1913, **27**: 136; April 2, 1913, **27**: 255; April 24, 1913, **27**: 354; June 13, 1913, **27**: 516; Jan. 19, 1914, **29**: 147; Feb. 16, 1914, **29**: 264; Feb. 19, 1914, **29**: 273; Feb. 25, 1914, **29**: 289; April 26, 1914, **29**: 509; May 2,

1914, **29:** 541; June 5, 1914, **30:** 155; June 26, 1914, **30:** 216; June 30, 1914, **30:** 230; Aug. 8, 1914, **30:** 360; March 20, 1915, **32:** 404; July 7, 1915, **33:** 482

George V, Aug. 12, 1916, **38:** 29

James Watson Gerard, June 30, 1913, **28:** 17; Dec. 8, 1914, **31:** 426; Jan. 24, 1915, **32:** 145; June 1, 1915, **33:** 297; June 8, 1915, **33:** 371; Aug. 24, 1915, **34:** 320; Aug. 28, 1915, **34:** 366; Sept. 4, 1915, **34:** 418; Sept. 7, 1915, **34:** 439; Sept. 8, 1915, **34:** 441; Sept. 9, 1915 (2), **34:** 452, 453; March 18, 1916, **36:** 341

James Cardinal Gibbons, Aug. 18, 1914, **30:** 399; May 12, 1916, **37:** 30

Francis van Gheel Gildemeester, June 7, 1915, **33:** 361

Samuel Gompers, Aug. 9, 1915, **34:** 148; July 5, 1916, **37:** 365; July 11, 1916, **37:** 402; July 17, 1916, **37:** 430; July 22, 1916, **37:** 465; July 27, 1916, **37:** 490

Edmund William Gosse, Aug. 7, 1914, **30:** 359

Charles Henry Grasty, March 3, 1914, **29:** 308; Jan. 3, 1916, **35:** 430

Benjamin Howell Griswold, Jr., April 10, 1915, **32:** 502

Delbert James Haff, May 12, 1913, **27:** 419

William Bayard Hale, May 3, 1913, **27:** 396; June 25, 1913 (2), **28:** 7, 8; July 9, 1913, **28:** 27; July 24, 1913, **28:** 69; Sept. 28, 1913, **28:** 339; Oct. 15, 1913, **28:** 411; Oct. 22, 1913, **28:** 423; Dec. 31, 1913, **29:** 90; Jan. 13, 1914, **29:** 130

James Alphonsus Hamill, March 5, 1914, **29:** 318; July 1, 1916, **37:** 344

Myron Timothy Herrick, Dec. 2, 1913, **29:** 11

Henry Lee Higginson, July 26, 1915, **34:** 28

Jacob Harry Hollander, March 22, 1913, **27:** 215; April 7, 1913, **27:** 265

Hamilton Holt, May 11, 1916, **37:** 75; May 29, 1916, **37:** 120

Herbert Clark Hoover, Feb. 26, 1915, **32:** 294

Edward Mandell House
May 1913–December 1914
May 6, 1913, **27:** 404; Jan. 23, 1914, **29:** 164; May 29, 1914, **30:** 108; June 3, 1914, **30:** 139; June 17, 1914, **30:** 189; June 11, 1914, **30:** 200; June 26, 1914, **30:** 214; July 3, 1914, **30:** 247; July 4, 1914, **30:** 255; June 6, 1914, **30:** 256; July 9, 1914 (2), **30:** 265, 271; July 17, 1914, **30:** 287; July 31, 1914, **30:** 323; Aug. 1, 1914, **30:** 327; Aug. 3, 1914, **30:** 341; Aug. 4, 1914, **30:** 343; Aug. 5, 1914, **30:** 349; Aug. 22, 1914, **30:** 432; Sept. 5, 1914, **30:** 488; Sept. 6, 1914, **31:** 5; Sept. 18, 1914, **31:** 45; Sept. 19, 1914, **31:** 55; Sept. 20, 1914, **31:** 60; Sept. 22, 1914, **31:** 76; Oct. 8, 1914, **31:** 137; Oct. 21, 1914, **31:** 204; Oct. 24, 1914, **31:** 228; Nov. 10, 1914, **31:** 295; Nov. 11, 1914, **31:** 296; Nov. 30, 1914, **31:** 369; Dec. 26, 1914, **31:** 535; Dec. 27, 1914, **31:** 540; Dec. 31, 1914, **31:** 553

January–March 1915

Jan. 8, 1915, **32:** 41; Jan. 15, 1915, **32:** 75; Jan. 18, 1915 (2), **32:** 83, 84; Jan. 20, 1915, **32:** 94; Jan. 21, 1915 (2), **32:** 98, 99; Jan. 22, 1915 (2), **32:** 107; Jan. 28, 1915, **32:** 147; Jan. 29, 1915 (3), **32:** 161, 162; Feb. 9, 1915, **32:** 204; Feb. 11, 1915 (2), **32:** 220; Feb. 12, 1915, **32:** 225; Feb. 13, 1915, **32:** 231; Feb. 15, 1915, **32:** 237; Feb. 17, 1915, **32:** 242; Feb. 18, 1915, **32:** 253; Feb. 20, 1915 (2), **32:** 266; Feb. 21, 1915, **32:** 267; Feb. 22, 1915, **32:** 268; Feb. 23, 1915, **32:** 276; Feb. 24, 1915, **32:** 285; Feb. 27, 1915 (3), **32:** 297, 299; Feb 28, 1915, **32:** 300; March 1, 1915, **32:** 303; March 5, 1915, **32:** 327; March 7, 1915, **32:** 335; March 8, 1915, **32:** 340; March 9, 1915 (2), **32:** 349; March 14, 1915, **32:** 372; March 15, 1915 (2), **32:** 376, 377; March 16, 1915, **32:** 393; March 20, 1915, **32:** 402; March 22, 1915, **32:** 411; March 23, 1915, **32:** 422; March 24, 1915, **32:** 429; March 26, 1915, **32:** 438; March 27, 1915 (2), **32:** 440, 441; March 29, 1915, **32:** 455; March 31, 1915, **32:** 458

April–June 1915

April 3, 1915, **32:** 475; April 5, 1915, **32:** 480; April 11, 1915 (2), **32:** 504; April 12, 1915, **32:** 513; April 14, 1915 (2), **32:** 521; April 16, 1915, **32:** 531; April 17, 1915, **33:** 10; April 18, 1915, **33:** 12; April 20, 1915, **33:** 47; April 22, 1915, **33:** 63; April 23, 1915, **33:** 65; April 30, 1915, **33:** 88; March 3, 1915, **33:** 100; May 5, 1915, **33:** 108; May 7, 1915, **33:** 121; May 9, 1915, **33:** 134; May 11, 1915, **33:** 158; May 13, 1915 (2), **33:** 189, 190; May 14, 1915 (2), **33:** 197, 198; May 18, 1915, **33:** 217; May 19, 1915, **33:** 222; May 20, 1915, **33:** 226; May 21, 1915, **33:** 229; May 21, 1915, **33:** 237; May 24, 1915, **33:** 247; May 25, 1915 (2), **33:** 253; May 27, 1915 (2), **33:** 266, 267; June 3, 1915, **33:** 321; June 16, 1915, **33:** 405

July–September 1915

July 1, 1915, **33:** 461; July 10, 1915, **33:** 490; July 12, 1915, **33:** 493; July 13, 1915, **33:** 501; July 15, 1915, **33:** 511; July 17, 1915, **33:** 516; July 18, 1915, **33:** 519; July 19, 1915 (2), **33:** 532, 533; July 22, 1915, **34:** 11; July 25, 1915, **34:** 24; July 28, 1915, **34:** 36; July 29, 1915 (2), **34:** 41, 42; Aug. 2, 1915, **34:** 62; Aug. 3, 1915, **34:** 80; Aug. 4, 1915, **34:** 84; Aug. 6, 1915, **34:** 106; Aug. 9, 1915 (2), **34:** 144, 146; Aug. 10, 1915, **34:** 158; Aug. 13, 1915, **34:** 186; Aug. 14, 1915, **34:** 200; Aug. 18, 1915, **34:** 238; Aug. 22, 1915 (2), **34:** 297, 298; Aug. 23, 1915 (2), **34:** 309, 310; Aug. 30, 1915, **34:** 368; Aug. 31, 1915, **34:** 388; Sept. 26, 1915, **34:** 520; Sept. 28, 1915, **34:** 536

October–December 1915

Oct. 1, 1915, **35:** 3; Oct. 4, 1915, **35:** 20; Oct. 17, 1915 (2), **35:** 78, 80; Oct. 19, 1915, **35:** 85; Oct. 29, 1915, **35:** 130; Oct. 31, 1915, **35:** 144; Nov. 10, 1915, **35:** 186; Nov. 11, 1915 (2), **35:** 191; Nov. 19, 1915, **35:** 220; Dec. 7, 1915, **35:** 310; Dec. 12, 1915, **35:** 346; Dec. 16, 1915, **35:** 362; Dec. 21, 1915, **35:** 380; Dec. 22, 1915, **35:** 381; Dec. 26, 1915, **35:** 391

January–March 1916
Jan. 7, 1916 (2), **35**: 453, 454; Jan. 10, 1916, **35**: 458; Jan. 11, 1916, **35**: 465; Jan. 13, 1916, **35**: 471; Jan. 15, 1916 (2), **35**: 483, 484; Jan. 16, 1916, **35**: 487; Jan. 17, 1916, **35**: 498; Jan. 25, 1916, **35**: 524; Nov. 14, 1915, **35**: 540; Jan. 30, 1916, **36**: 52; Feb. 1, 1916, **36**: 85; Feb. 3, 1916 (3), **36**: 122, 124, 125; Feb. 7, 1916, **36**: 138; Feb. 9, 1916 (2), **36**: 147, 150; Feb. 10, 1916 (2), **36**: 166; Feb. 11, 1916 (2), **36**: 170; Feb. 13, 1916, **36**: 173; Feb. 15, 1916, **36**: 180; Feb. 21, 1916 (2), **36**: 203; Feb. 25, 1916, **36**: 217; March 12, 1916, **36**: 294; March 15, 1916, **36**: 320; March 20, 1916, **36**: 346; March 22, 1916, **36**: 353; March 31, 1916, **36**: 398

April–June 1916
April 3, 1916, **36**: 405; April 7, 1916, **36**: 434; April 8, 1916 (2), **36**: 443, 446; April 13, 1916, **36**: 478; April 15, 1916, **36**: 486; April 19, 1916, **36**: 511; April 21, 1916, **36**: 524; April 22, 1916, **36**: 526; April 24, 1916, **36**: 541; April 25, 1916, **36**: 548; April 27, 1916, **36**: 559; May 5, 1916, **36**: 616; May 6, 1916, **36**: 628; May 7, 1916, **36**: 631; May 9, 1916, **37**: 6; May 10, 1916, **37**: 11; May 14, 1916 (2), **37**: 42, 45; May 17, 1916 (2), **37**: 62, 64; May 19, 1916, **37**: 77; May 21, 1916, **37**: 88; May 22, 1916, **37**: 94; May 26, 1916, **37**: 112; May 27, 1916, **37**: 116; May 31, 1916, **37**: 131; June 1, 1916, **37**: 134; June 7, 1916, **37**: 168; June 10, 1916, **37**: 201; June 14, 1916, **37**: 225; June 16, 1916, **37**: 238; June 18, 1916, **37**: 265; June 23, 1916, **37**: 289; June 25, 1916, **37**: 294; June 27, 1916, **37**: 311; June 28, 1916, **37**: 319

July–November 1916
July 3, 1916, **37**: 351; July 5, 1916, **37**: 364; July 12, 1916, **37**: 411; July 14, 1916, **37**: 422; July 15, 1916, **37**: 424; July 30, 1916, **37**: 502; Aug. 19, 1916, **38**: 53; Sept. 3, 1916, **38**: 141; Oct. 9, 1916, **38**: 376; Oct. 20, 1916, **38**: 494; Nov. 6, 1916, **38**: 619; Nov. 17, 1916, **38**: 668

Memorandum by Edward Mandell House on Wilson's forthcoming speech to the League to Enforce Peace, May 21, 1916, **37**: 88

Frederick Clemson Howe, Oct. 29, 1915, **35**: 132; June 28, 1916, **37**: 321; Aug. 5, 1916, **37**: 534

Arthur Hoag Howland, June 27, 1916, **37**: 310

Victoriano Huerta, March 4, 1913, **27**: 152

Paul Oscar Husting, Feb. 26, 1916, **36**: 221

William Moulton Ingraham, Oct. 9, 1916, **38**: 377

Edward Corbin Jenkins, March 14, 1913, **27**: 179

Charles Jenkinson, Sept. 8, 1914, **31**: 12

Hiram Warren Johnson, April 22, 1913, **27**: 347; April 23, 1913, **27**: 352; May 6, 1913, **27**: 405

Robert Underwood Johnson, Oct. 22, 1915, **35**: 103; June 27, 1916, **37**: 309

Thomas Davies Jones, March 22, 1913 (2), **27:** 214
William Atkinson Jones, June 26, 1914, **30:** 215
David Starr Jordan, March 19, 1913, **27:** 195; April 14, 1913, **27:** 309
Jean Jules Jusserand, April 1, 1915, **32:** 462

Francis Clement Kelly, Jan. 26, 1915, **32:** 128; Feb. 23, 1915, **32:** 279
William Kent, April 9, 1913, **27:** 280; April 24, 1914, **29:** 499; March 14, 1916, **36:** 310

Franklin Knight Lane, Aug. 2, 1914, **30:** 331; May 26, 1915, **33:** 258; July 2, 1915, **33:** 468; July 21, 1915, **34:** 6; Sept. 3, 1915, **34:** 411; Sept. 16, 1915, **34:** 477; March 13, 1916, **36:** 301; July 6, 1916, **37:** 370; Sept. 6, 1916, **38:** 153; Oct. 6, 1916, **38:** 355
Memorandum by Franklin Knight Lane of a conversation with General Snyman on Mexican affairs, May 26, 1915, **33:** 258
Memorandum by Franklin Knight Lane of a conversation with General Iturbide on Mexican affairs, May 25, 1915, **33:** 260
Memorandum by Franklin Knight Lane of a conversation with General Angeles on Mexican affairs, July 1, 1915, **33:** 463
Franklin Knight Lane and others, Sept. 6, 1916, **38:** 153
Robert Lansing
April–December 1914
April 14, 1914 (2), **29:** 436, 437; Aug. 22, 1914, **30:** 435; Aug. 24, 1914, **30:** 447; Sept. 26, 1914, **31:** 84; Sept. 27, 1914, **31:** 85; Sept. 28, 1914, **31:** 90; Oct. 8, 1914, **31:** 133; Oct. 15, 1914, **31:** 158; Oct. 19, 1914, **31:** 182; Oct. 20, 1914 (4), **31:** 188, 193; **35:** 536; Oct. 21, 1914, **31:** 197; Oct. 23, 1914 (3), **31:** 216, 217; Oct. 26, 1914, **31:** 235; Nov. 23, 1914, **31:** 347; Nov. 28, 1914, **31:** 359; Dec. 9, 1914, **31:** 432; Dec. 10, 1914, **31:** 450
January–June 1915
Jan. 11, 1915, **32:** 54; Feb. 5, 1915, **32:** 193; Feb. 7, 1915, **32:** 195; Feb. 10, 1915, **32:** 210; March 28, 1915, **32:** 449; April 10, 1915, **32:** 503; May 17, 1915, **33:** 214; June 1, 1915, **33:** 296; June 5, 1915, **33:** 344; June 12, 1915, **33:** 385; June 14, 1915, **33:** 395; June 15, 1915 (2), **33:** 400; June 17, 1915, **33:** 415; June 23, 1915, **33:** 445; June 24, 1915, **33:** 447; June 25, 1915 (2), **33:** 453, 454
July–September 1915
July 5, 1915, **33:** 475; July 6, 1915, **33:** 479; July 7, 1915, **33:** 480; July 8, 1915 (2), **33:** 487, 489; July 12, 1915, **33:** 493; July 14, 1915, **33:** 507; July 15, 1915, **33:** 509; July 16, 1915, **33:** 512; July 19, 1915 (2), **33:** 527, 529; July 21, 1915, **33:** 544; July 27, 1915 (2), **34:** 33; July 28, 1915, **34:** 34; July 29, 1915 (3), **34:** 43, 44; July 31, 1915 (2), **34:** 49, 51; Aug. 1, 1915, **34:** 54; Aug. 2, 1915 (4), **34:** 59, 60; Aug. 3, 1915 (2), **34:** 66, 69; Aug. 4, 1915, **34:** 83; Aug. 5, 1915, **34:** 98; Aug. 6, 1915 (4), **34:**

109, 110, 114; Aug. 7, 1915 (2), **34**: 121, 123; Aug. 8, 1915, **34**: 132; Aug. 9, 1915, **34**: 142; Aug. 10, 1915 (3), **34**: 156, 157; Aug. 13, 1915 (2), **34**: 183, 185; Aug. 14, 1915, **34**: 196; Aug. 18, 1915, **34**: 236; Aug. 20, 1915, **34**: 264; Aug. 21, 1915, **34**: 280; Aug. 25, 1915, **34**: 316; Aug. 24, 1915, **34**: 318; Aug. 26, 1915 (2), **34**: 329, 339; Aug. 27, 1915, **34**: 341; Aug. 30, 1915, **34**: 368; Aug. 31, 1915 (3), **34**: 382, 383, 385

September–December 1915

Sept. 1, 1915, **34**: 397; Sept. 2, 1915 (2), **34**: 403, 404; Sept. 3, 1915, **34**: 408; Sept. 4, 1915, **34**: 417; Sept. 6, 1915, **34**: 421; Sept. 7, 1915, **34**: 429; Sept. 8, 1915, **34**: 432; Sept. 9, 1915 (2), **34**: 435; Sept. 10, 1915, **34**: 444; Sept. 11, 1915 (3), **34**: 449, 452; Sept. 12, 1915 (2), **34**: 454, 455; Sept. 13, 1915 (2), **34**: 461, 462; Sept. 15, 1915, **34**: 472; Sept. 18, 1915, **34**: 487; Sept. 19, 1915, **34**: 492; Sept. 25, 1915, **34**: 519; Sept. 27, 1915, **34**: 528; Oct. 9, 1915, **35**: 45; Oct. 15, 1915, **35**: 68; Oct. 20, 1915, **35**: 88; Oct. 21, 1915 (2), **35**: 92, 93; Oct. 26, 1915, **35**: 111; Oct. 27, 1915, **35**: 115; Oct. 29, 1915 (2), **35**: 128, 129; Nov. 1, 1915, **35**: 147; Nov. 2, 1915, **35**: 158; Nov. 3, 1915, **35**: 162; Nov. 11, 1915 (4), **35**: 188, 189, 190; Nov. 12, 1915, **35**: 193; Nov. 18, 1915, **35**: 215; Nov. 19, 1915, **35**: 218; Nov. 22, 1915 (2), **35**: 235, 236; Nov. 24, 1915 (3), **35**: 244, 246, 247; Nov. 29, 1916, **35**: 264; Dec. 1, 1915 (2), **35**: 276, 277; Dec. 2, 1915, **35**: 281; Dec. 3, 1915 (4), **35**: 282, 284; Dec. 13, 1915, **35**: 349; Dec. 17, 1915, **35**: 364; Dec. 21, 1915 (3), **35**: 375, 378; Dec. 24, 1915, **35**: 389; Dec. 28, 1915 (4), **35**: 401, 402, 403; Dec. 30, 1915 (2), **35**: 409, 410

January–March 1916

Jan. 2, 1916, **35**: 420; Jan. 3, 1916, **35**: 422; Jan. 4, 1916, **35**: 425; Jan. 5, 1916, **35**: 432; Jan. 6, 1916 (2), **35**: 438, 446; Jan. 7, 1916 (3), **35**: 448, 450; Jan. 11, 1916 (2), **35**: 463 (2); Jan. 17, 1916, **35**: 495; Jan. 20, 1916, **35**: 505; Jan. 24, 1916 (3), **35**: 512, 516, 519; Jan. 25, 1916 (2), **35**: 521, 522; Jan. 27, 1916, **35**: 531; Jan. 31, 1916, **36**: 73; Feb. 4, 1916, **36**: 127; Feb. 5, 1916, **36**: 133; Feb. 8, 1916, **36**: 141; Feb. 16, 1916, **36**: 182; Feb. 18, 1916, **36**: 194; Feb. 19, 1916, **36**: 197; Feb. 28, 1916, **36**: 228; Feb. 29, 1916, **36**: 232; March 3, 1916, **36**: 245; March 6, 1916 (2), **36**: 251, 258; March 8, 1916, **36**: 269; March 9, 1916, **36**: 278; March 11, 1916, **36**: 292; March 13, 1916, **36**: 307; March 24, 1916, **36**: 361; March 27, 1916, **36**: 307; March 24, 1916, **36**: 361; March 27, 1916, **36**: 371; March 30, 1916, **36**: 383

April–June 1916

April 3, 1916, **36**: 404; April 4, 1916 (3), **36**: 411, 412, 413; April 7, 1916 (2), **36**: 429, 435; April 10, 1916 (2), **36**: 447, 452; April 12, 1916, **36**: 466; April 13, 1916, **36**: 480; April 15, 1916 (3), **36**: 485, 488; April 17, 1916, **36**: 498; April 22, 1916, **36**: 527; April 24, 1916 (2), **36**: 533, 540; April 25, 1916 (2), **36**: 546, 548; April 26, 1916, **36**: 556; April 27, 1916, **36**: 563; May 1, 1916, **36**: 577; May 2, 1916, **36**: 581; May 3, 1916, **36**: 594; May

4, 1916, **36:** 604; May 5, 1916, **36:** 613; May 6, 1916, **36:** 620; May 8, 1916 (2), **36:** 649, 654; May 9, 1916, **37:** 4; May 10, 1916, **37:** 13; May 15, 1916, **37:** 55; May 20, 1916, **37:** 83; May 24, 1916, **37:** 106; May 25, 1916, **37:** 106; June 15, 1916 (2), **37:** 231, 232; June 17, 1916, **37:** 240; June 21, 1916 (3), **37:** 271, 273, 275; June 23, 1916, **37:** 287

July–November 1916

July 3, 1916 (2), **37:** 348, 350; July 5, 1916 (2), **37:** 360, 361; July 6, 1916, **37:** 367; July 22, 1916, **37:** 464; Aug. 14, 1916, **38:** 33; Aug. 22, 1916 (3), **38:** 67, 71, 74; Aug. 23, 1916, **38:** 79; Aug. 26, 1916, **38:** 84; Sept. 6, 1916 (2), **38:** 148, 150; Sept. 18, 1916, **38:** 184; Sept. 21, 1916, **38:** 194; Sept. 22, 1916, **38:** 201; Sept. 30, 1916 (2), **38:** 313, 315; Oct. 2, 1916 (2), **38:** 320, 321; Oct. 13, 1916, **38:** 428; Oct. 17, 1916, **38:** 467; Oct. 26, 1916 (2), **38:** 544; Oct. 27, 1916, **38:** 548; Nov. 14, 1916, **38:** 641; Nov. 15, 1916 (2), **38:** 650, 653

Memorandum by Robert Lansing on America's role as a neutral, Nov. 19, 1914, **31:** 433

Memorandum by Robert Lansing on the status of armed merchant vessels, March 25, 1916, **36:** 534

Memorandum by Robert Lansing on the policy of the Central Powers in regard to submarine warfare against armed merchantmen, March 3, 1916, **36:** 252

Memorandum by Robert Lansing on German submarine warfare, July 19, 1915, **33:** 529

Memorandum by Robert Lansing about a conversation with Count von Bernstorff on submarine warfare against armed merchantmen, Feb. 17, 1916, **36:** 194

Memorandum by Robert Lansing on German submarine warfare as announced in the German *Sussex* note, May 5, 1916, **36:** 626

Memorandum by Robert Lansing on loans to belligerent governments, Oct. 23, 1914, **31:** 219

Memorandum by Robert Lansing on mediation in the Mexican crisis, June 26, 1916, **37:** 306

Suggested comment by Robert Lansing on the first German *Sussex* note, May 8, 1916, **36:** 654

David Lawrence, May 14, 1915, **33:** 199; May 27, 1915, **33:** 268; June 16, 1915, **33:** 409; Sept. 10, 1915, **34:** 448; Sept. 27, 1915, **34:** 530; Sept. 30, 1915, **34:** 540; Feb. 28, 1916, **36:** 229; March 13, 1916, **36:** 307; May 11, 1916, **37:** 15; June 2, 1916, **37:** 152; July 27, 1916, **37:** 485

Memorandum by David Lawrence on American policy toward the European belligerents, July 20, 1916, **37:** 448

Charles Herbert Levermore, March 24, 1916, **36:** 362

Memorandum by Charles Herbert Levermore on a possible league of nations, March 26, 1916, **36:** 363

John Lind, June 12, 1913, **27:** 513; Jan. 10, 1914, **29:** 118; Feb. 25, 1914, **29:** 289

Li Yüan-Hung, June 9, 1916, **37:** 182

Hamilton Wright Mabie, April 12, 1913, **27**: 298
Dudley Field Malone, Nov. 19, 1914, **31**: 333
Edmundo E. Martinez, Aug. 12, 1915, **34**: 174
George Thomas Marye, Jan. 25, 1916, **35**: 526
Shailer Mathews and others, Aug. 18, 1914, **30**: 396
William Gibbs McAdoo, Oct. 28, 1914, **31**: 244; Aug. 16, 1915, **34**: 218
William Frank McCombs, March 3, 1913, **27**: 148; April 3, 1913, **27**: 258; April 13, 1913, **27**: 300
Vance Criswell McCormick, Oct. 7, 1916, **38**: 368
Porter James McCumber, Jan. 27, 1914, **29**: 185
William Calhoun McDonald, May 12, 1916, **37**: 31; June 3, 1916, **37**: 159
Richard Lee Metcalfe, Aug. 14, 1915, **34**: 198
John Bassett Moore, April 14, 1913, **27**: 308; April 18, 1913, **27**: 327; May 6, 1913, **27**: 403; May 15, 1913 (2), **27**: 437, 441; June 29, 1913, **28**: 14; Aug. 22, 1913, **28**: 212; Oct. 9, 1913, **28**: 382; Oct. 28, 1913 (2), **28**: 458, 464; Nov. 19, 1913, **28**: 566; Dec. 29, 1914, **29**: 86
John Pierpont Morgan, Jr., Aug. 21, 1914, **30**: 426; Sept. 4, 1914, **30**: 483
Henry Morgenthau, June 12, 1913, **27**: 513
John R. Mott, March 21, 1913, **27**: 202; April 4, 1913, **27**: 261; Nov. 26, 1914, **31**: 358
James Mudge and others, April 20, 1914, **29**: 474
Hugo Münsterberg, April 13, 1915, **33**: 17

Richard Olney, March 10, 1913, **27**: 168; March 13, 1913, **27**: 176
John Eugene Osborne, June 30, 1915, **33**: 460
Harry Allen Overstreet and others, June 27, 1916, **37**: 308
Robert Latham Owen, May 13, 1915, **33**: 188

Ignace Jan Paderewski, Dec. 24, 1915, **35**: 391
Thomas Nelson Page, May 21, 1915, **33**: 230; July 19, 1916, **37**: 440
Walter Hines Page
1913–1914
Jan. 1, 1913, **27**: 5; April 1, 1913, **27**: 245; June 8, 1913, **27**: 503; Oct. 25, 1913, **28**: 442; Nov. 2, 1913, **28**: 484; Nov. 22, 1913, **28**: 575; Dec. 21, 1913, **29**: 51; Jan. 8, 1914, **29**: 111; Feb. 24, 1914, **29**: 285; Feb. 28, 1914, **29**: 300; March 6, 1914, **29**: 320; March 31, 1914, **29**: 388; April 7, 1914, **29**: 410; May 8, 1914, **30**: 9; June 5, 1914, **30**: 149; July 5, 1914, **30**: 257; July 19, 1914, **30**: 289; July 29, 1914, **30**: 314; Aug. 2, 1914, **30**: 329; Aug. 9, 1914, **30**: 366; Aug. 23, 1914, **30**: 438; Sept. 6, 1914, **31**: 6; Oct. 21, 1914, **31**: 199; Oct. 28, 1914, **31**: 244; Nov. 4, 1914, **31**: 262; Nov. 30, 1914, **31**: 370
1915–1916
Jan. 26, 1915, **32**: 129; Feb. 10, 1915, **32**: 211; March 10, 1915,

32: 357; May 8, 1915, 33: 129; May 25, 1915, 33: 255; July 7, 1915, 33: 483; July 2, 1915, 33: 549; July 22, 1915, 34: 32; July 23, 1915, 34: 17; Aug. 24, 1915, 34: 317; Sept. 8, 1915, 34: 440; Oct. 15, 1915, 35: 82; Oct. 16, 1915, 35: 74; Nov. 19, 1915, 35: 223; Dec. 31, 1915, 35: 412; Jan. 5, 1916, 35: 435; Jan. 15, 1916, 35: 483; Feb. 4, 1916, 36: 129; Feb. 15, 1916, 36: 181; March 26, 1916, 36: 369; March 30, 1916, 36: 384; April 7, 1916, 36: 436; May 6, 1916 (2), 36: 628; May 12, 1916, 37: 28; June 1, 1916, 37: 143; June 9, 1916, 37: 182; July 21, 1916, 37: 456; Oct. 11, 1916, 38: 392

Memorandum by Walter Hines Page about an interview with British politicians, April 7, 1916, 36: 436

Memorandum by Walter Hines Page on British-American relations, Sept. 23, 1916, 38: 257

John Clinton Parker, July 1, 1916, 37: 344

Frederic Courtland Penfield, June 28, 1914, 30: 222

James Duval Phelan, April 7, 1913, 27: 265

William Phillips, Jan. 28, 1914, 29: 187; Dec. 13, 1915, 35: 352

Memorandum by William Phillips on the possible destruction of Mexican oil wells in the event of a blockade, June 29, 1916, 37: 350

Amos Richards Eno Pinchot, June 28, 1916, 37: 320

Sir Horace Plunkett, June 4, 1915, 33: 338; Feb. 23, 1916, 36: 207

Raymond Poincaré, Aug. 23, 1916, 38: 79 (translation)

Address from the Polish Central Relief Committee, July 12, 1916, 37: 404

Frank Lyon Polk, March 15, 1916, 36: 318; March 17, 1916 (2), 36: 331, 333; March 20, 1916, 36: 342; March 21, 1916, 36: 350; May 22, 1916, 37: 93; May 31, 1916, 37: 130; June 1, 1916, 37: 138; June 3, 1916, 37: 157; June 6, 1916 (2), 37: 164; July 11, 1916 (2), 37: 400, 401; July 12, 1916, 37: 409; July 13, 1916, 37: 418; July 18, 1916, 37: 432; July 19, 1916, 37: 437; July 21, 1916, 37: 452; July 24, 1916, 37: 469; July 25, 1916, 37: 471; July 26, 1916, 37: 479; July 27, 1916 (2), 37: 482, 484; July 31, 1916, 37: 506; Aug. 3, 1916, 37: 521; Aug. 7, 1916, 37: 539; Aug. 8, 1916, 38: 10; Aug. 9, 1916, 38: 13

Manuel Castro Quesada, July 1, 1916, 37: 343

John Reed, June 15, 1914, 30: 186; June 18, 1914, 30: 192; June 27, 1914, 30: 219

Paul Samuel Reinsch, Oct. 5, 1914, 31: 284; Jan. 4, 1915, 32: 11; March 5, 1915, 32: 328; March 22, 1915, 32: 421; July 25, 1915, 34: 25; Oct. 14, 1916, 38: 439

Junius Benjamin Remensnyder and others, April 21, 1914, 29: 475

James Ford Rhodes, July 25, 1915, 34: 25

Elihu Root, April 23, 1913, 27: 352; March 11, 1914, 29: 331

Louis de Sadeleer, Oct. 2, 1914, **31:** 121

Jacob Henry Schiff, Nov. 19, 1914, **31:** 333

Charles Ernest Scott, May 31, 1913, **27:** 488

William Graves Sharp, June 20, 1914, **30:** 195; Oct. 11, 1916, **38:** 394

Morris Sheppard, July 22, 1915, **34:** 13

Furnifold McLendel Simmons, July 3, 1915, **33:** 472

Thetus Willrette Sims, Feb. 27, 1914, **29:** 298

Sir Cecil Arthur Spring Rice, Feb. 5, 1914, **29:** 226; Feb. 10, 1914, **29:** 244; March 20, 1914, **29:** 366; May 21, 1914, **30:** 58; May 28, 1914, **30:** 98; Sept. 30, 1914, **31:** 109; Oct. 1, 1914, **31:** 115; Oct. 5, 1914, **31:** 125; Oct. 12, 1914, **31:** 145; Oct. 15, 1914, **31:** 154; Oct. 16, 1914, **31:** 168; Oct. 20, 1914, **31:** 194; Oct. 22, 1914, **31:** 209; Oct. 24, 1914 (2), **31:** 228, 229; Oct. 25, 1914, **31:** 231; Dec. 21, 1914, **31:** 505; April 29, 1916, **36:** 569

William Joel Stone, March 25, 1915, **36:** 366; April 7, 1916, **36:** 430

Moorfield Storey, April 25, 1914, **29:** 508

Pleasant Alexander Stovall, May 9, 1916, **37:** 8; June 21, 1916, **37:** 278

Oscar Solomon Straus, April 30, 1915, **33:** 89

Sun Yat-sen, Nov. 30, 1914, **31:** 372

William Howard Taft, May 10, 1915, **33:** 150; April 11, 1916, **36:** 458; May 1, 1916, **36:** 578; May 9, 1916, **37:** 6

Thaddeus Austin Thomson, Feb. 2, 1916, **36:** 234

John Randolph Thornton, Feb. 21, 1914, **29:** 275; Feb. 25, 1914, **29:** 288

Haigazoun Hohannes Topakyan, Oct. 22, 1915, **35:** 104

Joseph Patrick Tumulty, Jan. 11, 1914, **29:** 128; July 2, 1915, **33:** 465; July 5, 1915, **33:** 474; July 14, 1915, **33:** 508; Aug. 21, 1915, **34:** 274; Sept. 10, 1915, **34:** 444; March 15, 1916, **36:** 317; May 16, 1916, **37:** 58; May 19, 1916, **37:** 75; June 20, 1916, **37:** 268; June 24, 1916, **37:** 291; July 20, 1916, **37:** 446

Sir William Tyrrell, Nov. 21, 1913, **28:** 573; Nov. 26, 1913, **28:** 592

Henry van Dyke, June 11, 1913, **27:** 509

Ambrose White Vernon, March 9, 1915, **32:** 346

Oswald Garrison Villard, April 23, 1914, **29:** 495; Aug. 27, 1914, **30:** 455; May 25, 1915, **33:** 254

Edward Charles Wade, Jr., April 28, 1916, **36:** 566

Henry White, Dec. 5, 1914, **31:** 404; April 5, 1915, **32:** 481

White House Staff, July 1, 1914, **30:** 241; Aug. 20, 1914, **30:** 407; Oct. 15, 1915, **35:** 69; Oct. 16, 1915, **35:** 73; Oct. 18, 1915, **35:** 84

Brand Whitlock, Oct. 19, 1914, **31:** 181

Joseph Edward Willard, May 11, 1916, **37:** 19
William II, Aug. 22, 1916, **38:** 64 (translation)
John Sharp Williams, April 24, 1914, **29:** 500; Aug. 17, 1914, **30:**
     392; June 29, 1915, **33:** 457
Henry Lane Wilson, July 1, 1913, **28:** 18
Huntington Wilson, March 19, 1913, **27:** 195
William Bauchop Wilson, July 2, 1915, **33:** 468; July 3, 1915, **33:**
     470; June 17, 1916, **37:** 245; July 1, 1916, **37:** 344
Simon Wolf, May 25, 1916, **37:** 109
John Downey Works, April 8, 1913, **27:** 275

Yoshihito, Nov. 15, 1916, **38:** 648

Personal correspondence

From Wilson to
Lyman Abbott, Aug. 20, 1914, **30:** 407
Herbert Adams, July 12, 1916, **37:** 409
Jane Addams, Feb. 1, 1915, **32:** 168; Dec. 13, 1915, **35:** 348
Cyrus Adler, June 23, 1902, **32:** 534
Hamilton Fish Armstrong, Nov. 8, 1915, **35:** 182
Stockton Axson, Aug. 5, 1914, **30:** 345; Aug. 6, 1914, **30:** 353;
     March 12, 1916, **36:** 297

Augustus Octavius Bacon, Feb. 5, 1914, **29:** 222
Newton Diehl Baker, Jan. 11, 1915, **32:** 53
Emilie Isabel Wilson Barrington, Sept. 18, 1914, **31:** 44; Sept. 27,
     1916, **38:** 282
Count Johann Heinrich von Bernstorff, Sept. 20, 1916, **38:** 191
Martha Berry, Nov. 21, 1914, **31:** 342; April 21, 1916, **36:** 522
Edward William Bok, Feb. 4, 1915, **32:** 191; April 28, 1915, **33:**
     86
Bertha Bolling, Aug. 29, 1915, **34:** 364
Sally White Bolling, Aug. 29, 1915, **34:** 363; Dec. 29, 1915, **35:**
     408
Helen Woodrow Bones, June 23, 1915, **33:** 445; Dec. 23, 1915, **35:**
     386
Robert Bridges, Jan. 28, 1914, **29:** 186; Aug. 21, 1914, **30:** 426
Herbert Bruce Brougham, May 10, 1915, **33:** 139
Jessie Bones Brower, Aug. 21, 1914, **30:** 425
Marjorie Brown, Sept. 16, 1916, **38:** 176
Mary Celestine Mitchell Brown, Nov. 26, 1914, **31:** 357
William Jennings Bryan, March 19, 1914, **29:** 357; June 25, 1914,
     30: 212; Aug. 25, 1914, **30:** 451; March 18, 1915, **32:** 396; Dec.
     28, 1915, **35:** 401
James Viscount Bryce, April 3, 1913, **27:** 257; Aug. 19, 1914, **30:**
     403; Oct. 9, 1914, **31:** 138

Charles August David Burk, Feb. 19, 1914, **29:** 272
Albert Sidney Burleson, June 7, 1916, **37:** 165
Joseph Green Butler, Jr., Nov. 18, 1915, **35:** 212
Wallace Buttrick, April 13, 1916, **36:** 478; April 21, 1916, **36:** 522
Richard Evelyn Byrd, Oct. 20, 1915, **35:** 87

Arthur Capper, Feb. 8, 1916, **36:** 140
Andrew Carnegie, March 13, 1914, **29:** 342; May 18, 1914, **30:** 43;
    May 22, 1914, **30:** 63
William Nesbitt Chambers, Dec. 13, 1915, **35:** 349
William Eaton Chandler, Dec. 30, 1914, **31:** 551
Winston Churchill, Oct. 22, 1915, **35:** 103
Champ Clark, March 6, 1916, **36:** 251
Genevieve Bennett Clark, Sept. 28, 1916, **38:** 283
Frances Moore Clarke, Oct. 3, 1916, **38:** 322
Frank Irving Cobb, March 4, 1915, **32:** 324
John Knox Coit, April 12, 1915, **32:** 509
Edwin Grant Conklin, Oct. 30, 1916, **38:** 563
Edward Samuel Corwin, April 19, 1913, **27:** 336
Admissions Committee of the Cosmos Club, Feb. 1, 1915, **32:** 167
Annie Wilson Howe Cothran, Sept. 16, 1916, **38:** 176
Ralph Adams Cram, Jan. 6, 1915, **32:** 23
Charles Richard Crane, Jan. 17, 1913, **27:** 60; May 26, 1913, **27:**
    474; June 23, 1915, **33:** 445; July 3, 1915, **33:** 471; June 1, 1916,
    37: 134; Aug. 28, 1916, **38:** 86
Anna Orme Crawford, Nov. 3, 1914, **31:** 259
Jabez Lamar Monroe Curry, Aug. 15, 1897, **36:** 657

Richard Heath Dabney, Jan. 4, 1915, **32:** 10; Oct. 13, 1915, **35:**
    56; April 26, 1916, **36:** 555; May 10, 1916, **37:** 10
Josephus Daniels, May 16, 1914, **30:** 37; Dec. 26, 1914, **31:** 533;
    July 2, 1915, **33:** 465; Sept. 7, 1915, **34:** 426; Dec. 30, 1915, **35:**
    409; May 18, 1916, **37:** 70; Nov. 9, 1916, **38:** 624
Edward Parker Davis, July 28, 1914, **30:** 312; March 30, 1916,
    36: 384; June 7, 1916, **37:** 165
Ellen Duane Davis, June 14, 1915, **33:** 395
Cleveland Hoadley Dodge, April 10, 1913, **27:** 283; July 21, 1913,
    28: 58; Aug. 25, 1913, **28:** 220; June 17, 1914, **30:** 189; July 12,
    1914, **30:** 277; July 19, 1914, **30:** 288; Aug. 21, 1914, **30:** 426;
    Oct. 23, 1914, **31:** 216; Nov. 3, 1914, **31:** 260; June 14, 1915,
    33: 395; July 27, 1915, **34:** 32; Sept. 1, 1915, **34:** 397; Oct. 13,
    1915, **35:** 57; Oct. 16, 1915, **35:** 73; Jan. 17, 1916, **35:** 492; Feb.
    7, 1916, **36:** 138; March 10, 1916, **36:** 280; July 3, 1916, **37:** 347;
    Sept. 7, 1916, **38:** 157
Theodore Dreiser, June 28, 1909, **37:** 541
Frederick A. Duneka, Aug. 2, 1915, **34:** 57; Feb. 14, 1916, **36:** 176
Jessie Kennedy Dyer, Jan. 28, 1915, **32:** 147; Dec. 30, 1915, **35:**
    409

Editor of the *New York Herald*, Sept. 2, 1915, **34**: 402

Henry Eitel, July 24, 1916, **37**: 469

Charles William Eliot, Sept. 17, 1913, **28**: 279; Feb. 18, 1914, **29**: 269

Edward Graham Elliott, Oct. 14, 1915, **35**: 60; Sept. 20, 1916, **38**: 190

Margaret Randolph Axson Elliott, Aug. 21, 1914, **30**: 425; Sept. 26, 1915, **34**: 523; Oct. 14, 1915, **35**: 61; Dec. 6, 1915, **35**: 293; Dec. 26, 1915, **35**: 392

James Fairman Fielder, Oct. 16, 1915, **35**: 72

David M. Flynn, June 24, 1913, **28**: 2

Henry James Ford, May 2, 1916, **36**: 581

John Franklin Fort, March 10, 1914, **29**: 327

Abel McIver Fraser, Jan. 3, 1913, **27**: 8

William Goodell Frost, March 17, 1914, **29**: 351; April 30, 1914, **29**: 537; May 22, 1914, **30**: 64

Edith Bolling Galt
April–May 1915
April 28, 1915, **33**: 87; April 30, 1915, **33**: 90; May 5, 1915 (2), **33**: 110, 111; May 6, 1915, **33**: 117; May 7, 1915 (2), **33**: 124, 126; May 8, 1915 (2), 128, 132; May 9, 1915 (2), **33**: 124, 126; May 8, 1915 (2), 128, 132; May 9, 1915 (2), **33**: 136, 137; May 10, 1915, **33**: 146; May 11, 1915 (2), **33**: 160, 162; May 12, 1915, **33**: 179; May 14, 1915 (2), **33**: 203, 204; May 15, 1915, **33**: 204; May 21, 1915 (2), **33**: 233, 234; May 22, 1915, **33**: 235; May 23, 1915, **33**: 243; May 24, 1915, **33**: 248; May 25, 1915, **33**: 256; May 26, 1915 (2), **33**: 262, 264; May 27, 1915, **33**: 273; May 28, 1915, **33**: 278; May 29, 1915, **33**: 284; May 30, 1915, **33**: 286; May 31, 1915, **33**: 289
June–July 1915
June 1, 1915, **33**: 301; June 2, 1915, **33**: 314; June 3, 1915, **33**: 334; June 4, 1915, **33**: 339; June 5, 1915, **33**: 345; June 6, 1915, **33**: 348; June 7, 1915 (3), **33**: 363, 364, 365; June 8, 1915, **33**: 366; June 9, 1915, **33**: 377; June 10, 1915 (2), **33**: 380, 381; June 11, 1915, **33**: 383; June 12, 1915, **33**: 388; June 13, 1915, **33**: 390; June 14, 1915 (2), **33**: 396, 397; June 15, 1915, **33**: 403; June 16, 1915, **33**: 411; June 17, 1915, **33**: 417; June 18, 1915 (2), **33**: 419, 420; June 19, 1915, **33**: 422; June 20, 1915 (2), **33**: 427, 428; June 21, 1915, **33**: 433; June 22, 1915, **33**: 442; June 23, 1915, **33**: 446; June 29, 1915, **33**: 458; June 30, 1915, **33**: 461; July 19, 1915, **33**: 534; July 20, 1915 (2), **33**: 537, 539; July 21, 1915, **34**: 8; July 23, 1915, **34**: 23
August 1915
Aug. 3, 1915, **34**: 72; Aug. 4, 1915, **34**: 87; Aug. 5, 1915, **34**: 101; Aug. 6, 1915, **34**: 117; Aug. 7, 1915, **34**: 126; Aug. 8, 1915, **34**: 137; Aug. 9, 1915, **34**: 150; Aug. 10, 1915 (2), **34**: 159; Aug.

11, 1915, **34:** 167; Aug. 12, 1915, **34:** 176; Aug. 13, 1915, **34:** 190; Aug. 14, 1915, **34:** 200; Aug. 15, 1915, **34:** 207; Aug. 16, 1915, **34:** 219; Aug. 17, 1915, **34:** 227; Aug. 18, 1915 (2), **34:** 240 (2); Aug. 19, 1915 (2), **34:** 253; Aug. 20, 1915 (2), **34:** 267, 268; Aug. 21, 1915 (2), **34:** 273, 280; Aug. 22, 1915 (2), **34:** 287; Aug. 23, 1915 (3), **34:** 296, 298, 300; Aug. 24, 1915 (4), **34:** 303, 308, 309, 311; Aug. 25, 1915 (6), **34:** 317, 318, 320, 321, 322; Aug. 26, 1915, **34:** 331; Aug. 27, 1915 (3), **34:** 339, 342; Aug. 28, 1915, **34:** 350; Aug. 29, 1915, **34:** 358; Aug. 30, 1915 (4), **34:** 366, 367, 374; Aug. 31, 1915, **34:** 391

September–October 1915

Sept. 2, 1915 (3), **34:** 405; Sept. 3, 1915 (3), **34:** 407, 413, 414; Sept. 4, 1915, **34:** 417; Sept. 5, 1915 (2), **34:** 418, 419; Sept. 6, 1915, **34:** 423; Sept. 7, 1915, **34:** 430; Sept. 8, 1915, **34:** 434; Sept 9, 1915, **34:** 437; Sept. 10, 1915 (4), **34:** 439, 440, 441, 446; Sept. 11, 1915 (2), **34:** 452, 453; Sept. 12, 1915 (2), **34:** 457, 458; Sept. 13, 1915 (2), **34:** 463, 465; Sept. 14, 1915 (2), **34:** 467, 468; Sept. 15, 1915, **34:** 474; Sept. 16, 1915, **34:** 479; Sept. 17, 1915, **34:** 485; Sept. 18, 1915, **34:** 489; Sept. 19, 1915 (2), **34:** 491, 492; Sept. 20, 1915, **34:** 494; Sept. 21, 1915, **34:** 497; Sept. 22, 1915, **34:** 508; Sept. 23, 1915, **34:** 510; Sept. 24, 1915, **34:** 517; Sept. 25, 1915, **34:** 519; Sept. 26, 1915 (2), **34:** 523, 524; Sept. 29, 1915, **34:** 538; Sept. 30, 1915, **34:** 543; Oct. 2, 1915, **35:** 15; Oct. 3, 1915 (2), **35:** 17, 18; Oct. 4, 1915, **35:** 21; Oct. 5, 1915, **35:** 27; Oct. 6, 1915, **35:** 34; Oct. 7, 1915, **35:** 40; Oct. 21, 1915, **35:** 93

November–December 1915

Nov. 1, 1915, **35:** 153; Nov. 2, 1915, **35:** 159; Nov. 3, 1915, **35:** 164; Nov. 15, 1916, **35:** 203; Nov. 17, 1915 (2), **35:** 208, 209; Nov. 29, 1915 (2), **35:** 263, 270; Nov. 30, 1915, **35:** 274; Dec. 1, 1915, **35:** 281; Dec. 10, 1915 (2), **35:** 321, 336; Dec. 18, 1915, **35:** 370

Harry Augustus Garfield, June 7, 1916, **37:** 165
Lindley Miller Garrison, Nov. 28, 1914, **31:** 358
John Palmer Gavit, April 9, 1915, **32:** 498
Carter Glass, Oct. 25, 1915, **35:** 107
John L. Golden, April 17, 1916, **36:** 497
Sophia Gompers, Aug. 6, 1915, **34:** 109
Samuel Gordon, March 22, 1913, **27:** 213
Thomas Watt Gregory, Nov. 4, 1915, **35:** 166
Sir Edward Grey, Aug. 19, 1914, **30:** 403
Lillian Baynes Griffin, Oct. 19, 1915, **35:** 84
David Wark Griffith, March 5, 1915, **32:** 325
Violet Sopwith Grubb, July 8, 1913, **28:** 26

William Bayard Hale, Jan. 1, 1913, **27:** 4; Jan. 2, 1913, **27:** 6
Benjamin Franklin Hall, Jan. 30, 1886, **37:** 541
Abram Woodruff Halsey, March 6, 1913, **27:** 156; Dec. 1, 1915, **35:** 279

Norman Hapgood, Feb. 10, 1913, **27**: 106; May 22, 1913, **27**: 464; Feb. 4, 1914, **29**: 219; Nov. 2, 1915, **35**: 156

Samuel Allen Harlow, May 14, 1915, **33**: 197

Belle Dunton Westcott Harper, Sept. 8, 1914, **31**: 13

George McLean Harper, Aug. 23, 1914, **30**: 438; Sept. 16, 1914, **31**: 36; March 8, 1916, **36**: 274

Karl Edwin Harriman, Feb. 12, 1915, **32**: 222

Azel Washburn Hazen, July 12, 1916, **37**: 409

Robert Randolph Henderson, Oct. 30, 1916, **38**: 563

Archer Wilmot Hendrick, Aug. 16, 1916, **38**: 39

Jenny Davidson Hibben, Jan. 23, 1913, **27**: 68; Sept. 18, 1914, **31**: 44

John Grier Hibben, April 1, 1914, **29**: 391; June 9, 1914, **30**: 163

Henry Lee Higginson, July 27, 1915, **34**: 32

Herbert Clark Hoover, March 19, 1915, **32**: 401; Sept. 20, 1915, **34**: 494

Herbert Clark Hoover and Lou Henry Hoover, Sept. 24, 1914, **31**: 80

Charlotte Everett Wise Hopkins, Nov. 10, 1914, **31**: 561; July 23, 1915, **34**: 16; Nov. 16, 1915, **35**: 205

Edward Mandell House, Jan. 6, 1913, **27**: 15; Jan. 23, 1913, **27**: 69; May 20, 1913, **27**: 458; July 17-18, 1913, **28**: 40; Feb. 16, 1914, **29**: 262; April 2, 1914, **29**: 395; June 16, 1914, **30**: 187; July 9, 1914, **30**: 264; Aug. 3, 1914, **30**: 336; Aug. 17, 1914, **30**: 390; Aug. 18, 1914, **30**: 395; Aug. 25, 1914, **30**: 450; Nov. 2, 1914, **31**: 258; Dec. 14, 1914, **31**: 462; Dec. 16, 1914, **31**: 468; Dec. 22, 1914, **31**: 508; Dec. 25, 1914, **31**: 523; Dec. 28, 1914, **31**: 541; Jan. 11, 1915, **32**: 53; Jan. 27, 1915, **32**: 135; Jan. 29, 1915, **32**: 159; March 8, 1915, **32**: 338; June 20, 1915, **33**: 423; June 22, 1915, **33**: 437; Aug. 31, 1915, **34**: 381; Sept. 22, 1915, **34**: 502; Sept. 29, 1915, **34**: 537; Oct. 4, 1915, **35**: 18; Oct. 8, 1915, **35**: 41; Oct. 29, 1915, **35**: 127; Nov. 1, 1915, **35**: 146; Nov. 4, 1915, **35**: 167; Nov. 10, 1915, **35**: 185; Dec. 14, 1915, **35**: 353; Dec. 17, 1915, **35**: 363; Dec. 25, 1915, **35**: 391; Dec. 27, 1915, **35**: 397; March 3, 1916, **36**: 244; April 20, 1916, **36**: 516; May 24, 1916, **37**: 101; Sept. 20, 1916, **38**: 191; Nov. 13, 1916, **38**: 637

David Franklin Houston, Feb. 17, 1915, **32**: 241; Feb. 16, 1916, **36**: 185

Annie Josephine Wilson Howe, Oct. 12, 1913, **28**: 396; Oct. 18, 1914, **31**: 175; Sept. 26, 1915, **34**: 521

Edward Howe, Oct. 10, 1916, **38**: 389

Frederic Clemson Howe, Nov. 1, 1915, **35**: 146

George Howe III, Oct. 16, 1916, **38**: 451

Florence Stevens Hoyt, Aug. 20, 1914, **30**: 406; Oct. 2, 1914, **31**: 118

Mary Eloise Hoyt, Aug. 25, 1914, **30**: 451; Nov. 18, 1914, **31**: 330; Sept. 26, 1915, **34**: 522

Sadie Cooper Hoyt, Dec. 1, 1914, **31**: 377

Wade Cothran Hoyt, Aug. 18, 1914, **30**: 395
Sarah Caruthers Park Hughes, Aug. 25, 1914, **30**: 452
Allen Schoolcraft Hulbert, June 22, 1913, **27**: 557
Mary Allen Hulbert,
1913
Jan. 1, 1913, **27**: 3; Jan. 5, 1913, **27**: 13; Jan. 19, 1913, **27**: 64; Feb. 2, 1913, **27**: 95; Feb. 9, 1913, **27**: 105; Feb. 16, 1913, **27**: 116; Feb. 23, 1913, **27**: 128; March 2, 1913, **27**: 146; March 9, 1913, **27**: 166; March 16, 1913, **27**: 189; March 23, 1913, **27**: 217; March 30, 1913, **27**: 241; April 8, 1913, **27**: 273; April 13, 1913, **27**: 298; April 21, 1913, **27**: 342; June 1, 1913, **27**: 490; June 9, 1913, **27**: 505; June 22, 1913, **27**: 555; June 29, 1913, **28**: 12; July 20, 1913, **28**: 46; July 27, 1913, **28**: 86; Aug. 3, 1913, **28**: 106; Aug. 10, 1913, **28**: 134; Aug. 24, 1913, **28**: 216; Sept. 7, 1913, **28**: 262; Sept. 21, 1913, **28**: 310; Sept. 28, 1913, **28**: 336; Oct. 12, 1913, **28**: 394; Nov. 2, 1913, **28**: 483; Nov. 19, 1913, **28**: 565; Nov. 30, 1913, **28**: 597; Dec. 8, 1913, **29**: 23; Dec. 23, 1913, **29**: 60
1914
Jan. 9, 1914, **29**: 112; Feb. 1, 1914, **29**: 210; Feb. 8, 1914, **29**: 238; March 15, 1914, **29**: 345; March 22, 1914, **29**: 371; April 26, 1914, **29**: 508; May 10, 1914, **30**: 12; May 24, 1914 (2), **30**: 72; June 7, 1914, **30**: 158; June 21, 1914, **30**: 196; July 12, 1914, **30**: 276; Aug. 2, 1914, **30**: 327; Aug. 7, 1914, **30**: 357; Aug. 23, 1914, **30**: 437; Sept. 6, 1914, **31**: 3; Sept. 20, 1914, **31**: 59; Oct. 11, 1914, **31**: 141; Oct. 18, 1914, **31**: 174; Oct. 30, 1914, **31**: 257; Nov. 8, 1914, **31**: 280; Nov. 22, 1914, **31**: 343; Nov. 23, 1914, **31**: 346; Dec. 6, 1914, **31**: 407; Dec. 23, 1914, **31**: 514; Dec. 27, 1914, **31**: 538
1915-1916
Jan. 10, 1915, **32**: 50; Jan. 17, 1915, **32**: 83; Jan. 31, 1915, **32**: 164; Feb. 14 1915, **32**: 232; March 14, 1915, **32**: 371; April 4, 1915, **32**: 475; April 21, 1915, **33**: 60; May 6, 1915, **33**: 120; May 23, 1915, **33**: 242; June 17, 1915, **33**: 416; June 25, 1915, **33**: 455; July 7, 1915, **33**: 482; Sept. 14, 1915, **34**: 469; Oct. 4, 1915, **35**: 23; Nov. 10, 1915, **35**: 187; Nov. 1, 1916, **38**: 589
Receipt for mortgages and bonds from Mary Allen Hulbert, July 19, 1915, **34**: 39

Melancthon Williams Jacobus, Aug. 20, 1914, **30**: 406; May 25, 1915, **33**: 253; July 20, 1915, **33**: 535; April 26, 1916, **36**: 555
John Franklin Jameson, Aug. 13, 1915, **34**: 185
George Sibley Johns, Oct. 30, 1913, **28**: 475
David Benton Jones, Oct. 14, 1915, **35**: 60; March 9, 1916, **36**: 278
Thomas Davies Jones, July 23, 1914, **30**: 300; Aug. 20, 1914, **30**: 405; Dec. 24, 1914, **31**: 520; Oct. 13, 1915, **35**: 57; Oct. 21, 1916, **38**: 510; Nov. 15, 1916, **38**: 649

Wesley Norwood Jones, April 3, 1916, **36:** 404

Jean Jules Jusserand, Sept. 20, 1916, **38:** 192

William Williams Keen, March 19, 1913, **27:** 195

Helen Adams Keller, Nov. 17, 1915, **35:** 210

Joseph Leland Kennedy, June 12, 1916, **37:** 208

Araminta Arabella Cooper Kern, Nov. 21, 1914, **31:** 342; Jan. 24, 1916, **35:** 521

James Kerney, Feb. 24, 1915, **32:** 285

Robert Brent Keyser, March 30, 1913, **27:** 240

Benjamin Mandeville King, March 22, 1914, **29:** 370

Robert Marion La Follette, May 23, 1913, **27:** 466; Oct. 22, 1914, **31:** 209

Joseph Rucker Lamar, May 20, 1915, **33:** 225; June 14, 1915, **33:** 394; Oct. 4, 1915, **35:** 19

Franklin Knight Lane, Sept. 24, 1914, **31:** 79; Jan. 11, 1915, **32:** 54

Robert Lansing, Dec. 29, 1915, **35:** 406; Oct. 9, 1916, **38:** 374

Harry Mower Lee, Oct. 24, 1916, **38:** 519

Henry Cabot Lodge, Aug. 26, 1914, **30:** 453

James Anderson Long, March 7, 1914, **29:** 322

Edgar Odell Lovett, Nov. 20, 1908, **27:** 574; June 19, 1909, **27:** 575

William Gibbs McAdoo, Dec. 23, 1913, **29:** 62; Dec. 27, 1913, **29:** 77; Dec. 31, 1913, **29:** 90; May 26, 1916, **37:** 111; Oct. 14, 1916, **38:** 439; Oct. 30, 1916, **38:** 563

William Frank McCombs, May 2, 1913, **27:** 386

Hervey McDowell, Jan. 6, 1914, **29:** 104

Charles Stedman Macfarland, Sept. 24, 1914, **31:** 80

Annie McIlvaine, Sept. 21, 1916, **38:** 194

Dudley Field Malone, Dec. 9, 1914, **31:** 428; June 22, 1916, **37:** 283

Shailer Mathews, Dec. 14, 1914, **31:** 461

George W. Megeath, July 12, 1916, **37:** 409

Elmer Truesdale Merrill, Jan. 19, 1915, **32:** 89

Rufus Wilder Miller, March 20, 1914, **29:** 361

Raleigh Colston Minor, Jan. 5, 1915, **32:** 18

George Campbell Morgan, Feb. 16, 1914, **29:** 263

John Pierpont Morgan, Jr., June 25, 1914, **30:** 213; Aug. 13, 1914, **30:** 378; May 20, 1915, **33:** 225

Henry Morgenthau, Oct. 28, 1915, **35:** 119

Robert Russa Moton, Dec. 28, 1915, **35:** 400

John R. Mott, Sept. 17, 1914, **31:** 40

Leroy Arthur Mullen, Oct. 25, 1915, **35:** 107

J. Edwin Murphy, Nov. 22, 1915, **35:** 235; Nov. 30, 1915, **35:** 273

Ida Houston Nelson, April 13, 1915, **32:** 517

James Hervey Neville and Susan Hart Neville, Jan. 3, 1914, **29:** 99

Newsboys of Baltimore, April 7, 1915, **32:** 488

Lucius William Nieman, Aug. 31, 1915, **34:** 388

Frank Mason North and others, Dec. 10, 1915, **35:** 328

William Henry Cardinal O'Connell, May 14, 1915, **33:** 196

Richard Olney, Feb. 7, 1916, **36:** 138

Richard Victor Oulahan, April 20, 1916, **36:** 516

Robert Latham Owen, May 20, 1915, **33:** 225

Walter Hines Page, March 28, 1913, **27:** 234; April 2, 1913, **27:** 254; June 21, 1913, **27:** 554; Sept. 11, 1913, **28:** 274; Sept. 26, 1913, **28:** 328; Nov. 21, 1913, **28:** 572; June 19, 1914, **30:** 195; Aug. 20, 1914, **30:** 407; Dec. 2, 1914, **31:** 380; July 22, 1915, **34:** 10; Sept. 10, 1915, **34:** 443; Nov. 2, 1915, **35:** 157; April 13, 1916, **36:** 477

Endicott Peabody, Jan. 5, 1916, **35:** 431

George Foster Peabody, Nov. 9, 1916, **38:** 625

Thomas Jones Pence, Nov. 6, 1914, **31:** 270

J. B. Phinney, Feb. 3, 1915, **32:** 188

Amos Richards Eno Pinchot and Gertrude Minton Pinchot, July 3, 1916, **37:** 348

Mahlon Pitney, Sept. 10, 1914, **31:** 19

Sir Horace Plunkett, June 17, 1915, **33:** 414

Raymond Poincaré, Jan. 27, 1914, **29:** 184

Frank Lyon Polk, Aug. 30, 1915, **34:** 368

Paul Wilkinson Pope, Nov. 13, 1914, **31:** 314

James Reese Price, April 14, 1914, **29:** 436

Robert Price, June 15, 1916, **37:** 231

Ralph Pulitzer, March 2, 1914, **29:** 303; May 18, 1916, **37:** 70; Sept. 15, 1916, **38:** 173

Herbert Putnam, May 22, 1913, **27:** 464

George Lawrence Record, Feb. 25, 1915, **32:** 287

William Cox Redfield, Dec. 26, 1914, **31:** 531; Dec. 28, 1915, **35:** 400

Edith Gittings Reid, Aug. 15, 1913, **28:** 160; April 15, 1914, **29:** 439; Aug. 21, 1914, **30:** 425; Oct. 5, 1915, **35:** 24; Dec. 5, 1915, **35:** 291

James Ford Rhodes, April 26, 1915, **33:** 69

Melvin A. Rice, June 8, 1916, **37:** 173; Aug. 25, 1916, **38:** 84

Franklin Delano Roosevelt, June 14, 1915, **33:** 394

Theodore Roosevelt, May 23, 1914, **30:** 65; Aug. 6, 1914, **30:** 351

Elihu Root, April 13, 1913, **27:** 298

Hugh Lawson Rose and Mary Francesca Granville Delaney Rose, Oct. 13, 1915, **35:** 56

Shosuke Satō, Jan. 13, 1914, **29:** 129

Francis Bowes Sayre, Oct. 9, 1916, **38:** 375; Nov. 9, 1916, **38:** 625

Jessie Woodrow Wilson Sayre, March 14, 1915, **32:** 370; Oct. 25, 1915, **35:** 109; Dec. 29, 1915, **35:** 408; July 30, 1899, **38:** 681; Aug. 21, 1902, **38:** 682; Aug. 28, 1902, **38:** 683; Sept. 26, 1907, **38:** 684; Oct. 21, 1907, **38:** 685; July 28, 1908, **38:** 686; Feb. 28, 1910, **38:** 687; Dec. 8, 1913, **38:** 688; Oct. 15, 1914, **38:** 688; Aug. 21, 1915, **38:** 689

Charles Ernest Scott, June 26, 1913, **28:** 10

Hugh Lenox Scott, May 7, 1915, **33:** 120

William Berryman Scott, April 13, 1916, **36:** 478

Charles Scribner, Jan. 6, 1913, **27:** 15

Edward Wallace Scudder, March 2, 1914, **29:** 302

Thomas Joseph Scully, Aug. 30, 1916, **38:** 118

Louis Seibold, Oct. 16, 1915, **35:** 73

William Arnold Shanklin, April 9, 1915, **32:** 499

Edward Wright Sheldon, Dec. 7, 1915, **35:** 310

Joseph Swagar Sherley, July 6, 1914, **30:** 260

Laura Jenks Shively, March 14, 1916, **36:** 309

John T. Brabner Smith, March 17, 1916, **36:** 331

Lucy Marshall Smith, Dec. 12, 1914, **31:** 453; May 23, 1915, **33:** 241; Sept. 15, 1915, **34:** 473

Lucy Marshall Smith and Mary Randolph Smith, Nov. 17, 1915, **35:** 211; Dec. 27, 1915, **35:** 399

Sir Cecil Arthur Spring Rice, Dec. 8, 1914, **29:** 24; Dec. 23, 1913, **29:** 61; Oct. 21, 1915, **35:** 95; June 9, 1916, **37:** 177; Sept. 20, 1916, **38:** 192

Pussy de Spoelberch and E. de Spoelberch, March 20, 1915, **32:** 408

James Sprunt, Feb. 16, 1916, **36:** 186

Henry Albert Stimson, May 14, 1915, **33:** 197

Pleasant Alexander Stovall, July 21, 1916, **37:** 455

Mark Sullivan, June 10, 1913, **27:** 507; Jan. 7, 1915, **32:** 25

Claude Augustus Swanson, Oct. 13, 1915, **35:** 57

William Howard Taft, Jan. 2, 1913, **27:** 5, Jan. 8, 1913, **27:** 18; Oct. 28, 1915, **35:** 120

James Henry Taylor, April 23, 1913, **27:** 351

Knox Taylor, Dec. 9, 1914, **31:** 429

Arthur W. Tedcastle, Jan. 3, 1913, **27:** 7; Jan. 17, 1913, **27:** 60; Dec. 31, 1914, **31:** 554

Stephen Seymour Thomas, Jan. 6, 1915, **32:** 23

Joseph Campbell Thompson, Feb. 17, 1916, **36:** 188

Samuel Huston Thompson, Jr., July 6, 1915, **33:** 479

Grace Elizabeth Titus, Sept. 9, 1914, **31:** 16

Nancy Saunders Toy, Sept. 6, 1914, **31:** 4; Oct. 15, 1914, **31:** 157; Nov. 9, 1914, **31:** 289; Dec. 12, 1914, **31:** 454; Dec. 23, 1914, **31:**

515; Dec. 26, 1914, **31:** 532; March 7, 1915, **32:** 334; May 23, 1915, **33:** 240; June 16, 1915, **33:** 411
Joseph Patrick Tumulty, Dec. 27, 1913, **29:** 77; May 5, 1915, **33:** 106; July 3, 1915, **33:** 470; Oct. 15, 1915, **35:** 68; Nov. 23, 1915, **35:** 240; Nov. 29, 1915, **35:** 263; Dec. 14, 1915, **35:** 353; Dec. 28, 1915, **35:** 401; Jan. 2, 1916, **35:** 419; Jan. 5, 1916, **35:** 431

Oscar Wilder Underwood, Jan. 21, 1913, **27:** 66; Jan. 27, 1913, **27:** 78

Oswald Garrison Villard, March 7, 1914, **29:** 323; May 20, 1915, **33:** 225; Sept. 2, 1915, **34:** 402; Sept. 16, 1915, **34:** 477; Oct. 18, 1915, **35:** 83

Henry Watterson, Sept. 21, 1914, **31:** 65; Sept. 28, 1914, **31:** 90
Thornton Whaling, March 27, 1916, **36:** 371; Sept. 20, 1916, **38:** 191
Benjamin Ide Wheeler, Jan. 13, 1915, **32:** 63
William Allen White, May 24, 1915, **33:** 247
Brand Whitlock, Dec. 29, 1915, **35:** 407
Whom it may concern (for Mary Allen Hulbert), Feb. 8, 1914, **29:** 239
Whom it may concern (for John R. Mott), Sept. 17, 1914, **31:** 41
John Sharp Williams, Feb. 5, 1914, **29:** 221
Ellen Axson Wilson: June 28, 1913 (2), **28:** 11; July 20, 1913, **28:** 44; July 24, 1913, **28:** 67; July 27, 1913, **28:** 84; Aug. 3, 1913, **28:** 104; Aug. 5, 1913, **28:** 113; Aug. 7, 1913, **28:** 129; Aug. 10, 1913, **28:** 132; Aug. 12, 1913, **28:** 144; Aug. 17, 1913, **28:** 179; Aug. 19, 1913, **28:** 190; Sept. 3, 1913 (2), **28:** 248; Sept. 7, 1913, **28:** 261; Sept. 9, 1913, **28:** 267; Sept. 17, 1913, **28:** 279; Sept. 21, 1913, **28:** 308; Sept. 28, 1913, **28:** 334; Oct. 1, 1913, **28:** 347; Oct. 5, 1913, **28:** 361; Oct. 9, 1913, **28:** 380; Oct. 12, 1913, **28:** 392; April 18, 1914, **29:** 460
John Adams Wilson, July 6, 1916, **37:** 370
Joseph R. Wilson, Jr., April 14, 1913, **27:** 307; April 22, 1913, **27:** 346; April 1, 1914, **29:** 391; July 24, 1914, **30:** 302; Aug. 6, 1914, **30:** 351; Sept. 26, 1915, **34:** 521; Nov. 30, 1915, **35:** 273; May 26, 1916, **37:** 112; Oct. 16, 1916, **38:** 451
Margaret Woodrow Wilson, Sept. 14, 1916, **38:** 171
William Bauchop Wilson, April 2, 1916, **36:** 401
Caleb Thomas Winchester, March 21, 1916, **36:** 349; April 4, 1916, **36:** 410
Charles Wesley Wisner, Jr., Dec. 5, 1899, **32:** 534
Felexiana Shepherd Baker Woodrow, Dec. 31, 1915, **35:** 412
James Woodrow, May 25, 1914, **30:** 74; April 4, 1916, **36:** 410
Hiram Woods, Jr., Sept. 17, 1913, **28:** 280; March 21, 1916, **36:** 349; March 31, 1916, **36:** 397
Lawrence Crane Woods, Sept. 15, 1915, **34:** 470

Emily Chapman Martin Yates, Aug. 4, 1915, **34:** 82
Frederic Yates, May 26, 1913, **27:** 474; March 7, 1914, **29:** 323;
    Aug. 20, 1914, **30:** 406; Sept. 4, 1914, **30:** 479; Oct. 25, 1915,
    35: 110

To Wilson from
Albert, King of the Belgians, Feb. 20, 1916, **36:** 201; translation,
    202
American Philosophical Society, March 7, 1913, **27:** 159
Hamilton Fish Armstrong, Nov. 1, 1915, **35:** 152
Stockton Axson, Oct. 6, 1915, **35:** 33; March 16, 1916, **36:** 329;
    Nov. 14, 1916, **38:** 644

Newton Diehl Baker, Oct. 4, 1913, **28:** 359; Jan. 6, 1915, **32:** 24
Bernard Mannes Baruch, Oct. 7, 1915, **35:** 39
Sylvester Woodbridge Beach, April 21, 1915, **33:** 61; Sept. 22,
    1916, **38:** 209
Count Johann Heinrich von Bernstorff, Oct. 7, 1915, **35:** 37; Sept.
    17, 1916, **38:** 180
Martha Berry, April 26, 1916, **36:** 558
William Warner Bishop, Nov. 14, 1914, **31:** 316
Mabel Thorp Boardmann, Aug. 5, 1915, **34:** 100
Edward William Bok, April 26, 1915, **33:** 69
Bertha Bolling, Aug. 26, 1915, **34:** 349
John Randolph Bolling, Sept 3, 1915, **34:** 416
William Archibald Bolling, Oct. 12, 1915, **35:** 56
Helen Woodrow Bones, May 29, 1915, **33:** 285; Aug. 27, 1915, **34:**
    379
Robert Bridges, Aug. 9, 1914, **30:** 366
Sydney Brooks, Oct. 7, 1913, **28:** 370
Jessie Woodrow Bones Brower, April 7, 1915, **32:** 493
William Jennings Bryan, Feb. 26, 1913, **27:** 137; March 19, 1914,
    29: 357; June 24, 1914, **30:** 207; Aug. 6, 1914, **30:** 355; March
    19, 1915, **32:** 401; Dec. 18, 1915, **35:** 371
James Viscount Bryce, Aug. 6, 1914, **30:** 356; Sept. 24, 1914, **31:**
    81
Albert Sidney Burleson, Oct. 7, 1915, **35:** 36; June 8, 1916, **37:**
    175
Wallace Buttrick, April 19, 1916, **36:** 512
Richard Evelyn Byrd, Oct. 18, 1915, **35:** 84

Andrew Carnegie, March 14, 1914, **29:** 351; May 21, 1914 (2), **30:**
    61, 62; Nov. 6, 1916, **38:** 621
William Nesbitt Chambers, Dec. 10, 1915, **35:** 337
William Eaton Chandler, Dec. 28, 1914, **31:** 543
Viscount Sutemi Chinda, Oct. 7, 1915, **35:** 36
Winston Churchill, Oct. 24, 1915, **35:** 106
Champ Clark, Dec. 9, 1914, **31:** 431; March 9, 1916, **36:** 279

CONTENTS   73

Genevieve Bennett Clark, Sept. 25, 1916, **38:** 277
Horace Herbert Clark, July 28, 1915, **34:** 39; Aug. 6, 1915, **34:**
    117; Jan. 19, 1916 (2), **35:** 503, 504
Frank Irving Cobb, March 8, 1915, **32:** 341
Annie Wilson Howe Cothran, Sept. 27, 1916, **38:** 283
Charles Richard Crane, May 23, 1913, **27:** 467; June 22, 1915,
    33: 441; June 26, 1915, **33:** 456; July 2, 1915, **33:** 469; May 29,
    1916, **37:** 119

Richard Heath Dabney, Jan. 1, 1915, **32:** 3; Oct. 10, 1915, **35:** 46;
    April 23, 1916, **36:** 532
Josephus Daniels, Feb. 25, 1913, **27:** 134; Aug. 6, 1914, **30:** 356;
    Dec. 25, 1914, **31:** 524; July 7, 1915, **33:** 486; Dec. 24, 1915, **35:**
    390; May 18, 1916, **37:** 71; Nov. 5, 1916, **38:** 616
Jo Davidson, June 13, 1916, **37:** 221
Edward Parker Davis, May 22, 1915, **33:** 235; March 27, 1916,
    36: 373; June 5, 1916, **37:** 163
Joseph Kossuth Dixon, June 10, 1913, **27:** 507
Thomas Dixon, Jr., Feb. 20, 1915, **32:** 267
Cleveland Hoadley Dodge, April 10, 1913, **27:** 284; July 18, 1913,
    28: 41; Aug. 21, 1913, **28:** 203; July 13, 1914, **30:** 281; July 24,
    1914, **30:** 303; Aug. 7, 1914, **30:** 359; Oct. 21, 1914, **31:** 204;
    Nov. 5, 1914, **31:** 266; June 11, 1915, **33:** 383; July 26, 1915,
    34: 28; Aug. 29, 1915, **34:** 358; Oct. 7, 1915, **35:** 39; Jan. 14,
    1916, **35:** 478; Feb. 4, 1916, **36:** 132; June 29, 1916, **37:** 330;
    Sept. 6, 1916, **38:** 154
Jessie Kennedy Dyer, Jan. 21, 1916, **35:** 508

Charles William Eliot, Sept. 10, 1913, **28:** 272; Sept. 22, 1913, **28:**
    317; Feb. 12, 1914, **29:** 246; May 14, 1915, **33:** 202
Edward Graham Elliott, Oct. 8, 1915, **35:** 41

Federal Council of the Churches of Christ in America, March 5,
    1913, **27:** 153
James Fairman Fielder, Oct. 13, 1915, **35:** 58
Henry Burchard Fine, Oct. 8, 1915, **35:** 42
John Miller Turpin Finney, Jan. 28, 1913, **27:** 90
William Goodell Frost, May 21, 1914, **30:** 63
Paul Fuller, May 10, 1915, **33:** 152

Edith Bolling Galt
    April–May 1915
    April 28, 1915, **33:** 87; May 5, 1915, **33:** 108; May 6, 1915, **33:**
    119; May 7, 1915, **33:** 127; May 8, 1915, **33:** 133; May 10, 1915
    (3), **33:** 145, 146; May 11, 1915 (2), **33:** 161, 163; May 12, 1915,
    33: 178; May 14, 1915, **33:** 203; May 15, 1915, **33:** 204; May 17,
    1915, **33:** 216; May 20, 1915, **33:** 228; May 22, 1915, **33:** 236;
    May 23, 1915 (2), **33:** 243; May 24, 1915, **33:** 249; May 25, 1915,
    33: 264; May 26, 1915, **33:** 263; May 27, 1915, **33:** 274; May 28,

1915, **33:** 278; May 29, 1915, **33:** 285; May 30, 1915, **33:** 286; May 31, 1915, **33:** 290

June 1915

June 1, 1915, **33:** 302; June 2, 1915, **33:** 315; June 3, 1915, **33:** 335; June 4, 1915 (2), **33:** 339, 340; June 5—6, 1915, **33:** 346; June 7, 1915 (2), **33:** 365, 366; June 8, 1915 (3), **33:** 366, 367, 373; June 9, 1915 (2), **33:** 378; June 10, 1915 (2), **33:** 380, 381; June 11, 1915, **33:** 384; June 12, 1915, **33:** 389; June 13, 1915, **33:** 391; June 14, 1915, **33:** 402; June 15, 1915, **33:** 404; June 17, 1915 (2), **33:** 418; June 18, 1915 (2), **33:** 421; June 19, 1915, **33:** 423; June 20, 1915, **33:** 426; June 21, 1915, **33:** 434; June 22, 1915, **33:** 443; June 29, 1915, **33:** 458

July–August 1915

July 17, 1915, **33:** 518; July 18, 1915, **33:** 525; July 20, 1915, **33:** 542; July 21, 1915, **34:** 7; July 22, 1915, **34:** 14; Aug. 2, 1915, **34:** 63; Aug. 3, 1915, **34:** 77; Aug. 4-5, 1915, **34:** 90; Aug. 5, 1915, **34:** 103; Aug. 7, 1915 (2), **34:** 124, 130; Aug. 8, 1915, **34:** 141; Aug. 9, 1915, **34:** 154; Aug. 11, 1915 (2), **34:** 165, 170; Aug. 12, 1915, **34:** 181; Aug. 13, 1915, **34:** 194; Aug. 15, 1915 (2), **34:** 205, 212; Aug. 16, 1915, **34:** 223; Aug. 17, 1915, **34:** 232; Aug. 18, 1915, **34:** 245; Aug. 19, 1915, **34:** 263; Aug. 20, 1915 (2), **34:** 269; Aug. 21, 1915, **34:** 285; Aug. 22, 1915 (2), **34:** 292; Aug. 24, 1915, **34:** 311; Aug. 25, 1915, **34:** 326; Aug. 26, 1915, **34:** 336; Aug. 27, 1915, **34:** 347; Aug. 28, 1915, **34:** 355; Aug. 29, 1915, **34:** 364; Aug. 30, 1915, **34:** 380; Aug. 31, 1915, **34:** 396

September–December 1915

Sept. 2, 1915, **34:** 406; Sept. 3, 1915, **34:** 415; Sept. 5, 1915, **34:** 420; Sept. 6, 1915, **34:** 424; Sept. 7, 1915, **34:** 431; Sept. 10, 1915, **34:** 447; Sept. 12, 1915, **34:** 459; Sept. 13, 1915, **34:** 464; Sept. 14, 1915, **34:** 469; Sept. 15, 1915 (2), **34:** 475, 476; Sept. 16, 1915, **34:** 480; Sept. 17, 1915, **34:** 486; Sept. 18, 1915 (2), **34:** 489, 490; Sept. 20, 1915, **34:** 495; Sept. 21, 1915 (2), **34:** 501; Sept. 22, 1915, **34:** 509; Sept. 24, 1915, **34:** 518; Sept. 26, 1915, **34:** 524; Sept. 27, 1915, **34:** 533; Sept. 30, 1915, **34:** 545; Oct. 1, 1915, **35:** 11; Oct. 3, 1915, **35:** 17; Oct. 4, 1915, **35:** 22; Oct. 6, 1915, **35:** 35; Oct. 7, 1915, **35:** 41; Nov. 1, 1915, **35:** 154; Nov. 2, 1915, **35:** 161; Nov. 3, 1915 (2), **35:** 162, 166; Nov. 28, 1915, **35:** 262; Nov. 30, 1915 (2), **35:** 271, 275; Dec. 1, 1915, **35:** 281; Dec. 9, 1915, **35:** 320

Harry Augustus Garfield, May 30, 1916, **37:** 130

John Palmer Gavit, April 7, 1915, **32:** 493

Carter Glass, Oct. 27, 1915, **35:** 117

Alice Gertrude Gordon, Oct. 4, 1915, **35:** 23

Charles Henry Grasty, June 13, 1913, **27:** 517

Thomas Watt Gregory, Nov. 8, 1915, **35:** 182

Sir Edward Grey, Aug. 7, 1914, **30:** 359

David Wark Griffith, March 2, 1915, **32:** 310

Abram Woodruff Halsey, March 5, 1913, **27:** 154

Norman Hapgood, Jan. 30, 1913, **27:** 92; Feb. 5, 1913, **27:** 102; May 20, 1913, **27:** 459; Oct. 31, 1915, **35:** 145

Samuel Allen Harlow, May 11, 1915, **33:** 160

George McLean Harper, Aug. 8, 1914, **30:** 364

Jenny Davidson Hibben, Aug. 15, 1914, **30:** 384

Jenny Davidson Hibben and John Grier Hibben, Aug. 19, 1914, **30:** 404

John Grier Hibben, June 6, 1914, **30:** 156

William Hitz, Jan. 30, 1915, **32:** 163

Herbert Clark Hoover, Sept. 3, 1915, **34:** 409

Charlotte Everette Wise Hopkins, Nov. 4, 1914, **31:** 560; June 21, 1915, **33:** 429

Edward Mandell House, May 21, 1913, **27:** 462; Sept. 10, 1913, **28:** 270; Nov. 20, 1913, **28:** 571; Feb. 12, 1914, **29:** 245; Feb. 21, 1914 (2), **29:** 277; June 12, 1914, **30:** 174; Aug. 7, 1914, **30:** 359; Aug. 16, 1914, **30:** 385; Jan. 26, 1915, **32:** 128; Jan. 29, 1915 (2), **32:** 162; Oct. 1, 1915, **35:** 15; Oct. 5, 1915, **35:** 24; Oct. 27, 1915, **35:** 118; Oct. 30, 1915, **35:** 137; Nov. 1, 1915, **35:** 152; Nov. 25, 1915, **35:** 254; May 9, 1916, **37:** 8; May 22, 1916, **37:** 95; Sept. 19, 1916, **38:** 186

David Franklin Houston, Feb. 17, 1915, **32:** 243; Feb. 17, 1916, **36:** 190

Annie Josephine Wilson Howe, April 13, 1915, **32:** 517

Florence Stevens Hoyt, Aug. 7, 1914, **30:** 358; Sept. 12, 1914, **31:** 27

Mary Eloise Hoyt, Aug. 11, 1914, **30:** 375; Jan. 21, 1915, **32:** 100; Nov. 1, 1916, **38:** 590

Mary Allen Hulbert, Aug. 7, 1914, **30:** 357; Aug. 23, 1914, **30:** 439; Feb. 12, 1915, **32:** 230; June 10, 1915, **33:** 382; June 16, 1915, **33:** 412; June 20, 1915, **33:** 424; Sept. 3, 1915, **34:** 412; Sept. 7, 1915, **34:** 430; Oct. 11, 1915, **35:** 53; Nov. 2, 1915, **35:** 237

Melancthon Williams Jacobus, May 21, 1915, **33:** 229; April 23, 1916, **36:** 531

John Franklin Jameson, Jan. 13, 1913, **27:** 45; Oct. 29, 1913, **28:** 470; Aug. 4, 1915, **34:** 87

George Sibley Johns, Oct. 28, 1913, **28:** 465

David Benton Jones, March 6, 1916, **36:** 260

Thomas Davies Jones, July 20, 1914, **30:** 292; July 27, 1914, **30:** 311; Oct. 7, 1915, **35:** 37; March 2, 1916, **36:** 244

Wesley Norwood Jones, March 29, 1916, **36:** 376

Jean Jules Jusserand, Oct. 7, 1915, **35:** 38; Sept. 17, 1916, **38:** 180

James Keeley, Feb. 17, 1915, **32:** 244

Benjamin Mandeville King, March 24, 1914, **29:** 375

George Mason La Monte, March 2, 1913, **27**: 146
Clarinda Huntington Pendleton Lamar, Oct. 7, 1915, **35**: 38; Feb. 22, 1916, **36**: 204
Joseph Rucker Lamar, May 14, 1915, **33**: 202
Franklin Knight Lane, Sept. 22, 1914, **31**: 77
Robert Lansing, Oct. 9, 1916, **38**: 376
Robert Lansing and others, Dec. 28, 1915, **35**: 401
Owen Reed Lovejoy, Feb. 10, 1913, **27**: 107
Abbott Lawrence Lowell, June 30, 1915, **33**: 458

William Gibbs McAdoo, Dec. 31, 1913, **29**: 89; Aug. 23, 1915, **34**: 294
Charles Stedman Macfarland, Dec. 14, 1915, **35**: 354
Anne McIlvaine, Sept. 17, 1916, **38**: 180
John Van Antwerp McMurray, April 18, 1916, **36**: 505
Thomas Riley Marshall, Aug. 6, 1914, **30**: 355
Elmer Truesdale Merrill, Jan. 15, 1915, **32**: 78
George Campbell Morgan, Feb. 18, 1914, **29**: 270
John Pierpont Morgan, Jr., May 14, 1915, **33**: 202
Frank Morrison, March 7, 1913, **27**: 159
John R. Mott, July 3, 1913, **28**: 22; May 30, 1914, **30**: 119
Leroy Arthur Mullen, Oct. 21, 1915, **35**: 95
J. Edwin Murphy, Nov. 25, 1915, **35**: 256

William Henry Cardinal O'Connell, May 11, 1915, **33**: 159
Richard Olney, Feb. 4, 1916, **36**: 132
Richard Victor Oulahan, April 18, 1916, **36**: 505

Walter Hines Page, July 20, 1913, **28**: 52; Sept. 12, 1913, **28**: 276; Nov. 7, 1913, **28**: 507; June 5, 1914, **30**: 149; March 6, 1916, **36**: 261
George Foster Peabody, Nov. 6, 1916, **38**: 620
Bliss Perry, Aug. 8, 1914, **30**: 363
Henry Means Pindell, May 23, 1913, **27**: 466
Raymond Poincaré, March 2, 1914, **29**: 304; Oct. 29, 1914, **31**: 247; translation, 247
Edward William Pou, July 10, 1916, **37**: 398
Paul Wilkinson Pope, Nov. 12, 1914, **31**: 310
The Princeton Alumni Weekly, June 21, 1915, **33**: 432
Princeton University, Board of Trustees, Jan. 9, 1913, **27**: 26
Henry Smith Pritchett, May 7, 1914, **30**: 6
Ralph Pulitzer, April 27, 1916, **36**: 565; May 23, 1916, **37**: 100

William Cox Redfield, Aug. 6, 1914, **30**: 356; Dec. 27, 1915, **35**: 398
Edith Gittings Reid, March 4, 1914, **29**: 310; Nov. 28, 1915, **35**: 262
Paul Samuel Reinsch, Oct. 5, 1914, **31**: 284

James Ford Rhodes, April 22, 1915, **33:** 64
Melvin A. Rice, June 6, 1916, **37:** 164; Aug. 23, 1916, **38:** 81
Franklin Delano Roosevelt, June 9, 1915, **33:** 377
Theodore Roosevelt, Aug. 5, 1914, **30:** 351

Willard Saulsbury, Jan. 11, 1913, **27:** 39
Francis Bowes Sayre, April 25, 1916, **36:** 552
Jessie Woodrow Wilson Sayre, Aug. 22, 1914, **30:** 436; Nov. 20, 1914, **31:** 341; Sept. 10, 1914, **31:** 556; March 1, 1915, **32:** 306; May 13, 1915, **33:** 190; Aug. 28, 1915, **34:** 378; Oct. 17, 1915, **35:** 79; Dec. 26, 1915, **35:** 393; Feb 9, 1916, **36:** 151; May 10, 1916, **37:** 14; May 19, 1916, **37:** 78; Aug. 30, 1916, **38:** 121; Oct. 11, 1916, **38:** 396
Louis Seibold, Oct.11, 1915, **35:** 52
Edward Wright Sheldon, Dec. 5, 1915, **35:** 292
Lucy Marshall Smith and Mary Randolph Smith, Dec. 20, 1915, **35:** 373; Jan. 7, 1916, **35:** 455
Marcus Aurelius Smith, Aug. 6, 1914, **30:** 357
Pussy de Spoelberch and E. de Spoelberch, Feb. 18, 1915, **32:** 257
Sir Cecil Arthur Spring Rice, Dec. 8, 1913, **29:** 24; Dec. 24, 1913, **29:** 75; Dec. 28, 1914, **31:** 541; Oct. 6, 1915, **35:** 32; Oct. 20, 1915, **35:** 89; June 10, 1916, **37:** 205; Sept. 17, 1916, **38:** 181
Joseph H. Stewart, March 13, 1913, **27:** 176
Henry Albert Stimson, May 11, 1915, **33:** 160
Mark Sullivan, June 12, 1913, **27:** 514
Claude Augustus Swanson, Oct. 7, 1915, **35:** 37

William Howard Taft, Jan. 6, 1913, **27:** 16
James Henry Taylor, April 24, 1913, **27:** 357
Knox Taylor, Dec. 7, 1914, **31:** 412
Arthur W. Tedcastle, Jan. 28, 1913, **27:** 90
Samuel Huston Thompson, Jr., July 3, 1915, **33:** 472
Nancy Saunders Toy, Jan. 22, 1915, **32:** 111; Jan. 13, 1915, **32:** 537; July 17, 1915, **33:** 517
Joseph Patrick Tumulty, Sept. 15, 1915, **34:** 471; Dec. 27, 1915, **35:** 397; Jan. 2, 1916, **35:** 419; Nov. 10, 1916, **38:** 629

Henry van Dyke, Aug. 9, 1914, **30:** 364; Sept. 6, 1916, **38:** 211
Oswald Garrison Villard, May 14, 1915, **33:** 201; Sept. 3, 1915, **34:** 411; Sept. 14, 1915, **34:** 466; Oct. 15, 1915, **35:** 69

Henry Watterson, Sept. 24, 1914, **31:** 83
Brand Whitlock, Dec. 19, 1914, **31:** 496; Dec. 24, 1915, **35:** 390
John Sharp Williams, Jan. 31, 1914, **29:** 208
Ellen Axson Wilson
   July–August 1913
   July 2, 1913, **28:** 20; July 15, 1913, **28:** 36; July 18, 1913, **28:** 42; July 20, 1913, **28:** 54; July 21, 1913, **28:** 61; July 22, 1913, **28:** 63; July 23, 1913, **28:** 66; July 24, 1913, **28:** 81; July 27,

1913, **28:** 88; July 28, 1913, **28:** 91; July 29, 1913, **28:** 95; July 30, 1913, **28:** 98; July 31, 1913, **28:** 101; Aug. 1, 1913, **28:** 102; Aug. 2, 1913, **28:** 103; Aug. 3, 1913, **28:** 108; Aug. 4, 1913, **28:** 112; Aug. 5, 1913, **28:** 119; Aug. 6, 1913, **28:** 126; Aug. 7, 1913, **28:** 129; Aug. 8, 1913, **28:** 131; Aug. 9, 1913, **29:** 562; Aug. 10, 1913, **28:** 138; Aug. 11, 1913, **28:** 143; Aug. 12, 1913, **28:** 145; Aug. 13, 1913, **28:** 149; Aug. 14, 1913, **28:** 159; Aug. 15, 1913, **28:** 165; Aug. 16, 1913, **28:** 178; Aug. 17, 1913, **28:** 181; Aug. 18, 1913, **28:** 189; Aug. 19, 1913, **28:** 194; Aug. 20, 1913, **28:** 199

September 1913

Sept. 3, 1913, **28:** 252; Sept. 4, 1913, **28:** 256; Sept. 5, 1913, **28:** 258; Sept. 6, 1913, **28:** 260; Sept. 7, 1913, **28:** 264; Sept. 8, 1913, **28:** 266; Sept. 9, 1913, **28:** 269; Sept. 10, 1913, **28:** 273; Sept. 15, 1913, **28:** 277; Sept. 16, 1913, **28:** 278; Sept. 17, 1913, **28:** 286; Sept. 18, 1913, **28:** 291; Sept. 19, 1913, **28:** 301; Sept. 20, 1913, **28:** 307; Sept. 21, 1913, **28:** 315; Sept. 22, 1913, **28:** 318; Sept. 23, 1913, **28:** 319; Sept. 24, 1913, **28:** 321; Sept. 25, 1913, **28:** 327; Sept. 26, 1913, **28:** 331; Sept. 27, 1913, **28:** 333; Sept. 28, 1913, **28:** 338; Sept. 29, 1913, **28:** 345

October 1913–April 1914

Oct. 3, 1913, **28:** 355; Oct. 4, 1913, **28:** 360; Oct. 5, 1913, **28:** 363; Oct. 6, 1913 (2), **28:** 367, 368; Oct. 7, 1913, **28:** 372; Oct. 8, 1913, **28:** 375; Oct. 9, 1913, **28:** 383; Oct. 10, 1913, **28:** 387; Oct. 11, 1913, **28:** 391; Oct. 12, 1913, **28:** 398; Oct. 13, 1913, **28:** 400; Oct. 16, 1913, **28:** 413; April 18, 1914, **29:** 460

John Adams Wilson, July 4, 1916, **37:** 359

Joseph R. Wilson, Jr., Jan. 14, 1913, **27:** 55; Jan. 27, 1913, **27:** 82; May 22, 1916, **37:** 95

Margaret Woodrow Wilson, Aug. 16, 1915, **34:** 217; Oct. 5, 1915, **35:** 27; Dec. 23, 1915, **35:** 386; Jan. 3, 1916, **35:** 423; c. June 17, 1916, **37:** 246; July 9, 1916, **37:** 382; Aug. 9, 1916, **38:** 15; Sept. 19, 1916, **38:** 186

Margaret Woodrow Wilson and others, Sept. 2, 1915, **34:** 407

William Bauchop Wilson, April 3, 1916, **36:** 406

Caleb Thomas Winchester, March 31, 1916, **36:** 399

Felexiana Shepherd Baker Woodrow, March 3, 1913, **27:** 147; Dec. 28, 1914, **31:** 542; Dec 28, 1915, **35:** 404

James Woodrow, March 31, 1916, **36:** 398

Charles Albert Woods, April 22, 1913, **27:** 348

Hiram Woods, Jr., March 23, 1916, **36:** 359; March 29, 1916, **36:** 377

Frederic Yates, Aug. 18, 1914, **30:** 401

Telephonic messages

From Wilson to
Alexander Graham Bell, Jan. 25, 1915, **32:** 118

Charles Cadwell Moore, Jan. 25, 1915, **32:** 118
Thomas Augustus Watson, Jan. 25, 1915, **32:** 118

Interviews, conferences, and dialogues

Interview on the banking and currency bill, June 23, 1913, **27:** 565
Wilson's policy toward Mexico, Jan. 1914, **29:** 92; April 27, 1914, **29:** 516
Draft of an article by John Reed, June 30, 1914, **30:** 231
Dialogues with William Monroe Trotter about segregation in governmental departments, Nov. 6, 1913, **28:** 496; Nov. 12, 1914, **31:** 301; 308
Interview on Mexico by Samuel G. Blythe, Dec. 5, 1914, **31:** 390
Memorandum of an interview on the European war by Herbert Bruce Brougham, Dec. 14, 1914, **31:** 458
Memorandum by Gabriel Alphaud about an interview with Wilson on America's neutrality, April 1, 1915, **32:** 463
Memorandum by Henry Skillman Breckinridge about an interview with Wilson on the intended resignation of Lindley Miller Garrison, Feb. 4, 1915, **32:** 538
Account by Arch Wilkinson Shaw of a talk with Wilson on relations between business and government, Jan. 14, 1915, **32:** 69
An interview with Thomas Beaumont Hohler, Oct. 21, 1915, **35:** 97
A memorandum by Andrew Clerk Imbrie about a conversation with Wilson on antidumping legislation, March 8, 1916, **36:** 274
A colloquy with a group of antipreparedness leaders, May 8, 1916, **36:** 634
A memorandum by Ray Stannard Baker about a conversation with Wilson, May 12, 1916, **37:** 31
A memorandum by Franz Hugo Krebs about a conversation with Wilson regarding the fate of Sir Roger Casement, July 7, 1916, **37:** 379
A dialogue with John Franklin Smulski, July 12, 1916, **37:** 407
A memorandum by Homer Stillé Cummings about a talk with Wilson on the presidential campaign, Aug. 7, 1916, **38:** 5
A memorandum by Homer Stillé Cummings about a conference of the Democratic National Committee with Wilson, Aug. 15, 1916, **38:** 36
A coloquy with members of the American Neutral Conference, Aug. 30, 1916, **38:** 108
A memorandum by Homer Stillé Cummings about a talk with Wilson on the political situation in Connecticut, Sept. 11, 1916, **38:** 168
A memorandum by Walter Hines Page about a talk with Wilson on British-American relations, Sept. 23, 1916, **38:** 241
An account of an interview with Wilson by Ida Minerva Tarbell, Oct. 3, 1916, **38:** 323
An interview with Henry Noble Hall on the presidential campaign, Oct. 31, 1916, **38:** 564

A memorandum by Homer Stillé Cummings about an interview with Wilson on the aftermath of the election, Nov. 17, 1916, **38:** 669

Press Conferences

March 22, 1913, **27:** 210; April 7, 1913, **27:** 263; April 11, 1913, **27:** 284; April 14, 1913, **27:** 301; April 18, 1913, **27:** 323; April 21, 1913, **27:** 337; April 24, 1913, **27:** 352; April 28, 1913, **27:** 359; May 5, 1913, **27:** 397; May 8, 1913, **27:** 408; May 12, 1913, **27:** 415; May 15, 1913, **27:** 430; May 19, 1913, **27:** 449; May 22, 1913, **27:** 463; May 26, 1913, **27:** 471; May 29, 1913, **27:** 483; June 5, 1913, **27:** 495

June 9, 1913, **27:** 504; June 12, 1913, **27:** 509; June 16, 1913, **27:** 522; June 23, 1913, **27:** 558; June 26, 1913, **28:** 8; July 17, 1913, **28:** 37; July 21, 1913, **28:** 55; July 28, 1913, **28:** 89; Aug. 11, 1913, **28:** 139; Aug. 14, 1913, **28:** 151; Sept. 18, 1913, **28:** 287; Sept. 25, 1913, **27:** 322; Oct. 6, 1913, **28:** 364; Oct 9, 1913, **28:** 378; Oct. 20, 1913, **28:** 417; Oct. 30, 1913, **28:** 471; Nov. 3, 1913, **28:** 485; Nov. 10, 1913, **28:** 516; Nov. 17, 1913, **28:** 559; Nov. 20, 1913, **28:** 568

Jan. 3, 1914, **29:** 98; Jan. 13, 1914, **29:** 128; Jan. 18, 1914, **29:** 138; Jan. 26, 1914, **29:** 174; Jan. 29, 1914, **29:** 198; Feb. 2, 1914, **29:** 212; Feb. 5, 1914, **29:** 222; Feb. 9, 1914, **29:** 240; Feb. 16, 1914, **29:** 261; Feb. 26, 1914, **29:** 291; March 2, 1914, **29:** 302; March 5, 1914, **29:** 313; March 12, 1914, **29:** 333; March 16, 1914, **29:** 347; March 19, 1914, **29:** 353; March 23, 1914, **29:** 373; March 26, 1914, **29:** 377; March 30, 1914, **29:** 384; April 2, 1914, **29:** 397; April 6, 1914, **29:** 406; April 9, 1914, **29:** 414; April 13, 1914, **29:** 424; April 16, 1914, **29:** 450; April 20, 1914, **29:** 468; April 23, 1914, **29:** 488

June 1, 1914, **30:** 126; June 8, 1914, **30:** 158; June 11, 1914, **30:** 170; June 15, 1914, **30:** 181; June 18, 1914, **30:** 190; June 25, 1914, **30:** 208; June 29, 1914, **30:** 222; July 2, 1914, **30:** 243; July 6, 1914, **30:** 259; July 9, 1914, **30:** 267; July 13, 1914, **30:** 279; July 23, 1914, **30:** 296; July 27, 1914, **30:** 307; July 30, 1914, **30:** 317; Aug. 3, 1914, **30:** 331; Aug. 17, 1914, **30:** 387; Aug. 20, 1914, **30:** 404; Aug. 24, 1914, **30:** 440; Sept. 3, 1914, **30:** 469; Sept. 21, 1914, **31:** 63; Sept. 24, 1914, **31:** 78; Sept. 28, 1914, **31:** 87

Oct. 1, 1914, **31:** 111; Oct. 8, 1914, **31:** 132; Oct. 12, 1914, **31:** 142; Oct. 15, 1914, **31:** 149; Oct. 19, 1914, **31:** 176; Oct. 22, 1914, **31:** 206; Oct. 26, 1914, **31:** 233; Nov. 10, 1914, **31:** 292; Nov. 17, 1914, **31:** 322; Nov. 24, 1914, **31:** 350; Dec. 1, 1914, **31:** 373; Dec. 8, 1914, **31:** 413; Dec. 15, 1914, **31:** 463; Dec. 22, 1914, **31:** 507; Dec. 29, 1914, **31:** 543; Jan. 5, 1915, **32:** 13; Jan. 12, 1915, **32:** 54; Jan. 19, 1915, **32:** 87; Jan. 26, 1915, **32:** 122; Feb. 2, 1915, **32:** 171; Feb. 9, 1915, **32:** 199; Feb. 16, 1915, **32:** 239; Feb. 23, 1915, **32:** 273; March 2, 1915, **32:** 306; March 9, 1915, **32:** 342; March 30, 1915, **32:** 456; April 13, 1915, **32:** 516; April 27, 1915, **33:** 70;

May 11, 1915, **33:** 153; May 25, 1915, **33:** 251; June 1, 1915, **33:** 292; June 8, 1915, **33:** 367; June 15, 1915, **33:** 397; June 22, 1915, **33:** 435; Sept. 29, 1916, **38:** 286

News Reports

Opposes inaugural ball, Jan. 17, 1913, **27:** 59

Confers with social workers, Jan. 27, 1913, **27:** 75

Discourses on cabinet posts, Jan. 31, 1913, **27:** 93

Conversation with newspapermen in Trenton, Feb. 3, 1913, **27:** 96

Confers with senators at Capitol, April 9, 1913, **27:** 278

Plan for currency legislation adopted, July 28, 1913, **28:** 90

Discusses diplomatic problems with the Senate Foreign Relations Committee, Jan. 26, 1914, **29:** 178, 180

Receives a delegation of suffragists, Feb. 2, 1914, **29:** 213

Endorses some labor measures as part of antitrust legislation, April 13, 1914, **29:** 425

Briefs congressional leaders on plans to meet the Mexican crisis, April 15, 1914, **29:** 440

Confrontation with labor leaders and their supporters in Congress, April 30, 1914, **29:** 537

Says army will stay in Mexico until peace is guaranteed, May 18, 1914, **30:** 39

Refuses plea of businessmen's delegation to limit antitrust legislation, May 28, 1914, **30:** 93

Confers with congressional leaders on shipping crisis, July 31, 1914, **30:** 324

Confers with House leadership on progress of the shipping bill, Aug. 1, 1914, **30:** 325

Opposes valorizing of cotton, Oct. 7, 1914, **31:** 129

Administration position on loans by American bankers to belligerent nations, Oct. 15, 1914, **31:** 153

Receives Negro delegation on segregation in governmental departments, Nov. 12, 1914, **31:** 308; Nov. 13, 1914, **31:** 311

Opposes congressional investigation on the state of national preparedness, Dec. 7, 1914, **31:** 409

Speaks to railroad presidents about plan for settling the strike crisis, Aug. 21, 1916, **38:** 55

Confers with the Mexican members of the Joint Commission, Sept. 12, 1916, **38:** 169

Discusses strategy and issues of the presidential campaign, Sept. 29, 1916, **38:** 291

Remarks on woman suffrage, Oct. 5, 1916, **38:** 336

Reacts to election returns, **38:** Nov. 7, 1916, 621; Nov. 9, 1916, 623; Nov. 10, 1916, 625

Writings

A paper about the workings of the Constitution, May 17, 1884, **38:** 680

Tribute to the women of the South, Jan. 1, 1910, **27:** 574
Preface to *The New Freedom*, Jan. 2, 1913, **27:** 6
Epitaph for his father's tombstone, May 25, 1914, **30:** 74
An estimate of his father, May 25, 1914, **30:** 75
A draft of the National Democratic platform of 1916, June 10, 1916, **37:** 190
America's Opportunity, July 30, 1916, **37:** 500
The Mexican Question, Aug. 1, 1916, **37:** 508

COLLATERAL MATERIALS

Political correspondence, reports, memoranda, and aide-mémoire

William Charles Adamson to Franklin Knight Lane, March 12, 1916, **36:** 302
Joshua Willis Alexander to Joseph Patrick Tumulty, April 28, 1916, **36:** 567
Elias Milton Ammons to Joseph Patrick Tumulty, April 25, 1914, **29:** 502
Peirce Anderson to Oscar Wenderoth, Oct. 23, 1913, **28:** 502
Bernard Mannes Baruch to Edward Mandell House, April 24, 1916, **36:** 544
Louis Dembitz Brandeis to Frank Lyon Polk, Aug. 9, 1916, **38:** 14
Desha Breckinridge to William Frank McCombs, March 7, 1914, **29:** 343
Herbert Janvrin Browne to William Jennings Bryan, Aug. 4, 1914, **30:** 346
Frank Buchanan to Joseph Patrick Tumulty, July 28, 1915, **34:** 39
William Edwin Chilton to Joseph Patrick Tumulty, April 5, 1914, **29:** 405
Henry D. Clayton on Wilson's patronage policies, April 22, 1913, **27:** 344
Alfred B. Cosey to Joseph Patrick Tumulty, Aug. 22, 1913, **28:** 209
Margaret Blaine Damrosch to Joseph Patrick Tumulty, March 27, 1915, **32:** 455
Memorandum by Josephus Daniels on the Council of National Defense, Sept. 25, 1916, **38:** 272
Hywel Davies and W. R. Fairley, draft of a possible adjustment of the Colorado coal strike, Sept. 5, 1914, **30:** 486
Alice Chipman Dewey to Norman Hapgood, Sept. 14, 1916, **38:** 175
Thomas Dixon, Jr., to Joseph Patrick Tumulty, Jan. 27, 1915, **32:** 142
William Edward Burghardt Du Bois to Joseph Patrick Tumulty, Oct. 24, 1916, **38:** 522
Charles William Eliot to Joseph Patrick Tumulty, Sept. 11, 1916, **38:** 167; Sept. 25, 1916, **38:** 279
Mary Field to Frederic Clemson Howe, Aug. 15, 1916, **38:** 59

Edward Aloysius Flannery to Joseph Patrick Tumulty, Aug. 24, 1916, **38:** 83

Lindley Miller Garrison to Francis Burton Harrison, Jan. 11, 1915, **32:** 535; Jan. 12, 1915, **32:** 536

Lindley Miller Garrison to Joseph Patrick Tumulty, Aug. 7, 1914, **30:** 360; Oct. 19, 1915, **35:** 85; Nov. 1, 1915, **35:** 149

Memorandum by Lindley Miller Garrison on conversation with Wilson about Mexican situation, May 9, 1914, **30:** 11

John Palmer Gavit to Oswald Garrison Villard, Sept. 26, 1913, **28:** 332; Oct. 1, 1913, **28:** 348

Samuel Gompers and others to the officers of all organized labor, Oct. 14, 1916, **38:** 469

Thomas Watt Gregory to Joseph Patrick Tumulty, May 31, 1914, **30:** 123

Memorandum by Thomas Watt Gregory on the Clayton bill, Sept. 4, 1914, **30:** 480

Henry Noble Hall to Joseph Patrick Tumulty, March 13, 1914, **29:** 344

Norman Hapgood to Cary Travers Grayson, May 4, 1916, **36:** 606

Norman Hapgood to Raymond Robins, July 6, 1916, **37:** 373

Norman Hapgood to Joseph Patrick Tumulty, Jan. 28, 1916, **36:** 25; Feb. 1, 1916, **36:** 86; May 27, 1916, **37:** 117

Joseph Wright Harriman to Frank Lyon Polk, March 3, 1916, **36:** 249

Karl Edwin Harriman to Joseph Patrick Tumulty, April 26, 1916, **36:** 559

Francis Burton Harrison to Lindley Miller Garrison, Jan. 12, 1915, **32:** 535

Francis Burton Harrison to Joseph Patrick Tumulty, Aug. 31, 1915, **34:** 389

James Hay to Albert Sidney Burleson, July 27, 1915, **34:** 38

J. L. Hegler to Morris Sheppard, Oct. 24, 1914, **31:** 248

Gilbert Monell Hitchcock to Joseph Patrick Tumulty, Jan. 11, 1916, **35:** 466

Herbert Clark Hoover to Edward Mandell House, Feb. 26, 1915, **32:** 293

John Appleton Haven Hopkins to Vance Criswell McCormick, Nov. 14, 1916, **38:** 642

Memorandum by Edward Mandell House on the successful settlement of the railroad controversy, Sept. 8, 1916, **38:** 165

Edwin Walter Kemmerer and Royal Meeker on banking reform, March 21, 1913, **27:** 204

John Worth Kern to William Gibbs McAdoo, July 5, 1916, **37:** 366

James Kerney to Joseph Patrick Tumulty, May 7, 1913, **27:** 407

Franklin Knight Lane to Edward Mandell House, Jan. 26, 1913, **27:** 81

Robert Lansing to William Gibbs McAdoo, Sept. 14, 1916, **38:** 197

Robert Lansing to Joseph Patrick Tumulty, Jan. 23, 1915, **32:** 116; Sept. 29, 1916, **38:** 300

Robert Lansing to Brand Whitlock, Feb. 1, 1916, **36:** 86

James Hamilton Lewis to Joseph Patrick Tumulty, Sept. 5, 1916, **38:** 146

Benjamin Barr Lindsey to Joseph Patrick Tumulty, May 16, 1914, **30:** 38

Walter Lippmann to Newton Diehl Baker, Aug. 2, 1916, **37:** 525; Aug. 21, 1916, **38:** 62

Walter Lippmann to Norman Hapgood, Aug. 23, 1916, **38:** 87; Sept. 22, 1916, **38:** 274

William Luke Marbury to Albert Sidney Burleson, July 13, 1916, **37:** 420

Thomas Riley Marshall to Joseph Patrick Tumulty, April 9, 1914, **29:** 418; Aug. 23, 1916, **38:** 81

William Gibbs McAdoo to George Earle Chamberlain, Sept. 22, 1915, **34:** 504

William Gibbs McAdoo to collectors and other officers of the Customs Service, Feb. 12, 1915, **32:** 226

William Gibbs McAdoo to Oswald Garrison Villard, Oct. 27, 1913, **28:** 453

Statement by William Gibbs McAdoo on the ship purchase bill, March 8, 1915, **32:** 336

Charles McCarthy to Norman Hapgood, June 3, 1914, **30:** 161

William Calhoun McDonald to Joseph Patrick Tumulty, May 4, 1916, **36:** 606

Frank McIntyre to Joseph Patrick Tumulty, Nov. 11, 1916 (2), **38:** 632, 633; Nov. 15, 1916, **38:** 656; Nov. 18, 1916, **38:** 674

Michael M. de La Mora to James Cardinal Gibbons, Aug. 14, 1914, **30:** 399

Paul Ferdinand Mueller to William Gibbs McAdoo, Sept. 26, 1916, **38:** 351

May Childs Nerney to Oswald Garrison Villard, Sept. 30, 1913, **28:** 402

Memorandum of statements by John T. Owen and E. G. Quamme before the Federal Farm Loan Board, Sept. 7, 1916, **38:** 160

Thomas Nelson Page to Carter Harrison FitzHugh, Sept. 6, 1916, **38:** 441

William Phillips to Joseph Patrick Tumulty, June 6, 1914, **30:** 156

Amos Richards Eno Pinchot to Norman Hapgood, Feb. 1, 1916, **36:** 86

Gifford Pinchot to Edward Mandell House, Nov. 18, 1915, **35:** 231

Sir Horace Plunkett to Edward Mandell House, Oct. 28, 1913, **29:** 115

Clarence Poe to Josephus Daniels, Oct. 5, 1914, **31:** 126

Louis Freeland Post to Joseph Patrick Tumulty, Nov. 15, 1913, **28:** 546; Nov. 22, 1913, **28:** 580

John Herbert Quick to William Gibbs McAdoo, Sept. 2, 1916, **38:** 158

Memorandum by the railroad presidents on Wilson's proposal for a settlement of the railroad controversy, Aug. 29, 1916, **38:** 93

Proposal by the railroad presidents for a settlement of the impending railroad strike, Aug. 29, 1916, **38:** 95

Henry Thomas Rainey to Joseph Patrick Tumulty, Oct. 25, 1914, **31:** 232

George Lawrence Record to Joseph Patrick Tumulty, Feb. 23, 1915, **32:** 281

William Cox Redfield to William Jennings Bryan, Dec. 19, 1914, **31:** 493

John Reed to William Phillips, June 4, 1914, **30:** 157

John Reed to Joseph Patrick Tumulty, June 30, 1914 (2), **30:** 231

Joseph Taylor Robinson to Joseph Patrick Tumulty, July 20, 1916, **37:** 451

Wilbur Fisk Sadler, Jr., to Joseph Patrick Tumulty, Oct. 23, 1915, **35:** 105

Hugh Lenox Scott to Leonard Wood, Sept. 1, 1915, **34:** 401

Anna Howard Shaw to Norman Hapgood, Sept. 16, 1916, **38:** 178

Arch Wilkinson Shaw to Joseph Patrick Tumulty, Jan. 14, 1915, **32:** 68

Furnifold McLendel Simmons to Joseph Patrick Tumulty, Dec. 31, 1914, **31:** 554

Lincoln Steffens to Joseph Patrick Tumulty, May 22, 1914, **30:** 64

Ethelbert Stewart to Louis Freeland Post, Nov. 21, 1913, **28:** 580

William Joel Stone to Joseph Patrick Tumulty, Sept. 25, 1916, **38:** 277; Oct. 1, 1916, **38:** 318

Ida Minerva Tarbell to John Robertson Dunlap, Aug. 21, 1916, **38:** 172

Charles Willis Thompson to Reuben Adiel Bull, March 8, 1913, **27:** 164

Samuel Huston Thompson, Jr., to Cary Travers Grayson, July 18, 1916, **37:** 435

Joseph Patrick Tumulty to Carrie Clinton Lane Chapman Catt, Sept. 1, 1916, **38:** 125

Joseph Patrick Tumulty to Lindley Miller Garrison, Aug. 8, 1914, **30:** 360

Joseph Patrick Tumulty to Samuel Gompers, Nov. 17, 1915, **35:** 211

Joseph Patrick Tumulty to James Kerney, May 5, 1913, **27:** 402

Joseph Patrick Tumulty to Vance Criswell McCormick, July 7, 1916, **37:** 378

Joseph Patrick Tumulty to Amos Richards Eno Pinchot, Jan. 28, 1916, **36:** 23

Joseph Patrick Tumulty to Edward William Pou, Feb. 25, 1916, **36:** 218

Press release by Joseph Patrick Tumulty on the development of the merchant marine, Aug. 19, 1914, **30:** 402

An unknown person to Joseph Patrick Tumulty, July 18, 1916, **37:** 434

Walker Whiting Vick to William Jennings Bryan, May 30, 1914, **30:** 165
Oswald Garrison Villard to Robert Hayne Leavell, May 15, 1913, **27:** 442
Oswald Garrison Villard to Joseph Patrick Tumulty, Nov. 17, 1914, **31:** 328
Hugh Campbell Wallace to Edward Mandell House, Aug. 2, 1915, **34:** 135; Aug. 31, 1916, **38:** 139
Alexander Walters to Joseph Patrick Tumulty, Jan. 30, 1914, **29:** 204; Jan. 10, 1916, **35:** 461
Booker Taliaferro Washington to Oswald Garrison Villard, Aug. 10, 1913, **28:** 186
Jessie Floyd Welborn to Joseph Patrick Tumulty, Sept. 17, 1914, **31:** 43
Edward Douglass White to Joseph Patrick Tumulty, April 5, 1915, **32:** 486
Brand Whitlock to Robert Lansing, Feb. 5, 1916, **36:** 135
Louis Wiley to Joseph Patrick Tumulty, Sept. 30, 1915, **34:** 542
George Fred Williams to William Jennings Bryan, April 22, 1914, **30:** 25
John Sharp Williams to Walter O. Borcherdt, Jan. 27, 1916, **36:** 21

*Diplomatic correspondence, reports, memoranda, and
aide-mémoire*

Jesús Acuña to Robert Lansing and others, Aug. 24, 1915, **34:** 321
Alvey Augustus Adee on his conversation with Chang Yin Tang, March 25, 1913, **27:** 224
Alvey Augustus Adee to Joseph Patrick Tumulty, Dec. 28, 1915, **35:** 405
Emilio Aguinaldo to William Jennings Bryan, Nov. 15, 1912, **27:** 10
Memorandum by the American members of the Joint Commission on the withdrawal of American troops from Mexico, Nov. 11, 1916, **38:** 634
Memorandum by the American members of the Joint Commission with regard to control of the Mexican-American border, Nov. 11, 1916, **38:** 634
Memorandum by Chandler Parsons Anderson on German-American relations, July 13, 1915, **33:** 501
Memorandum by Chandler Parsons Anderson on the Thrasher case, April 7, 1915, **32:** 490
Thomas Jackson Anketell to Robert Lansing, April 26, 1916, **36:** 435
Eliseo Arredondo to Robert Lansing, May 1, 1916, **36:** 582; June 24, 1916, **37:** 292; July 4, 1916, **37:** 360
Eliseo Arredondo to Frank Lyon Polk, July 12, 1916, **37:** 410
Stockton Axson's draft of an announcement of the engagement of Edith Bolling Galt to Woodrow Wilson, Oct. 2, 1915, **35:** 16

Charles Johnston Badger to Josephus Daniels, April 15, 1914, **29:** 454

Arthur Bailly-Blanchard to William Jennings Bryan, Dec. 12, 1914, **31:** 483; Dec. 15, 1914, **31:** 485

Newton Diehl Baker to Tasker Howard Bliss, Sept. 23, 1916, **38:** 235

Newton Diehl Baker to Frederick Funston, March 13, 1916, **36:** 298; March 15, 1916, **36:** 313

Newton Diehl Baker to Robert Lansing, Sept. 25, 1916, **38:** 271

Newton Diehl Baker to Joseph Patrick Tumulty, June 6, 1916, **37:** 171

Memorandum for the Adjutant General by Newton Diehl Baker about the formation of our expeditionary force to Mexico, March 10, 1916, **36:** 285

Memorandum for the Adjutant General by Newton Diehl Baker on initial objectives in Mexico in the event of open hostilities, June 22, 1916, **37:** 283

Memorandum for the Chief of Staff by Newton Diehl Baker on the dispatch of troops to Mexico, March 10, 1916, **36:** 285

Memorandum for the Chief of Staff by Newton Diehl Baker on possible confrontation between American troops and Mexican forces, March 16, 1916, **36:** 323

George Bakmet'ev (Bakhméteff) to Robert Lansing, Oct. 20, 1914, **35:** 537

Emily Greene Balch to Jane Addams, Aug. 19, 1915, **34:** 250

Arthur James Balfour to Edward Mandell House, Sept. 12, 1915, **35:** 5; March 2, 1916, **36:** 346

Colville Barclay to William Jennings Bryan, Nov. 25, 1913, **28:** 591

Colville Barclay to Sir Edward Grey, Aug. 16, 1914, **30:** 386

John Barrett to Joseph Patrick Tumulty, Jan. 6, 1916, **35:** 439

James Whitford Bashford to William Jennings Bryan, April 19, 1915, **33:** 31

Benjamin Franklin Battin to Pieter Wilhelm Adriaan Cort van der Linden and Jonkheer John Loudon, Oct. 4, 1915, **35:** 20

John William Belt to Robert Lansing, Oct. 19, 1915 (2), **35:** 94, 95

William Shepherd Benson to Robert Lansing, Aug. 9, 1915, **34:** 158

Memorandum by William Shepherd Benson on American politics in Haiti, Aug. 7, 1915, **34:** 122

Herman Bernstein to Joseph Patrick Tumulty, May 8, 1916, **36:** 655

Count Johann Heinrich von Bernstorff to Theobald von Bethmann Hollweg, March 11, 1913, **27:** 170, translation, 171; May 29, 1915, **33:** 279, translation, 283; Nov. 23, 1915, **35:** 240, translation, 241

Count Johann Heinrich von Bernstorff to the German Foreign Office, Sept. 7, 1914, **31:** 9, translation, 10; Feb. 19, 1915, **32:** 264, translation, 264; June 2, 1915, **33:** 316, translation, 318; Oct. 10, 1916, **38:** 390, translation, 391

Count Johann Heinrich von Bernstorff to Edward Mandell House, July 10, 1915, **33:** 494; July 27, 1915, **34:** 37; Aug. 21, 1915, **34:**

297; Aug. 28, 1915, **34:** 372; Sept. 11, 1915, **34:** 468; March 31, 1916, **36:** 405; April 14, 1916, **36:** 486; April 26, 1916, **36:** 558; May 8, 1916, **36:** 656; July 14, 1916, **37:** 425; Oct. 18, 1916, **38:** 494

Count Johann Heinrich von Bernstorff to Robert Lansing, Aug. 6, 1915, **34:** 123; Aug. 24, 1915, **34:** 308; Aug. 26, 1915, **34:** 330; Sept. 1, 1915, **34:** 400; Sept. 3, 1915, **34:** 417; Sept. 8, 1915 (3), **34:** 436; Sept. 25, 1915, **34:** 519; Oct. 2, 1915 (3), **35:** 13, 14; Oct. 5, 1915, **35:** 26; Dec. 31, 1915, **35:** 418; Jan. 7, 1916 (3), **35:** 451, 452; Jan. 10, 1916, **35:** 464; Jan. 22, 1916 (3), **35:** 514, 515; Jan. 26, 1916, **35:** 528; Feb. 16, 1916, **36:** 183; Feb. 29, 1916, **36:** 232; April 27, 1916, **36:** 577

Memorandum by Count Johann Heinrich von Bernstorff on the conduct of submarine warfare, March 8, 1916, **36:** 270

Tasker Howard Bliss to Newton Diehl Baker, Oct. 11, 1916, **38:** 397

Tasker Howard Bliss to Hugh Lenox Scott, Nov. 15, 1916, **38:** 675

Memorandum by Tasker Howard Bliss on the protection of the Mexican-American border, Sept. 18, 1916, **38:** 220

Proposed agreement by Tasker Howard Bliss for protection of the Mexican-American border, Sept. 23, 1916, **38:** 233

Victor Blue to Frank Friday Fletcher, April 13, 1914, **29:** 432

Redraft by the Brazilian and Chilean governments of a proposed Pan-American treaty, June 16, 1916, **37:** 241

Charles Henry Brent to Edward Mandell House, Dec. 28, 1913, **29:** 165

Statement by the British government in response to a Senate resolution on clemency for Irish political prisoners, Aug. 28, 1916, **38:** 92

The British embassy to Sir Edward Grey, Nov. 14, 1913, **28:** 543

Constantin Brün to Robert Lansing, Dec. 27, 1915, **35:** 403; Jan. 22, 1916, **35:** 508

Constantin Brün to Frank Lyon Polk, July 29, 1916, **37:** 506

William Jennings Bryan to Emilio Aguinaldo, Jan. 2, 1913, **27:** 10

William Jennings Bryan's peace plan, April 8, 1913, **27:** 276

William Jennings Bryan on French loans to Mexico, May 23, 1913, **27:** 478; May 26, 1913, **27:** 479

William Jennings Bryan to Arthur Bailly-Blanchard, Dec. 11, 1914, **31:** 457; Dec. 18, 1914, **31:** 486; Feb. 27, 1915, **32:** 297

William Jennings Bryan to William Wesley Canada, April 21, 1914, **29:** 477; Dec. 9, 1914, **31:** 431

William Jennings Bryan to Viscount Sutemi Chinda, April 27, 1915, **33:** 82; May 5, 1915, **33:** 102

William Jennings Bryan to Henry Prather Fletcher, March 31, 1915, **32:** 542

William Jennings Bryan to John Franklin Fort, Feb. 27, 1915, **32:** 295

William Jennings Bryan to Paul Fuller, Jr., May 6, 1915, **33:** 116

William Jennings Bryan to George Wilkins Guthrie, Feb. 18, 1915,

32: 247; Feb. 18, 1915, **32:** 248; April 2, 1915, **32:** 467; May 6, 1915 (2), **33:** 113, 114

William Jennings Bryan to William Bayard Hale, Nov. 19, 1913, **28:** 568; Nov. 24, 1913, **28:** 588

William Jennings Bryan to Robert Lansing, Sept. 2, 1915, **34:** 404

William Jennings Bryan to John Lind, Aug. 15, 1913, **28:** 162; Aug. 20, 1913, **28:** 205; Dec. 13, 1913, **29:** 34; Jan. 17, 1914, **29:** 137

William Jennings Bryan to Ernest Lister, March 23, 1913, **27:** 221

William Jennings Bryan to Nelson O'Shaughnessy, April 13, 1914, **29:** 426; April 19, 1914, **29:** 464; April 19, 1914 (2), **29:** 466; April 21, 1914, **29:** 478

William Jennings Bryan to Thomas Nelson Page, May 13, 1915, **33:** 182

William Jennings Bryan to Walter Hines Page, Oct. 1, 1914, **31:** 113; Jan. 12, 1915, **32:** 59; March 3, 1915, **32:** 311

William Jennings Bryan to Walter Hines Page, William Graves Sharp, and David Rowland Francis, May 6, 1915, **33:** 114

William Jennings Bryan to Don Juan Riaño y Gayangos, April 28, 1914, **29:** 524

William Jennings Bryan to Paul Samuel Reinsch, Feb. 18, 1915, **32:** 246; March 31, 1915, **32:** 460; April 2, 1915, **32:** 467; April 9, 1915, **32:** 500; April 15, 1915, **32:** 520; April 16, 1915, **32:** 528; May 6, 1915, **33:** 114

William Jennings Bryan to Arnold Shanklin, April 21, 1914, **29:** 478

William Jennings Bryan to the special commissioners, May 20, 1914, **30:** 49; May 30, 1914, **30:** 119; May 31, 1914, **30:** 122; June 23, 1914, **30:** 204

William Jennings Bryan to Sir Cecil Arthur Spring Rice, March 10, 1914, **29:** 341

William Jennings Bryan to Eduardo Suárez-Mujica, April 27, 1915, **33:** 77

William Jennings Bryan to James Mark Sullivan, Jan. 12, 1915, **32:** 76; April 19, 1915, **33:** 27

William Jennings Bryan to Joseph Patrick Tumulty, April 8, 1913, **27:** 276; May 2, 1913, **27:** 381; Aug. 24, 1914, **30:** 449; Dec. 2, 1914, **31:** 381

William Jennings Bryan to John Campbell White, Dec. 3, 1914, **31:** 383

James Viscount Bryce to Sir Edward Grey, Feb. 21, 1913, **27:** 124; March 24, 1913, **27:** 221; April 14, 1913, **27:** 310; April 24, 1913, **27:** 357

James Viscount Bryce to Edward Mandell House, July 30, 1915, **34:** 187; Nov. 26, 1915, **35:** 347; May 31, 1916, **37:** 239; June 8, 1916, **37:** 289; June 12, 1916, **37:** 312; Aug. 26, 1916, **38:** 85; Oct. 2, 1916, **38:** 454

Baron Stephan Burián von Rajecz to Robert Lansing, Dec. 20, 1915 (2), **35:** 379, 380; Dec. 23, 1915, **35:** 389

Baron Stephan Burián von Rajecz to Frederick Courtland Penfield, Dec. 15, 1915, **35**: 365

Noel Buxton to Edward Mandell House, Aug. 19, 1916, **38**: 54

Noel Buxton to Franklin Knight Lane, July 5, 1916, **37**: 370

Memorandum by Noel Buxton on the settlement of the European conflict, July 5, 1916, **37**: 370

De Rosey Carroll Cabell to George C. Saffarrans, June 17, 1916, **37**: 319

Luis Cabrera to William Phillips, Jan. 27, 1914, **29**: 187; Jan. 28, 1914, **29**: 191; Jan. 30, 1914, **29**: 205

Luis Cabrera and others to Franklin Knight Lane and others, Oct. 6, 1916, **38**: 357

Memorandum by Luis Cabrera on control of the Mexican-American border, Nov. 11, 1916, **38**: 635

William Wesley Canada to William Jennings Bryan, Jan. 5, 1914, **29**: 101; April 20, 1914, **29**: 477; April 21, 1914, **29**: 480

William Wesley Canada to the Department of State, April 18, 1914, **29**: 464

William Wesley Canada to Robert Lansing, June 30, 1915, **33**: 459; Aug. 29, 1915, **34**: 383; Aug. 30, 1915, **34**: 386; Sept. 1, 1915, **34**: 408

Bishop Warren Akin Candler to Josephus Daniels, Oct. 9, 1915, **35**: 45

William Banks Caperton to Josephus Daniels, Aug. 3, 1915, **34**: 70

Report by Lionel Carden on his interview with Huerta, May 20, 1914, **30**: 59

George C. Carothers to William Jennings Bryan, April 22, 1914, **29**: 483; April 23, 1914, **29**: 494; April 25, 1914, **29**: 504; June 18, 1914, **30**: 193; July 27, 1914, **30**: 311

Venustiano Carranza to Eliseo Arredondo, June 2, 1915, **33**: 307; Sept. 26, 1915, **34**: 532; April 24, 1916, **36**: 540

Proclamation by Venustiano Carranza concerning the policy of the provisional Mexican government, April 20, 1915, **33**: 44

Clifford Nickels Carver to Edward Mandell House, Aug. 23, 1915, **34**: 310

Viscount Sutemi Chinda to Baron Takaaki Katō, Oct. 29, 1914, **31**: 254, translation, 256

Viscount Sutemi Chinda to Robert Lansing, Oct. 27, 1915, **35**: 115

Viscount Sutemi Chinda to Baron Nobuaki Makino, March 7, 1913, **27**: 161, translation, 162; April 16, 1913, **27**: 315, translation, 318; June 6, 1913, **27**: 498, translation, 501; Sept. 19, 1913 (2), **28**: 303, translation, 305; 307, translation, 307; Sept. 21, 1913, **28**: 312, translation, 314

Memorandum by Viscount Sutemi Chinda on Japan's policy toward China, March 22, 1915, **32**: 416

Chinese Foreign Office to the Chinese Legation, Sept. 2, 1916, **38**: 151

Zach Lamar Cobb to Robert Lansing, March 6, 1916, **37**: 316

Duke of Connaught to Sir Cecil Arthur Spring Rice, Oct. 23, 1914, **31:** 229

"Criminal correspondence with foreign governments," Section 5335, Revised Statutes of the United States, May 5, 1916, **36:** 618

Jacques Davignon to Emmanuel Havenith, Aug. 28, 1914, **30:** 458

Robert Beale Davis, Jr., to Robert Lansing, July 31, 1915, **34:** 61

Jacob McGavock Dickinson to Robert Lansing, Feb. 6, 1915, **32:** 217

Willoughby Hyett Dickinson to Benjamin Franklin Battin, Aug. 9, 1916, **38:** 207

Charles Alexander Douglas to William Jennings Bryan, Jan. 19, 1914, **29:** 142

Charles Alexander Douglas on proposed convention between the United States and Nicaragua, June 16, 1913, **27:** 527

Michael Francis Doyle to Joseph Patrick Tumulty, July 6, 1916, **37:** 446; Sept. 29, 1916, **38:** 316

Constantin Theodor Dumba to Baron Stephan Burián von Rajecz, Aug. 20, 1915, **34:** 403

Maurice Francis Egan to Robert Lansing, Aug. 19, 1915, **34:** 280; Dec. 12, 1915, **35:** 350

Bradley Allen Fiske to Josephus Daniels, April 13, 1914, **29:** 430

Henry Prather Fletcher to William Jennings Bryan, July 5, 1914, **30:** 259

Henry Prather Fletcher to Edward Mandell House, April 12, 1916, **36:** 479; May 4, 1916, **36:** 605; June 15, 1916, **37:** 238; June 24, 1916, **37:** 292; July 10, 1916, **37:** 398; Aug. 9, 1916, **38:** 17

Henry Prather Fletcher to Robert Lansing, Sept. 9, 1915, **34:** 444; Jan. 21, 1916, **35:** 519; Jan. 21, 1916, **36:** 198; June 16, 1916, **37:** 241; Aug. 9, 1916, **38:** 18

James Berwick Forgan to Frederick Adrian Delano, Aug. 17, 1915, **34:** 316

Rudolph Forster to Joseph Patrick Tumulty, May 1, 1913, **27:** 371; May 2, 1913, **27:** 381

David Rowland Francis to Robert Lansing, Sept. 2, 1915, **34:** 405; July 25, 1916, **38:** 67

Memorandum by the French government on the policy of the Allies toward belligerent merchant and neutral submarines, Aug. 21, 1916, **38:** 148

Paul Fuller to William Jennings Bryan, Aug. 17, 1914, **30:** 392

Paul Fuller, Jr., to William Jennings Bryan, May 27, 1915, **33:** 277

Frederick Funston to Newton Diehl Baker, March 10, 1916 (4), **36:** 281, 282, 283; March 31, 1916, **36:** 397; May 12, 1916, **37:** 38; Oct. 25, 1916, **38:** 547

Frederick Funston to Henry Pinckney McCain, March 14, 1916, **36:** 312; March 21, 1916 (2), **36:** 352, 353; April 17, 1916, **36:** 501; June 21, 1916, **37:** 280; June 26, 1916, **37:** 307; June 27, 1916 (2), **37:** 315, 317; Aug. 17, 1916, **38:** 44

Report by Ernest Albert Garlington on the Carrizal incident, Oct. 2, 1916, **38:** 378

Percy Norman Furber to Sir Edward Grey, May 14, 1914, **30:** 246

Domicio da Gama to William Jennings Bryan, May 18, 1915, **33:** 221

Domicio da Gama to Edward Mandell House, Dec. 24, 1914, **31:** 536

Domicio da Gama to Robert Lansing, July 29, 1915, **34:** 43

Domicio da Gama, Rómulo Sebastian Naón and Eduardo Suárez-Mujica to William Jennings Bryan, April 25, 1914, **29:** 505

Federico Gamboa to John Lind, Aug. 16, 1913, **28:** 168

Alfred George Gardiner to Edward Mandell House, June 15, 1916, **37:** 313

Lindley Miller Garrison to Frederick Funston, April 26, 1914, **29:** 510

Memorandum by Lindley Miller Garrison about cabinet meetings, June 1, 1915, **33:** 294; July 20, 1915, **33:** 536

Memorandum by Lindley Miller Garrison on certain diplomatic exchanges between the United States, Germany, and Great Britain, March 20, 1915, **32:** 405

Memoranda by Lindley Miller Garrison on the ship purchase bill, Feb. 5, 1915, **32:** 192; Feb. 9, 1915, **32:** 207

Lázaro de la Garza to Felix A. Sommerfield, June 27, 1914, **30:** 220

John Palmer Gavit to Joseph Patrick Tumulty, June 27, 1916, **37:** 313; June 28, 1916, **37:** 323

James Watson Gerard to William Jennings Bryan, Aug. 14, 1914, **30:** 382; Sept. 1, 1914, **30:** 467; Feb. 19, 1915, **32:** 262; May 26, 1915, **33:** 265

James Watson Gerard to the Department of State, July 24, 1916, **37:** 480

James Watson Gerard to the German Foreign Office, Sept. 8, 1914, **31:** 14

James Watson Gerard to Edward Mandell House, Dec. 26, 1914, **31:** 536; Feb. 15, 1915, **32:** 255; March 6, 1915, **32:** 351; June 1, 1915, **33:** 407; June 16, 1915, **33:** 477; July 6, 1915, **34:** 12; July 27, 1915, **34:** 187; Aug. 3, 1915, **34:** 238; May 3, 1916, **36:** 595; June 28, 1916, **37:** 319

James Watson Gerard to Robert Lansing, June 24, 1915, **33:** 453; July 27, 1915, **34:** 44; July 13, 1915, **34:** 46; Aug. 2, 1915, **34:** 83; Oct. 25, 1915, **35:** 193; Dec. 14, 1915, **35:** 355; Feb. 16, 1916, **36:** 258; March 14, 1916, **36:** 413; April 11, 1916, **36:** 563; May 2, 1916, **36:** 594; May 3, 1916, **36:** 613; June 7, 1916, **37:** 272; July 18, 1916, **37:** 507; Aug. 8, 1916, **38:** 71; Sept. 25, 1916, **38:** 313

German Foreign Office to Count Johann Heinrich von Bernstorff, Sept. 8, 1915, **34:** 436

Memorandum by the German government on the *Lusitania* case, Feb. 4, 1916, **36:** 128

Two notes from the German government on the sinking of *Arabic*, Aug. 24, 1915, **34:** 308; Sept. 7, 1915, **34:** 439

German note on the *Frye* case (extract), Nov. 29, 1915, **35:** 453

Note by the German government in reply to the third *Lusitania* note, Feb. 16, 1916, **36:** 183

Note verbale by the German government on the inauguration of submarine warfare against armed merchantmen, Feb. 28, 1916, **36:** 228

Note by the German government on the *Sussex* case, May 4, 1916, **36:** 621

Walter Rockwell Gherardi to Edward Mandell House, Oct. 11, 1915, **35:** 131

Lawrence Godkin to Joseph Patrick Tumulty, March 26, 1914, **29:** 380

Samuel Gompers to Venustiano Carranza, July 27, 1916, **37:** 490

John Temple Graves to Joseph Patrick Tumulty, June 29, 1916, **37:** 331

Thomas Watt Gregory to William Jennings Bryan, April 15, 1915, **32:** 525

Sir Edward Grey to Colville Barclay, July 2, 1914, **30:** 245; Aug. 21, 1914, **30:** 435

Sir Edward Grey to Sir Lionel Carden, Nov. 11, 1913 (2), **28:** 528; Nov. 17, 1913, **28:** 562

Sir Edward Grey to Edward Mandell House, April 15, 1915, **33:** 13; April 24, 1915, **33:** 124; June 2, 1915, **33:** 408; June 6, 1915, **33:** 462; July 14, 1915, **34:** 145; Aug. 10, 1915, **34:** 370; Nov. 10, 1915, **35:** 186; Nov. 11, 1915, **35:** 254; Dec. 15, 1916, **35:** 362; Dec. 22, 1915, **35:** 382; March 24, 1916, **36:** 443; April 8, 1916, **36:** 444; March 23, 1916, **36:** 445; April 7, 1916, **36:** 511; May 12, 1916, **37:** 43; May 22, 1916, **37:** 94; May 25, 1916, **37:** 113; May 27, 1916, **37:** 116; May 29, 1916, **37:** 131; June 28, 1916, **37:** 412; Aug. 28, 1916, **38:** 89

Sir Edward Grey to Sir Cecil Arthur Spring Rice, May 27, 1913, **27:** 482; July 11, 1913, **28:** 34; Oct. 28, 1913, **28:** 467; Nov. 17, 1913, **28:** 561; Dec. 1, 1913, **28:** 601; Jan. 21, 1914, **29:** 162; March 13, 1914, **29:** 344; May 20, 1914, **30:** 59; Sept. 3, 1914, **30:** 473; Sept. 19, 1914 (paraphrase), **31:** 58; Sept. 29, 1914, **31:** 110; Sept. 30, 1914, **31:** 116; Oct. 4, 1914, **31:** 125; Oct. 9, 1914, **31:** 146; Oct. 14, 1914, **31:** 155; Oct. 17, 1914 (2), **31:** 191, 192; Oct. 24, 1914 (2), **31:** 229, 230; Oct. 25, 1914, **31:** 231; Nov. 11, 1914, **31:** 297; Dec. 21, 1914 (2), **31:** 505, 506; June 8, 1915, **33:** 372; Feb. 3, 1916, **36:** 133; Feb. 17, 1916, **36:** 193; Sept. 17, 1916, **38:** 184

Sir Edward Grey to Sir William Tyrell, Nov. 20, 1913, **28:** 573

Delbert James Haff on conditions in Mexico, May 12, 1913, **27:** 419

William Bayard Hale to William Jennings Bryan, Aug. 20, 1913, **28:** 200; Aug. 22, 1913, **28:** 207; Nov. 11, 1913, **28:** 527; Nov. 12, 1913, **28:** 529; Nov. 14, 1913 (5), **28:** 541, 542; Nov. 15, 1913, **28:** 545; Nov. 16, 1913, **28:** 558; Nov. 17, 1913, **28:** 561; Nov. 18, 1913 (2), **28:** 563; Nov. 19, 1913 (3), **28:** 567, 568; Nov. 22, 1913, **28:** 579

William Bayard Hale on the Huerta coup, June 18, 1913, **27:** 536

Henry Noble Hall to Joseph Patrick Tumulty, March 13, 1914, **29:** 344

Francis Burton Harrison to Lindley Miller Garrison, Oct. 18, 1913, **28:** 415

Francis Burton Harrison to Newton Diehl Baker, April 3, 1916, **36:** 414

Emmanuel Havenith to William Jennings Bryan, Aug. 28, 1914, **30:** 457

Myron Timothy Herrick to William Jennings Bryan, July 28, 1914, **30:** 313

Memorandum by Thomas Beaumont Hohler on a conversation with Bryan on Mexico, Feb. 9, 1914, **29:** 251

Memorandum by Thomas Beaumont Hohler on a conversation with Wilson and Bryan on Mexico, Feb. 11, 1914, **29:** 255

Thomas Snell Hopkins to Rudolph Forster, July 21, 1913, **28:** 59

Edward Mandell House to James Watson Gerard, Dec. 4, 1914, **31:** 387; Feb. 17, 1915, **32:** 256; Feb. 18, 1915, **32:** 257

Edward Mandell House to Sir Edward Grey, Oct. 17, 1915, **35:** 81; March 7, 1916, **36:** 266; May 7, 1916, **36:** 652; May 10, 1916, **37:** 7; May 11, 1916, **37:** 21; May 14, 1916, **37:** 44; May 17, 1916, **37:** 63; May 23, 1916, **37:** 100; June 8, 1916, **37:** 178; July 15, 1916, **37:** 422

Edward Mandell House to Robert Lansing, July 18, 1915, **33:** 520; Oct. 12, 1915, **35:** 54; Oct. 27, 1915, **35:** 119; Oct. 30, 1915 (2), **35:** 137, 143

Edward Mandell House to Walter Hines Page, Dec. 4, 1914, **31:** 388; July 18, 1915, **33:** 520; Aug. 4, 1915, **34:** 85

Edward Mandell House to William II, July 8, 1914, **30:** 266

Edward Mandell House to Arthur Zimmermann, July 8, 1914, **30:** 265; Sept. 5, 1914, **30:** 488; Feb. 17, 1915, **32:** 256

Roy Howard to William Waller Hawkins, Oct. 20, 1916, **38:** 496

Victoriano Huerta to Count Johann Heinrich von Bernstorff, July 26, 1915, **34:** 56

Aletta Henrietta Jacobs to Jane Addams, Sept. 15, 1915, **34:** 473

Gottlieb von Jagow to Count Johann Heinrich von Bernstorff, April 17, 1916, **36:** 498

Hiram Warren Johnson to William Kent, April 8, 1913, **27:** 281

Jean Jules Jusserand to Aristide Briand, Nov. 4, 1915, **35:** 174, translation, 174

Jean Jules Jusserand to Gaston Doumergue, Feb. 7, 1914, **29:** 233, translation, 236

Jean Jules Jusserand to the French Foreign Ministry, Sept. 8, 1914, **31:** 15, translation, 15; Dec. 27, 1914, **31:** 539, translation, 539; Aug. 29, 1916 (2), **38:** 106, translation, 106; 107, translation, 107; Oct. 12, 1916, **38:** 405, translation, 408

Jean Jules Jusserand to Stéphen Pichon, June 17, 1913, **27:** 532, translation, 533

Kai Fu Shah to Robert Lansing, Oct. 29, 1915, **35:** 128

Baron Takaaki Katō to William Jennings Bryan, July 10, 1914, **30:** 273; Aug. 16, 1914, **30:** 391

Baron Takaaki Katō to Viscount Sutemi Chinda, June 10, 1914, **30:** 169

Daniel Fiske Kellogg to Robert Lansing, June 1, 1915, **33:** 296

William Kent to William Jennings Bryan, April 7, 1913, **27:** 265

William Kent to Hiram Warren Johnson, April 7, 1913, **27:** 281

William A. Kincaid to Joseph Patrick Tumulty, Feb. 11, 1916, **36:** 172

Julius Kruttschnitt to William Jennings Bryan, May 26, 1913, **27:** 479

Joseph Rucker Lamar to William Jennings Bryan, June 30, 1914, **30:** 239; July 1, 1914, **30:** 241

Baron Oscar von der Lancken Wakenitz to Count Adolf von Montgelas, Jan. 16, 1916, **35:** 489, translation, 490

Franklin Knight Lane to Robert Lansing, Sept. 9, 1916, **38:** 167; Sept. 29, 1916, **38:** 300; Nov. 11, 1916, **38:** 633

Franklin Knight Lane and others to Luis Cabrera and others, Sept. 22, 1916, **38:** 356; Oct. 6, 1916, **38:** 357

Memorandum by Franklin Knight Lane on the Mexican position with regard to the negotiations of the Joint Commission, Oct. 6, 1916, **38:** 358

Robert Lansing to Eliseo Arredondo, July 6, 1916, **37:** 368

Robert Lansing to John William Belt, Oct. 19, 1915, **35:** 93

Robert Lansing to William Jennings Bryan, Oct. 16, 1914, **31:** 163; Dec. 26, 1914, **31:** 534; Jan. 1, 1915, **32:** 4; Feb. 10, 1915, **32:** 223; March 1, 1915, **32:** 302; March 1, 1915, **32:** 322; April 2, 1915, **32:** 465; April 5, 1915, **32:** 483; April 11, 1915, **32:** 510; April 20, 1915, **33:** 42; April 27, 1915, **33:** 72; May 1, 1915, **33:** 91; May 3, 1915, **33:** 94; May 5, 1915, **33:** 107; May 7, 1915, **33:** 140; May 10, 1915, **33:** 144; May 12, 1915, **33:** 168; May 14, 1915, **33:** 193; May 15, 1915, **33:** 206; June 1, 1915, **33:** 312; June 2, 1915, **33:** 313; June 3, 1915, **33:** 327; June 5, 1915, **33:** 344; June 7, 1915, **33:** 355

Robert Lansing to Count Johann Heinrich von Bernstorff, Dec. 15, 1915, **35:** 355; March 24, 1916, **36:** 361

Memoranda by Robert Lansing on conversations with Count Johann Heinrich von Bernstorff, Oct. 5, 1915, **35:** 25; Dec. 31, 1915, **35:** 417; Jan. 26, 1916, **35:** 528

Memorandum by Robert Lansing on a conversation with Constantin Brün, Nov. 15, 1915, **35:** 202

Robert Lansing to William Banks Caperton, Aug. 9, 1915, **34:** 143

Robert Lansing to Viscount Sutemi Chinda, Nov. 4, 1915, **35:** 173

Memorandum by Robert Lansing on a conversation with Viscount Sutemi Chinda, Nov. 3, 1915, **35:** 163

Robert Lansing to James Watson Gerard, Jan. 26, 1916, **35:** 529; Jan. 31, 1916, **36:** 74; April 26, 1916, **36:** 556

Robert Lansing to Edward Viscount Grey, Sept. 22, 1916, **38**: 202

Robert Lansing to Edward Mandell House, Oct. 6, 1915, **35**: 34; Oct. 14, 1915 (3), **35**: 65, 66, 67; Oct. 28, 1915, **35**: 126; Jan. 7, 1916, **35**: 446; Jan. 19, 1916, **35**: 504

Robert Lansing to Jean Jules Jusserand, April 7, 1916, **36**: 383

Robert Lansing to Franklin Knight Lane, Sept. 8, 1916, **38**: 166; Oct. 3, 1916, **38**: 361

Robert Lansing to William Gibbs McAdoo, Aug. 26, 1915, **34**: 330

Robert Lansing to Rómulo Sebastian Naón, Oct. 20, 1915, **35**: 111

Robert Lansing to Walter Hines Page (draft), Sept. 28, 1914, **31**: 90

Robert Lansing to Walter Hines Page, Oct. 19, 1914, **31**: 183; June 12, 1915, **33**: 387; July 14, 1915, **33**: 509; July 16, 1915, **33**: 515

Robert Lansing to Frederic Courtland Penfield, Nov. 16, 1915, **35**: 209

Robert Lansing to Frank Lyon Polk, July 28, 1916, **37**: 495

Robert Lansing to John Reid Silliman, June 17, 1915, **33**: 415

Robert Lansing to Sir Cecil Arthur Spring Rice, Oct. 2, 1914 (2), **31**: 133, 135; Jan. 17, 1916, **35**: 495; March 31, 1916, **36**: 427

Robert Lansing to Joseph Patrick Tumulty, June 17, 1915, **33**: 416

Robert Lansing to Frank Arthur Vanderlip, Sept. 1, 1915, **34**: 401

Robert Lansing to Joseph Edward Willard, Aug. 23, 1916, **38**: 82

Memorandum by Robert Lansing on a conversation with Baron Erich Zwiedinek, Dec. 13, 1915, **35**: 351

Memorandum by Robert Lansing on a reply to a British note and Order in Council, March 24, 1915, **32**: 428

Draft by Robert Lansing of the first article of the Colombian treaty, July 31, 1915, **34**: 51

Memorandum for the German government by Robert Lansing on the position of the United States with regard to the conduct of belligerent naval vessels toward merchant ships, April 24, 1916 (outline), **36**: 541; April 26, 1916, **36**: 556

Draft by Robert Lansing of a note to Great Britain, May 15, 1915, **33**: 207

Draft by Robert Lansing of a note to Japan and China, May 7, 1915, **33**: 141

Memorandum by Robert Lansing on loans to the belligerents, Oct. 23, 1914, **31**: 219

Memorandum by Robert Lansing on the sinking of the *Lusitania* May 10, 1915, **33**: 142

Redraft by Robert Lansing of the first *Lusitania* note, May 12, 1915, **33**: 169

Draft by Robert Lansing of the third *Lusitania* note, July 16, 1915, **33**: 527

Memorandum by Robert Lansing on the policy of the United States toward merchant submarines, Aug. 31, 1916, **38**: 149

Draft by Robert Lansing of a proposed Pan-American treaty, April 4, 1916, **36**: 412

Draft by Robert Lansing of a proposed note to Germany on the *Sussex* affair, April 6, 1916, **36**: 448

Memorandum by Robert Lansing on the Thrasher case, April 5, 1915, **32:** 484

Comments by Robert Lansing on Chandler Parsons Anderson's memorandum on the Thrasher case, April 7, 1915, **32:** 492

Draft by Robert Lansing of a reply to Count Johann Heinrich von Bernstorff's memorandum on the sale of American arms to the Allies, April 12, 1915, **32:** 511

Draft of a note to the Latin American governments on the purpose of the American troops in Mexico, June 21, 1916, **37:** 276

David Lawrence to Robert Lansing, Aug. 29, 1915, **34:** 383; Aug. 30, 1915, **34:** 386; Sept. 1, 1915, **34:** 408; Sept. 27, 1915, **34:** 530; Sept. 30, 1915, **34:** 540

Marion Letcher to William Jennings Bryan, Feb. 21, 1914, **29:** 278; April 22, 1914, **29:** 486; April 23, 1914, **29:** 495

John Lind to William Jennings Bryan, Aug. 14, 1913, **28:** 157; Aug. 16, 1913, **28:** 167; Aug. 18, 1913, **28:** 188; Aug. 19, 1913, **28:** 195; Aug. 20, 1913, **28:** 201, 205; Aug. 21, 1913, **28:** 204; Aug. 23, 1913, **28:** 208; Aug. 27, 1913 (2), **28:** 232; Sept. 16, 1913, **28:** 282; Sept. 19, 1913, **28:** 293; Sept. 23, 1913, **28:** 326; Oct. 3, 1913, **28:** 356; Oct. 4, 1913, **28:** 357; Oct. 8, 1913, **28:** 376; Oct. 9, 1913, **28:** 382; Oct. 10, 1913, **28:** 386; Oct. 23, 1913, **28:** 428; Oct. 25, 1913, **28:** 444; Oct. 29, 1913, **28:** 471; Dec. 5, 1913, **29:** 14; Dec. 9, 1913, **29:** 30; Jan. 28, 1914, **29:** 190; Feb. 24, 1914, **29:** 286; March 10, 1914, **29:** 328; March 12, 1914, **29:** 338; March 19, 1914, **29:** 357; March 29, 1914, **29:** 382; May 5, 1914, **29:** 549; April 16, 1915, **33:** 3

John Lind to Nelson O'Shaughnessy, April 5, 1914, **29:** 405

Memorandum by John Lind on the Mexican situation, April 30, 1914, **29:** 539

Memorandum by John Lind on recognition of the provisional Mexican government, April 20, 1915, **33:** 45

Louis Paul Lochner to the American Peace Society, Nov. 12, 1915 (2), **35:** 195, 199

Boaz Walton Long to William Jennings Bryan, April 13, 1914, **29:** 429

Robert Threshie Reid, Earl Loreburn, to Edward Mandell House, June 26, 1915, **33:** 521; June 13, 1916, **37:** 351

Henry Pinckney McCain to Hugh Lenox Scott, April 23, 1916, **36:** 540

James P. McDonald to Robert Lansing, Aug. 2, 1915, **34:** 66

Charles Kenneth McIntosh to Robert Lansing, Oct. 24, 1914, **31:** 236

Memorandum by Frank McIntyre on the Philippine situation, Jan. 17, 1914, **29:** 147

Baron Nobuaki Makino to Viscount Sutemi Chinda, April 11, 1913, **27:** 293; Aug. 19, 1913, **28:** 284

Thomas Riley Marshall to Joseph Patrick Tumulty, April 9, 1914, **29:** 418

Adolph Caspar Miller to William Jennings Bryan, June 3, 1915, **33:** 332

John Bassett Moore on recognition of the Huerta government, May 14, 1913, **27:** 437

John Henry Morehead to William Jennings Bryan, May 18, 1915, **33:** 336

Lewis S. Morey to John Joseph Pershing, June 25, 1916, **37:** 317

John R. Mott to Cleveland Hoadley Dodge, March 1, 1913, **27:** 144; April 1, 1913, **27:** 248

Rómulo Sebastian Naón to Henry Prather Fletcher, June 27, 1916, **37:** 399

Rómulo Sebastian Naón to Edward Mandell House, Dec. 26, 1914, **31:** 536

Rómulo Sebastian Naón to Robert Lansing, Oct. 21, 1915, **35:** 113

Rómulo Sebastian Naón to the Minister of Foreign Affairs, June 21, 1914, **30:** 197, translation, 198

Declaration by Rómulo Sebastian Naón on the recognition of the *de facto* Mexican government, Aug. 6, 1915, **34:** 112

Redraft by Rómulo Sebastian Naón of a Pan-American treaty, June 17, 1916, **37:** 244

Charles James O'Conner to Robert Lansing, June 24, 1915, **33:** 448

Nelson O'Shaughnessy to William Jennings Bryan, Aug. 27, 1913, **28:** 233; Sept. 19, 1913, **28:** 292; Oct. 3, 1913, **28:** 363; Oct. 14, 1913, **28:** 410; Oct. 20, 1913, **28:** 420; Nov. 13, 1913 (2), **28:** 537, 539; April 12, 1914, **29:** 426; April 14, 1914, **29:** 438; April 15, 1914, **29:** 446; April 16, 1914, **29:** 455; April 17, 1914, **29:** 458; April 18, 1914, **29:** 462; April 19, 1914, **29:** 467

Thomas Nelson Page to William Jennings Bryan, March 23, 1915, **32:** 432

Walter Hines Page to William Jennings Bryan, Oct. 21, 1913, **28:** 421; Oct. 28, 1913, **28:** 465; Nov. 8, 1913, **28:** 515; Nov. 11, 1913, **28:** 525; Nov. 13, 1913, **28:** 536; Jan. 14, 1914, **29:** 131; Jan. 9, 1914, **29:** 144; Jan. 28, 1914, **29:** 195; May 6, 1914, **30:** 4; July 29, 1914, **30:** 316; July 31, 1914, **30:** 325; Sept. 10, 1914, **31:** 21; Sept. 11, 1914, **31:** 26; Sept. 29, 1914, **31:** 99; Sept. 30, 1914, **31:** 105; Oct. 15, 1914, **31:** 159; Oct. 20, 1914, **31:** 195; Jan. 15, 1915, **32:** 81; Jan. 18, 1915, **32:** 91; Feb. 17, 1915, **32:** 251; March 3, 1915, **32:** 313; March 15, 1915, **32:** 378; March 21, 1915, **32:** 409; May 7, 1915, **33:** 131; May 16, 1915, **33:** 214; June 10, 1915, **33:** 386

Walter Hines Page to the Department of State, July 7, 1916, **37:** 401

Walter Hines Page to Sir Edward Grey, Feb. 18, 1915, **32:** 258

Walter Hines Page to Edward Mandell House, Oct. 26, 1913, **28:** 447; Nov. 23, 1913, **28:** 586; Nov. 26, 1913, **28:** 593; June 30, 1915, **33:** 522; May 30, 1916, **37:** 226; June 2, 1916, **37:** 227; June 28, 1916, **37:** 319

Walter Hines Page to Robert Lansing, Oct. 19, 1914, **31:** 189; July 15, 1915, **33:** 512; July 19, 1915, **33:** 534; July 27, 1915 (2), **34:**

33, 35; July 31, 1915, **34:** 54; Sept. 1, 1915, **34:** 403; Sept. 25, 1915, **34:** 528; Jan. 3, 1916, **35:** 425; Jan. 22, 1916, **35:** 517; Jan. 25, 1916, **35:** 533; March 23, 1916, **36:** 411; July 3, 1916, **37:** 353; Oct. 18, 1916, **38:** 472

Memorandum by Walter Hines Page on British attitudes toward the United States, Sept. 23, 1916, **38:** 242

Memorandum by Walter Hines Page of a conversation with James Viscount Bryce, July 31, 1916, **38:** 249

Memorandum by Walter Hines Page of a conversation with Edward Viscount Grey, Sept. 23, 1916, **38:** 251

Memorandum by Walter Hines Page of a conversation with Herbert Henry Asquith, Sept. 23, 1916, **38:** 255

Frederick Courtland Penfield to Robert Lansing, Nov. 16, 1915, **35:** 208; Dec. 24, 1915, **35:** 394; Dec. 29, 1915, **35:** 410; April 15, 1916, **37:** 4; June 3, 1916, **37:** 273; July 3, 1916, **37:** 464; Aug. 1, 1916, **38:** 74

John Joseph Pershing to Frederick Funston, March 21, 1916, **36:** 353; April 14, 1916, **36:** 584; May 12, 1916, **37:** 38; June 25, 1916, **37:** 307; June 26, 1916, **37:** 317

William Phillips to Frank Lyon Polk, July 13, 1916, **37:** 414; July 18, 1916, **37:** 433

William Phillips to Joseph Patrick Tumulty, Sept. 30, 1914, **31:** 108; Oct. 27, 1915, **35:** 118

Proposed agreement by the members of the Pan-American conference to recognize a *de facto* Mexican government, Sept. 18, 1915, **34:** 489

Sir Horace Plunkett to Edward Mandell House, Sept. 17, 1915, **35:** 4; Oct. 1, 1915, **35:** 8; March 7, 1916, **36:** 347; April 20, 1916, **36:** 519; May 29, 1916, **37:** 137; June 7, 1916, **37:** 295

Frank Lyon Polk to the American Embassy, Santiago, May 29, 1916, **37:** 122

Frank Lyon Polk to Eliseo Arredondo, Aug. 8, 1916, **38:** 11

Frank Lyon Polk to Constantin Brün, July 28, 1916, **37:** 496

Frank Lyon Polk to Rudolph Forster, July 24, 1916, **37:** 470

Frank Lyon Polk to Robert Lansing, July 21, 1916, **37:** 452; July 25, 1916, **37:** 476; July 28, 1916, **37:** 495

Frank Lyon Polk to James Linn Rodgers, July 21, 1916, **37:** 453

Frank Lyon Polk to William Worthington Russell, June 3, 1916, **37:** 158

Frank Lyon Polk to Joseph Patrick Tumulty, Aug. 2, 1916, **37:** 516; Aug. 7, 1916, **38:** 5; Oct. 5, 1916, **38:** 350

Memorandum by Frank Lyon Polk of a conversation between Edward Mandell House and Count Johann Heinrich von Bernstorff on submarine warfare, April 25, 1916, **36:** 547

Manuel Luis Quezon to William Jennings Bryan, Aug. 16, 1913, **28:** 192

Paul Samuel Reinsch to William Jennings Bryan, Nov. 28, 1914, **31:** 364; Dec. 22, 1914, **31:** 509; Dec. 26, 1914, **31:** 547; Jan. 26,

1915, **32**: 137; Feb. 1, 1915, **32**: 169; March 30, 1915, **32**: 459; March 31, 1915, **32**: 461; April 14, 1915, **32**: 519; May 4, 1915, **33**: 104

Paul Samuel Reinsch to Robert Lansing, Nov. 9, 1915 (2), **35**: 203; Nov. 13, 1915, **35**: 204; Nov. 16, 1915, **35**: 209; Dec. 4, 1915, **35**: 289; May 27, 1916, **37**: 234; June 14, 1916, **37**: 235; June 15, 1916 (2), **37**: 235, 236

Ernst Richard to the Secretary of State, Sept. 24, 1914, **31**: 85

James Linn Rodgers to the Secretary of State, March 19, 1916, **36**: 338

Hugh Lenox Scott to Newton Diehl Baker, April 22, 1916, **36**: 528; May 12, 1916, **37**: 39

Hugh Lenox Scott to Robert Lansing, Sept. 8, 1916, **38**: 166

Hugh Lenox Scott and Frederick Funston to Newton Diehl Baker, May 3, 1916, **36**: 592; May 11, 1916, **37**: 22

Hugh Lenox Scott and Frederick Funston to Robert Lansing, April 30, 1916, **36**: 570; May 1, 1916, **36**: 579

Statement by Hugh Lenox Scott, Frederick Funston, and Álvaro Obregón on the suspension of their conferences, May 11, 1916, **37**: 24

Jefferson D. Short to John Hall Stevens, March 30, 1916, **36**: 407

John Reid Silliman to William Jennings Bryan, June 8, 1914, **30**: 167; Aug. 24, 1914, **30**: 449; Sept. 5, 1914, **30**: 489; Sept. 8, 1914, **31**: 18

John Reid Silliman to Robert Lansing, Aug. 24, 1915, **34**: 321

Special Commissioners to William Jennings Bryan, May 20, 1914, **30**: 55; May 21, 1914, **30**: 57; May 22, 1914, **30**: 64; May 23, 1914 (3), **30**: 66, 67, 68; May 25, 1914, **30**: 75; May 26, 1914, **30**: 87; May 28, 1914, **30**: 96; May 29, 1914 (3), **30**: 100, 101, 114; May 30, 1914, **30**: 117; May 31, 1914, **30**: 123; June 1, 1914, **30**: 132; June 2, 1914, **30**: 136; June 24, 1914, **30**: 207; June 29, 1914, **30**: 225

Sir Cecil Arthur Spring Rice to the Foreign Office, Dec. 2, 1913, **29**: 13; Jan. 29, 1914, **29**: 203; May 18, 1916, **37**: 73; Sept. 16, 1916, **38**: 179

Sir Cecil Arthur Spring Rice to Sir Edward Grey
May 1913–June 1914
May 6, 1913, **27**: 405; June 12, 1913, **27**: 514; Nov. 18, 1913, **28**: 565; Nov. 28, 1913, **28**: 594; Jan. 23, 1914, **29**: 168; Jan. 31, 1914, **29**: 209; Feb. 17, 1914, **29**: 266; March 12, 1914, **29**: 340; March 16, 1914, **29**: 347; May 13, 1914, **30**: 29; May 15, 1914, **30**: 33; May 25, 1914 (2), **30**: 77, 78
June–December 1914
June 1, 1914, **30**: 133; June 3, 1914, **30**: 141; Sept. 3, 1914, **30**: 472; Sept. 8, 1914, **31**: 13; Sept. 20, 1914, **31**: 62; Sept. 28, 1914 (4), **31**: 96, 97, 98; Sept. 29, 1914, **31**: 100; Oct. 1, 1914, **31**: 117; Oct. 2, 1914, **31**: 136; Oct. 10, 1914, **31**: 140; Nov. 9, 1914, **31**: 292; Nov. 11, 1914, **31**: 298; Nov. 13, 1914, **31**: 315; Dec. 19, 1914, **31**: 499; Dec. 24, 1914, **31**: 522

January 1915–May 1916
Jan. 1, 1915, **32:** 6; Jan. 18, 1915, **32:** 87; Jan. 22, 1915, **32:** 112;
    March 8, 1915, **32:** 342; June 3, 1915, **33:** 333; June 6, 1915, **33:**
    347; June 7, 1915, **33:** 362; Aug. 8, 1915, **34:** 137; Aug. 23, 1915,
    34: 295; Oct. 31, 1915, **35:** 145; Feb. 10, 1916, **36:** 169; Feb. 17,
    1916, **36:** 192; March 7, 1916, **36:** 269; May 4, 1916, **36:** 607
Sir Cecil Arthur Spring Rice to Edward Mandell House, Dec. 31,
    1914, **31:** 553; Jan. 20, 1915, **32:** 99; Jan. 22, 1915, **32:** 107; July
    17, 1915, **33:** 519; Oct. 15, 1915, **35:** 79
Sir Cecil Arthur Spring Rice to Robert Lansing, Oct. 27, 1915, **35:**
    117; Jan. 27, 1916, **35:** 532
Sir Cecil Arthur Spring Rice to Sir William Tyrrell, Dec. 14, 1913,
    29: 34; Dec. 22, 1913, **29:** 59; Feb. 3, 1914, **29:** 217; March 9, 1914,
    29: 324
Memorandum by Sir Cecil Arthur Spring Rice on neutral trade,
    Aug. 13, 1915, **34:** 188
Memorandum by George Owen Squier of an interview with Field
    Marshal Earl Kitchener on the desirability of American inter-
    vention in the European war, April 27, 1916, **37:** 97
Lincoln Steffens to Edward Mandell House, Aug. 7, 1915, **34:** 147
John Hall Stevens to Joseph Patrick Tumulty, April 3, 1916, **36:**
    407
Eduardo Suárez-Mujica to William Jennings Bryan, April 21, 1915,
    33: 55
Eduardo Suárez-Mujica to Edward Mandell House, Jan. 19, 1915,
    32: 98
Draft by Eduardo Suárez-Mujica of a communication to the warring
    factions in Mexico, Aug. 6, 1915, **34:** 113
James Mark Sullivan to William Jennings Bryan, Jan. 13, 1915,
    32: 77; April 18, 1915, **33:** 26
George Thomas Summerlin to William Jennings Bryan, April 2,
    1915, **32:** 474
Charles Lee Swem to Rudolph Forster, April 13, 1914, **29:** 432; Jan.
    30-31, 1916, **36:** 52
Herbert Bayard Swope to Maximilian Harden, Sept. 1, 1916, **38:**
    126
Charles Willis Thompson to Reuben Adiel Bull, May 22, 1913, **27:**
    465
Thaddeus Austin Thomson to William Jennings Bryan, Sept. 23,
    1913, **28:** 330
Joseph Patrick Tumulty to Herman Bernstein, May 20, 1916, **37:**
    84
Joseph Patrick Tumulty to Michael Francis Doyle, Oct. 14, 1916,
    38: 443
Joseph Patrick Tumulty to Rudolph Forster, July 3, 1916, **37:** 353
Joseph Patrick Tumulty to Robert Lansing, Sept. 30, 1916, **38:** 315;
    Oct. 11, 1916, **38:** 396
Joseph Patrick Tumulty to Frank Lyon Polk, Aug. 2, 1916, **37:** 516

Memorandum by Joseph Patrick Tumulty on the sinking of *Hesperian*, Sept. 7, 1915, **34:** 428

Memorandum by Joseph Patrick Tumulty on the *Persia* incident, Jan. 4, 1916, **35:** 424

Resolution by the United States Senate requesting clemency for Irish political prisoners, July 29, 1916, **37:** 516

Unknown person to Count Johann Heinrich von Bernstorff, April 17, 1916, **36:** 503

Unknown person to James Watson Gerard, Aug. 27, 1915, **34:** 239

Samuel Untermeyer to William Gibbs McAdoo, June 19, 1915, **33:** 438

Henry van Dyke to Robert Lansing, April 6, 1916, **36:** 429

Frederic Collin Walcott to Vance Criswell McCormick, Oct. 6, 1916, **38:** 369

Memoranda by Duval West on interviews with Francisco Villa, March 4, 1915, **32:** 383; March 6, 1915, **32:** 385; March 16, 1915, **32:** 389

Memorandum by William II about a possible peace initiative by Wilson, Oct. 20, 1916, **38:** 495

Edward Thomas Williams to William Jennings Bryan, Jan. 27, 1915, **32:** 135; Feb. 2, 1915, **32:** 177; Feb. 26, 1915, **32:** 319; March 12, 1915, **32:** 368

Memorandum by Edward Thomas Williams on Japanese designs on China, Jan. 28, 1915, **32:** 148

Charles Stetson Wilson to the Secretary of State, Oct. 16, 1914, **31:** 182

Arthur Zimmermann to Edward Mandell House, Dec. 3, 1914, **31:** 540; Feb. 4, 1915, **32:** 254; March 2, 1915, **32:** 351

Personal correspondence

Helen Woodrow Bones to Jessie Woodrow Bones Brower, Feb. 12, 1913, **29:** 553; Feb. 23, 1913, **29:** 553; March 1, 1913, **29:** 555; April 12, 1913, **29:** 556; May 3, 1913, **29:** 557; June 1, 1913, **29:** 559; June 7, 1913, **29:** 561

Helen Woodrow Bones to Mary Allen Hulbert, May 29, 1915, **33:** 286

Edward Thomas Brown to Mary Celestine Mitchell Brown, June 8, 1915, **33:** 373

Edith Bolling Galt to Annie Stuart Litchfield Bolling, March 23, 1915, **32:** 423

Edith Bolling Galt, "A Pledge," June 29, 1915, **33:** 458

Charles Henry Grasty to Joseph Patrick Tumulty, June 20, 1913, **27:** 554

Cary Travers Grayson to Edith Bolling Galt, Aug. 25, 1914, **31:** 563

Norman Hapgood to Edward Mandell House, Aug. 1, 1914, **30:** 385

Edward Mandell House to Walter Hines Page, Sept. 4, 1914, **30:** 489

William Luke Marbury to Albert Sidney Burleson, Jan. 3, 1916, **35:** 429

George W. Megeath to John Adams Wilson, July 4, 1916, **37:** 360

Walter Hines Page to Joseph Patrick Tumulty, April 4, 1916, **36:** 415

Ralph Pulitzer to Joseph Patrick Tumulty, April 27, 1916, **36:** 565

Sir Cecil Arthur Spring Rice to Ellen Axson Wilson, Dec. 2, 1913, **29:** 12

Charles Lee Swem to the White House Staff, July 25, 1915, **34:** 24

William Howard Taft to Ellen Axson Wilson, Jan. 3, 1913, **27:** 12

Joseph Patrick Tumulty to Horace Herbert Clark, Dec. 14, 1915, **35:** 355

Announcement by Joseph Patrick Tumulty about the alleged break between Wilson and Colonel House, Aug. 31, 1915, **34:** 381

Comment about Wilson by an unknown person, May 23, 1915, **33:** 244

Edith Bolling Wilson to Sallie White Bolling, Dec. 19, 1915, **35:** 371

Ellen Axson Wilson to Helen Herron Taft, Feb. 26, 1913, **27:** 138

Ellen Axson Wilson to William Howard Taft, Jan. 10, 1913, **27:** 28; Jan. 23, 1913, **27:** 69

Joseph R. Wilson, Jr., to Kate Wilson and Alice Wilson, Aug. 11, 1914, **30:** 373

Margaret Woodrow Wilson to Edith Bolling Galt, Aug. 16, 1915, **34:** 268

Frederic Yates to Emily Chapman Martin Yates and Mary Yates, March 5, 1913, **27:** 155

Diaries and reminiscences

Chandler Parsons Anderson, Jan. 9, 1915, **32:** 44

Josephus Daniels, March 6, 1913, **27:** 157; March 7, 1913, **27:** 160; March 11, 1913, **27:** 169; March 12, 1913, **27:** 174; March 18, 1913, **27:** 194; March 21, 1913, **27:** 210; March 28, 1913, **27:** 235; April 1, 1913, **27:** 248; April 4, 1913, **27:** 261; April 8, 1913, **27:** 267; April 11, 1913, **27:** 290; April 15, 1913, **27:** 312; April 18, 1913, **27:** 328; April 22, 1913, **27:** 348; May 13, 1913, **27:** 425; May 15, 1913, **27:** 441; May 16, 1913, **27:** 442; May 17, 1913, **27:** 446; May 20, 1913, **27:** 459; Jan. 26, 1915, **32:** 133

Edward Mandell House
January–June 1913
Jan. 8, 1913, **27:** 20; Jan. 15, 1913, **27:** 57; Jan. 17, 1913, **27:** 61; Jan. 24, 1913, **27:** 69; Feb. 13, 1913, **27:** 109; Feb. 14, 1913, **27:** 112; Feb. 18, 1913, **27:** 117; Feb. 21, 1913, **27:** 125; Feb. 23, 1913, **27:** 129; Feb. 24, 1913, **27:** 132; Feb. 26, 1913, **27:** 137; Feb. 27, 1913, **27:** 139; Feb. 28, 1913, **27:** 140; March 1, 1913, **27:** 145; March 4, 1913, **27:** 152; March 8, 1913, **27:** 163; March 20, 1913, **27:** 198; March 22, 1913, **27:** 215; March 24, 1913, **27:** 223; March

25, 1913, **27:** 227; March 26, 1913, **27:** 232; March 28, 1913, **27:** 234; April 1, 1913, **27:** 250; April 3, 1913, **27:** 259; April 4, 1913, **27:** 262; April 11, 1913, **27:** 292; April 18, 1913, **27:** 333; May 1, 1913, **27:** 372; May 2, 1913, **27:** 383; May 7, 1913, **27:** 407; May 11, 1913, **27:** 413; May 19, 1913, **27:** 457

July–December 1913
Aug. 10, 1913, **28:** 139; Aug. 16, 1913, **28:** 178; Oct. 30, 1913, **28:** 476; Nov. 11, 1913, **28:** 527; Nov. 12, 1913, **28:** 530; Nov. 18, 1913, **28:** 564; Nov. 28, 1913, **28:** 594; Dec. 2, 1913, **29:** 12; Dec. 12, 1913, **29:** 32; Dec. 22, 1913, **29:** 55; Dec. 23, 1913, **29:** 74

January–June 1914
Jan. 16, 1914, **29:** 135; Jan. 21, 1914, **29:** 159; Jan. 22, 1914, **29:** 163; March 25, 1914, **29:** 377; April 15, 1914, **29:** 447; April 16, 1914, **29:** 456; April 17, 1914, **29:** 459; April 18, 1914, **29:** 462; April 27, 1914, **29:** 515; April 28, 1914, **29:** 530; April 29, 1914, **29:** 535; May 7, 1914, **30:** 6; May 11, 1914, **30:** 21

July–December 1914
Aug. 30, 1914, **30:** 461; Sept. 5, 1914, **30:** 490; Sept. 27, 1914, **31:** 86; Sept. 28, 1914, **31:** 91; Sept. 29, 1914, **31:** 100; Sept. 30, 1914, **31:** 108; Oct. 2, 1914, **31:** 122; Nov. 4, 1914, **31:** 263; Nov. 5, 1914, **31:** 268; Nov.6, 1914, **31:** 274; Nov. 7, 1914, **31:** 279; Nov. 8, 1914, **31:** 281; Nov. 14, 1914, **31:** 317; Nov. 25, 1914, **31:** 354; Dec. 3, 1914, **31:** 384; Dec. 16, 1914, **31:** 468; Dec. 17, 1914, **31:** 481; Dec. 18, 1914, **31:** 489; Dec. 19, 1914, **31:** 497; Dec. 20, 1914, **31:** 499; Dec. 23, 1914, **31:** 517; Dec. 29, 1914, **31:** 548; Dec. 30, 1914, **31:** 552

1915
Jan. 12, 1915, **32:** 61; Jan. 13, 1915, **32:** 63; Jan. 24, 1915, **32:** 117; Jan. 25, 1915, **32:** 119; Sept. 22, 1915, **34:** 505; Sept. 23, 1915, **34:** 509; Sept. 24, 1915, **34:** 513; Oct. 8, 1915, **35:** 42; Oct. 9, 1915, **35:** 46; Oct. 13, 1915, **35:** 59; Oct. 14, 1915, **35:** 61; Oct. 15, 1915, **35:** 69; Nov. 4, 1915, **35:** 175; Nov. 5, 1915, **35:** 178; Nov. 18, 1915, **35:** 217; Nov. 22, 1915, **35:** 239; Nov. 27, 1915, **35:** 257; Dec. 10, 1915, **35:** 320; Dec. 15, 1915, **35:** 355

1916
March 6, 1916, **36:** 262; March 7, 1916, **36:** 266; March 17, 1916, **36:** 335; March 28, 1916, **36:** 375; March 29, 1916, **36:** 377; March 30, 1916, **36:** 387; April 2, 1916, **36:** 401; April 5, 1916, **36:** 416; April 6, 1916, **36:** 421; April 11, 1916, **36:** 459; May 3, 1916, **36:** 596; May 24, 1916, **37:** 103; Sept. 23, 1916, **38:** 257; Oct. 11, 1916, **38:** 411; Oct. 18, 1916, **38:** 474; Oct. 19, 1916, **38:** 493; Nov. 2, 1916, **38:** 606; Nov. 14, 1916, **38:** 645; Nov. 15, 1916, **38:** 656; Nov. 19, 1916, **38:** 678

Walter Lippmann, March 22, 1916, **36:** 658
Nancy Saunders Toy, Jan. 2, 1915, **32:** 7; Jan. 3, 1915, **32:** 8; Jan. 4, 1915, **32:** 12; Jan. 5, 1915, **32:** 21; Jan. 6, 1915, **32:** 21
Brand Whitlock, Dec. 1, 1915, **35:** 280
Reminiscences about Ellen Axson Wilson, Sept. 12, 1914, **31:** 27

ILLUSTRATIONS

Illustrations appear in the center section of each volume

WOODROW WILSON

Leaving Princeton, 27
A happy President with his successor, 27
The inaugural parade, 27
The inaugural address (2), 27
After the inauguration, 27
With Joseph P. Tumulty, 27
With his cabinet, 27
At Harlakenden, 28
Reading his tariff message to Congress, 28
"Going down?" "Not if I know it," 29
Big paleface chief, 29
Diplomacy: making friends with President Wilson, 29
On with the dance, 29
"Look out, Mr. President, your worst enemies are behind," 29
The Professor, 29
"Stop the ship! I've dropped a penny overboard!", 29
"Don't mind them, William, they're really trying to hit me," 29
With Joseph P. Tumulty in the Oval Office, 31
With Colonel House at Cornish, September, 1914, 31
With the Secretary of State, 31
In the Oval Office, 32
At a baseball game with Helen Bones, 32
Wilson's shorthand draft of the second *Lusitania* note, 33
With Francis Bowes Sayre and Francis, Jr., 34
At the World Series Game with Mrs. Galt in Philadelphia, 34
Ready for Business, 35
Ripping It Out, 35
Wiping Away His Tears, 35
The Class in Reading and Writing, 35
"Obstructing Traffic, Your Honor," 35
With the White House Press Corps, 36
With Mrs. Wilson in St. Louis on the Preparedness Tour, 36
Addressing Congress on the *Sussex* crisis, 36
With his granddaughter, Ellen Wilson McAdoo, 37
Bust of Wilson by Jo Davidson, 37
The Wilsons leaving Memorial Continental Hall in Washington, 37
Signing the Federal Farm Loan Act, July 17, 1916, 37
Leading the Flag Day parade, June 14, 1916, 37
A momentary distraction at Shadow Lawn, September 2, 1916, 38

Delivering the acceptance speech, **38**
On the hustings in Albany, **38**
The happy campaigner, **38**
The Cabinet, **38**

COLLATERAL

Jessie, Ellen, Eleanor, and Margaret, **28**
Ellen Axson Wilson, **28**
South side of the White House, **28**
Francis Bowes Sayre and Jessie Wilson Sayre, **28**
John Lind, **28**
Victoriano Huerta, **28**
The Rev. Dr. Isaac Stockton Keith Axson, **30**
The Rev. Dr. Joseph Ruggles Wilson, **30**
William Ewart Gladstone, **30**
Prospect Gate, **30**
Prospect Gardens, **30**
Scene Near Old Lyme, Connecticut, **30**
Autumn, 1910, **30**
Pastoral, **30**
Woods and Fields, 1911, **30**
Apple Orchard, **30**
Moonlight Scene, **30**
Landscapes, **30**
Sir Edward Grey, **31**
Sir Cecil Arthur Spring Rice, **31**
Francisco Villa, **31**
Venustiano Carranza, **31**
William Monroe Trotter, **31**
The Secretary of State is Amused (Bryan with Albert S. Burleson),
    32
Walter Hines Page, **32**
Edward Mandell House, **32**
Constantin Theodor Dumba, **32**
Count Johann Heinrich von Bernstorff, **32**
Jean Jules Jusserand, **32**
William Jennings Bryan, **33**
Photographic Portrait of Edith Bolling Galt by Arnold Genthe, **33**
Edith Bolling Galt's letter to Wilson of August 3, 1915, **34**
Robert Lansing, **34**
Theobald von Bethmann Hollweg, **34**
The Employment Agent, **35**
"The German Government believes that it was acting in justified
    self-defense," **35**
"To Arms! To Arms!", **35**
Claude Kitchin, **36**
James Hay, **36**

Lindley M. Garrison, **36**
Newton D. Baker, **36**
General Pershing in Mexico, **36**
Villa on the Move, **36**
Bust of Colonel House by Jo Davidson, **37**
Louis Dembitz Brandeis, **37**
James Watson Gerard, **37**
Charles Evans Hughes, **38**
The Speaker of the House under cover, **38**
Joseph Patrick Tumulty, **38**
Charles Lee Swem, **38**

INDEXES BY VOLUME

INDEX FOR VOLUMES 27–38

A. Jaeckel and Co. (New York, **35:** 272-n2
A. Mitchell Palmer: Politician (Coben), **27:** 22n2; **29:** 223n2; **34:** 24n1
A. W. Shaw Co. (Chicago), **32:** 68n1
ABC powers: *see* Mexico and the United States—ABC mediation
Abbott, Frederick H., **27:** 469n1
Abbott, Gordon, **29:** 278,n3
Abbott, Lyman, **30:** 407,n1
Abendpost (Chicago); *see* Chicago *Abendpost*
Abendpost Co. (Chicago), **38:** 351n1
Aberdeen, Scotland, **29:** 389
Abraham Lincoln (Charnwood), **34:** 21n7
Académie des Beaux Arts, **37:** 42n1
Academy of Arts and Letters: *see* American Academy of Arts and Letters
Achievement of the Democratic Party and Its Leader since March 4, 1913 (Eliot), **37:** 535,n2; **38:** 319,n1
Acosta, Julio, **36:** 586,n2
Acree, Sterling N., **29:** 208, 221
Across the Years (Macfarland), **35:** 354n2
Acuña, Jesús, **34:** 321, 386,n1, 455n1, 531; **35:** 95; **36:** 308n1, 313n1
Adair, Henry R., **37:** 318,n1; **38:** 378, 380, 384, 386
Adair, John Alfred McDowell, **38:** 457,n1
Adamowska, Antoinette Szumowska, **38:** 371,n2
Adams, Adeline Valentine Pond (Mrs. Herbert), **28:** 45,n3, 146, 166, 252, 328; **34:** 178,n2
Adams, Annette Abbott (Mrs. Martin H.), **30:** 172,n1
Adams, Alva, **27:** 383; **28:** 584n1
Adams, Charles Francis, **27:** 200; **29:** 401n1; **31:** 258, 267-68
Adams, Fred, **28:** 376,n2, 377, 378, 445, 446; **29:** 146,n2, 329
Adams, Graham, Jr., **27:** 77n6,7
Adams, Granger, **38:** 238,n1
Adams, Herbert, **28:** 45n3, 146, 166, 392; **37:** 247,n1, 409
Adams, John, **27:** 159, 268, 273; **37:** 105n4
Adams, John Quincy, **27:** 159
Adamson, Robert, **38:** 591n1
Adamson, William Charles, **29:** 139-40, 152-53, 183, 461, 462,n1, 478, 542; **30:** 224,n1, 245, 289, 324, 348-49, 351, 433; **32:** 241, 252; **36:** 277, 301; **38:** 103, 199, 666-67; and Covington bill, **29:** 139-40, 173-74, 496-97; and Panama Canal tolls exemption bill, **29:** 162, 171, 182, 233, 265-66,n2, 269, 282-83, 288, 297,n1, 383, 394; and water-power bill, **29:** 281,n2; **30:** 222-23, 224,n1, 244-45; **31:** 178, 450; opposed by W. Kent, **30:** 217-19,n2; **35:** 232; **36:** 302-304, 304-306, 322; congratulates WW on Mexican policy, **30:** 286-87; and safety-at-sea-legislation, **31:** 508; on railroad labor situation, **36:** 415, 428-29; and Interstate Commerce Commission, **36:** 612,n1
Adamson Act (Eight-Hour Act), **38:** 56, 174,n1,3, 280, 354, 457, 466, 516n1, 657; Chambers on, **38:** 48-49, 199-200; WW on, **38:** 49-50, 96-101, 167, 193, 215-19, 293, 333, 516,n1, 554, 571-72,n1, 586-87, 600; N. D. Baker on, **38:** 177; H. Ford on, **38:** 187,n2; S. H. Thompson, Jr. on, **38:** 192-93; R. Hudspeth on, **38:** 197-98; T. R. Marshall on, **38:** 212; W. Lippmann on, **38:** 274-75; and Endicott Johnson Co., **38:** 461n2, 483; S. Gompers on, **38:** 471; *see also* Eight–Hour Commission
Adamson water-power bill, **36:** 241, 243, 244, 306
Adana, Turkey, **35:** 337
Addams, Jane, **27:** 9; **32:** 20, 53, 168, 516n2; **33:** 331,n1, 469,n2,3, 471, 472; **34:** 110n1, 243, 250-52,n2,6,8, 260, 473; **35:** 196, 199, 200,n1, 348-49,n1; **37:** 308, 316, 515, 527-28; **38:** 34, 460,n1, 481n1; requests interview with WW, **32:** 20; praises WW veto of immigration bill, **32:** 162; meets European leaders, **33:** 300, 469,n2; E. M. House on visit to Europe of, **33:** 516, 522-23; on preparedness, **35:** 134-35, 158
Address of the President of the United States . . . April 8, 1913, **27:** 272n
Address of the President of the United States . . . June 23, 1913, **27:** 573n
Address of President Wilson Delivered at Swarthmore College, Oct. 25, 1913, **28:** 442n
Address of President Wilson at the Brooklyn Navy Yard, May 11, 1914, **30:** 15n
Address of President Wilson at the Unveiling of the Statue to the Memory of Commodore John Barry, May 16, 1914, **30:** 36n
Address of President Wilson to the Graduating Class of the United States Naval Academy, June 5, 1914, **30:** 148n

Address of President Wilson at Independence Hall, July 4, 1914, **30**: 255n
Address Delivered before the American Bar Association, Oct. 20, 1914, **31**: 186n
Address of the President of the United States . . . January 29, 1915, **32**: 157n
Address of the President of the United States before the United States Chamber of Commerce, Feb. 3, 1915, **32**: 187n
Address of the President . . . at Convention Hall, Philadelphia, Pa., May 10, 1915, **33**: 147n
Address of the President . . . at the Luncheon Tendered to Him by the Mayor's Committee, May 17, 1915, **33**: 209n
Address of the President . . . at the Pan American Financial Conference, May 24, 1915, **33**: 247n
Address of President Wilson at Arlington National Cemetery, May 31, 1915, **33**: 287n
Address of President Wilson at the Pan American Scientific Conference, Jan. 6, 1916, **35**: 446n
Address of President Wilson at the First Annual Banquet of the Motion Picture Board of Trade (Jan. 27, 1916), **36**: 19n
Address of President Wilson at the Gridiron Dinner, Feb. 26, 1916, **36**: 220n
Address of President Wilson at Arlington National Cemetery, May 30, 1916, **37**: 128n
Address of President Wilson . . . Flag Day, June 14, 1916, **37**: 225n
Address of President Wilson . . . June 29, 1916, **37**: 328n
Address of President Wilson to the Citizenship Convention, July 13, 1916, **37**: 418n
Address of President Wilson at Suffrage Convention, Sept. 8, 1916, **38**: 164n
Address of President Wilson Before the Grain Dealers' Association, Sept. 25, 1916, **38**: 270n
Addresses and Papers of John R. Mott, **27**: 131n
Addresses of President Wilson January 27-February 3, 1916, **36**: 7n, 16n, 35n, 41n, 48n, 63n, 73n, 85n, 96n, 110n, 114n, 120n2, 121n
Addresses of President Wilson at Detroit, Mich. . . . (July 1916), **37**: 387n, 395n
Addresses of President Wilson at Omaha, Oct. 5, 1916, **38**: 342n, 343n, 349n
Addresses of President Wilson at Indianapolis, Oct. 12, 1916, **38**: 419n, 427n
Addresses of President Wilson at Cincinnati, Oct. 26, 1916, **38**: 533n, 537n, 543n
Adee, Alvey Augustus, **27**: 195, 224-25; **35**: 405
Adkins, Jesse Corcoran, **37**: 176,n1
Adler, Cyrus, **32**: 534-35,n1
Adler, Felix, **27**: 107; **29**: 170

Administration and Mexico (Woolsey), **29**: 121n1
Admirals, Generals, and American Foreign Policy, 1898-1914 (Challener), **27**: 441n1, 448n1, 518n2
Admiralty House, Bermuda, **28**: 135
Adna Brown Hotel, Springfield, Vt., **34**: 63, 101, 125
Adventure in Constructive Finance, An (Glass), **27**: 535n1
Aeolian Hall, N.Y., **36**: 7n1
Affair of Honor: Woodrow Wilson and the Occupation of Veracruz (Quirk), **29**: 420n2, 476n1
Africa, **32**: 277; **33**: 100-101; **35**: 466, 486
African Methodist Episcopal Zion Church, **36**: 481n2
Afro-Americans, **28**: 492, 494; **31**: 298-99
Against the Spector of a Dragon: The Campaign for American Military Preparedness 1914-1917 (Finnegan), **37**: 321n1
Age of Industrial Violence, 1910-1915: The Activities and Findings of the United States Commission on Industrial Relations (Adams), **27**: 77n6,7
Agger, Eugene Ewald, **27**: 206-207
Aglen, Mr. (Inspector General of Customs in China), **31**: 510
Agricola, Georgius (Georg Bauer), **31**: 332,n1
agricultural credit: *see* rural credit
Agricultural Credit: Land-Mortgage or Long-Term Credit (S. Doc.), **29**: 69n1
agriculture: improvement in production, **27**: 50-51, 150; rural credits, **28**: 146-48,n1; **29**: 5-6; movement of crops, **28**: 156,n1; **29**: 6; Federal Reserve bill, **29**: 5-6; D. F. Houston on land mortgage banking system, **29**: 69-74; H. Plunkett on, **29**: 115-17; Bacon-Bartlett bill, **29**: 413n1, 425, 538; Smith-Lever Act, **30**: 8n1; sundry civil appropriations bill, **30**: 205, 284; Clayton bill, **30**: 205-207,n2, 272; **31**: 25-26; effect of war on farmers, **30**: 420; aid to cotton farmers, **31**: 126-29; appropriation bill (March 1915), **35**: 97; farmers and preparedness, **36**: 637-38,n15; and 1916 platform, **37**: 197-98; WW signs rural-credits bill, **37**: 427-28; WW on legislative accomplishments for, **38**: 24-27, 130; farmers and 1916 election, **38**: 159-61, 260-61; WW's addresses on, **38**: 261-70, 419-27, 500-509, 637-40
Agriculture, Department of, **29**: 6, 115, 116, 117; **30**: 153, 217; **32**: 181; **35**: 232, 238n4; **37**: 198; **38**: 24, 130, 421, 422, 504, 505, 569-70, 638, 639; WW on Houston as Secretary, **29**: 270; and cotton crisis, **31**: 212
Agriculture Committee (House of Reps.), **35**: 97; Farmers' Union, **29**: 116
Agriculture and Forestry Committee (Senate), **35**: 97

Agua Prieta, Sonora, Mex., **38:** 401
Aguascalientes, Mex., **29:** 539; **33:** 29, 187; convention at, **31:** 179,n3, 206, 313, 322,n1; **32:** 355,n6; **33:** 239n1, 271
Aguilar (mining camp, Colo.), **28:** 512, 523
Aguilar, Cándido, **31:** 72, 178; **36:** 340,n2, 540n1; **37:** 360-61, 367, 410-11, 437-38
Aguilar Oil Co. Ltd. (Mexican Eagle), **27:** 331,n2; **28:** 376n2; **29:** 18, 146n1; **30:** 246n2
Aguinaldo, Emilio, **27:** 9, 10, 58, 468; **28:** 242n1; **32:** 535n1
Aguirre Benavides, Luis, **30:** 413,n8, 417; **32:** 355,n4, 356
Ahnelt, William Paul, **30:** 173n1
Ahumada, Chihuahua, Mex.: *see* Villa Ahumada
Ainslie, Peter, **29:** 476
Aitken, Harry E., **32:** 445,n2
Alabama: federal patronage in, **27:** 344,n1, 345; Gov. O'Neal and senatorial appointee, **28:** 160,n2, 391; Underwood nomination, **29:** 410n1
Alabama, U.S.S., **30:** 345, 427
Alabama Claims, **31:** 369, 425
Alabama Great Southern Railroad Co. *v* United States, **36:** 196
Alabama Merchants Association, **34:** 373
Alaska, **35:** 232, 233; **37:** 200n3; **38:** 130; appointment of governor, **27:** 285-86; conservation, **29:** 9-10; railroad project and bill, **29:** 400, 536; **30:** 332,n1; **32:** 231, 366; **33:** 541; coal-leasing bill, **30:** 20, 27, 31; **35:** 231-32,n1; development board bill, **30:** 31; survey of coastline, **31:** 419-20; transit of war material, **31:** 444; purchase, **33:** 34
Alaska coal-leasing bill, **37:** 197
Alaska purchase, **33:** 34
Alaska Railroad, **34:** 6n1
Alaska Railroad (Fitch), **29:** 332n1
Albano, Angelo: lynching in 1910: WW recommends indemnity: Congress approves, **28:** 115,n2
Albany (ship), **27:** 426n2
Albany, N.Y., **34:** 233, 247, 261, 263, 269, 285, 288, 433
Albany Hospital, N.Y., **38:** 182n8
Albemarle Orchard Co. (Charlottesville, Va.), **27:** 73n1
Albert I (of Belgium), **30:** 383, 470n1; **31:** 33; **35:** 391-92,n2, 499; **36:** 150, 201-202; **38:** 392, 653
Albert, Heinrich Friedrich, **34:** 74n5, 158,n1, 278, 430n1; **35:** 264n1, 281, 282, 282-83, 290-91
Albert Ballin: Business and Politics in Imperial Germany, 1888-1918 (Cecil), **33:** 298n1
Albion Hotel (Baltimore, Md.), **28:** 397
Albright, John J., **29:** 401n1
alcoholic beverage tax, **31:** 32
Alcott, Louisa May, **36:** 132n1
Alderman, Edwin Anderson, **36:** 481

Aldrich, G. B., **28:** 344n2
Aldrich, Nelson Wilmarth, **38:** 307-308, 331, 435
Aldrich bill: *see* Aldrich plan
Aldrich plan, **27:** 79,n1, 457; **28:** 122n4; **38:** 497
Aldrich-Vreeland Act (1908), **30:** 325,n1, 326, 335; **38:** 498
Aleshire, James B., **30:** 8,n1
Alexander, Archibald Stevens, **27:** 95,n1
Alexander, Caroline Bayard Stevens, **27:** 75, 76, 95, 109
Alexander, Charlton Henry, **34:** 108,n4, 226
Alexander, John White, **28:** 62,n6, 67
Alexander, Joshua Willis, **29:** 280,n1, 282; **35:** 345,n1, 459,n1; **36:** 567, 575-76; **37:** 451; **38:** 52-53,n1, 77, 335,n4, 456; safety-at-sea convention and treaty, **30:** 317; **31:** 491, 492; seamen's bill, **30:** 223,n1, 317; and ship-purchase bill, **30:** 402, 454; **31:** 87, 88; **32:** 197, 242
Alexander, Julian Power, **34:** 108,n4, 226
Alexander Brown and Sons (banking firm of Baltimore), **32:** 502n1
Alexander Hamilton: An Essay on American Union (Oliver), **37:** 34,n5
Alexandra Fýodorovna (Empress of Russia), **38:** 68,n3
Alexis, Nord, **31:** 485
Alfonso XII (of Spain), **33:** 47n1; **37:** 274n2
Alfonso XIII (of Spain), **32:** 350, 504,n1; **33:** 47, 123n6; **35:** 88n4, 130, 144, 176; **37:** 19-20,n1, 274,n3; **38:** 34, 82, 392
Alfred Nobel, S.S., **31:** 477
Algara, Don A. de Terreros, **29:** 254
Algeria, **31:** 562,n3
Algonquin Hotel, N.Y., **34:** 357, 366, 376
Alice's Adventures in Wonderland (Carroll), **37:** 53
alien land bill (California), **31:** 236
All for the Ladies (Blossom), **29:** 558,n4
All in a Life-Time (Morgenthau), **36:** 425n3
All in a Life-Time . . . The Campaign of 1916 (Morgenthau), **36:** 425n3
Allemagne, et les Problèmes de la Paix pendant la Première Guerre Mondiale: Documents extraits des archives de l'Office allemand des Affaires étrangères (Scherer and Grunewald, eds.), **38:** 314n2
Allen, Alfred Gaither, **31:** 446n1; **38:** 524n1
Allen, Anjenett Holcomb (Mrs. Charles Sterling), **27:** 3,n1, 555; **31:** 142; **34:** 430; **35:** 237
Allen, Arthur M., **34:** 382n1
Allen, C. Loomis, **32:** 149,n2
Allen, Henry Tureman, **36:** 587,n6, 591
Allen, William Vincent, **35:** 153,n1
Allied Blockade of Germany 1914-16 (Siney), **36:** 387n2

Allied Economic Conference, **36:** 387n2; **37:** 287,n1, 397n1, 459, 525

Allnutt Memorial Methodist Protestant Church, Baltimore, **32:** 494n2

Almy, Frederic, **27:** 244

Alphaud, Gabriel, **32:** 462,n1,2, 463-64

Alsace: *see* Alsace-Lorraine

Alsace-Lorraine, **30:** 190; **31:** 294n1, 459, 518; **32:** 44, 45, 81, 205, 212, 341, 349; **33:** 18, 298, 347, 462; **35:** 71n3, 466, 484; **36:** 148n1, 180n2; **37:** 135n2, 179, 412, 507n1; **38:** 69, 647

Altrude: *see* Gordon, Alice Gertrude

Alvarez, Francisco, **36:** 653

Amador, Juan Neftali, **37:** 22,n1, 39, 254-55

Amalgamated Council of New Orleans, **27:** 185-86

Ambleside, Westmorland, **28:** 286n1

America, Asia and the Pacific, With Special Reference to the Russo-Japanese War and its Results (Schierbrand), **33:** 32,n3

American Academy of Arts and Letters, **31:** 247, 248n2; **32:** 16

American Aid for Assassins (London *Financial News*), **29:** 331n1

American Anti-Congestion League, **32:** 96, 97

American Association for Labor Legislation, **35:** 184, 185n1

American Association of Foreign Language Newspapers, **32:** 14n1

American Bankers' Association, **27:** 79; **28:** 3,n1, 8n1, 346; **35:** 322, 325

American Bar Association, **38:** 585; WW welcoming remarks: outline, **31:** 183-84; text, 184-86,n1

American Belgian Relief Committee: *see* Commission for Relief in Belgium

American Bible Society, **36:** 465n1, 481; WW remarks to, **36:** 629-31

American Board of Commissioners for Foreign Missions, **27:** 65n1, 179n1; **35:** 337n1

American Can Co., **30:** 482

American Chemical Society, **36:** 275,n3

American Citizens' Relief Committee (London), **30:** 367, 438

American College of Surgeons, **38:** 182,n1,4

American Commission for the Relief of East Prussia, **38:** 177n2

American Constitutional Law (Hare), **32:** 534,n2

American Diplomacy and the Furtherance of Commerce (Schuyler), **32:** 534,n4

American-Dominican Convention (1907), **27:** 272n1; **30:** 203,n1

American Economist, **38:** 20n1

American Electric Railway Association: WW address to, **32:** 149-57

American Embargo Conference, **36:** 576n1

American Epic, An (Hoover), **31:** 206n1

American Express Co., **28:** 328, 397

American Federation of Catholic Societies, **37:** 476n3

American Federation of Labor, **35:** 184; **36:** 24, 567; **38:** 468-73, 671-72,n1; and union exemption from Sherman Act, **27:** 366-69; **29:** 347, 425, 535, 537-38; executive council confers with WW, **28:** 317-18, 319n1; **32:** 78, 87; and Sec. Wilson, **28:** 590,n1; on Supreme Court justices, **30:** 309-10; and Clayton Act, **31:** 131; and California alien land law, **31:** 237; and immigration bill, **32:** 95, 96; and seamen's bill, **32:** 305; **35:** 458,n1; and recognition of Carranza, **34:** 512n1; and Hillstrom case, **35:** 206-207, 211, 214; and vocational education bill, **36:** 357,n1; WW's address at dedication of new building of, **37:** 353-58; and Mexican-American labor conferences, **37:** 365-66,n1

American Federationist, **30:** 264

American flag: and Wanamaker expedition to Indian tribes, **27:** 508n2; WW on, **30:** 146, 184-86, 252, 254; **33:** 391-93

American Food in the World War and Reconstruction Period (Surface and Bland), **31:** 206n1

American Group of the Six-Power Consortium, **32:** 329; **37:** 233, 271

American Hebrew, **36:** 656

American Heritage, **34:** 491n1

American Heroine: The Life and Legend of Jane Addams (Davis) **34:** 251n8

American Historical Association, **28:** 470; **38:** 655

American Historical Review, **36:** 280n1

American Indian Portraits from the Wanamaker Expedition of 1913 (Reynolds), **27:** 508n2

American Indians, **37:** 213; **38:** 227-29; WW message to, **27:** 469-70, 507-508,n1,2; government appointments, **28:** 187,n2, 410n4; Navajo revolt, **29:** 36,n1; Montana band to remain neutral in European war, **31:** 77-78

American International Corp., N.Y., **35:** 347n2

American Jewish Relief Committee, **35:** 412n1

American Labor Legislation Review, **35:** 184n1

American Luncheon Club of London, **31:** 380

American Machinist, **33:** 497,n1, 506, 511,n1

American Manufacturers Export Association, **29:** 435

American Medical Association, **38:** 182n8

American National Red Cross, **31:** 334; **32:** 397, 525; **35:** 120, 243-44, 316,n1, 367, 472; **36:** 380,n1; **37:** 405; WW appeal for funds, **27:** 229; and Mexico, **31:**

12n1, 13, 68-69; **33:** 258, 275, 334, 447, 448,n1, 461, 466; WW remarks to, **31:** 430,n1; and *Eastland* disaster, **34:** 27n1

American Neutral Conference Committee, **38:** 104-105, 123; WW's colloquy with members of, **38:** 108-17

American Newspaper Publishers' Association: WW's address to, **36:** 560-61,n1

American Note (*New Statesman*), **35:** 223,n1

American Peace Movement and Social Reform 1898-1918 (Marchand), **36:** 632n1; **37:** 291n2

American Peace Society, **35:** 195n1

American Philosophical Society, **27:** 159, 195

American Revolution, **27:** 307; **30:** 34-36, 233; **34:** 535; **35:** 47-48; **36:** 72, 97, 489

American Revolution (Trevelyan), **32:** 8

American Smelting and Refining Co., **27:** 481n2

American Society in London, **29:** 111n2; **30:** 367

American Society of International Law, **29:** 331

American Society of Mining and Metallurgy, **31:** 332

American Sugar Refining Co., **30:** 482; **37:** 427n3

American Syndicalism: The I.W.W. (Brooks), **27:** 481,n1

American Telephone and Telegraph Co., **36:** 152n2; agrees to reduce holdings and adjust to antitrust laws, **29:** 45,n1, 141n1; possibility of federal acquisition of, **29:** 58; WW on first transcontinental hookup, **32:** 118-19

American Tobacco Co., **28:** 255n1; **29:** 68

American Truth Society, **38:** 285,n1, 286n1

American Union Against Militarism, **36:** 632-33,n1; **37:** 75, 291n1,2; WW's colloquy with leaders of, **36:** 634-49

American Unitarian Association, **27:** 80n1

American University: WW address at opening of, **30:** 89-91, 162

American Women's War Hospital (Paignton, England), **35:** 77n2

American Woolen Co., **27:** 321

America's Traditional Isolation (Bryce), **37:** 76n1, 77n1, 290,n1

Amerika: Allgemeine Zeitung für Wahrheit und Recht, **38:** 279,n2

Amherst College, **33:** 296n1

Ammons, Elias Milton, **28:** 426,n4, 507, 519-20, 521, 524, 555, 581, 584; **30:** 60,n1; **31:** 49, 143, 215, 309, 353, 373, 449, 464, 545; requests federal troops in Colorado coal strike, **29:** 501-502, 502-503, 511, 526, 527-28; request granted, 528-29; exchanges with WW about settling coal strike, **30:** 37-38, 45-46, 48-49, 422, 452-53; requests federal troops remain longer, **31:** 272-

73,n2, 452; plan for withdrawal of troops, 334-35, 517; withdrawal, 548, 557-59

Amory, Browne and Co., Boston, **29:** 401n1

Amsterdam, Netherlands, **34:** 251n2

Anaconda Copper Mining Co., **38:** 182n3

Analysis of the trust question, particularly as to industrials, as shown by proposed bills and other suggestions, arranged by topics, submitted by Joseph E. Davies, Commissioner of Corporations, **29:** 78n1

Anatolia, Turkey, **36:** 148n1

Ancient Order of Hibernians of Connecticut, **38:** 83,n1

Ancon, Treaty of, **32:** 474,n4

Ancona incident: *see* Austria-Hungary and the United States

Anderson, Chandler Parsons, **30:** 369,n4; **31:** 100, 103, 111, 160, 192, 196, 201, 230, 372; **32:** 44, 75, 91, 112, 490; on Allied war objectives, **32:** 44-50, 66, 67; memorandum on British interference with trade, **32:** 48,n1; on *Falaba* case, **32:** 490-92, 492-93; memorandum on submarine warfare, **33:** 501-504

Anderson, Charles Williams, **28:** 211; **30:** 491,n2

Anderson, George Weston, **27:** 334,n1; **36:** 611n3; **37:** 152, 267

Anderson, Peirce, **28:** 501, 502

Anderson, Roy S., **31:** 287-88

Andonaegui, Juan Luis Sanfuentes, **36:** 198,n4

Andover Theological Seminary (Cambridge, Mass.), **28:** 54n1

Andrássy, Countess Ella Zichy, **38:** 71,n2

Andrássy, Count Gyula (1823-1890), **38:** 71,n3

Andrássy, Count Gyula (1860-1929), **38:** 71,n1

Andrew Furuseth, Emancipator of the Seamen (Weintraub), **27:** 188n2; **30:** 223n1; **31:** 458n1

Andrews, John Bertram, **35:** 184,n1

Andrews, Mary Raymond Shipman, **31:** 316,n2

Ángeles, Felipe, **28:** 541; **29:** 551,n2; **30:** 57,n1, 97, 339, 393, 409, 413, 414, 416, 417, 418; **32:** 355,n7, 383,n1, 384, 387, 390; **34:** 118, 119; differences with Carranza, **30:** 410; quoted on religious freedom, **32:** 279; Villa on, **32:** 386; talks with F. K. Lane in Washington, **33:** 463-64, 468; talks with J. R. Garfield in Mexico, **33:** 533n1

Angell, Norman, **30:** 236; **34:** 135-36,n1, 217; **37:** 77, 294n1

Anglo-American relations: *see* Great Britain and the United States

Anhui Province, China, **32:** 137

Anketell, Thomas Jackson, **36:** 435,n1, 435-36, 464

Annabel Lee (Poe), **28:** 465, 475

Ann May Memorial Hospital, Spring Lake, N.J., **38**: 118n3

Annapolis: *see* United States Naval Academy

Annexionistische Deutschland (Grumbach), **34**: 47n6

Annin, Robert Edwards, **29**: 386,n2

Annual Report of the Attorney General of the United States for the year 1913, **29**: 67n2

Annual Report of the Commissioner General of Immigration to the Secretary of Labor . . . 1914, **32**: 56,n1

Another Attack on the Banking Centres (New York *Sun*), **30**: 50,n1

Ansonia Hotel, N.Y., **33**: 89

Answer to a Child's Question (Coleridge), **29**: 460n1

Anthracite Bureau of Information, **38**: 297n2

Anthracite Coal Strike Commission of 1902, **28**: 555,n2; WW compares its settlement to Colorado situation, **31**: 503-504

Anthracite Coal Strike of 1902 (Cornell), **28**: 555n2

anthracite coal strikes of 1900 and 1902: and Mother Jones, **28**: 509n1

antidumping legislation, **35**: 502, 511; **36**: 274-76, 366n1; **38**: 529; Redfield on, **35**: 427-29; Owen on, **35**: 434; McAdoo on, **35**: 476

Anti-Imperialist League, **28**: 301; **29**: 508; **38**: 19,n1

Anti-Militarism Union Works for Peace in Mexico (New York *World*), **37**: 291n1

Antisdale, Louis Marlin, **28**: 64,n1; **29**: 136; **38**: 546,n2

antitrust laws: New Jersey, **27**: 90,n2, 120-22, 178; **28**: 420

antitrust legislation, **28**: 532, 560; **29**: 138,n1,2, 163, 175, 212, 261-62, 315-16, 335-37, 347, 374, 378, 399, 407,n2, 424, 486, 535; **30**: 44, 94, 126, 182-83, 194, 219, 243, 268, 312n1, 319n3; **32**: 184; **37**: 192, 397-98; **38**: 129, 340; amendments to Sundry Civil bill exempting labor, **27**: 530; L. Brandeis articles on, **29**: 30n1; WW on consent decrees, **29**: 141,n1; address to Congress, **29**: 153-58; and labor, **29**: 356, 535, 537-38; Bacon-Bartlett bill, **29**: 425; Export Association urges recognition of differences between interstate and foreign trade, **29**: 435n1; J. T. Robinson on stock watering, **29**: 456; business efforts to delay, **30**: 173n1; C. R. Van Hise on, **30**: 272; F. Newlands on, **30**: 296; U.S. Chamber of Commerce protests exemption of labor, **30**: 205; WW on role of C. A. Culberson in, **31**: 21; T. W. Gregory on, **31**: 24-26

Antitrust Legislation: Conference Report on H.R. 15657, **31**: 30n2

Antung, China, **32**: 321

Antwerp, Belgium, **30**: 459n1, 460, 467, 471; **33**: 18; **35**: 74, 466

Apache Indians, **38**: 227, 228

Appam affair, **36**: 134,n2, 216

Appleton, Margarett S., **31**: 454,n4

Appleton, Mary W., **31**: 454,n4

Appleton, William Worthen, **31**: 454,n4

appropriations bills, **32**: 227, 228, 240

Appropriations, Committee on (House of Reps.), **27**: 44, 369; **36**: 330; on anniversary of Emancipation Proclamation, **27**: 15; W. H. Taft on funds for president's military aide, **27**: 17; and flood relief, **27**: 229,n1; WW on aid for Americans stranded in Europe, **30**: 337, 337-38,n1; WW on working with, **32**: 62-63

Appropriations, Committee on (Senate), **30**: 337, 337-38,n1; and flood relief, **27**: 229,n1

Arabia, S.S., **38**: 658n1

Arabic crisis: *see* Germany and the United States

Arcadia (Georgetown, S.C.), **29**: 89,n1

Arcadia Hall, Detroit, **37**: 383n1

Arcadian Adventures with the Idle Rich (Leacock), **31**: 468,n1

Archer, A. M., **30**: 165

Archibald, James Francis Jewell, **31**: 338; **34**: 403,n1, 404, 429, 528; **35**: 277n1

Arecibo, P.R., **36**: 568,n1

Arellano, Cayetano Simplicio, **29**: 165,n2

Argentina, **27**: 478; **28**: 95n1; **30**: 23, 41-42, 121; **31**: 152,n5, 218; **35**: 54-55, 254, 520; **36**: 197, 199-201, 445, 461, 479, 605; **37**: 238, 241-44, 486; **38**: 19, 116; and ABC mediation in Mexican situation, **28**: 141,n2; **29**: 135, 505-506,n1, 506-507, 518, 525, 534, 539-40; **30**: 87; **32**: 117-18; **34**: 43, 80, 81, 487-88; and Mexico, **28**: 412, 516; **32**: 117-18, 263, 398n1; **33**: 305-306, 437, 455, 487, 488; J. Bryce on, **28**: 506-507; **29**: 47; and Peru, **29**: 244; Bryan conciliation treaty with, **29**: 342; refuses to recognize Huerta, **29**: 484; R. S. Naón on meeting with WW, **30**: 197-99; WW thanks for ABC mediation, **30**: 262,n1 and Pan-Americanism, **30**: 271; and Pan-American Pact, **31**: 470, 471-72,n1, 497, 540, 548-49; **32**: 64, 338-39, 339-40, 474, 478, 542; **33**: 52, 55, 62, 63, 65, 68, 80,n1, 221-22; WW address aboard *Mareno*, **32**: 451-53

Argumedo, Abel Ortiz, **33**: 261,n2

Argumedo, Benjamín, **32**: 387

Arias, Desiderio, **32**: 76,n1, 77; **33**: 27; **37**: 157n1, 158

Arica: *see* Tacna-Arica dispute

Aristocrats of the Labor World, **36**: 204n1

Arizona, **27**: 361; **29**: 393, 408; **34**: 192; **37**: 300, 321n1; **38**: 515n1

Arkansas, **27**: 457,n1,2; diplomatic appointments from, **28**: 5, 111-12

Arlington Confederate Memorial Association, **30:** 141n2

Arlington Memorial Amphitheater, **35:** 11n1

Arlington National Cemetery, **30:** 110,n1, 113,n4, 141,n1; **31:** 561n1; **33:** 286n1, 287,n1, 290n1; **37:** 123n1

Armed Merchantmen, International Relations of the United States, **36:** 226n2

Armenia, **36:** 148n1; **38:** 539, 652

Armenians: plight of, **35:** 3, 104-105, 119, 337, 348, 349

Armes, Lucy Hamilton Kerr (Mrs. George A.), **32:** 22,n1, 23

armor-plate, bill, **36:** 60, 68-69, 174, 175, 278-79, 311, 376, 396,n1, 545-46,n1,2

armor trust, **35:** 434n1, 446, 456; **36:** 82-83

Armour and Co., Chicago, **33:** 509n1

Armstrong, Hamilton Fish, **35:** 152,n1, 182

Armstrong Academy, Okla., **28:** 187n2

Army (U.S.): *see* United States Army

army appropriation bill, **37:** 380-81, 491; **38:** 40, 102, 181

army reorganization bill (militia bill, Hay bill), **36:** 178-79,n1,2,4, 217,n1,2, 240, 518,n1, 640, 643; **37:** 27n1, 156; **38:** 41, 52n1, 102, 636; and nitrate plant resolution, **36:** 344, 348, 619-20,n1; **37:** 66-67, 94; passes in the House, **36:** 360,n1; J. Hay compares Senate and House bills, **36:** 514-15

Army War College, **34:** 235, 250, 482-83,n1, 484; **35:** 106; **38:** 238n3,4

Arnold, Charlotte Bruce, **28:** 159,n1

Arnold, Frances Bunsen Trevenen, **28:** 286,n1; **35:** 110,n2

Arnold, Grace, **28:** 159,n1, 199

Arnold, Julean Herbert, **27:** 465,n1, 466

Arnold, Matthew, **28:** 286n1; **30:** 22; **33:** 161; **38:** 259

Arnold, Olney, **35:** 360,n5

Around the Tea Table—Afternoon Tea (Hulbert), **32:** 50n1

Arredondo, Eliseo, **33:** 3-10, 307-308, 416,n1; **34:** 448, 488, 530, 531-33, 542; **35:** 93, 94, 95, 101, 103, 501, 505; **37:** 19, 130, 250, 293-94, 306n1, 348, 360-61, 368,n1, 437, 452, 453, 476, 482-83, 497; **38:** 10, 11, 13, 19, 79; and Punitive Expedition, **36:** 342-43,n2, 343-44, 350,n2, 382n2, 540, 581-83; and Parral incident, **36:** 480,n1; as ambassador to the U.S., **36:** 603, 604, 608; on need for U.S. troop withdrawal from Mexico, **37:** 152-53; on Carrizal incident, **37:** 292; and Joint High Commission, **37:** 367, 400-401, 409, 410-11; D. Lawrence on, **37:** 485, 489

Art Students' League, **28:** 195,n3; **36:** 415n1

As I Remember (Genthe), **28:** 355n2

As One Woman Sees the Issues (Hamilton), **38:** 275,n3

Asama (Japanese cruiser), **32:** 525, 528n1

Asbury, Francis: WW address on, **36:** 391-94

Asbury Park, N.J., **34:** 293; **38:** 622

Ascutney, Mount, Vt., **28:** 363

Ascutneyville, Vt., **34:** 160

Asheville, N.C., **28:** 382,n2

Ashurst, Henry Fountain, **27:** 326; **30:** 261; **36:** 311,n1

Asia Minor, **31:** 471; **35:** 466, 484

Aspirantes Military Academy, Mexico, **27:** 537

Asquam House (Holderness, N.H.), **28:** 104, 132

Asquith, Emma Alice Margaret (Margot) Tennant (Mrs. Herbert Henry), **30:** 247; **35:** 413; **38:** 256-57,n5

Asquith, Herbert Henry, **28:** 443-44,n2, 525,n1, 536, 544, 576, 577; **29:** 52, 244, 301; **30:** 215, 247, 258, 266; **31:** 372, 397; **32:** 225, 231, 268, 406; **33:** 372n1, 519, 520, 523; **34:** 18, 506; **35:** 74, 356, 413, 414, 485, 499; **36:** 320n1, 436, 444, 512; **37:** 5,n1, 42, 75n2, 77,n1, 89, 95, 182-83, 294n1, 371, 372, 502; **38:** 54, 104, 255-57, 472; WW reads Gardiner's sketch of, **31:** 482,n1; meetings with E. M. House, **32:** 238n1, 242, 251, 253, 277; W. H. Page on, **32:** 362; **33:** 550-51; and House's peace mission, **36:** 148, 166, 167, 170, 173, 180n1, 266n1

Assault on the Senate (Sullivan), **27:** 507n1

Associated Advertising Clubs: WW remarks to, **37:** 324-28

Associated Press, **27:** 119, 539; **28:** 472, 488; **29:** 103; **30:** 203; **31:** 339, 411, 550, 560; **32:** 14, 15, 170, 195, 206; **33:** 454n1, 490; **34:** 189, 333,n1; **36:** 308, 332, 364n1, 368; **37:** 75, 204n2, 452, 473, 525; **38:** 107, 548; WW's remarks to, **33:** 37-41, 61

Association for the Relief and Protection of Jewish Immigrants, **32:** 97n12

Association of Chambers of Commerce (London), **29:** 333n1

Association of Commerce (Chicago), **29:** 500-501

Association of the Polish Clergy, **37:** 406n1

Association to Resist British Domination of American Commerce, **38:** 562n1

Astor Theater, N.Y., **28:** 597

Atchison, Topeka, and Santa Fe Railroad, **32:** 383

Athens, Greece, **36:** 358

Atlanta, Ga., **28:** 402,n1

Atlanta Journal, **28:** 4n2; **33:** 457n1

Atlantic City, N.J., **28:** 3n1; **34:** 240, 270, 292, 328, 356; **37:** 539, 540; **38:** 20, 609; WW talk with N.J. senators, **27:** 85-90; WW's address on woman suffrage, **38:** 161-64

Atlantic City Daily Press, **38:** 432n3

Atlantic City Evening Union, **38:** 432n3

Atlantic Coast Line Railroad Co., **31:** 149n1

Atlantic Communication Co., **33:** 486n2

Atlantic County, N.J., **38:** 432,n3

Atlantic Fruit Co., **38:** 455n2

Atlantic Monthly, **31:** 370,n2, 386; **32:** 24; **36:** 581,n2; **37:** 201n1, 424, 535,n2; **38:** 319,n1, 460,n2

Atlantic Transport Line, **38:** 455n1

Atrocity Propaganda 1914-1919 (Read), **33:** 485n1

Attila the Hun, **31:** 121

Auchincloss, Gordon, **27:** 145; **28:** 597,n3; **30:** 461,n1; **31:** 318,n1, 384; **32:** 341; **33:** 448, 452; **34:** 426; **35:** 44, 178,n1; **36:** 335, 389, 416, 422; **37:** 177-78, 238,n1; 290; **38:** 616

Auchincloss, Janet House (Mrs. Gordon), **28:** 597; **31:** 384,n1, 387, 410, 427, 453; **34:** 426; **35:** 44; **38:** 55; appendectomy, **35:** 118, 127, 137, 152, 155

Auchincloss, Louise, **31:** 387, 410, 427, 453

Auchincloss, Reginald La Grange, **28:** 597,n3

Austin, Tex., **27:** 228n2; **29:** 277

Australia, **31:** 218; **32:** 277; **34:** 19, 20; **35:** 427, 428, 486; **37:** 103n1; and Japan, **31:** 513

Austria-Hungary, **27:** ix; **31:** 459; **32:** 49, 50, 81, 440, 522; **33:** 12, 63, 81n1, 88, 482n2, 489, 504, 511; **34:** 18, 59,n1, 145, 159, 188-89, 333; **35:** 131, 484, 507; **36:** 124; **37:** 4-5, 19, 319; **38:** 71,n1, 74, 107; ambassador to, **27:** 24, 70, 110,n1, 127, 228, 361-62; and Mexico, **27:** 439, 540; **28:** 460; appointments to, **28:** 4; ambassador to U.S., **29:** 74,n3; Count Karolyi visits the U.S., **29:** 404, 409; and expenses of ambassador in London, **29:** 411, 412; **30:** 152; E. M. House on relations with Germany, **30:** 109; and assassination of archduke, **30:** 222, 315; and outbreak of war, **30:** 314; and Germany, **30:** 323, 327; and E. Grey's attempt to prevent war with Serbia, **30:** 325; W. H. Page on background to war, **30:** 330; Grey says no cause for war with, **30:** 368; Page fears war between Great Britain and, **30:** 369; Kaiser explains Germany's commitment to, **30:** 382-83; and Russia, **30:** 457; House on C. Dumba and, **31:** 5-6, 296; and peace moves, **31:** 95, 137, 140, 385; and Declaration of London, **31:** 113-14, 118n1, 134, 135, 136, 163; British military or war settlement and, **31:** 294n1; and H. Münsterberg on U.S. lack of neutrality, **31:** 336, 337, 434, 437; Page on Austrians, **31:** 372; and conditional contraband, **31:** 438, 439; and transshipment of reservists, **31:** 444; and Belgian relief, **31:** 559; and China, **32:** 135, 415, 418; and Italy, **33:** 230-31;

and U.S. export of munitions, **34:** 92-98, 114-16, 126, 142, 156, 264, 276; and Dumba's plan for disruption of U.S. munitions production, **34:** 403,n1, 403-404,n3, 429,n1; and Dumba's recall, **34:** 432,n1, 432-33,n1, 503,n1; and armed merchantmen controversy, **36:** 229,n2, 233, 252-57, 383; public opinion and peace moves in, **37:** 272, 273-74; and new ambassador to U.S., **38:** 544-45, 560

Austria-Hungary and the United States: WW on archduke's assassination, **30:** 222; E. Grey asks about U.S. good offices, **30:** 325; C. W. Eliot on crisis, **30:** 353-55, 419; and loans problem, **30:** 372; and resolutions of Federal Council of Churches, **30:** 396, 397; reply to WW mediation offer, **30:** 457n1; negotiations concerning *Ancona* sinking, **35:** 192,n1, 208-209, 222, 234, 235-37,n2, 244, 245, 282, 286-88,n2, 311n1, 351,n1, 362, 364-66, 368-70, 378-80, 381-82, 389, 391, 394-95, 403-404, 406-407, 410, 411, 415, 420, 425, 426, 430-31, 446-47; **36:** 124, 616; and possible severance of diplomatic relations, **35:** 260, 404, 406-407, 426-27, 435; and recall of Von Nuber, **35:** 265, 276-77,n1, 379, and *Persia* sinking, **35:** 420, 446-47; and armed merchant vessels, **35:** 448-49, 495; E. M. House urges continuance of diplomatic relations, **35:** 483, 491

Austria-Hungary after Two Years of War (Penfield), **38:** 75,n1

Austrian Americans, **38:** 140

Austrian Fear of Serb Empire is Real War Cause (Hart), **30:** 343,n1

Austrians: in Colorado mining industry, **28:** 522

Average Wage of Enginemen and Trainmen $1253 a Year, **36:** 204n1

Ávila, Fidel, **30:** 409

Avon, N.J.: J. P. Tumulty vacation in, **28:** 85, 87, 133, 135

Axson, Edward William, brother of EAW, **31:** 27,n1

Axson, Samuel Edward, father of EAW, **31:** 29; **38:** 590

Axson, Stockton (Isaac Stockton Keith Axson II), brother of EAW, **28:** 308-309, 318, 327,n1, 333, 335, 337, 345, 362; **29:** 277, 554,n4; **30:** 345,n1, 436; **31:** 28,n2, 91, 94, 341; **34:** 87, 185, 485, 506, 517, 523; **35:** 393, 394, 455; **38:** 191,n2, 644-45, 681n2, 688; and death of EAW, **30:** 353,n1; at funeral of EAW, **30:** 374; drafts engagement announcement for WW and EBG, **35:** 16-17, 33-34; and Wesleyan University, **36:** 297,n1,2, 329-30, 349, 399-400

Ayala, Plan of, **31:** 12,n4

Ayarragaray, Lucas, **36:** 199-200,n7

Aycock, Charles Brantley, **31:** 127n1
Aycock, Cora Lily Woodard (Mrs. Charles Brantley), **31:** 127,n1
Aylward, John Arthur, **36:** 315,n1, 316,n3, 482, 500-501, 510-11

B. S. Moss Motion Picture Corp., **35:** 431-n1
Babcock, Mrs., daughter of Mr. Kennedy of Cornish, N.H., **28:** 62,n5
Babson, Roger Ward, **38:** 393,n1
Bachmann, Gustav, **34:** 453; **35:** 131n1
Bacon, Augustus Octavius, **27:** 276,n1, 300, 470, 526; **28:** 223, 484; **29:** 213,n1, 222, 225, 245, 266, 305; private secretary, **28:** 4,n4; and Fall resolution, **28:** 68, 82; Nicaraguan treaty, **28:** 100; Mexico, **28:** 162, 163, 194, 488,n1, 500, 501,n1; WW on the death of, **29:** 248,n1
Bacon, Sir Francis, **29:** 56
Bacon, Robert, **35:** 525,n2; **37:** 42,n2; **38:** 275, 364,n3
Bacon-Bartlett bill, **29:** 347, 413,n1, 425
Bad Times (Hannay), **31:** 316,n2
Badger, Charles Johnston, **29:** 442, 453, 454-55; **34:** 17, 267n1
Bagehot, Eliza Wilson (Mrs. Walter), **31:** 44,n3
Bagehot, Walter, **28:** 276; **31:** 44,n1, 279; **38:** 282
Baguio, P. I., **27:** 189, 370; **28:** 242n1
Bailey, Joseph Cannon, **27:** 50n8
Bailey, Thomas Andrew, **33:** 127n1, 135n3
Bailey, Warren Worth, **33:** 494-95, 506, 511; **37:** 342-43, 346-47
Bailly-Blanchard, Arthur, **27:** 449,n1; **31:** 483-85, 485-86; **32:** 27, 76, 288, 295, 296, 297, 437n2, 479, 487n1; W. J. Bryan on recall of, **32:** 471-72
Baizley, John H. **30:** 248,n1
Baker, Bernard Nadal, **38:** 455,n1, 456
Baker, Elizabeth Leopold (Mrs. Newton Diehl), **36:** 260,n1; **38:** 178,n4
Baker, James M., **37:** 516
Baker, Newton Diehl, **27:** 24, 57, 70, 112, 116, 117, 118-19, 120; **28:** 69, 359; **32:** 24, 53, 324; **35:** 134, 193; **36:** 41n1, 214, 227, 274, 379, 560n1, 612; **37:** 9, 22, 38, 65, 74, 76, 97, 218, 467, 522, 537; **38:** 37, 40n1, 62-63, 119, 142n1, 155, 159, 166, 177-78, 237n1, 238, 271, 275, 312, 335, 438, 523, 560, 675
offered Secretary of War position, **36:** 251,n1,2; accepts appointment, **36:** 259-60; and water-power legislation, **36:** 265-66, 277, 301; on Columbus Raid, **36:** 280, 281; and Punitive Expedition, **36:** 284, 286-87, 295-96, 298, 313, 317n1, 322-24,n1,2, 397, 416, 456-58, 463-64, 519, 528-29, 540n1, 584; W. F. Sadler on, **36:** 292, 300; on A. B. Fall and the Mexican situation, **36:** 395,n1, 416; and the Philippines, **36:** 414, 583;

E. M. House meets with on German crisis, **36:** 423-24, 425; memorandum on preparedness as a policy, **36:** 431-34; and Scott-Obregón conference, **36:** 592-94, 603-604, 618; WW on, **37:** 33; on Ohio politics, **37:** 84, 96; as possible vice-presidential candidate, **37:** 105, 210; on Mexican situation, **37:** 121-22, 248, 263, 283-86, 291, 296-98, 316; **38:** 361, 362, 386, 397-405, 546-47, 548; on U.S. Constitution and calling out militia, **37:** 156; on German Americans, **37:** 156-57, 175; on fate of Columbus raiders, **37:** 171-72; and 1916 platform, **37:** 190n1; suggested as Democratic national chairman, **37:** 211, 230; on T. W. Gregory for the Supreme Court, **37:** 278; on British oil interests in Mexico, **37:** 305-306; on duty of American soldier in Mexico, **37:** 337, 359; on Senate amendment to army appropriations bill, **37:** 380-81; on J. H. Clarke and antitrust laws, **37:** 397-98; on Porto Rico bill, **37:** 455-56; on C. E. Hughes' speech, **37:** 524; on Council of National Defense appointments, **38:** 181-83, 272-73, 386-87, 439; on Joint High Commission, **38:** 219-20, 235-37; on promotions for brigadier and major generals, **38:** 238-39; offers to resign, **38:** 636; WW retains as Secretary of War, **38:** 663; photograph, **36:** *illustration section*
Baker, Ray Stannard, **27:** xv, 133n1; **37:** 31-38, 286,n1; **38:** 445n1
Baker, William John, **27:** 251n1
Bakhmet'ev (Bakhméteff), George, **27:** 249,n1, 261-62; **31:** 473,n1; **32:** 64; **35:** 358,n2, 536-37
balance of trade, **34:** 421-23
Balch, Emily Greene, **34:** 58,n1, 110,n1, 243, 250-52, 260, 350, 397-99, 399; **37:** 515, 527-28
Baldwin, Abram Martin, **29:** 383,n1, 390
Baldwin, Simeon Eben, **33:** 151, 219
Baldwin Bay, Alaska, **33:** 35
Baldwin-Felts Detective Agency, **30:** 17
Balfour, Arthur James, **32:** 327,n2; **33:** 89, 100, 122, 214, 227n4, 484; **34:** 514; **35:** 3, 4,n1, 5, 9, 279, 356, 382n1, 413; **36:** 519; **37:** 77,n1, 90, 294n1; **38:** 104; defends British blockade, **32:** 449; conference with E. M. House, **33:** 190; W. H. Page on, **33:** 255; House on, **33:** 268; on armed merchantmen, **35:** 5-7, 19; and House's trip to London, **35:** 453, 454, 465, 473, 484, 485, 486, 487; and House's peace mission, **36:** 148, 166, 167, 170, 173, 180n1, 266n1, 346
Balfour Defends British Order in Council (*New York Tribune*), **32:** 449n2
Balkan States, **28:** 4, 5; **33:** 267, 549; **34:** 239, 304, 405n1, 419, 493, 506; **35:** 8, 75, 83, 185, 194, 226, 245, 255, 348,

Balkan States (*cont.*)
413; **37:** 89, 135n2; **38:** 454, 647; *see
also* under the names of the individual
countries
Balkan States, Confederation of, **27:** 70
Balkan wars, **34:** 94
Ball, Thomas H., **27:** 27
Ballin, Albert, **33:** 298n1; **34:** 47,n2, 453;
36: 235,n4
Ballinger, Richard Achilles, **37:** 270
Balliol College, **30:** 278n1
Baltic Sea, **34:** 188; **35:** 483
Baltimore, Md., **28:** 321,n1; **29:** 439n1;
31: 330n2; **35:** 153,n3; postmastership,
27: 192; segregation protest in, **28:** 343;
J. R. Wilson, Jr., takes position in, **28:**
396-97; newspaper stories about visit
of WW and family to restaurant, **29:**
561; WW's address in, **38:** 261
Baltimore, U.S.S., **28:** 188n1
Baltimore and Ohio Railroad, **38:** 38n1
Baltimore *Commonwealth*, **35:** 240n1
Baltimore Convention (1912): *see* Dem-
ocratic National Convention of 1912
Baltimore *Evening Sun*, **34:** 312,n1,
445,n1
Baltimore *Sun*, **27:** 25n1, 141n3, 517, 554;
29: 308, 311; **35:** 412n2; **37:** 27,n2
Banco Central (Mex.), **29:** 192
Banco Nacional (Mex.), **28:** 428
Banco Nacional de Santo Domingo, **30:**
165
Banco Oriental (Puebla state), **29:** 328
Banda, General, **32:** 383
Banish Thoughts of War (*Springfield
Republican*), **33:** 142,n1
bank deposits: WW on guarantee of and
currency reform, **27:** 453
Bank of California, **31:** 235
Bank of China, **31:** 287
Bank of the United States, Second, **31:**
460
Bankers Trust Co. of New York, **28:** 428;
30: 366,n1
Bankhead, John Hollis, **29:** 274; **30:** 261;
32: 173n2; **33:** 540,n1; **37:** 316, 330
banking: loans and credits, **34:** 295, 373,
401,n1, 421, 422, 481, 504; **37:** 191, 389;
McAdoo on credits to belligerents, **34:**
275-80; WW on, **36:** 112, 157-58, 473;
and Chinese loan, **37:** 232-33; achievements during WW's first term, **37:** 191;
and 1916 platform, **37:** 186-87, 189-90;
see also World War: economic impact
on United States
Banking and Currency, Committee on:
see U.S. Congress, House; Senate
banking and currency reform, **27:** 33, 34,
566, 571-72; **28:** 84-85, 108, 128,n1,
146n2, 151, 257,n2, 261, 336n2, 351-
52, 381, 395, 421; **29:** 5-6, 61; discusses with E. M. House, **27:** 21, 227,
292, 413-14; writes C. Glass about, **27:**
25; tells businessmen credit must be
expanded, **27:** 33; says system obso-
lete, **27:** 150; urges Congress to plan
for, **27:** 272; discusses bills in press
conferences, **27:** 340-41, 397-99, 408,
484-86, 496-97, 504-505, 509-11, 522-
25, 558-64; **28:** 8-10, 89-90, 364-65, 378-
79, 412-18, 485, 517-18, 600; **29:** 53-
54; explains proposed federal reserve
currency, **27:** 560, 568-69; views sum-
marized by J. C. O'Laughlin, **27:** 565-
70; address to joint session of Congress, **27:** 570-73; and agriculture, **28:**
45,n1; on opposition to bill in Congress, **28:** 84-85; intervenes in conference committee discussions, **28:** 90-91;
remarks to delegation of southern
bankers, **28:** 127-28; and rural credits,
28: 146-48,n1; remarks to delegation
of western bankers, **28:** 156; hopes for
quick passage of bill, **28:** 267; bill
passed by House of Reps., **28:** 301,n1;
cautions against Senate delay, **28:** 389;
bill passed by Senate, **29:** 48,n1
ΔC. Glass, **27:** 11, 79-80; E. M. House,
27: 21, 199, 227, 292, 413-14, 458;
R. Meeker and E. W. Kemmerer, **27:**
204-209; P. U. Kellogg, **27:** 243; W. J.
Bryan, **27:** 413-14, 436, 457, 458, 523;
S. Untermyer, **27:** 457; P. M. Warburg, **27:** 476; L. D. Brandeis, **27:** 520-
21; R. J. Bulkley, **28:** 69,n1; J. W.
Ragsdale, **28:** 121-23,n4; R. L. Owen,
28: 200,n1; G. M. Hitchcock, **28:** 241;
R. L. Henry, **28:** 255; E. A. Wilson, **28:**
260, 273, 308, 384; J. R. Gray, **28:** 271;
D. V. Stephens, **28:** 346-47; J. A. Reed,
28: 369-70,n1, 425,n1; W. J. Stone, **28:**
374; **29:** 48-49, 63; Boston and Chicago
bankers, **28:** 379,n1; R. Pulitzer, **28:** 385;
J. S. Williams, **28:** 389, 425, 560; H. F.
Hollis, **28:** 414-15,n1; B. F. Shively, **28:**
415; J. A. O'Gorman, **28:** 421,n1; F. J.
Wade, **28:** 444; E. F. Goltra, **29:** 51; *see
also* Federal Reserve Act
banking lobby, **28:** 373n1
banks: and N.J. corporations, **27:** 121; and
Clayton antitrust bill, **31:** 75-76; and
cotton crisis, **31:** 251, 271
Banks, James Arthur, **33:** 496,n4
Banks, William, **33:** 496
Banque de Paris y Pays Bas, **29:** 381n1
Baptist Ministers' Conference of New
London and Vicinity, **36:** 139-40,n1,
140
Baralong affair, **34:** 368,n1; **35:** 421; **36:**
134,n1
Barclay, Colville Adrian de Rune, **28:**
566-67, 571, 591; **29:** 24; **30:** 245-47,
386-87, 435-36; **35:** 420; **37:** 350
Barclay, Florence Louisa, **31:** 316n2, 317
Baring, Evelyn, 1st Earl of Cromer, **34:**
20,n5, 22; **37:** 143,n1
Bark, Petr L'vovich, **32:** 206,n2, 276; **38:**
70
Barker, Lewellys Franklin, **35:** 118,n1
Barker, Wharton, **38:** 103,n1, 122

Barnes, Charles L., **28:** 41
Barnes, William, **37:** 162,n1, 174, 340
Barnett, Mrs. (buys pictures from EAW in Cornish, N.H.), **28:** 308, 331
Barnett, George Ernest, **27:** 206-207
Barnhart, Henry A., **36:** 187-88,n1,2
Barnum, Gertrude, **38:** 247,n1
Barr, Captain, **27:** 538
Barra, Francisco Léon de la, **27:** 548; **28:** 69,n1, 71, 341; **29:** 91,n3, 253; **33:** 194n1
Barrera, Atilano, **28:** 77
Barrett, D. Milton, **37:** 383n1, 387n1
Barrett, Don Carlos, **27:** 206-207
Barrett, John, **28:** 95,n1; **33:** 33; **35:** 395, 439,n1
Barrie, Sir James, **31:** 137
Barrie, James Matthew, **28:** 286, 355,n4,6
Barringer, Daniel Moreau, **32:** 190
Barrington, Emilie Isabel Wilson (Mrs. Russell Henry), **31:** 44,n1,3; **38:** 282
Barry, John: WW address at unveiling of statue of, **30:** 34-36
Barthmann, Mr., **38:** 73
Bartholdt, Richard, **31:** 426,n1; **32:** 24n1, 101, 174
Bartholdt resolution, **32:** 24n1, 102
Bartlett, Adolphus Clay, **30:** 33,n1, 53, 54
Bartlett, Charles Lafayette, **29:** 413n1
Bartlett, Ruhl Jacob, **33:** 368n1
Bartlett-Bacon bill: *see* Bacon-Bartlett bill
Barton, Dante, **38:** 445n1
Barton, James Levi, **27:** 179,n1; **28:** 82
Baruch, Bernard Mannes, **35:** 39-40; **36:** 479, 518, 523, 611-12, 612; **37:** 9, 238; **38:** 43-44, 50-51; on mobilization of business, **36:** 544,n1; and Council of National Defense, **38:** 182, 183, 387
Bashford, James Whitford, **27:** 27-28,n1, 58; **33:** 23-26, 31-37, 80
Bass, Elizabeth (Mrs. George), **38:** 481n1
Bates, James Leonard, **36:** 464n1; **37:** 140n2
Bates, Lindon, **37:** 542,n1,2
Bath County, Va., **32:** 494n2
Bathrick, Elsworth Raymond, **27:** 327-28,n1; **31:** 462
Batten, Clare W., **34:** 73,n1, 74, 101, 119, 128, 138, 153; **38:** 16,n3
Batten, Loring Woart, **34:** 73n1; **38:** 16,n3
Battenberg, Beatrice of (wife of Prince Henry Maurice of Battenberg), **33:** 484
Battin, Benjamin Franklin, **35:** 20-21,n1; **36:** 482; **38:** 104,n2, 207, 207-208
Battle, George Gordon, **27:** 72,n3, 115,n2; **33:** 370,n1
Battle Creek, Mich.: mention of T. Roosevelt's speech in, **38:** 318,n1
Bauer, Georg: *see* Agricola, Georgius
Bavaria, **33:** 371; **38:** 73
Bay St. Louis, Miss., **29:** 86
Bayer, Philip, **35:** 238
Baylies, Walter Cabot, **29:** 401,n1
Baynes, Ernest Harold, **28:** 320,n1, 392

Beach, Edward Latimer, **34:** 71,n1
Beach, Sylvester Woodbridge, **33:** 61; **37:** 270, 305; **38:** 209
Beal, Howard Walter, **35:** 77,n2
Beals, Carleton, **27:** 64n2
Beaman, Charles Cotesworth, **28:** 165n1
Beaman, Hettie Sherman Evarts (Mrs. Charles Cotesworth), **28:** 165,n1
Beard, James Thom, **38:** 441,n2
Beard, Mary Ritter (Mrs. Charles Austin), **36:** 3n1
Beaufort, S.C., **27:** 283-84,n1
Beaulieu (Pass Christian, Miss.), **29:** 77,n1
Beautiful Mountain, N. Mex., **29:** 36,n1
Beck, Emanuel L., **36:** 364,n1
Beecher, Norman Buckingham, **29:** 404,n1, 409
Beer, William C., **31:** 253,n3; **33:** 219
Behncke, Paul L. Gustav, **34:** 47,n1; **35:** 131,n2
Beirut (Lebanon), Turkey, **31:** 471,n8
Belasco, David, **37:** 352,n2
Belasco Theater, N.Y., **27:** 112; **29:** 558n4
Belasco Theater, Wash. D.C., **34:** 467-n1
Belcher, George, **30:** 17
Belgian Congo, **32:** 262; **36:** 150
Belgian Relief Commission: *see* Commission for Relief in Belgium
Belgium, **28:** 516; **31:** 7, 154; **32:** 81, 120, 133, 161, 375, 441, 455, 506; **33:** 361, 407, 478, 516, 523; **34:** 47, 48, 62, 85, 189, 214, 236, 238, 409-10; **35:** 8, 71n3, 197, 221n2, 261, 348, 367, 466, 484, 495; **36:** 88-89, 443, 532, 615; **37:** 28n2, 43n1, 88, 89, 104, 135n2, 137, 145, 272n1; **38:** 69, 89, 90, 194-95, 242, 250, 254, 294, 298, 371, 647, 669
ministerial appointment, **27:** 110, 228, 259; **28:** 4, 354,n4; and Mexico, **28:** 171, 411, 460; and Peru, **29:** 244; William II on neutrality of, **30:** 383; and Germany's disregard of treaty with, **30:** 457-58; and alleged German atrocities in, **30:** 457-58, 459, 459-61, 471,n1; **31:** 17, 21, 22, 26-27, 58, 121-22,n1; **32:** 379; **33:** 485,n1, 486, 513, 514; and destruction of Louvain, **30:** 458, 467; commission on German atrocities seeks U.S. help, **30:** 459n1, 470,n1; commission in U.S., **31:** 16,n2; WW remarks to commissioners, **31:** 33-34,n1,2; WW comments to J. R. Mott on meeting, **31:** 40n1; E. M. House on peace settlement for, **31:** 45; and question of indemnity for, **31:** 61, 62, 385, 490, 501, 518,n2, 522-23; **32:** 17n1, 44, 211, 231, 237, 254, 255, 267, 276, 335, 359; **33:** 18, 48, 63, 371; **34:** 370-71; WW on fund drive in U.S., **31:** 84,n1; plan to display Belgian atrocity victims in U.S., **31:** 85, 89-90; and Declaration of London, **31:** 104; and importation of foodstuffs, **31:** 197,n1; Field Marshal

Belgium (*cont.*)
French on war settlement and, **31:** 294n1; WW on aid to, **31:** 321; WW appeal for relief for, **31:** 559-60; German invasion: U.S. attitude toward, **32:** 42,n2, 60,n1, 92, 222; English attitude toward, **32:** 107,n1, 109; **34:** 145; children thank WW for food, **32:** 257-58; and financial problems of relief commission, **32:** 294; economic conditions in, **33:** 523-24; and Edith Cavell case, **35:** 147-48,n1,2,3; and House's mission, **35:** 391-92; 499; and Lansing's *modus vivendi re* armed merchant ships, **35:** 498; WW receives gift from association in, **35:** 520-21; Bethmann Hollweg on peace terms, **36:** 123n, 444n1; B. Whitlock wishes to remain minister to, **36:** 136, 231, 409; House meets with King Albert, **36:** 150-51, 202; and House-Grey Memorandum, **36:** 180n2; J. W. Gerard on peace terms and, **36:** 341; protests against deportation of Belgians to Germany, **38:** 650-53, 656-57; Brussels suburb to name street after WW, **38:** 661-62; *see also* Whitlock, Brand
Belgium: A Personal Narrative (Whitlock), **35:** 280n3
Belgrade, Yugoslavia, **30:** 382
Bell, Alexander Graham, **32:** 118-19,n1
Bell, Edward, **34:** 403,n1
Bell, Edward Price, **34:** 370,n1; **37:** 43,n4; **38:** 90
Bell, George, Jr., **37:** 280,n1, 315
Bell, Thomas Montgomery, **27:** 239n1
Bell System, **29:** 45n1; *see also* American Telephone and Telegraph Company
Belle: *see* Hagner, Isabella A.
Belleville, Countess Jeanne de, **35:** 88,n1,2,3,4, 103n1, 107, 118, 127, 174-75
Bellevue-Stratford Hotel, Phila., **34:** 258-59
Bellows Falls, Vt., **28:** 345
Belmont, Alva Erskine Smith Vanderbilt (Mrs. Oliver Hazard Perry), **37:** 167n4
Belmont College, Nashville, **28:** 397
Belo and Co., A. H. (Dallas and Galveston), **29:** 263n2
Belt, John W., **33:** 306,n1; **35:** 93, 94-95, 95; **36:** 318n1
Bemis, Samuel Flagg, **36:** 371n1
Benavides, Luis Aguirre: *see* Aguirre Benavides, Luis
Benckendorff, Count: *see* Constantovich, Alexander
Benedict XV, **32:** 14, 516,n1, 521, 522,n1; **33:** 47; **34:** 31,n2; **35:** 82n2,4; **36:** 124, 652, 655, 656; **37:** 19, 30, 54, 55, 56, 73, 84,n1, 85, 87, 95, 274
Benedict, Elias Cornelius, **38:** 670,n1
Benham, Edith, **35:** 154n6; **38:** 17

Benighted Mexico (Smith), **36:** 364n1
Benjamin Harrison: Hoosier President (Sievers), **28:** 188n1
Bennet, William Stiles, **38:** 285
Bennett, Hiram D., **30:** 200,n2
Bennett, J. O., **31:** 338-39
Bennett, James Gordon, **34:** 471,n1
Benson, Allan Louis, **36:** 634,n5; **38:** 522n1
Benson, Clarence C., **36:** 281,n3
Benson, Godfrey Rathbone, 1st Baron Charnwood, **34:** 21,n7
Benson, William Shepherd, **34:** 17, 121,n1, 143, 157, 158, 267,n1; **37:** 158; **38:** 473n2
Benton, William Smith: disappearance and murder, **29:** 285-86,n1,3, 291, 293, 293-94, 300-301,n2, 320n1; **34:** 175: *see also* Mexico and the United States
Benton, Mrs. William Smith, **29:** 285n1
Benton affair: *see* Mexico and the United States; Benton, William Smith
Berea College, **29:** 342, 350, 537n1; **30:** 6, 43-44, 62-63; WW address on, **32:** 282-84
Berea Quarterly, **32:** 284n
Beresford, Charles William de la Poer, 1st Baron Beresford, **38:** 472n1
Bergheimer, Henry Christian, **33:** 402,n1; **34:** 533,n1
Berle, Adolf Augustus, **36:** 524, 635-36,n9, 644
Berlin, Germany, **29:** 13; **30:** 266, 325; **31:** 167, 340; **32:** 64, 221; **34:** 47-48, 403n1
Berlin *Continental Times*, **36:** 563n2; **37:** 106n1
Berlin *Deutsche Tageszeitung*, **34:** 187n1
Berlin *Die Zukunft*, **37:** 86n4; **38:** 126n1
Berlin Lokal Anzeiger, **37:** 507,n2
Berlin *National Zeitung*, **37:** 319,n2
Berlin *Tageblatt*, **32:** 145, 442n2, **34:** 419
Bermuda, **27:** 13, 116, 129; **28:** 134, 135, 337; **30:** 73; **31:** 456
Bermudez Castro, Colonel, **31:** 67
Bern, Switzerland, **35:** 20n1, 196,n2
Bern, University of, **37:** 86n5
Bernabé, Luis Polo de, **37:** 19,n2
Bernard (Barnett), Sam, **29:** 558,n4
Bernhardi, Friedrich Adam Julius von, **31:** 27,n1; **34:** 510,n1
Bernstein, Eduard, **34:** 47,n5
Bernstein, Herman, **28:** 4, 5, 111; **30:** 162-63; **32:** 97, 148; **36:** 355-56, 356; **37:** 84-88; **38:** 188-89
Bernstorff, Christian Günther von, **29:** 218
Bernstorff, Jeanne Luckemeyer, Countess von, **38:** 180,n1, 191
Bernstorff, Count Johann Heinrich von, **27:** 170,n1, 171; **29:** 218, 254; **30:** 457, 469; **31:** 9-10,n1, 10, 14, 21n1, 295, 296, 336, 533, 540,n1, 552; **32:** 41, 67, 94, 98, 147-48, 161, 193,n1, 201,n1, 220, 231, 235,n1, 251, 252,n2, 264-65, 268,

309, 349; **33:** 93, 124, 171, 213, 215, 254, 257, 347, 348, 372, 497; **34:** 187, 218, 272, 278, 296, 297-98, 337, 372-73, 425n1, 427, 435, 442, 445, 455, 466, 486,n2; **35:** 79,n2, 85, 137-38, 191, 224, 244, 310n1, 391; **37:** 45, 58, 64, 425-26, 480, 535; **38:** 139,n1, 140,n2,3, 195, 246, 314,n2, 320, 352, 372, 397, 494, 652, 657
and peace moves, **31:** 15, 45, 55, 60, 62, 76, 95, 140, 469, 498-99, 500, 518, 519; **36:** 656; **38:** 411, 494-96,n1,3; claims that Gerard is anti-German, **31:** 404-405; and coaling of German war vessels, **31:** 521; on withdrawal from and compensation for Belgium, **31:** 522; Spring Rice on, **31:** 550; **35:** 62-66; protests U.S. arms trade, **32:** 509-10,n1, 516, 516-17, 524, 526,n1, 531; **33:** 143,n2; WW reply, **33:** 20-23, 41-43, 52,n1, 65; and *Lusitania* crisis, **33:** 143,n2, 165, 168, 191n1, 199-201, 311, 313, 333, 335; **34:** 37; **35:** 14-15, 158-59,n1,3, 176, 218-19,n1, 220-21, 233, 244-45,n1, 278, 355, 362, 417-19, 450, 463-64,n1, 512-15, 516, 521, 522-23, 528-29,n1; **36:** 73n1, 74, 127, 129, 141, 182, 183-84, 184, 194-95; **38:** 315; receives WW's peace conditions in secret interview, **33:** 279-80,n1, 283-84; EBG fears WW's meeting with, **33:** 315, 334, 339, 341; reports on meeting with WW, **33:** 316-20; and E. M. House, **33:** 407,n1, 493-94, 494, 505, 511, 516; **34:** 36, 44, 505, 506, 520-21, 536; **36:** 294, 378, 398, 405, 446,n1, 547-48, 548-49, 558, 559, 599, 629; **37:** 135; **38:** 141-42, 669; and Huerta's appeal for protection, **34:** 56,n1, 73-74; offers to buy U.S. cotton, **34:** 123, 142, 178-79; possible recall of, **34:** 260, 274, 290, 299, 408, 426; **35:** 3, 43, 224, 260, 387, 513; **36:** 372-73, 388; WW on, **34:** 303, 381; **38:** 294-95; and *Arabic* crisis, **34:** 304, 305, 308-309, 315, 320, 324-25, 329, 330, 333, 339-40, 340-41, 341,n1, 400-401, 407,n1, 417, 428, 436, 449, 461-62, 465, 468-69, 492, 493, 503, 519, 527, 537, 539; **35:** 13,n1, 14, 25-26, 26-27; and *Hesperian* incident, **34:** 436, 436-37; congratulates WW on his engagement, **35:** 37; on House's mission, **35:** 240-43, 381; on recall of attachés, **35:** 264, 276, 277-78; W. H. Page on British view of, **36:** 130, 385; on armed merchantmen controversy, **36:** 228, 232-33, 237, 251-52, 255, 256; memorandum on submarine warfare question, **36:** 269-72; R. Lansing reply, **36:** 361-62; suggests temporary suspension of German submarine warfare, **36:** 524, 526-27,n1; and State Dept. memorandum on submarine warfare, **36:** 541-42; and continued use of submarines, **38:** 184, 185, 390-92, 411, 473,n3,

494-95; and *Sussex* crisis, **36:** 372-73, 389,n8, 417, 451-52, 471, 486-87; and Irish rebellion, **36:** 503; and Von Igel case, **36:** 529, 577-78; on death of WW's sister, **38:** 180, 191-92; and Polish relief, **38:** 368, 369
Berrera, Alberto Calzadiaz: *see* Calzadiaz Berrera, Alberto
Berry, Joseph Flintoft, **37:** 148n1
Berry, Lucy Lindabury (Mrs. Robert Lawrence), **34:** 345,n1
Berry, Martha McChesney, **28:** 308n2; **31:** 342; **36:** 478, 512-13, 522, 558; **37:** 247
Berry, Robert Lawrence, **32:** 21,n1; **34:** 345,n1
Berry, William H., **27:** 286n4, 333, 338-39
Berry School, Mount Berry, Ga., **28:** 308,n2, 331; **31:** 259, 342; **36:** 478, 512-13, 522, 558
Bertie, Francis Leveson, 1st Baron of Thame, **33:** 124
Bertoni, Senior, **36:** 312,n1
Bertron, Caroline Harding (Mrs. Samuel Reading), **31:** 317
Bertron, Samuel Reading, **29:** 219-20,n1, 226; **31:** 291, 317; **35:** 347
Bertron, Griscom and Co., **29:** 219n1
Berwindvale case, **36:** 483n1, 486
Beseler, Hans Hartwig von, **38:** 369,n1, 371
Betancourt, Julio, **28:** 197,n3, 572,n1; **29:** 128; **35:** 375-78
Bethlehem, N.H., **28:** 132
Bethlehem Steel Corp., **27:** 216n4, 538; **31:** 310n1, 425n1; **32:** 177, 415; **35:** 434n1; C. Dumba's plan for disruption of munitions production in, **34:** 404,n3
Bethmann Hollweg, Martha Elisa (Frau Theobald von), **30:** 139
Bethmann Hollweg, Theobald von, **27:** 170,n2, 171; **30:** 138; **31:** 9n1, 37, 427, 519, 535; **32:** 206, 214, 351, 352, 403, 441, 455, 514; **33:** 279-80,n1, 283-84, 298n1, 299, 347, 454, 511; **34:** 47,n6, 187, 238, 239, 320, 370, 442, 454; **35:** 74, 240-43, 245n1; **36:** 122, 123,n1, 341, 354, 414; **37:** 5,n1, 43,n1, 45n1, 75n2, 106n1, 272, 379n1, 480, 507; **38:** 91, 314n2, 453n1, 495n1, 651, 652; on *Arabic* crisis, **34:** 333,n1, 342n1, opposition of Junkers to, **36:** 258; speech in Reichstag in defense of submarine warfare, **36:** 441,n1; meets with Gerard and William II, **36:** 613-16; possible removal of, **37:** 424, 425-26
Bethmann Hollwegs Kriegsreden (Thimme), **37:** 43n1
Bettis, E. G., **29:** 549
Between Sittings: An Informal Autobiography (Davidson), **36:** 415n1; **37:** 221n1
Bevans, Charles I., **38:** 228n1
Beveridge, Albert Jeremiah, **32:** 349
Beveridge, Ray, **34:** 528,n3

Bey, Ahmed Rustem, **31:** 16,n1, 20, 32, 56; **32:** 510; **35:** 438
Biarritz, France, **32:** 442, 475, 480
Bibeau, Henry C., **32:** 94,n3
Bicknell, Grace Vawter (Mrs. Ernest Percy), **28:** 20n6
Bielaski, Alexander Bruce, **34:** 266,n1
big business: *see* business
Big Men and Little Business (Brandeis), **29:** 30n1
Big Steel Profits in Defense Plan (New York *Evening Mail*), **35:** 146,n3
Bigelow, Herbert Seely, **36:** 524, 634,n3, 635
Bigge, Arthur John, 1st Baron Stamfordham, **32:** 303; **33:** 123; **35:** 499,n2
Bigham, John Charles, 1st Baron Mersey, **33:** 89,n2
Bilibid Prison, P.I., **32:** 536n2
bill of lading, **38:** 102
Bill of Rights (U.S.), **28:** 436
Bill to create a National Waterways Commission, and for other purposes (draft, Lane), **36:** 290,n1
Bill to Provide a Civil Government for Porto Rico, and for Other Purposes, **29:** 273n1
Billard, John Leander, **37:** 203,n3
Billinghurst, Guillermo, **29:** 244n2
Billings, Edmund, **28:** 270-71, 271,n2; suggested as Democratic national chairman, **37:** 129-30, 131, 133, 143,n1, 151, 164
Biltmore Hotel, N.Y., **33:** 212n1; **34:** 112, 196n1, 529; **35:** 13n1, 178, 258; **36:** 16n1; **37:** 373
Bingham, Robert, **27:** 267,n3
Bingham School (Mebaneville, N.C.), **27:** 267,n3
Binghamton, N.Y., **38:** 461n1
Biography of Joseph T. Robinson (Neal), **27:** 457n2
Birch, Thomas Howard, **28:** 4,n1
Bird, Francis W., **30:** 491
Birdsall-Thompson bill: *see* Thompson-Birdsall bill
Birdseye, George, **33:** 404,n1
Birmingham, Ala., **29:** 308, 309, 322; **34:** 296
Birmingham, George A. [James Owen Hannay], **31:** 316n2
Birnbaum, Karl Edward, **33:** 279n1; **37:** 45n1
Birrell, Augustine, **36:** 6
Birth of a Nation, **32:** 142n1, 267,n1, 310n1, 455,n2, 486,n1,3; **33:** 68,n1, 86,n1, 431; sequel to, **34:** 426n1
Birth of a Nation (MacKaye), **32:** 267n1
Bishop, William Warner, **31:** 316,n1
Bishop Brent on the Philippines (Milwaukee *Wisconsin*), **36:** 172n2
Bishop Burnet's History of His Own Time, **37:** 35n7
Bishop McConnell's View (*Denver Post*), **38:** 520n2
Bismarck-Schönhausen, Otto Eduard

Leopold von, **30:** 201; **31:** 459; **32:** 381-82; **33:** 14; **34:** 46
Bittner, Harvey, **38:** 117,n1
Bjornsen, S.S. (*Björnstjerne Björnson*), **31:** 477
Black, Frank, **36:** 497n2
Black, John, **38:** 637,n1
Black, Van Lear, **29:** 401n1
Black Is White (McCutcheon), **31:** 316n2, 317
Black Jack, the Life and Times of John J. Pershing (Vandiver), **36:** 285n2, 335n2
Black Sea, **32:** 212
Blackett, Basil B., **31:** 252, 315
Blackett, Charles W., **29:** 474,n1
Blackmon, Frederick Leonard, **32:** 231-32,n1, 241-42
Blackstone Hotel, Chicago, **27:** 29n1; **38:** 489n1
Blackton, James Stuart, **36:** 16n1
Blagden, Samuel P., **38:** 626
Blaine, James Gillespie, **27:** 288n6; **32:** 455,n1
Blalock, Aaron C., **28:** 402,n1, 413-14
Blanchard, Arthur: *see* Bailly-Blanchard, Arthur
Blanco, Lucio, **28:** 77; **32:** 355,n5
Bland, Ewing Charles, **32:** 325,n1,2
Bland, John Randolph, **30:** 375,n3
Bland, Raymond LeRoy, **31:** 206n1
Bland, Richard Parks ("Silver Dick"), **32:** 325n1
Blankenburg, Rudolph, **28:** 435,n2; **33:** 147n2
Blanquet, Aureliano, **27:** 539, 542; **28:** 473, 482,n1; **29:** 429; **30:** 236
Blatch, Harriot Eaton Stanton (Mrs. William Henry), **37:** 426,n2, 427n4
Blauvelt, James Gilmore, **32:** 272
Bleistein, George, **35:** 460,n1
Bliss, Robert Woods, **33:** 451
Bliss, Tasker Howard, **29:** 278, 295,n3; **34:** 482,n5, 484; **36:** 295,n1, 322, 618; **38:** 219, 237n1, 271, 361, 362, 373; memorandum on border protection, **38:** 220-32, 397-405, 675-78; on agreement for Joint High Commission, **38:** 233-35
Blocksom, Augustus P., **36:** 352
Bloedel, Henry C., **34:** 116n2
Blokland, Jonkheer F. Beelaerts van, **37:** 236,n1
Blossom, Henry Martyn, **29:** 558n4; **34:** 467n1
Blue, Victor, **29:** 432,n1,2
Blum, John Morton, **31:** 277n3; **38:** 674n1
Blumenthal, Maurice B., **38:** 562,n1
Blythe, Samuel George, **29:** 516,n3; **30:** 320; **32:** 69; **34:** 57n1; interviews WW, **29:** 516-24; **31:** 390-403
B'nai B'rith, **32:** 97; **37:** 109
Board of Mediation and Conciliation: *see* United States Board of Mediation and Conciliation

Board of Public Utility Commissioners, N.J., **27:** 48-49, 58

Boardman, Florence Sheffield (Mrs. William Jarvis), **34:** 100,n1

Boardman, Mabel Thorp, **29:** 561; **32:** 20; **33:** 239, 258, 266, 334, 448; **34:** 100-101

Boardman, William Jarvis, **34:** 100,n2

Bobo, Rosalvo, **31:** 483,n5, 484, 485-86; **34:** 70, 71, 143, 165; reported resignation, **34:** 142-43

Boemeke, Manfred, **27:** xxii

Boer War, **31:** 337, 437; **33:** 457; **34:** 94, 96

Bogotá, Colombia, **28:** 197, 198, 292, 329, 342; **29:** 40n1

Bohemia, Austria, **38:** 71

Böhm, Clara, **37:** 164-65,n2, 173-74; **38:** 81, 84

Bohn, Frank, **27:** 476-77, 481

Bohn, William E., **27:** 476

Bok, Cary, **33:** 69-70, 86

Bok, Edward William, **32:** 50,n1, 191-92; **33:** 69-70, 86; **37:** 130,n1, 508, 534-35; **38:** 27

Bok, Mary Louise Curtis (Mrs. Edward William), **33:** 70, 86

Bolce, Harold, **33:** 34,n5

Bolivia, **28:** 412, 448n1, 458; **34:** 157n1, 488; **35:** 54; **36:** 461; and Mexico, **33:** 455, 487, 488

Bolling, Annie Stuart Litchfield (Mrs. Rolfe E.), **32:** 423-24,n2; **34:** 124-25,n4, 131, 137-38, 167, 234, 241, 323, 345, 349, 354-55, 425,n1

Bolling, Bertha, sister of EBG, **33:** 287,n1, 340-41, 345, 346, 366, 391, 422; **34:** 156, 171, 207, 221, 246, 260, 283-84, 300-301, 312, 313, 314, 324, 326, 328, 329, 336, 347, 356, 361-62, 364, 365, 376, 394, 395, 424, 431, 459, 464, 487; **35:** 270, 274, 372; and sister's engagement to WW, **34:** 347, 348; welcomes WW into family, **34:** 347, 348; WW on, **34:** 351, 354, 380

Bolling, Elizabeth, niece of EBG, **34:** 124,n4, 131, 140, 151, 167, 178, 234, 253, 254, 260, 323-24, 328,n1, 329, 332-33, 357, 447; marriage, **34:** 312, 348-49, 354-55; *see also* Bolling family: crisis in

Bolling, John Randolph, brother of EBG, **33:** 385,n1, 542; **34:** 8-9, 15, 207, 221, 225, 246, 347, 354, 397, 431, 459, 464, 467, 487; **35:** 274, 372; welcomes WW as his brother, **34:** 416

Bolling, Julian B., **38:** 7,n2

Bolling, Mrs. Julian B., **38:** 7,n2

Bolling, Rolfe E., brother of EBG, **33:** 542,n3; **34:** 91, 119, 124,n4, 131, 137, 151, 167, 178, 221, 225, 234, 241, 245, 253, 254, 312, 323, 328, 332, 348-49, 355; WW to try to further career of, **34:** 255, 345-46

Bolling, Sallie White (Mrs. William Holcombe), mother of EBG, **32:** 423,n1; **33:** 87, 119, 366, 385n1; **34:** 156, 171, 207, 221, 234, 246, 260, 283-84, 293, 300-301, 313, 314, 324, 326, 328n1, 329, 332, 356, 361-62, 376, 377, 394, 395, 396, 425, 431, 459, 464, 469, 487, 501; **35:** 18, 43, 44, 274, 275, 371-72; reaction to daughter's engagement to WW; **34:** 347-48, 350; WW's letter of introduction to, **34:** 363, 379; and EBG's marriage to WW, **35:** 371n1; WW thanks for birthday wishes, **35:** 408-409

Bolling, William Archibald, brother of EBG, **35:** 56,n1

Bolling, William Holcombe, father of EBG, **32:** 423n1; **33:** 385n1; **34:** 425; **35:** 16, 32, 372

Bolling family: crisis in, **33:** 365n1; **34:** 91, 124-25, 131,n3, 137-38, 139, 140, 151-52, 167, 221, 225, 234, 241, 245, 253-55, 255, 260, 284, 312, 322, 323-24, 328, 332, 345-46, 348-49, 354-55, 357, 447; and Byrd family, **35:** 84, 87-88

Bombay, India, **28:** 82

Bond, Thomas, **30:** 375,n4

bonds (corporate): A. O. Stanley on, **29:** 29; J. E. Davies on, **29:** 82; W. C. Adamson on, **29:** 139; *see also* stocks

Bones, Helen Woodrow, **28:** 45, 61, 67, 103, 104, 106, 108, 134, 143, 150, 182, 183, 189, 249, 258, 260, 265, 266, 269, 277, 308, 310, 318, 320, 331, 335, 360, 387, 598; **29:** 159, 440, 449, 516; **30:** 276; **31:** 59, 94, 119, 141, 142, 158, 175, 341, 454, 500, 556; **32:** 7, 8, 21, 111, 190, 335; **33:** 111, 137, 162, 163, 178-79,n2, 180, 203, 204, 228, 234, 236, 240, 274, 278n1, 279n1, 285, 286,n1, 290, 334, 339, 341, 346, 379, 382, 384-85, 388, 402, 403, 418, 421, 423, 434, 435, 442, 444, 445, 447, 525, 526, 543; **34:** 7, 8, 14, 15, 64, 72, 73, 77, 89, 91, 104, 163, 171, 192, 201, 232, 263, 286, 289, 293, 359, 365, 377, 378, 379-80, 393-94, 394, 397, 407, 414, 416, 420, 424, 430, 432, 447, 469, 473, 474, 485, 486, 490, 500, 506, 509, 517, 519, 521, 522, 543, 545; **35:** 11, 12, 15, 16, 18, 23, 24, 25, 32, 41, 43, 44, 59, 110, 154, 386, 423; **36:** 151, 417, 463; **37:** 78, 247, 382, 383, 534; **38:** 17, 186, 481n1, 590, 623, 627, 661, 689n3; hospitalization and operation, **28:** 319, 320, 327, 328, 333, 393; letters to sister, **29:** 553-62; attends baseball game with WW, **29:** 559-60; and Edith Bolling Galt, **32:** 423,n3; **35:** 127, 155-56, 161, 162, 261, 262, 271, 272, 273, 275, 276; and Mrs. Hulbert, **35:** 238,n3

Bonillas, Ignacio, **30:** 57,n1; **38:** 83n1, 153, 153-54, 356, 358

Bonillas, Manuel, **28:** 542, 563, 580; **33:** 260,n1, 400, 464, 488

Bonser, Frederick Gordon, **32:** 282n1

Bontz, L. E., **27:** 487n1

Bonzano, Giovanni, **37**: 30,n2, 54, 55n1, 95

books: duty on foreign, and book publishers, **28**: 579

Boquillas del Carmen, Coahuila, Mex., **37**: 22

Borah, William Edgar, **28**: 162,n1, 163, 224; **30**: 242, 261, 274n1; **32**: 123, 286; **33**: 518

Borcherdt, Walter O., **36**: 21,n1, 137

Bordas Valdés, José, **29**: 20, 21; **30**: 308

Borden, Sir Robert Laird, **29**: 60,n2, 204; **36**: 203

Borland, Solon, **29**: 437

Borno, Louis, **31**: 485,n1, 486

Bosnia (Austria-Hungary): assassination of Archduke Franz Ferdinand in, **30**: 222

Boston, Mass., **28**: 598, 599; **29**: 113; **32**: 118n1; district attorney appointment in, **27**: 334; **28**: 270-71, 275,n1,2,3,4; segregation protest planned in, **28**: 343; bankers on Federal Reserve bill and Act, **28**: 379,n1; **29**: 86-87; American Union Against Militarism meeting in, **36**: 635

Boston and Maine Railroad, **29**: 338-40,n2, 345, 369, 374; **30**: 85-87, 163n1, 293n3, 294-95, 302, 308; **37**: 203n3

Boston Audubon Society, **28**: 291

Boston Congregational Club, **30**: 119,n1

Boston Daily Advertiser, **28**: 498n1

Boston Elevated Railway Co., **36**: 610

Boston *Guardian*, **28**: 491n2, 494n3, 498n1

Boston Herald, **31**: 276n2; **36**: 606

Boston Jewish Voice, **32**: 97

Boston Journal, **38**: 171n1

Boston Post, **28**: 271n1; **37**: 526n1

Boston Railway Holding Co., **30**: 85, 163n1

Boston Traveler, **32**: 178n2

Boughton, Edward J., **30**: 60,n1

Bouillon, Franklin, **33**: 12-13

Boulder, Colo., **31**: 334

Boulder County, Colo., **29**: 529

Boulton, Alfred J., **37**: 316n1

Bourand, Darius, **34**: 143,n1

Bowen, Charles Synge Christopher, **35**: 37,n1

Bowen, J. V., **29**: 549

Bowen, Thomas S., **36**: 353,n2

Bowers, John S., **32**: 494n2

Bowers, LaMont Montgomery, **28**: 426,n3, 427, 507-14, 518, 546-56, 563, 581, 583, 589-90,n1; **29**: 46, 87-88

Bowman, A. Llewellen, **35**: 68,n2

Boxer Rebellion, **27**: 237, 488-89; **29**: 292, 331; **32**: 177

Boy Scouts of America: WW's remarks to, **32**: 165-16

Boyce, Everett Robert, **27**: 55n3

Boyd, Charles T., **37**: 277n1, 300, 307, 309n2, 317, 318, 319, 348; **38**: 227, 378-86

Boyd, Elizabeth Bolling (Mrs. Jorge Eduardo); *see* Bolling, Elizabeth

Boyd, Jorge Eduardo, **34**: 124n4, 131,n3, 140, 167, 221, 234, 253, 254, 323, 328, 332, 345, 348-49, 355, 357; meets with WW, **34**: 447; *see also* Bolling family: crisis in

Boy-Ed, Karl, **34**: 266,n2; **35**: 43,n1, 264,n1, 265, 276, 277n1, 277-78, 291n1

Boylston Manufacturing Co., Boston, **30**: 400n1

Boynton, Albert E., **27**: 343-44,n2

Bradford, Mary Field Conover (Mrs. Willard Hall), **28**: 62,n4

Bradford, Willard Hall, **28**: 62n4

Bradley, Mahlon, **29**: 23,n1

Braeman, Roselius: *see* Breman, Roselius

Braid, Mr., **31**: 380

Braisted, William Clarence, **33**: 486,n1

Braisted, William Reynolds, **32**: 528n1

Brake, Edwin V., **28**: 426,n7

Braman, Dwight, **31**: 291,n4

Branagan, Frank A., **28**: 300-301

Brand, Herman L., **33**: 361

Brand, Horace L., **33**: 185

Brand, Katharine Edith, **27**: xxii; **29**: viii; **30**: viii; **31**: x; **32**: x; **33**: x; **34**: x; **35**: x

Brandegee, Frank Bosworth, **30**: 181,n1

Brandeis, Louis Dembitz, **27**: 8, 106, 138, 188,n4; **28**: 271, 275, 392n3; **29**: 7n2, 30n1, 481,n1; **30**: 110, 134, 161, 166,n2, 296; **31**: 239; **35**: 132, 535; **37**: 264, 310, 314, 330, 363, 436, 522; **38**: 13, 14, 19, 34; as possible cabinet appointee, **27**: 23, 27, 61, 62, 112, 130, 137-38; E. M. House on, **27**: 23, 27, 62, 71, 110, 130; N. Hapgood on, **27**: 60-61; J. M. Head on, **27**: 67-68; suggested by WW for Solicitor General, **27**: 71; J. W. Westcott on, **27**: 92,n1; R. M. La Follette on, **27**: 107-108; C. R. Crane on, **27**: 108; on unfinished legislation, **27**: 244; and appointments to Industrial Relations Commission, **27**: 353-54, 365, 456, 465, 476-77, 481, 487; and purchase of *Harper's Weekly*, **27**: 436; and currency legislation, **27**: 520-21; and membership in Cosmos Club, **32**: 163, 167,n1; suggested for Supreme Court, **36**: 19-20, 22-23; and nomination to Supreme Court, **36**: 23, 25-26, 51, 86, 136,n1, 137, 140, 191, 359, 609-11; controversy over nomination of, **36**: 250, 606-607; **37**: 9-10, 25, 34, 56, 72, 78n1, 101, 102, 103; Morgenthau's plan for Brandeis to enter Mass. Senate race, **36**: 425,n3; Court nomination confirmed, **37**: 151,n1; comments praising confirmation of, **37**: 151, 152, 162, 163, 165; and Hapgood on Supreme Court appointments, **37**: 372-73, 446, declines position on Joint High Commission, **38**: 22, 33; photograph of, **37**: *illustration section*

Brandeis: A Free Man's Life (Mason), **36:** 25n1, 26n2, 611n3; **37:** 72n1
Brandt, Louis E., **37:** 219n3
Braniff, Oscar, **33:** 259,n1, 261
Braschi, Victor M., **36:** 364
Brassey, Thomas, 1st Earl Brassey, **37:** 371,n1
Braucher, Howard S., **27:** 244
Braun, Marcus, **32:** 97; **34:** 528
Braz Pereira Gomes, Wenceslao **31:** 536
Brazil, **27:** 540; **28:** 412, 516; **30:** 23, 121; **34:** 80, 81; **35:** 54-55, 215, 254, 520; **36:** 197, 199-201, 445, 461, 479, 605; **37:** 8-9, 122, 138, 239, 241-44, 292; **38:** 19, 116; and China, **27:** 267; and conciliation treaties, **27:** 478; **29:** 342; and ABC mediation, **28:** 117-18, 141,n2; **29:** 135, 505-506,n1, 506-507, 507, 518, 525, 534, 539-40; **30:** 41-42, 87, 121, 262,n1; **33:** 305-306; and Bolivian concessions to foreign investors, **28:** 458; and L. Carden, **29:** 103, 366; **31:** 16; and Mexico, **29:** 484; **32:** 263, 398n1; **33:** 437, 455, 487, 488; **34:** 487-88; and Pan-American Pact, **30:** 271; **31:** 470, 471-72,n1, 498, 536, 552; **32:** 64, 338-39, 339-40, 474, 478, 542; **33:** 52, 55, 62, 63, 65, 68, 80,n1, 220; **34:** 448; and Germany, **31:** 355; **32:** 505
Breaking the Money Trust (Brandeis), **29:** 30n1
Breceda, Alfredo, **30:** 409,n5
Breckinridge, Desha, **28:** 290n4; **29:** 326, 342, 343
Breckinridge, Henry Skillman, **27:** 274,n1; **28:** 130; **29:** 326; **34:** 192, 235; and Garrison's proposed resignation, **32:** 168,n1, 538-40; on Jones bill, **36:** 139; resignation of, **36:** 165
Breckinridge, Roeliff Morton, **27:** 206-207
Breckinridge, Sophonisba Preston, **35:** 134-35,n1, 158; **37:** 308, 316
Breitung, Edward Nicklas, **32:** 89n3, 102
Breman, Roselius, **36:** 564,n5
Bremen, Germany, **32:** 102; **35:** 62
Brenham, Tex., **29:** 417n2
Brent, Charles Henry, **27:** 516,n1, 526; **29:** 164, 165-67
Briand, Aristide, **35:** 174-75,n1,2; **36:** 354, 387n1, 444, 511-12; **37:** 42, 412; and House's meetings with, **36:** 125, 138,n1, 147, 148,n1, 180n2
Bridges, Robert, **29:** 171, 186-87; **30:** 156, 282; **35:** 262n3, 274, 275; on death of EAW, **30:** 366; WW acknowledgement, **30:** 426
Bridgewater, N.H., **28:** 129
Bridgman, Howard Allen, **28:** 256,n1, 265-66, 277-78,n1
Brieux, Eugène, **31:** 248,n2, 410; **32:** 16
Bright, John, **29:** 320; **36:** 320n1
Brightwood Citizens' Association, **31:** 192
Brindilla, S.S., **31:** 176, 193, 206, 209, 214, 229, 234, 347
Bristow, Joseph Little, **28:** 414; **29:**

272,n1, 275, 482,n1, 495; **30:** 226,n2; opposes nomination of T. D. Jones to Federal Reserve Board, **30:** 299n1
Bristow-Mondell resolution, **30:** 226,n2
Britain: *see* Great Britain
Britain's Clandestine Submarines, 1914-1915 (Smith), **31:** 310n1, 425n1
British Honduras, **37:** 112
British National Committee for Relief in Belgium, **37:** 28n2
British Press on Benton's Fate (*Literary Digest*), **29:** 301n2
British Response to President Wilson's Peace Efforts (Oxman), **33:** 372n1
British Royal Mail Steam Packet Co., **34:** 439
Britt, Philip J., **35:** 167,n1
Britten, Frederick Albert, **36:** 362,n2
Brockdorff-Rantzau, Countess Juliane, **29:** 531; mother of Ulrich Karl Christian, Count Brockdorff-Rantzau
Brockman, Fletcher Sims, **28:** 23,n1
Broesamle, John Joseph, **28:** 156n1; **37:**, 187n4
Bromo-Seltzer, **29:** 89n1
Bronson Alcott's Fruitlands (Sears), **36:** 132n1
Brook Chapel, Hillburn, N.Y., **31:** 237n1
Brook Farm, **36:** 132
Brooklyn Navy Yard: WW memorial address at, **30:** 13-15,n1, 21n1
Brooklyn, N.Y. (Kings County), **29:** 402,n1, 403, 423; **31:** 349; political appointments in, **35:** 319
Brooklyn Daily Eagle, **31:** 252; **37:** 27,n2
Brooks, Arthur, **27:** 12, 28; **29:** 558,n3; **34:** 24; **35:** 155, 372
Brooks, Florence Fenn (Mrs. Sydney), **35:** 258,n1; **36:** 402
Brooks, John Graham, **27:** 456, 476, 477, 481,n1
Brooks, Sydney, **28:** 370-71,n1,2,3; **29:** 74,n1; **30:** 192,n2, 287; **32:** 299, 328,n3, 340, 341,n4; **33:** 244,n1; **35:** 320-21,n1, 346, 357; **36:** 402
Brophy, J. P., **33:** 497n4
Brotherhood of Locomotive Engineers, **30:** 305; **36:** 204n1
Brotherhood of Locomotive Enginemen and Firemen, **30:** 305; **36:** 204n1; **37:** 434
Brotherhood of Railroad Trainmen, **36:** 204n1; **37:** 434
Brougham, Herbert Bruce, **31:** 458-60; **33:** 139
Brower, Jessie Woodrow Bones (Mrs. Abraham Thew H.), first cousin of WW: letters from her sister Helen, **29:** 553-62; **30:** 425; **32:** 493-94,n1
Brown, Arthur Judson, **29:** 476
Brown, Benjamin Henry Innes, **37:** 264,n4
Brown, David W., **28:** 518,n1, 519, 581, 583

Brown, Edward Norphlet, **27:** 252,n2; **28:** 7; **36:** 364,n1

Brown, Edward Thomas, first cousin of EAW, **30:** 395; **31:** 357n1; **32:** 66, 423; **33:** 373-75, 538; **34:** 231, 335, 353, 359-60, 360, 467, 470, 474, 479, 485, 506, 511; **35:** 33

Brown, Marjorie (daughter of Edward T. Brown), first cousin once removed of EAW, **30:** 376; **38:** 176

Brown, Mary Celestine (Mimi) Mitchell (Mrs. Edward Thomas), **28:** 355,n1; **31:** 357,n1; **33:** 373-75; **34:** 467, 470, 474, 479, 485; **35:** 33,n1, 161,n1; **38:** 176

Brown, Meyer L., **32:** 97

Brown, Norris, **38:** 342n3

Brown, Sevellon Ledyard, **37:** 141,n4

Brown, William Carey, **36:** 528,n1, 586,n4

Brown, William Garrett, **27:** 140, 465

Brown, William Gay, Jr., **28:** 90,n1; **30:** 10,n1

Brown Brothers (New York): and Nicaraguan loan, **28:** 176, 184, 251, 353, 354, 358-59

Browne, Herbert Janvrin, **30:** 346,n1, 346-48; **38:** 445n1

Browning, Elizabeth Barrett (Mrs. Robert), **33:** 373,n1, 380

Browning, Robert, **28:** 126; **30:** 459; **33:** 111; **34:** 464,n4; **38:** 259,n2

Brownsville, Tex., **37:** 249, 255, 284, 285

Bruère, Henry, **38:** 276,n7

Brumbaugh, Martin Grove, **38:** 430n2

Brün, Constantin, **37:** 476, 484, 495, 496, 497, 506, 521; and Danish West Indies, **35:** 202-203,n1, 401-403, 407, 432,n1, 508-509

Brush, Edward, **27:** 481,n2, 482

Brush, George De Forest, **28:** 195,n2

Brussels, Belgium, **31:** 197,n1; suburb to name street after WW, **38:** 661-62

Brussels, S.S., **38:** 72n9, 251

Bryan, Charles Wayland, **38:** 372

Bryan, Mary Elizabeth Baird (Mrs. William Jennings), **27:** 414; **30:** 207, 212, 355; **31:** 118; **33:** 337, 422; **34:** 135; **35:** 371, 401; **38:** 372

Bryan, Nathan Philemon, **27:** 418

Bryan, Ruth: *see* Owen, Ruth Bryan

Bryan, William Jennings, **27:** xvi, xxi, 28, 57-58, 64, 67, 71, 102, 111-12, 120, 128, 137, 138, 196, 198, 253, 265-66, 272, 444, 462, 494-95, 534; **28:** 195, 247, 477, 491, 527, 530, 588,n4; **30:** 29, 89n1, 171, 184n1, 188, 241, 283, 390, 404, 470, 493-94; **31:** 40n1, 43, 112, 118, 450, 530, 545, 550; **32:** 8,n2, 9, 24, 25, 65, 67-68, 100-105, 188,n1, 198, 496,n3; **33:** 3, 12, 20-23, 23, 28-29, 31, 41-43, 51, 52, 61, 65, 67, 68, 69, 71, 81, 82, 88, 91, 108, 139, 139-40, 140, 140-41, 142, 154, 185-86, 192-93, 194, 195, 205-206, 223, 224, 237, 239, 257, 264, 266, 279n1, 287n1, 295,n4, 302-303, 308, 314, 331, 332-33, 333, 335, 336, 337-38, 344, 349, 375, 375-76, 425n1, 449, 452, 511, 523; **34:** 13, 15n1, 42, 49, 85, 107, 114, 158, 187, 197n2, 225, 241, 278, 288, 486n1, 493, 515; **35:** 60, 65, 70, 185n2, 200, 218, 266, 380n1, 387, 492; **36:** 187, 211, 288, 335, 564, 657; **37:** 33, 35, 42, 76,n1, 118, 130, 429; **38:** 243, 256, 280, 607, 668, 670; papers of, **27:** xi; and Philippines, **27:** 8-10; **28:** 192, 192-93, 382; and diplomatic appointments, **27:** 14, 124, 126, 131, 167, 169, 218-19, 311-12, 314, 341, 474, 492; **28:** 4-5, 111-12, 175, 184, 197, 320, 326-27, 354; and appointment as Secretary of State, **27:** 23, 26, 62, 70, 93-94, 96, 110, 111-12; and single term for President, **27:** 103n1, 104-105, 114; **28:** 57 *and Mexico:* general, **27:** 158n1, 202, 330-32, 479-80, 481; **28:** 6-7,n1,2, 246-47, 410-11, 516; **29:** 144, 381, 498; **30:** 59, 80; **31:** 322n1, 380, 411; **32:** 477-78; **33:** 258, 302-304,n1, 304-306; **37:** 291,n1,2; on Huerta, **27:** 158n1, 330-32, 481; **28:** 27, 145n1, 281, 363, 399, 423, 431-32,n1,2, 433n1, 537-40; **29:** 13, 137-38, 237, 325, 497-98; **30:** 78-79; **32:** 468,n2; on appointment of ambassador to, **27:** 163, 228; on Madero, **27:** 202; on Carranza and Constitutionalists, **28:** 6-7,n1,2, 325; **29:** 34, 142, 143, 231, 483-85, 486, 491, 495, 497-98, 525; **30:** 297-98, 449-50; **31:** 431; **32:** 326-27,n1, 331-32, 352-53, 355-56, 367, 369, 369-70,n1; **33:** 29, 43-45, 69, 343-44,n1; on H. L. Wilson, **28:** 26-27, 83-84,n2; offers plans for restoring peace in, **28:** 49-52, 136-136-37; **29:** 530; and Lind mission, **28:** 148-49, 157-59, 162, 167-68, 188-89, 191, 195-96, 200-201, 201-202, 224-27, 232-39, 241, 281-82, 293-300, 324-25, 347-48, 356-57, 365, 376-78, 382-83, 386-87, 423, 428-29, 444-47, 471; **29:** 14-19, 30-31, 101, 190-91, 328-31, 338, 357-60, 382-83; **30:** 47-48, 166-67; **33:** 45-47; and Senate comment on administration policies, **28:** 162-63, 205, 206-207, 208-209, 223-24,n1; arms shipments to, **28:** 193-94; **29:** 206-207,n1, 210; and WW's message on, **28:** 231; on Hale mission, **28:** 339, 340, 505, 529, 541-43, 545-46, 557,n1, 558-59, 561, 563-64, 567-68, 579-80, 588; criticizes L. Carden on, **28:** 433; **29:** 209; **31:** 61n1; and T. B. Hohler on, **29:** 230-31, 248, 251-55, 255-61, 266; and Benton affair, **29:** 285n1; on Tampico affair and occupation of Veracruz, **29:** 420-21, 426-29, 432, 436, 438-39,n1, 446-47, 455, 456-57, 458-59, 460-61, 462-64, 464-65, 466, 466-67, 467-68, 476-78, 480, 524-25; **31:** 23-24; and ABC mediation, **29:** 505-506, 525; **30:** 45, 47, 49-50 58, 64, 75-77, 87-88, 91-93, 99-100, 100-101, 101-103, 113, 114-18, 119, 120-21, 122, 123-26, 132-33, 135, 136, 137-39, 198-

99, 203, 204, 207-208, 225-26, 228-29, 239-40, 241-42; transmits WW's position to E. Grey, **30:** 9-10; on J. R. Silliman as emissary, **30:** 166-67, 167-69, 297-98; **32:** 363-64; on L. J. Canova as emissary, **30:** 180; and G. C. Carothers, **30:** 301,n1, 193-94, 297-98, 311; **33:** 29; and Sen. B. Lee's visit to Cardinal Gibbons, **30:** 340-41,n1, 342; and P. Fuller mission, **30:** 392-93, 443-44, 489-90; **31:** 18-19; and Catholics in, **32:** 134,248-49,259,365,392,393,398,404; **33:** 30-31,n1; and D. West mission, **32:** 202-203, 203, 507,n1; **33:** 187-88,n1, 217-18,n1

and Japan: controversy over California alien land legislation, **27:** 162, 220, 221, 282, 318-21,n1, 326, 348-51, 352, 360, 361, 362-64, 365, 371-72, 372, 381, 382-83, 384, 395, 396, 397, 403, 404, 405, 412-13, 415-17, 426, 448-49, 450, 459-60; **28:** 16-17, 18, 21-22, 268, 274, 282-83,n1, 284-85, 305-306, 314-15; **29:** 133; **30:** 169-70, 273-74; **31:** 256-57,n5; **32:** 113-14; movement of the fleet in Pacific, **27:** 444; imperialistic designs of Japan in China, **30:** 390-92, 396, 402; **31:** 546-47; **32:** 139,n2, 169-71,n4, 177-78, 246-47, 247, 248, 269-71, 287, 322-23, 333,n1, 353-54, 367,n1, 368, 391, 414-15, 434-35, 435-36, 436-37,n1, 458, 459, 466, 499-500, 501, 519-20, 520-21, 524-25, 527-28, 529-30, 531; **33:** 80, 82-84, 85, 95-99, 101, 102-104, 104-105, 113-15, 120, 131; **32:** 500,n1,2

greets diplomatic corps, **27:** 171; and China, **27:** 174, 175, 218, 237, 248, 249-50, 261, 262, 267, 328, 329, 330; **28:** 401, 490; **30:** 362-63; **31:** 364-67, 381-82, 509-13; **32:** 500,n1,2; **33:** 99-100, 349; Huntington Wilson resignation, **27:** 197-98,n1, 199, 210; and Champ Clark, **27:** 268-69; and conciliation ("cooling off") treaties, **27:** 276-77, 352-53,n1, 359-60, 448, 477-79, 482, 504, 515; **28:** 477n3; **29:** 136, 179, 218, 340-41, 349-50; **30:** 397, 472; **31:** 64; **37:** 479, 480; and Panama Canal tolls controversy, **27:** 310-11, 312-13, 332-33, 357, 512-13; and currency reforms, **27:** 413-14, 436,n1, 457, 458, 523, 554-55; **28:** 9, 121-23,n2, 369-70; and Nicaragua, **27:** 470, 526-30, 552; **28:** 175-77, 184-85, 216, 250-51, 353, 354, 358-59; **29:** 134-35, 152, 171, 172-73, 204, 221, 245, 274-75; **30:** 174-75; **31:** 102, 115; **32:** 59-60, 68; and Dominican Republic, **27:** 518-20, 531; **28:** 124,n2; **29:** 20; **31:** 382-84; **32:** 353-54, 466; **33:** 26-27, 218-20; and Haiti, **27:** 518-20,n3; 531, 553, 557-58; **31:** 456-57, 482; **32:** 27-28, 62, 75-76, 80, 288-89, 295, 437,n2, 438, 439-40, 458, 471-73, 479; **33:** 115, 116-17, 275-76, 276-77, 278; and Latin American policy, **28:** 47-48, 123-25, 455-57;

29: 244, 360; **32:** 469-70,n3; and Colombia, **28:** 197-98, 292, 329-30, 342, 533-36, 572-73; **29:** 36-37, 39-40; on loyalty to the administration, **28:** 255, 257; on Chautauqua lecturing, **28:** 292, 302,n3; Mr. Dooley on, **29:** 56n2; and patronage, **29:** 159, 162; **31:** 500, 501; WW on, **29:** 220-21, 449, 557-58; **30:** 464; **31:** 384-85, 386; **32:** 10, 65-66; **33:** 363, 366, 377-78, 384, 388, 395, 398, 449, 452-53; and Illinois politics, **29:** 261,n1,2; and New York politics, **29:** 395,n1,2, 395-96,n2; congratulates WW and EAW on wedding anniversary, **30:** 207, 212

and Great Britain: offers U.S. good offices, **30:** 314-15, 316-17, 325; and protest about interference with neutral trade, **31:** 476-80, 521, 524-30; **33:** 106-10; and *Dacia* affair, **32:** 91; and total blockade of Germany, **32:** 301,n1, 311-12, 317-19, 409-11, 412-13, 421-22, 427, 432, 451; and Order in Council, **32:** 453-54, 457-58; on EAW's death, **30:** 355, 451; and loans to belligerents, **30:** 372-73, 386; **34:** 422, 478; and consorship of wireless, **30:** 407-408; and Joint State and Navy Neutrality Board, **30:** 435; and responses of belligerents to mediation offers, **30:** 456-57; *and Germany:* alleged atrocities, **30:** 457-58, 459, 459-61, 467; **31:** 26-27, 85, 121,n1; on bombing of cities, **30:** 471, 478; on invasion of Belgium, **32:** 42-43, 58-59, 60, 222-23; and strict accountability note, **32:** 207,n1, 207-10, 237, 249-51,n1; on proposed *modus vivendi,* **32:** 235-36, 250, 259-60, 260-62; and *Falaba* sinking, **32:** 464, 487, 489-90, 490, 497-98, 527; **33:** 66-67, 71-72, 72-73, 85-86, and Bernstorff on arms exports, **32:** 509-10,n1, 526; and peace moves, **31:** 10, 15, 16, 21-22,n1, 37, 55n1,3, 56-57, 140, 295, 378-79, 385; and Turkish ambassador, **31:** 16,n1, 56; and leaks in State Department, **31:** 29-30,n1; and Liberia, **31:**102, 114; and Declaration of London, **31:** 103, 113-14; against large increase in army, **31:** 281, 355; on sale of unassembled submarines, **31:** 310, 359; on prohibition as a party measure, **31:** 355-56; and W. W. Vick allegations on appointments, **31:** 447-48, 453, 467; and seamen's bill, **31:** 458, 490-93, 493; **32:** 302, 309-10; and Americans in Turkey, **31:** 471; and new commercial treaty with Russia, **31:** 473,n1; and conference of neutral nations, **31:** 480-81; and Pan-American Pact, **31:** 497; **32:** 99, 146, 159-60, 338-39, 339-40, 474, 478, 542; **33:** 52-54, 55-60, 77-80, 220-21; **35:** 55, 59, 163; and sale of arms to belligerents, **31:** 533-34; thinks JPT caused news leaks, **31:** 549-50; replies to charges U.S. is

Bryan, William Jennings (*cont.*)
unneutral, **32**: 26n1, 218,n2, 281; allegedly distrusted by German Americans, **32**: 90,n1; and ship-purchase bill, **32**: 106, 114-15; and access of newsmen to State Dept. offices, **32**: 245-46, 541, 542; and French loan, **32**: 451,n1 *and Lusitania crisis*: sinking and first note, **33**: 134-35, 155, 164, 165-66, 167-69, 174-78, 180, 181, 186, 212-13, 247,n1, 333, 424-26,n1; and alleged postscript, **33**: 173-74, 181-82, 182-83, 183-84, 191; **38**: 559n2; and second note, **33**: 309, 310-13, 321-26, 326-27, 342-43, 343, 351-55, 355, 368, 424-26,n1; resignation, **33**: 370,n1, 374, 375, 375-76, 376, 378,n1, 383, 387-88, 401, 421,n1, 422, 427, 478, 480n2; EBG on, **33**: 346, 364, 366, 380, 382, 421,n1; **34**: 172,n2, 192, 407, 486, 509; meets with H. C. Wallace, **34**: 133, 135, 146,n1, congratulates WW on *Arabic* pledge, **34**: 404, meets with F. K. Lane, **34**: 477-78, 481; meeting with WW, **34**: 510-11; wedding congratulations to WW, **35**: 371, 401; and Chile, **36**: 199; D. B. Jones on, **36**: 260; House on presidential hopes of, **36**: 267; on WW's campaign progress, **38**: 372; congratulates WW on victory, **38**: 629; photographs, *see illustration sections*, **27**; **31**; **33**
Bryan and World Peace (Curti), **27**: 277n1
Bryan-Chamorro Treaty: *see* Nicaragua and the United States
Bryant, William Cullen, **33**: 452
Bryce, Elizabeth, Lady Bryce, **27**: 254, 257; **28**: 506, 572; **30**: 356-57; **38**: 249
Bryce, James, Viscount Bryce, **27**: 124, 203, 213, 221-23, 254-55, 257, 276, 292, 310-11, 357-58, 406, 482; **28**: 506-507,n1, 507, 571-72, 587; **30**: 195, 385, 385-86, 395; **31**: 81-82, 138; **32**: 299; **34**: 21, 187-88, 515; **35**: 64, 83, 259, 347-48, 356, 473, 484; **36**: 203, 354, 654; **37**: 76,n1, 77,n1, 265, 289-90, 440; **38**: 247, 258, 282, 453, 454; and Panama Canal tolls, **27**: 312-13, 322-33; **30**: 260; on EAW's death, **30**: 356-57, 403; on alleged German atrocities, **33**: 485,n1; Gardiner on, **36**: 320n1; on British feelings about peace moves, **37**: 239-40; on WW's speech to League to Enforce Peace, **37**: 312; on future plans of League to Enforce Peace, **38**: 85-86; Page on conversation with, **38**: 249-51; congratulations to WW, **38**: 665
Bryn Mawr, Pa., **37**: 541
Bryn Mawr College, **28**: 63n1; **30**: 375n1; **38**: 526
Bryn Mawr School, Baltimore, **30**: 375n1
Buchanan, Frank, **34**: 39-40,n1, 52,n1, 64-65, 116,n1, 120
Buchanan, James, **27**: 159; **28**: 463
Buckingham Palace, **30**: 143n1, 370

Buckler, William Hepburn, **27**: 517,n1, 554,n1
Buckner, George Washington, **34**: 504
Buddhism, **32**: 466, 467; **33**: 23, 24
Buenaventura, Colombia, **34**: 50
Buenos Aires, Argentina, **36**: 267n1, 367; **37**: 187n4, 197
Buffalo, N.Y., **35**: 27n1, 460; post office appointments, **28**: 589; and American Union Against Militarism meeting in, **36**: 635; WW's addresses in, **38**: 572-79, 580-89
Buffalo Courier, **35**: 460n1
Buffalo Daily Times, **35**: 460n1
Buffalo Enquirer, **35**: 460n1
Bukovina, Austria, **38**: 74, 75
Bulgaria, **28**: 4n2; **32**: 204, 220; **33**: 232, 267, 501, 505, 511; **35**: 76, 174n1; **38**: 75
Bulgin, Myra, **32**: 509,n3
Bulkley, Robert Johns, **27**: 535,n2; **28**: 69,n1, 90; **30**: 10
Bulkley-Hollis bill: *see* Hollis-Bulkley bill
Bull, Reuben Adiel, **27**: 164-66, 465
Bull Moose party: *see* Progressive party
Bullard, Arthur, **37**: 201,n1, 225, 411
Bullard, William Hannum Grubb, **33**: 486,n4
Bulletin of the Metropolitan Museum of Art, **27**: 72n1
Bullock, Amy Isabel Thomson, Lady Bullock, **28**: 150,n4
Bullock, Sir George Mackworth, **28**: 150,n3, 159
Bülow, Bernhard Heinrich Martin Karl, Prince von, **32**: 285,n1; **33**: 28n1, 299; **37**: 86
Bund Neues Vaterland, **34**: 47,n6; **35**: 198,n3
Bunker Hill, Battle of, **36**: 97
Bunsen, Sir Maurice William Ernest de, **36**: 445,n2
Bunty Pulls the Strings (Moffat), **28**: 355,n5
Bureau of: *see under the latter part of the name*, such as Engraving and Printing
Bureaucracy Convicts Itself: The Ballinger-Pinchot Controversy of 1910 (Mason), **36**: 26n3
Burgard, Henry P., **28**: 64,n1
Burgess, George Farmer, **31**: 103,n1, 207
Burgess, John William, **33**: 18,n2
Burián von Rajecz, Count Stephan (Stefan), **33**: 481,n2; **34**: 403; **37**: 5, 289; **38**: 71, 75; and *Ancona* case, **35**: 365-66, 368, 379, 380, 389
Buried Life (Arnold), **33**: 161, 164
Burke, Edmund, **31**: 279, 403; **36**: 645; **38**: 291, 449
Burke, James Francis, **36**: 26n1, 35n1
Burke, John: as cabinet possibility, **27**: 21,n1, 27, 71, 126
Burlasque, James, **28**: 367-68,n1, 384; **34**: 201,n2, 258

Burlasque, Mrs. James, **28:** 367-68,n1, 384

Burleson, Adele Steiner (Mrs. Albert Sidney), **34:** 53; **35:** 36,n1

Burleson, Albert Sidney, **27:** 15, 17, 72, 123, 127, 129, 130, 131, 136-37, 163, 238-39, 251, 260, 268, 444, 487, 491-92; **28:** 476, 498n1, 589; **29:** 32, 56, 58, 277, 373, 456, 542; **30:** 464; **31:** 139, 274, 275, 384, 411, 500; **32:** 94, 134, 193; **33:** 449, 536; **34:** 6, 38-39, 42, 44, 53, 192; **35:** 61, 65, 338, 347, 361, 398, 401, 429-30, 431-32; **36:** 178-79, 239, 263, 267, 376, 377, 400-401, 513; **37:** 379, 420-21; **38:** 5, 6, 85,n1, 124,n2, 159, 664; and cabinet post, **27:** 21, 44-45, 61, 62, 70, 111, 112, 127, 133, 135; and Democratic National Convention of 1912, **27:** 22n2; postmasters and civil service, **27:** 160; code name for, **27:** 164; and segregation in government offices, **27:** 290-91; **31:** 308, 328,n3; and Panama Canal tolls question, **27:** 313, 373; and Mexico, **27:** 332; and shipping bill, **31:** 100-101; congratulations to WW on his engagement, **35:** 36; and I.W.W investigation, **36:** 189n1, 190n3; on bills Congress should pass, **36:** 249-50; on Punitive Expedition, **36:** 335, 462; WW's birthday wishes to, **37:** 165, 175; on platform suggestions, **37:** 169; photographs: *see illustration section,* **27:** 32

Burlingame, Anson, **33:** 34

Burlingham, Charles Culp, **27:** 244; **33:** 89

Burlington Railroad: *see* Chicago, Burlington and Quincy Railroad

Burner, David, **37:** 542n1

Burnet, Gilbert, **37:** 35,n7

Burnett, Frances Hodgson, **31:** 316n2, 317

Burnett, John Lawson, **30:** 273n1

Burnett immigration bill, **30:** 273n1; **31:** 234, 373-74, 463-64, 545; **32:** 14, 15-16, 26, 56, 78, 82, 87, 88, 122-23; **37:** 428; J. H. Schiff on, **32:** 77-78; C. W. Eliot on, **32:** 93, 105; hearings on, **32:** 95-98; WW's veto, **32:** 142-44; H. Bernstein on, **32:** 148; J. Addams on, **32:** 162; F. Trumbull on, **32:** 162-63; F. L. Blackmon on, **32:** 231

Burns, Allen T., **27:** 244

Burns, John, **32:** 350,n1

Burns, William John, **34:** 63, 79

Burnside, R. H., **35:** 258n1

Burnside, William A., **28:** 196,n2, 204, 224, 233

Burroughs, John, **38:** 545,n1

Burt, Andrew Sheridan, **28:** 60,n2

Burton, Ernest DeWitt, **27:** 28,n2; **28:** 22-23

Burton, Theodore Elijah, **28:** 162,n1, 163, 412,n1; **38:** 201n1

Burton, Walter C., **35:** 319,n4

business, **27:** 41-42, 88, 122, 270; **28:** 351; **29:** 7, 65, 93, 95, 97, 102, 103, 176, 337; **30:** 93-96, 110, 128-29, 190, 243-44, 249-50, 263, 282, 476; **31:** 39, 45-47, 169, 325; **32:** 34-35, 40, 149-57; **34:** 40, 52; **35:** 321-28, 427-29,n1; **36:** 111, 153-60, 475; **37:** 25-27, 191, 193; **38:** 51, 129-30, 137, 212-19, 262-70, 340-42, 591-96, 614; address to Commercial Club of Chicago, **27:** 29-39; on signing Seven Sisters bill, **27:** 120-22; remarks to southern bankers, **28:** 127-28; remarks to western bankers, **28:** 156; on use of consent decrees, **29:** 141; address on antitrust legislation, **29:** 154-58; on need for trade commission, **29:** 184-85; remarks on outlook, **30:** 128-29, 210-12; meets with National Trade Association of Wholesalers, **30:** 318-19,n3; remarks to delegation of businessmen, **30:** 378-79,n1; remarks to cotton interests, **30:** 441-42; annual message and, **31:** 415; address to Chamber of Commerce, **32:** 178-87; on defeat of ship-purchase bill and, **32:** 69-75, 316; on Tariff Commission and, **36:** 11-12; address to Associated Advertising Clubs, **37:** 324-28; addresses in Detroit on, **37:** 383-87, 387-95; and tariff bill, **27:** 301, 339-40, 410, 565-66; **30:** 129; and currency legislation, **27:** 524-25, 571; and credit, **27:** 572; and Federal Reserve bill, **28:** 378, 379, 389; interests in Mexico, **28:** 443; and resignations from corporate directorships by J. P. Morgan and associates, **29:** 101-103; and antitrust legislation, **29:** 212; **30:** 110, 173n1, 182, 183, 211-12; opposes exemption of labor and agricultural workers from antitrust legislation, **30:** 284; and emergency currency, **30:** 325-26; and federal trade commission bill, **30:** 348, 429; impact of war on, **31:** 143-44, 378; and preparedness, **36:** 60, 69; Chamber of Commerce recommendations for maintenance of world peace, **36:** 168-69,n1; and corporate tax, **38:** 51n1; B. M. Baruch on, **38:** 43-44

Δ L. D. Brandeis on, **27:** 521; F. Buchanan on, **34:** 39-41, 52; E. F. Goltra on, **29:** 50-51; S. Gompers on, **27:** 367-68; E.R.L. Gould on, **29:** 76; J. R. Gray on, **28:** 271; H. L. Higginson on, **31:** 213, 215; H. F. Hollis on, **30:** 110; E. M. House on, **29:** 103; R. S. Lovett on, **38:** 377n2; J. P. Morgan on, **31:** 82-83; W. C. Redfield on, **29:** 40, 443-46; **31:** 45-47; J. T. Robinson on trust legislation, **29:** 457-58; A. Shaw on, **32:** 68-75; JPT on, **29:** 102; **31:** 388-89; **38:** 20-21; cartoon: *see illustration section,* **29:** *see also* World War - economic impact on the United States

Business Men's League, **38:** 178n3; WW's address to, **36:** 110-14

Butler, Joseph Green, Jr., **35:** 212,n1
Butler, Nicholas Murray, **31:** 247,n1, 413,n3
Butler, Thomas Stalker, **36:** 362,n2
Butler, William Tobias, **36:** 276-77,n1
Butt, Archibald Willingham, **27:** 17,n2
Butterfield, Kenyon L., **27:** 201
Butternuts (house, Cornish, N.H.), **28:** 159n1
Buttrick, Wallace, **36:** 478,n1, 512-13, 522, 558
Buxton, Noel (Noel-Buxton, Noel Edward), **37:** 294,n2, 311-12, 345, 364, 370, 370-72, 375, 402; **38:** 54-55, 85, 258
Buzzards Bay, Mass., **30:** 303
By the Fireside (Browning), **34:** 464,n4
Byers, Tracy, **28:** 308n2
Byrd, Elinor Bolling (Mrs. Richard Evelyn), **35:** 84
Byrd, Richard Evelyn, **35:** 84, 87-88
Byrd, Thomas Bolling, **35:** 84
Byrne, James, **36:** 402; **37:** 264,n3, 268
Byrne, James Patrick, **35:** 8,n2
Byrne and Cutcheon, New York, **37:** 264n3
Byrnes, James Francis, **27:** 284,n2
Byron, George Gordon, 6th Baron Byron, **36:** 260,n2

Cabell, De Rosey Carroll, **37:** 319,n3
Cabot, Richard Clarke, **27:** 244
Cabral, Juan G., **28:** 77; **31:** 66
Cabrera, Luis, **30:** 57,n1, 118,n2, 208, 340; **31:** 66; **33:** 65; **34:** 530-31; **37:** 401; **38:** 83n1, 153, 153-54, 169, 170, 300, 301, 355, 356, 358; on border protection, **38:** 633, 635-36
cacos (Haitian insurgents), **34:** 70-71
Cadiz, Spain, **32:** 468n1
Cadwalader, Wickersham and Taft, N.Y., **38:** 566n6
Caffey, Francis Gordon, **34:** 31,n1, 42, 134; **36:** 599
Caird, Edward, **31:** 28
Calaban, **28:** 583
Calais, France, **32:** 81; **34:** 44, 84; **35:** 413
Calderón, Fernando Iglesias, **30:** 340,n1
Calderón, Ignacio, **33:** 454, 455, 487, 488; **34:** 111,n1, 157n1,2, 321, 488; **37:** 306n1
Caldwell, Anne, **35:** 258n1
Caldwell, Charles Pope, **37:** 404,n1, 413-14, 428
Caldwell, Frank Congleton, **36:** 63n1
Calero, Manuel, **28:** 339, 340; **33:** 261
Calhoun, William James, **27:** 28
California, **27:** 188, 487,n1; **28:** 107; **38:** 58, 59-60, 458, 624; and controversy with Japan over alien land legislation, **27:** 220,n4, 261, 265, 265-66, 275-76,n1, 277, 280-82, 283, 286-88, 293-94, 298, 299, 304-305, 309-10, 318-21, 323-24, 326, 338, 343n1, 344, 347, 348-

51, 360-61, 363-64, 365,n1, 371-72, 381, 382, 384, 396, 405, 415-17, 425-26, 428-30, 442-43, 448-49, 449-50, 453-55, 459, 484, 496, 501-502; **28:** 14n1, 283, 284, 305, 355n7; **30:** 169; **31:** 235-36, 236-37, 256-57,n5, 323, 463; **32:** 113-14, 171n4, 321, 322, 323; in 1916 election, **27:** 492n2; and women in politics, **30:** 172,n1; immigration and the Raker bill, **30:** 273,n1; and relief to Belgian refugees, **31:** 332; and water-power development, **36:** 51; and I.W.W. investigation, **36:** 188-90; and Chinese immigration, **36:** 515-16, 549-52, 576; oil reserves in, **37:** 65-66,n1, 111, 172,n2
California, University of, **32:** 63; **34:** 87
Call a Neutral Conference Now (Fisher), **38:** 111,n2
Callahan, Patrick Henry, **37:** 402,n1
Callaway, Fuller Earle, **31:** 524,n3, 531
Callaway, Oscar, **36:** 175,n1, 362,n2
Calles, Plutarco Elías, **28:** 77, 246,n1; **30:** 412n6, 418; **36:** 579
Calls on Germans to Vote for Hughes; New Yorker Herold Says Wilson or T. R. Supporters Merit Kicking (New York *World*), **37:** 219n3
Calvert, Peter, **28:** 429n1, 544n1, 593n2
Calzadiaz Berrera, Alberto, **36:** 280n1
Camargo, Chihuahua, Mex.: *see* Ciudad Camargo
Camb, John Adam, **31:** 7,n5
Cambon, Jules Martin, **35:** 525n3; **37:** 42; meetings with House, **36:** 125,n1, 138, 147-48,n1, 180n2, 387n1,3; Grey on peace plans and, **36:** 443, 444, 512
Cambridge, England, **38:** 681
Cambridge, Mass., **31:** 515
Cambridge Springs, Pa., **30:** 196; **36:** 337
Camden, Johnson Newlon, **32:** 173n2
Cameno, S.S., **31:** 332
Camera Club of New York, **35:** 84n1
Cameron County, Tex., **37:** 255n6
Caminetti, Anthony, **27:** 220,n3, 275; **28:** 99n4; **31:** 256-57,n3; **36:** 516, 550, 551
Caminetti, Farley Drew, **28:** 99n4
Caminetti bill, **27:** 349
Camp, John Lafayette, **27:** 227; **33:** 474
Camp Abneki, **38:** 565,n5
Camp Emery, Washington, D.C., **34:** 534n1
campaign contributions, **30:** 202
Campaign Literature Issued by the Democratic National Committee, **38:** 465n
Campaigns for Progressivism and Peace 1916-1917: see Wilson: Campaigns for Progressivism and Peace
Campbell, Henry Colin, **37:** 220,n4
Campbell, John McLeod, **31:** 28
Campbell, Richard Kenna, **37:** 414n1
Campeche (state), Mex., **28:** 31, 73, 76, 77, 341
Can the Kaiser Defeat the President? (New York *World*), **37:** 219n3

Canada, **27:** 203, 222, 464; **28:** 463; **31:** 218, 229, 425, 501, 513; **32:** 118; **35:** 427, 428, 534; **36:** 57, 66, 320n1, 368, 445; and Mexico, **28:** 573-74, 575; and Ship Registry Act of 1914, **30:** 326; and cable messages, **30:** 389; Prime Minister, *see* Borden, Sir Robert Laird

Canada, William Wesley, **28:** 219,n1, 225, 300; **31:** 431n1; **33:** 459-60, 460; **34:** 383-85, 386-87, 408-409

Canadian Boundaries Commission, **27:** 71

Canadian Industrial Disputes Investigation Act, **38:** 94

Canadian Pacific Railroad, **30:** 295; **31:** 444

Canadian Vickers, Ltd., **31:** 425n1

Cananea, Mex., **27:** 424-25

Cananea Consolidated Copper Co., Mex., **28:** 278n3

Candelaria Mining Co., Mex., **28:** 41n1

Candler, Warren Akin, **32:** 429,n2, 431; **35:** 45-46

Canning, George, **36:** 320n1

Cannon, Joseph Gurney, **35:** 339,n2; **36:** 212; **37:** 174

Canova, Leon Joseph, **30:** 148,n2, 180, 188, 283n1, 285-86,n1, 303n1, 348; **33:** 448, 467,n1; and Villa-Carranza break, **30:** 383n1

Canton, S.S., **31:** 477

Cap Haïtien, Haiti, **34:** 61, 70, 142, 165

Cape May County, N.J., **27:** 379; **34:** 292, 326-27

Caperton, William Banks, **34:** 45,n1, 61, 70, 121, 133, 143, 144, 164-65; **37:** 157, 158,n3

capital: S. Gompers on, **27:** 183

Capmany, Rafael Zubarán: *see* Zubarán Capmany, Rafael

Capper, Arthur, **36:** 87n1, 89n2, 96n1, 100n1, 140n2

Capper, Florence Crawford (Mrs. Arthur), **36:** 140,n1,2

Caprivi, Count Leo von, **32:** 381, 382

Carbajal, Francisco S., **30:** 97,n2, 285n2, 290, 360,n1

Carden, Anne Eliza Lefferts, Lady Carden, **28:** 411

Carden, Sir Lionel Edward Gresley, **28:** 376,n1, 384, 388, 420-21, 428-29,n1, 433, 434, 444, 447, 461, 465-66, 468, 469, 471, 477, 516, 526, 528, 529, 530, 537, 539, 562, 565, 566, 573, 578,n1, 587, 591-92, 601; **30:** 4, 58, 59, 79, 82, 134; **31:** 61,n1, 145-46

Cardenas, Francisco, **27:** 549

Cardenas, Miguel, **30:** 167, 168

Cardoso de Oliveira, José Manuel, **30:** 80, 290,n1, 291; **31:** 18,n1; **32:** 326n1, 331-32, 427n1,2, 437n1; **33:** 239,n1, 343n1, 344n1, 459-60, 460, 465n1

Cardozo, Benjamin Nathan, **37:** 264,n5

Carib, S.S., **36:** 615

Caribbean Construction Company, **34:** 66n1

Carlin, Charles Creighton, **30:** 210,n2; **31:** 43, 138; **34:** 466n1

Carlisle, Cumberland, England: illuminated address from, **29:** 12, 24, 34, 59, 61, 75

Carlson, George Alfred, **31:** 273n2, 474, 503, 517, 545; **35:** 537-38

Carlyle, Thomas, **27:** 461; **30:** 90; **31:** 28; **34:** 140; **38:** 532

Carmichael, Otto, **31:** 274

Carnegie, Andrew, **27:** 216; **29:** 29, 351-52, 417; **30:** 334; **31:** 143, 152n3; **38:** 549, 562, 621, 625; and Berea College, **29:** 342, 351, 537,n1; **30:** 6, 43-44, 62-63, 63; on withdrawing forces from Mexico, **30:** 61-62; on ship-purchase bill, **32:** 167

Carnegie Corporation, **30:** 6

Carnegie Endowment for International Peace, **30:** 354,n1, 435n1; **38:** 314n2

Carnegie Foundation, **27:** 240-41; **30:** 62

Carnegie Hall, N.Y., **33:** 469n3; **35:** 120,n1, 141; **36:** 186n1, 635; **37:** 519n1; **38:** 284; Jane Addams' speech in, **34:** 251,n6,8

Carnegie Institution of Washington, **27:** 45n1

Carnegie, Phipps and Co., **35:** 434n1

Carnegie Steel Co., **27:** 216,n1

Carolina Hotel, Pinehurst, N.C., **36:** 435,n1

Caroline Islands, **32:** 277

Carothers, George C., **28:** 570,n1; **29:** 334,n2, 375, 450,n1, 480-81, 490, 498; **30:** 29,n2, 148, 180, 230n1, 285, 290, 297-98, 301n1; **31:** 313n1; **32:** 383,n2, 384, 386n2, 387, 388; **33:** 29,n2, 305; **36:** 282-83; and Benton affair, **29:** 285n1; and translation of Carranza's reply to W. J. Bryan, **29:** 483-85; on meeting with F. Villa, **29:** 494-95; **30:** 311; note from Villa, **29:** 504-505; on Carranza and Villa, **30:** 193-94, 339-40, 340, 383n1; friendship with Villa, **30:** 347; and Fuller report, **30:** 413, 416, 417

Carr, Clyde Mitchel, **27:** 29,n2

Carrancistas, **28:** 57, 141, 340; **29:** 110n1, 182; **30:** 48, 69, 70, 71, 92, 98, 199, 230n1, 301n1; **32:** 388; **33:** 65n1, 239n1, 459, 460, 475; **34:** 147, 287, 382n1, 401, 455, 456; **36:** 395n1, 397, 407n1, 457,n2; **37:** 38, 249, 250, 251n4, 261, 263n2, 277n1, 280,n3, 306, 350n1; **38:** 225, 381; recapture Torreón, **29:** 382n1

Carranza, Venustiano, **27:** 422n1; **28:** 6, 29, 31, 59, 72, 73, 76, 77, 80, 141, 178, 196, 213, 216, 298, 340, 342, 486, 505, 529, 558, 559-60,n1, 563-64, 567, 569, 579-80; **29:** 169, 331, 334, 338; **30:** 39, 42, 47, 57,n1, 208, 389; **31:** 179, 206, 233, 380, 431; **32:** 202,n3, 280, 331, 342,

Carranza, Venustiano (*cont.*)
343, 355-56, 389, 390, 398n1, 404; **33:**
12, 29, 43, 69n1, 71, 259, 260, 261, 271-
72, 295, 305, 409-10, 448, 459-60, 463,
464, 476, 488; **34:** 41n2, 160, 241-42,
273,n1, 338-39, 346, 378n2, 382n1, 388,
427, 437, 488, 530; **35:** 45, 134, 359;
36: 280n1; **37:** 15, 19, 121, 153, 154,
250, 300, 309n1, 310, 322, 331-32, 344,
346, 362, 452, 482, 483, 497; **38:** 223,
230, 300, 355, 356, 359,n2, 360, 362,
408, 633
Escudero memorandum on, **28:** 70n1;
military plans, **28:** 541-43; and U.S.
intervention, **28:** 543; desires not too
early a triumph, **29:** 90; sends L. Cabrera to Washington, **29:** 142, 187-89,
191-95; and U.S. note on possible intervention, **29:** 143; and communications between Mexico City and Veracruz, **29:** 161; and raising the arms
embargo, **29:** 205-206; Cabrera's pam-
phlet and, **29:** 249n2; and T. B. Hohler
memorandum, **29:** 252, 253, 260; and
Benton affair, **29:** 293, 320n1; rejects
idea of a northern republic, **29:** 295;
and finances, **29:** 296-97; tries to appear independent of U.S., **29:** 348; and
Spaniards in Mexico, **29:** 416, 417; and
U.S. landing at Veracruz, **29:** 480; on
Huerta, **29:** 484; statement on U.S. intervention, **29:** 484-85, 489, 490-91,
504-505; seeks to avoid armed conflict,
29: 486; and F. Villa, **29:** 494; **30:**
303n1, 340, 346-48, 441, 450; **31:** 73;
36: 301, 310; asks WW for meeting of
representatives, **29:** 495; U.S. desires
neutrality of, **29:** 497-98; and W. J.
Bryan on mediation, **29:** 524-25; and
peace mediation, **29:** 552; British views
of, **30:** 9, 42, 131
ABC mediation: plans, **30:** 45, 50, 66,
67, 76, 88, 99, 101n2, 113, 118,n1,2,
120-21; letter to mediators, **30:** 101-102,
114; objects to mediation except of
Tampico incident, **30:** 114; and discussion of entire Mexican situation, **30:**
122, 123-26, 132-33; WW wants representative of at talks, **30:** 135,n1,2;
may send representative on mediators' terms, **30:** 136; and membership
in possible provisional government, **30:**
83, 199
desires to take Mexico City, **30:** 81;
W. J. Bryan on provisional presidency
and, **30:** 138, 139; WW on, **30:** 143; and
L. J. Canova, **30:** 148,n2, 180, 285; and
break with Villa, **30:** 193-94,n1, 383n1;
and Zacatecas affair, **30:** 193n2; and
advance toward Mexico City, **30:** 285n1;
and reconciliation with Villa, **30:** 285-
86n1; willing to meet with representatives of F. S. Carbajal, **30:** 290; agrees
to suspend military operations during
conference, **30:** 290, 291

U.S. recognition: conditions important
to, **30:** 297; and importance of, **30:** 321-
22; E. M. House on, **30:** 463-64; seeks
U.S. recognition, **33:** 9-10; J. Lind recommends, **33:** 45-47; possibilities of, **33:**
414, 415, 415-16, 419, 436n2; pros and
cons of, **34:** 112, 149n1, 198-200,
242,n1, 385, 509-10, 512,n1, 540-41; **35:**
93-94, 94, 95, 97-103, 254; recognized
as First Chief of the Constitutionalists, **30:** 301n1
Villa fears Torreón agreement will not
be honored, **30:** 311, 339; personal
wealth, **30:** 340; Cardinal Gibbons
critical of, **30:** 341; and H. J. Browne,
30: 346n1; demands arms from Carbajal, **30:** 360,n1; causes apprehension
in Mexico City, **30:** 361; Villa on support for presidency of, **30:** 393; and
F. Angeles, **30:** 410; and J. M. Maytorena, **30:** 412; desires A. Obregón to
accompany Villa to Sonora, **30:** 417;
and decree establishing claims commission, **30:** 443,n1; and Division of the
North, **30:** 447; assumes executive authority, **30:** 449-50; and P. Fuller, **30:**
463, 495; and plans for permanent
government, **30:** 489-90; and E. Zapata, **30:** 490; **31:** 68-69, 70n1; on
evacuation of U.S. troops, **31:** 18, 313;
reply to WW, **31:** 74-75; WW on retirement, **31:** 322; and U.S. ultimatum on
safety of Americans, **32:** 332, 346-49,
353, 363; and Progreso blockade, **32:**
367,n1, 369-70,n1, 408-409; and Menocal, **32:** 408n1; and food supply, **33:**
307-308, 447, 466; and Declaration to
the People of Mexico, **33:** 308n1,
398,n1, 417,n2; and Gonzalez Garza,
33: 343n1, 344; and armistice possibilities, **33:** 465-66,n2; and Japan, **33:**
467n1; plan for deposition of, **33:** 533n1;
WW against elimination from provisional government, **34:** 164,n1; and
mediation proposals, **34:** 321, 383n1,
383-85, 448, 455,n1; and National City
Bank, **34:** 401,n1; and constituent assembly, **34:** 531; and programs for
Mexico, **34:** 532; and Punitive Expedition, **36:** 308,n1, 313,n1, 318-19,n1,
340, 342,n2, 343, 343-44, 434, 456, 464,
502; desires withdrawal of U.S. troops,
36: 540,n1, 581, 582; on Obregón-Scott
conferences, **36:** 541, 580, 603; U.S.
warning to, **37:** 248-63; and Joint High
Commission, **37:** 400, 401, 490;
P. Fuller on, **31:** 66; P. N. Furber on, **30:**
246; H. A. Garfield on, **29:** 496; W. B.
Hale on, **29:** 130; R. Lansing on, **33:**
475; D. Lawrence on, **37:** 486, 487, 489;
M. Letcher on, **29:** 280; J. Lind on, **29:**
17-18, 31, 550, 551; **30:** 113,n2; E. E.
Martinez on, **34:** 174, 175; J. L. Portillo y Rojas on, **29:** 358; J. Reed on,

30: 42n1; E. Root on, **36:** 186n1; J. R. Silliman on, **30:** 166-67, 167-69; L. Steffens on, **34:** 147-48; F. Villa on, **30:** 194, 220-21, 411-12, 415, 445; D. West, **33:** 65n1; photograph: *illustration section,* 31

Carratalá, Alfredo de Mariatequi y: *see* Mariatequi y Carratalá, Alfredo de

Carrizal incident: *see* Mexico and the United States

Carroll, Francis, **28:** 275,n1, 289

Carroll, Henry King, **30:** 398

Carson, Edward Henry, Sir, **33:** 227n4, 484

Carson, James S., **36:** 364,n1

Cartegena, Colombia, **34:** 50

Carter, Alice Henry (Mrs. John Franklin), **28:** 20,n4, 63; **34:** 73,n2, 89, 101

Carter, Edward Broadway, **27:** 39,n1

Carter, Henry, **28:** 20n4

Carter, John, **28:** 20n4

Carter, John Franklin, **28:** 20n4; **34:** 73,n2, 89, 101; **38:** 628,n3

Carter, Lawrence, **28:** 20n4

Carter, Lewis, **28:** 20n4

Carter, Paul, **28:** 20n4

Carter, Percival, **28:** 20n4

Carter, Sallie, **28:** 20n4

Carter, Wade H., **31:** 313

Carter, William Samuel, **38:** 30, 31n1, 48, 93, 94

Carteret Club of Jersey City, **27:** 386n1

Carver, Clifford Nickels, **34:** 42,n1, 310, 315

Carver, Thomas Nixon, **29:** 352

Caryll, Ivan, **35:** 258n1

Casa Obrero Mundial, **37:** 245

Casas Grandes, Chihuahua, Mex., **36:** 339, 352, 353, 571; **37:** 251

Case for Wilson (Lippmann), **38:** 275,n4

Casement, Sir Roger David, **36:** 563,n1,2, 566,n2; **37:** 106n1, 344, 353,n1, 379-80,n2, 446, 446-47, 516n1, 517n1; **38:** 5, 255, 256, 315, 316, 350, 443-45

Casenave, Jean Marie Maurice, **32:** 377,n1; **34:** 69,n1, 184

Casey, John Joseph, **29:** 538

Caso, Ángel, **31:** 69

Castillo, Juan, **36:** 653

Castillo Brito, Manuel, **28:** 73, 76

Castine, U.S.S., **34:** 165

Castle Point (Hoboken, N.J.), **27:** 75, 76

Castrejón, Martin, **28:** 77

Castrillo, Salvador, Jr., **27:** 470,n3

Castro, Cipriano, **27:** 145,n1; **28:** 107, 543, 544

Castro, Rafael, **37:** 251,n3

Castro Quesada, Manuel: *see* Quesada, Manuel Castro

Castro Ruiz, Carlos, **32:** 474,n2; **37:** 238,n1, 239, 242-43, 243

Catholic Church: *see* Roman Catholic Church

Catholic party (Mex.), **28:** 324n1, 325, 334; **29:** 120, 328, 329, 359

Catholic University of America, **37:** 475

Catlin, Mr. (American in Mex.), **28:** 296,n4

Catt, Carrie Clinton Lane Chapman (Mrs. George William), **34:** 251,n3; **35:** 30; **37:** 237, 266, 490, 491, 513n1, 539-40; **38:** 7, 19-20, 30-31, 87, 125, 161,n1,2

Caucasus, **35:** 104

Causes Behind Mexican Revolution (Reed), **30:** 42,n1

Cavazos, José, **36:** 586,n3

Cavell, Edith Louisa, **35:** 103,n1,2, 147-48,n1,2,3, 491

Cecil, Lord Robert (Edgar Algernon Robert Gascoyne–), **35:** 471,n1,2; **37:** 459,n3, 462; **38:** 54

Cecil, Robert Arthur Talbot, Gascoyne, 3rd Marquess of Salisbury: *see* Salisbury, Robert Arthur Talbot Gascoyne–Cecil, 3rd Marquess of

Cecil, Lamar, **33:** 298n1

Cedar Hill Coal and Coke Co., **29:** 549

Celaya, Guanajuato, Mex., **33:** 272; battles in, **33:** 7,n1, 29n1

Celebration of the Rededication of Congress Hall . . . , **28:** 439n

censorship: and cable and wireless messages, **30:** 388-89, 407-408; **31:** 506; of mails, **31:** 443, 443-44; Lansing on State Department and, **36:** 254-55, 257

Census Bureau, **27:** 337-38; segregation in, **28:** 60, 403

Central America, **27:** ix, 145, 169, 172, 215, 335,n1; **28:** 48, 55, 56, 110, 125, 170-71, 228, 231, 434, 464, 543, 577, 585, 587, 588; **29:** 52, 53, 134, 230, 231, 524; **30:** 209, 235, 287; **31:** 355, 416; **33:** 454; **35:** 254, 294-95; **37:** 181; and European interests, **29:** 11; E. G. Lowry on WW's policy in Mexico, **29:** 92-98; and Bryan-Chamorro treaty, **29:** 152, 172; T. R. Marshall on U.S. policy in, **29:** 419; McAdoo and Pan American Financial Conference, **31:** 244, 258; WW and EBW feted by diplomats from, **35:** 372-73, 396

Central Federated Labor Union of New York, **37:** 316n1

Central News Service, **36:** 308, 332

Central Organization for a Durable Peace, **35:** 20n1, 196,n2

Central Park, N.Y., **28:** 321n2

Central Presbyterian Church, Wash., D.C., **27:** 351,n1, 357; **28:** 263, 362; **29:** 44-45; **33:** 49n1; **35:** 371n1

Central Railroad (Mex.), **30:** 220

Central Relief Committee, **32:** 97n13

Central Trust Company of New York, **29:** 67n2

Century, The, **27:** 411; **37:** 201n1

Century Cyclopedia of Names, **30:** 142; **36:** 161

Century Dictionary, **30:** 142

Century of Disagreement: The Chamizal Conflict 1864-1964 (Liss), **27:** 437n1

Cervantes, Federico, **29:** 18; **36:** 280n1
Céspedes y Quesada, Carlos Manuel de, **35:** 129-30,n1, 176; **37:** 343-44,n1, 358
Chadbourn, Philip H., **35:** 520-21,n1
Challener, Richard Delo, **27:** xxi, 441n1, 448n1, 518n2
Challenging Years: The Memoirs of Harriot Stanton Blatch (Blatch and Lutz), **37:** 427n4
Chalmers, Hugh, **30:** 318-19,n2,3
Chamber of Commerce of Cleveland, **36:** 41n1
Chamber of Commerce of New York, **29:** 93
Chamber of Commerce of the United States: *see* United States Chamber of Commerce
Chamberlain, George Earle, **27:** 276n1, 337, 513, 515, 534; **29:** 333n1; **31:** 458; **34:** 58,n1, 481,n1, 503, 504, 512; **35:** 106, 138; **36:** 311,n1; **37:** 381
Chamberlain, Joseph, **32:** 21n1, 66
Chamberlain, (Joseph) Austen, **33:** 89,n3, 227n4, 484; **35:** 436-37, 484
Chamberlain bill, **36:** 640, 643; *see also* Army reorganization bill
Chambers, F. R., **37:** 211,n1
Chambers, Laura Ligon Clopton (Mrs. William Lea), **34:** 249,n1
Chambers, William Lea, **30:** 305-307,n1, 313-14, 314, 343-44; **32:** 429,n3; **34:** 248, 249, 274; **37:** 438-39, 525,n1; **38:** 12,n1, 30-31, 32, 48-49, 199-200
Chambers, William Nesbitt, **35:** 337,n1, 349
Chamizal case, **27:** 437,n1
Chamorro, Emiliano, **27:** 470,n3; **28:** 101,n1, 250; **29:** 134, 172, 204
Chancellor, Sir John Robert, **36:** 607n1; **37:** 73,n2
Chandler, Appleton P., Jr., **33:** 430n2
Chandler, William Eaton, **27:** 178,n1; **31:** 543,n1, 551
Chandler, William Marion, **32:** 97
Chandler-Dunbar Water Power Co. (Michigan), **30:** 218,n3
Chang-chia-k'ou, China, **32:** 418
Chang Yin Tang, **27:** 224,n1
Chanler Brothers Bankers (Philadelphia), **34:** 279
Chao, Manuel, **28:** 213; **32:** 384
Chapultepec, Federal District, Mex., **31:** 69
Chapultepec Castle, **29:** 280, 446
Character of Democracy in the United States (Wilson), **27:** 15-16
Charles, Arthur, **31:** 232
Charles Evans Hughes (Pusey), **37:** 203n5
Charles Francis Adams, by His Son, Charles Francis Adams (Morse, ed.), **38:** 179,n3
Charles Francis Joseph (Charles I of Austria), **38:** 71,n4
Charleville, France, **38:** 495,n1, 496n3

Charlotte, N.C., **37:** 67n1; WW address in, **37:** 79-83
Charnwood, 1st Baron: *see* Benson, Godfrey Rathbone, 1st Baron Charnwood
Chase, John, **30:** 49,n1, 60,n1; **31:** 335
Chase National Bank, N.Y., **27:** 79n2; **31:** 139n2,4
Chasing Villa (Tompkins), **36:** 280n1
Chatham County, Ga., **28:** 179n1
Chattanooga, U.S.S., **29:** 443
Chautauqua, **27:** 58,n2; **28:** 292, 302,n3; **33:** 431, 472
Chefoo, China, **27:** 465,n1
Chekiang Province, China, **32:** 137, 421
Chemnitz, Germany, **35:** 194,n2
Cheng-hsiang, Lu, **35:** 204,n2
Chengchia Tun affair, **38:** 150,n1, 151-52
Chernovtsy, Russia: *see* Czernowitz, Rumania
Cherokee Indians, **27:** 469, 507-508
Chesapeake and Ohio Railway Co., **31:** 21n1, 531; **37:** 439n1
Chester, Mass., **34:** 63
Chester, U.S.S., **29:** 86, 98,n1
Chesterton, Gilbert Keith, **28:** 531; **38:** 331, 593
Chestnut Hill, Mass., **31:** 453
Chevalley, Daniel Abel, **29:** 11,n2
Chevy Chase, Md., **36:** 572n1
Chevy Chase Club, Wash., D.C., **30:** 103-n1
Chiao-chou Wan, China, **32:** 248
Chicago, Ill., **28:** 547; **31:** 471; WW address to Commercial Club, **27:** 29-39; bankers on Federal Reserve bill, **28:** 379,n1; reaction to Federal Reserve bill in, **29:** 76; and *Eastland* disaster, **34:** 27,n1, 65,n1, 217; WW's address on preparedness in, **36:** 63-73; and I.W.W. investigation, **36:** 189; and postmaster appointment, **36:** 576-77,n1, 602-603,n1; **38:** 146,n1, 181; primary elections in, **38:** 275,n5; WW's addresses in, **38:** 481-89, 489-93
Chicago, University of, **27:** 208; **28:** 22; **29:** 352; **30:** 396n1; **32:** 20n1, 78n1; **35:** 135n1; **38:** 182n1, 518,n1
Chicago *Abendpost*, **33:** 361; **38:** 46, 64, 351n1
Chicago and Alton Railroad, **29:** 140,n3
Chicago Association of Commerce, **29:** 500-501
Chicago, Burlington and Quincy Railroad, **30:** 344; **38:** 38n2
Chicago Chamber of Commerce, **30:** 243, 244, 267,n1, 268
Chicago *Daily Journal*, **27:** 241n1
Chicago *Daily News*, **34:** 65n1, 370n1,2; **35:** 525n3; **37:** 43,n4; **38:** 73, 90
Chicago Daily Tribune, **34:** 377n1; **36:** 63n, 73n; **38:** 146n1, 481n1, 489n,n1, 493n
Chicago Defender, **31:** 301n

Chicago Federation of Labor, **34:** 27n1, 136n2; **37:** 402,n2

Chicago Herald, **30:** 311,n1; **32:** 244n1,2; **33:** 28n1; **36:** 287

Chicago Nipple Manufacturing Co., **38:** 146n1

Chicago Press Club: WW's address to, **38:** 475-81

Chicago *Sonntagpost*, **38:** 351n1

Chicago Tribune, **27:** 565n1; **31:** 338; **34:** 27n1, 437, 443

Chihuahua, Chihuahua, Mex., **30:** 311, 339, 408, 413, 416; **31:** 69, 73; **32:** 384; **33:** 260; **36:** 457,n1,2, 503, 591; **37:** 121, 263,n2, 277n1, 285, 293, 315; **38:** 271,n1, 293, 362, 398, 399, 546, 547

Chihuahua state, Mex., **27:** 422,n1; **28:** 30, 41, 101, 213, 341; **29:** 252; **30:** 221, 347; **34:** 531; **35:** 478n1; **36:** 503, 519n1, 554; **37:** 250, 255, 256; **38:** 230-31, 232, 233, 234, 235, 373, 404, 676; M. Letcher report on conditions in, **29:** 278-80; F. Villa and, **29:** 279-80; and Benton affair, **29:** 285n1, 293, 334

Chilbert, Joseph, **28:** 427

Child, Clifton James, **34:** 116n2

child labor, **27:** 78; **28:** 509n1; **29:** 170,n1; and 1916 platform plank, **37:** 175, 198, 200n3; O. R. Lovejoy, **27:** 107; A. J. McKelway, **27:** 108

child-labor bill: *see* Keating-Owen child-labor bill

Children's Bureau, **27:** 76,n1, 78, 108-109,n1, 233n2; **29:** 400, 417-18; **38:** 123n1, 161n2

Children's Emancipation Day (McKelway), **38:** 284n1

Childs, Mary M., **31:** 329-30,n1

Childs, Ralph David, **28:** 108,n1

Childs, Richard Spencer, **27:** 244

Chile, **28:** 506; **29:** 47, 135, 524; **30:** 23, 41-42, 121; **34:** 80, 81, 444, 448, 488; **35:** 254; **36:** 198-201, 229-30, 278, 333, 380, 398, 403, 445, 461, 479, 596-97, 605; **37:** 122, 238, 241-44, 486; **38:** 18-19, 116; and Mexico, **27:** 540, 546, 548; **28:** 141,n2, 412, 516; **32:** 117-18, 263, 398n1; **33:** 305-306, 437, 455, 487, 488; ministerial possibilities, **27:** 110,n2, 385; crisis with U.S., **28:** 188,n1; and conciliation treaty, **29:** 342; appointments to, **29:** 449; will not recognize Huerta, **29:** 484; and ABC mediation offer, **29:** 505-506,n1, 507, 518, 525, 534, 539-40; on recognition of provisional government of Mexico, **30:** 87; WW and telegram of thanks to, **30:** 259; **30:** 262,n1; Pan-American pact: and House's negotiations for, **30:** 271; **31:** 470, 498, 540, 549, 552; draft sent to, **31:** 471-72,n1; negotiations for, **32:** 64, 338-39, 339-40, 474, 478, 542; **33:** 52, 56-57, 62, 63, 65, 68, 77-80, 220; **35:** 54-55, 111, 126, 162-63, 215-16, 519, 519-20; and Peru, **32:** 474,n3,4; **33:** 53-54, 63; **35:** 55, 126, 216; talk of new U.S. ambassador to, **35:** 64; *see also* Mexico and the United States—ABC mediation; Pan-American Conferences on Mexico

Chile and the United States, 1800-1962 (Pike), **28:** 188n1

Chillicothe, Ohio, **38:** 524

Chilton, Mary Elizabeth Wilson (Mrs. William Edwin, Sr.), **29:** 405, 410

Chilton, William Edwin, **29:** 405, 410; **36:** 86,n1, 606; **38:** 277, 457

Chin-Chin, or a Modern Aladdin, **35:** 258n1

China, **30:** 238; **34:** 84; asks for Christian prayers, **27:** 328-30

and Japan: general, **27:** 305, 452; **28:** 268, 287; **30:** 362-63; **36:** 411, 428; and Japanese customs appointments in, **31:** 547; and 21 demands on China, **32:** 120,n2, 135-37, 137-38, 139,n1, 148, 169-71, 273, 287, 333n1, 353, 367,n1, 368, 415, 416-21, 426, 434-35, 435-36, 436-37,n1, 460, 461, 466-67, 499-500, 500-501, 524-25; Japanese military preparations in, **32:** 433,n1 and Japan's ultimatum to, **33:** 104-105; and further Japanese demands, **38:** 150-52

and Russia, **27:** 488-89; and recognition of Mexico, **28:** 460; Philippine Islands and Chinese, **29:** 148; P. S. Reinsch on, **31:** 364-67, 509-13; **38:** 439-40; and Great Britain, **33:** 121, 131-32,n1; W. Kent suggests commission for better understanding, **36:** 546; and Russo-Japanese treaty, **37:** 382, 408; new president of, **37:** 167,n1

China and the United States, **27:** ix, 224-25, 285, 488-90; **28:** 401, 490; **29:** 118; **30:** 238; **31:** 283,n1; **33:** 70, 80, 81, 85, 153-54; **34:** 25-26; **37:** 181; J. W. Bashford on, **27:** 27-28n1; C. R. Crane on, **27:** 203; gift scroll sent to WW, **27:** 465-66; investments for American business, **27:** 489; D. S. Jordan on immigration, **27:** 309-10; proposed movement of U.S. ships, **27:** 441, 443, 444, 446-47; and U.S. recognition of, **27:** 144-45, 249-50, 261-62, 267,n2, 273, 330, 340, 381-82; resolutions of Federal Council of the Churches of Christ in America, **27:** 231,n3; selection of minister to, **27:** 14, 28, 58, 62, 65, 70, 110, 124, 131, 167,n1, 179, 190, 203n1, 214-15, 247,n2, 259, 262-63, 275, 283, 492; **28:** 4, 5, 15n1, 22-23; Six-Power loan, **27:** 174-75, 192-94, 210, 218, 237, 248-49, 439, 495,n1; Huntington Wilson on, **27:** 196-97, 210; Boxer Rebellion, **29:** 292, 331; and neutrality, **30:** 362-63, 470; and Japan, **30:** 391, 396n1; **35:** 115-16, 128,n1, 128-29, 143-44, 163-64, 173-74, 289-90, 517; treaty between, **31:** 64,n1; harassment of Chinese students, **31:** 101; and immigration, **31:**

China and the United States (*cont.*)
283n1; P. S. Reinsch on, **31:** 284-88, 366-67, 511-13; **32:** 328-30; Sun Yat-sen and Morgan loan, **31:** 372-73, 381; Bryan on Sun Yat-sen and Yüan Shih-k'ai conflict, **31:** 381-82; and U.S. loan, **31:** 508; **32:** 502; **33:** 99-100, 349, 350-51; **37:** 19, 232-33, 234-36, 271, 534, 537; and crisis over Japan's 21 demands, **32:** 139,n1, 169-71, 177, 197, 246-47, 247, 248, 269-71, 319-22, 322-23, 391, 421, 458-59, 459-61, 517, 519, 519-20, 520-21, 529,n1; **33:** 23-26, 31-37, 82-84, 95-99, 102-104, 113-15, 131,n1; American missionaries on situation in, **32:** 508,n1, 529; WW feels need to defend, **32:** 531; on trade possibilities between, **33:** 31-35; WW on religion and, **33:** 51; Bryan's caveat, **33:** 101,n1, 140-41, 141; WW on death of Yüan Shih-k'ai, **37:** 167,n2, 182
China, S.S., **36:** 269n1; **37:** 184n2
Chinchou, Manchuria, **31:** 510
Chinda, Viscount Sutemi, **27:** 161-62, 288, 293-94, 305, 315-21, 403, 412, 415, 428-30, 432, 441, 448, 450, 453-55,n1, 459, 460,n1, 493n1, 494, 495-96, 498-502; **28:** 16, 17, 268, 274, 282-83, 284-86, 287, 303-307, 312-15; **29:** 91; **30:** 169-70, 273n1; **31:** 235-36, 254-57; **32:** 433, 519, 531; **33:** 81-82,n2, 82-84, 95, 97, 99, 102-104, 105, 107, 113, 131; **35:** 115-16, 163-64; and California alien land legislation, **27:** 425-26,n1, 442, 450-51; **32:** 113-14; and Japan's 21 demands on China, **32:** 246,n2, 269, 270, 414, 415, 416-21, 426, 499; and news leaks, **32:** 500,n1; congratulates WW on his engagement, **35:** 36
Chinese-American relations: *see* China and the United States
Chinese immigration, **36:** 549-52, 576
Chinese Maritime Customs Service, **31:** 509
Chinese National Railway Corp., **27:** 237n1
Ching, Hsu Shan, **36:** 551,n2
Choate, Joseph Hodges, **27:** 222; **29:** 93, 410, 412; **30:** 152, 154; **33:** 17, 18; **38:** 275
Choate, Rufus, **37:** 121
Chosen: *see* Korea
Christ Church, Suffern, N.Y., **38:** 396n1
Christian X (of Denmark), **30:** 143n1; **35:** 350,n1
Christian Science, **35:** 151
Christian Science Monitor, **32:** 174
Christmas, Its Unfinished Business (Crothers), **35:** 343,n3
Chronicle of a Generation: An Autobiography (Fosdick), **29:** 327n1
Church of England: in Wales, **30:** 61,n2
Church Peace Union of New York, **38:** 276n1
Churchill, Mabel Harlakenden Hall (Mrs.

Winston), **28:** 360,n1, 368,n1; **34:** 178,n1, 195
Churchill, Thomas William, **27:** 246; **38:** 602n1
Churchill, Winston (American author), **27:** 189n1, 200; **28:** 360,n1, 368,n1; **33:** 452n3, 543; **35:** 103, 106
Churchill, Winston Leonard Spencer, **32:** 361,n1; **33:** 121, 255, 268, 484
Churchill Inn, Cornish, N.H., **28:** 55,n7, 368
cientificos (Mex.), **27:** 537; **28:** 75, 78; **29:** 118; **30:** 40, 92, 131; **33:** 4, 5; **34:** 242
Cincinnati, Ohio: segregation protest in, **28:** 343; and American Union Against Militarism meeting in, **36:** 636; WW speeches in, **38:** 524-25, 526-33, 534-37, 537-43
Cincinnati, U.S.S., **27:** 426n1; **30:** 385
Cincinnati, University of, **38:** 526n1
Cincinnati Enquirer, **31:** 446n1; **38:** 525n, 526n1, 533n, 534n1, 537n,n1, 543
Cincinnati *Times-Star*, **38:** 177n2
Citizen Soldiers: The Plattsburgh Training Camp Movement, 1913-1920 (Clifford), **34:** 133n1, 337n1
citizenship, **37:** 219; and California alien land legislation, **27:** 281, 304, 309-10, 320, 326, 338,n3, 343n1, 344, 347, 360, 363-64, 365,n1, 371-72, 416, 448, 496; and A. B. Fall resolution, **28:** 68, 82,n1; and Japanese, **28:** 14n1, 16-17, 18, 21; **29:** 199; **31:** 257n5; Negroes and, **28:** 492; Porto Rico and, **28:** 366,n2; **29:** 264n1, 273; **37:** 455-56; Kaneko case in California, **29:** 243; WW on, **35:** 39,n3, 306-307; **38:** 489-93; Higginson on dual, **35:** 217; Swedish-Americans and Hillstrom case, **35:** 283n1; and Chinese, **36:** 550-51
Citizenship Convention: WW's address to, **37:** 414-18,n1
Citrus Growers Association of Florida: *see* Florida Citrus Exchange
City of Marseilles, S.S., **36:** 232-33
Ciudad Camargo (Santa Rosalia), Chihuahua, Mex., **30:** 392,n1, 409, 411, 416
Ciudad Juárez, Chihuahua, Mex., **28:** 28; **29:** 285,n1,3, 294-95, 494, 495; **30:** 220, 290, 339, 408, 416; **33:** 474; **34:** 530, 531; **36:** 570; **37:** 251n4, 280n3, 315, 360; **38:** 45, 547
Ciudad Victoria, Tamaulipas, Mex., **28:** 570; **31:** 24
Civic Club of New York, **37:** 308n2
Civic League of St. Louis, **36:** 110,n2
Civic Service House, Boston, **32:** 97
civil service, **29:** 23, 449; and fourth-class postmasters, **27:** 160; and segregation, **28:** 117, 408; WW on, **36:** 504
Civil Service Act of 1883, **28:** 272n1
civil service bill, **36:** 640
Civil Service Commission, **27:** xvi, 434; **29:** 100, 309,n1; **36:** 503,n2, 504
Civil War (U.S.), **27:** 228; **28:** 214, 348,

414; **30:** 110-11, 185, 472; **31:** 140, 154, 196, 279; **32:** 218, 445, 449n1, 506; **33:** 267, 288, 289, 457; **34:** 22, 29, 84, 534-35; **35:** 131, 223n1, 532; **37:** 124, 175, 184,n2, 222-23; **38:** 109; monument to women of the Confederacy, **29:** 322-23; WW's remarks at unveiling of memorial to Confederate veterans, **30:** 141-42; WW on, **36:** 109, 160-61

Clafin, John, **28:** 375,n1

Clansman, The (Dixon), **32:** 142n1

Clapham, Ashton G., **33:** 542,n2; **34:** 221, 241

Clapp, Moses Edwin, **29:** 227; **32:** 172n1; **37:** 101-102

Claremont, N.H., **34:** 89, 153

Clarendon Press, Oxford, **32:** 534

Clark, Mr. (of Mexican National Railroad), **29:** 127

Clark, A., **28:** 294,n2

Clark, Champ (James Beauchamp), **27:** 19, 22n2, 157; **29:** 515; **30:** 110n1; **31:** 431-32, 448; **33:** 387; **35:** 114; **36:** 211, 315, 366n1, 378; **37:** 118, 119, 128; **38:** 103, 125, 276, 666; and W. J. Bryan, **27:** 268-69; and Panama Canal tolls, **29:** 335, 389, 391n1; and Negro appointments, **29:** 540-41, 543; ship purchase bill and, **32:** 197, 221-22n1,2, 240n1; and "sunrise conference," **36:** 238n1, 287-90; WW's birthday greetings to, **36:** 251, 279; is not presidential candidate, **36:** 288,n2; on legislative program, **36:** 306-307; photograph: *illustration section,* **38**

Clark, Clarence Don, **36:** 328,n4

Clark, Edgar Erastus, **38:** 297,n1, 354n1

Clark, Elmer T., **36:** 391n2

Clark, Genevieve Bennett (Mrs. Champ), **36:** 179; **38:** 125, 277, 283

Clark, Horace Herbert, **34:** 39,n1, 117, 412, 469; **35:** 237-38, 355, 503-504,n1

Clark, James T., **33:** 185

Clark, Mary Charlotte Woodrow (Lottie) (Mrs. Melton), **31:** 542

Clark, Melton, **31:** 542

Clark, Walter Eli, **27:** 286,n2

Clark, Walter Ernest, **27:** 206-207

Clark-Kennedy, Archibald Edmund, **35:** 103n1

Clarke, Frances Moore (Mrs. James Paul), **38:** 322

Clarke, George Washington, **36:** 77n1

Clarke, James Paul, **28:** 111,n4, 204,n2, 245; **29:** 178; **30:** 324, 402; **31:** 458; **32:** 173n2, 286; **36:** 606; **37:** 15, 27-28, 54-55; and shipping bill, **35:** 345,n2, 396, 459,n1, 471, 475; and amendment to Jones bill, **35:** 466,n1, 467n1, 508, 509; death of, **38:** 322,n1

Clarke, John Hessin: Supreme Court appointment of, **37:** 397-98,n1, 428,n2, 431, 446, 467, 475

Clarke amendment: *see* Jones bill

Clarksville, Tenn., **30:** 280n2; **37:** 231n1

Claypool Hotel, Indianapolis, **38:** 412n2

Clayton, Henry De Lamar, **27:** 97,n2, 103, 344n1; **28:** 160n2, 385,n1, 391, 420; **29:** 185, 282, 443; **30:** 44; WW defends his appointment of, **30:** 28,n1

Clayton, William McK., **31:** 192

Clayton Antitrust Act, **29:** 175, 185, 316,n4, 443-46, 487; **30:** 134, 181, 183, 404, 423,n1, 454; **31:** 21n1, 29, 75-76, 78-79, 88-89, 130, 143, 149, 170, 271; **32:** 73, 74; **37:** 329, 356-57, 439n1; labor exemption clause, **30:** 126, 272, 281; U.S. Chamber of Commerce opposes labor exemption clause, **30:** 205-207,n2; compared to federal trade commission bill (Newlands bill), **30:** 321; and shoe machinery industry, **30:** 400-401,n4; T. W. Gregory's objection to, **30:** 480-83; and tying contract section, **31:** 30,n1,2; and interlocking directorates, **31:** 75-76,n1, 89, 171; WW on Reed and Culberson and, **31:** 122; Gompers requests pen after WW's signing of, **31:** 131, 138, 168; C. C. Carlin on, **31:** 43; C. A. Culberson on, **30:** 433; J. E. Davies on, **30:** 320-21; J. C. Floyd on, **31:** 41-42,n2,3; S. Gompers on, **31:** 168; T. W. Gregory on, **31:** 24-26; C. McCarthy on, **30:** 161; J. P. Morgan, Jr., on, **30:** 484; **31:** 39; F. G. Newlands on. **30:** 261, 262; W. C. Redfield on, **31:** 45; G. Rublee on, **30:** 274n1; C. R. Van Hise on, **30:** 272; W. B. Wilson on, **31:** 131; wholesalers' associations on, **30:** 319n3

Claxton, Philander Priestly, **29:** 418,n3

Cleary, Peter J., **35:** 319,n3, 338

Clemenceau, Georges Eugène Benjamin, **33:** 48,n4,5

Clemenceau, Mary A. Plummer (Mrs. Georges Eugène Benjamin), **33:** 48,n6

Clendenen, Clarence Clemens, **30:** 230n1

Cleveland, Frances Folsom: *see* Preston, Frances Folsom Cleveland

Cleveland, Grover, **28:** 96; **29:** 59, 319, 348; **31:** 118, 168; **33:** 478; **34:** 168, 433n1; **36:** 249, 408, 644; **38:** 327-28,n1, 478,n3; and Monroe Doctrine, **28:** 455; Negroes, **28:** 88, 186n1, 493, 497

Cleveland, Ohio, **27:** 118; **31:** 471; WW's address on preparedness in, **36:** 41-48; American Union Against Militarism meeting in, **36:** 635

Cleveland, U.S.S., **29:** 443

Cleveland Automatic Machine Co., **33:** 497-98,n1,4, 506, 507

Cleveland *Plain Dealer,* **36:** 48n

Cleveland *Szabadság,* **34:** 403

Cleveland *Waechter und Anzeiger,* **38:** 177,n1

Cliff House (San Francisco), **36:** 152n2

Clifford, John Garry, **34:** 133n1, 337n1

Clifton, N.H., **38:** 682

Clinical Congress of Surgeons of North America, **38:** 182n7

Clore, Leonard B., **38:** 419,n1

Clothier, Isaac Hallowell, **28:** 439,n2
clothing and the tariff; *see* Underwood-Simmons Tariff Act
Clough, Arthur Hugh, **28:** 361,n1
Coahuila state, Mex., **27:** 422,n1, 423; **28:** 30, 72, 73, 76, 77, 213; **29:** 485; **30:** 167, 220, 285n1, 445; **32:** 383, 384; **33:** 261; **34:** 382n1; **35:** 94; **37:** 250, 285; **38:** 223
coal-leasing bill: *see* Alaska coal-leasing bill
coal strikes: Colorado, **28:** 518-24, 546-56, 580-84, 589-90; of 1902, **28:** 555,n2
Coast and Geodetic Survey: *see* United States Coast and Geodetic Survey
Coates (butler), **28:** 36,n2, 143, 291
Cobb, Frank Irving, **29:** 344; **31:** 361,n2; **32:** 324, 341-42; **33:** 233, 320; **34:** 158n1, 186; **35:** 178; **37:** 129, 203; **38:** 329
Cobb, Irvin Shrewsbury, **37:** 332,n1
Cobb, James A., **30:** 491,n3
Cobb, Zach Lamar, **30:** 194, 290,n1, 408, 417, 418; **33:** 29n2; **36:** 480,n2; **37:** 316
Coben, Stanley, **27:** 223n2; **34:** 24n1
Cochranton, Pa., **36:** 337
Cockran, Anne Ide (Mrs. William Bourke), **36:** 402,n1
Cockran, William Bourke, **32:** 97; **36:** 402,n1
Coffeyville, Kan., **28:** 6,n1,2
Coffeyville *Sun*, **28:** 6n2
Coffin, Howard Earle, **36:** 432,n1; **38:** 182,n2, 336, 387, 439
Coffin, William Carey, **37:** 374
Cohalan, Daniel Florence, **36:** 503,n1
Cohan, George Michael, **28:** 597n1
Cohan's Theater, N.Y., **28:** 595
Cohen, Myer, **32:** 97
Coit, John Knox, **32:** 509,n1
Colby, Bainbridge, **37:** 329,n1, 332,n1, 333, 335n3, 352, 523n1, 524,n2; **38:** 121, 123, 179, 189
Colby, Everett, **28:** 97
Colcock, Franklin Pierce, **27:** 284,n3
Colegrove, A. D., **36:** 337
Coleridge, Samuel Taylor, **29:** 460n1
Coletta, Paolo E., **27:** 277n1; **28:** 302n3; **33:** 370n1, 425n1
Colgate University, **27:** 208
Colima state, Mex., **32:** 387
Coliseum, Des Moines, **36:** 77n1
collective bargaining: W. B. Wilson on, **28:** 590n1
College Men's League: *see* National Woodrow Wilson College Men's League
College of the City of New York, **27:** 206; **29:** 245, 262, 277,n1; **37:** 308n1
Collier, Robert Joseph, **38:** 142n1
Collier's Weekly, **27:** 61, 90, 93, 418,n1, 507,n1; **36:** 600; **37:** 38n10; **38:** 322, 334n
Collins, Wilkie, **35:** 374n1
Colombia: recognition of Mexico, **28:** 460; Lord Cowdray and, **28:** 593, 600; **29:** 111; suggestions for appointment to, **38:** 317

Colombia and the United States, **28:** 197-98,n1,2,4, 292,n1,2, 533-36, 572-73; **29:** 128, 180, 182; **33:** 57; **34:** 49-51, 55-56, 393; **35:** 375-78, 394; **36:** 230, 233-34; **37:** 269; minister to, **28:** 95n1, 197n1,4; concessions and treaty settlement, **28:** 329-30, 342, 535; **29:** 36-37, 39-40,n1, 181, 182, 183, 238, 415-16; **30:** 29, 160, 175, 209,n1, 317; **32:** 245, 286; **36:** 234-36; Cardinal Gibbons' views on, **30:** 341
Colombia and the United States, 1765-1934 (Parks), **28:** 197n2
Colonel House's Journey (*Le Temps*), **35:** 525n3
Colonel House's Mission (*La Libre Parole*), **35:** 525n3
Colonel House to Go Again to Europe (Lawrence), **35:** 380,n1
Color Line, The (*La Follette's Weekly*), **28:** 403,n2
Colorado, **37:** 435-36, 515; **38:** 376n1, 515n1, 520; Peabodyism in, **28:** 584,n1
Colorado Coal Commission, **31:** 356, 368-69, 373, 389-90, 446, 474-75, 503-504, 513-14, 523, 530; **32:** 18, 532-33; **35:** 317, 348, 492,n1; report of, **35:** 537-40; **36:** 237,n1, 245; termination of, **36:** 291, 299; *see also*, Colorado coal strike
Colorado Coal Operators' Association, **30:** 17
Colorado coal strike, **28:** 426-27,n1,8, 475, 507-14, 518-24, 540, 546-56, 563, 580-84, 589-90, 599; **29:** 14, 25, 31-32, 46,n1, 87-88, 512, 515, 533, 546-49; **30:** 16-20, 23, 29, 37-38, 48-49, 49,n1, 160, 171, 191, 485-86; **31:** 87,n1, 112, 124-25, 142-43, 150, 178, 215-16, 233-34, 324, 352-53, 356, 424, 463, 464, 481, 503-504, 523, 530; **32:** 84, 532; **33:** 26, 49 Ludlow massacre, **29:** 479,n1, 479-80; federal troops: request for and withdrawal, **29:** 501-502, 502-503, 503-504, 511,n1, 514, 528-29, 529; **30:** 37; **31:** 50; L. M. Garrison on, **29:** 525-28, 541-42; Gov. E. M. Ammons on, **30:** 45-46; **31:** 272-73,n2, 334-35, 452, 517, 545, 557-59; J. P. White on, **30:** 46; WW wants withdrawal, **30:** 422; **31:** 309; WW orders withdrawal, **31:** 449, 547-48; and J. D. Rockefeller, Jr., **29:** 513; **31:** 77; state legislature and, **30:** 37-38, 45, 48; B. B. Lindsey's suggestion of arbitration, **30:** 38-39; and National Guard, **30:** 60-61; and state finances, **30:** 452-53; workers and WW's settlement, **31:** 31-32, 37, 40, 81; coal operators on settlement, **31:** 43, 48-54, 78, 106-108; union on operators' modifications, **31:** 99; state election results and, **31:** 273,n2; UMW leaders wish to see WW, **31:** 310; and AF of L resolution, **31:** 330-31,n1; WW on AF of L resolution, **31:** 340-41; and S. Low, **31:** 363, 474-75; WW's statement on, **31:** 367-69; WW appoints commission, **31:**

368-69, 373, 389, 389-90; weapons of state militia, **31**: 406-407; miners accept commission, **31**: 446; union claims operators not hiring strikers, **31**: 488; S. Low meets with Rockefeller, **31**: 548; reports on in Colorado newspapers, **31**: 556-57,n1,2

Colorado Fuel and Iron Co., **29**: 46, 87-88, 504, 512, 514, 546; **31**: 48, 51, 77, 78; **35**: 317,n2, 538-39; **36**: 237n1; **37**: 310; and strike, **28**: 426-27,n1,8, 475, 507-14, 518-24, 540, 546-56, 563, 580, 580-84, 589-90, 599; *see also* Colorado coal strike

Colorado Industrial Commission, **32**: 532; **33**: 26

Colorado National Guard, **30**: 48, 49, 60-61,n1; **31**: 215, 558

Colorado River, **27**: 437

Colquitt, Oscar Branch, **30**: 7,n2; **33**: 474

Colton, George Radcliffe, **27**: 199,n1

Columbia, S.C., **29**: 391; **30**: 374; **33**: 495; **36**: 371; **38**: 191n1; tombstone of J. R. Wilson in, **30**: 74n1

Columbia, S.C. *Evening Record*, **33**: 496

Columbia Theological Seminary, S.C., **36**: 371n1; **38**: 191,n1

Columbia University, **27**: 191n1, 206, 554n1; **29**: 216n2; **31**: 84n1, 413; **32**: 9, 282n1; **33**: 18n2; **35**: 184n1; **36**: 601n4

Columbia University School of Law, **34**: 15n1

Columbus, N.M., **36**: 352; **38**: 45, 230; *see also* Mexico and the United States—Columbus Raid

Columbus, Ohio, **29**: 270; WW's speeches in: to Federal Council of Churches, **35**: 79n2, 328, 329-36, 354; to Chamber of Commerce, **35**: 253, 321-28

Columbus, Ohio, *Dispatch*, **36**: 172n2

Columbus, Christopher, **28**: 449

Columbus Memorial: C. W. Eliot, **28**: 502

Comanche Indians, **38**: 227, 228

Comment on Congress (Sullivan), **27**: 418n1, 507

Commentaries on the Constitution of the United States: With a Preliminary Review of the Constitutional History of the Colonies and States, Before the Adoption of the Constitution (Story), **36**: 226n1

commerce, **27**: 121, 271; **28**: 448-49; **30**: 95; **31**: 39n1; **35**: 268, 302, 321-22, 324-25, 442, 526; segregation and, **28**: 407, 408; American Telephone and Telegraph Co., **29**: 45,n1, and federal trade commission bill, **30**: 274n1, 349, 430; and U.S. fear of blockade, **30**: 324-25; and Ship Registry Act, **30**: 325-26; and surplus crops to Europe, **30**: 332; and conversion of coastwise ships to transatlantic vessels, **30**: 333; and neutralization of ships, **30**: 335-36; E. M. House on shipping bill, **30**: 345; and decline in customs revenue, **30**: 467-68; and

Clayton bill, **30**: 481; **31**: 42,n3, 46n2, 78; and foreign credits in the U.S., **31**: 217-19, 219-20; WW on, **36**: 32, 43, 112, 153-60; **38**: 136, 339-40, 528; WW on shipping bill, **36**: 374-75; U.S. note to Britain on blacklist, **37**: 476-79; WW on international trade, **37**: 383-87, 393-94, 492-93; and platform plank, **37**: 160, 166, 193-94; and Revenue Act, **38**: 179n1; W. C. Adamson on, **29**: 139; J. E. Davies on, **29**: 78, 80-81, 84; D. B. Jones on, **29**: 67-68; R. Lansing on, **37**: 287-88; R. L. Owen on, **35**: 433-34; W. H. Page on, **37**: 460; W. C. Redfield on, **29**: 435n1, 443-46, 544-45; **35**: 427-29,n1; A. O. Stanley on, **29**: 25, 27; W. J. Stone on, **36**: 366-68

Commerce, Department of, **30**: 175, 210; **31**: 39; **32**: 57; **35**: 229; **36**: 154-55; **38**: 264; and *Eastland* disaster, **34**: 27,n1

Commerce Act of 1887: *see* Interstate Commerce Act of 1887

Commerce and Finance, **34**: 296n2

Commerce Commission: *see* Interstate Commerce Commission

Commerce Committee (Senate), **30**: 324, 402; **32**: 173n2; **37**: 27-28, 54, 375

Commerce Court, **27**: 325

Commercial Bank of Canada, **38**: 529

Commercial Club of Chicago, **27**: 29-39; **29**: 76

Commercial Club of Omaha: WW's address to, **38**: 336-42

Commercial Code, **29**: 106, 109

Commercial National Bank of Washington, **33**: 542n2,3; **34**: 255, 345,n2

Commission for Prevention and Relief of Distress (on conditions in London), **32**: 350n1

Commission for Relief in Belgium, **31**: 206,n1, 296-97, 323, 356, 377; **32**: 293,n1, 294, 358, 379, 401; **33**: 408; **34**: 409-10, 494; **35**: 165, 520n1; **37**: 405, 433, 541-42,n1; **38**: 72n8, 455n3, 653

Commission for Relief in Belgium, **32**: 293n1

Commission for Relief in Poland, **37**: 433

commission government (N.J.), **27**: 49, 390

Commission on Industrial Relations: *see* United States Commission on Industrial Relations

Commission on National Aid to Vocational Education, **36**: 357n1

Commission on National Historical Publications, **28**: 470

Comité France Amérique, **31**: 426n2

Committee of American Physicians for Medical Preparedness, **38**: 182,n4, 10

committee on: *see under the latter part of the name, such as* Industrial Arts and Expositions, Committee on

Common Counsel Club, **36**: 263, 388; WW's speech to, **36**: 472-76,n1

Commoner, The, **27**: 58n2, 219,n2; **29**:

Commoner, The (cont.)
261n1; **33:** 453,n4
Commons, John Rogers, **27:** 244n1,
291n2; **28:** 82,n1; **32:** 189, 199
Common Sense in the White House
(Johnson), **27:** 411
competition, **27:** 35, 121, 122, 177, 236,
270, 302; **29:** 176, 337; **31:** 169, 170,
171; **32:** 72; **35:** 322, 427n1, 511; in for-
eign markets, **32:** 184-85; **35:** 527
*Compilation of the Messages and Papers
of the Presidents 1789-1897* (Richard-
son), **29:** 292n1
Computing Scale Co. of America, **37:**
492n1
Condé (French cruiser), **31:** 176n1
*Conditions in the Coal Mines of Colorado.
Hearings before a Subcommittee of the
Committee on Mines and Mining . . . ,*
29: 46n1
Conditions prevailing in Torreón from
Sept. 25 to Oct. 11, inclusive (Caroth-
ers), **28:** 570n1
Condon, Randall Judson, **38:** 526n1
Confalonieri, Cusani, **28:** 461,n2; **35:** 498
Conférence navale de Londres (Renault),
31: 191,n2
Confessions of an Undergraduate
(Whipple), **34:** 470,n1
*Conflict of Laws; or, Private Interna-
tional Law* (Minor), **32:** 4,n3
*Confusions and Crises: see Wilson: Con-
fusions and Crises*
Conger, Kenyon B., **35:** 503n1
Conger, Seymour Beach, **33:** 454,n1
Congo: *see* Belgian Congo
Congregational Club of Boston, **30:** 119-
20,n1
Congregationalist and Christian World,
28: 256n1, 278n1, 290
Congress: *see* United States Congress
Congress Hall, Phila., **28:** 435-39,n1,4
Congress of Physicians and Surgeons of
North America, **38:** 182n6
*Congressional Government: A Study in
American Politics* (Wilson), **27:** 284; **32:**
8; **33:** 421,n1; **38:** 680
Congressional Record, **36:** 310; **38:** 328;
62d Congress, 2d sess., **27:** 225, 226;
63d Congress, 1st sess., **28:** 68n1, 99n4,
115n3, 141n3, 160n2, 163n4, 208n2,
255n1, 259n2, 272n1; 63d Congress, 2d
sess., **29:** 272n1, 349n2, 355n1, 409n1,
471n1, 482n1; **30:** 219, 226n2, 261, 262,
273n1, 338n, 342n1, 400n2; **31:** 103n1,
152n3, 176n1, 180n6, 208n2, 414,
448n1; **32:** 15n3, 197n1; **36:** 288n2; 63d
Congress, 3d sess., **30:** 273n1; **32:** 24n1,
41n, 81n1, 172n1, 197n1, 222n1; **33:**
431,n6; 64th Congress, 1st sess., **36:**
20n1, 211n1, 238n1, 242, 250n1, 500n1,
515n3, 546n2, 576n1, 612n1; **37:** 203n5,
359n1, 530n1; **38:** 14n1, 27n1, 36n1,
85n1, 87n1, 444; 64th Congress, 2d
sess., **37:** 359n1.
Congressional Union for Woman Suf-

frage, **30:** 226,n1,4; **35:** 292n1; **36:** 3n1;
37: 208, 376n1, 426n2, 427n3, 491, 515;
38: 5, 78, 175n1
Congressman Eagle Analyzes and Op-
poses the Glass Banking and Cur-
rency Bill (press release), **28:** 122n4
Conkin, Paul Keith, **32:** 56n2
Conklin, Edwin Grant, **38:** 147,n2, 563
Connaught and Strathearn, Luise Mar-
garethe Alexandra Victoria Agnes,
Duchess of, **31:** 501
Connaught and Strathearn, Duke of
(Prince Arthur William Patrick Al-
bert), **30:** 88n2; **31:** 229, 501, 502
Connecticut, **35:** 176; **38:** 376n1, 518;
H. S. Cummings' senatorial quest, **38:**
165n2, 168, 624
Connecticut, U.S.S., **34:** 45, 61, 71, 165
Conners, William James, **35:** 460,n1
Connor, Ralph (Charles William Gor-
don), **37:** 48,n3
Connors, Richard J., **27:** 494n1
Conover, Helen Field (Mrs. Francis Ste-
vens), **28:** 62,n4
Conover, Juliana, **28:** 62,n4
Conrad, Joseph, **36:** 415
conscription, **34:** 84; **36:** 197; **38:** 52n1;
Villard on L. Wood and, **31:** 475-76; in
Britain, **37:** 28
consent decrees, **30:** 423, 480,n1
conservation, **27:** 31, 51, 52, 150; **29:** 9-
10; **31:** 173, 178, 354, 416; **35:** 176, 231-
33, 308; **36:** 250, 366n1; **37:** 197, 329;
38: 137; G. Pinchot on, **36:** 48-51; WW
on, **36:** 360, 464-65,n1, 521-22, 603;
F. K. Lane on, **36:** 518
conservation bills and programs, **30:** 27-
28, 126, 160, 183, 222, 476; **32:** 35;
F. K. Lane on, **30:** 3-4; S. Ferris on, **30:**
20-21; bills pending in the Senate, **30:**
31; and Chandler-Dunbar decision, **30:**
218n3
Conservative, A (Gilman), **30:** 22,n2
Constantine I (of Greece), **38:** 107n1
Constantine Bay (Cape Constantine),
Alaska, **33:** 35
Constantinople, Turkey, **31:** 518; **32:** 45,
67, 81, 205, 377; **33:** 501, 511; **34:** 310;
35: 75, 77, 226; **38:** 647
Constantovich, Alexander, Count
Benckendorff, **33:** 122,n4, 523,n2, 550
Constitution (U.S.): *see* United States
Constitution
*Constitution of the United States: A Crit-
ical Discussion of Its Genesis, Devel-
opment, and Interpretation* (Tucker), **36:**
226n1
*Constitutional Government in the United
States* (Wilson), **32:** 9, 13, 15n4; **37:**
35,n6
*Constitutional Politics in the Progressive
Era: Child Labor and the Law* (Wood),
29: 170n1
Constitutional Union (Kadet) party, **37:**
90n2
Constitutionalists (Mex.), **28:** 6n1, 8, 39,

57, 136, 141-42, 241n1, 322-23, 333, 370, 391, 423, 429n1, 486n1, 541, 543, 557, 558-59, 559, 561, 563-64, 568, 569-70; **29:** 169, 196, 197, 229, 359, 470, 484, 490, 512; **30:** 59, 69, 81, 134; **31:** 66, 67, 68-69; **32:** 279, 332, 348; **33:** 7, 30, 43, 65n1, 69n1, 272, 308,n1, 398n1, 416, 463, 533; **34:** 273n1, 456, 532; **35:** 98; **38:** 360; W. J. Bryan on arms to, **28:** 193-94; Durango, **28:** 7,n1; F. Escudero on, **28:** 59, 73-81; F. Gamboa on union with, **28:** 171; W. B. Hale report on, **28:** 27-30; plans of, **28:** 545-46; Torreón incident, **28:** 382-83,n1, 602,n1; possibility of recognition of, **28:** 477-78, 517; atrocities against, **29:** 15; F. Villa and, **29:** 278-80; **30:** 220-21, 408-19, 445-46, 446-47; U.S. and, **29:** 17, 34, 98n1, 138, 160, 249, 266; **30:** 10, 11-12, 92, 228; and rumors of graft, **29:** 30; and cost of ammunition, **29:** 74, 130, 489; claim forces are strengthened, **29:** 90; success in San Luis Potosí, **29:** 101n1; J. Lind on, **29:** 110n1, 123-24, 126, 287, 290, 540; and Tampico, **29:** 111n1; **30:** 246; L. Cabrera and, **29:** 142, 187-89, 191-95, 249n2; WW note about sending guards to Mexico City, **29:** 143; and Lord Cowdray, **29:** 144; fear support of U.S. will unite Huerta forces, **29:** 159; and communications between Mexico City and Veracruz, **29:** 161; and raising of the arms embargo, **29:** 178, 185-86; and monetary support, **29:** 189; civil policy of, **29:** 189; agrarian reforms, **29:** 192; finances of, **29:** 193; and repayment of loans, **29:** 194; and war damages, **29:** 194-95; and policy on Huerta concessions and contracts, **29:** 195; and T. B. Hohler memorandum, **29:** 252, 257, 259, 260; against formation of northern republic, **29:** 295; desire to be independent of U.S., **29:** 348; and distrust of Spaniards, **29:** 416-17; on neutrality in Veracruz incident, **29:** 481; Huerta seeks union with against U.S., **29:** 498; W. Kent on, **29:** 499-500

and ABC mediation: general, **29:** 525, 550-51, 552; **30:** 55, 56, 57, 58, 78, 96, 99, 100, 101, 113, 115, 120, 133, 136, 237, 242; W. J. Bryan on cessation of hostilities during mediation talks, **30:** 47; mediators on renewing invitation to, **30:** 64; WW on basic terms of, **30:** 71, 72; Commissioners on plan acceptable to, **30:** 76; and WW comments on mediation plans, **30:** 83; and mediation proposals, **30:** 87, 88, 207-208; Carranza wishes representatives at negotiations, **30:** 101,n2; mediators seek cessation of hostilities before conferring with Constitutionalists, **30:** 117-18, 123-26; mediators await arrival of representatives of, **30:** 208, 226; British attitude toward, **30:** 42, 59; provisional government's plan and, **30:** 71, 75, 77, 98
enter Tampico, **30:** 79, 80; C. A. Spring Rice on effects of Huerta's retirement, **30:** 78-80; and massacre in Tepic, **30:** 82; and elections, **30:** 116, 117; WW prefers Constitutionalists to Huerta, **30:** 130; Bryan on attitude of mediators toward, **30:** 137; and agreement with Huerta on the establishment of provisional government, **30:** 199; and W. R. Hearst, **30:** 283n1; WW urges avoidance of cruelty and revenge in victory, **30:** 285-86,n2; WW on harmony among, **30:** 290; willing to meet with Carbajal's representatives, **30:** 290, 291; and need of U.S. recognition, **30:** 297-98; Carranza recognized as First Chief of, **30:** 301,n1; WW indicates excesses will risk U.S. recognition, **30:** 321-22; demand arms from Carbajal, **30:** 360,n1; views of F. Angeles, **30:** 410; and the Catholic Church, **30:** 424; WW on Villa's reform proposals, **30:** 450; *see also* Carranza, Venustiano; Mexico; Mexico and the United States
Construction and Repair, Bureau of (U.S.N.), **32:** 21n2
consular and diplomatic appropriations bill, **30:** 42
consular service, **28:** 280; **29:** 23; C. W. Eliot comments on, **28:** 272, 317; *see also* Wilson, Woodrow: Appointments, *diplomatic suggestions and appointments*
consuls general: and civil service, **27:** 434
Consumer's League, Washington, D.C., **30:** 226n3
Continental and Commercial National Bank of Chicago, **27:** 79n2
Continental Army plan, **35:** 105-106, 139-41, 149-50,n1, 469, 500, 503; Hay on, **36:** 135, 141-42; WW on, **36:** 145, 146, 163; Scott on, **36:** 197
Continental Memorial Hall, Washington, D.C., **36:** 629n1
Contreras, Calixto, Mex., **28:** 77
Conty, A. R., **35:** 203,n2
Convention Hall, K.C., Kansas, **36:** 100n1
Convention Hall, Phila., **33:** 147n1
Conventions of Auction Bridge (Whitehead), **31:** 316n2, 317
Cook, George W., **36:** 364
Cook, Raymond Allen, **32:** 267n1
Cooke, Charles Berkley, **30:** 210,n2
Cooksey, George Robert, **34:** 294,n1
Coolidge, John Gardner, **38:** 317,n2
Cooper, Henry Allen, **29:** 440,n1, 441; **36:** 517n1
Cooper, John Milton, Jr., **27:** xxii; **30:** viii; **34:** 55n1; **38:** 241n1
Cooper, Robert Muldrow, **33:** 496,n5
Cooper Union, **35:** 221n1; WW's speeches at, **38:** 602-605, 606

Cooperative Agricultural Extension Act, **38:** 25
Cooperative Education Association of Virginia, **31:** 261n2
Coosa River bill, **36:** 49
Cope, Edward D., **38:** 574n3
Copeland, William Adams, **30:** 400-401,n1
Copenhagen, Denmark, **34:** 188; **35:** 62
Copp, Charles C., **29:** 421, 440
Copper, H. E., **28:** 427
copper, **32:** 102, 130, 131, 132, 215; and shipment to Krupp, **31:** 111, 116, 231; and Italy, **31:** 527
Corbins Park, N.H., **28:** 320
Corcoran, Brewer, **28:** 181n3
Cordoba, Veracruz, Mex., **29:** 329
Corey, Herbert, **31:** 339
Corliss engine, **30:** 186
Corn Products Refining Co., **30:** 482; **37:** 363,n2
Cornell, Robert J., **28:** 555n2
Cornish, N.H., **27:** 189n1, 200, 511, 556; **28:** 12, 13, 87, 95, 133, 161, 263, 334; **30:** 93, 277, 436, 489; **31:** 59, 141, 158; **33:** 366, 396, 423, 436n2, 444, 445, 447, 452, 471, 472, 477, 483, 525, 543; **34:** 3,n1, 14-15,n1, 23, 58, 181, 205, 215, 233, 246, 257, 270, 283, 294, 313, 379, 473; **35:** 16, 32, 103; society in, **28:** 43,n4, 5, 6, 7, 98-99, 119-20,n2, 3, 4, 145-46, 159,n1, 165-66, 181,n3, 195,n1, 252, 278, 320; **34:** 101-102, 128,n1, 178; WW on being with EAW in, **28:** 45, 46; Wilson family reunion in, **34:** 83
Cornish (N.H.) Center Congregational Church, **28:** 54,n1, 199
Cornish—The Summer Capital (Corcoran), **28:** 181,n3
Corona (yacht), **28:** 203, 221; **30:** 189, 303; **33:** 383; **37:** 331; **38:** 154
Corona, Ramon, **29:** 427
Coronel, Chile, **36:** 235n6
corporation tax bill, **29:** 177
corporations and corporate finance, **27:** 40; **29:** 175, 177; **30:** 482; **31:** 325; New Jersey, **27:** 47, 87, 88, 120-22; New Hampshire, **27:** 178; commissionership of, **27:** 345; **29:** 28, 29-30; and D. B. Jones, **29:** 67; and WW address on antitrust legislation, **29:** 155; C. W. Eliot on, **29:** 339; S. Gompers on, **27:** 184; W. C. Redfield on, **29:** 444, 445; J. T. Robinson on, **29:** 457-58, 479, 487-88; A. O. Stanley on, **29:** 26, 28-29
Corporations, Bureau of, **29:** 28, 79, 83, 84, 184, 227n1, 481; **32:** 57; **36:** 410n1
Corralitos Co., Mex., **28:** 41n1
Corregidor Fort, P.I., **27:** 441, 444, 446
Correspondence Respecting the European Crisis (British Foreign Office), **30:** 359,n2
Corrupt Practices Act (N.J.), **27:** 233
corrupt-practices bill, **35:** 433,n1, 447, 456, 474; **36:** 250; **38:** 58, 657, 670
Corry, Pa., **36:** 337

Corsicana, Tex.: post office appointment, **27:** 238, 239,n1; **29:** 311-12
Cort van der Linden, Pieter Wilhelm Adriaan, **38:** 104,n1
Cort Theatre, N.Y., **27:** 63,n4
Cortés, Enrique, **35:** 376,n1
Corwin, Edward Samuel, **27:** 299, 336
Cosby, Spencer, **27:** 16,n1, 18, 405; **28:** 268
Cosey, Alfred B., **28:** 209-12
Cosmopolitan Magazine, **30:** 156
Cosmos Club, Wash., D.C., **37:** 370: L. D. Brandeis nomination for admission to, **32:** 163-64; WW letter of support, **32:** 167,n1
Coss, Francisco, **28:** 77
Costa Rica, **28:** 448n1; **31:** 498; **36:** 235; Lord Cowdray and, **29:** 111
Costigan, Edward Prentiss, **37:** 435,n1
Cothran, Annie Wilson Howe (Mrs. Perrin Chiles), niece of WW, **28:** 398,n3; **31:** 175; **32:** 518; **33:** 178,n2; **34:** 73, 83, 101-102, 128, 178, 217, 268; **35:** 393n1; **37:** 382; **38:** 283, 451,n1, 690; WW on death of mother, **38:** 176
Cothran, Josephine, **28:** 398,n3; **31:** 176; **33:** 178n2; **34:** 73, 102, 128, 153, 167, 178, 217, 246; **35:** 393,n1; **38:** 283, 690
cotton, **36:** 20n1, 93
cotton crisis, **31:** 12,n1, 157-58, 326; **32:** 102, 174, 314, 359, 410; **33:** 239, 267, 386, 445n1, 453, 457-58; **34:** 6-7,n1,3, 12, 13, 30, 32, 34, 42, 58, 98, 123, 126, 137, 180, 186,n2, 188, 200, 238, 253n1, 267, 298, 382; **35:** 506,n2; WW remarks to delegates from cotton interests, **31:** 79; WW responds to questions on, **31:** 132, 144, 149, 177, 180, 207-208, 233, 234-35, 324; and foreign trade, **31:** 150-51; and Federal Reserve Banks, **31:** 208,n2; WW on British permission for shipments, **31:** 243; and British position on, **31:** 246; **33:** 526, 534, 535-36, 538; **34:** 294-95,n1, 296,n1; in Texas, **31:** 248, 248-49; **34:** 53-54; and passing of shipping bill, **31:** 276; and France, **31:** 370-71; and Japan, **32:** 321; and Georgia, **33:** 457,n1; and South Carolina, **33:** 495-96; and B. Strong on, **34:** 106; and German offer to purchase cotton, **34:** 123, 142; W. J. Bryan on, **31:** 378; L. M. Garrison on, **31:** 210-12; E. Grey on, **31:** 231; **34:** 371; R. Henry on, **31:** 119-20,n1, 205; H. L. Higginson on, **31:** 213; E. M. House on, **34:** 36, 62; R. Lansing on **31:** 217-19, 219-20; **34:** 34-35; W. G. McAdoo on, **31:** 250-52, 271-72, 272; J. L. McLaurin on, **34:** 99-100, 121, 400,n1; W. H. Page on, **34:** 21, 22; C. Poe on, **31:** 126-29; F. A. Sayles on **31:** 139-40; C. A. Spring Rice on, **31:** 230; **34:** 295-96,n1,2; *see also* cotton fund; Crawford plan
Cotton Crisis, the South, and Anglo-

American Diplomacy, 1914-1915 (Link), **31:** 12n1
cotton exchanges, **30:** 441-42
Cotton Futures Act, **37:**197; **38:** 26
Cotton Goods Export Association of New York, **32:** 321
cotton loan fund, **31:** 129,n1, 148, 167, 268-69, 271-72, 272, 275, 321, 328, 467
Cotton. The American Point of View (London *Times*), **34:** 21,n6
Couden, Henry Noble, **37:** 123n1
Coudert, Frederic René, **31:** 426,n2, 447n1, 450, 461
Coudert Brothers, **30:** 346, 408n1, 443n3; **31:** 426n2; **32:** 479; **33:** 115n1
Coughlin, John William, **38:** 36
Coulter, John Lee, **27:** 201
Council of Executive Information, **37:** 381
Council of National Defense, **37:** 381, 473, 491; appointments to advisory board of, **38:** 47, 181-83, 272-73, 297, 387-88, 429, 439; WW on appointments, **38:** 386-87, 479-80, 507; chief functions of, **38:** 387-88
Country Life Commission, **31:** 343
Courier Co., Buffalo, N.Y., **35:** 460n1
Courier Herald Co. (Lincoln, Ill.), **34:** 405n1
Court of Assessors of New York, **29:** 349
Courtney, William Leonard, **28:** 576
Covington, James Harry, **29:** 496; **30:** 404, 429, 430, 433-34, 442, 454-55, 455
Covington bill: *see* Federal Trade Commission Act
Cowdray, 1st Baron: *see* Pearson, Weetman Dickinson, 1st Baron Cowdray
Cowing, Cedric B., **30:** 312n1
Cox, James Middleton (incorrectly identified as James McMahon Cox in earlier volumes), **28:** 354,n4; **37:** 84, 428; **38:** 457; and Ohio floods, **27:** 229n1, 230, 232, 234
Cox, Kenyon, **28:** 43,n4, 143, 146, 276
Cox, Louise Howland King (Mrs. Kenyon), **28:** 146
Cox, Victor Eastman, **36:** 200,n9
Coyoacan, Mex., **28:** 27
Cradock, Sir Christopher George Francis Maurice, **29:** 111,n1, 119; **36:** 235,n6
Craig, Donald Alexander, **34:** 402,n2, 471, 471-72,n1; **37:** 141,n4
Craig, Locke, **36:** 503n2; **37:** 79n1
Craik, Dinah Maria Mulock (Mrs. George Lille), **34:** 431,n2
Cram, Ralph Adams, **32:** 23,n1; **38:** 333n3
Crampton, Charles Albert, **37:** 374, 473
Crampton, Henry Edward, **36:** 601,n4
Crandall, John J., **30:** 104,n3
Crane, Allan D., **32:** 96,n4
Crane, Charles Richard, **27:** 60, 179, 203, 244; **28:** 4, 111,n1, 353,n1; **29:** 401; **30:** 31, 33, 58, 343; **31:** 161, 291,n1, 318; **32:** 25, 52-53, 75; **33:** 441-42, 445, 456, 469, 471, 516; **34:** 91n1, 271n1, 369; **35:** 132, 178, 483, 535; **36:** 20, 185, 348-49, 401, 518; **37:** 46, 119-20, 134, 206,

228, 377, 402; **38:** 15, 86, 591n1; as cabinet possibility, **27:** 23, 26, 27, 61, 62, 70; on L. D. Brandeis, **27:** 92-93, 107-108; and Russian ambassadorship, **27:** 228, 259, 262; **30:** 46; and purchase of *Harper's Weekly*, **27:** 467, 474; appointment suggestions, **36:** 177-78, 191-92, 202-203
Crane, Cornelia Workman Smith (Mrs. Charles Richard), **30:** 343,n2; **33:** 441-42,n3, 445, 456, 469, 471
Crane, William Iler, **38:** 352n1
Crane, Winthrop Murray, **37:** 340
Crane Co., Chicago, **31:** 291n1
Cranston, Earl (Bishop Cranston), **30:** 89n1; **33:** 206; **36:** 391,n1,2; WW remarks on retirement of, **37:** 148-50,n1
Crawford, Anna Orme (Mrs. C. P.), **31:** 259-60,n1
Crawford, Coe Isaac, **28:** 162,n1, 163; **30:** 299n1
Crawford, Sir Richard Frederick, **34:** 32,n1, 106,n4, 186,n2, 200, 295, 296; **35:** 362n1
Crawford County, Pa., **36:** 337
Crawford House, White Mts., N.H., **28:** 102, 104, 138, 150, 159; **29:** 562,n1
Crawford Notch, N.H., **28:** 104, 144; **29:** 562
Crawford plan, **34:** 21n6, 106n4
credit: *see* banking and currency; corporations; rural credits
credit associations, **29:** 73
Creel, Blanche Lyon Bates (Mrs. George), **38:** 15-16,n1
Creel, George, **30:** 39n1; **33:** 452-53,n4; **38:** 15-17,n1,2, 427n1
Creel, Macedo Enrique, **29:** 18
Cress, George Oscar, **38:** 378,n3
Crewe-Milnes, Robert Offley, 1st Marquess of Crewe and Earl of Madeley, **30:** 214-15,n1, 257, 266; **33:** 268,n1, 372n1, 386, 484, 550
Crimean War, **34:** 94
Criminal correspondence with foreign governments, Section 5335, *Revised Statutes of the United States*, **36:** 617-18
Cripps, Thomas, **32:** 455n3; **33:** 68n1
Crisis, The, N.Y., **28:** 60,n4; **38:** 24n2, 522,n1
Crisp, Charles Robert, **29:** 381, 387
Croly, Herbert David, **28:** 120,n3
Croly, Louise Emory (Mrs. Herbert David), **28:** 120,n3
Cromer, 1st Earl of: *see* Baring, Evelyn, 1st Earl of Cromer
Crompton, Lillian Sheridan (Mrs. David Henry), **31:** 454,n6
Cromwell, Oliver, **27:** 114
Cronon, Edmund David, **27:** xii
Crosby, Oscar Terry, **28:** 192,n1; **38:** 455,n3, 456
Crothers, Samuel McChord, **35:** 343-44,n3
Crowded Years: The Reminiscences of William G. McAdoo, (McAdoo), **28:**

Crowded Years: The Reminiscences of William G. McAdoo (McAdoo) (*cont.*) 156n1; **34:** 74n5, 158n1; **37:** 187n4

Crozier, Mary Williams (Mrs. William), **32:** 12,n1

Crozier, William, **32:** 12,n1

Crump, Edward Hull, **27:** 55n3

Cuadra, Pedro Rafael, **27:** 470,n1; **28:** 101,n3, 250; **29:** 172

Cuatro Cienegas, Coahuila, Mex., **30:** 167

Cuba, **27:** 112; **28:** 124, 412, 432, 442, 456, 466, 468, 484, 576, 586; **29:** 134, 169, 222, 275, 484; **31:** 339, 476; **35:** 129-30, 144, 176, 247, 438; **38:** 346; W. E. Gonzales appointed minister, **27:** 14,n2, 531; and Mexico, **27:** 540, 546; and sugar exports to U.S., **27:** 340; L. J. Canova in, **30:** 148n2

Cuba (Cuban gunboat), **27:** 546

Cuba and the United States, **36:** 94; and Haiti, **34:** 60, 67

Cudworth, Ralph, **31:** 316,n2

Cuernavaca, Morelos, Mex., **27:** 539; **30:** 47n1; **31:** 12, 13; **32:** 387, 507

Cueva, Arturo de la, **27:** 330,n1

Cuff, Robert Dennis George, **36:** 432n1, 601n4

Culberson, Charles Allen, **27:** 61-62; **28:** 160, 181; **30:** 194, 320, 423, 433; **31:** 21, 93, 122, 282, 499-500, 500, 524; **36:** 387, 609

Culberson, William Smith, **38:** 3n2

Culebra Cut, Panama Canal, **29:** 307,n2

Cullop, William Allen, **29:** 140,n2, 173, 174; **37:** 92

Culp, Julia, **36:** 268n4

Cumberland, Charles Curtis, **27:** 64n1, 422n1; **28:** 391n1, 482n1; **30:** 193n1; **32:** 202n3; **33:** 7n1

Cumberland County, England: *see* Carlisle, Cumberland, England

Cummings, Charles E., **36:** 364

Cummings, Homer Stillé, **38:** 5-8, 36-37, 517-18, 669-71; and Democratic National Committee, **37:** 45-46, 163, 177-78, 203,n3, 206, 211, 227, 229, 475; and Connecticut senatorial race, **38:** 165,n2, 168-69, 518, 624

Cummins, Albert Baird, **27:** 483,n1; **29:** 227; **30:** 261, 380; **32:** 189, 190; **33:** 518; **36:** 242-44; **38:** 103, 146n2, 174,n2,3, 284

Cummins resolution, **27:** 483-84,n1

Cunard Line, **32:** 176; **33:** 127n1, 290n1; **34:** 315n1

Curley, James Michael, **32:** 97; **33:** 68n1, 86n1

Currency and Banking Committees: *see* Banking and Currency Committees

currency bill: *see* Federal Reserve Act

Currency Commission (American Bankers' Association), **28:** 3,n1, 8n1

currency reform: *see* banking and currency reform

Currier, Charles Warren, **32:** 392,n1, 395-96

Curry, Jabez Lamar Monroe, **36:** 657

Curry, Roy Watson, **27:** 175n1

Curse of Bigness (Brandeis), **29:** 30n1

Curti, Merle Eugene, **27:** 277n1

Curtin resolution (California Senate), **27:** 382

Curtis, Charles B., **34:** 50,n1

Curtis, Cyrus Hermann Kotzschmar, **31:** 524,n2, 531; **32:** 6-7

Curtis, James L., **34:** 504-505, 511,n1; **35:** 68,n1

Curtis, Oakley Chester, **38:** 174,n1

Curtis Publishing Co., **31:** 524n2

Curtiss Aeroplane Co., **34:** 224

Curzon, George Nathaniel, 1st Marquess Curzon of Kedleston, **33:** 227n4; **35:** 414; **36:** 386

Cushing incident: *see* Germany and the United States

Cusi Mines, Mex., **37:** 250

customs: decline in revenues due to war, **30:** 467-68, 471-72, 473; and publication of ships' manifests, **32:** 226, 227

customs laws, **37:** 192; and control by tariff board, **35:** 510

Cyane, U.S.S., **29:** 437

Cycle of Power: The Career of Jersey City Mayor Frank Hague (Connors), **27:** 494n1

Czernowitz, Bukovina, Rumania, **38:** 74

Czolgosz, Leon Franz, **28:** 117,n4

D. C. Heath and Co., Boston, **32:** 534

D. H. Burnham and Co., **28:** 501

Da Gama, Domicio: *see* Gama, Domicio da

Dabney, Richard Heath, **32:** 3-4, 10-11, 18; **35:** 46-47, 56; **36:** 532-33, 555; **37:** 10,n2; **38:** 526n1

Dacia affair, **32:** 89,n3, 91-93,n2,3, 102-105, 106, 119, 130, 337; Kaiser and Gerard on, **36:** 615

Dade City, Fla., **32:** 188,n1

Dahlman, James Charles (Cowboy Jim), **38:** 342n3

Daily Courier (Lincoln, Ill.), **34:** 405n1

Daily Princetonian, **30:** 176n1; **35:** 152,n1, 182,n1,2,3

Dallas, Tex.: and preparedness, **36:** 165-66

Dallas *Evening Journal*, **29:** 263n2

Dallas Morning News, **29:** 263n2

Dalrymple, James, **29:** 547; **31:** 51

Dam, Milton, **37:** 12,n2

Damrosch, Margaret Blaine (Mrs. Walter Johannes), **32:** 455,n1

Damrosch, Walter Johannes, **32:** 455n1

Daniel, Samuel, **33:** 345n1

Daniels, Addie Worth Bagley (Mrs. Josephus), **30:** 356; **31:** 524, 533; **33:** 486; **38:** 441, 617

Daniels, Frank Arthur, **31:** 524; **33:** 486

Daniels, Joan Robertson (Mrs. Winthrop More), **37:** 129,n1

Daniels, Jonathan Worth, **31:** 524; **33:** 486

Daniels, Josephus, **28:** 130-31, 142,

486n2, 498n1; **29:** 392n1; **30:** 13n1, 34n1, 37, 89n1, 184n1; **31:** 126-29, 131, 270, 276, 524, 533; **32:** 133-34, 274, 331; **33:** 209, 210, 216n1, 287n1, 295, 465, 486-87, 537; **34:** 4-5, 17, 99, 109, 173, 177, 195, 197, 208, 233, 267, 412, 426, 432n1, 478, 514; **35:** 45-46, 299, 300, 316-17, 401; **36:** 296, 391n1, 417n1, 426; **37:** 66, 76, 78n1, 148n1, 264, 431, 481n1, 518; **38:** 35-36, 38, 173, 181, 183, 258, 272, 276, 386,n1, 387, 441, 450, 498, 624, 659;

cabinet appointment, **27:** 21, 23, 24, 27, 62, 70, 111, 112, 128, 133, 134-35,n1; selects F. D. Roosevelt as Assistant, **27:** 157-58; on cabinet meetings, **27:** xii, 160, 169-70, 174-75, 194, 210, 235-38, 248-50, 261-62, 267-69, 290-92, 312-13, 328-33, 348-51, 425-26, 442-45, 459-62; **32:** 133-34; code name, **27:** 164; and Joint Board of the Army and Navy, **27:** 441-42, 446-48; on Military Order of the Carabao incident, **29:** 37-39, 54-55; on Tampico incident and occupation of Veracruz, **29:** 420, 421, 429, 430-32, 440, 442-43, 453, 454-55, 476n1, 509; **30:** 26, 27 and continuing education for sailors, **30:** 145,n3; on EAW's death, **30:** 356; and Joint State and Navy Neutrality Board, **30:** 435; quotes WW on W. M. Trotter incident, **31:** 309n2; and O. Gardner resolution, **31:** 411; **32:** 501,n3; and "Tipperary" song incident, **32:** 21,n3; and Turtle Bay incident, **32:** 528n1; and *Eastland* disaster, **34:** 45,n1, 56-57,n1; and Haiti, **34:** 45, 61-62, 70-71, 79, 81; congratulates WW on *Arabic* pledge, **34:** 410-11; campaign to improve public image of, **34:536,n1, 537; Christmas greetings to WW, **35:** 390, 409; on jeopardy to oil reserves by general leasing bill, **37:** 39-41, 65-66, 141, 142, 143, 172,n2, 269; WW's birthday greetings to, **37:** 70-71, 71; and Santo Domingo, **37:** 157-58,n3; on naval appropriations bill, **37:** 267; urges passage of child-labor and workmen's compensation bills, **37:** 428-29; on E. Keating and woman suffrage, **37:** 515; on WW's campaign, **38:** 545, 616-17; photograph: *illustration section,* 27
Daniels, Josephus, Jr., **31:** 524; **33:** 486
Daniels, Robertson Balfour, **27:** 129,n2
Daniels, Roger, **27:** 220n3
Daniels, Winthrop More, **27:** 58, 66; **28:** 119; **29:** 406,n1; **30:** 103,n2, **31:** 247, 269
Daniels, Worth Bagley, **31:** 524; **33:** 486
Danish West Indies: and U.S. purchase of, **33:** 405,n1, 465,n1; **34:** 280, 462-63; **35:** 202-203, 284-85, 290, 349, 350, 401-403, 407, 432n1, 447, 508-509; **36:** 292; **37:** 452, 476, 484, 485, 495, 496-97, 506, 512, 539; **38:** 10,n1; and Monroe Doctrine, **35:** 246-47

Dansville, N.Y., **34:** 125, 140, 141, 152, 154, 166, 168, 178
D'Antin, Louis, **27:** 545; **28:** 232,n1
Dardanelles, **32:** 45, 225n1, 266, 300, 360, 475, 480; **33:** 17, 18, 122, 189, 230, 232, 405, 407, 501, 522, 549, 551; **34:** 18, 42, 310, 311; **35:** 8, 75, 83, 185, 413
Dare, Susan, **35:** 155,n1, 162
Darien, China, **31:** 509; **33:** 321
Daring, Hope: *see* Johnson, Anna
Dark Invader (Rintelen), **33:** 437n1
Darnielle, E. E., **36:** 364
Dartiguenave, Philippe Sudre, **34:** 143,n2, 158, 311n1; elected president of Haiti, **34:** 256-57,n1
Dartmouth College, **37:** 363n3
Darwin, Charles III, **28:** 52
Darwin, Maud, Lady Darwin (widow of Sir George Howard Darwin), **28:** 52
Daughters of Liberty, **32:** 96
Daughters of the American Revolution, **27:** 306-307; **33:** 14-16, n1,2, 149n3, 431; **35:** 19; **36:** 629n1; **37:** 482n1: WW address to, **35:** 47-51; WW welcome to, **36:** 489-90
Daughters of the Confederacy: *see* United Daughters of the Confederacy
Davenport, Ia.: WW's remarks in, **36:** 75
David, Marion L. (later Mrs. Ralph Kingsbury), **32:** 518,n2; **34:** 217; **35:** 28, 109
David, Ross, **28:** 398,n1; **32:** 518,n1; **34:** 217; **35:** 28, 423; **37:** 246
David, Mrs. Ross, **34:** 217; **35:** 28, 109; **37:** 246
Davidson, Jo, **36:** 415,n1, 565, 565-66; **37:** 70, 100-101, 221,n1; busts of WW and E. M. House by: *illustration section,* 37
Davidson, Randall Thomas, **35:** 499,n1
Davidson College, **30:** 37; yearbook dedicated to WW, **35:** 95-96
Davies, Clarence, **34:** 412
Davies, Emlen Knight, (Mrs. Joseph Edward), **29:** 79
Davies, Hywel, **30:** 488,n1; **31:** 51, 53
Davies, Joseph Edward, **32:** 61, 116; **35:** 200; **36:** 274, 401, 410,n1; as cabinet possibility, **27:** 21; as possible Governor General of Philippines, **27:** 255-57, 259, 274; **28:** 595; WW appoints Commissioner of Corporations, **27:** 345,n1; and trust legislation, **29:** 78-88, 99; on Clayton bill, **29:** 320-21; on proposed trade commission, **30:** 427-31; **31:** 500-501, 531, 548; appointed chairman, Federal Trade Commission, **32:** 271,n1; and J. A. Aylward, **36:** 315-16, 482, 500-501, 510-11; and Federal Trade Commission, **37:** 117n1, 204-205,n2,3, 268
Davignon, Jacques, **30:** 458,n1
Davis, Allen Freeman, **34:** 251n8
Davis, Ben G., **27:** xi; **30:** 49, 404; **32:** 245, 369, 459, 542
Davis, Charles Russell, **37:** 101-102,n2
Davis, Edward Parker, **28:** 320,n2, 335,

Davis, Edward Parker (*cont.*)
393; **30:** 312; **32:** 117; **33:** 235, 395; **35:** 275; **36:** 373, 384; **37:** 163, 165, 523; **38:** 689n1
Davis, Ellen Duane Gillespie (Mrs. Edward Parker), **31:** 454,n2; **33:** 395; **37:** 522-23, 529
Davis, Harry L., **36:** 41n1
Davis, James Harvey (Cyclone), **36:** 175,n1
Davis, Jefferson, **33:** 550
Davis, John Warren, **27:** 141n1, 190-91
Davis, John William, **33:** 491,n1, 492, 493, 501; **34:** 53,n1, 134; **37:** 139, 365; suggested as Democratic national chairman, **37:** 129, 131, 151, 206
Davis, Katherine Bement, **38:** 161n2, 162
Davis, Richard Harding, **34:** 251n8
Davis, Robert Beale, Jr., **34:** 61,n1, 311n1, 367, 437-38
Davis, Mrs. Seymour (of Philadelphia), **28:** 310
Davison, Henry Pomeroy, **28:** 428, 430; **30:** 373,n1; **31:** 148,n2
Dawson, Else Münsterberg (Mrs. William Harbutt), **33:** 19,n3
Dawson, Francis Warrington, **28:** 397,n2
Dawson, Robert MacGregor, **35:** 317n2
Dawson, William Harbutt, **33:** 19,n3
Day, Frank Miles, **28:** 435,n4
Day, William Rufus, **29:** 25, 517
Day, The, N.Y., **36:** 656
Dayton, Ohio, **31:** 119-20
De Conde, Alexander, **27:** 288n6
De Forrest, Robert Weeks, **31:** 291, 295
De La Barra, Francisco León, **33:** 194n1
De la Rosa, Luis: *see* Rosa, Luis de la
De Lacy, William Henry, **27:** 109,n2
De Peña, Carlos Maria: *see* Peña, Carlos Maria de
De re metallica (Agricola), **31:** 332,n1
De Saulles, John Gerard Longer, **27:** 110,n2, 385; **28:** 4, 5
Declaration of Independence, **28:** 436; **30:** 248,n1, 250, 253, 254; **37:** 82, 120, 334; **38:** 541-42
Declaration of Interdependence (Holt), **37:** 120,n2
Declaration of London, **31:** 85, 86-87, 90-91, 96-97, 97-98, 98, 99-100, 103-105, 105-106, 109, 110, 113-18, 125-26, 133-36, 138, 146-47, 154-55, 155-56, 158, 159-66, 160n1, 188-92, 197-204, 216, 229, 230,n1, 231, 244, 294, 438, 444, 445-46, 489; **32:** 46, 130, 255, 358, 359, 412,n1,2, 414, 425, 445; **33:** 320; **35:** 453; **36:** 129-30, 131, 270, 537; **37:** 460, 462; **38:** 243,n2, 410
Declaration of Paris (1856), **32:** 445
Declaration of Policy (Levermore), **36:** 374n1
Declaration of Rights, **28:** 436-37
Declaration to the Nation by the First Chief of the Constitutionalist Government of Mexico and Depository of the

Executive Power of the Republic (Carranza), **33:** 308n1, 398n1, 417,n2
Deemer, Jesse, **37:** 22n4
Defender of the Faith, William Jennings Bryan: The Last Decade 1915-25 (Levine), **33:** 370n1
Degen, Mary Louise, **32:** 516n2
Del Valle, Reginaldo Francisco, **28:** 6-7,n1,2, 10, 26, 40
Deland, Margaret Wade, **31:** 316n2, 317
Delaney, John Pope, **34:** 156,n4, 205, 213
Delano, Frederic Adrian, **36:** 192, 203; **37:** 463, 467-68, 472, 479; on Federal Reserve Board, **30:** 344,n1, 350, 353; **34:** 278, 316-17; as possible cabinet member, **33:** 441, 445
Delano, Matilda Annis Peasley (Mrs. Frederic Adrian), **33:** 441,n2, 445
Delaware, **38:** 376n1, 515n1; senatorial election, **27:** 25,n1, 39,n3; and woman suffrage, **37:** 503
Delaware and Hudson Railroad, **30:** 295
Delaware, Lackawanna, and Western Railroad Co., **27:** 116,n1
Delbrück, Clemens Gottlieb Ernst von, **33:** 332,n2, 361; **34:** 47; **35:** 197
Delbrück, Hans, **37:** 86
Delcassé, Théophile, **32:** 205, 220,n1, 276, 335, 341, 373, 378, 422, 521, 522, 523; **33:** 11, 63; **35:** 381
Delineator, The, **31:** 490; **37:** 541,n1
Demi-Gods (Stephens), **34:** 287,n1
democracy, **27:** 36; **30:** 142
Democratic Bulletin, **37:** 378, 379n1
Democratic Congressional Campaign Committee, **30:** 466n4
Democratic Fair Play Association: *see* National Democratic Fair Play Association
Democratic National Committee, **32:** 175; **33:** 420, 421; **35:** 239, 291, 460n1; **36:** 480; **38:** 16n2, 27, 46n1, 139-41,n1, 197n1, 284n1, 296n1, 637; WW's talk to, **35:** 312-16; and death of T. J. Pence, **36:** 371,n1; suggestions for chairman of, **36:** 378, 597-98; **37:** 206, 210, 227; and McCombs resignation, **36:** 479, 480, 525-26, 543; new quarters for, **36:** 518,n1; House's suggestions for executive committee, **37:** 45-46, 56, 57, 76-77, 117-18, 119, 128-29, 129-30, 133, 151, 203, 236; WW's suggestions, **37:** 118,n1, 156, 163-64, 206, 229, 230; executive committee named, **37:** 229, 230, 231; F. L. Polk declines to serve, **37:** 245; J. P. Tumulty on campaign, **37:** 378-79,n1; D. C. Roper named assistant chairman, **37:** 474-75,n1; WW sends check to, **37:** 508; Progressives associated with, **37:** 513; *see also* Democratic party; Democratic platform; Democratic presidential campaign and election, 1916
Democratic National Convention of 1912 (Baltimore Convention), **27:** 22,n2, 74,

222; **28:** 221; **37:** 279; single-term plank, **27:** 104

Democratic National Convention of 1916 (St. Louis Convention), **36:** 378,n1; **37:** 155-56, 228, 282n1; and R. Wagner, **36:** 530; McCombs on, **36:** 543; WW asks J. Wescott to give nominating speech, **36:** 580-81; M. H. Glynn to be temporary chairman of, **36:** 601; and WW draft of platform, **36:** 602; and M. H. Glynn speech, **37:** 56, 61, 133; WW thanks Glynn, O. James and Wescott, **37:** 282, 286

Democratic party and Democrats, **27:** 41, 42, 43, 68, 148, 275, 374-75, 387; **28:** 255, 257; **29:** 302n1; **30:** 232, 234, 477-78; **31:** 59, 145, 271, 292, 403; **32:** 10, 30-31, 32, 33, 37, 40, 79n2, 112, 192, 539; **33:** 326; **34:** 131n2, 242; **35:** 151, 178, 239, 271, 286, 312, 323, 434; **37:** 269; **38:** 3n4, 179; E. Aguinaldo on victory of, **27:** 10; S. Gompers on labor and, **27:** 187; and M. Dies amendment to free wool bill, **27:** 322n1; tariff, **27:** 418n1, 524; **28:** 35n2; **35:** 433, 476-77; and currency reform bill, **27:** 524, 525; **28:** 90,n1, 91, 373n1, 375, 518; **29:** 64, 65; **30:** 291, 299,n2; and patronage, **28:** 94; **29:** 100n2, 162; and Negroes and segregation, **28:** 98, 115-16, 209-12, 221-22, 223, 240, 349; **30:** 491-93; **31:** 297, 300, 308; **35:** 461; and printing contracts, **28:** 272,n2; and renomination of WW, **29:** 57; and antitrust legislation, **29:** 78, 109, 538; **30:** 110; and woman suffrage, **29:** 213-15; **30:** 227; **36:** 484-85; **37:** 208-209; **38:** 4-5, 9, 9-10, 28; and Panama Canal tolls controversy, **29:** 240-41, 272n1, 298-99, 373-74, 376, 386, 387, 418

and platform: foreign affairs, **29:** 271; interlocking directorates, **31:** 89; presidential term, **27:** 97-101; **31:** 152,n4 and early adjournment of Congress, **29:** 404, 409; and business, **30:** 95; **32:** 34-35, 71; and 1914 congressional campaign and elections, **30:** 466,n4, 477; **32:** 37-38; T. R. Marshall on WW renomination, **31:** 23,n1; WW on, **31:** 171, 173-74, 265; **32:** 375; **37:** 388, 408,n1, 442, 443; **38:** 286-87, 302-303, 311, 328-29, 363, 367, 432, 449-50, 463, 552-53, 578; C. H. Dodge on, **31:** 266-67; H. Münsterberg on, **31:** 277-78; WW on western support for, **31:** 290; N.Y. *World* on 1914 fall elections, **31:** 295n1; and legislative successes, **31:** 326; F. C. Howe on social and economic program of, **31:** 342-43; R. Lansing on German Americans and, **31:** 534-35; Catholics and Mexican situation, **32:** 86; and ship-purchase bill, **32:** 134n1, 173,n2, 222,n2, 227-29, 232, 239, 240,n1, 275, 313, 315; **37:** 366; and L. M. Garrison's threatened resigna-

tion, **32:** 168; and possibility of Bryan's candidacy, **34:** 135, 146n2; Filipinos and, **34:** 389-90; and war-revenue bill, **35:** 370n1; and corrupt-practices bill, **35:** 433, 456; and preparedness, **35:** 479, 494; **36:** 32, 83-84, 143; Tumulty on E. Root's speech and, **36:** 186, 187; Rainey bill and, **36:** 206-207; McLemore resolution and, **36:** 212-13; and Congress on armed-ship controversy, **36:** 214; and water-power legislation, **36:** 328; Tumulty on platform of, **36:** 333-34; C. H. Levermore on, **36:** 362, 363; T. J. Anketell on break with Germany and, **36:** 435; WW on, **36:** 474-76; **38:** 611; W. F. McCombs and, **36:** 525-26, 543; and controversy over Brandeis nomination, **36:** 606-607; and child-labor bill, **37:** 429, 431,n1, 451; achievements compared to Progressive platform of 1912, **37:** 429-30,n1; and Rublee and Brandeis nominations, **38:** 34; W. Stone on senatorial elections, **38:** 277-79; and 1912 election and Progressives, **38:** 446; J.A.H. Hopkins on, **38:** 643; *see also*, Democratic National Committee; Democratic platform

Democratic party and Democrats in Alabama, **29:** 410n1

Democratic party and Democrats in California, **27:** 220n1,3,4, 382, 396; **29:** 373n2

Democratic party and Democrats in Colorado, **31:** 273n2; **37:** 435-36

Democratic party and Democrats in Connecticut, **38:** 168

Democratic party and Democrats in Delaware, **27:** 25n1, 39,n3

Democratic party and Democrats in Illinois, **29:** 261,n1,2; **31:** 232,n2; **37:** 373, 522,n1; **38:** 146n1

Democratic party and Democrats in Kentucky, **29:** 343,n2; **35:** 88

Democratic party and Democrats in Maine, **28:** 149,n1; **38:** 105-106,n1, 170, 173-74, 175

Democratic party and Democrats in Massachusetts, **28:** 275,n2,3; **29:** 247

Democratic party and Democrats in Missouri, **35:** 183, 185, 191

Democratic party and Democrats in New Hampshire, **27:** 158,n1,2

Democratic party and Democrats in New Jersey, **27:** 40,n1, 42-43, 190-91,n1, 375, 380n5, 387, 388, 389, 456, 494n1; **28:** 42n3, 65-66,n1, 83, 93, 96-97,n1, 373,n1,2, 490n2; **38:** 35,n3, 285,n2

Democratic party and Democrats in New York, **28:** 64,n1; **29:** 136,n1, 240,n1, 382, 387, 395,n1, 395-96,n1, 402-404, 422-23, 447-48; **31:** 11-12,n1, 93, 112, 116-17,n1, 123, 139,n1, 148, 161, 167, 252-54, 349,n1; **35:** 398; **37:** 155-56, 290; **38:** 189, 190; and city and state elections, **28:** 490n2; and Sulzer impeach-

Democratic party and Democrats in New
York (*cont.*)
ment, **28:** 149,n1,2, 181; and Negro
support, **30:** 491-92; WW endorses
Glynn, **35:** 156-57; and postmaster-
ship, **35:** 318, 338, 346; E. S. Harris
and W. C. Osborn and, **36:** 458,n1;
R. F. Wagner and, **36:** 530
Democratic party and Democrats in Ohio,
35: 193; **37:** 84, 96,n1
Democratic party and Democrats in
Pennsylvania, **27:** 406; **29:** 222-23,n1,2,
305,n1; **30:** 319; **31:** 188; **37:** 373; and
W. B. Wilson and Senate contest, **36:**
23-25, 137; and M. Liebel's complaints
about appointments, **36:** 336-38
Democratic party and Democrats in
Tennessee, **27:** 55n3
Democratic party and Democrats in
Texas, **31:** 249
Democratic party and Democrats in Vir-
ginia, **27:** 73-74, 200n2; **37:** 228-29,n1
Democratic party and Democrats in
Wisconsin, **30:** 161, 161-62; **31:** 346,n2,
406; **32:** 19
Democratic platform of 1912, **37:** 188,
189, 190, 338
Democratic platform of 1916: A. J.
McKelway on, **37:** 65,n1; endorses
WW's speech before League to Enforce
Peace, **37:** 121, 423; R. L. Owen and
progressive planks, **37:** 151, 161, 162,
174-75; and foreign trade, **37:** 160, 166;
suggestions from five senators, **37:**
169,n1; F. C. Howe on imperialism
planks, **37:** 180-81; Pou on navy and,
38: 181-82, 207, 230; McAdoo on, **37:**
186-90; draft of, **37:** 190-200; and
budget plank, **37:** 211,n1; Tumulty on
German-American issue, **37:** 217-21;
and woman suffrage, **37:** 237,n1, 266,
375-76,n1, 513n1, 529; and peace, **37:**
311-12
Democratic presidential campaign and
election (1916): **38:** 3n2,4, 23-24, 59-
60, 287-88, 293, 302, 318, 319, 321, 334,
349, 376-77,n1,2, 429, 452, 457-58, 513-
14, 515,n1, 610-11; acceptance speech,
38: 9, 27, 63, 66,n1, 126-39, 145, 154,
288, 325, 454; House on Marshall
speeches and, **38:** 11, speeches at
Shadow Lawn, **38:** 212-19, 257-58, 362-
68; on resigning if election is lost, **38:**
493, 494, 617-18, 678-79; refuses to
concede defeat, **38:** 621-22; learns of
victory, **38:** 623-24; congratulatory
messages and replies, **38:** 629-30, 631,
631-32, 632, 633, 642, 648, 649, 656,
664, 665-66; geographical gains made,
38: 645n1; photographs: *illustration
section*, **38:** *see also* under the names
of the individual states
Democratic Record (Taft), **38:** 497,n1
Democratic Revenue Bill (Lippmann), **38:**
87n2
Democratic Text-book 1914, **35:** 137n3

Democratic Text-book 1916, **38:** 27n1,
514n2
Denby, Edwin, **37:** 387-88,n1
Denison, Winfred T., **30:** 156
Denman, William, **27:** 280n1; **38:** 428,n3,
454, 455
Denmark, **31:** 201, 203, 294n1, 480, 526;
32: 46; **33:** 144, 215, 524; **34:** 86, 188,
189, 251n4, 253n1, 398; **35:** 416-17; **38:**
116; *see also* Danish West Indies
Denmark and the United States: and
Danish West Indies, **36:** 292,n1,2, 373
Dennis, Alfred Lewis Pinneo, **37:** 381,n1
Dennison, J. E., **36:** 364
Denny, Austin Flint, **34:** 266
Densmore, John B., **36:** 550,n1, 551
Denton, Frances B., **32:** 117, 119, 442n3;
36: 422; **37:** 103
Denver, Colo., **28:** 512, 589
Denver, University of, **37:** 148n1
Denver Express, **31:** 557,n2
Denver Post, **38:** 520n2
Department of: *see under the latter part
of the name, such as* Justice, Depart-
ment of
depression (business) *see* business
Derby, Edward George Villiers Stanley,
17th Earl of; **35:** 414,n4
Dercum, Francis Xavier, **36:** 297,n2
Dernburg, Bernhard, **31:** 96,n1, 336, 433,
434, 496; **32:** 11; **33:** 48, 69; **34:** 238;
35: 197
Des Moines, Ia., **27:** 198n1; WW's ad-
dress in, **36:** 77-85; American Union
Against Militarism meeting in, **36:** 635,
639
Des Moines, U.S.S., **35:** 337
Des Moines *Register and Leader*, **36:** 85n;
38: 174,n1, 190
Desvernine y Galdós, Pablo, **35:** 130,n3
Detroit, Mich.: and American Union
Against Militarism meeting in, **36:** 635;
WW's addresses in, **37:** 383-87, 387-95
Detroit Athletic Club, **37:** 387n1
Detroit Free Press, **37:** 383n1, 387n, 395n1
Detroit News, **37:** 395n
Deutsch Ohnmachtspolitik im Weltkriege
(Von Tirpitz), **37:** 45n1
Deutsche Bank, **34:** 320; **38:** 18
Deutsche Tageszeitung, **34:** 187n1
Deutschland (commercial submarine), **37:**
425,n2, 461; **38:** 148n1
*Deutschland, Diaz und die mexikanische
Revolution* (Katz), **33:** 298n1
Deutschland und der nächste Krieg
(Bernhardi), **31:** 27n1
Devil Baby at Hull House? (Addams), **38:**
460,n2
Devil's Acre (London *Pall Mall Gazette*),
29: 320,n1
Devine, Edward Thomas, **27:** 244; **29:** 170
Devol, Edmond, **28:** 259,n1; **35:** 272n6;
38: 16
Dewey, Alice Chipman (Mrs. John), **38:**
175, 175-76, 189
Dewey, Davis Rich, **27:** 206-207, 301n1

Dewey, George, **33:** 216n1
Dewey, John, **38:** 445n1
Díaz, Adolfo, **29:** 204, 221, 222, 274-75
Díaz, Felix, **27:** 119, 252n2, 383, 537, 538, 538-39, 542, 545, 548, 551; **28:** 18, 78, 101, 157, 201n2, 268,n2, 298, 377, 423, 429; **29:** 126, 257, 330; **32:** 343; **35:** 501n1, 505
Díaz, José de la Cruz Porfirio (1830-1915), **27:** 64,n2, 119n1, 141, 331, 421, 537; **28:** 59, 69n1, 70-71, 72, 74, 75, 77, 206, 213, 298, 341, 422, 460, 506; **29:** 18, 47, 97, 122, 123, 167, 253, 255, 459, 519, 520, 522; **30:** 25, 42n1, 97, 234, 237, 443n1, 445; **32:** 39, 386,n1; **33:** 89; **34:** 148, 242; **36:** 600; **37:** 341, 510
Díaz, Porfirio, Jr., **29:** 18
Díaz Lombardo, Miguel, **31:** 66, 69, 71; **32:** 383,n, 384; **33:** 398n1
Dickey Memorial Presbyterian Church of Baltimore, **33:** 49n1
Dickinson, George L., **35:** 237,n2, 355
Dickinson, Jacob McGavock, **27:** 126; **32:** 217-19,n1
Dickinson, Lowes, **32:** 24, 53
Dickinson, Willoughby Hyett, **38:** 207,n1, 207-208
Dickinson High School, Jersey City, **27:** 386n1
Dickson, Mr., **34:** 153,n1
Dickson, Bessie Louise, **28:** 333,n1
Diego, José de, **37:** 455-56,n1
Diéguaz, Manuel, **32:** 388
Dies, Martin, **27:** 322n1; **36:** 175,n1, 186n2
Digby, Margaret, **29:** 60n4
Digest of International Law (Moore), **36:** 226n2
Digest of the Proceedings of the Council of National Defense during World War (Martin), **38:** 182n1
Diggs, Maury I., **28:** 99n4
Diggs-Caminetti cases, **28:** 99,n4
Dill, Clarence Cleveland, **37:** 12,n2
Dillard, James Hardy, **31:** 464n1
Dimmick, J. Benjamin, **29:** 401n1
Dinant, Belgium, **31:** 16
diplomatic corps in Washington: greeted by WW and WJB, **27:** 171; desires to congratulate WW and EBW, **35:** 352-53, 397
Diplomatic Dealings of the Constitutionalist Revolution of Mexico, **36:** 350,n2, 496n1
diplomatic service, **27:** 69-70, 300, 326, 434, 462; **28:** 272, 280, 317; **36:** 175-76,n1; *see also* Wilson, Woodrow: appointments, diplomatic
Dissatisfactions (New York *Globe*), **35:** 221n2
direct election of senators, **27:** 54; **37:** 174
direct presidential preference primary, **37:** 338-39
disarmament: E. M. House on, **29:** 12-13
discrimination: Japan and California alien land legislation, **27:** 344, 360, 416,

463; **28:** 283, 284, 344; *see also* Negroes; segregation
Disentangling Alliance (London *Nation*), **37:** 294n1
District of Columbia: *see* Washington, D.C.
Dividing Line (New York *Globe*), **29:** 515,n2
Dixon, Frederick, **32:** 174,n3
Dixon, Joseph Kossuth, **27:** 507-508,n1,2
Dixon, Thomas, Jr., **28:** 88-89, 94; **32:** 142,n1, 267,n1, 310, 486n3; **34:** 426-27,n1,2
Dodd, George Allan, **36:** 283,n1, 397, 585
Dodd, Townsend F., **36:** 353,n4
Dodge, Arthur Murray, **30:** 257n1
Dodge, Cleveland Earl, **37:** 331
Dodge, Cleveland Hoadley, **27:** ix, 23, 92,n1, 103, 110, 144-45, 167, 168, 175, 179, 190, 247-48, 263, 274-75, 283, 284, 290; **28:** 58, 203, 220-21; **29:** 456, 554; **30:** 189, 303-304; **31:** 204-205, 216, 260, 266-67, 320, 358, 454; **33:** 383, 395; **34:** 28, 32-33, 358, 397; **35:** 39, 57, 73, 137, 146, 152, 155, 160, 176, 178, 179, 274-75, 492; **36:** 132, 138, 191, 280, 377, 518; **37:** 42, 330-31, 347; **38:** 154-55, 157-58, 591n1, 597n2, 649; on recognition of Mexico, **28:** 41-42; on murder of Americans in, **35:** 478; provides funds to keep W. H. Page in London, **30:** 277-78, 281-82, 288,n1, 490; **31:** 122; on EAW's death, **30:** 359, 426
Dodge, Elizabeth Wainwright, **31:** 454,n3; **35:** 39,n1, 57; **37:** 331
Dodge, Grace Parish (Mrs. Cleveland Hoadley), **30:** 282; **31:** 320; **35:** 39; **37:** 331; **38:** 155
Dodge, Henry Percival, **30:** 39, 138n2
Dodge, Josephine Marshall Jewell (Mrs. Arthur Murray), **30:** 257,n1
Dodge, Mary Hoadley, **34:** 28,n1
Dodge, Randolph, **32:** 97
Doerries, Reinhard R., **27:** xxii; **33:** 473n1; **35:** 43n1; **36:** 503n1
Dogger Bank incident, **35:** 395,n3
Doheny, Edward Lawrence, **27:** 404n1
dollar diplomacy, **27:** 195, 423, 488; **28:** 177; **29:** 93, 419; **30:** 251; **37:** 180, 181, 510
Dolphin, U.S.S., **29:** 421, 429, 430, 431, 440, 454, 463, 464, 468, 471, 484; **33:** 249; **37:** 157n3
Dominican Republic, **28:** 48, 124,n2, 221n1; **29:** 20,n1, 94; **30:** 165, 203,n1, 213, 260, 296, 307-309, 319, 346, 363, 493; **32:** 457; **33:** 440, 451, 452; **34:** 78; **35:** 188, 247, 259; **37:** 157-59; and Mexico: **28:** 412
Dominican Republic and the United States, **27:** 215,n1, 219, 265, 272,n1, 385, 495, 518-20, 531; and Sullivan scandal, **31:** 382-84,n2, 403-404,n2, 410, 411, 414,n4, 447-48, 453, 467; and Haiti, **31:** 457, 485, 487; **32:** 353-54,n1, 466, 469; **33:** 218-20; compared to Haiti,

Dominican Republic and the U.S. (*cont.*) **32:** 27, 28, 62, 288, 289, 295,n1, 473, 479; **34:** 67; political crisis in, **32:** 76-77,n1; **33:** 26-27; and appointments to, **34:** 24-25

Dominici, Santos Anibal, **31:** 480,n1, 481

Donald, John A., **38:** 455,n2, 456

Donald, Robert, **35:** 473, 524,n1

Donald Steamship Co., **38:** 455n2

Donk, Benjamin de Jong van Beek en, **37:** 75,n1

Donnersmarck, Prince: *see* Henckel von Donnersmarck, Count Guido

Dooley, Mr. (Dunne), **30:** 259

Doremus, Frank Ellsworth, **27:** 225-26, 244; **29:** 282, 298; **30:** 475-78; **31:** 112,n1; **36:** 211

Dorr, Rheta Louise Childe (Mrs. John Pixley), **30:** 227,n4, 228

Dorsey, George Amos, **38:** 170n1

Doshisha University (Kyoto), **29:** 243n1

Doubleday, Page and Co., **37:** 324n1

Douglas, Charles Alexander, **27:** 526-30,n1; **28:** 358, 359; **29:** 142, 143, 172, 173, 525; **30:** 118; **33:** 3, 4, 295,n2, 409-10, 419; **34:** 531

Douglas, Lee, **27:** 84; **29:** 304, 317, 322

Douglas, William Lewis, **38:** 197-98,n2, 468, 591n1

Douglas, Ariz., **29:** 91, 130; **37:** 284

Douglas, Baker, Ruffin and Obear, Washington, D.C., **27:** 526n1

Doumergue, Gaston, **29:** 180n1, 233-38,n1

Dover, N.H., **30:** 400

Dowling, Robert, **36:** 542

Dowling, Victor James, **27:** 102; **35:** 178; **38:** 429

Downes, Edward Olin, **37:** 526-27,n1, 538

Downes, Edward Olin Davenport, **37:** 526n1

Downey, George E., **29:** 54

Doyle, Arthur Conan, **27:** 464; **37:** 447

Doyle, Ed L., **29:** 479, 479-80; **31:** 37

Doyle, James, **27:** 465

Doyle, Michael Francis, **36:** 566,n1, 580n1; **37:** 353, 446-47; **38:** 316, 350, 443-45

Doyle, W. H., **38:** 574,n3

draft: *see* conscription

Draper, Eben Sumner, **29:** 401n1

Dreicer, Jacob, **35:** 19,n2, 42

Dreicer and Co., N.Y., **35:** 192,n2

Dreiser, Theodore, **37:** 541,n1

Dresselhuys, Hendrik Coenraad, **37:** 75,n1

Dressler, Marie, **28:** 178,n2

Drexel Institute, **31:** 16; **36:** 601n4; **38:** 182n3, 386

Droppers, Garrett, **27:** 206-207, 492; **28:** 320, 326; **36:** 358-59; **37:** 60, 97; **38:** 523-24

Druid Oak Belting Co. (Baltimore), **27:** 192

Drummond, Sir (James) Eric, **33:** 462n; **35:** 346n1

Drummond, Michael J., **27:** 245, 246

Dublán, Mex., **37:** 315; **38:** 45, 379, 380, 399, 404-405

Dublin, N.H., **28:** 108,n1, 291, 447, 477; **35:** 64

Dubofsky, Melvyn, **34:** 539n2

DuBois, James Taylor, **28:** 198,n4; **36:** 235

DuBois, William Edward Burghardt, **28:** 165, 344, 350; **38:** 459-60, 522,n1

Dubose, Rosalie Anderson (Mrs. Mc-Neely), **28:** 400,n3

Dubose, McNeely, **28:** 400,n5

Duff-Gordon, Lady (dress designer), **35:** 162,n2

Dumba, Constantin Theodor, **29:** 74,n3; **31:** 5-6, 10, 140, 296, 385; **32:** 94, 99, 235,n1, 462; **33:** 88, 223; **34:** 187, 430, 452,n1; **35:** 43,n1, 193, 438; **36:** 124; **38:** 298, 544; and Bryan, **33:** 212-13, 247,n1, 333, 335; **34:** 158,n3; plots disruption of munitions production, **34:** 403n1, 403-404,n3, 428, 429,n1; recall of, **34:** 408, 426, 432,n1, 432-33,n1, 433, 435, 445n5, 471, 503,n1, 515

Dumont, Frederick Theodore Freling-huysen, **34:** 546,n2

Dumont, Mary Wolfe (Mrs. Frederick Theodore Frelinghuysen), **34:** 546,n2

Duncan, John Steele, **38:** 517,n1

Duneka, Frederick A., **33:** 149n3; **34:** 57,n1; **36:** 176-77, 516, 543, 600-601

Dunlap, John Robertson, **29:** 395,n1; **34:** 536,n1, 537; **38:** 172-73

Dunne, Edward Fitzsimons, **27:** 9,n2; **36:** 63n1; **37:** 522,n1; **38:** 457, 489n1, 491

Dunne, Finley Peter, **28:** 181,n1; **29:** 56n2, 333n1; **30:** 259

Dunning, James Edward, **33:** 194n1

Dunsley, S.S., **34:** 265, 305, 340, 417, 439, 449

DuPont de Nemours, Pierre Samuel (1739-1817), **35:** 133

DuPont factory (E. I. duPont de Ne-mours and Co.), **35:** 355

Durango, Durango, Mex., **28:** 7,n1, 28, 30, 163,n3, 213, 341; **30:** 101n3

Durango, state, Mex., **28:** 31, 77; **29:** 30; **37:** 251

Durbin, William W., **28:** 354,n3; **37:** 84, 96,n1

Dutch Harbor, Alaska, **33:** 34-35

Dutch Minister to the United States: *see* Rappard, Willem Louis Frederick Christiaan van

DuVivier, Ulrich, **33:** 467n1

Dwight Braman and Co., N.Y., **31:** 291n4

Dyer, Edith LaBau (Mrs. E. Tiffany), **36:** 3n1

Dyer, Jessie Kennedy (Mrs. Harvey), niece of WW, **32:** 147; **35:** 409, 508

dyestuffs industry, **36:** 261,n2,3, 274-76, 406, 410, 487

E. P. Dutton and Co., N.Y., **28:** 390n1

Eagle, Joe Henry, **28:** 122,n4, 128

Eagle, U.S.S., **34:** 165
Eagle Pass, Tex., **37:** 245, 284
Eagle Point, S.S., **36:** 449, 483n1, 486
East River, New York, **37:** 15, 27, 54
East St. Louis, Ill.: WW's remarks in, **36:** 121-22
Eastland Disaster (Taylor), **34:** 27n1
Eastland disaster and investigation, **34:** 27,n1, 45,n1, 48-49, 56-57,n1, 65, 71-72, 81-82,n1, 136, 217
Eastland Disaster Relief, American Red Cross, 1915-1918, **34:** 27n1
Eastman, Crystal, **36:** 632n1
Eastman, John Coates, **27:** 241,n1
Eastman, Max, **36:** 635,n7, 639
Eastman Kodak Co., **30:** 482
Eberle, Edward Walter, **37:** 147,n1
Eccles, Silas Wright, **27:** 481,n2, 482
Echo Lake, Vt., **34:** 161
Eckhardt, Heinrich von, **35:** 100,n2
Economist, The, **28:** 276,n1; **37:** 352,n1
Ecuador, **28:** 177; **35:** 520; **36:** 200; appointments to, **28:** 4, 4-5,n3, 175; loans to, **28:** 123-25
Edge, Walter Evans, **38:** 432n3, 609,n2
Edison, Thomas Alva, **35:** 29n1; **38:** 166
Edison Hotel, Schenectady, N.Y., **34:** 77
Edith Bolling Wilson: First Lady Extraordinary (Hatch), **32:** 423n1
Edith Cavell (Ryder), **35:** 88n4, 103n1
Edith Cavell, Pioneer and Patriot (Clark-Kennedy), **35:** 103n1
Edmunds, George Franklin, **27:** 182, 183, 322,n2
education: WW on preparedness and, **36:** 13, 29-30; *see also* vocational education bill
Edward VII (of Great Britain), **33:** 484
Edward Pierce, S.S., **31:** 477
Edwards, Agustin, **36:** 445,n1
Edwards, Bessie Rochester Porter (Mrs. Clarence Ransom), **34:** 125,n6
Edwards, Clarence Ransom, **34:** 125,n6, 137, 138, 140, 323
Edwards, Edward Irving, **28:** 96,n1
Edwards, J. H., **33:** 218,n4
Edwards, Thomas D., **29:** 285n1, 295
Edwards, William Hanford ("Big Bill"), **38:** 362n1
Eells, Mrs. Stillman Witt, **27:** 106
Efficiency Society, **32:** 133n1
Egan, Maurice Francis, **27:** 507, 517; **33:** 465n1; **34:** 280,n1, 462-63,n1; **35:** 196, 285,n2, 349, 350, 402; **37:** 476
Egerton, George William, **38:** 207n1
Egypt, **28:** 576, 586; **29:** 47; **33:** 230; **35:** 104, 226, 360, 466; M. A. Hulbert's trip to, **29:** 371
Ehrgott, Mr., **37:** 237n1
Eight-Hour Commission, **38:** 38, 95, 278, 429; appointments made to, **38:** 354n1
eight-hour law: *see* Adamson Act
Eight Years with Wilson's Cabinet, 1913 to 1920 (Houston), **33:** 295n4; **35:** 512n2
Einicke, Paul, **34:** 97

Eitel Friedrich, Prince (of Germany), **38:** 71,n5
Eitel, Henry, **37:** 469,n1
Ekengren, Wilhelm August Ferdinand, **27:** 477,n1; **33:** 279n1, 284,n1; **34:** 539,n2; **35:** 529n1; and Hillstrom case, **35:** 3, 58, 69, 73-74, 84, 207, 213
El Paso, Tex., **29:** 494, 498; **30:** 193, 230n1, 283n1, 290n1, 408, 413, 418; **31:** 64; **33:** 29, 471, 474, 482; **34:** 56; **36:** 296,n2, 339, 395n1, 407,n2, 408; **37:** 231, 253, 254, 255, 284, 285, 291n1, 315, 360-61; **38:** 547; Villa and customs revenues, **30:** 347
El Paso *Times*, **30:** 413; **37:** 159n1
El Salvador, **27:** 439, 540; **28:** 56, 460; **29:** 132; **32:** 470,n1,2,3
El Valle, Mex., **38:** 45, 399
Eleanora of Bulgaria, **30:** 22
Elberon, N.J., **38:** 154, 155, 157, 209
Election of Reserve Bank Directors (New York *Sun*), **30:** 50n1
election reform, **29:** 7-8
elections of 1914, **31:** 403; **32:** 37-38; WW on Republican victories, **31:** 264-65; and Colorado coal strike, **31:** 273,n2; H. Münsterberg on, **31:** 277; WW on support from the West, **31:** 290; C. A. Spring Rice on, **31:** 292, 315; New York *World* on, **31:** 295,n1; R. Pulitzer on, **31:** 314; L. Nieman on Democratic victory in Wisconsin, **38:** 406
electoral reform (N.J.), **27:** 376
Electric Power Development in the United States (Houston), **36:** 50,n2
Electric Railway Association: *see* American Electric Railway Association
Elegy Written in a Country Churchyard (Gray), **31:** 279; **38:** 524,n1
Elevated Railway Co., **30:** 86
Elguero, Luis, **30:** 45, 47, 66, 77, 115, 119, 228
Elguero, Rafael, **30:** 115
Elias, Francisco, **37:** 22,n2
Eliot, Charles William, **28:** 272, 279-80, 317; **29:** 246-47, 269, 270, 367, 369, 544; **30:** 73-74, 432, 434-35; **31:** 109, 455; **32:** 105, 238-39, 263-64, 275-76; **33:** 100, 226; **34:** 11, 29-30, 45, 251; **35:** 486, 500-501, 506-508, 535; **36:** 261,n1, 477; **37:** 269, 314, 322, 336, 535,n2; **38:** 34, 86,n1, 117, 167-68, 193,n1, 279-80, 319,n1, 352-54
possible appointee: minister to China, **27:** 28, 62, 65, 69, 70, 71, 80, 92, 110, 124; ambassador to England, **27:** 194, 198, 199, 228; and inscriptions for Post Office building, **28:** 366n1, 501, 502, 505; on Federal Reserve Board appointments, **29:** 247,n1; on government and railroads, **29:** 338-40, 345; **30:** 305, 309; on Mexican situation, **29:** 533-34; **30:** 5-6; and European war, **30:** 353-55, 379-80, 403, 418-20; on immigration bill, **32:** 93; on formation of

Eliot, Charles William (*cont.*)
   mediation committee, **33:** 17-20; on
   Lusitania notes, **33:** 202, 513-15
Eliot, George, **38:** 256
Eliot, Grace Mellen Hopkinson (Mrs.
   Charles William), **27:** 70n1
Eliot, Samuel Atkins, **27:** 80,n1
Elkus, Abram Isaac, **27:** 244, 384-85; ap-
   pointed ambassador to Turkey, **36:**
   378n3
Ellen, S.S. **31:** 477, 479
Ellen Wilson Fund for Christian Edu-
   cation of Mountain Youth, **30:** 452; **31:**
   259-60,n1, 260, 266
Ellen Wilson Memorial, **33:** 429-32; **35:**
   153n2
Ellen Wilson Memorial Homes, **33:**
   431,n6; **34:** 16-17; **35:** 205-206,n1
Ellicott Club, Buffalo, **38:** 572n1
Elliott, Edward Graham, **27:** 91,n2,
   239n1; **29:** 245,n1, 246, 262, 277; **34:**
   523; **35:** 41, 60-61, 293, 393; **36:** 329;
   38: 190-91
Elliott, Howard, **29:** 368-69; **30:** 295
Elliott, John Lovejoy, **36:** 632n1
Elliott, Margaret Graham Johnston (Mrs.
   William Yandell), **27:** 239,n1,3
Elliott, Margaret Randolph Axson (Mrs.
   Edward Graham), sister of EAW, **28:**
   318; **30:** 425; **34:** 523; **35:** 41, 60-61, 61,
   293, 392-93; **36:** 329; **38:** 190-91, 688
Ellis (Henry) Havelock, **36:** 415n1
Ellis, William Thomas, **27:** 247,n2, 263
Ellis Island, **27:** 95; **32:** 124
Ellison, William B., **27:** 246
Elm Lawn Inn, N.H., **28:** 132
Eltinge Theatre, N.Y., **27:** 140n2
Ely, Carl, **38:** 278
Ely, Matthias Cowell, **27:** 456, 480, 482-
   83, 494; **32:** 272
Elzina, S.S. **36:** 429, 430
Emancipation Proclamation, **27:** 15
emergency currency: and cotton crop, **31:**
   127, 128
Emergency Currency Act, **30:** 325,n1,
   326, 334-35; *see also* Aldrich-Vreeland
   Act
emergency revenue bill: *see* war-reve-
   nue bill
Emerson, Edwin, Jr., **34:** 528,n4; **36:**
   563,n2
Emerson, Isaac Edward, **29:** 89,n1, 90
Emerson Drug Co., Baltimore, **29:** 89n1
Emery, Sloan M., **28:** 295,n3, 296
Emigrant Industrial Savings Bank, N.Y.,
   27: 245, 246
*Emissaries to a Revolution: Woodrow
   Wilson's Executive Agents in Mexico*
   (Hill), **28:** 6n1; **29:** 98n1, 285n1, 450n1;
   30: 47n1,2, 166n1, 193n1, 230n1; **32:**
   202n2
Emory College, **35:** 45
Empey, Charles, **28:** 398
Empire Coal Mining Co., Colo., **29:** 549
Empire Theater, N.Y., **35:** 19n1, 44

*Employes' Representation in Coal Mines:
   A Study of the Industrial Representa-
   tion Plan of the Colorado Fuel and Iron
   Company* (Selekman and Van Kleeck),
   35: 317n2
*Employees Not Asking Real Eight-Hour
   Day*, **36:** 204n1
employment bureau bills, **32:** 54-55
Emporia Kan. *Gazette*, **30:** 32,n1; **33:**
   247,n1
End of Huerta Regime (London *Times*),
   30: 287n1
Endicott, Caroline Seward (Mrs. Rob-
   ert), **34:** 182,n1, 245
Endicott, Henry Bradford, **38:** 461,n1,
   591n1
Endicott, Johnson and Co., **38:** 483, 510,
   571-72
Endless Chain, Interlocking Director-
   ates (Brandeis), **29:** 30n1
*Enemy Within: The Inside Story of Ger-
   man Sabotage in America* (Landau), **36:**
   527n2
Enforcement of Peace (*New Statesman*),
   37: 294n1
Engineering Magazine, **29:** 395n1; **34:**
   536,n1
England: *see* Great Britain
England, 1870-1914 (Ensor), **27:** 251n1
English, Harry David Williams, **27:** 244
English Channel, **32:** 193n1, 194, 196n1,
   201n1, 208; **34:** 15n1
English Review, **28:** 371n3; **30:** 192n2
Englishman, S.S., **36:** 378,n2, 449, 483n1,
   486
Engraving and Printing, Bureau of: seg-
   regation in, **28:** 60, 403-404, 408, 409,
   454, 492, 498n1; **31:** 299, 312, 361n2
Enríquez, Ignacio Perches, **30:** 408,n2
Ensor, Robert Charles Kirkwood, **27:**
   251n1
Entente powers, **36:** 253, 383-84
*Enterprise Denied: Origins of the Decline
   of American Railroads, 1897-1917*
   (Martin), **29:** 140n3
Epistle Containing the Strange Medical
   Experience of Karshish, the Aram
   Physician (Browning), **38:** 259,n2
Epoch Producing Co., **32:** 455n2
Equinox Hotel, Manchester, Vt., **34:** 63,
   64
Erie, Pa., **36:** 336
Erie County, Pa., **34:** 211; **36:** 337
Erie Railroad, **38:** 466n1
Erie (Pa.) *Times*, **36:** 336,n2
Errera, Paul, **38:** 662
Escandón, Pablo (Governor of Morelos),
   29: 18
Esch, John Jacob, **36:** 301,n2
Escudero, Francisco, **28:** 59, 59-60, 340,
   342, 563-64, 568, 580; memorandum,
   28: 70-81; aide mémoire, **28:** 370
Eshleman, John Morton, **37:** 140-41,n3
Espinosa, Martin, **28:** 77
Essen, Germany, **31:** 155

Essex County, N.J., **27:** 373-74,n1, 378, 379, 387-88, 456, 483; **28:** 373n2
Essig, Joseph I., **31:** 183
Estañol, Jorge Vera, **27:** 545; **28:** 292
estate taxes, **38:** 51n1
Esteva, Gonzalo A., **32:** 431,n1, 432
Esteva Ruiz, R. A., **29:** 428
Ethiopia (ship), **27:** 348,n1
Eulalia (Infanta of Spain), **33:** 47,n1
European Tragedy (*Atlantic Monthly*), **31:** 370n2
Eustis, William Corcoran, **27:** 59, 61
Evangeline (Longfellow), **28:** 291
Evans, Charles (Chick), **38:** 374-75,n1
Evans, Elizabeth Gardiner (Mrs. Glendower), **29:** 214; **37:** 9-10
Evans, Powell, **31:** 187-88,n1.
Evans, Robert Kennon, **38:** 238,n7
Evarts, Mary, **28:** 102-103,n1
Evarts, Maxwell, **28:** 165, 387,n1
Evarts, William Maxwell, **28:** 62n3, 102-103,n1, 387n1
Evarts family, **28:** 62,n3, 66, 92, 103
Evening Star Club, **36:** 375n1
Ewing, Harriet Hoyt (Hattie) (Mrs. Robert), **31:** 83
Ewing, Robert (of Nashville), **31:** 83, 377
Ewing, Robert (of New Orleans), **27:** 286,n3; **31:** 180n5
Executive Office appropriations bill, **36:** 330,n1
Exit President Huerta (London *Times*), **30:** 287n1
Expansion of Trade in China (Whitehead), **33:** 32,n2
Exposition Music Hall, Pittsburgh, **31:** 220n1
Eysinga, W.J.M., **36:** 226n2

Fabela, Isidro, **31:** 19, 66, 68, 69, 70, 72
Fabian Society, **35:** 223n2
Fagan, Mark, **27:** 494n1
Fahey, John Henry, **32:** 178,n2; **36:** 152n1, 168-69, 267n1
Fahnestock, Carolyn Andrews (Mrs. Gibson), **36:** 572,n2
Fair Play, **32:** 97; **34:** 528
Fair Play (*Boston Herald*), **31:** 276n2
Fairchild, Fred Rogers, **27:** 208-209; **32:** 96
Fairchild, Henry Pratt, **29:** 352,n1
Fairley, W. R., **30:** 488,n1; **31:** 51, 53
Falaba incident (Thrasher case), **32:** 464-66,n1, 468-69, 477, 483-86, 487, 487-88, 488-90, 490-92, 497, 498, 503,n1, 527; **33:** 61-62, 66-67, 71-72, 72-77, 85-86, 91-93, 93, 94, 108, 155, 169, 174-75, 194, 290n1, 309, 322, 329, 352, 357; **34:** 288
Falkenhayn, Erich von, **30:** 140,n1; **32:** 352,n2, 506; **33:** 299, 406; **34:** 47; **36:** 122
Fall, Albert Bacon, **28:** 68n1; and Punitive Expedition, **36:** 395,n1, 407-408,n1,2,3, 416

Fall in, for Your Mother Land (march), **36:** 497,n2
Fall of a Railroad Empire: Brandeis and the New Haven Merger Battle (Staples and Mason), **36:** 26n3
Fall of a Nation: A Sequel to the Birth of a Nation (Dixon), **34:** 426,n1
Fall resolution, **28:** 68n1, 82,n1
Falmouth, England, **32:** 381n2; **34:** 403n1
Fanny's First Play (Shaw), **31:** 316,n2
Far Eastern Policy of the United States (Griswold), **27:** 175n1
Farewell Address (Washington), **33:** 335
Fargo, N.D., **38:** 159
Farley, John Murphy Cardinal, **36:** 7n1; **37:** 421-22
Farm and Fireside, **38:** 158n1
farm credit, **27:** 570
Farm Land Banks, Bureau of, **29:** 70
Farm Loan Act: see Federal Farm Loan Act of 1916
farmers: and credits, **29:** 5; associations: and exemption from antitrust legislation, **27:** 475; **29:** 413n1, 425, 538
Farmer's Day, **38:** 500n1
Farmers' Educational and Cooperative Union: see Farmers' Union
Farmers' National Congress of the United States, **38:** 511n1
Farmers' National Union, **32:** 96
Farmers' Union, **29:** 115
farming: see agriculture
Farmington Shoe Manufacturing Co. (Dover, N.H.), **30:** 400
Farnham, Roger Leslie, **31:** 220,n2; **32:** 437, 438, 439-40,n1; **34:** 60, 69
Farquhar, Arthur Briggs, **38:** 428,n4, 456
Farquhar, Horace Brand, 1st Baron Farquhar, **33:** 555,n2
Farrand, Livingston, **27:** 244
Farrar, Edgar Howard, **27:** 67
Farrar, Fred, **31:** 273n2, 335
Farrell, James Augustine, **27:** 216,n3; **30:** 128,n1
Farwell, John Villiers, **37:** 499,n1, 512
Fatherland, The, **31:** 337,n4
Fatigue and Efficiency: A Study in Industry (Goldmark), **27:** 76,n2
Fava, Saverio, **33:** 215,n1
Federal Board of Vocational Education, **37:** 173n1
Federal Council of the Churches of Christ in America, **27:** 153-54, 231,n1,3; **29:** 243n1, 476; **30:** 396-98,n1; **31:** 80, 461,n2; **35:** 79n2, 328, 354,n2; **37:** 422; WW's speech to, **35:** 329-36
Federal Employers Liability Act, **27:** 77
Federal Farm Loan Act of 1916, **37:** 208n2, 351n1; **38:** 27, 197; photograph of WW signing: *illustration section*, 37
Federal Farm Loan Board, **38:** 158n1,2, 160,n5,6, 197,n1, 423, 429
Federal Health Service, **27:** 76-77,n3
Federal Highway Act (good roads bill), **37:** 316, 330,n1; **38:** 26, 412-19

Federal Land Banks, **37:** 208n2

Federal Reporter, **33:** 398n3

Federal Reserve Act, **27:** xix, xxi; **29:** 91, 102, 153, 448; **31:** 169, 354; **32:** 32, 70, 72, 73; **34:** 276, 277, 369; **35:** 309, 313, 322, 325; **37:** 160, 187, 191, 338, 389, 427; **38:** 165, 299, 513, 545; WW thanks supporters of: C. Glass, **29:** 62; R. L. Owen, **29:** 62; W. G. McAdoo, **29:** 62, 77-78; remarks on signing, **29:** 63-66,n1, on acceptance by bankers, **30:** 211, 250; remarks to Federal Reserve Board, **30:** 376-77; evaluates, **31:** 171-72; remarks upon inauguration of Federal Reserve System, **31:** 196-97,n1; and rediscount facilities, **31:** 208,n2; and rural credits, **32:** 13, 14; and the farmer, **38:** 26, 420, 423-24, 503-504; WW on, **38:** 32, 129, 130, 131, 219, 263, 331, 449, 512, 594; reaction of business, **30:** 211; E.R.L. Gould on, **29:** 75-77; H. L. Higginson on, **29:** 370; **31:** 212-13; E. M. House on, **29:** 49; D. F. Houston on, **29:** 73-74, 86-87; T. B. Love on, **29:** 48; W. G. McAdoo on, **29:** 66, 89; **30:** 50, 53, 84; W. J. Stone, **29:** 66-67; W. H. Taft on, **38:** 497-98; and U.S. Chamber of Commerce, **30:** 205; *see also* banking and currency reform; Federal Reserve Board

Federal Reserve Bank of Kansas City, **38:** 188n3

Federal Reserve Bank of New York, **34:** 6n2

Federal Reserve Bank of Philadelphia, **38:** 158n2

Federal Reserve Bank of the U.S.: F. A. Vanderlip plan, **28:** 428n1

Federal Reserve banks of the U.S., **30:** 51-52; **31:** 321, 324, 326, 327; **34:** 276, 277, 278

Federal Reserve bill: *see* banking and currency reform

Federal Reserve Board, **27:** 535,n1, 560, 563, 564, 567, 568-69; **28:** 8, 69n1, 123, 375n1, 594; **29:** 54, 57, 92, 129, 135, 203, 226, 316-17, 377, 399, 417; **30:** 129, 160, 334; **31:** 172, 177,n2, 196n1, 207; **33:** 245n1; **34:** 36, 100, 107, 276, 278, 279, 369, 382; **35:** 64; **38:** 35, 39, 360, 498, 660

WW on: selection process and authority of, **27:** 558-64, 568-69; **28:** 8; **29:** 54, 57, 92, 203, 226, 399; **30:** 201-202, 334; five nominees, **30:** 181n1; T. D. Jones and P. M. Warburg nominations, **30:** 263, 270-71, 279-80, 288, 298-300, 304,n1, 317; remarks to, **30:** 376-77; W. G. McAdoo on quality of men needed, **29:** 49-50; **30:** 50

nominees and appointees: **29:** 56,n1, 159, 219-20, 247,n1,2,3, 263, 270, 277-78, 288, 308-309, 322, 380, 383,n1, 390, 401,n1, 448, 483,n1, 500-501, 515, 532; **30:** 7, 23, 27, 30,n1, 33, 53-55, 181,n1;

F. A. Delano, **30:** 344,n1, 350, 353; C. S. Hamlin, **30:** 188; **37:** 489-90; W.P.G. Harding, **29:** 543,n1; T. D. Jones, **30:** 149, 164, 173, 179, 203,n1, 260, 263, 270-71, 278, 279-80, 282, 288, 291-92, 292-93; A. C. Miller, **29:** 543n1; R. Olney, **29:** 536, 543-44; **30:** 3; Warburg, **29:** 536-37, 541; **30:** 263, 270, 279-80, 282, 288, 304,n1, 353; **31:** 386,n1; H. A. Wheeler, **29:** 543n1

and cotton crisis, **31:** 130, 132, 133, 148, 251, 271-72, Spring Rice on domination of by Warburg, **31:** 315; authorizes lower interest rate, **31:** 466-67; and governorship controversy, **37:** 105, 291, 345-46, 364, 463, 467-68, 472; appointments of governor and vice-governor, **38:** 22,n1, 32-33,n1

Federal Reserve Bulletin, **34:** 276n1

Federal Reserve System, **30:** 334-35; **34:** 36; **35:** 313; **36:** 154, 157-58; **38:** 307-308, 341, 366, 497, 498, 529-30, 540; W. G. McAdoo on, **30:** 50-55; J. P. Morgan, Jr., on, **30:** 484

Federal Reserve System (Willis), **27:** 535n1

federal shipping board, **36:** 366n1

Federal Trade Commission, **31:** 170-71, 326; **32:** 17, 32, 37, 57, 70, 73, 74, 175, 202; **33:** 245,n1; **35:** 177, 384; **36:** 154, 401, 406; **37:** 26, 192, 291, 392, 493; **38:** 129, 136, 265, 269-70, 297n1, 308, 341, 478-79; C. W. Eliot on, **30:** 434-35; suggestions for commissioners, **31:** 93-94, 176, 269, 293, 318, 353,n1,2,3, 500, 518, 524,n4, 531, 548, 552; **32:** 6-7, 19, 61n2, 271,n1,2; and cotton-loan fund, **31:** 271; and G. L. Record, **32:** 272, 281-82, 287; and party politics, **32:** 273; and coal-mining industry, **36:** 237,n1, 245, 291; and G. Rublee nomination and defeat, **37:** 20, 25, 70, 362-63, 374-75, 475, 512-13, 517-18; **38:** 4; Davies and Hurley controversy, **37:** 117,n1, 204,n2,3, 268; and Gallinger resolution, **38:** 87n1; *see also* Federal Trade Commission Act

Federal Trade Commission Act, **29:** 78-79, 105-10, 155-56, 184-85, 219, 281, 316,n3, 481,n3, 535n1; **30:** 94-95, 130, 219, 243, 267-68,n1, 404, 423n1, 427-31, 454-55,n1; **37:** 341, 363n2

WW on: Stevens bill, **30:** 166n2; Section 5 and unfair competition, **30:** 320, 348-49, 389, 454-55,n1; urges passage, **30:** 400n4, 424; confers with F. G. Newlands and J. H. Covington, **30:** 442; signing of bill (Sept. 26, 1914), **31:** 78-79; functions compared to those of Dept. of Justice, **29:** 175-77

Newlands bill, **29:** 219, 227,n1, 317-18, 326n2, 535,n1, 544-45; **30:** 261-62, 267-70, 433-34; Covington bill, **29:** 316,n3, 481-82, 486-87; Stevens bill, **29:** 481-

82,n2,3, 496, 535; **30:** 166,n1,2, 170-71, 181; wholesalers association and, **30:** 319,n3; C. A. Culberson amendment, **30:** 320; and Clayton bill, **30:** 320-21, 400,n2, 480-81; **31:** 43; foreign competition and, **30:** 455; and C. C. Carlin, **31:** 43; W. C. Adamson on, **29:** 496-97; **30:** 351; W. C. Copeland and, **30:** 400-401; J. E. Davies on, **29:** 83-85; **30:** 321, 427-31; J. C. Floyd on, **31:** 42; H. F. Hollis on, **30:** 110; J. P. Morgan, Jr., on, **30:** 483-84; W. C. Redfield on, **29:** 443; **31:** 45-47; J. T. Robinson on, **29:** 486-88; G. Rublee on, **30:** 274,n1; **36:** 203n2; C. R. Van Hise on, **29:** 326,n2; **30:** 272; *see also* Federal Trade Commission

federal warehouse bill: *see* Lever-Smith warehouse bill

Federalist, The, **38:** 162

Federalist party, **38:** 303

Federation of Labor: *see* American Federation of Labor; Chicago Federation of Labor

Federation of Women's Clubs, **27:** 108; **30:** 226n1

Federico, Ojo, **37:** 319

Feeling in Washington is Strongly Hopeful of Peace (*New York Times*), **33:** 191n1

Felix Frankfurter Reminisces; Recorded in Talks with Dr. Harlan B. Phillips, **27:** 133n1

Felts, Albert C., **30:** 17

Fendall, Annie A. Galt (Mrs. Reginald), **35:** 272,n4

Fendall, Reginald, **35:** 272n4

Fenn, Harry, **35:** 258n1

Ferdinand I (of Bulgaria), **33:** 267

Ferdinand I (of Rumania), **37:** 464,n1

Ferguson, Charles, **27:** 117,n1, 118, 464-65

Ferguson, James Edward, **37:** 237,n1

Fern, U.S.S., **28:** 59n2

Ferrero, Guglielmo, **31:** 370,n2, 386

Ferris, Scott, **30:** 3,n1, 20-21, 27-28, 224,n1, 245; **36:** 265, 277, 301, 464n1, 619; **37:** 92, 140, 142, 313, 328

Ferris leasing bill: *see* general leasing bill

Ferris water-power bill, **30:** 21, 27, 222, 224,n1; **35:** 232; **36:** 518n3; **37:** 313, 480; W. Kent on, **30:** 217n2, 218; G. Pinchot on, **36:** 48n1, 50, 51; F. K. Lane on, **36:** 243, 244, 290; T. J. Walsh on, **36:** 311-12, 324-29; WW on, **36:** 316

Fetherling, Dale, **28:** 509n1

feudalism: S. Gompers, **27:** 181, 182

Fidelity Trust Co. of Baltimore, **29:** 401n1

Field, Marshall, **29:** 401n1

Field, Mary, **38:** 58, 59-60,n1, 78

Field, Sara Bard, **35:** 292n1; **37:** 208-209,n1, 237, 375-76

Fielder, James Fairman, **27:** 54, 141n1, 191n1, 233, 235, 240, 386n1; **28:** 65, 83, 97, 373, 490n2; **31:** 561n1, 562; **35:** 58-59,n1, 72; **38:** 591n1, 608,n1

Fierro, Rudolfo, **29:** 285n1; **32:** 384,n3

Fifth Avenue Presbyterian Church, N.Y., **31:** 320,n1

Figaro, Le (Paris), **33:** 48; **35:** 525n3

Fight for the Panama Route: The Story of the Spooner Act and the Hay-Herrán Treaty (Miner), **33:** 46n3

Filibusters and Financiers: The Story of William Walker and His Associates (Scroggs), **33:** 46n1

Filipinos: *see* Philippine Islands and Filipinos

Finance Committee (Senate), **27:** 261, 264n1, 278-80, 282, 296, 433, 498; **28:** 336n2; **30:** 402; **35:** 459; **36:** 207; **38:** 51n1; income tax; **28:** 247, 254

Financial History of the United States (Dewey), **27:** 301n1

Financial News (London), **29:** 331n1

Fine, Henry Burchard, **28:** 119; **30:** 277; **35:** 42; **38:** 518n1; and presidency of The Johns Hopkins University, **27:** 90-91, 240-41, 554; and German ambassadorship, **27:** 110, 167, 169, 173-74, 175, 188, 214, 219, 225, 228, 247, 263, 290

Fine, Philena Fobes (Mrs. Henry Burchard), **28:** 20; **35:** 42

Finland, S.S., **35:** 93

Finnegan, John Patrick, **37:** 321n1

Finney, Edward Clingan, **30:** 224n1; **36:** 301,n3

Finney, John Miller Turpin, **27:** 90-91; **38:** 182n4

Fire from the Flint: The Amazing Careers of Thomas Dixon (Cook), **32:** 267n1

First Baptist Church of Washington, **31:** 309n1

First Congregational Church (Unitarian), Cincinnati, **38:** 534n1

First National Bank of Birmingham, Ala., **29:** 278n4, 308

First National Bank of Boston, **29:** 86

First National Bank of Chicago, **27:** 79n2; **34:** 316n1

First National Bank of Great Bend, Kan., **38:** 160n5

First National Bank of Jersey City, **28:** 96,n1

First National Bank of Princeton, **27:** 142n1

First National Bank of Rome, Ga., **30:** 452n1

First Presbyterian Church, Columbia, S.C., **30:** 74n1

First Presbyterian Church, Wilmington, N.C., **37:** 541n1

First Presbyterian Church of Mercer, Pa., **38:** 517n1

First Reformed Episcopal Church of New York, **38:** 686n1

Fischer, Fritz, **33:** 279n1

Fishel, Martin, **38:** 427,n1

Fisher, Boyd Archer, **27:** 476,n1; **28:** 259,n1, 264-65
Fisher, Irving, **27:** 208; **35:** 151n1; **37:** 308-309,n1, 316n1, 531-33,n1; **38:** 9-10, 110, 111,n2, 115, 362n1, 510
Fisher, John Arbuthnot, 1st Baron Fisher of Kilverstone, **31:** 7,n4; **34:** 42-43; **35·** 413
Fisher, Walter Lowrie, **27:** 93,n2
Fisher, Willard, **27:** 208
Fiske, Bradley Allen, **27:** 426-28,n3, 441-42,n2, 446, 447, 448; **29:** 429n1, 430-32, 454
Fitch, Albert Parker, **28:** 54,n1, 108-109, 113, 182-183, 256, 277, 309; **32:** 8; **33:** 543,n3; **34:** 9, 14
Fitch, Edwin M., **29:** 332n1
Fitch, Flora May Draper (Mrs. Albert Parker), **28:** 54,n2, 256, 277; **33:** 543,n3; **34:** 9, 14
Fitch, John Andrews, **38:** 445n1
Fitts, William Cochran, **38:** 297,n3
Fitzgerald, John Francis, **28:** 270-71, 275,n1
Fitzgerald, John Joseph, **27:** 22n2, 229,n1, 303, 369, 410-11; **29:** 282; **30:** 337; **32:** 62; **35:** 319; **36:** 380; **37:** 8,n1
FitzHenry, Louis, **37:** 217,n1, 218
FitzHugh, Carter Harrison, **38:** 441-43,n1
FitzHugh-Luther Co., Chicago, **38:** 441n1
Fitzpatrick, John, **37:** 402
Flag Day: WW address on, **33:** 391-94,n1,3; **37:** 221-25, 221n6, 236; proclamation on, **37:** 122-23; WW leading parade: *illustration section*, **37**
Flanders, Belgium and France, **34:** 311; **35:** 8
Flannery, Edward Aloysius, **38:** 83,n1, 84
Fleming, Robert F., **33:** 49n1
Fletcher, Duncan Upshaw, **27:** 201; **28:** 448,n2; **29:** 114-17, 129, 132-33, 139, 141; **31:** 458, 554-55,n1; **35:** 68, 96-97, 106, 345,n1, 459; **36:** 267n1; **37:** 366, 375,n1; **38:** 77
Fletcher, Frank Friday, **28:** 130, 142, 295, 300, 376; **29:** 111n1, 144, 174n1, 291, 295; **30:** 41, 147; **33:** 209; **36:** 68; Tampico affair, **29:** 421, 432,n1,2; J. Daniels on, **29:** 453; and Veracruz intervention, **29:** 476n1, 477, 480, 484, 509,n2, 510
Fletcher, Henry Prather, **29:** 449,n1, 533; **30:** 259, 262; **32:** 542; **33:** 533; **34:** 444, 448; **36:** 606; **38:** 13, 17, 18-19, 409; as ambassador to Mexico, **35:** 64, 359; **36:** 603, 604, 605, 608; and Pan-American Pact, **35:** 163, 519-20; **36:** 197, 198-201,n1,12, 398, 402-403, 423, 426, 461, 478, 479, 595n1, 596-97, 605; **37:** 238, 240-41, 241-44, 265, 271,n1, 292-93, 398-400; and Mexican situation, **37:** 18, 138, 331, 398-400, 489
Flexner, Abraham, **36:** 513,n1, 522
Flint and Co., N.Y., **30:** 347

Flood, Henry De La Warr, **27:** 73, 74; **28:** 95; **29:** 440, 441, 471,n1; **31:** 448-49,n1; **33:** 337, 349; **35:** 423n1; **36:** 209, 211, 462; and "sunrise conference," **36:** 238n1, 288, 289; WW confers with about speech to Congress, **36:** 517n1
flood control, **31:** 446-47; **36:** 366n1
Florence, Italy, **34:** 546n2
Flores Magón, Jesús, **28:** 339, 340
Florida: lynching, **28:** 115n2
Florida Citrus Exchange, **27:** 418,n1
Flournoy, Mrs., **35:** 262,n4
Floyd, John Charles, **31:** 41-42,n1,2, 43
Flume House (Franconia Notch, N.H.), **28:** 102, 104, 131
Fly Fishing (Grey), **37:** 32,n3, 457,n1
Flynn, David M., **27:** 142n1; **28:** 3; **38:** 608,n1
Flynn, William James, **30:** 21n1; **34:** 74n5, 235; **35:** 24, 42
Folk, Joseph Wingate, **27:** 252, 414, 492; **28:** 505, 506; **30:** 23,n4; **34:** 515; **35:** 179, 183, 185, 191, 192; **38:** 142n1
Folks, Homer, **27:** 76-77, 244
Fonseca, Gulf of, **27:** 528; **28:** 100, 176, 184; **29:** 134; **30:** 174; **32:** 60, 470n2
Fontenelle Hotel, Omaha, **38:** 343n
food investigation, **30:** 432,n1
Fools Prayer (Sill), **30:** 22
Forbes, William Cameron, **27:** 256,n1, 370; **36:** 436-42
Forbes-Robertson, Johnston, **28:** 400,n1
Ford, Cornelius, **29:** 100,n1,2
Ford, Henry, **36:** 260, 616; **37:** 395,n1; **38:** 112, 146, 166, 187,n1,2, 554; on railroad crisis, **38:** 125
Ford, Henry Jones, **28:** 227, 288,n1, 329; **29:** 137,n1, 164; **30:** 243,n2, 244, 267; **34:** 486n1, 510; **35:** 279n1, 373; **36:** 581,n1,2; **37:** 76; and Philippines, **27:** 6n1, 188-89, 256, 370-71, 468; **28:** 242,n1
Ford, James, **33:** 430
Ford, John Howard, **27:** 371,n2; **28:** 242n1
Ford Motor Co. (Detroit), **38:** 125; WW remarks to employees of, **37:** 395,n1; women granted equal wages at, **38:** 187n2
Ford peace expedition, **35:** 279,n1, 349n1, 373, 380n1; **37:** 87
Fore River Shipbuilding Co., **31:** 310n1, 425
Foreign Affairs Committee: *see* U.S. Congress, House of Representatives
Foreign and Domestic Commerce, Bureau of, **32:** 57, 182; **35:** 177; **36:** 154, 402n2; **38:** 137, 264
foreign exchange: **27:** 204; H. L. Higginson on, **30:** 420-22
Foreign Relations Committee: *see* U.S. Congress, Senate
foreign trade, **27:** 271; **30:** 94; **31:** 150-51, 155, 218; and lumber, **30:** 4; W. C. Redfield on Clayton bill and, **31:** 46-

47; R. Lansing on credits, **31:** 217-19, 219-20; WW on, **38:** 262-70, 293, 339-40, 528; *see also* commerce

Foreign Trade Convention: *see* National Foreign Trade Convention

forest preservation, **27:** 51

Forest Service, **32:** 164

Forgan, James Berwick, **27:** 79,n2; **31:** 75-76; **34:** 316, 316-17,n1, 330

Formosa, **33:** 36

Forster, Rudolph, **27:** 371-72, 381-82; **28:** 59-60, 70n1, 262,n3; **29:** 130, 432; **33:** 456; **34:** 65n1, 267; **36:** 52, 330; **37:** 353, 470; **38:** 238

Fort, John Franklin, **29:** 327,n1; **30:** 307n1, 363; **32:** 76, 80, 288, 297, 439n1, 457,n2, 471,n1

Fort Bliss, Tex., **29:** 494; **33:** 482

Fort Corregidor: *see* Corregidor Fort

Fort Leavenworth, Kan., **30:** 374

Fort Lewis, Va., **32:** 494,n2

Fort Myer, Va., **31:** 561n1

Fort Sam Houston, Tex., **29:** 295n3; **36:** 503n1, 540n1

Fort Worth Star-Telegram, **36:** 186,n1,2

Fortnightly Review, **28:** 576

Forty-two Years in the White House (Hoover), **35:** 371n1

Fosdick, Raymond Blaine, **29:** 327,n1; **35:** 317n2

Foster, John Watson, **32:** 12, 219,n4; **37:** 497

Foster, Martin David, **29:** 503,n2, 504, 512, 513, 513-14, 533; **36:** 619; **37:** 92, 337, 347-48, 359,n1

Foster, Mary Parke McFerson (Mrs. John Watson), **32:** 219,n4; **37:** 497

Foulois, Benjamin Delahouf, **36:** 353,n5, 585

Foundry Methodist Episcopal Church, Washington, D.C., **38:** 157n1

Fowler, Harold, **35:** 416

Fowler, Robert, **28:** 255,n1

Fowler, Wilton B., **27:** xxii

Fox, Edward Lyall, **37:** 408,n1

Fox, John, **36:** 465,n1, 481, 488

Fox, Stephen R., **31:** 322n1; **33:** 68n1

Fox, Thomas, **27:** 487,n1, 491n1

Fox How (Westmorland), **28:** 286n1

Fram, S.S., **31:** 477

France, **27:** 439, 448, 540; **29:** 244, 411, 412; **30:** 152; **31:** 7, 16n1, 154, 218, 340; **32:** 255, 358; **33:** 123, 347, 371, 405, 407, 485,n1, 516, 517, 522, 524; **34:** 18, 19, 20, 22, 42, 62, 84, 85, 145, 236, 371; **35:** 8, 71n3, 74, 75, 77, 204, 255, 348, 413, 466, 484, 495, 504, 517; **37:** 20, 21, 88, 98, 185, 311, 411, 423-24, 458

and Mexico, **28:** 70, 411, 445-46, 460, 465, 471, 526; **29:** 92, 121-22, 194, 381n1, 442, 451; **30:** 246; **31:** 352; **33:** 194-95,n1; and Panama Canal tolls, **29:** 180; and Great Britain, **30:** 214, 248, 267, 323, 327; **31:** 161; and Germany,

30: 382, 383, 457; **31:** 26-27, 38-39, 54, 145; **32:** 301,n1, 379, 521-22; **33:** 514; and war atrocities, **31:** 26-27, 38-39, 54, 145; **32:** 379; **33:** 514; and Japan, **31:** 511; and Haiti, **32:** 437, 438, 439n1, 440, 472; **33:** 452; **38:** 339-40; F. Bouillon on war preparations, **33:** 12-13; public opinion in, **33:** 122; strength of army, **33:** 189, 190; strategic battles in, **34:** 310-11; cabinet changes in, **35:** 174,n1,2; J. H. von Bernstorff on, **30:** 457; T. von Bethmann Hollweg on, **36:** 123n1; A. G. Gardiner on, **36:** 320n1; E. Grey on, **36:** 443-44, 444, 511-12; **38:** 251; E. M. House on, **30:** 109, 190, 214, 266, 267, 342; **32:** 349; H. H. Kitchener on, **36:** 438; William II on, **30:** 382, 383; **36:** 614

France and the United States, **27:** ix; **29:** 11; **30:** 209, 233-34, 419; **35:** 354n2, 430, 498; **38:** 405-10; ambassadorship, **27:** 110, 127, 148, 198, 217,n1, 218, 228, 250, 258, 384; **28:** 111, 597; **29:** 11n1, 32, 159, 242, 373, 401n1, 531-32; **30:** 152, 153, 195-96; **31:** 283; conciliation treaties, **27:** 448, 478, 514; **29:** 136, 238, 341, 342, 349, 350; **31:** 64,n1; and Mexico, **28:** 8, 455n1, 515, 516; **29:** 11; **38:** 359,n2, 408-409; and revision of commercial treaty, **30:** 200,n1,2, 201; and seamen's bill, **30:** 280n1; **32:** 305

WW on: mediation, **30:** 342, 352, 457n1; shipping bill views, **31:** 345-46, 347-49; and R. Poincaré, **31:** 410, 461-62, 539-40; war settlement, **31:** 459; response to U.S. aid, **32:** 523; and discussion with E. M. House, **38:** 646, 658

W. H. Page on Americans in, **30:** 369; and loans, **30:** 372-73, 386, 396; **31:** 153, 217; **34:** 279, 478; and ship-purchase bill, **30:** 469; **31:** 280; and peace talks prospects, **31:** 10, 15-16, 61, 518, 541; **32:** 300; illegal search of U.S. ship, **31:** 176,n1; and cotton as contraband, **31:** 370-71; and Gen. P. Kearny, **31:** 562,n3,4; and House peace mission, **32:** 276-77, 335,n1, 341, 372-74, 402, 455, 504, 522, 531-32; **33:** 10-11, 12-13, 47-48, 63-64; **35:** 357, 499, 524-25,n3; **36:** 125-26,n1, 138, 147-48,n1, 180n2; W. J. Bryan on Anglo-French blockade, **32:** 311-12; public opinion on U.S. motives, **32:** 377-78; and Japan, **32:** 391; G. Alphaud on meeting with WW, **32:** 462-64; and Haiti, **34:** 61, 69, 70, 184; case of Countess de Belleville and Louise Thuliez, **35:** 88,n1,2,3,4, 118, 127, 174-75,n1,2; C. W. Eliot on, **35:** 486, 501, 506-508; **38:** 353; E. M. House on, **36:** 463; and the mails, **37:** 102, 103,n1, 112, 116-17; **38:** 640-41, 641-42; displeased over prospect of U.S. mediation moves, **37:** 93, 100, 103n2, 104, 134-35,n2, 164,

France and the United States (*cont.*)
178-79, 202, 240; Grey and peace moves, **37:** 132, 412; and peace terms, **38:** 69, 91, 253; and belligerent submarines in neutral waters, **38:** 148-50

France, S.S., **35:** 236-37

Francis, David Rowland, **34:** 404-405; **37:** 419, 470; **38:** 67-71, 350; appointed ambassador to Russia, **36:** 202,n1, 401-402

Francis Ferdinand (Archduke of Austria), **30:** 222, 315: **37:** 5

Francis Joseph I (Emperor of Austria, King of Hungary), **37:** 464-65; **38:** 71, 75, 458, 544; WW message to, **30:** 222; W. H. Page on, **30:** 330; WW's offer of good offices, **30:** 342; and aid to Poland, **37:** 414, 445n1, 470; **38:** 62

Francisco I. Madero: Apostle of Mexican Democracy (Ross), **27:**64n1

Francisco Villa y la Revolucion (Cervantes), **36:** 280n1

Franco-Prussian War, **31:** 177, 439

Franconia (ship), **30:** 215

Franconia Notch, N.H., **28:** 102, 104, 114, 131

Frankel, Moritz, **38:** 72

Frankfurter, Felix, **27:** 133n1

Frankfurter Zeitung, **34:** 366, 418; **37:** 507

Franklin, Benjamin, **30:** 153; **32:** 283; **33:** 6; **35:** 132, 133; **36:** 418, 472-73

Franklin, John, **27:** 228

Franklin, N.H., *Journal Transcript*, **27:** 178

Franklin Park, Washington, D.C., **30:** 34n1

Franklin Street Presbyterian Church, Baltimore, **35:** 153n3

Fraser, Abel McIver, **27:** 8

Fraser, Douglas de Saussure, **27:** 8n2

Fraser, Jean Blanding, **27:** 8n2

Fraser, Margaret McIver, **27:** 8n2

Fraser, Nora Blanding, **27:** 8n2

Fraser, Octavia Blanding (Mrs. Abel McIver), **27:** 8n1

Frazier, Arthur Hugh, **32:** 341,n2; **35:** 525n3

Frazier, Robert Thomas, Jr., **38:** 119-20,n1, 122-23

Freidenwald, Harry, **35:** 412,n1

Frelinghuysen, Frederick Theodore, **38:** 228n1

Fremont County, Colo., **31:** 334, 335, 517, 558

French, Francis Henry, **38:** 238,n8

French, Sir John Denton Pinkstone, **31:** 294,n1; **32:** 81-82,n1, 214; **34:** 18

French Academy, **31:** 248,n2, 539; **32:** 16

French Alliance of the United States, **31:** 426n2

French Americans, **28:** 164, 492; and 1912 and 1916 vote, **38:** 140

French Lick Springs, Ind., **29:** 384n1, 398, 408; **37:** 242

French Revolution, **30:** 362; **35:** 132-34, 146

Freschi, John J., **27:** 81,n2

Freshwater Fisheries Treaty, **27:** 203

Frick, Henry Clay, **27:** 215,n1, 223, 227, 232, 259

Friedland, S.S., **31:** 477

Friedman, Jacob Alexis, **28:** 149n1,2

Friedman, Samuel, **32:** 96, 97

Friends, the Society of, **28:** 441

Friends of Irish Freedom, **38:** 5n1

Friends of Poland Society, **38:** 371n2

Friends of Russian Freedom, **32:** 96

Frissell, Hollis Burke, **31:** 261-62

From Sea to Sea, Letters of Travel (Kipling), **36:** 191n1

From Slavery to Public Service: Robert Smalls, 1838-1915 (Uya), **27:** 283n1

Frost, William Goodell, **29:** 342, 351, 537; **30:** 6, 43n1, 63, 64; **32:** 282,n1, 284

Fruitlands: see Bronson Alcott's Fruitlands

Fruth, G., **31:** 54n1

Frye case, **32:** 380n1; **33:** 370, 436, 502; **34:** 89, 124,n3, 288, 330,n1; **35:** 417-18, 450, 453; **36:** 73n1, 133, 558, 614, 615

Fukien Province, China, **32:** 149, 177, 248, 270, 320, 414-15, 417, 418, 418-20, 426, 434, 436-37,n1, 459n1, 460, 499-500, 501, 519, 524; **33:** 98, 103

full-crew bill, **27:** 49,n6, 58, 66, 323

Fullam, William Freeland, **30:** 145,n2

Fuller, Cynthia, **38:** 500n1

Fuller, Dorothy, **38:** 500n1

Fuller, Henry Brown, **34:** 128,n1

Fuller, Leonie Coudert (Mrs. Paul), **30:** 443,n5, 444

Fuller, Lucia Fairchild (Mrs. Henry Brown), **34:** 128,n1

Fuller, Melville Weston, **36:** 610,n2, 611n3

Fuller, Paul, Sr., **30:** 209, 346,n2, 363,n2, 392-93, 441, 443-44,n7, 459, 489; **31:** 18, 63, 89, 426, 447n1, 448, 450, 461; **32:** 128, 129, 479; memorandum on Mexico, **30:** 408-18; Villa on, **30:** 444; as ambassadorial possibility, **30:** 463; WW letter of introduction to Villa, **30:** 494; WW letter of introduction to Carranza, **30:** 495; report on Mexico, **31:** 65-74; Carranza on, **31:** 74-75; and Nicaragua, **32:** 59, 60, 68; on *Lusitania* crisis, **33:** 52; and appointment as liaison with the Mexican factions, **33:** 477, 479, 487, 487-88; on Carranza and recognition, **34:** 98, 111, 148, 164n1, 199, 242

Fuller, Paul, Jr.: and Haitian mission, **33:** 115,n1, 116-17, 275-76,n1, 276-77, 278, 395-96, 400, 467,n1; **34:** 60, 69

Fuller, Roslind, **38:** 500n1

Funston, E. M., **36:** 364

Funston, Frederick, **29:** 509,n1,2, 510, 541,n1; **30:** 28, 79, 360,n1; **31:** 375-76; **37:** 121, 254, 323; **38:** 166,n2, 523, 548n1, 560, 677; on Villa's Columbus raid, **36:** 280, 281, 282-83, 283; and Punitive Expedition, **36:** 284, 285, 286, 287, 295, 298, 312-13, 313, 323, 352-53, 387, 416, 457, 501-503, 519, 528; and Scott-Obregón agreement, **36:** 540n1, 541, 554, 570-71, 579-80, 592-94, 607-608; and meetings with Obregón, **37:** 18n1, 22-24, 38-39; on Carrizal incident, **37:** 280, 307-308; on strategic plans, **37:** 315, 319; on troop withdrawal and border patrol, **38:** 44-45; recommendations should Villa capture Chihuahua, **38:** 546, 547

Furber, Henry Jewett, Jr., **33:** 231,n1
Furber, Percy Norman, **30:** 245-47,n1, 2,4
Furuseth, Andrew, **28:** 15-16,n1,2, 204n1, 469-70; **30:** 93,n1, 171,n1, 223n1; **32:** 295n1, 304-305, 309, 309-10, 357; **35:** 338, 339n1; thanks WW for signing the seamen's bill, **32:** 333
Furuya, Jun, **27:** xxii
Future, The (Arnold), **38:** 259
Fyfe, Henry Hamilton, **28:** 559,n1; **29:** 17

Gaboriau, Émile, **27:** 464
Gadski, Johanna, **37:** 425n1
Gaffney, Thomas St. John, **36:** 563n2
Galicia, **33:** 18; **37:** 404: *see also* Poland
Gaillard, David Dubose, **28:** 400,n2; **29:** 307,n2
Gaillard, Katherine Ross Davis (Mrs. David Dubose), **28:** 400,n4
Gaillard Cut, Panama Canal, **29:** 307n2
Gainesville, Ga.: post office, **27:** 239,n1
Galbraith, J. N., **27:** 544
Galdós, Pablo Desvernine y: see Desvernine y Galdós, Pablo
Gallatin, Albert, **36:** 418
Gallauner, Edmund, **36:** 276,n1, 291, 320
Gallinger, Jacob Harold, **35:** 213n2; **36:** 395,n1, 416; **37:** 25, 67, 363, 366, 428-29, 429, 431; **38:** 87,n1, 146n2
Gallipoli Peninsula, Turkey, **32:** 225n1; **34:** 42n2
Gallivan, James Ambrose, **31:** 297; **32:** 96
Galt, Alexander Hunter, **32:** 423n1
Galt, Edith Bolling: *see* Wilson, Edith Bolling Galt (Mrs. Woodrow)
Galt, Gertrude Bolling (Mrs. Alexander Hunter), **32:** 423n1
Galt, Norman, **32:** 423n1; **35:** 272n4
Galt and Brothers (Wash., D.C.), **34:** 553n1
Galveston, Tex., **29:** 127, 492; **30:** 8, 11, 33, 441; **31:** 353; **32:** 258
Galveston News, **29:** 263n2
Gama, Domicio da, **29:** 505-506,n1, 506-507, 539-40; **30:** 68, 78, 98, 101, 136, 242, 493; **33:** 64, 338; **34:** 43, 157n1,2, 321, 487-88, 540-41, 542; **37:** 122, 241; **38:** 18; and negotiations concerning Pan-American pact, **31:** 470, 498, 535, 536; **32:** 54, 55, 56, 220, 221; **35:** 54-55, 189, 215, 519; **36:** 199, 461, 479, 597, 605, 654; and Mexico, **33:** 437, 454-55, 487, 488; and soirée in honor of WW and EBW, **35:** 372-73, 386, 396

Gamboa, Federico, **28:** 145n1, 162, 167, 188, 196, 219, 220, 224n1, 298, 299, 326, 331; **29:** 329, 358-59; **33:** 392,n1; and J. Lind, **28:** 157-59, 168-75, 191, 224-27, 233-39; on Constitutionalists, **28:** 171-72; W. B. Hale on, **28:** 200; proposed trip to Washington, **28:** 204, 205, 207, 208, 209; presidential candidacy, **28:** 322, 323, 324-25,n1, 333, 334, 339, 340, 356, 377

Garcia, Andres G., **37:** 280,n2
Garcia, Paurino, **36:** 653
Garcia Granados, Alberto, **35:** 99
Gardiner, Alfred George, **31:** 482,n1; **33:** 8,n1,2, 21,n1, 61, 66,n1, 117, 206, 207; **34:** 476,n1, 510,n1; **35:** 465; **36:** 320,n1, 379, 380; **37:** 265,n1, 313
Gardner, Augustus Peabody, **31:** 455; **33:** 501,n1,3, 516; and resolution regarding preparedness, **31:** 152,n3, 293, 357-58, 373, 375, 409, 411, 413, 423n6; and ship-purchase bill, **33:** 114
Gardner, Obadiah, **27:** 27, 126; **37:** 498-99; **38:** 51, 173-74, 189
Gardner, Robert, **38:** 374-75,n1
Gardner, Washington, **30:** 141n1
Gardner resolution, **32:** 501,n3
Garfield, Belle Hartford Mason (Mrs. Harry Augustus), **31:** 341
Garfield, Harry Augustus, **29:** 496, 499, 512-13; **31:** 341; **36:** 247, 264, 358, 359, 544-45, 562; **37:** 60, 97, 130,n1, 165; **38:** 145-46, 201,n1, 375,n1, 626, 627, 628
Garfield, James Rudolph, **27:** 93; **33:** 517, 533,n1
Garfield, Garfield and Howe, Cleveland, **30:** 282n1
Garford, A. L., **33:** 497
Garlington, Ernest Albert: report on Carrizal incident, **38:** 378-86
Garner, John Nance, **32:** 222
Garraty, John Arthur, **29:** 272n1; **37:** 203n4
Garretson, Austin Bruce, **38:** 30, 31n1, 32n1, 48, 93, 94
Garrett, Alice Warder (Mrs. John Work), **38:** 317,n3
Garrett, Finis James, **36:** 306
Garrett, John Work, **29:** 380, 401n1; **35:** 358; **38:** 317,n1, 350
Garrison, Lindley Miller, **27:** 268, 292; **28:** 300-301, 329, 390, 401, 595; **29:** 147, 168, 264-65, 269, 281, 284-85, 289, 476n1, 509-11,n2, 516, 517, 530; **30:** 79, 80, 81; **31:** 411, 447; **32:** 207, 234, 285;

Garrison, Lindley Miller (*cont.*)
34: 192; 35: 150, 401; 36: 176, 379, 424; 37: 33
cabinet appointment, 27: 133,n1, 136; code name, 27: 164; on Philippines, 27: 255-57, 274, 282-83, 354-56, 516, 527; 28: 415-17; on recognizing China, 27: 330; on Mexico, 27: 331, 332, 460-61; and California alien land legislation, 27: 349; on moving ships from China to Philippines, 27: 443, 444-45; on F. B. Harrison, 28: 192; on Porto Rican bill, 28: 366-67; 29: 273-74; 30: 216; no segregation in War Department, 28: 498n1; and incident concerning Military Order of the Carabao, 29: 37-39, 54-55; and Colorado coal strike, 29: 525-28, 541-42; 30: 49, 60-61; 31: 309, 517, 545, 547-48; on Veracruz incident and aftermath, 30: 7-8, 11-12, 28; 31: 33, 360, 360-61, 362, 375-76; 33: 294-95, 482-83, 517, 533; and Jones bill, 30: 144, 155-56, 160, 172, 213, 216, 225, 230, 245; 32: 291-92, 293; on water-power bill, 30: 224,n1; offers solutions to cotton crisis, 31: 210-12, 249-50; and army promotions, 31: 328,n4; birthday greetings from WW, 31: 358-59; and Gen. L. Wood, 31: 475, 502, 506-507; 34: 337n1, 353; and resignation intentions, 32: 168-69, 538-40; 33: 450-51; on ship-purchase bill, 32: 192-93; reviews diplomatic exchanges among U.S., Germany and Great Britain, 32: 404-408; and case of M. Noriel, 32: 535-36; on *Lusitania* correspondence, 33: 295,n3, 536-37, 540; and preparedness, 34: 3, 4, 173-74,n1, 195, 208, 216, 227, 232, 235, 240,n1, 248, 250, 264, 412, 482-85, 514; 35: 105-106, 138-41, 149-50,n1, 169-70, 173, 180, 478-80, 481-82, 499-500; 36: 139,n1, 143-44, 144-45, 145-47, 162-64; WW on, 34: 392; F. K. Lane on, 34: 478; and Tumulty, 34: 515; transmits message from Philippine legislature, 35: 85-87; and resignation, 35: 479, 481; 36: 164, 164-65, 192; C. R. Crane on, 36: 177; photographs: *illustration section*, 27; 36
Gary, Elbert Henry, 27: 216, 232; 29: 29; 30: 128; 36: 267n1
Garza, Lázaro de la, 30: 220-21,n1
Garza, Roque González: *see* González Garza, Roque
Garza Aldape, Manuel, 28: 168, 445, 446, 537-38; 29: 190
Gascoyne-Cecil, (Edgar Algernon) Robert: *see* Cecil, Robert
Gaskill, Nelson Burr, 27: 240,n1
Gasparri, Pietro Cardinal, 34: 31n2; 36: 655; 37: 84n3, 85, 86
Gates, F. P., 28: 427
Gates, Robert M., 36: 241
Gatun Dam, Gatun Lake, 29: 307

Gatzke, Hans Wilhelm, 37: 507n4
Gaulois, Le (Paris), 35: 525n3
Gaunt, (Reginald Archer) Guy, 35: 310n1; 37: 103,n1, 112; 38: 377,n3, 388
Gavira, Gabriel, 37: 251,n4, 316
Gavit, John Palmer, 28: 332, 348-50,n1; 32: 493, 498-99; on Mexico, 37: 313-14, 314-15, 323-24
Gaynor, John Jay, 27: 246
Gaynor, William Jay, 28: 211; 35: 346
Geer, William Montague, 38: 560n1
Geier, S.M.S., 31: 444
Geiger, Louis George, 30: 23n4
General Board of the Navy, 27: 160; 29: 430; 34: 17, 267,n1, 427n2, 514; 35: 300; and Haiti, 34: 143-44
general dam bill: *see* Shields water-power bill
General Education Board, 30: 153; 36: 478,n1, 513, 522, 558,n1
General Federation of Women's Clubs, 37: 535n1
General Film Co., 33: 431
general leasing bill, 30: 20, 27, 31; 31: 234, 450; 35: 232; 36: 464,n1, 518,n3, 521, 570; 37: 39-41, 140-41, 172n1, 269, 313, 480
General Theological Seminary, N.Y., 34: 73n1; 38: 16n3
Genesee Valley, N.Y., 34: 166
Geneseo, N.Y., 34: 166n2
Geneva, N.Y., 34: 63n1, 64, 77, 117, 119, 155, 178, 244, 245, 263, 284, 289, 357, 362
Genthe, Arnold, 28: 355,n2; 33: 264,n1; 37: 32
George V (of Great Britain), 27: 503; 28: 52; 29: 195, 196, 301, 320, 411; 30: 370; 32: 6,n1, 303-304,n1; 33: 123, 198, 483; 34: 10n1; 35: 142, 359, 499; 36: 385; 38: 458; and WW's offer of peace mediation, 30: 342; and William II, 30: 382; and aid to Poland, 37: 407, 414, 445,n1, 470; 38: 29-30
George, Henry, Jr., 27: 9, 342,n1
George, James Zachariah, 27: 182, 183
George, Joseph Warren, 34: 108,n2, 273
George Hawley, S.S., 31: 477
George von Lengerke Meyer: His Life and Public Services (Howe), 31: 55n1
George Washington, S.S., 28: 596; 31: 193
George Washington University, 32: 259n1
Georgetown, S.C., 29: 89,n1, 92
Georgetown, Wash., D.C., 34: 513
Georgia, 33: 431; *see also* Bacon, A. O.
Geran Law (N.J.), 27: 233
Gerard, James Watson, 27: 63, 110, 200; 28: 4, 17; 29: 74; 30: 265; 31: 17, 181, 468, 537; 32: 145, 195, 200, 207-10, 260-62, 301,n3,4, 421,n1, 483-86; 33: 63, 107-108, 251, 297-301, 371-72, 375, 406, 407-408, 425, 436, 479, 505n1, 511; 34: 6,n2, 12-13, 44, 46-48, 83-84, 186,

187, 238,n1, 238-39, 260, 272, 333, 342,n1, 372, 405,n1, 418-19, 454, 492; **35:** 192, 193-94, 220, 355, 382, 398; **36:** 52, 126, 129, 258, 273, 350, 353-54, 413-14, 482, 529, 599; **37:** 106,n1, 202, 271, 345, 470, 479-80, 507; **38:** 64-65, 429, 494n2, 494-95,n1, 497
and William II message to WW, **30:** 382-83,n1; on destruction of Louvain, **30:** 467; and mediation, **31:** 10, 14, 15; and N.Y. senatorial race, **31:** 139,n1, 167, 267, 426; warned of nonneutral statements, **31:** 385-86, 387-88; Spring Rice on, **31:** 405; on meetings with Bethmann Hollweg, **31:** 426-27, 535-36; **36:** 340-41, 613-16; on hostility for U.S. in Germany, **31:** 426-27, 535-37; on peace prospects in Germany, **32:** 75, 234, 255-56, 351-52; **37:** 45,n1, 272, 319,n2, 507; **38:** 313-14,n2; and House peace mission, **32:** 238, 253, 262, 268, 340, 374, 375, 439, 480n1, 514; H. White's evaluation of, **32:** 481-82; and *Falaba* incident, **33:** 73-77; and proposal for Anglo-German renewal of *modus vivendi,* **33:** 222, 223, 227, 229, 237, 238, 239, 253, 264, 265-66; and Bryan-Dumba exchange on *Lusitania* crisis, **33:** 247-48,n1, 257; and *Lusitania* correspondence, **33:** 328, 355, 356, 453-54, 466, 477-78, 480,n1,2,3, 490, 527, 545; **35:** 523, 529-30; **36:** 73-74,n1; and *Nebraskan* case, **33:** 369n3; possible recall of, **34:** 274, 290, 299; **35:** 191, 192, 219; **36:** 417, 451, 460, 471; and *Arabic* crisis, **34:** 306, 320, 366-67; 439-40, 461; William II refuses to see, **34:** 441-42; on German attitude regarding submarine warfare, **34:** 452-53; opens Bernstorff despatches to German Foreign Office, **34:** 528; and case of Countess de Belleville and Louise Thuliez, **35:** 88; WW criticism of, **35:** 178-79, 192, 201; interview with Kaiser, **35:** 193-94, 359; on Von Jagow reaction to possible recall of attachés, **35:** 291,n1; wedding gift to WW, **35:** 380, 387; and *Sussex* crisis, **36:** 447,n1, 448-52, 452-56, 466-71, 491-96, 556n1, 620-26; on dissent in Germany and German Americans in, **36:** 563-64; reports Bethmann Hollweg's hopes for another House mission, **36:** 595; interview with William II and Bethmann Hollweg, **36:** 613-16; on situation in Germany, **38:** 71-74; talk of return to U.S., **38:** 141-42, 259, 292; meets with WW at Shadow Lawn, **38:** 452-53,n1; photograph of, *illustration section;* **37**
Gerard, Mary Daly (Mrs. James Watson), **31:** 388,n2, 405; **32:** 482; **35:** 179, 380, 387; **38:** 142
Gerard, Sumner, **38:** 445n1

Gerhard, Anton Meyer: *see* Meyer Gerhard, Anton
German Allegations Regarding *Lusitania* (Lansing), **33:** 327n1
German-American Alliance: *see* National German American Alliance
German Americans, **28:** 492; **31:** 426n1, 434, 441, 501, 533, 534; **32:** 90,n1, 101, 102, 108, 477n1, 526; **33:** 28n1, 185, 201, 229, 255, 297, 299, 299-300; **34:** 25, 62, 116,n2, 319, 418-19; **35:** 221-22, 524n1; **36:** 187, 361,n1, 542,n1, 563; **37:** 156-57, 175; **38:** 389, 492, 497; H. Münsterberg on administration and, **31:** 276-78, 336; and propaganda campaign, **32:** 4-6, 19-20, 116, 510-11; in Wisconsin, **32:** 19, 58; C. A. Spring Rice on WW and vote of, **32:** 87, 120n1; E. Grey on, **32:** 107n1, 109; and *Falaba* case, **32:** 489; and Mexico, **33:** 321; and 1916 campaign, **37:** 135n2, 217-21, 279, 364-65; **38:** 46, 66, 140, 188, 277, 278-79, 289-91, 293,n2; and Chicago, **38:** 146n1, 275,n5; and W. Heinecke, **38:** 427,n1
German-Americans in Politics 1914-1917 (Child), **34:** 116n2
German Information Service, **31:** 96n1
German Involvement in Northern Mexico, 1915-1916: A New Look at the Columbus Raid (Sandos), **36:** 280n1
German-Irish Central Legislative Committee, **33:** 185
German propaganda in the United States, **32:** 4-6, 19-20, 116, 129n2, 130-33, 160, 161, 358, 510-11; **34:** 62-63, 79, 109-10, 158-59,n1, 206, 209, 234, 266, 528; **35:** 221,n2, 222; **36:** 294, 617-18; and Albert incident, **34:** 74n5, 158,n1; J. P. Tumulty on, **34:** 116; W. G. McAdoo on, **34:** 218,n1
German Propaganda in the United States, 1914-1917 (Hirst), **31:** 27n1; **34:** 74n5; **37:** 425n2
German Proposals (*Springfield Republican*) **33:** 505,n1
German Purchasing Commission (N.Y.), **34:** 74n5
German Red Cross, **31:** 96n1; **33:** 317n2, 319; **34:** 528,n3
German Submarine Warfare (Woolsey), **36:** 452,n1
German White Book, **31:** 8n8
Germans Generally Pleased with Naming of Hughes; Alliance and Its Allied Societies Will Conduct Campaign for Him from Chicago (New York *World*), **37:** 219n3
Germany, **28:** 53; **30:** 152, 209; **31:** 195, 419; **33:** 11, 524; **34:** 20, 46-48, 84, 145, 186, 188, 188-89, 238-39, 239; **35:** 8, 74, 75, 194, 415, 466, 488; **36:** 383; **37:** 20, 100, 507,n4; and Mexico, **27:** 424, 540; **28:** 411, 445, 446, 460, 465, 526;

Germany (*cont.*)
29: 92, 190, 196, 267, 285, 441-42, 451, 464, 476n1, 477; **33:** 194n1, 298,n1, 321; **34:** 56,n1, 73-74; **35:** 100; and claims on Venezuela in 1901, **28:** 459; and Nicaraguan treaty, **29:** 172, 173; and Great Britain, **29:** 180, 285; **30:** 315, 323, 359,n2, 401, 426-27; **31:** 6-8, 58-59, 155-56, 159, 196, 201, 282, 297-98, 371, 372, 427; **32:** 358-60, 480,n1; **36:** 123n1; E. M. House on, **30:** 140, 190; **31:** 5, 265-66; **33:** 12-13, 405; and France, **30:** 200, 266, 267, 313; **31:** 38-39, 54; E. Grey on, **30:** 247-48, 325; **31:** 21-22,n1, 58-59, 518,n2; **32:** 44-50; **33:** 13-14, 372; **34:** 370; and Austria, **30:** 323, 327; invades Luxembourg, **30:** 330; delcares war against Russia, **30:** 330; W. H. Page on, **30:** 330, 368-69, 370, 371; **31:** 6-8, 55n3, 263; William II message for WW, **30:** 382-83; and Japan, **30:** 391; **31:** 511; **33:** 82; C. W. Eliot on, **30:** 419
and alleged atrocities in Belgium, **30:** 457-58, 458, 470,n1; **31:** 16, 26-27, 85, 121-22,n1, 145; and Russia, **30:** 463,n2; **32:** 458, 480,n1; and Haiti, **31:** 34-36,n2; **32:** 439n1, 440, 472; **34:** 70; and Holland, **31:** 100, 156; and Declaration of London, **31:** 110, 113-14, 116, 118n1, 125-26, 134, 135, 136, 154, 161; and Belgium, **31:** 207, 559; **32:** 42,n1, 60,n1; Field Marshal French on war settlement and, **31:** 294,n1; and Austria-Hungary, **31:** 296; G. Ferrero on military caste in, **31:** 370,n2; William II as pacifist, **31:** 370,n2; Gerard on political situation in, **31:** 426-27; **32:** 351-52; **33:** 407; **34:** 453-54; **36:** 341; **38:** 71-74; WW says not solely responsible for war, **31:** 459; and raids on English coastal towns, **31:** 489; **32:** 98; and China, **31:** 509; **32:** 135, 138, 415, 418, 434; **35:** 203-205; H. Metz on conditions in, **31:** 536-37; and House peace mission, **32:** 17,n1, 42, 75, 81, 98, 120,n1, 204-207, 212-15, 220, 220-21, 234, 237, 242, 254-55, 255-56, 257, 265, 267, 268, 276-78, 340, 341, 374, 375, 411-12, 438-39, 455-56, 504-507; C. P. Anderson on, **32:** 44-50, 48,n1; public opinion and press in, **32:** 145, 456; **33:** 73, 89, 299; **34:** 48, 297-98; **36:** 558; submarine campaign, **32:** 145, 217, 250, 264-65, 307, 412; **35:** 418-19; **36:** 125n1, 128, 208-209, 429, 429-30; war-zone proclamation, **32:** 193,n1,3, 200-201,n1, 217-19; and British blockade, **32:** 301,n1, 317-19; **35:** 62, 418-19, 463-64, 471-72,n2, 517-18; **36:** 128-29; WW on peace terms of, **33:** 81-82; Lord Loreburn on land in Africa for, **33:** 100-101; and Italy, **33:** 231, 232; F. Gildemeester on political situation in, **33:** 332; C. A. Spring Rice on peace plan of, **33:** 362-63; and Spain as mediator, **35:** 130; W. R. Gherardi on, **35:** 131-32; and dissent in Reichstag, **36:** 341,n1; T. von Bethmann Hollweg defends submarine warfare, **36:** 444,n1

Germany and the United States, **27:** ix, 130; **29:** 180, 325; **31:** 355, 530; **32:** 449n1; **33:** 91,n3, 91-93, 107-108, 141n1, 153, 154, 231, 408, 511, 516; **34:** 6-7, 12, 15n1, 146, 319, 329, 330, 363, 381, 388, 400, 405n1, 418-19; **35:** 137-38, 354n2, 490-91; **36:** 52, 482, 483; and U.S. ambassador to, **27:** 62, 110, 167, 173-74, 214, 228, 240, 263, 334; **28:** 4, 17; **29:** 74; and conciliation treaty, **27:** 478; **29:** 136; **32:** 65; WW to William II on anniversary, **27:** 521; and seamen's bill, **28:** 412-13, 463; **30:** 280n1; and Mexico, **28:** 455n1, 486n3, 515, 516, 567,n2, 571, 585; **29:** 168; **36:** 434; and House peace missions, **29:** 12, 462, 531; **30:** 23, 108-109, 139-40, 200-201, 214, 258, 247-48, 265, 266-67, 323, 342; **36:** 122-23; and Ship Registry Act of 1914, **30:** 326; and liners in U.S. ports, **30:** 335,n3; and loans to belligerents, **30:** 372; House on possible victory of Central Powers, **30:** 432-33; and U.S. purchase of ships, **30:** 435, 436, 447-49, 451, 469-70; **31:** 345-46, 347-49; **32:** 106; and Americans in Belgium, **30:** 461; WW on Germany's role in coming of war, **30:** 462-63; military spending compared, **30:** 464; American sentiment toward, **31:** 13-14, 228, 276-78, 292, 336-40, 386
peace discussions and prospects, **31:** 14, 21n1, 37, 45, 62, 76-77, 94-95, 137, 140-41, 385, 387, 428,n1, 490, 518-19, 523, 540, 540-41; **37:** 3,n2, 179, 272, 411, 412, 507; **38:** 69, 91-92, 294-95, 313-14,n1,2, 454, 494-96, 619, 646, 647, 658; and U.S. export of food to Belgium, **31:** 197n1; credit in U.S., **31:** 218; and cotton imports, **31:** 233; H. Münsterberg and German propaganda, **31:** 276-78, 293, 336-40, 376, 432-46, 523, 534-35; arms trade, **31:** 426-27, 521-22, 533-34, 545; **32:** 509-13; **33:** 20-23, 52,n1; **34:** 92-98, 114-16, 142; and censorship of mails, **31:** 443, 443-44; and fraudulent naturalization papers, **31:** 471; C. A. Spring Rice on German spy system, **31:** 505; *Dacia* affair, **32:** 91-93,n1,2,3, 102-105, 106; strict accountability note, **32:** 194-95, 195-96,n1, 207-10, 249-51,n1, 374n5; and violations of Hague conventions, **32:** 223, 223-25; proposal for Anglo-German *modus vivendi*, **32:** 235-36, 259-60, 260-62, 301,n2,3; **33:** 198, 205, 222,n1, 223, 226-27, 229, 237-38, 238, 253-54, 265-66; M. Rice on peace possibilities, **32:** 300; L. M. Garrison on diplomatic exchanges, **32:** 404-408; obstacles to trade between, **32:** 421n1,

425; and *Falaba* incident, **32:** 464-66,n1, 468-69, 477, 483-86, 487, 487-88, 488-90, 490-92, 492-93, 497, 498, 503,n1, 527; **33:** 61-62, 66-67, 73-77, 85; R. Lansing on possible war between, **32:** 477,n1; H. White on Gerard, **32:** 481-82

Lusitania crisis: newspaper warning on *Lusitania*, **33:** 28-29,n1; *Lusitania* sinking and reactions, **33:** 127,n1, 129,n1, 134, 134-35,n3,4, 138-39, 142n1, 142-43, 144-45, 150-52, 153n1, 158-59, 169, 174, 175, 184,n1, 188, 194, 214-15, 247,n1, 279n1, 290n1, 296-97, 299, 318, 323, 326, 327, 328-29, 337, 353, 357-58, 407, 462, 473,n1, 494, 501-504, 505n1, 509, 514, 527, 528, 530, 544, 547; **38:** 89, 560n1, 570n1, 689; first *Lusitania* note, **33:** 139, 155-58, 165-66, 167-68, 168-73, 174-78, 180, 186, 187, 190, 191n1, 197-98, 199-201, 201-202,n1, 202, 202-203, 214, 214-16, 224, 229-30, 244, 251-53, 335n1, 424-25, 516n1; *Lusitania* postscript, **33:** 173, 181-82, 182-83, 183-84,n1, 186, 191n1, 192-94; **38:** 559,n2, 559-69,n2; C. Dumba on *Lusitania* negotiations, **33:** 212-13; F. von Papen on *Lusitania* negotiations, **33:** 233; German reply of May 28 to first *Lusitania* note, **33:** 290n1, 292, 295,n3,4, 297, 312-13, 313, 316-20, 327-28, 369-70; second *Lusitania* note, **33:** 309, 310-13, 314, 321-26, 328-31, 334, 342-43, 344, 344-45, 346, 351-55, 355-60, 368, 369, 371, 374, 378n1, 383, 398, 424-25, 477-78; Bernstorff on interview with WW on *Lusitania* crisis, **33:** 319, 323, 507; F. Gildemeester's visit to U.S. on *Lusitania* crisis, **33:** 347-48, 361-62; German reply of July 8 to second *Lusitania* note, **33:** 436, 453-54, 480,n3, 481,n3, 490, 498, 499-500,n1, 505,n1, 507-508,n1, 513-15; third *Lusitania* note, **33:** 490, 492, 498-99, 499-500, 507-508,n1, 509-10, 513-15, 527-29, 530-32, 536, 538, 540, 544, 545-48,n1,5; continuing negotiations, **34:** 8, 15n1, 24, 25, 28, 29, 29-30, 33, 37, 44, 52n2, 85, 86, 264, 288, 299, 333n1, 339, 340, 372, 373, 418, 428, 441, 445n3, 449; **35:** 14-15, 75, 158-59, 176, 189-90, 208, 218-19,n1, 222, 233-34, 244-45,n1, 278, 355, 362, 417-19, 430-31, 450, 452, 457-58, 462n2, 463-64,n1, 504, 512-15, 516, 521, 522-23, 528-29; **36:** 73-74,n1, 122, 123, 125n1, 127-29, 129, 141, 148,n1, 181-82, 182, 183-84, 186,n2, 194-95, 205-206, 215, 252, 254, 256, 341, 373, 450-51, 470, 616, 629; **37:** 135n2; **38:** 294, 315, 352; Lansing on how to answer WW's critics on *Lusitania* case, **38:** 195, 320; Hughes on U.S. reaction to *Lusitania* sinking, **38:** 298, 513n1

Cushing incident, **33:** 91,n1, 91-93, 93-94,n1, 94, 108, 155, 165, 169, 175, 194, 290n1, 321, 322, 328, 351, 356, 357, 369; and *Gulflight* incident, **33:** 93-94, 94, 108, 130, 155, 165, 169, 175, 194, 290n1, 321, 322, 328, 351, 352, 356, 357, 369; Gerard on German attitudes, **33:** 297-301, 371; predictions of war between, **33:** 406, 483; and cotton crisis, **33:** 457-58; **34:** 123, 137, 142, 186,n2; C. P. Anderson memorandum on submarine warfare, **33:** 501-504; and German intrigues in the Americas, **34:** 249, 309, 315, 528-29

Arabic crisis: sinking and reactions, **34:** 257,n2, 259, 260, 261, 264-66, 269-70, 271, 272, 274, 279, 282, 285, 288, 290, 297, 304, 305-306, 315, 318-19, 339-40, 342n1, 366-67, 372-73, 393, 418, 428, 452-53, 453-54, 492, 493; initial German responses, **34:** 308-309, 324-25, 330; J. W. Gerard confers with Von Jagow, **34:** 320, 342n1; Bethmann Hollweg on, **34:** 333n1, 342n1; WW and Lansing on German responses, **34:** 339-41; delay in official German report on, **34:** 393, 417; *Arabic* pledge, **34:** 400-401; congratulations on *Arabic* pledge, **34:** 404-405, 407,n1, 410, 410-11, 411, 411-12, 415; Bernstorff on instructions to submarine commanders, **34:** 436; German report on *Arabic* sinking, **34:** 438,n2, 439-40, 445,n3, 453; Lansing on German report, **34:** 449, 449-51; Lansing suggests Bernstorff broaden *Arabic* pledge, **34:** 461-62; Bernstorff alarmed at U.S. press reports on, **34:** 468-69; WW insistence on disavowal, **34:** 493, 537, 539; House and Bernstorff confer on possible disavowal, **34:** 520-21; German disavowal, **35:** 13,n1, 14-15, 25-26, 26-27, 34; referred to, **35:** 75, 158; **36:** 73n1, 183, 184, 470, 616; **38:** 689

Orduna incident, **34:** 315,n1; *Hesperian incident,* **34:** 423,n1, 425, 426, 427, 428-29, 433, 436, 436-37, 441, 444-45,n1,2,3,4, 453; and possibility of severance of relations, **35:** 43, 219, 221, 260, 426-27, 435, 483, 491, 512-13, 516, 523, 529n1, 530; German intrigues in the U.S., **35:** 43,n1, 220, 222, 230-31, 264,n1, 265, 276-77,n1, 278, 282-83, 290-91,n1, 306-307, 355; **36:** 250, 527,n1, 529, 577-78; **37:** 218-19, 223; and Cavell case, **35:** 147-48,n1,2,3, 149; and *Frye* case, **35:** 417-18, 450, 453; Germany defends submarine warfare, **35:** 418-19, 451, 452-53, 464; and *Baralong* case, **35:** 421-22; and *Persia* case, **35:** 446, 450; Lansing's *modus vivendi re* armed merchantmen, **35:** 448-49, 495, 531-33, 534; **36:** 133-34, 182-83,n1, 184, 192-93,n3, 215-16, 216-17, 221-25, 225-26, 228-29, 232-33, 239, 245-46, 252-57, 258-59, 267-68,n1; and treat-

Germany and the United States (*cont.*)
ment of prisoners in Russia, **36:** 125-
26; W. C. Redfield on postwar dumping of goods, **36:** 127; and House-Grey
Memorandum, **36:** 180,n2; WW asks for
vote on McLemore resolution, **36:** 231-
32; and German activities in Colombia, **36:** 234n1, 234-36; and "sunrise
conference," **36:** 238n1; and dyestuffs,
36: 261,n2; German memorandum on
submarine controversy, **36:** 270-73, 273,
361-62; Bernstorff meets with House,
36: 294; Bethmann Hollweg on possible WW mediation, **36:** 341; suggestion of special ambassador to the U.S.,
36: 341, 353-54, 414, 428
Sussex crisis: attack, **36:** 371-73,n1;
reactions, **36:** 375, 381-82, 389n8, 416-
17,n1, 446n1, 447,n1, 483,n1, 485-86,
486-87, 488, 497, 532-33, 545,n1; preliminary instructions, **36:** 448-52; draft
of note, **36:** 452-56; House meets with
WW on drafting of *Sussex* note, **36:** 466-
71; first draft of *Sussex* note, **36:** 466-
71; final draft of *Sussex* note, **36:** 490-
96; Von Jagow's instructions to Bernstorff on *Sussex* note, **36:** 498-99; WW's
message to Congress, **36:** 506-10;
Bernstorff on suspension of submarine
warfare, **36:** 526,n1; Lansing memorandum on status of armed merchantmen, **36:** 533-39; House and Bernstorff
meet on, **36:** 547-48; Lansing on naval
operations against merchant ships, **36:**
556-57,n1; Germany on submarine
warfare during negotiations, **36:** 558,
559; German reply to *Sussex* note, **36:**
608,n1, 620-26; Gerard report of meeting with William II and Bethmann
Hollweg, **36:** 613-16; House on rejoinder, **36:** 616-17, 629; Lansing's memorandum on German reply, **36:** 626-27;
WW's draft of rejoinder and Lansing's
redraft, **36:** 649-51; press statement on
German reply, **36:** 654-55; *Sussex* crisis mentioned, **38:** 315; German pledge,
37: 13, 61-62; **38:** 453n1
L. H. Woolsey on German submarine
warfare, **36:** 452,n1; antiadministra-
tion Americans in Germany, **36:** 563-
64; Bernstorff on relations between, **37:**
45, 425-26; H. H. Kitchener on, **37:** 98,
98-99; House on, **37:** 423; D. Lawrence
on, **37:** 448-51; and Bryan arbitration
treaty, **37:** 479, 480; and *U-53* affair,
38: 374,n1, 386,n1, 390-92, 409-10, 452-
53,n1, 472-73,n1,2,3, 646, 647; British
opinion on relationship between, **38:**
246-47; O'Leary on pro-German voices,
38: 285,n1; and Polish relief question,
38: 369-72; and *Marina* incident, **38:**
570-71,n1,2, 607-608; U.S. protests
against German deportation of Belgians, **38:** 650-53, 656-57

*Germany's Drive to the West (Drang nach
Westen): A Study of Germany's West-
ern War Aims During the First World
War* (Gatzke), **37:** 507n1
Germany's Just Cause, **31:** 338
Geronimo, **29:** 279
Gespräch mit Oberst House (Bethmann
Hollweg), **36:** 123n1
Get Behind Wilson or Come Home and
Stay There (Mooney), **36:** 240,n1
Gettysburg, Battle of, **28:** 164; **37:** 460-
61, 462; fiftieth anniversary, **28:** 11, 11-
12, 13; WW's address on, **28:** 23-26
Gettysburg Address, **29:** 55; **33:** 160; **37:**
130
Gherardi, Neville S. Taylor (Mrs. Wal-
ter Rockwell), **35:** 132,n3
Gherardi, Walter Rockwell, **34:** 452,n1;
35: 130, 131-32; **37:** 65,n1
Giaour, A Fragment of a Turkish Tale
(Byron), **36:** 260,n2
Gibboney, Stuart Gatewood, **27:** 223, 227;
29: 136n1; **31:** 117, 123, 252, 253, 254
Gibbons, James Cardinal, **30:** 340-41,n1,
399, 399-400, 424; **33:** 17; **34:** 199,n1;
37: 30, 55,n1, 56n1
Gibraltar, **33:** 123n6
Gibson, Hugh Simons, **35:** 148n3; **37:**
71,n1
Gibson, Idah McGlone, **35:** 353,n1
Gibson Hotel, Cincinnati, **38:** 526n1
Gilbert, Newton Whiting, **28:** 301
Gilday, Patrick, **31:** 369,n2, 376n1, 424,
474, 475, 503, 523; **35:** 540; **36:** 237,
245
Gildemeester, Francis van Gheel, **33:**
279n1, 319, 332-33,n1, 347, 361-62,
362,n1
Gilford, Anna R., **34:** 452n1
Gillespie, George J., **27:** 246
Gillette, Cassius Erie, **28:** 357,n1
Gilman, Charlotte Perkins, **30:** 22,n2
Gilman, Joseph, **38:** 321-22,n1, 334
Gilman and Clucas, N.Y., **38:** 321n1
Glacier National Park, **34:** 87
Glad Adventure (Sayre), **28:** 20n1, 565n1;
38: 590n2
Gladden, (Solomon) Washington, **35:**
344,n1, 353; **37:** 314; **38:** 517,n1
Gladstone, William Ewart, **37:** 89
Glasgow, Scotland, **28:** 540
Glasgow, University of, **37:** 149
Glass, Carter, **27:** 4, 11, 21, 24-25, 79-80,
84, 199, 227, 292, 408, 409, 413, 430,
431, 436, 453, 457, 485,n2, 522-23, 525,
535,n1, 536,n1; **28:** 3,n1, 90,n1, 91, 257;
29: 62, 63n1, 77, 278; **30:** 10, 24, 325;
31: 130, 264; **32:** 13; **33:** 427, 442; **35:**
107, 117-18, 501; **36:** 472n1, 474; **37:**
46; **38:** 37, 660; and Democratic National Committee, **37:** 37, 229, 231, 238
Glass, Franklin Potts, **28:** 160n2; **29:** 274;
30: 28
Glass, Montagne Marsden, **28:** 595,n2

Glass-Owen Currency Act: see Federal Reserve Act
Glasson, William Henry, 27: 208-209
Gleaves, Albert, 38: 386n1
Gleeson, James Knox Polk, 30: 110n1
Glenconner, Edward Priaulx, 1st Baron Glenconner, 30: 315
Glenconner, Pamela Adelaide Genevieve Wyndham, Lady Glenconner, 30: 316
Glencove, West Paget, Bermuda, 27: 13, 218
Glenn, John Mark, 27: 244
Glen Springs, Tex., 37: 22n4, 254, 255, 258, 261
Glick, Frank, 31: 412,n4
Globe Theater, N.Y., 35: 258
Glory of Russia, Alaska, 33: 35
Glynn, Martin Henry, 28: 596; 29: 240,n1, 414,n1, 422, 423; 30: 65; 31: 117n1, 139, 148,n1, 156-57, 161, 167, 253, 267; 35: 347; 36: 378, 471-72, 497; 37: 61, 104; 38: 429, 515, 597n1; supports preparedness program, 36: 263,n1; temporary chairman of 1916 Democratic convention, 36: 601; 37: 156; and speech at Democratic convention, 37: 56-57, 76, 128, 133, 135,n3, 168, 282
Glynn, Mary Magrane (Mrs. Martin Henry), 36: 472,n2
Godfrey, Hollis, 36: 601,n4; 37: 374, 473; and Council of National Defense, 38: 182n3, 297, 386, 387, 439
Godkin, Lawrence, 27: 60,n2,4; 29: 380-81
Godwin, Harold, 33: 452,n2
Görlitz, Walter, 33: 299n2
Goethals, George Washington, 27: 488; 29: 306-308,n1; 32: 134; 36: 178; 38: 297,n1, 354n1
Golden, John L., 36: 497,n1,2
Golden, Colo., 31: 215
Goldfogle, Henry Mayer, 32: 96; 35: 319
Goldmark, Josephine Clara, 27: 76,n2, 244; 28: 63,n1
Gollan, Henry Cowper, 29: 562,n5
Gollan, Marie Louise Norris (Mrs. Henry Cowper), 29: 562,n3
Goltra, Edward Field, 29: 50-51; 37: 46
Gomez, Félix Uresti, 37: 277n1, 280, 300, 307; 38: 378, 382, 383
Gomez Palacio, Durango, Mex., 29: 15
Gompers, Samuel, 27: 160, 180-87, 191-92, 366-69, 403; 28: 317-18, 319,n1; 29: 425, 537; 30: 264, 313; 31: 257,n4, 330-31, 340-41; 32: 78, 87; 34: 174, 175; 35: 462; 37: 170, 346, 353-54,n1, 356, 357, 494; 38: 468-73, 671-72,n1, 673; on Supreme Court justices, 30: 309-10; desires pen with which WW signs Clayton bill, 31: 131, 138; thanks WW for pen, 31: 168; nephew killed in Haiti, 34: 109n3; on interview with Martinez, 34: 148-49, 164; and recognition of Carranza, 34: 512,n1; on Hillstrom case, 35: 206-207, 211, 214; and Seamen's Act, 35: 338-39,n1, 458,n1; urges WW to retain W. B. Wilson as labor secretary, 36: 23-25, 137; on labor rights in Porto Rico, 36: 567-68, 569, 570n1; on Mexican-American joint labor union convention, 37: 245-46, 267, 365-66,n1, 369; and release of Carrizal prisoners, 37: 344,n1; comments on Mexican-American Joint High Commission, 37: 402-403, 430-31, 436, 465-66, 470, 490; and Council of National Defense, 38: 182, 387
Gompers, Sophia, 34: 109,n1, 173
Gompers, William C., 34: 109,n3
Gonzáles, Ambrosio José, 27: 14,n2
Gonzáles, Francisco, 37: 280,n3
Gonzales, William Elliott, 27: 14, 531
González, Pablo, 29: 551,n2; 30: 194, 220; 32: 355,n5, 390; 33: 7, 307, 436n2, 459
González Garza, Roque, 28: 77; 32: 404; 33: 187n1, 239,n1, 343,n1, 344, 349, 461,n1
Good Comrade (Silberrad), 31: 316,n2
Good Evening! (Swing), 34: 370n2
Good Government League of Massachusetts, 28: 271
Good Hope, H.M.S., 36: 235n6
Goodhue, William Fletcher, 27: 208-209
Goodnow, Frank Johnson, 27: 554; 31: 381,n1; 32: 502,n3; 33: 99, 337
Goodrich, James Putnam, 38: 412n1
Goodwin, Augusta MacDonald (Mrs. Clarence Norton), 38: 47,n6
Goodwin, Clarence Norton, 38: 47,n5, 489n1
Goodwin, Elliot Hersey, 27: 530,n1; 30: 205-207,n1
Goodwin, Forrest, 28: 149n1
Goodyear, Anson Conger, 28: 112,n1,2, 278n1
Goodyear, Charles, 28: 112n2
Goodyear, Mary Martha Forman (Mrs. Anson Conger), 28: 112,n1
Gorchakov, Aleksandr Mikhailovich, 38: 68,n4
Gordon, Alice Gertrude (Altrude), 31: 563; 33: 178,n2, 339,n1, 363, 364,n1, 373, 525, 526,n1, 543; 34: 181, 193, 201, 211, 215; 35: 17, 23; 38: 258; in New York with EBG, 35: 155, 161, 162, 262n1, 272; marriage of, 37: 92,n1, 103, 106, 111,n1
Gordon, Charles William: see Connor, Ralph
Gordon, Samuel, 27: 213,n1,2; 33: 434,n1
Gordon, William, 36: 240,n1
Gore, Sir Edward Arthur, 36: 644,n19
Gore, Thomas Pryor, 27: 55, 61, 71, 82, 83, 107, 201, 251; 28: 10, 20, 41; 32: 197,n2; 36: 211, 311,n1; claims WW wants war, 36: 238n1

Gore resolution, **36:** 238n1, 240n1; tabled, **36:** 250,n1, 278,n1
Gore shipping bill, **32:** 197,n2
Gorgas, William Crawford, **28:** 125,n3; **29:** 307; **38:** 182
Gorham, N.H., **38:** 682,n1
Goricar, Josef, **35:** 277,n1, 281
Gorrell, Edgar Staley, **36:** 353,n3
Goshorn, Denny D., **36:** 337,n4
Gosse, Edmund William, **30:** 359,n1
Gothenburg (Göteborg), Sweden, **31:** 96
Gould, Elgin Ralston Lovell, **29:** 75-77
Gould, George J., **28:** 427
Gould, Lewis Ludlow, **36:** 175n1
Gracchus, Tiberius, **30:** 41
Grace and Co.: *see* W. R. Grace and Co.
Graham, James McMahon, **27:** 93,n1
Graham, Samuel Jordan, **29:** 50-51, 105-110, 111; **38:** 499-500
Grain Dealers' National Association: WW's address to, **38:** 261-70
Grain Grades Act, **37:** 197; **38:** 26, 426
Granados Campina, Enrique, **36:** 268n4
Grand Army of the Republic, **30:** 141n1; **37:** 123n1; WW address to, **34:** 534-36,n1,2; **36:** 160-62
Grand Central Station, N.Y., **38:** 591n1
Grand Rapids, Mich.: T. Roosevelt's speech at mentioned, **38:** 394,n2
Grant, Jesse Root, **27:** 62,n1
Grant, Ulysses Simpson, **27:** 159, 278; **30:** 466; **31:** 439
Grant, William W., **34:** 141,n1, 154
Grant, Mrs. William W., **34:** 141,n1
Grantham, Dewey Wesley, Jr., **34:** 62n1; **36:** 357n1
Granville, George, 2nd Earl Granville, **31:** 104,n1
Grasty, Charles Henry, **27:** 192,n1, 517, 554; **29:** 308, 311, 380, 515; **30:** 285; **35:** 429-30, 430-31, 432, 446
Graves, John Temple, **37:** 331-32,n1
Gray, George, **33:** 219; and Joint High Commission, **36:** 654; **38:** 79n1, 122n1, 153, 166, 355, 356, 357, 360, 362, 677
Gray, James Richard, **28:** 4,n2, 271
Gray, John G., **32:** 353, 466; **33:** 218
Gray, John Henry, **30:** 434-35
Gray, Thomas, **31:** 279; **38:** 524,n1
Graydon, Fannie Arnold (Mrs. Clendenen), **28:** 159,n1
Grays' Armory, Cleveland, **36:** 41n1
Grayson, Alice Gertrude Gordon (Mrs. Cary Travers): *see* Gordon, Alice Gertrude
Grayson, Cary Travers, **28:** 45,n2, 67, 85, 86, 104, 113, 133-34,n1, 135, 161, 199, 252, 261, 264, 331, 333, 360, 387, 395, 595, 596, 597; **29:** 99n2, 159, 377, 456, 516, 536, 558; **30:** 22, 23, 374n1, 436, 467; **31:** 59, 279, 318, 341, 354, 384, 387, 392, 517, 540, 548, 556, 563; **32:** 7, 21, 61, 67, 117, 121, 494; **33:** 178n2, 274, 339, 346, 373, 383, 442, 450, 452, 525n1, 538, 540, 542, 543; **34:** 74, 77,

91, 101, 119, 126, 128, 138, 150, 153, 177, 193, 201, 211, 213, 215, 221, 255, 256, 259, 287, 289, 291, 302, 305, 335, 337, 345, 353, 360, 447, 474, 485, 490, 508; **35:** 23, 25, 44, 153, 155, 162, 165, 166, 270, 272, 360, 460; **36:** 178, 402, 463, 606-607; **37:** 435-36; **38:** 258, 623, 628; EAW's last words to, **30:** 353n2; and Edith Galt's first meeting with WW, **32:** 423,n3; WW seeks promotion for, **33:** 465, 486; Mrs. Galt on, **34:** 181-82; and WW's crisis concerning Mrs. Hulbert, **34:** 500, 505; marriage of, **37:** 92,n1, 111n1
Great Britain, **27:** 130; **28:** 593; **32:** 42, 101-102, 259; **33:** 100-101, 405, 407, 408, 512-13, 522-24; **34:** 17-23, 42, 86, 145, 310-11, 319; **37:** 88, 104; **38:** 69; H. Plunkett and agricultural reform in, **27:** 60,n3,4; labor laws in, **27:** 186-87; and Mexico, **27:** 325, 331, 383, 424, 439, 478, 540; **28:** 158, 220, 376-78, 388, 410-11, 420-21, 421-23, 429, 443, 444-45, 445-46, 460, 462, 465, 466, 477, 484-85, 526,n2, 528, 529, 536-37, 543-45, 562, 564-65, 567, 575-76, 587; **29:**16-17, 91, 92, 119, 121, 190, 195, 210, 252, 253, 256, 320,n1, 381n1, 441-42, 540; **31:** 352; **33:** 298,n1; **35:** 100; and Japan, **27:** 448, 452; **29:** 183; **30:** 391; **31:** 511, 512; **33:** 114, 121-22, 131-32,n1, 139-40; **34:** 19; **35:** 289, 517, 518; and China, **27:** 488; **31:** 365; **33:** 114, 121-22, 131-32,n1, 139-40; **35:** 117, 203, 204, 289; and Bermuda, **28:** 135; W. Tyrrell on Germany and, **29:** 13; and Nicaraguan treaty, **29:** 172, 173; W. H. Page on conditions in, **29:** 285; **30:** 329-31, 438-39; **31:** 6-7, 55n3, 263; **32:** 129-33, 213-14, 313, 357-63, 426; **33:** 555; **35:** 74-77, 413-17; and Spain, **29:** 417
House peace mission (1914) and, **30:** 109, 140, 247-48, 256-57, 265, 266-67, 323, 342; prewar relations with Germany, **30:** 140, 315; and Pan-Americanism, **30:** 255, 256, 271-72; E. Grey on conference to avoid war, **30:** 315; agreements with France and Russia, **30:** 327; issues White Book on coming of war, **30:** 359,n2; and Germans in London, **30:** 368-69; William II on relations with, **30:** 382-83; and Turkey, **31:** 16n1; and wool exports, **31:** 292; and restrictions on neutral commerce, **31:** 371-72, 521; WW on cabinet system, **31:** 397; and trade with Central and South America, **31:** 416; and safety-at-sea convention, **31:** 419; and Italy, **31:** 524-25; **36:** 125; and House peace mission (1915), **32:** 204-207, 211-15, 220-21, 265, 267-68, 268, 276-78, 349-50, 402-403, 455, 514, 523; E. Grey on peace terms, **32:** 44-50; **33:** 124; **34:** 370; and public opinion in, **32:** 92, 99, 106, 107, 107-10,n1, 206, 268, 340,

480,n1; **33:** 14, 88, 122, 129-30, 139, 214, 255, 387-88, 512-13; **34:** 17-23, 33-34, 317, 440-41; **35:** 9, 11, 82-83, 138, 223,n1, 415, 517; **36:** 129-31, 181, 347,n1, 369, 384-87, 628; and far eastern crisis, **32:** 138, 170-71, 178, 197, 391; and German war-zone declaration, **32:** 193,n1, 194-95, 195-96,n1; and Gallipoli campaign plans, **32:** 225,n1; economic conditions in, **32:** 350; and German conduct of war, **32:** 378-79; **33:** 189-90; H. H. Kitchener on distribution of forces, **33:** 189; London air raids, **33:** 400, 414; and German propaganda in U.S., **34:** 200; and U.S. exports to Scandinavia, **34:** 253n1; and arming of merchantmen, **35:** 4-8; and Dogger Bank incident, **35:** 395,n3; German defense of submarine campaign against, **35:** 418-19, 451, 458, 463-64; **36:** 183-84; and *Persia* sinking, **35:** 419,n1; and *Baralong* case, **35:** 421-22; and negotiating concessions, **35:** 462, 464; declares blockade of Germany effective, **35:** 483, 517-18; Bethmann Hollweg on peace conditions with, **36:** 123n1; and *Brussels* case, **38:** 72n9, 91

Great Britain and the Caribbean, 1901-1913: A Study in Anglo-American Relations (Kneer), **28:** 578n1

Great Britain and the Creation of the League of Nations: Strategy, Politics and International Organization, 1914-1919 (Egerton), **38:** 207n1

Great Britain and the United States, **27:** ix, 124-25, 405-406, 482, 503-504, 554; **28:** 576; **29:** 12, 33, 52-53, 103, 112, 171, 180, 182, 201-202, 203, 217, 236, 241, 244, 321; **32:** 6, 9, 12, 59, 67-68, 107n1, 217-18, 249-51,n1, 443-49, 451, 453-54, 456, 457-58; **33:** 130, 251, 265-66, 362-63, 483-86; **34:** 42, 189; **35:** 144-45, 186, 187, 310,n1, 354n2, 504; **37:** 20, 57, 98-99; and Sir. W. Wiseman, **27:** xii-xiii; and Panama Canal tolls, **27:** 71, 203, 226, 310-11, 312-13, 332, 357-58, 512; **28:** 462, 531, 545; **29:** 160-61, 180, 224-25, 231-33, 237, 267-68, 312, 314-15, 348, 380, 385, 418-20; **30:** 141, 195, 248n1; **35:** 223, 224; WW on discovery of U.S. and, **28:** 449

ambassadorship: and R. Olney, **27:** 110, 167, 168-69, 176, 177; and C. W. Eliot, **27:** 194, 199; and W. H. Page, **27:** 200, 228, 234, 245; Hay-Pauncefote Treaty, **27:** 221-22; and arbitration treaty, **27:** 358, 514, 515, 534; **28:** 532-33; **29:** 52, 53, 162, 179, 182-83, 267-68; WW greeting to Spring Rice, **27:** 395; and conciliation treaty, **27:** 448, 477,n1; **29:** 136, 146-47, 340-42, 349-50; **31:** 64,n1; and Mexico, **28:** 34, 167-68, 433,n1, 434, 442-44,n1, 447-48, 455n1, 467-69, 515, 525-26,n1,2, 527, 530-31, 536-37, 537, 539, 561-62, 566-67, 573, 592, 601; **29:**

16-17, 131, 195-96, 228, 230, 256-57, 259, 267; **34:** 106,n2; Sydney Brooks on, **28:** 370; and seamen's bill, **28:** 412-13, 463; **30:** 280n1; oil interests in Mexico, **28:** 428-29; **30:** 237-38, 245-47; **37:** 305-306, 350; W. Tyrrell visits U.S., **28:** 447; fisheries treaty, **28:** 463; WW praises J. Bryce, **28:** 506n1, 507; and British subjects in Mexico, **28:** 571; changed attitude toward U.S. policy in Mexico, **29:** 111; Lord Cowdray's suggestion of joint intervention in Mexico, **29:** 144-46,n1; L. Carden's proposed visit to Washington, **29:** 209; Spring Rice on T. B. Hohler visit, **29:** 248-49; Hohler interview with WW and Bryan, **29:** 255-61; and Benton affair, **29:** 285-86,n1,3, 293, 300-301, 320,n1; W. H. Page on Monroe Doctrine, **29:** 333,n1, 389; L. Carden's interview in newspapers, **29:** 347,n1; and Canadian food fisheries treaty, **29:** 349n2; and expenses of U.S. ambassador in London, **29:** 410-13; **30:** 42, 149-55; and nationals in Mexico, **30:** 4, 9, 33, 130; fear of U.S. confidence in Villa, **30:** 29; Spring Rice on WW's interest in reforms in Mexico, **30:** 77-78; Spring Rice on ABC mediation, **30:** 133-34; WW on English view of Villa, **30:** 143; WW requests Page to remain ambassador, **30:** 195; House meets with Grey, Lord Haldane, and Earl of Crewe, **30:** 214, 214-15; House meets with H. H. Asquith, **30:** 247; and Pan-Americanism, **30:** 255-56, 271-72

Page on House peace mission, **30:** 258; C. H. Dodge's financial aid to ambassador, **30:** 277-78, 281-82; and views of WW's Mexican policy, **30:** 287-88,n1,2; WW grateful to Dodge, **30:** 288,n1, 490; and reaction to Huerta's abdication, **30:** 289; Page's offer of assistance in crisis, **30:** 316-17; and Ship Registry Act of 1914, **30:** 326, 387; Page on London on eve of war, **30:** 329-31; C. W. Eliot proposes blockade of Germany and Austria-Hungary, **30:** 353-55; American embassy during early days of war, **30:** 366-71; *U.S.S. Tennessee* to bring tourists back, **30:** 369,n7; and loans to belligerents, **30:** 372; resolution of the Federal Council of the Churches of Christ in America, **30:** 396, 397; C. W. Eliot on neutrality, **30:** 419; and British on purchase of German ships, **30:** 426-27, 431, 435-36, 469, 470; Eliot on position of England, **30:** 434; Page on Anglo-American relations, **30:** 438-39; Lansing on transfer of German merchant ships, **30:** 447-49; and WW's offer of mediation, **30:** 457n1; House on Anglo-American relations, **30:** 462; U.S. maintains neutrality, **30:** 472; Grey on relations between, **32:**

Great Britain and the United States
(*cont.*)
46-50; Spring Rice on American sentiment, **31:** 13-14
and peace discussions, **31:** 45, 61, 62, 76-77, 94-95, 385, 428,n1, 541; **36:** 652, 652-53; and Carden on U.S. troop evacuation from Mexico, **31:** 61n1; and Declaration of London, **31:** 85-86, 86-87, 90-91, 96-98,n1, 99-100, 103-105, 133-35, 136; Grey on new list of contraband and Declaration of London, **31:** 105-106, 125-26; and Order in Council, **31:** 109-11, 112-13, 115, 154-55; and new proclamation on contraband, **31:** 116; Spring Rice on Lansing's suggestions on Declaration of London, **31:** 136; and Germany's desire for peace negotiations, **31:** 140; and conditional contraband, **31:** 144, 528-59; and neutral trade, **31:** 154, 155-56; Page on accepting new Order in Council, **31:** 159-60; will not admit war materials to Germany, **31:** 159-60; U.S. on proposed Order in Council, **31:** 161-63, 163-66; Lansing seeks understanding on Declaration of London, **31:** 166; Spring Rice on relations between, **31:** 168; and visit of Sir G. Paish, **31:** 177,n2; Grey refuses U.S. proposal, **31:** 189-90, 191, 192
and seizure of U.S. ships bound for neutral ports, **31:** 193, 194; and export of foodstuffs to Belgium, **31:** 197n1; U.S. on British adherence to Declaration of London, **31:** 198, 216; Page on U.S. demands on Great Britain, **31:** 201-202; Page on proposed compromise, **31:** 202-204; seizure of *Brindilla*, **31:** 209; and debt, **31:** 212; and credits, **31:** 217, 218; Grey on new proclamation, **31:** 230,n1; and cotton situation, **31:** 230, 231, 233, 243; WW rebukes Page on U.S. perspective, **31:** 242-43; British reaction after U.S. withdraws demands regarding Declaration of London, **31:** 244-46; hopes for improving cotton situation and foreign exchange, **31:** 252; Münsterberg on pro-British feelings in U.S., **31:** 277, 336-40; and German ships in U.S. ports, **31:** 297-98; and sale of submarine parts, **31:** 310,n1; and shipping bill, **31:** 345-46, 347-49; Page on shipping problems, **31:** 370; importance of good relations between, **31:** 372; and seizure of ships bound for neutral ports, **31:** 439; and censorship of mail, **31:** 443, 443-44; WW on war settlement and, **31:** 459; and commercial treaty with Russia, **31:** 473; proposed instruction to Page, **31:** 477-80; House on release of U.S. ships, **31:** 489; Spring Rice reports on U.S. reaction to detention of ships, **31:** 499; and prize court proceedings, **31:** 505, 505-506; censorship of cables, **31:** 506; and Chinese customs management, **31:** 509; Grey's essential terms of peace, **31:** 518,n2; U.S. note of protest, **31:** 525-30; and China and Japan, **31:** 546-47; leak of protest note, **31:** 549-50; Spring Rice believes U.S. becoming pro-German, **31:** 550; J. P. Morgan, Jr., and, **32:** 87; and *Dacia* affair, **32:** 89,n3, 91-93,n2,3, 102-105; and German influence in the U.S., **32:** 92; and ship purchase bill, **32:** 192-93; use of American flag on British ships, **32:** 210,n2, 231, 249n1, 250; *modus vivendi* proposal, **32:** 235-36,n1,2,3, 249-50, 251-52, 259-60; **33:**28, 198, 205, 222,n1, 223, 226-27, 229, 237-38; **36:** 193,n3, 427-28; response to American note of Dec. 26, 1914, **32:** 237,n1; and British blockade of Central Powers, **32:** 301,n1, 307, 311-12, 399,n1, 399-401, 409-11, 412-13,n1, 414, 421,n2, 425, 427-29, 433; *Wilhelmina* affair, **32:** 380-81,n2; and *Falaba* incident, **32:** 488-90, 490-92, 492-93, 503; and interference with U.S. trade, **33:** 105-106, 239, 255, 257, 342, 472, 489, 508,n1, 509, 515-16, 517, 520
Lusitania sinking and immediate repercussions, **33:** 134n4, 193-94; and *Lusitania* correspondence, **33:** 166, 354, 359, 502-504, 507-508, 510, 531; and *Transylvania*, **33:** 185, 186n1; and proposed protest to Britain, **33:** 206, 206-207, 207-209, 215, 217, 223-24, 295n4, 385-86, 387, 394, 537; Dumba on, **33:** 212-13; House peace mission and, **33:** 267-68, 321, 406; **35:** 240-43, 356-58, 359, 381-82,n1, 453-55, 458-59, 471-73,n2, 483, 484-86, 487-88, 491, 498-99; **36:** 148n1, 166-68, 173, 180; H. Plunkett on, **33:** 338; **36:** 347n1, 519-20; and cotton crisis, **33:** 386, 445,n1, 453, 457-58, 526, 533n1, 534, 535-36; **34:** 6,n1, 11-12, 13, 30, 32, 34-35, 53-54, 100, 106-107,n4, 123, 137, 297; and British mining of North Sea, **34:** 15n1; and reply to U.S. note of March 30, 1915, **34:** 33,n1; and extending credit to Great Britain, **34:** 275-80; cotton declared absolute contraband, **34:** 295,n3, 296,n1; Bernstorff on, **34:** 298; and proposed loan to Britain, **34:** 316-17, 329, 478; and *Baralong* affair, **34:** 367, 368,n1; and armed British merchant vessels, **34:** 454-55, 460; Bernstorff on *Arabic* case and, **34:** 468-69; House on seeking British naval advice, **34:** 514; U.S. note on the blockade, **35:** 45, 60, 62-64, 85, 91,n1, 92, 93,n1, 223,n1, 255-56; and public opinion, **35:** 78, 223,n1, 362n1, 425-27, 430, 435-38; T. B. Hohler memorandum on Mexico, **35:** 97-103; and China, **35:** 117; and Cavell case, **35:** 147-

48,n1,2; and American shipping in Far East, **35:** 362n1; and Lansing's *modus vivendi re* armed merchant ships, **35:** 495-98,n1, 531, 532-33, 534; **36:** 129-31, 133, 133-34, 185; H. Smith on, **36:** 20n1; and *Appam* case, **36:** 134,n2; and House-Grey Memorandum, **36:** 180,n2, 261; **37:** 21, 62-63, 100, 179, 422-24, 502; and armed-merchantmen controversy, **36:** 192,n1, 193-94, 203, 207-209, 209-11, 215-16, 221-25, 225-26, 228-29, 232-33; WW asks for vote on McLemore resolution, **36:** 231-32; H. A. Garfield on dealing firmly with Britain, **36:** 247; WW on correspondence between, **36:** 264; and *Laurentic* incident, **36:** 269n1; **37:** 184,n2 A. G. Gardiner on returning Bryce to U.S., **36:** 320n1; W. J. Stone on, **36:** 366-68; H. H. Kitchener on, **36:** 436-42; House on, **36:** 548, 549; **38:** 258-59; and Pan-American Pact, **36:** 601-602; and detention of mail and blacklist, **37:** 83, 102, 103,n1, 112, 116-17, 450,n1, 467,n1, 469-70, 471, 476, 476-79, 480, 495-96; **38:** 202-206, 248-50, 315, 410, 467, 562,n1, 640-41, 641-42; Page on public opinion in, **37:** 143-44, 226-27, 227, 319-20, 456-62; and WW's speech to League to Enforce Peace, **37:** 143-44, 226-27, 227, 289-90, 294-95,n1; British on peace moves, **37:** 143-44, 202, 226-27, 239-40, 311, 411, 412-13; and blockade of food to Germany, **37:** 183, 184; A. Bullard on, **37:** 201-202; House on Pan-American Pact and, **37:** 265; N. Buxton on peace prospects, **37:** 370-72; and Casement case, **37:** 380, 446-47, 500, 516, 517; **38:** 350, 443-45; Page wishes to return to U.S. for discussions, **37:** 401-402; Germany's feelings on relations between, **37:** 425-26; T. N. Page on, **37:** 440-41; D. Lawrence on, **37:** 448-51; and aid to Poland, **38:** 29-30; and belligerent submarines in neutral waters, **38:** 149; British public opinion on German submarine warfare, **38:** 184-85; growing anti-British sentiment in U.S., **38:** 202, 204, 205, 315; Page memorandum on British feeling toward U.S., **38:** 241, 242-57; Grey on Anglo-French relations and, **38:** 251; J. A. O'Leary on WW's pro-British policies, **38:** 285,n1; WW on, **38:** 294, 388; P. F. Mueller on WW inaction and British "outrages," **38:** 351-52; British public opinion on *U-53* incident, **38:** 472-73,n3; House records WW annoyance with Allies, **38:** 646, 658
Great Britain's Vicious Plea (*St Louis Post-Dispatch*), **32:** 90n1
Great Coalfield War (McGovern and Guttridge), **28:** 426n1; **29:** 479n1, 511n1; **30:** 39n1, 49n1, 60n1; **31:** 273n2

Great Corn and Little Corn Islands, **27:** 528
Great Danger (*London Spectator*), **32:** 129, n2
Great Lake of Nicaragua, **27:** 527, 528
Great Northern Railway Co., **36:** 326
Greble, Edwin St. John, **38:** 238,n2
Greece, **32:** 203, 475; **33:** 12, 231, 232, 267, 501; **34:** 81; **35:** 194, 245; **37:** 89, 464; **38:** 107n1, 108, 114, 298; diplomatic appointments, **28:** 4, 5, 320, 326-27; resolutions of Federal Council of Churches and, **30:** 397; and Turkey, **31:** 56; G. Droppers considers resigning post in, **36:** 358; **37:** 97
Green, Constance McLaughlin, **29:** 240n2; **33:** 430n2
Green, John, **33:** 511
Green, Lawrence, **38:** 566
Green, Richard, **31:** 312
Green, William, **30:** 485-86,n1; **31:** 32, 99, 310; **36:** 639n16
Green Briar, S.S., **36:** 615
Green Mountains, Vt., **28:** 260, 320, 321
Greene, Sir Conyngham, **27:** 441n1
Greene, Daniel Crosby, **27:** 65,n1
Greene, Jerome Davis, **31:** 291,n3; **37:** 433,n1; **38:** 371,n3
Greene, Warwick, **38:** 72, 371,n4
Greene Cananea Copper Co., **27:** 404n1
Greenland, Denmark, **35:** 285,n2, 290, 350, 402, 403; **36:** 292n1; **37:** 484, 485, 495, 496, 497, 506; **38:** 10
Greenwood, Miss., **29:** 208
Greenwood Memorial Methodist Church, Boston, **29:** 474n1
Gregg, Alexander White, **36:** 151,n1, 175
Gregg, Mary Brooks (Mrs. Alexander White), **36:** 151,n2
Gregory, Ross, **29:** 333n1
Gregory, Thomas Watt, **27:** 23, 24, 27, 64, 127, 130, 163, 223, 228; **28:** 595; **29:** 67n2, 278, 530, 531; **31:** 93, 467-68, 500, 507, 552; **32:** 87, 325,n1,2; **33:** 342, 449, 450, 456, 493; **34:** 73,n3, 107-108, 134, 235, 266, 273, 516; **35:** 46, 65, 166, 182-83, 336, 359-60, 398, 401, 502; **36:** 240, 263, 267, 335, 376, 377, 425, 430, 602; **37:** 203, 398, 475, 481; **38:** 258, 494, 660; Clayton bill and New Haven Railroad suit, **30:** 123,n1, 423, 480-83; and attorney general appointment, **30:** 285,n1, 464, 468; and Clayton bill, **31:** 24-26, 29; on cotton-pool plan, **31:** 268-69, 271, 275; on Bryan's resignation, **33:** 424-26; and J. W. Davis as Solicitor General, **33:** 491,n1, 492; on third *Lusitania* note, **33:** 536, 537; on I.W.W. investigation, **36:** 188-90; on militia, **36:** 195-96; on army reorganization bill, **36:** 217,n1,2; on L. D. Brandeis, **36:** 611,n3; F. K. Lane on oil reserves and, **37:** 139-40, 142, 172,n2; and Pan-American Pact, **37:** 265; suggested for Supreme Court ap-

Gregory, Thomas Watt (*cont.*)
   pointment, **37:** 267,n1, 268, 278, 373, 467
Greil, Cecile L., **35:** 236,n1
Grella, E. M., **32:** 97
Grenfell, Wilfred Thomason, **29:** 51,n1
Grew, Joseph Clark, **31:** 404,n1; **33:** 451; **36;** 613,n1; **37:** 135n2; **38:** 141, 651, 652, 653
Grey, Albert Henry George, 4th Earl Grey, **32:** 211,n2; **38:** 472n1, 473
Grey, Sir Edward (Viscount Grey of Fallodon), **27:** 124,n1, 221-23, 310-11, 357-58, 405-406, 482, 503-504, 514; **28:** 530-31, 586-87, 588; **29:** 12, 19, 52, 53, 60, 103, 111, 162, 168-69, 195, 196, 209-10, 228, 228-33, 244,n1, 248-50, 256, 260, 266-68, 320n1, 324, 340-42, 344, 347-50; **31:** 8,n6, 100, 235, 243, 245, 292, 371, 372, 489, 549; **32:** 6, 41, 42, 53n1, 99, 112-13, 236,n3, 318n3, 342, 378-82, 406, 425; **33:** 64, 105, 130, 215, 217, 255,n1, 279n1, 333-34, 347-48, 361, 362, 407, 452, 470, 484, 515, 516, 519, 519-20, 550-52; **34:** 5, 32, 33,n1, 54, 62, 84, 85, 137, 163, 172, 186, 295-96, 297, 381, 506; **35:** 4,n2, 11, 74, 76, 78-79, 144, 145, 176, 191, 257, 259, 346, 356, 362, 388, 413, 414; **36:** 169-70, 193-94, 269, 294, 354, 405, 607, 652; **37:** 3, 6, 57, 58, 71, 76, 77,n1, 88, 90, 93, 94-95, 112, 144, 168, 182-83, 201, 294n1, 320, 371, 372, 440; **38:** 54, 89-93, 104, 181, 192, 201, 202, 206, 244, 247, 256, 258, 313n1, 319,n1, 472,n1, 647
   and Mexican situation, **28:** 34, 388, 421, 422, 429n1, 443, 447, 448, 465-66, 467-69, 477,n3, 515, 516, 525-26, 527, 528, 529, 536, 543-45, 561-62, 562, 565, 566, 573-74, 575-76, 577, 587,n1, 591, 592, 594, 601; **30:** 11, 59, 82; **34:** 106; fears for nationals in Mexico, **30:** 4, 9; and WW on protection of foreigners in Mexico, **30:** 9-10; and Spring Rice on Mexico, **30:** 29, 33, 77-78; on P. N. Furber and oil interests in Mexico, **30:** 245-47
   Panama Canal tolls, **28:** 531, 532-33; **29:** 315; **30:** 248n1; Page on, **31:** 7, 263; **32:** 362; **36:** 386; **37:** 457; conference with L. Carden, **29:** 131; **31:** 145; and conciliation treaty, **29:** 285,n3, 300; and L. Carden, **29:** 366,n1; Spring Rice on ABC mediation, **30:** 78-82, 133-34; Spring Rice to visit, **30:** 98; E. M. House hopes to meet with William II and, **30:** 140; Spring Rice on Panama Canal tolls, **30:** 141; House meets with, **30:** 189, 190, 200, 214-15; wishes House to convey impressions to Germany, **30:** 247-48; and Pan-Americanism, **30:** 255; W. H. Page on House and, **30:** 258
   House missions, **30:** 266; **32:** 117, 120, 161, 204-207, 211, 231, 238,n1, 242, 251, 252,n2, 253-54, 257, 265, 266, 267, 268, 277, 278, 285-86, 335, 340, 350, 373, 374, 377, 504, 513-14; **33:** 12, 13-14, 88, 89, 100, 121, 122, 123, 198, 205, 226, 229, 239, 248, 253, 254, 257, 267-68, 321, 408, 409, 451, 462-63, 533; **35:** 279, 382,n1, 453, 454, 465, 484, 485, 486, 487; **36:** 148, 166-67, 170, 173, 180n1
   Page's offer of good offices to, **30:** 314, 315, 316-17, 330; effect of war on, **30:** 315, 316, 370, 438-39; House on European situation and, **30:** 323, 327; ambassadorial conference plans fail, **30:** 325; note on EAW's death, **30:** 359, 403; warns Page of what is to come, **30:** 366; and Austrian embassy in London, **30:** 368; William II on George V and, **30:** 382; never took William II's offer seriously, **30:** 382, 383; and C. Barclay on U.S. loan policy, **30:** 386-87; use of German ships, **30:** 435-36; and transfer of German merchantships, **30:** 447-48; and House, **30:** 462, 463; fears Prussian militarism, **30:** 473; and peace discussions, **31:** 21-22, 58, 58-59, 60, 61, 62, 64, 95, 140-41, 501, 518,n2, 519, 522-23; **36:** 631-32, 652-53; **37:** 131-32, 202, 412-13; Page on State Department leaks and, **31:** 30n1; and Declaration of London, **31:** 90, 92, 96, 96-97, 97-98, 98, 99, 103, 105, 109, 113, 115, 116, 117-18, 125, 126, 135, 146, 154-55, 155-56, 158, 161, 162, 163, 165, 189-90, 191, 192, 230,n1
   and seizure and detention of American ships, **31:** 194, 229, 499; Page on new proposal of, **31:** 195-96; fears German ships in U.S. ports, **31:** 297-98; WW reads A. Gardiner's sketch of, **31:** 482,n1; and prize court hearings, **31:** 505; on Allied peace objectives, **32:** 44-50, 66; and Lansing on reply of Jan. 7, 1915, **32:** 54, 59; and *Dacia* affair, **32:** 89n3, 91-93; on public opinion, **32:** 104, 105, 107n1; W. Tyrrell on, **32:** 225; and order regarding publication of ships' manifests, **32:** 258; and correspondence with T. Roosevelt, **32:** 300; on consequences of defeat, **32:** 361; on freedom of the seas, **32:** 124, 372; and Japan and China, **33:** 131-32, 139-40; **36:** 411,n1; on *Lusitania* incident, **33:** 197-98; and renewal of *modus vivendi*, **33:** 222, 237-38; and cotton crisis, **33:** 534; **34:** 13, 30, 34, 126; Page's tribute to, **33:** 551-52; on war and peace, **34:** 145-46; on Germany's peace terms, **34:** 370-72; replies to mediation inquiries, **35:** 71,n3; and House's proposal, **35:** 81-82, 85, 186, 187, 254-56; on German blockade, **35:** 471-72,n2; reaction to *modus vivendi re* armed merchantmen, **35:** 531, 532-33, 534; **36:** 133-34,

192,n1; and House-Grey Memorandum, **36:** 180n2, 262, 266; **37:** 21, 42, 43-44,n4, 62-63, 100, 178-80, 411, 422-24; and Pan-American Pact, 203, 445, 601, 602; House informs of possible break with Germany, **36:** 421,n1, 422; on France and Britain, **36:** 443, 443-44, 511-12; on rudeness to McAdoo party in Trinidad, **36:** 569, 580; ennobled, **37:** 32,n2, 458n2; and mail seizures, **37:** 102, 103,n1, 116-17; **38:** 641; and *Laurentic* affair, **37:** 182n2; on German submarine warfare, **38:** 184-85; Page meets with, **38:** 251-55; photograph: *illustration section,* 31
Greytown, Nicaragua, **29:** 437, 452, 468
Gridiron Club, **27:** 294-97, 299; WW remarks to, **35:** 339-44; **36:** 218-20,n1, 317n1
Griff nach der Weltmacht (Fischer), **33:** 279n1
Griffen, S.C., **36:** 364
Griffin, Lillian Baynes, **35:** 84,n1
Griffin, Solomon Bulkley, **38:** 389
Griffin, Walter, **28:** 183,n6
Griffith, David Wark, **32:** 142n1, 310-11,n1, 325
Grimke, Archibald H., **28:** 498n1
Grinnell, Ia.: WW remarks in, **36:** 76
Griswold, Alfred Whitney, **27:** 175n1
Griswold, Benjamin Howell, Jr., **27:** 517,n2; **32:** 502,n1,3; **33:** 99, 337, 349, 350-51
Grogan, Edward Wesley, **33:** 196
Grosscup, Edward E., **27:** 40n1; **28:** 65, 83
Grosvenor, Edwin Prescott, **30:** 203,n1
Groton School, Groton, Mass., **35:** 431,n1
Grove Cottage, Gorham, N.H., **38:** 682n1
Grove Park Inn, Asheville, N.C., **28:** 382,n2
Grozier, Edwin Atkins, **28:** 271,n1, 275
Grubb, Edward Burd, **28:** 26,n1
Grubb, Violet Sopwith (Mrs. Edward Burd), **28:** 26
Grumbach, Salomon, **34:** 47n6
Grumpy (Hodges and Percyval), **35:** 19,n1, 25, 44
Grunewald, Jacques, **38:** 314n2
Guadalajara, Mex., **28:** 28, 72; **29:** 90, 286, 357
Guadalajara, University of, **28:** 59
Guadalupe, Plan of, **27:** 422n1; **28:** 73, 561; **29:** 189; **30:** 410, 445, 449, 490; **31:** 68; **33:** 65n1
Guadalupe-Hidalgo, Treaty of, **29:** 439
Guanajuato, state, Mex., **28:** 77
Guantánamo, Cuba, **30:** 296; **32:** 343
Guaranty Trust Co., N.Y., **32:** 135, 162
Guardian of Boston: William Monroe Trotter (Fox), **31:** 322n1; **33:** 68n1
Guatamala, **27:** 439, 474,n1, 540; **32:** 470,n2,3; **33:** 455, 487, 488; **34:** 157n1, 488; and Mexico, **28:** 7, 460; **35:** 501-

502,n1, 505; diplomatic appointments to, **28:** 112, 354; L. Carden, **28:** 411; *see also* Pan-American Conferences on Mexico
Guayaquil, Ecuador, **28:** 123, 124, 125, 177
Guaymas, Sonora, Mex., **27:** 331; **28:** 29, 157; **29:** 539; **37:** 284, 285
Gude, William Frederick, **34:** 534,n2
Guerrero, state, Mex., **28:** 77; **29:** 459; **31:** 13; **32:** 387; **36:** 397, 502, 585
Guerre Sous-Marine, La (Spindler), **36:** 483n1
Guest, G. N., **31:** 287
Guild, Mary Lyman Eliot (Mrs. Charles Eliot), **27:** 80n2
Gulf Oil Co., **30:** 246n2
Gulflight incident: *see* Germany and the United States
Gulfport, Miss., **29:** 98,n1, 99n1
Gulick, Sidney Lewis, **29:** 243,n1,2,3; **30:** 398; **31:** 80, 256,n2, 461n2; **37:** 308n2
Gummere, William Stryker, **27:** 141n1
Gunboat Diplomacy in the Wilson Era: The U.S. Navy in Haiti, 1915-1916 (Healy), **34:** 45n1
Gunner, Byron, **31:** 237,n1, 308
Guthrie, George Wilkins, **27:** 134, 228, 364; **28:** 16, 18, 282,n1, 284, 285-86; **30:** 396n1; **31:** 546; **32:** 246n2, 269,n3, 270, 414, 418, 426, 435,n1, 460, 466; **37:** 418-19
Gutiérrez, Eulalio, **31:** 313, 322,n1, 374, 380, 382, 411n2, 431; **32:** 355, 356, 404
Gutiérrez, Luis, **36:** 308n1, 457,n2, 579, 585-86, 590, 591
Guttridge, Leonard F., **29:** 479n1, 511n1; **30:** 39n1, 49n1, 60n1; **31:** 273n2
Guyot, Arnold Henry, **36:** 418
Gwinner, Arthur von, **33:** 478,n1; **34:** 47,n3, 48, 320

H. B. Clafin Co., **30:** 244,n3
H. K. Porter Co., Pittsburgh, **31:** 220n3
Haase, Hugo, **34:** 47,n5
Haff, Delbert James, **27:** 404n1,3, 419-25,n1; **28:** 41, 58
Haggard, Henry Rider, **31:** 316n2, 317
Hägglund, Joel: *see* Hillstrom, Joseph
Hagner, Isabella Louisa: *see* James, Isabella Louisa Hagner
Hague, The, Netherlands, **27:** 509, 515; **30:** 467n1; **32:** 205, 516,n2; **37:** 59; flag at half staff for EAW, **30:** 365; and International Conference on Women, **33:** 314,n1; **34:** 58n1, 251n2, 397,n1; and Central Organization for a Durable Peace, **35:** 196n2
Hague, Frank, **27:** 456, 480, 482, 494n1
Hague Conference (1899), **30:** 460; **33:** 152
Hague Conference (1907), **31:** 38, 54, 153; **32:** 198; **33:** 321, 347; **34:** 96-97; **36:** 134n2, 363, 483n1, 486; **38:** 112; and ABC mediation, **30:** 119, 124; and Ar-

Hague Conference (1907) (*cont.*)
ticle Three on mediation, **30:** 311, 342, 396; and use of airships, **30:** 460; and Münsterberg on contraband, **31:** 337, 437, 438, 444; and Germany's invasion of Belgium, **32:** 42n1, 92, 211n2, 223, 224-25; and *Lusitania* case, **35:** 14, 419, 452

Hague Conference (Third: proposed), **29:** 225; **30:** 460-61

Hague Tribunal: *see* Permanent Court of Arbitration

Haig, Sir Douglas, **38:** 253,n1

Haimhausen, Edgar Haniel von, **31:** 34n2

Haiti, **27:** 518-19, 531, 553, 557-58; **28:** 48; **29:** 242,n3; **30:** 200, 209, 213, 241,n1, 244, 296, 319, 493; **31:** 482, 483-85, 485-86, 486-87; **35:** 188, 247, 259; diplomatic appointments, **28:** 4, 221n1; customs control in, **31:** 34-36,n2; Bryan on, **31:** 456-57; France and, **38:** 339-40, 530

Haiti and the United States, **32:** 27-28, 62, 75-76, 288-89, 295-96, 297, 437,n1, 457, 479, 487,n1; **33:** 395-96, 440, 452; **34:** 60, 61, 61-62, 78-79, 80, 81, 89, 139, 142-44, 144, 157-58, 158, 163, 173, 233, 338; U.S. financial interests in, **32:** 437,n2, 458, 472-73; Bryan on recall of A. Bailly-Blanchard, **32:** 471-72; and Fuller mission, **33:** 115, 116-17, 275-76, 276-77, 278, 467,n1; U.S. occupation of, **34:** 45,n1; J. P. McDonald on solving problems in, **34:** 66-68; Lansing on, **34:** 69-70, 121-22; J. Daniels on, **34:** 70-71; and *cacos*, **34:** 70-71; U.S. instructions to W. B. Caperton in, **34:** 122; elections to be held, **34:** 164-65; and treaty, **34:** 183-84,n1, 208-209, 256-57, 311,n1, 367, 437-38

Haiti and the United States 1714-1938 (Montague), **34:** 67n1

Haldane, Richard Burdon, 1st Viscount of Cloan, **28:** 587,n3; **29:** 111,n2; **30:** 214-15,n1, 257, 258, 359; **32:** 91n3, 225; **33:** 227, 524, 552; **37:** 447

Haldeman, William Birch, **33:** 196,n1

Hale, Eugene, **38:** 174n2

Hale, Frederick, **38:** 170,n1, 174,n3

Hale, George Ellery, **37:** 472-74,n1, 494

Hale, Mary Douglass Chandler (Mrs. Eugene), **38:** 174,n2

Hale, Matthew, **37:** 523n1, 524,n2; **38:** 171,n1

Hale, William Bayard, **27:** 145, 335,n1, 396,n1, 483; **28:** 38-39, 140, 145n1, 200-201, 206, 207, 218n1, 219, 259,n2, 300, 334n1, 505, 506, 527, 557, 559, 560, 579-80, 588; **29:** 90-91, 121; **31:** 496; report on Mexican situation, **27:** xix, 536-52; *The New Freedom*, **27:** 4,6; recall of H. L. Wilson, **28:** 7, 8, 22, 26, 27,n1; H. L. Wilson on, **28:** 18-20; memoranda on Mexican affairs, **28:** 27-34; **29:** 130-31; and Americans in Mex-

ico, **28:** 32-33; De la Barra request to meet with WW, **28:** 69; B. Penrose and, **28:** 163,n4, 185; report on Mexican political situation, **28:** 339-40; suggestions on objection to Huerta's presidency, **28:** 411-12; proposes secret meeting with the Constitutionalists, **28:** 423, 431; WW orders to avoid intervention, **28:** 525; considered as Third Assistant Secretary of State, **28:** 527-28; secret meetings with Carranza, **28:** 529, 541-43, 545-46; Carranza and the Constitutionalists, **28:** 558-59, 561, 563, 564, 567-68, 568-69; WW recalls to Washington, **28:** 600; submits resignation because of poor health, **29:** 130; WW accepts resignation, **29:** 133-34

Half an Hour (Barrie), **28:** 355,n4

Half Bitter, Half Sweet: An Excursion into Italian-American History (De Conde), **27:** 288n6

Halifax, Nova Scotia, **31:** 229, 340, 347

Hall, Benjamin Franklin, **37:** 541,n1

Hall, Granville Stanley, **27:** 306n1

Hall, Henry Clay, **31:** 269,n2, 356

Hall, Henry Noble, **29:** 344,n1; **38:** 564-70,n1

Hall, Henry R., **32:** 355, 356

Hall, Hubert L., **30:** 47,n1, 113,n3; **31:** 13,n6

Hall, Margaret Tannahill Sprunt (Mrs. Benjamin Franklin), **37:** 541,n2

Hall, Mary Hepburn Hough (Mrs. William Richardson), **28:** 61n2, 146,n1, 252

Hall, Ruth Preble, **28:** 61,n2, 66, 81, 102, 252, 266, 269, 273, 355

Hall, William Edward, **29:** 432; **32:** 543n3

Hallett, Alice Morrell, **38:** 511,n1

Hallinan, Charles T., **36:** 632n1

Halsey, Abram Woodruff, **27:** 154, 156-57, 168; **30:** 176,n1; **35:** 274, 279-80

Ham, Clifford D., **29:** 245,n1

Hamburg, Germany, **32:** 381n1; **35:** 62

Hamburg-American Line, **29:** 477; **31:** 345; **32:** 89n3; **33:** 333; **34:** 47,n2, 266, 453; **36:** 235

Hamburg-Colombian Banana Co., **36:** 234-35

Hamerton, Philip Gilbert, **33:** 87,n1, 364

Hamill, Ernest Alfred, **31:** 76

Hamill, James Alphonsus, **27:** 180, 303n2; **29:** 318-19, 323; **33:** 219; **37:** 344

Hamilton, Allan McLane, **31:** 316,n2

Hamilton, Alexander, **27:** 391; **29:** 448; **38:** 303, 326

Hamilton, Alice, **38:** 275,n3

Hamilton, C. A., **27:** 544

Hamilton, Edith, **29:** 439n1

Hamilton, Franklin Elmer Ellsworth, **37:** 148n1

Hamilton, Sir Ian Standish Monteith, **34:** 42n2

Hamilton, Jean Miller Muir (Mrs. Ian Standish Monteith), **34:** 42,n2

Hamilton, John William, **37:** 148n1

Hamilton, Peter Joseph, **38:** 633,n1

Hamish (dog), **31:** 454; **32:** 9

Hamlet (Shakespeare), **28:** 400,n1; **36:** 260,n1

Hamlin, Charles Sumner, **28:** 498n1; **29:** 401n1, 532; **31:** 196; **34:** 107, 277, 278, 316, 330, 369; **36:** 171-72, 177; **38:** 35, 198, 336, 512; as candidate for Federal Reserve Board, **30:** 7, 27, 53, 54, 181n1; accepts Federal Reserve Board position, **30:** 188; and decision to accept reappointment on Federal Reserve Board, **37:** 105, 291, 346, 463, 467-68, 489-90, 498; on Federal Reserve Act, **38:** 497-99

Hamm, T. C., **28:** 163n3

Hammerling, Louis Nicholas, **32:** 14,n1, 96

Hammond, John Hays, **32:** 17,n2; **37:** 167

Hampden, John, **28:** 52

Hampshire, H.M.S., **37:** 179n1

Hampton (estate) Baltimore, **28:** 291,n2

Hampton Institute, **29:** 537n1; **30:** 43; **31:** 261,n1

Hancock, John, **30:** 248,n1

Hancock, Lewis, **27:** 228,n1

Hancock, U.S.S., **29:** 454; **31:** 383, 486

Hand, Frances Amelia Fincke (Mrs. Learned), **28:** 43,n6, 63, 150

Hand, Learned, **28:** 43, 150; **37:** 363,n2; **38:** 14-15, 27

Handy, Parker, **30:** 189

Hangchow, China, **32:** 248

Hangchow College, **33:** 51n2

Hanger, Grossbrenner Wallace William, **30:** 305,n2, 313-14, 314

Hankow, China, **31:** 365; **32:** 135, 530

Hanna, Charlotte Augusta Rhodes (Mrs. Marcus Alonzo), **32:** 12,n2

Hanna, Marcus Alonzo, **32:** 12n2; **35:** 433; **38:** 3n4, 310-11, 331, 434-35

Hanna, Philip C., **29:** 522-23; **30:** 290

Hannay, James Owen: see Birmingham, George A.

Hannibal National Democratic League, **38:** 156,n1

Hanover, N.H., **28:** 102, 108, 150, 252; **30:** 436; **34:** 89, 119

Hanover National Bank, N.Y., **31:** 139n4

Hanson, Ole, **37:** 432,n1, 524n2

Han-ye-p'ing Iron and Coal Co., China, **32:** 169, 321, 333n1, 461, 466-67, 529-30, 531; **33:** 83-84, 96-97, 102-103

Hapgood, Norman, **27:** 102, 106, 112, 259, 262-263; **28:** 112, 301-302; **29:** 74n1, 219, 481-82, 483, 496; **30:** 161, 161-62, 162, 285, 385, 385-86; **31:** 161, 291, 318, 353n3; **32:** 9, 128; **33:** 122, 516,n1; **35:** 145, 156; **37:** 535; **38:** 3, 12, 14-15, 23-24, 27, 29, 34-35, 42-43, 78, 117, 175, 178-79, 189, 273, 274-76, 281, 564; and L. D. Brandeis, **27:** 61, 92-93; **36:** 25-26, 86, 606-607; *Harper's Weekly*, **27:** 436, 459, 464-65, 467, 474; appointment suggestions, **36:** 191-92; on Fed-

eral Trade Commission appointment, **37:** 117,n2, 204n3, 268, 362-63,n1, 374-75, 475; and H. L. Wilson suit against, **37:** 176; suggestions for Democratic National Committee officers, **37:** 206-207, 210-11, 230; and Supreme Court appointments, **37:** 264, 372-73, 446; and Robins support of Wilson in 1916, **37:** 321-22, 328-30, 373-74, 522, 528; on campaign and woman suffrage, **38:** 86-87, 87; desire for a diplomatic appointment, **38:** 350

Hapgood, Ruth, **28:** 302,n2; **36:** 86,n2

Happy Acres (Turpin), **28:** 318,n1

Happy Warrior (Wordsworth), **37:** 37

Harbaugh, William Henry, **27:** xxii; **30:** viii

Harbison, Elmore Harris, **31:** 220n2

Harbison, Frederick Harris, **31:** 220n2

Harbison, Ralph Warner, **31:** 220n2

Harbison-Walker Refactories Co., Pittsburgh, **31:** 220n2

Harden, Maximilian Felix Ernst, **37:** 86,n4; **38:** 126,n1

Harding, Alfred, **37:** 123n1

Harding, Earl, **31:** 403,n1

Harding, Warren Gamaliel, **36:** 219,n2; **37:** 167,n1, 168

Harding, William Procter Gould, **29:** 278,n4, 288, 308, 322, 383, 390, 532, 543; **31:** 269,n1, 271; **34:** 99, 100, 200, 267, 272, 277, 278, 295, 296, 373, 400; **37:** 463, 467; **38:** 22,n1, 566n7; and Federal Reserve Board nomination, **30:** 7, 30n1, 52, 54, 181n1; and cotton situation, **34:** 186n2

Hardinge, Charles, 1st Baron Hardinge of Penshurst, **36:** 386,n2

Hardware Manufacturers' Association, **30:** 127

Hardwick, Thomas William, **27:** 239,n1; **32:** 173n2, 222,n2, 366, 375-76; **33:** 134; **36:** 606; **37:** 429

Hardy, Rufus, **27:** 239n1; **29:** 312

Hare, Augustus John Cuthbert, **28:** 93,n5

Hare, Constance Parsons (Mrs. Montgomery), **35:** 258,n2

Hare, John Innes Clark, **32:** 534,n2

Hare, Montgomery, **35:** 258,n2

Hargreaves, Grace Dexter Bryan (Mrs. Richard Lewis), **33:** 205n1

Hargreaves, Richard Lewis, **33:** 205,n1

Harkins, Miss (household help), **32:** 306

Harlakenden House, Cornish, N.H., **27:** 189n1; **28:** 12, 360n1, 368n1; **30:** 461, 464; **33:** 452n3, 525; **34:** 64, 169, 202, 204, 213, 247, 257, 294, 306, 354; **35:** 103; Wilson family reunion at, **34:** 72-73, 83; WW on time spent with Mrs. Galt at, **34:** 177; WW at: *illustration section,* 28

Harlan, John Marshall: Interstate Commerce Commission v. Brimson, **29:** 85

Harlow, Samuel Allen, **33:** 160, 197

Harmon, Judson, **27:** 74; **38:** 537n1

Harmsworth, Alfred Charles William, 1st Baron Northcliffe, **31:** 204,n1; **32:** 328, 340; **35:** 83; **37:** 226, 371, 447; **38:** 619

Harper, Mr., **30:** 164

Harper, Belle Dunton Westcott (Mrs. George McLean), **30:** 364,n2, 401, 479; **31:** 13, 36

Harper, George McLean, **31:** 36; **36:** 274,n1; condolence on EAW's death, **30:** 364; WW acknowledges, **30:** 438

Harper and Brothers, N.Y., **33:** 149n3; **34:** 57n1; **36:** 177n2, 516

Harper's Magazine, **36:** 516, 600-601

Harper's Weekly, **27:** 140,n1, 436, 459, 464-65, 467, 474; **29:** 7n2, 30n1, 219,n1, 327,n1; **30:** 161,n1; **32:** 128n1, 211; **33:** 149n3; **37:** 176n2

Harriet Lane, C.S.S., **27:** 228

Harriman, Edward Henry, **29:** 140,n3

Harriman, Ethel Borden, **33:** 462,n2; **34:** 136,n4

Harriman, Florence Jaffray Hurst (Mrs. Jefferson Borden), **28:** 42, 44; **29:** 449, 456; **33:** 461-62,n2, 470, 477; **34:** 135-36, 216-17; **37:** 427; **38:** 6, 7

Harriman, Jefferson Borden, **29:** 456; **33:** 462n2

Harriman, Joseph Wright, **36:** 249,n1

Harriman, Karl Edwin, **32:** 222,n1; **36:** 559-60

Harriman and Co., N.Y., **36:** 249n1

Harriman National Bank and Trust, N.Y., **36:** 249n1

Harrington, D. M. **29:** 549

Harris, Edwin S., **36:** 458,n1; **37:** 155, 156, 533; **38:** 8, 429

Harris, Frank, **36:** 415n1

Harris, Frederick Robert, **36:** 279,n2

Harris, Heaton W., **32:** 402,n2, 505,n1

Harris, Joel Chandler, **31:** 316n2, 317

Harris, William Julius, **32:** 61,n1, 271n2; and Federal Trade Commission, **37:** 117, 204,n2,3, 268, 363

Harrison, Benjamin, **28:** 188,n1; **37:** 520

Harrison, Fairfax, **31:** 20,n3

Harrison, Francis Burton, **28:** 175, 184, 192, 197, 203, 301, 323-24,n1, 372, 415-17, 595; **29:** 147, 148; **30:** 156; **32:** 330-31, 457; **34:** 389-91; **35:** 52, 72, 85-97; **36:** 414, 583; **38:** 119, 155, 438, 632, 648, 656, 674; M. Quezon on, **28:** 192-93; and Noriel case, **32:** 535,n1, 535-36, 536,n1,2

Harrison, Jane Serumgard, **27:** xxii

Harrison, Leland, **29:** 128,n1; **34:** 50-51, 55; **37:** 158

Hart, Albert Bushnell, **30:** 343,n1; **33:** 229

Hart, William Howard, **28:** 166,n2, 178, 195

Harts, William Wright, **37:** 474,n5

Hartford Theological Seminary, **35:** 39n2

Hartman, Charles Sampson, **28:** 5,n3, 175

Harvard Club of Boston, **30:** 5n1

Harvard Law School, **28:** 355n3

Harvard Medical School, **38:** 182n7

Harvard University, **27:** 206; **28:** 375,n2;

29: 367; **30:** 5n1, 156n1; **31:** 108, 276,n1; **32:** 25, 538n3; **33:** 430; **35:** 216-17, 383; **36:** 156n3; **37:** 541; **38:** 3n3, 510n2, 687n3; and Princeton football, **31:** 412n2; Twenty-Fifth Anniversary Report (class of 1910), **27:** 476n1

Harvey, George Brinton McClellan, **27:** 72; **28:** 597; **29:** 32, 121,n1, 159; **31:** 468,n2; **36:** 226n2

Harvey, Roland Bridendall, **37:** 272,n2

Harvey-Watterson affair, **27:** 72; **31:** 83

Hastings, Samuel Miles, **37:** 492-93,n1

hat manufacture: *see* millinery manufacture

Hatch, Alden, **32:** 423n1

Hatton, Fanny Locke, **27:** 112n1

Hatton, Frederic, **27:** 112n1

Hatzfeldt-Trachenberg, Prince von, Hermann (1848-1933), **31:** 336,n2

Haultain, Theodore Arnold, **31:** 19n1

Havana, Cuba, **27:** 518-19; **30:** 148n2

Havelberg, Prussia, **37:** 507n3

Havemeyer, Louisine Waldron Elder (Mrs. Henry Osborne), **37:** 427,n3

Haven, William I., **27:** 154

Havenith, Emmanuel, **30:** 457-58,n1; **31:** 16, 89-90, 291, 295, 317; **35:** 498; **38:** 651, 653; collection of funds for Belgium in the U.S., **31:** 84,n1

Havenith, Mrs. Emmanuel, **31:** 317

Haverford College, **27:** 206

Hawaii, **27:** 426-28, 443, 446, 447; **29:** 8; **33:** 35, 134n1; **35:** 123, 169, 298; **37:** 200n3; and sugar, **27:** 340; and Japan, **29:** 218

Hawkins, William Waller, **38:** 494,n1

Hay, James, **27:** 73,n3, 74; **32:** 86n1; **34:** 38,n1, 38-39, 58; **36:** 134-35, 141-43, 146, 163, 170-71, 178, 513-15; **37:** 381; on preparedness and Garrison plan, **35:** 138-39, 173, 180, 469-71, 479, 480, 481, 482, 499-500, 502-503, 512; WW comments on army reorganization bill of, **36:** 178-79,n1,2,4; and Lever amendment, **36:** 345, 354-55; WW congratulates on House passage of army reorganization, **36:** 360,n1; on difference between Senate and House preparedness bills, **36:** 514-15; on nitrate plant construction provision, **36:** 619-20; photograph: *illustration section,* **36;** *see also* army reorganization bill

Hay, John Milton, **27:** 237; **28:** 317, 459; **29:** 331; **30:** 152, 404; **32:** 7, 414, 426; **33:** 34; **36:** 440; **37:** 32, 109

Hay bill: *see* army reorganization bill

Hay-Pauncefote Treaty, **27:** 221-22, 225, 337; **29:** 112, 179, 182, 220, 232, 237, 271, 276, 310n1, 408, 420; **30:** 159n1

Hayden, Lewis A., **29:** 549

Hayden Brothers (Juniper Mine), Colo., **29:** 549

Hayes, Dr. (aide to Lord Cowdray), **29:** 144

Hayes, Frank J., **29:** 25; **30:** 17, 485-86,n1;

31: 32, 37, 99, 106-108, 124-25, 215-16, 310, 446, 449, 488; and Colorado coal strike, **28:** 426,n8, 509, 513, 519-20, 520-21, 554, 583
Hays, Isaac Minis, **27:** 159
Hays, Samuel Augustus, **27:** 333,n1
Hays, Will H., **38:** 412n1
Hazen, Azel Washburn, **28:** 355n3; **37:** 409
Hazen, Maynard Thompson, **28:** 355,n3
Head, James Marshall, **27:** 67-68,n1
Health, Department of: suggestion for creation of, **35:** 151, 183-84; R. L. Owen on establishing, **37:** 161
health care: Juliet B. Rublee on, **30:** 93, 135
health insurance, **36:** 248; **37:** 532
Healy, David, **34:** 45n1
Healy, Timothy, **38:** 445n1
Hearst, William Randolph, **27:** 11,n1, 24; **29:** 389, 459; **30:** 283n1; **37:** 290,n1
Hearst newspapers, **27:** 117n1, 118, 334, 464; **28:** 105; **34:** 81n1; **37:** 331n1; **38:** 244
Hebrew Immigrant Aid Society of Massachusetts, **32:** 97n1
Hebrew Sheltering and Immigrant Aid Society of America, **32:** 97
Hebron, N.H., **28:** 129
Heckscher, August, **27:** xxi, xxii
Hedry de Hedri et de Genere Aba, Stephen, **29:** 248
Heflin, James Thomas, **28:** 117
Hegel, Georg Wilhelm Friedrich, **31:** 28
Hegler, J. L., **31:** 248, 248-49
Heimke, William, **31:** 456,n1
Heinecke, William, **38:** 427,n1
Helen: *see* Bones, Helen Woodrow
Helfferich, Karl, **37:** 379n1
Helgoland, Germany, **35:** 350
Heller, Isaac, **32:** 97,n11
Heller, Joseph Milton, **29:** 38,n1
Helm, J. D., **36:** 364
Henckel von Donnersmarck, Count Guido, **33:** 298
Henderson (household help), **28:** 392; **32:** 7
Henderson, Robert Randolph, **35:** 262n3, 275; **38:** 563
Henderson, Theodore Sommers, **36:** 391n1, 393
Hendrick, Archer Wilmot, **38:** 39,n1
Hendrick, Burton Jesse, **38:** 241n1, 445n4
Hendricks, Thomas M., **28:** 289n1; **37:** 324n1
Hendrix, Eugene Russell, **35:** 328
Heney, Francis Joseph, **27:** 93; **37:** 338-42, 358, 524n2
Hennessy, David C., **27:** 288n6
Hennessy, John A., **31:** 11n1, 116,n1, 123, 252
Henríquez y Carvajal, Federico, **37:** 158,n1
Henry (Heinrich Albert Wilhelm), Prince of Prussia, brother of William II, **30:** 382

Henry, Robert Lee, **27:** 14,n3, 62, 96; **28:** 122, 255, 257; **30:** 454; **31:** 411; **32:** 197; **34:** 180, 208; **36:** 231; currency bill, **27:** 485,n3, 486, 523-24; and cotton crisis, **31:** 79n1, 119-21, 129-30, 205, 324; and Porto Rico bill, **31:** 465, 466, 474
Henry Cabot Lodge: A Biography (Garraty), **29:** 272n1
Henry V (Shakespeare), **28:** 351-52; **36:** 92
Henry Street Settlement, **36:** 632n1
Hensley, Walter Lewis, **36:** 362,n2, 374n1
Hensley resolution, **36:** 374n1
Hepburn, Alonzo Barton, **27:** 79,n2; **28:** 3; **30:** 51; **31:** 139,n4
Heraux, Edmond, **31:** 485
Herbert, Hilary Abner, **30:** 141,n2
Herbert, Victor, **34:** 467n1
Herbert Hoover: A Public Life (Burner), **37:** 542n1
Hercules, **28:** 438
Herford, Oliver, **28:** 439
Hermione, H.M.S., **29:** 416
Hermosillo, Sonora, Mex., **28:** 342, 370, 423, 567; **30:** 417
Hernandez, Eliseo, **36:** 397,n1
Hernandez, Gabriel, **27:** 544-45
Herrera, Luis, **36:** 457,n1, 584-85
Herrick, Myron Timothy, **29:** 11,n1, 401n1; **30:** 152, 200, 313, 369, 457n1; **31:** 21n1, 283, 348; **32:** 372; **35:** 460; **37:** 441, 519; loses Senate race, **37:** 441n2
Herring, D. W., **28:** 354,n2
Herring, Pendleton (Edward), **27:** xxi
Hershey, Omer Fenimore, **29:** 515,n1; **30:** 27, 54
Herty, Charles Holmes, **36:** 275,n3
Hesperian affair, **34:** 423,n1, 425, 426, 427, 428-29, 433, 436, 436-37, 441, 453; public opinion on, **34:** 444-45,n1,2,3,4
Hetch Hetchy bill, **30:** 217
Hewitt, C. H., **29:** 190-91
Hexamer, Charles John, **34:** 116,n2
Hibben, Elizabeth Grier (Beth), (afterwards Mrs. Robert Maxwell Scoon), **30:** 385; **31:** 44; **38:** 682,n4
Hibben, Jenny Davidson, **27:** 68-69, 72; **29:** 392; **31:** 44; **38:** 682n1; condolence note on EAW's death, **30:** 384-85, 404
Hibben, John Grier, **27:** 72; **28:** 335, 337; **29:** 171, 554; **30:** 156, 163-64, 176n1, 385; **31:** 44, 205; **33:** 432n1; **38:** 682n1; and Panama Canal tolls controversy, **29:** 391-92,n1; condolence note on EAW's death, **30:** 404
Hicks Beach, Sir Michael Edward, **33:** 34,n4
Hidalgo, state, Mex., **28:** 77, 78
Hidalgo de Parral, Chihuahua, Mex.: *see* Parral
Higginson, Henry Lee, **29:** 367-70; **30:** 294, 294-95, 302, 338, 432; **31:** 215, 320-21, 516; **32:** 140-41, 167-68, 176, 238; **34:** 28-29, 32; **35:** 216-17, 235; **36:** 218, 250, 265; on foreign exchange, **30:** 420-

Higginson, Henry Lee (*cont.*)
22; on achievements of WW and Congress, **31:** 212-14; on railroad situation, **31:** 238-41, 247
Highcourt (estate, N.H.), **28:** 278,n1
Higher Realism of Woodrow Wilson and Other Essays (Link), **31:** 12n1
Highland Park, Ill., **37:** 492n1
highway bill: *see* good roads bill
Hill, David Jayne, **33:** 17
Hill, Ebenezer, **36:** 261n3, 275; **38:** 498,n2
Hill, James Jerome, **30:** 190; **33:** 17,n1
Hill, Larry D., **28:** 6n1; **29:** 98n1, 285n1, 450n1; **30:** 47n1,2, 166n1, 193n1, 230n1; **32:** 202n2
Hill bill, **36:** 261n3, 275,n2, 406,n1
Hill Publishing Co., **33:** 497n4
Hillburn, N.Y., **31:** 237n1, 308
Hillstrom, Joseph (Joe Hill), **34:** 539,n2; **35:** 3, 58, 69, 73, 73-74, 84, 206,n1,2, 206-207, 210, 211, 213-15, 283n1,2, 290
Hinchey, Margaret, **29:** 214
Hindenburg, Paul von, **32:** 506,n1; **38:** 314n2, 369
Hinojosa, Ramón H., **29:** 428, 438
Hintze, Paul von, **27:** 540; **29:** 405
Hioki, Eki, **31:** 367,n3; **32:** 137,n3; **38:** 152,n2
Hirst, David Wayne, **31:** 27n1; **34:** 74n5; **37:** 425n2
Hirst, Francis Wrigley, **28:** 276,n1; **32:** 340,n1; **38:** 110
Hispanic American Historical Review, **36:** 280n1
Historian, The, **28:** 97n1
Historical Society of Nebraska, **38:** 337n2, 342-43
Historische Zeitschrift, **36:** 503n1
History of Labour in the United States (Commons *et al.*), **27:** 291n2
History of the American People (Wilson), **27:** 368; **31:** 109, 118, 397-98; **32:** 7; **33:** 525n1; **34:** 57,n1; **38:** 327
History of the Christian Church (Schaff), **29:** 361n2
History of the Marconi Company (Baker), **27:** 251n1
History of Woman's Peace Party (Degen), **32:** 516n2
Hitch, Calvin Milton, **28:** 4,n4, 5
Hitchcock, Gilbert Monell, **27:** 356; **29:** 162; **30:** 216, 225, 230, 245; **31:** 414, 426, 500, 501; **32:** 173n2; **35:** 466-67, 467,n1,2; **36:** 311,n1, 583; **37:** 406n1; **38:** 342n3; and Federal Reserve bill, **28:** 241,n2, 261, 269, 336n2, 355, 360, 361, 369n1, 373n1, 391, 414, 435, 600-601; and nominations to the Federal Reserve Board, **30:** 270n4, 279, 288, 299n2, 317; and Philippine bill, **32:** 291-92
Hitchcock bill for arms embargo, **31:** 414, 426; Stone on, **32:** 290-91
Hitler, Adolf, **30:** 108n2
Hity, Mrs. **35:** 272,n7

Hitz, William, **32:** 163-64,n1; **38:** 275,n6
Hoar, William D., **27:** 183
Hoboken, N.J., **27:** 75-76, 109; **28:** 595
Hobson, Richmond Pearson, **33:** 186n1
Hodgenville, Ky., **38:** 142n1
Hodges, Harry Foote, **29:** 307,n4
Hodges, Horace, **35:** 19n1
Hoffman, Arthur, **35:** 405,n1
Hohenberg, Sophie, Countess von (wife of Francis Ferdinand, Archduke of Austria), **30:** 222
Hohenzollern, Friedrich Wilhelm Viktor August Ernst, Crown Prince of Germany, **31:** 519; **32:** 171n1, 506, 522; **34:** 48
Hohler, Thomas Beaumont, **28:** 544,n2; **29:** 209, 230, 231, 248, 330; **32:** 342; **35:** 83, 89, 97-103; **37:** 36,n8, 350; memorandum on meeting with WW and W. J. Bryan, **29:** 251-55, 255-61; C. A. Spring Rice on Washington visit of, **29:** 266, 267; WW on, **29:** 284
Hoke Smith and the Politics of the New South (Grantham), **34:** 62n1; **36:** 357n1
Holbrook, Lucius Roy, **29:** 541,n2, 542
Holden, Hale, **31:** 20,n3; **38:** 38n2
Holden Pierce Williams Insurance Co., Boston, **29:** 238n1
Holderness, N.H., **28:** 104
holding companies, **27:** 122; **29:** 26, 78, 79, 81, 82, 157, 175, 335-37
Holdsworth, John Thom, **27:** 208-209
Holland: *see* Netherlands, The
Holland-America Line, **35:** 390
Holland House, N.Y., **33:** 214, 444
Hollander, Jacob Harry, **27:** 206-207, 215,n1, 219, 265, 272,n1
Hollender Hotel, Cleveland, **36:** 41n1
Hollis, Henry French, **27:** 158,n1,2, 178, 492; **28:** 414-15, 418; **30:** 113; **35:** 530,n1; **36:** 472n1; **37:** 166, 212; **38:** 22, 29, 376, 624; on antitrust legislation, **30:** 110, 134; and Stevens amendment, **30:** 166n2, 181, 187; on Rublee defeat, **37:** 101-102, 128, 363; on 1916 platform, **37:** 169n1
Hollis, William Stanley, **31:** 471,n8
Hollis-Bulkley bill; *see* rural credits: Hollis-Bulkley bill
Hollis-Lever bill, **35:** 530,n1
Hollister, Howard Clark, **38:** 534n1
Hollister, W. R., **36:** 518,n1
Holmes, John Haynes, **36:** 524
Holmes, Oliver Wendell, Sr., **37:** 328; **38:** 487
Holmes, William Fowler, **28:** 187n4; **34:** 108n4
Holt, Hamilton, **29:** 476; **36:** 524; **37:** 75, 76, 120,n2, 166-67, 168; **38:** 104, 108-109
Holt, Henry Chandler, **37:** 120,n1
Holtzendorff, Henning von, **34:** 453,n1; **35:** 131,n1; **36:** 341
Holyoke, Mass., **27:** 489
Home-Maker of the White House, Mrs.

Woodrow Wilson's Social Work in Washington (Bicknell), **28:** 20n6

Home Missions, Board of (Presbyterian Church), **31:** 259, 260

Homer, Charles C., **29:** 390, 401n1

Homme Enchaîné, **33:** 48n4,5

Homme Libre, **33:** 48n4

Honduras, **29:** 94; **32:** 470,n3; and recognition of Mexico, **28:** 460

Honduras and the United States, **28:** 56; appointments, **28:** 4, 4-5

Hong Kong and Shanghai Banking Corp., **33:** 32

Honolulu Co., **37:** 139

Honolulu incident, **31:** 340,n5, 439, 444

Honorable Senator Sage-brush (Lynde), **31:** 316,n2

Hood, Louis, **27:** 373n1, 376,n4

Hooker, Della E. (Mrs. J. W.), **37:** 376,n1

Hooper, Ben Walter, **27:** 55n3

Hoover, Herbert Clark, **31:** 80, 206,n1, 331-32,n1, 341; **32:** 214, 293, 294, 401; **33:** 523, 553-54; **34:** 409-10, 494; **35:** 165; **37:** 405, 541-42,n1; **38:** 72, 368n1, 371, 392

Hoover, Irwin Hood (Ike), **28:** 182,n4, 262, 393; **29:** 532; **31:** 91; **32:** 119, 524; **33:** 279n1, 421, 434; **34:** 156, 171, 176, 194, 196, 211, 219, 224, 234, 240, 259, 261-62, 262, 322, 374, 378, 379, 396, 425; **35:** 41, 164, 371n1, 372; **36:** 262; **37:** 143, 513

Hoover, Lou Henry (Mrs. Herbert Clark), **31:** 80, 332,n1

Hopeful Tone in Washington Regarding Berlin Government's Reply to Wilson Note (New York *Evening Post*), **33:** 191n1

Hopkins, Archibald, **28:** 21n5

Hopkins, Charles A., **36:** 364

Hopkins, Charles F., **31:** 561n1

Hopkins, Charlotte Everett Wise (Mrs. Archibald), **28:** 21,n5; **31:** 560,n2, 561; **33:** 429-32,n1,6; **34:** 16-17; **35:** 205-206,n1

Hopkins, John Appleton Haven, **37:** 524n2; **38:** 35,n3, 642, 642-44, 663

Hopkins, Sherburne Gillette, **28:** 59,n2, 59-60

Hopkins, Thomas Snell, **28:** 59,n1, 70n1

Hopkins and Hopkins (Washington, D.C. law firm), **28:** 59n1

Horace Plunkett: An Anglo-American Irishman (Digby), **27:** 60n4

Horacistas, **32:** 76n1

Hornibrook, William Harrison, **38:** 209,n1

Horodyski, Jean (Jan), Marie de, Count, **38:** 564,n1

Horst, E. Clemens, **36:** 515,n1, 549

Horst, Louis Aton von, **38:** 244-45,n3

Horton (H.L.) and Co., N.Y., **27:** 245

Horton, William Edward, **29:** 36,n1

Hosford, Hester Eloise, **32:** 95

Hosoya, Chihiro, **27:** xxii

Hostetter, Louis, **30:** 417

Hot Springs, Va., **28:** 484; **29:** 395; **32:** 230; **33:** 242, 243; WW and EBW spend honeymoon in, **35:** 368, 371-72, 399

Houghton, William Stanley, **28:** 355,n4

Houghton, Mifflin and Co., Boston, **28:** 261

Hourwich, Isaac A., **32:** 97

House, Edward Mandell, **27:** xi-xii, xiv, xvii, 15, 20, 69, 94, 101-102, 139, 140-41, 252-54, 458, 462-63; **28:** 40, 54, 139, 178, 288-89, 419, 447-48, 476-78, 490, 527-28, 530-32, 532-33, 543, 545, 564-65, 571, 586-88, 593-94; **29:** 12-13, 32-34, 35, 52, 55-59, 60, 74, 99, 102, 103, 135-36,n1, 159-62, 163, 219, 226, 245-46, 262-63, 270, 288, 377, 383, 395, 447-49, 456, 459, 515, 530-33, 535-36, 541; **30:** 21-23, 242, 385, 395, 450

31: 10, 91-96, 100-101, 108-109, 122, 140, 196, 258, 263-66, 268-69, 274-75, 279, 281-83, 291, 292,n1, 295, 349-50, 354-57, 376, 377, 384-87, 462, 468, 468-71, 481-82, 489-90, 499-501, 502, 508, 548-51, 552-53, 553; **32:** 41-42, 75, 81-82, 99, 107-10,n1, 119-21, 128, 135, 144-45, 147-48, 254-55, 265, 267-68, 276-77, 480; **33:** 16-17, 85, 93, 105-106, 223, 239, 257, 264, 265, 274, 279n1, 342, 372,n1, 407-408, 408-409, 423-24, 424-26, 437, 441, 445, 446, 462-63, 469, 477-78, 479-80, 483, 485, 492, 501, 505, 506, 511, 516-17, 519, 521-22, 522-24, 526, 532-33, 533, 538, 540; **34:** 5-6, 11-12, 24-25, 29, 31, 32, 36-37, 41-42, 42-43, 44, 53, 62-63, 79-80, 80, 84-85, 85-86, 98, 106-107, 121, 130, 133-34, 145-46, 146-47, 151, 158-59, 186, 187, 187-88, 194-95, 200, 209, 238, 238-39, 247, 251, 271-72, 278, 302, 303, 305, 310-11, 315, 346, 350, 351, 368-69, 370-72, 372-73, 381-82, 388, 425-26, 493, 509-10, 513-17, 527, 536, 539; **35:** 3-5, 5-7, 8-11, 12, 20, 34, 59-60, 61-65, 78-79, 82, 82-83, 85, 118, 130, 131-32, 144-45, 185, 191, 191-92, 217-18, 231, 234, 239, 244, 257-62, 270, 276, 279, 346-48, 353, 355-61, 362, 391, 437, 446-47, 462, 504, 519, 523, 534; **36:** 52, 85, 194, 262-63, 266-68, 340, 346, 375-76, 377-81, 387-89, 395n2, 401-402, 416-17, 421-26, 443, 459-63, 477, 482, 511-12, 519-20, 520, 567, 596-602; **37:** 8, 24, 35, 65, 68, 68-69, 94-95, 101, 103-104, 116-17, 168, 204n3, 225-26, 226, 269, 280-81, 294, 319, 337-38, 345-46, 351, 364-65, 373, 424-25, 425-26, 466-67, 474-75, 480, 535; **38:** 34, 54-55, 85-86,n1, 89-93, 139-41, 257-59, 296, 313, 314n2, 376-77, 388, 395, 410, 411, 453, 454, 494-97, 516, 561-62, 591n1, 606-608, 618-19, 637, 656-61, 668-69

appointment suggestions: cabinet, domestic and diplomatic, **27:** 11-12, 21-24, 26-27, 57, 61-64, 69-73, 80-81, 102-103, 109-11, 112, 115-16, 117-20, 126-

House, Edward Mandell (*cont.*)
27, 129-31, 132-33, 137-38, 152-53, 163-
64, 199-201, 223-24, 228-29, 234, 259,
262-63, 292, 333-34, 372-73, 383-86,
396-97, 407; **28:** 271, 275, 288-89, 527-
28, 594-95; **29:** 247, 277-78, 308-309,
380, 390, 401,n1; **30:** 285; **32:** 6-7, 19,
243; **33:** 397, 409; **36:** 485, 488-89, 523,
525, 530, 542; **37:** 268, 402, 420; **38:**
317-18, 659-60

mission to Europe (1914): proposed visit
to Germany, **29:** 12-13, 462, 531; on
peace mission, **30:** 30, 200-201;
impressions of European situation, **30:**
108-109; meets with Kaiser and German representatives, **30:** 139-40; WW
on mission of, **30:** 187, 264-65, 336;
meets with officials in Great Britain,
30: 189-90, 214-15, 247-48, 255-57;
W. H. Page on mission of, **30:** 258; com-
municates to Kaiser through A. Zimmermann, **30:** 265; letter to William
II, **30:** 266-67; meets with H. Plunkett
and S. Brooks, **30:** 287; on conditions
in Europe, **30:** 323-24, 327, 432-33; on
negative feelings in Europe toward
W. J. Bryan, **30:** 327

peace mission (1915): decides to go to
Europe, **32:** 61, 63-67, 94, 117-18, 161-
62; WW's letter of introduction and instructions to, **32:** 82, 83-84, 84-85, 157-
58; farewell to WW, **32:** 121, 128, 162;
WW on mission of, **32:** 199-200, 230-
31, 234, 265, 338, 462; in England, **32:**
204-207, 211, 220, 220-21, 225-26, 242,
253-54, 266, 300, 327-28, 335, 340-41;
33: 88-89, 100-101, 108, 121-23, 124,
189-90, 205, 217, 229, 247-48, 253-54,
266-68, 321; on second convention for
postwar security and international organization, **32:** 205, 238, 300, 327, 376,
402-403, 422-23, 438, 440-41, 456, 504,
514; **33:** 63, 64; and Germany, **32:** 231,
237-38, 256-57, 265, 299, 351; proposed Italian trip and meeting with
T. N. Page, **32:** 285-86, 287, 297, 475;
devises new code, **32:** 297-99; on meeting with George V, **32:** 303-304; on
M. Rice's trip to Germany, **32:** 366; in
France, **32:** 372-75, 376-77, 521-23, 531-
32; **33:** 10-11, 12-13, 47-48, 63-64; in
Germany, **32:** 393, 402-403, 411-12,
429, 438-39, 440-41, 441-42, 455-56,
457, 458, 504-507; and Spain, **32:** 504;
33: 123n6; and plans for "paper campaign" between Germany and England, **32:** 513-14; returns to U.S., and
renewal of *modus vivendi*, **33:** 222,n1,
226-27, 237-38; **33:** 394, 398

peace mission (1916): general, **35:** 240-
43, 260-61, 279, 356-58, 359, 362, 363,
363-64, 380,n1, 381-82,n1, 387-88, 391-
92, 397; **36:** 122-23,n1, 124, 125-26,n1,
138, 147-48,n1, 150-51, 166-68, 170,
173, 180, 185, 192,n1, 202, 203, 217;

on financial compensation for trip
abroad, **35:** 398; meetings in London,
35: 453, 454-55, 457, 458-59, 465-66,
471-73,n2, 483, 484-86, 486, 487-88,
491, 498-99, 516; in Paris, **35:** 524-
25,n3; and House-Grey Memorandum,
36: 180,n2, 262-63, 266; **37:** 21, 42,
100,n1, 411, 422, 422-24, 502; WW
welcomes home and thanks for service
abroad, **36:** 244, 276, 291; J. W. Gerard on success of mission, **36:** 258

currency, **27:** 21, 227, 292, 413, 436,
445, 457, 459, 476; Senate secretaryship, **27:** 55, 82, 83, 113-14; on W. F.
McCombs, **27:** 125-26, 140, 153, 198;
inauguration, **27:** 145, 152; Steel Trust
suit, **27:** 215-16, 223, 232, 252, 414;
tariff, **27:** 250-51; **28:** 270; **35:** 177; on
Mexico, **27:** 383, 404-405; **29:** 135; **33:**
461-62, 477; and WW's photographic
memory, **28:** 452n4; WW spends weekend with, **28:** 595-97; congratulates
WW on passage of Federal Reserve Act,
29: 49; letter from H. Plunkett, **29:** 115-
17; letter from C. H. Brent on Philippines, **29:** 164-67; on presidency of the
College of the City of New York, **29:**
277; on wedding of E. Wilson and
W. G. McAdoo, **30:** 6-7; and Federal
Reserve Board suggestions, **30:** 7, 27,
30, 33, 54; congratulates WW on passage of Sims bill, **30:** 174; and commercial treaty with France, **30:** 200,
201; on Pan-Americanism, **30:** 255-56,
271-72; on loans to underdeveloped
countries, **30:** 256-57; on WW's Mexican policy and Great Britain, **30:** 287-
88; and C. H. Dodge's payments to
Page, **30:** 288,n1, 303, 489, 490; and
use of WW good offices for peace, **30:**
341-42, 342, 343, 349, 349-50; WW informs message sent, **30:** 345; fears over
Ship Registry Act, **30:** 345, 352; condolence message on EAW's death, **30:**
359; WW acknowledges condolence
message, **30:** 390; visits WW in Cornish, **30:** 461-67; wants nations to have
frequent meetings to prevent disas-
ters, **30:** 462, 463

letter to A. Zimmermann with WW's
offer of mediation, **30:** 488; meeting
with C. Dumba, **31:** 5-6, 296-97; on
peace moves, **31:** 7, 45, 55, 60-61, 62,
76-77, 94, 137, 385, 490, 517-19, 522-
23; **37:** 3, 6-7, 11, 45, 57-58, 62-63, 92,
112-13; on Lansing's proposed instructions to Page, **31:** 86-87, 91-93; code
name for, **31:** 93; suggests British
concessions, **31:** 96-98; and New York
politics, **31:** 139-40, 148, 161, 167, 252,
349; and Page, **31:** 214, 228, 246; **32:**
350; on importance of reserve army, **31:**
265-66; and Colorado coal strike, **31:**
363, 462-63, 474, 523-24; encourages
WW to strengthen foreign policy, **31:**

369-70, 379; to Gerard and Page on necessity of neutrality, **31**: 387-88; on WW's message to Congress, **31**: 388, 414n1, 427, 452-53; on Dominican Republic scandal, **31**: 403-404, 410; WW suggests peace mission by, **31**: 468-70; plan for all nations meeting as prelude to peace negotiations, **31**: 480-81; on Pan-American pact, **31**: 497-99, 535, 536, 536-37, 549, 552; **32**: 98, 98-99, 474, 478; **33**: 55, 56, 62, 62-63, 65, 68, 77; **35**: 54-55, 60, 64-68, 69-71, 119, 126-27, 143; **36**: 398, 403, 445, 478, 605; **37**: 238, 239-40, 265-66, 398-99; Christmas greetings from WW, **31**: 523; A. Zimmermann on peace plans, **31**: 540, 540-41; would replace Spring Rice, **31**: 550; appeal to A. Zimmermann for statement of peace terms, **32**: 17,n1; praises WW's Indianapolis speech, **32**: 43, 53; on *Lusitania* incident, **33**: 134, 158-59, 197-98, 198-99; **36**: 73-74, 205-206

Plunkett on, **33**: 338, 414; on war developments, **33**: 405-406; WW discusses possible marriage to Mrs. Galt, **33**: 450; on German reply of July 8 to second *Lusitania* note, **33**: 490-91; and Bernstorff, **33**: 493-94; on cotton crisis, **33**: 533,n1; **34**: 137; unauthorized intimation to Page to return to U.S., **34**: 55,n1; and interview with Spring Rice, **34**: 109; WW on, **34**: 190, 352-53; on *Arabic* crisis, **34**: 297, 297-98, 298-99, 468-69, 520-21; fears German outbreak in U.S., **34**: 309; and Mrs. Galt, **34**: 338, 356, 516, 518-19, 519-20; and alleged break with WW, **34**: 377-78,n1,2, 381, 402,n2, 437, 442-43, 471, 471-72,n1, 517; and WW's crisis concerning Mrs. Hulbert, **34**: 500, 502, 505, 506-508, 509, 510; WW discusses engagement and wedding plans with, **34**: 508, 537; **35**: 15-16, 18-19; WW visits New York and meets with, **35**: 24-25, 41, 42, 46, 127, 146, 152, 153, 155, 160, 165, 167, 175-77, 178-79, 257-62; discusses mediation idea with WW and Lansing, **35**: 43-44, 59-60, 61-62; proposal of mediation to Grey and reactions to, **35**: 80-82, 186, 187, 192, 254; meetings with Bernstorff, **35**: 137-38, 220-21; **36**: 294; **38**: 141-42; on Democratic politics in Missouri, **35**: 183; and W. Vick, **35**: 285-86; on Spring Rice, **35**: 320-21,n1, 380

on talk with Plunkett, **35**: 310-11,n1; on New York politics, **35**: 398, 460; **37**: 290; on A. Gardiner article on WW, **36**: 320; on Punitive Expedition, **36**: 335, 434-35; on special German ambassador to the U.S., **36**: 353-54; on breaking diplomatic relations with Germany, **36**: 405, 421,n1, 421-22, 446, 460; and Democratic National Committee, **36**: 479, 518, 523; **37**: 45-46, 56-57, 76-77, 117-18, 118, 128-29, 129-30, 131, 133, 151, 163-64, 177-78, 203, 206, 211, 236-37; on Bernstorff, **36**: 486; WW asks to write article for *Harpers*, **36**: 516-17, 543, 600-601; negotiations with Bernstorff, **36**: 524, 526,n1, 541-42, 547-48, 548-49, 558, 559; Gerard on German desire for another peace mission from, **36**: 595, 616; and controversy over L. D. Brandeis nomination, **36**: 607,n2; advises WW on rejoinder to *Sussex* reply, **36**: 608, 616-17, 628-29; on renewed interest in peace proposal, **36**: 631-32, 652-53, 656; criticism of Page, **37**: 11-12, 42, 61, 71-72; on strengthening the navy, **37**: 64-65, 68, 105; on WW's speech to League to Enforce Peace, **37**: 68, 77, 88-91, 104, 105, 121, 289; on Tumulty, **37**: 104-105; meets with Jusserand, **37**: 134-35; Page on British gossip about peace mission of, **37**: 145; on A. Bullard's suggestions regarding Britain, **37**: 201-202; on Federal Reserve Board governor, **37**: 291; on Britain's change regarding peace moves, **37**: 311-12; on political campaign strategy, **37**: 364-65; and National Research Council, **37**: 374; criticizes C. E. Hughes' acceptance speech, **37**: 518-21,n1; suggestions for WW's acceptance speech, **37**: 521; on T. R. Marshall, **38**: 11; meets with W.L.F.C. van Rappard, **38**: 53,n2; on railroad crisis, **38**: 165-66; on death of WW's sister, **38**: 186, 191; suggestions for Eight-Hour Commission, **38**: 297; on 1916 campaign, **38**: 317, 349-50, 429, 474-75, 515, 545-46, 616; on WW's plans to resign if election is lost, **38**: 493, 494, 678-79; on some ministers' desire for war, **38**: 560-61; on WW's desire for mediation before break with Germany occurs, **38**: 645-47; Page on mission of, **38**: 258; photograph: *illustration section*, **31**

House, Loulie Hunter (Mrs. Edward Mandell), **27**: 15, 20, 27, 152; **28**: 40, 595, 596, 597; **29**: 245n2, 449, 456; **30**: 7, 201, 265, 386; **31**: 246, 258, 263, 274, 281, 317, 523; **32**: 119, 352; **33**: 408, 441, 470; **34**: 426; **35**: 15, 44, 46, 132, 155, 162, 178, 179, 185, 257, 258, 261, 272, 276, 348, 358, 364, 380, 387, 391; **36**: 340, 346, 354, 389; **37**: 106; **38**: 55

House-Grey Memorandum, **36**: 180n2, 262-63, 263; *see also* House, Edward Mandell; Grey, Sir Edward (Viscount Grey of Fallodon)

House Mission in Paris (*Le Gaulois*), **35**: 525n3

House of Representatives (U.S.), **27**: 100, 123, 148: *see also* United States Congress, and under the names of the in-

House of Representatives (U.S.) (*cont.*)
dividual committees, such as Ways and
Means Committee
Housekeepers' Alliance, **30**: 226n3
Houston, David Franklin, **27**: 163, 198;
28: 498n1, 595; **29**: 32, 52, 56, 74, 86-
87, 91-92, 114, 115, 116, 132, 246, 355,
383, 449; **30**: 53-54, 434; **31**: 101, 356;
32: 52, 241, 243; **33**: 295,n4, 397, 469,
471, 516, 536-37; **34**: 31, 42, 369; **35**:
401, 512n2, 530n1; **36**: 177, 190-91,
267, 335, 344-45, 348, 387, 424, 425,
462, 599; **37**: 105, 345, 420; **38**: 181,
183, 275, 335, 660; cabinet possibility
and selection, **27**: 21, 22, 23, 24, 27,
61, 62, 70, 102, 112; WW code name
for, **27**: 164; on J. E. Davies and the
Philippines, **27**: 259; Panama Canal
tolls, **27**: 313; on movement of U.S.
fleet, **27**: 444; and Federal Reserve
Board, **29**: 54, 247,n1, 270, 278, 401,
531; on land-mortgage banking system, **29**: 69-74; and water-power legislation, **36**: 50,n2; WW's congratulations on birthday, **36**: 185; on lowering
income-tax exemptions, **37**: 376-77;
photograph: *illustration section*, **27**
Houston, Helen Beall (Mrs. David
Franklin), **32**: 243
Houston, Herbert Sherman, **37**: 324n1
Houston, William Cannon, **27**: 239,n2
Houston Chronicle, **31**: 12n1
How Do I Love Thee? (E. B. Browning),
33: 373,n1, 380
How Mr. Dooley Recuperated at Ely-
sium-by-the-Lake (Dunne), **28**: 181,n1
*How Russia and her Ruler Betrayed
Germany's Confidence and Thereby
Caused the European War* (German
Foreign Office), **31**: 8n8
How the Combiners Combine (Bran-
deis), **29**: 30n1
How to Find the Size of the Average
American, Split the Difference (car-
toon), **34**: 432n1
Howard, Clarence Henry, **36**: 110n1,
114n1
Howard, Edward Percy, **37**: 332n1, 377-
78, 468
Howard, Roy Wilson, **38**: 313n1, 392, 494,
496, 619,n1
Howard, William Marcellus, **34**: 134
Howard University, **32**: 272,n1
Howe, Annie Josephine Wilson (Mrs.
George, Jr.), sister of WW, **28**: 315, 328,
336, 396-98; **30**: 451; **31**: 175-76, 456;
32: 517, 517-18; **33**: 178,n2; **34**: 73, 75,
77, 83, 102, 119, 128, 138, 167, 178,
521-22; **35**: 12,n4, 18; **36**: 373; **37**: 382;
38: 168n1, 169, 171, 172, 180, 277,
519,n1, 690; death of, **38**: 176; funeral,
38: 191n1; WW offers to pay outstand-
ing interest on loans of, **38**: 389, 451
Howe, Edward, **38**: 389, 451

Howe, Edward Leavitt, **27**: 6n1, 485,n4;
28: 127, 328, 336
Howe, Frederic Clemson, **30**: 282,n1,2,
283; **31**: 342-43; **32**: 19; **35**: 279,n1; **37**:
230, 321, 336; **38**: 58, 58-59,n5, 61, 63,
78, 84; on Mexico and suggestions for
ambassador to, **35**: 132-34, 146; on de-
mocracy or imperialism, **37**: 180-81; on
Chinese loan, **37**: 534, 537
Howe, George III, nephew of WW, **30**:
374; **34**: 73, 101, 102, 119, 127, 522;
38: 283,n1, 451
Howe, Harry, **29**: 401n1
Howe, James Wilson, nephew of WW, **28**:
328; **31**: 531; **32**: 7; **34**: 522
Howe, Louis McHenry, **37**: 141,n4
Howe, Margaret Smyth Flinn (Mrs.
George III), **34**: 127,n1
Howe, Marjorie Frances, **28**: 291,n4,
355n3
Howe, Mark Anthony DeWolfe, **31**: 55n1
Howland, Arthur Hoag, **37**: 310-11,n1
Howland, Harold Jacobs, **34**: 307,n3
Howland, William Bailey, **37**: 168,n2
Howze, Robert Lee, **36**: 591,n8; **37**: 307,
318
Hoyt, Abraham, **28**: 132
Hoyt, Florence Stevens, first cousin of
EAW, **28**: 43, 63; **30**: 358, 406; **31**: 118-
19, 330n2; **34**: 522; **38**: 683n3; memo-
ries of EAW, **31**: 27-29
Hoyt, Margaret Bliss, first cousin of
EAW, **34**: 522
Hoyt, Mary Eloise, first cousin of EAW,
30: 375-76,n1, 451-52; **31**: 27, 330,n2;
32: 100; **34**: 522, 546; **38**: 590, 683n3,
684,n2
Hoyt, Meribah Perkins (Mrs. Nathan),
28: 129,n2, 131
Hoyt, Nathan, **28**: 129,n1,2, 131
Hoyt, Sadie Cooper (Mrs. Thomas Alex-
ander), aunt-in-law of EAW, **31**: 377
Hoyt, Wade Cothran, first cousin of EAW,
30: 395,n1
Hoyt, Mrs. William Dana, **28**: 291
Hsun, Chang, **31**: 364
Huai River (China), **31**: 286-87
Huang Hsing, General, **31**: 381; **33**: 36
Hubbard, C. A., **32**: 508,n1
Hübscher, Carl P., **38**: 53n2
Hudson, N.Y., **35**: 347
Hudson, C. R., **27**: 544
Hudson, Paul, **27**: 460,n2, 461
Hudson County, N.J., **27**: 387-88, 392, 394
Hudson Motor Car Co., Detroit, **36**:
432n1; **38**: 182n2
Hudspeth, Robert Stephen, **27**: 19, 40n1,
386,n1; **28**: 41, 83; **30**: 492; **37**: 46; **38**:
197-98
Huerfano Coal Co., Colo., **29**: 549
Huerfano County, Colo., **29**: 524; **31**: 334,
558, 559
Huerta, Victoriano, **27**: xxi, 119n1, 152,
158,n1, 252n2, 330, 331, 332, 383,

404n2,3, 421, 422,n1, 423-25, 435-36, 440, 460-61, 465, 481, 518,n1, 538, 542, 543, 545, 546, 547, 548, 551; **28:** 27, 30, 37, 41n3, 50, 58, 69, 92n1, 137,n1, 141, 144, 145n1, 148, 153-56, 178, 190, 200, 201,n2,3, 204, 205, 206, 208, 216, 219, 226, 232, 234, 235-36, 297, 381, 382,n1, 445-46, 466, 476, 486n1, 488n2, 515, 517, 536, 565, 568, 573, 574-75, 575, 585-86, 594; **29:** 47, 74, 97, 111, 120, 121, 123, 124, 125, 159-60, 169, 174n1, 191, 206, 209, 210, 231, 237, 249,n2, 251-52, 253, 258, 260, 469, 520; **30:** 9, 12, 48, 64, 259, 445; **31:** 51; **32:** 369, 468,n2; **33:** 9, 44, 47, 71, 187n1, 258, 259, 260, 261, 307, 435, 456, 488; **34:** 56,n1, 91; **35:** 100, 102, 278; **36:** 186n1; **37:** 257, 301, 519; **38:** 66, 134, 230, 292, 299

and resignation: **28:** 7, 101; WW plans to force retirement of, **28:** 566; proposal to resign and run for reelection, **29:** 190; Great Britain's plan to request resignation of, **29:** 195; would retire if European powers had requested it, **29:** 254-55; elimination necessary for settlement, **29:** 507; G. F. Williams on peaceful removal of, **30:** 25; ABC delegates and others agree on necessity of removal, **30:** 33, 39, 41, 49, 55, 67, 69, 70, 71, 75, 78, 92, 93, 137, 138, 143n2; ways of selecting a successor to, **30:** 57; will resign if firm government established, **30:** 68; mediators propose resignation of, **30:** 87; J. Lind against successor being appointed by, **30:** 113; U.S. hopes for resignation of, **30:** 118; if retires may appoint successor who will surrender to mediators' choice, **30:** 119; refuses to retire unless participates in new plans, **30:** 133; abdication of, **30:** 285n2, 287,n1,2, 289, 290; WW on eliminating, **31:** 351-52

U.S. recognition question, **28:** 8, 34, 39, 41,n3, 42, 57, 84n3, 92n2, 140n1, 152, 167, 174, 195-96,n1, 206-207, 455,n1; **29:** 228, 229, 381, 464, 468; candidacy and noncandidacy, **28:** 27,n1, 172, 173, 236-37, 239, 241,n1, 322, 323, 325, 326, 334, 348, 356,n1, 363, 377, 423; change of sentiment of people, **28:** 31; W. B. Hale's description of, **28:** 31-32; Carranza and the Constitutionalists, **28:** 59, 541, 546, 561; Escudero memorandum, **28:** 72, 73, 75, 77, 78, 79, 80; EAW on, **28:** 108, 195, 331, 400; U.S. terms for negotiation and settlement, **28:** 111, 481, 482, 539, 562; WW's drafts and notes to the powers, **28:** 130, 502-504, 504; WW on, **28:** 133, 135, 161, 307, 479, 484; **29:** 4-5, 211, 302; W. J. Bryan on, **28:** 136; **29:** 131; and Urrutia resignation, **28:** 278n2, 282; and elec-

tions, **28:** 281, 340, 376, 431n2, 473, 517n1, 567n2, 602; and Chamber of Deputies, **28:** 292,n1, 293; Lind and, **28:** 298, 299, 386; **29:** 16, 17, 286-87, 338, 405, 406, 539; endorses F. Gamboa for president, **28:** 324-25,n1; and Lord Cowdray, **28:** 378, 526,n2, 530, 544,n1

dissolves Congress, **28:** 387, 391n1, 399, 431n2; recognition by European and South American nations, **28:** 411-12; and L. Carden, **28:** 420-21, 428-29,n1, 465-66, 516, 601; **29:** 325; **30:** 79-80; financial changes decreed by, **28:** 428; and power in Mexico, **28:** 431-32,n2; and Great Britain, **28:** 442-44,n1, 469, 525-26,n1,2, 528, 529, 537; **29:** 259, 366; statement of intent, **28:** 591; WW finds proposals of absurd, **29:** 13; and Japan, **28:** 268n2; **29:** 91n3, 181; E. G. Lowry on WW's policy toward, **29:** 92, 93; and ammunition, **29:** 110n1, 198; reversal of sentiment toward, **29:** 118, 119, 126; support from foreign bankers, **29:** 130; and financial situation, **29:** 137-38, 161, 194, 296, 359, 382, 442; and U.S. raising of arms embargo, **29:** 178-79, 205; P. J. McCumber's fear of Constitutionalist slaughter of, **29:** 185-86; L. Cabrera on, **29:** 187; proposal to resign and run again, **29:** 190; Constitutionalists on concessions and contracts made by, **29:** 195; U.S. view of British policy toward, **29:** 267; U.S. desire to remove, **29:** 324; gains converts since Benton case, **29:** 328-29; and Carden interview, **29:** 347,n1; **30:** 81, 82; A. Carnegie on recognition of, **29:** 352; Portillo y Rojas on, **29:** 358-59; gains confidence, **29:** 360

Tampico affair: **29:** 426-29, 472; refuses demand of twenty-one gun salute to U.S. flag, **29:** 428-29, 434-35, 438-39,n1; claims marines violated law at Tampico, **29:** 432; and simultaneous gun salute, **29:** 446-47, 449, 450, 455, 456-57, 458-59, 460, 460-61; accepts demands and protocol for gun salute, **29:** 463; must trust U.S. regarding gun salute, **29:** 466, 466-67; refuses to salute unconditionally, **29:** 467-68; and U.S. resolution supporting use of armed forces to enforce demands, **29:** 471n1, 482n1; affronts are retaliation for failure of U.S. to recognize, **29:** 473

V. Carranza on activities of, **29:** 484; F. Villa on, **29:** 494, 504-505; H. A. Garfield on, **29:** 496; hopes Constitutionalists will join against U.S., **29:** 497-98; accepts ABC mediation offer, **29:** 518, 525, 550, 551; and Bryan and occupation of Veracruz, **29:** 524-25; opinions on U.S. nonrecognition, **30:** 5-6, 115, 157, 234, 235-36, 238, 298;

Huerta, Victoriano (*cont.*)
  promises Carden will cooperate with
  mediation settlement, **30:** 58, 59; and
  Lobos Island, **30:** 78,n1; title of representatives of disturbs American commissioners, **30:** 121; compared to Constitutionalists, **30:** 130; WW acknowledges patriotism of, **30:** 134; should
  yield to mediators' plans, **30:** 137;
  suspends order for blockade of
  Tampico, **30:** 159; Carranza refuses to
  acknowledge government of, **30:** 168;
  and mediators' thoughts on provisional government, **30:** 199; U.S. signing protocol might seem like recognition, **30:** 241; thanks Chile for
  participation in mediation, **30:** 259; and
  Catholic clergy, **30:** 301n1; Villa on
  loan from Catholic Church, **30:** 417;
  and Veracruz occupation, **31:** 67, 71;
  on loan from Church, **31:** 74,n2; meets
  with Straus, **33:** 89-90, 106; arrest of
  in U.S., **33:** 456, 468,n1, 470-71, 473,
  474, 482; desires German protection,
  34: 73-74; photograph and cartoon: *illustration section*, **28; 29**
Huerta: A Political Portrait (Meyer), **28:**
  391n1, 482n1; **31:** 74n1; **33:** 456n1
Huerta and the Two Wilsons (Murray),
  37: 176n2
Huerta is the Man, Says British Envoy
  (*New York Herald*), **29:** 347n1
Huertistas, **33:** 4
Hughes, Antoinette Carter (Mrs. Charles
  Evans), **38:** 63,n1
Hughes, Charles Evans, **32:** 282n1; **34:**
  536, 537; **36:** 425,n3, 446; **37:** 37, 152,
  203,n4, 206, 207, 210, 237, 264, 320,
  345, 346, 362, 374, 375, 398, 429-30,
  441, 523,n1, 531; **38:** 3n4, 7, 24, 34-35,
  50-51, 59, 66, 73, 140, 145, 146, 147n2,
  169, 170n1, 172, 173, 174, 177, 186,
  196-97, 209, 212, 260, 274,n2, 275, 282,
  287, 290, 292, 293, 319, 349, 353, 392,
  394, 395, 410, 429, 452, 457, 475, 499,
  513, 522n1, 564, 620-21, 645n1; resigns from Supreme Court to become
  Republican candidate, **37:** 186,n1; and
  income tax, **37:** 203,n3; German-
  American vote and, **37:** 217, 219,n3;
  R. Robins and, **37:** 329, 330, 522; F. J.
  Heney states opposition to, **37:** 338,
  340; and woman suffrage, **37:** 503, 514,
  515, 523, 529, 535; **38:** 28; comments
  on acceptance speech of, **37:** 516, 518-
  19,n1, 522, 524, 525, 528, 532; J. P.
  Tumulty on industrial preparedness
  and, **38:** 20, 21; B. Baruch on, **38:** 43;
  W. Lippmann on, **38:** 62; refuses to take
  stand on issues, **38:** 298-99; T. N. Page
  on, **38:** 442, 443; WW's plan to resign
  if election won by, **38:** 493, 494, 617-
  18; and Federal Reserve system, **38:**
  498; election night, **38:** 621, 622; re-

ported winner, **38:** 630; delay in con-
  gratulating WW, **38:** 670; photograph:
  illustration section, **38**
Hughes, Dudley Mays, **36:** 357n1
Hughes, Sarah Caruthers Park (Mrs.
  Benjamin Isbell), **30:** 452,n1
Hughes, William, **27:** 22, 81, 180, 198,
  282, 369; **28:** 204, 245, 246; **29:** 356;
  32: 94-95; **37:** 431n1; **38:** 444
Hughes, William Morris, **37:** 459,n4
Hughes Acceptance (*New Republic*), **38:**
  3n4
Hughes-Hamill amendment, **27:** 303,n2
Hughes National College League, **38:**
  201n1, 518,n1
Hulbert, Allen Schoolcraft, **27:** 105, 117,
  146, 166, 241, 343, 506, 557; **28:** 47,
  108, 134, 136, 217, 218, 262, 336, 338,
  394, 396, 483, 484, 598; **29:** 23, 113,
  210, 238, 239, 345, 508; **30:** 358, 437;
  31: 3, 142, 174, 175, 345, 346, 407, 456;
  32: 51, 164, 230, 233, 476; **33:** 243, 382,
  412, 413, 416, 424, 455, 482; **34:** 412,
  430, 507; **35:** 23, 53, 187, 238, 503n1;
  WW concerned over illness of, **31:**
  257,n1, 280, 343; loses family fortune,
  31: 514-15, 515
Hulbert, Mary Allen, **27:** viii, xiv, 3-4,
  13-14, 64-65, 95-96, 105-106, 116-17,
  128-29, 146, 166-67, 189-90, 217-18,
  241-42, 273, 298-99, 342-43, 490-91,
  505-506, 555-57; **28:** 12-14, 46-47, 86-
  87, 103, 106-108, 134-36, 216-18, 262-
  64, 310-12, 336-38, 394-96, 483-84, 565-
  66, 597-99; **29:** 23, 60-61, 112-14, 210-
  12, 238-39, 345-47, 371-72, 508; **30:** 12-
  13, 72-73, 158, 196-97, 276-77, 327-28,
  357, 357-58, 437, 439; **31:** 3-4, 59-60,
  141-42, 174-75, 280-81, 343-45, 346-47,
  407-409, 514-15; **32:** 50-52,n1, 83, 164-
  65, 230, 232-33, 371-72, 475-77, 538;
  33: 60-61, 242-43, 286,n1, 382,n2, 412-
  13, 416, 424, 455; **34:** 412-13, 430, 469;
  35: 53, 187; **38:** 589,n1
WW concerned over illness of son, **31:**
  257,n1; WW asks Mrs.Toy to call upon,
  31: 455-56; Mrs. Toy meets, **31:** 515;
  WW seeks employment for, **31:** 515-16,
  538-39, 554; **32:** 23,n1; WW attempts
  to find publisher for writings of, **32:**
  191-92,n1; article accepted by *Ladies
  Home Journal*, **32:** 222,n1; WW helps
  in having cookbook published, **33:** 120;
  leaves for California, **33:** 482; WW
  purchases mortgages of, **34:** 39,n1,
  117,n1; WW's statement of admission
  about, **34:** 496-97; WW confides in
  House concerning, **34:** 506-507; WW
  informs of his engagement, **35:** 23-24;
  on financial affairs in California, **35:**
  237-38, 503-504,n1; **38:** 589,n1
Hull, Cordell, **27:** 314,n1, 322; **37:** 528-
  29
Hull, Mr. (of Dreicer and Co.), **35:** 42

Hull-House, **32:** 162; **38:** 460,n2
Human Nature in Politics (Wallas), **31:** 316n2, 317
Hummel, G. F., **33:** 185
Hunan Province, China, **32:** 322, 368, 418
Hungary, **38:** 71n1; Count Károlyi visits U.S., **29:** 404, 409
Huntington, George Herbert, **35:** 39,n2, 57
Huntington-Wilson, Francis Mairs: *see* Wilson, Huntington
Hupeh Province, China, **32:** 322, 368, 418
Hurlbut, Byron Satterlee, **38:** 687,n3
Hurley, Edward Nash, **32:** 271n2; **38:** 297,n1; and Federal Trade Commission, **37:** 25-27,n1, 117n1, 204n2,3, 268, 363; mentioned for Democratic National Committee chairman, **37:** 206
Hurst, Elmore W., **28:** 4,n1
Husband, W. W., **32:** 56,n1
Husting, Paul Oscar, **31:** 346,n2, 406; **32:** 19-20, 58, 116; **36:** 239, 307, 316n2, 464n1, 501, 576,n1; **37:** 143, 220, 221; **38:** 450; offers solution to armed-ship controversy, **36:** 221-25, 239-40; on German propaganda in U.S., **36:** 617-18
Hustis, James H., **30:** 293
Hutchins, Agnes Swan (Mrs. Waldo), **34:** 225,n3
Hutchins, Waldo, **34:** 225,n3
Hutchinson, Kan., **38:** 196
Hutchinson, George, **29:** 401n1
Huttig, William, **38:** 187-88,n1,3
Huxley, Thomas Henry, **38:** 574-75,n4
Hymans, Paul, **30:** 470n1; **38:** 392,n1
Hymen's Triumph (Daniel), **33:** 345n1
hyphenate question: *see* German Americans

I Myself (O'Connor), **34:** 215n2
I Took Chances, From Windjammers to Jets (Furber), **30:** 246n2
I.W.W.: *see* Industrial Workers of the World
Idaho, **38:** 458
Idzumo (Japanese warship), **29:** 181
If America Backs the Bill (London *Nation*), **37:** 294n1
If I Were Wilson (Harden), **38:** 126,n1
If War Should Come (*Washington Post*), **33:** 166,n2
Igel, Wolf von, **36:** 527,n2, 529, 548, 577-78; **37:** 45, 135n2
Igorotes (of P.I.), **28:** 242n1
Ikaria, S.S., **35:** 7
Ike: *see* Hoover, Irwin Hood
Illinois, **27:** 462, 466-67,n2; **29:** 223; **30:** 333n2; **38:** 260, 376,n1, 457, 515n1, 630; Negro vote and 1912 presidential election, **28:** 222; and farm mortgages, **29:** 71; senatorial race, **29:** 261,n1,2; Democratic senatorial primary in, **31:** 232,n2; Republican victories in, **31:**

264n3; WW's preparedness speeches in, **36:** 52-53, 63-73, 121-22; Democratic party in, **37:** 373, 522n1; and postmaster controversy, **38:** 146,n1; WW's addresses in Chicago, **38:** 475-81, 481-89, 489-93; and Polish Americans, **38:** 564
Illinois, University of, **27:** 208
Illinois Central Railroad, **30:** 305
Illinois Manufacturers' Association, **30:** 94, 95, 128; **37:** 117n1, 492n1
Illinois Staats Zeitung, **33:** 361
Imbrie, Andrew Clerk, **36:** 261,n1,2, 274-76
immigration, **27:** 37, 76, 95, 243-44, 463; D. S. Jordan on, **27:** 301-10; Japan, **28:** 284; C. W. Eliot on restriction of, **29:** 246; search for commissioner of Port of New York, **29:** 327; H. P. Fairchild wishes to see WW on, **29:** 352; J. E. Raker and, **30:** 273n1; appointment of commissioner of Port of New York, **30:** 282,n1,2; and treatment of Chinese students entering U.S., **31:** 101; F. C. Howe on improvements in immigration service, **31:** 343; and employment, **32:** 56; WW on, **36:** 12; Jusserand on effect on American spirit, **36:** 387n1; and Chinese in California, **36:** 515-16, 549-52, 576; *see also* Burnett immigration bill
Immigration Act of 1903, **32:** 143n1
Immigration and Naturalization, Committee on (House of Reps.), **30:** 273n1
immigration bill: *see* Burnett immigration bill
Immigration Commission, **29:** 352
Immigration Committee (Senate), **29:** 243
Immigration Restriction League, **32:** 96n5
Impeachment of Governor William Sulzer (Friedman), **28:** 149n1,2
Imperiali, Guglielmo, **34:** 19,n1; **35:** 414,n1, 426
Imperator, S.S., **30:** 30
Imperial Palace, Tokyo, **29:** 91n3
Imre, Thomas, **38:** 521
In the Senate—in Executive Session—Executive Document D, **38:** 10n
Inaugural Addresses of President Woodrow Wilson and Vice President Thomas R. Marshall, **27:** 152n
inauguration: *see* under Woodrow Wilson entry
Inauguration of President Wilson (Lawrence), **27:** 154n1, 155n2
Inauguration Smoker (anon.), **27:** 147n1
income tax, **27:** 54, 301,n1, 314n1, 322; **28:** 247-48, 253-54, 254, 258, 272,n1; **31:** 32, 170; **35:** 305; **37:** 169n1, 192, 203,n5, 341; **38:** 51,n1, 130, 299; B. Tillman on preparedness and, **37:** 288; D. F. Houston on lowering exemptions, **37:** 376-77; O. Gardner on, **37:** 498-99

Independence Hall, Phila., **30:** 248,n1; **37:** 324n1, 325

Independence Square, Phila., **30:** 248n1, 252-53

Independent, The, **29:** 121n1; **34:** 307,n3; **37:** 120,n2, 168,n1,2, 535; **38:** 111,n2

Independent Order of King Solomon (Newark), **32:** 97

Independents: and 65th Congress, **38:** 666,n1

India, **28:** 576, 586; **29:** 47; **32:** 358; **34:** 189; **35:** 466, 486; American missionaries in, **28:** 82

Indian Affairs, Bureau of, **29:** 399, 533

Indian Affairs, Committee on (House of Reps.), **29:** 399

Indiana, **30:** 333n1; **38:** 296, 317, 376n1, 457, 494, 499; floods, **27:** 229,n1, 230, 232, 233-34; Negro vote and 1912 presidential election, **28:** 222; WW's remarks in Richmond, **32:** 28-29; address in Indianapolis, **32:** 29-41; **38:** 411-12, 412-19, 419-27

Indianapolis, Ind., **28:** 540; **34:** 266; **37:** 523,n1; WW addresses in, **32:** 29-41; **38:** 411-12, 412-19, 419-27

Indianapolis *Freeman,* **28:** 455,n2

Indianapolis News, **32:** 41n; **38:** 412n1,2

Indians, American: *see* American Indians

Industrial Arts and Expositions, Committee on (House of Reps.), **29:** 401n2

Industrial Club, Chicago, **36:** 63n1

Industrial Commission: *see* United States Commission on Industrial Relations

Industrial Commission of Colorado, **38:** 520n1

industrial education, **35:** 308; WW on, **36:** 13, 29

Industrial Preparedness, Committee on, **38:** 387

Industrial Relations Act, **27:** 477

Industrial Relations Commission: *see* United States Commission on Industrial Relations

industrial revolution, **27:** 182

Industrial Workers of the World (I.W.W.), **27:** 456, 465, 476-77, 481, 487; **30:** 21; **34:** 539n2; **35:** 206n1; federal investigation of, **36:** 188-90,n1,2,3

Inefficiency of the Oligarchs (Brandeis), **29:** 30n1

inflation, **27:** 559-60, 563, 569

Ingersoll, Charles Henry, **38:** 516,n2, 591n1

Ingersoll-Rand Co., N.J., **28:** 42n3

Ingersoll-Sergeant Drill Co., N.J., **28:** 42n3

Ingling, Clarence E., **32:** 507,n3

Inglis, Brian, **36:** 563n1

Ingraham, William Moulton, **36:** 300,n1; **38:** 377-78

inheritance tax, **37:** 169n1

Inner Mongolia, **31:** 365; and Japan's 21 demands on China, **32:** 169, 320, 321,

323,n1, 333n1, 367n1, 368, 416, 417, 418, 434, 435, 460

Inouye, Kaoru, **34:** 19n3

Inouye, Katsunosuke, **33:** 121,n1, 131; **34:** 19,n2

Inouye, Suye Ozawa (Mrs. Katsunosuke), **34:** 19,n3

Institut de France, **37:** 42n1

Insular Affairs, Bureau of (Dept. of War), **27:** 133n1; **29:** 147; **30:** 392

Insular Affairs, Committee on (House of Reps.), **30:** 144, 215; **36:** 306; **37:** 455

Insurgent Mexico (Reed), **30:** 157,n1

Interior, Department of the, **30:** 217, 224n1; **35:** 229, 232; **37:** 269-70; segregation in, **28:** 498n1; **31:** 361n2

internal revenue taxation: W. G. McAdoo on need for, **30:** 468

International Commission of Jurists, **27:** 191n1

International Conference on Safety of Life at Sea, **28:** 469; **29:** 10, 268, 280-81,n1,2, 500; **30:** 284, 286, 318; **31:** 375, 419, 457, 461, 464, 490-93, 493-96, 508; *see also* seamen: safety at sea; seamen's bill

International Conference on Safety of Life at Sea, **29:** 281n2

International Congress of Women, The Hague, **32:** 516,n2; **33:** 314,n1,2, 469n; **34:** 58n1, 251n2, 397,n1; **35:** 200n1

International Harvester Co., **34:** 148; T. D. Jones' Federal Reserve Board nomination and, **30:** 164, 191-92, 203,n1, 270,n4, 278, 288, 301; and T. W. Gregory on antitrust cases; **30:** 481, 482

International High Commission: *see* Pan American Financial Conference and International High Commission

International High Commission on Uniformity of Laws Relating to Foreign Trade (Buenos Aires), **36:** 267n1, 367

International Ladies Garment Workers' Union, **38:** 274n1

international law, **28:** 68, 189; **30:** 184; and Mexican problem, **29:** 430-32, 437, 452, 453; and contraband, **31:** 144, 337, 438-39; and loans to belligerents, **31:** 152,n6, 153; and Declaration of London, **31:** 165, 190, 192, 200, 216; and seizure of ships, **31:** 176; and altering laws of neutrality during warfare, **31:** 426; and Britain's restrictions on neutral ships, **31:** 527; and use of neutral flags by belligerents, **32:** 200, 201; WW on, **36:** 65, 80, 92-93, 94, 116-17, 214; Chamber of Commerce on, **36:** 169n1; W. Kent on, **36:** 208-209; P. O. Hustings on, **36:** 221, 222-23, 224; and submarine warfare, **36:** 246n2, 270-73

International Law, A Treatise (Oppenheim), **29:** 432, 437

International Law Digest (Moore), **29:** 432

International News Service, **36:** 308, 332

International Relief Committee in Mexico, **32:** 427n2
International Review, **38:** 680
International Seamen's Union, **28:** 15n1; **30:** 171n1
International Socialist Review, **27:** 476, 477
international trade: *see* commerce
International Union of Bridge and Structural Iron Workers, **34:** 39n1
Interoceanic Canals, Committee on (Senate), **29:** 274, 397n1, 405
Interoceanic Railroad, **30:** 8n2
Interstate and Foreign Commerce Committee (House of Reps.), **29:** 184, 282-83, 298, 299, 318, 461-62; **30:** 224n1, 324; **36:** 301, 304; **37:** 359n1
interstate commerce, **29:** 25, 27, 106
Interstate Commerce Act, **27:** 567; **29:** 28; **30:** 274n1
Interstate Commerce Commission, **27:** 152,n1, 365, 564; **28:** 594; **29:** 43-44, 51, 83, 108, 139, 173, 174, 177, 356, 406, 419, 497, 544; **30:** 103,n2, 173n1, 269; **31:** 46, 213, 247, 258; **32:** 72; **33:** 446n1; **35:** 261; **36:** 306, 401, 415, 612,n1; **37:** 291, 420; **38:** 129, 297n1, 333; railroads and, **29:** 140n3, 155-56; and freight rate increase, **29:** 400,n2; and New Haven Railroad, **30:** 23n4, 129; and Rayburn bill, **30:** 162n2; and railroad rate case, **30:** 270; G. Rublee compares Federal Trade Commission to, **30:** 274n1; and railway securities bill, **30:** 296; and freight rate increase, **30:** 333n2; and Shreveport rate cases, **30:** 482n7; J. P. Morgan, Jr., on railroads and, **30:** 483; H. L. Higginson on railroads and, **31:** 239, 240; C. F. Adams on railroads and, **31:** 267-68; and appointments to, **31:** 269, 356; **38:** 158, 158-59; and railroad crisis of 1916, **37:** 435, 499, 530n1, 531; **38:** 32n1, 38n2, 50, 95, 98, 100, 166, 516n1
Interstate Commerce Commission *v.* Brimson, **29:** 85
Interstate Commerce Committee (Senate), **28:** 204,n2; **29:** 227, 317,n1, 318, 486, 535; **31:** 458; **32:** 173n2; **35:** 345; **37:** 530n1; **38:** 146n2; and Federal Trade Commission bill, **30:** 171, 181, 187, 219, 243, 427
Interstate Trade Board: *see* Federal Trade Commission
Interstate Trade Commission: *see* Federal Trade Commission
Interstate Trade Commission bill: *see* Federal Trade Commission Act
Interstate Trade Commission: Hearings before the Committee on Interstate Commerce, United States Senate, **29:** 317n1
Interstate Trade Commission Bill Amendment in the nature of a substitute, **29:** 535n1

Interstate Trust and Commerce Act of 1890 (Edmunds), **27:** 322n2
Intervention (H. L. Wilson), **28:** 84,n3
Intervention and Dollar Diplomacy in the Caribbean, 1900-1921 (Munro), **27:** 470n2,5,6; **28:** 124n2; **29:** 20n1; **30:** 165n1; **34:** 66n2; **35:** 252n1
Interview with Mark Twain (Kipling), **36:** 190-91,n1
Intimate Life of Alexander Hamilton (Hamilton), **31:** 316,n2
Intimate Papers of Colonel House (Seymour), **27:** xvii; **35:** 471n2
Invincible, H.M.S., **37:** 185
Iowa, **38:** 260; WW addresses on preparedness in, **36:** 75, 76, 77-85; and woman suffrage, **37:** 503, 523
Ipswich Mills (Mass.), **29:** 401n1
Irarrázaval Zañartu, Alfredo, **36:** 199,n6, 200
Ireland, **30:** 143, 154, 397; **32:** 358; **34:** 310n1; **38:** 5,n1, 90, 244n3, 255, 256, 444; H. Plunkett on, **27:** 60n3; Germany and rebellion in, **36:** 503, 563-64,n1,2; Britain and Irish Rebellion, **37:** 57, 137-38, 168, 502; **38:** 90, 92; and Casement case, **37:** 106n1, 447, 516n1, 517n1; *see also* Casement, Sir Roger
Ireland, Alleyne, **27:** 487-88,n1
Ireland, John, **37:** 476,n3
Irish Agricultural Organization Society, **35:** 8n2
Irish Americans, **28:** 492; **30:** 35-36, 63, 141; **31:** 277, 278; **32:** 101, 102; **33:** 28n1; **38:** 316, 492; and Panama Canal tolls, **29:** 349, 419
Irish Catholics, **38:** 83
Irish Fellows Club, **33:** 185
Irish Sea, **34:** 450
Irvin, Elliott, **28:** 6n1
Irwin, May, **34:** 517,n2
Irwin, Noble E., **32:** 528n1
Is Vardaman President? (New York News), **29:** 205n2
Isaac, Paul E., **27:** 55n3
Isaacs, Rufus Daniel, *see* Reading, 1st Marquess of
Isabella McCosh Infirmary, **28:** 333n1
Ise, John, **36:** 464n1
Ishii, Kikujiro, **35:** 115-16,n1, 204
Italian-American Alliance of the United States, **32:** 97
Italian Americans, **28:** 164, 492; **38:** 140, 349; New Orleans, **27:** 288n6
Italian Press Publishing Association, **32:** 97
Italy, **28:** 598; **30:** 152, 234, 353-55; **31:** 7, 202, 203, 355, 478, 521, 524, 527; **32:** 45-46, 204, 237; **33:** 12, 130, 145, 182-83, 198, 215, 233, 371, 407, 408, 522; **34:** 22, 31,n2, 62, 94, 145, 253n1; **35:** 75, 226, 407, 495, 498; **36:** 125, 147, 148n1, 169, 320n1, 439; **37:** 20, 21, 104, 179, 274; **38:** 91; and Mexico, **28:** 460, 461-62; Nicaragua treaty,

Italy (*cont.*)
29: 172, 173; and Great Britain, 29: 180; and Peru, 29: 244; expenses of ambassador in London, 29: 411; E. M. House's visit to, 32: 221, 256, 278, 285, 297; 35: 486, 499; House meets with T. N. Page, 32: 423, 475; and Pope's involvement in peace negotiations, 32: 522; Page on war situation, 33: 230-32; entrance into war, 33: 254, 279n1; and *Ancona* sinking, 35: 208-209, 235-37,n2, 244, 245
Italy and the United States, 27: ix; ambassadorship, 27: 70, 110, 228, 259; California land law, 27: 324; conciliation treaty, 27: 448, 477; renewal of arbitration treaty, 27: 534; Albano case, 28: 115n2; and Mexico, 28:461-62, 516
It's a Long, Long Way to Tipperary song incident, 32: 21,n3
It's Permissible (song), 29: 558n4
Iturbe, Ramón, 28: 77
Iturbide, Eduardo, 31: 18,n2; 33: 258,n1, 259, 260-62, 461, 470, 477, 488
Iturbide Bridge (Tampico), 29: 427, 428, 471, 472

J. P. Morgan and Co., N.Y., 28: 428; 29: 29, 74n1, 101,n1, 103, 381n1; 30: 372, 386; 31: 148n2, 153, 220n1, 372, 381; 32: 329, 451n1; 33: 194-95, 296n1; 37: 42
Jackson, Miss., 34: 108n3,4
Jackson, Tenn., 29: 332
Jackson, Andrew, 27: 438; 31: 279; 32: 30, 39-40, 79n2; 35: 327
Jackson, Charles Samuel, 29: 271,n1; 37: 463, 469
Jackson, Giles B., 34: 16; 38: 156-57
Jackson, John Brinckerhoff, 38: 72,n6
Jackson, Sir Thomas, 33: 32
Jackson, William Purnell, 37: 218n2, 219
Jackson Health Resort, Dansville, N.Y., 34: 154
Jacobs, Aletta Henriette, 34: 251,n2, 350, 397-99, 399, 473; 35: 20, 21
Jacobs, I. H., 36: 364
Jacobus, Melancthon Williams, 30: 406; 31: 204-205; 33: 229-30, 253, 535; 36: 531-32, 555
Jaeckel and Co.: *see* A. Jaeckel and Co.
Jaffray, Elizabeth (Mrs. L. A.), 27: 12,n1,2,3, 16, 28; 28: 62, 108, 143, 360, 367-68, 368, 375-76, 384; 29: 210-11
Jaffray, Reginald, 27: 189,n2
Jagow, Gottlieb von, 30: 109, 140; 31: 426, 518; 32: 206, 351, 373, 442n4; 33: 63, 253, 265-66, 298n1, 355, 369n3, 371, 478, 480n3, 499,n1, 511, 516, 527; 34: 46, 238, 290, 366, 454; 35: 291n1, 355; 36: 122, 413, 414; 37: 319, 379n1, 507; 38: 104, 314, 453n1; and *Arabic* crisis, 34: 306, 320, 342n1; and *Orduna*, 34: 315n1; on *Sussex* crisis, 36: 447n1; and *Sussex* note, 36: 452, 467-71, 483,n1,

491-96, 556n1; instructions to Bernstorff *re Sussex*, 36: 498-99; and German reply to *Sussex* note, 36: 621-26
Jalapa, Veracruz, Mex., 29: 328, 464; 32: 348, 353
Jalisco, state, Mex., 28: 77; 32: 387
James, Henry (author), 30: 152; 33: 552
James, Henry (son of William James), 33: 441,n1
James, Isabella Louisa Hagner, 28: 143,n1, 182, 183, 189, 195, 258, 259, 262, 319, 320, 327, 331, 333, 368; 29: 555; 35: 154,n6
James, Jesse, 38: 335n3
James, Norman, 35: 154n6
James, Ollie Murray, 27: 93; 29: 161, 343,n2,3; 34: 337; 35: 88; 36: 328, 355n1; 37: 118, 128, 156, 282, 367, 431n1; 38: 8, 126,n1, 671
James, William, 33: 228, 441n1
James River bill, 36: 49
Jameson, John Franklin, 27: 45-46,n1; 28: 470,n1; 34: 87, 185; and National Archives, 38: 654-56, 664
Jane Jefferson Club of Colorado, 37: 536-37
Japan, 28: 53; 31: 8, 64n1; 34: 19, 22, 370; 35: 203-204, 209-10, 517-18; 36: 148n1; 38: 69, 70, 149
and China, 27: 28; 36: 411, 428; 38: 150-52, 440n1; and Chinese laborers, 28: 14n1; attack on Tsingtau, 31: 364; designs upon China, 31: 364-67, 512-13; and customs appointments in, 31: 509, 547; and 21 demands, 32: 120,n2, 135-37, 137-38, 148, 169-71, 197, 287, 353, 368, 418-20, 434-35, 435-36, 436-37,n1, 460, 461, 466-67, 499-500, 500-501, 529, 531; and military preparations in, 32: 433,n1; Bryan suggests China confer directly with U.S. on matters involving, 32: 524-25; and ultimatum to China, 33: 104-105; and Chinese loan, 37: 232-33, 234, 235
and Mexico, 27: 439, 540; 29: 91,n3, 182, 183, 198, 201, 267, 442, 493; 33: 467,n1; F. Díaz in, 28: 268,n2; and recognition of Mexico, 28: 460; and F. L. de la Barra reception in, 29:91n3
Russo-Japanese War, 27: 451-52; 38: 314,n1; and the Philippines, 29: 148; and Great Britain, 29: 183; 31: 512; 33: 121, 131-32,n1, 139-40; ambassador in London, 29: 411; 30: 152; and treaty of alliance with Great Britain, 30: 391-92; becomes involved in European war, 30: 391-92, 432; and Russia, 31: 137, 469n4; Germany fears Allies will bring troops of into Europe, 31: 500; and Germany, 31: 511, 541; 33: 82; E. Grey's statement on peace terms and, 32: 45; and Russo-Japanese Treaty, 37: 134,n1, 135n2, 283, 408, 418-19
Japan and the United States, 27: ix, 162,

511; **28:** 54, 274, 287-88, 361; **29:** 175, 180, 182, 204, 218, 236, 315, 325; **30:** 29; **33:** 70, 81, 85, 153-54, 467,n1; **35:** 224-25, 289-90; **36:** 546; controversy over California alien land legislation, **27:** xxi, 220,n4, 261, 265, 265-66, 275-76,n1, 280-82, 286-88, 293-94, 298, 304-305, 309-10, 318-21, 324, 326, 338, 343-44, 348-51, 360-61, 362-63, 365, 372, 403-404, 412-13, 415-17, 425-26, 428-30, 432, 442-43, 449-53, 453-55, 459-60, 463-64, 484, 495-96, 501-502; **28:** 14,n1, 16, 18, 21-22, 355,n7; **29:** 179, 180-81, 183, 198-99, 238; **30:** 169-70; **31:** 235-36, 236-37, 256-57,n5, 323; **32:** 113-14, 171n4; ambassadorship, **27:** 14, 58, 65,n1, 259, 364,n1,2; Six-Power loan, **27:** 237-38; Commercial Treaty of 1911, **27:** 287n5; **30:** 274; S. Chinda's protest, **27:** 425-26; possibility of war, **27:** 426-28, 441; proposed movement of U.S. ships, **27:** 441-42, 443, 446-47; aide-mémoire from Japanese government, **27:** 493-94; naturalization question, **28:** 16-17, 18, 21; proposed most-favored-nation treaty, **28:** 282-83,n1, 284-86, 303-307, 314, 314-15, 355,n7, 364; **29:** 133,n1; and Mexico, **28:** 516; and F. L. de la Barra reception in Tokyo, **29:** 91n3

best conditions under which to expand empire, **29:** 181; U. Kaneko citizenship case, **29:** 243; Straits of Shimonoseki incident, **29:** 437; and war loans, **31:** 154; wishes to end negotiations, **30:** 170; and immigration bill, **30:** 273-74,n1; **31:** 283n1; C. W. Eliot proposes blockade of Austria-Hungary and Germany by, **30:** 353-55; and relations with China, **30:** 362, 396,n1, 402; **31:** 546; enters war, **30:** 387, 391-92; wants U.S. to represent interests in Germany, **30:** 390; impact of Japanese policy in China, **31:** 364-67; ships removed from Honolulu, **31:** 439; and Federal Council of Churches of Christ in America, **31:** 461,n2; P. S. Reinsch on Japanese plans to dominate China, **31:** 509-13; and 21 demands on China, **32:** 139,n2, 169-71, 177, 246-47,n2, 247, 248, 269,n1, 269-71, 273, 319-22, 322-23, 333,n1, 367n1, 368, 391, 414-15, 416-21, 426, 434-35, 436-37,n1, 459-60, 460-61, 508,n1; **33:** 23-26, 31-37, 82-84, 95-99, 131; Y. Uchida on Japanese emigration, **32:** 320-21; P. S. Reinsch on rumors of U.S. favoring Japan, **32:** 519-20, 520-21; Turtle Bay incident, **32:** 525,n1, 528,n1; and Bryan's caveat, **33:** 101,n1, 102-104, 104-105, 113-15, 140-41; alleged Japanese purchase of land in Panama, **34:** 185n1, 216, and Japan's concern over reestablishment of Chinese monarchy, **35:** 115-16, 128,n1, 143-44, 163-64, 173-74, 203-204

Japanese-American Commercial Treaty of 1911, **28:** 14n1
Japanese minister in Stockholm: *see* Uchida, Y.
Japanese people, **27:**451-52, 493; in California, **27:** 266, 319
Japanese Problem (Gulick), **29:** 243n2
Japanese Russian War: *see* Russo-Japanese War
Jarvis, Samuel Miller, **28:** 124,n2, 184, 185, 250-51
Jason, U.S.S., **34:** 61
Java, **32:** 473
Jeanes Fund, **31:** 464n1
Jefferson, Charles Edward, **29:** 476
Jefferson, Joseph, **30:**106
Jefferson, Thomas, **27:** 63, 268n4, 391; **28:** 369n2; **29:** 438; **32:** 82, 86n1; **33:** 553; **35:** 132, 133; **36:** 59, 263-64, 387; **37:** 82-83, 105n4, 482, 520; **38:** 326, 450, 647; and American Philosophical Society, **27:** 159; American Indians, **27:** 469, 470, 507-508
Jefferson Hotel, St. Louis, **36:** 110n1
Jefferson Image in the American Mind (Peterson), **32:** 86n1
Jefferson Medical College, Phila., **35:** 423n1; **36:** 552,n1
Jeffery, E. P., **28:** 427
Jekyll Island, Ga., **32:** 118n1, 119
Jellicoe, Admiral Sir John Rushworth, **31:** 7,n3; **33:** 553,n1; **37:** 186
Jenkins, Edward Corbin, **27:** 168,n1, 179, 190
Jenkins, John Murray, **37:** 307,n1
Jenkinson, Charles, **30:** 490,n1; **31:** 12,n1, 68; **32:** 507,n2
Jenks, Almet Francis, **37:** 268,n2
Jenks, Jeremiah Whipple, **27:** 179,n2, 275, 283; **29:** 352
Jennings, Charles E., **29:** 476
Jersey City, N.J., **27:** 384, 456, 483; WW address on jury reform, **27:** 386-94; city commission election, **27:** 494,n1
Jersey City, *Jersey Journal,* **27:** 191n1
Jervis, Mr. (household help), **33:** 435; **35:** 155, 156, 161, 262, 272
Jewish Agricultural and Industrial Aid Society, **37:** 351,n1
Jewish Americans, **27:** 457; **28:** 164, 492; **29:** 180; **30:** 162-63; **31:** 277, 278, 315-16, 473n1; **36:** 348, 356; **37:** 109-11, 264, 351; **38:** 140, 188-89, 349; C. R. Crane on L. D. Brandeis, **27:** 108; H. Morgenthau on, **27:** 513; diplomatic appointments, **28:** 5; and Russian treaty, **29:** 217, 218
Jewish National Workers Alliance of America, **32:** 97
Jews, **35:** 412; in Russia, **30:** 434; in Prussia, **33:** 298; S. Wolf's concern for European, **37:** 109-11; Gerard on condition of in Germany, **38:** 73
Jiménez, Enrique, **32:** 76,n2
Jiménez, Juan Isidro, **31:** 383-84,n2; **32:**

Jiménez, Juan Isidro (*cont.*)
76,n3; **33:** 27; **37:** 157,n1
Joe Tumulty and the Wilson Era (Blum),
38: 674n1
Joffre, Joseph Jacques Césaire, **32:**
522,n2; **33:** 123, 130; **38:** 253
John D. Rockefeller, S.S., **31:** 193, 206,
207, 209, 214
John D. Rockefeller, Jr.: A Portrait (Fosdick), **35:** 317n2
*John Purroy Mitchel, The Boy Mayor of
New York* (Lewinson), **27:** 384n1
John V. Farwell Co., Chicago, **37:** 499n1
Johns, George Sibley, **28:** 465, 475-76; **32:**
90; **33:** 443,n2
Johns Hopkins University, The, **27:** 90-
91,n1, 206, 215n1, 240-41, 272, 306n1,
517,n1,2, 554,n1; **29:** 129n3; **30:** 282n1;
31: 381n1, 393; **32:** 502n3, 534n1; **35:**
118n1; **36:** 362n1; **37:** 492; **38:** 182n6,
680; medical school, **37:** 468n1
Johns Hopkins University Hospital, **35:**
118n1
Johnson, Alice, **27:** 238, 239,n1; **29:** 311-
12
Johnson, Anna, **38:** 520,n1
Johnson, Charles Fletcher, **30:** 3,n2, 381;
38: 106,n1
Johnson, Cone, **32:** 269; **33:** 193, 206,n2,
224; **37:** 469; and draft of proposed telegram to Page, **31:** 476, 477-80, 489,
525n1
Johnson, Edwin Stockton, **36:** 311,n1;
37:20,n1, 70
Johnson, George Francis, **38:** 461,n1,
591n1
Johnson, Harry Leonard, **38:** 510
Johnson, Henry Lincoln, **28:** 211; **30:**
491,n4
Johnson, Hiram Warren, **30:** 65; **31:**
257n5; **32:** 171n4; **36:** 152n2, 188-
90,n1,2,3; **38:** 59, 458; and California
alien land legislation, **27:** 220,n5,
276n1, 280, 281-82, 320, 326, 343-44,
347, 349, 350-51, 351, 352, 365, 366,
372, 397, 403-404, 404, 405, 412-13,
416, 432,n2, 441, 450, 484
Johnson, Jesse H., **31:** 23,n1; **33:** 69n3
Johnson, Joseph, **35:** 346,n1, 361, 363,
503, 505; and New York postmastership, **36:** 376, 380-81, 463, 523, 542
Johnson, Joseph French, **27:** 208-209
Johnson, Robert Underwood, **27:** 411-12;
31: 461-62; **35:** 103; **37:** 309
Johnson, Warren Forman, **27:** 165,n1; **32:**
171n4; **33:** 68,n1
Johnson City, N.Y.: WW's remarks in,
38: 571-72,n1
Johnson *v.* Sayre, **36:** 196
Johnston, John Thomas Morris, **29:**
263,n1, 277
Johnston, Joseph Forney, **28:** 138,n2,
160n2
Johnstown, Pa., **33:** 494
Joint Board of the Army and Navy, **27:**

441,n1, 443, 444, 445, 446, 447, 448ᴸ.,
32: 501, 516
Joint High Commission: *see* Mexico and
the United States
Joint State and Navy Neutrality Board,
30: 435,n1,2; **31:** 86, 359; **32:** 276,n1,
503,n1
Joliet, Ill., **29:** 71
Joliffe, Frances, **35:** 292n1
Joline, Adrian Hoffman, **36:** 564,n4
Jolo, P. I., **27:** 370
Jones, Andrieus Aristieus, **38:** 458,n4
Jones, David Benton, **29:** 67-68, 90, 483,
501; **30:** 270n4, 405; **31:** 81, 520; **32:**
401; **34:** 136; **35:** 60; **36:** 244, 260, 278;
38: 510,n1,2, 649
Jones, Ernest Lester, **36:** 417n1
Jones, Frederick, **29:** 243
Jones, Gwethalyn, **35:** 60,n2
Jones, Herbert, **35:** 60,n2
Jones, Lewis Pinckney, **27:** 14n2
Jones, Mary Harris (Mrs. George E.),
"Mother Jones," **28:** 509,n1, 512, 548-
50; **31:** 556n1, 557; and W. B. Wilson,
28: 550
Jones, Owen Barton, **35:** 60,n2; **38:** 510,n2
Jones, Paul A., **28:** 6,n2
Jones, Thomas Davies, **27:** 214-15, 219;
29: 483, 500-501, 501; **30:** 311; **31:** 520;
33: 397; **34:** 136; **35:** 37-38, 57, 60; **36:**
244, 245; **38:** 456, 510, 649; WW asks
to serve on Federal Reserve Board, **30:**
149; explains situation as director of
International Harvester Co., **30:** 164;
candidacy for Federal Reserve Board,
30: 173, 179, 181,n1, 191-92,n1, 202,
203,n1, 260, 263, 279-80, 288; appearance before Senate Banking Committee, **30:** 270,n4, 271; C. McCormick, Jr.,
on, **30:** 278, 301; C. H. Dodge on, **30:**
282, 303; requests that his name be
withdrawn, **30:** 291-92, 292-93; WW
regrets Federal Reserve Board incident, **30:** 298-300, 300, 312, 353; WW
on successor to, **30:** 317; suggests F. A.
Delano for Federal Reserve Board, **30:**
344-45, 350; offers home to WW for
vacation, **30:** 405; declines position on
Joint High Commission, **38:** 12, 22-
23,n1, 28, 43
Jones, Wesley Livsey, **28:** 344-45,n1,
346,n1; **36:** 325,n3
Jones, Wesley Norwood, **36:** 376-77,n1,
404
Jones, William Atkinson, **27:** 356; **28:**
175; **29:** 149, 164, 289; **30:** 144, 155,
159, 160-61, 172, 208-209, 259; **31:** 466,
474; **32:** 291; **36:** 145, 146, 163, 555,
583; and Porto Rican bill, **30:** 213, 215-
16
Jones bill (Philippine bill), **27:** 356; **29:**
166, 289; **30:** 155-56, 159, 160, 160-67,
172, 208-209, 213, 216, 259; **31:** 88, 89,
234, 354, 375, 417; **32:** 15,n3,4, 57-58,
291-92, 293; **34:** 389-91; **35:** 52, 86, 176;

36: 250, 545; **38:** 19,n1, 102, 119, 438; WW urges passage of, **32:** 285; reasons for delay in passage, **32:** 330-31; and Clarke amendment, **35:** 466,n1, 467,n1,2, 509n1; **36:** 139,n1, 144-45, 145, 146, 162-63, 172n2, 414, 583-84,n1; WW hopes for adoption of, **36:** 555,n1

Jones Bill (Porto Rico), **36:** 250,n2, 306; **38:** 649,n1

Jordan, David Starr, **27:** 195, 309-10, 342; **35:** 195-99,n1, 218, 373; **37:** 291n1; **38:** 108n1, 112-13, 116

Jordan, Harvie, **27:** 201

Jordan, Sir John Newell, **33:** 131,n1; **35:** 203,n3

Jordan Stabler Co., Baltimore, **37:** 29,n5

Joseph W. Folk of Missouri (Geiger), **30:** 23n4

Journal and Letters of Francis Asbury, **36:** 391n2

Journal of Proceedings of the National Grange of the Patrons of Husbandry, Forty-Ninth Annual Session, Oakland, California 1915, **36:** 638n15

Journal of Southern History, **27:** 291n1

Journal of the American Bankers Association, **28:** 3n1

Journal of the Sixty-Ninth Senate of the State of New Jersey . . . , **27:** 53n11, 54n, 134n

Jowett, John Henry, **31:** 320,n1; **35:** 176, 231, 258

Juárez, Mex.: *see* Ciudad Juarez

Juárez, Benito Pablo, **28:** 325, 561; **29:** 120; **33:** 5, 30, 46

Judaism, **30:** 162

Judgment of the People in the Congressional Elections (*The Fatherland*), **31:** 337-38,n4

judicial appointments, **27:** 194, 335-36, 348

judicial reform, **32:** 36

Judiciary Act of 1911, **27:** 348

Judiciary Committee (House of Reps.), **28:** 385; **29:** 378, 407, 424, 425, 462, 486, 535; **35:** 184

Judiciary Committee (Senate), **29:** 487; **30:** 187, 261, 262; **31:** 21n1, 499; and L. D. Brandeis nomination, **36:** 86n1, 606, 609; **37:** 56, 102,n3

jury reform (N.J.), **27:** 48,n3, 133-34, 190-91,n1, 235, 240; WW address in Newark, **27:** 373-81; WW address in Jersey City, **27:** 386-94

Jusserand, Elise Richards (Mrs. Jean Jules), **38:** 180,n1, 192

Jusserand, Jean Adrien Antoine Jules, **27:** 170-71,n3, 460n1, 477, 478, 479, 512, 514, 532-35; **29:** 180n1, 233-38, 254, 350; **30:** 80, 256, 272; **31:** 15-16, 21n1, 145, 345, 347-48, 539-40; **32:** 64, 89n3, 106, 462,n1,2; **33:** 14n1, 497; **34:** 184; **35:** 38, 79,n3, 259, 352, 397, 498, 499; **36:** 148n1, 383-84, 443, 463; **37:**

42, 104, 118, 131, 289, 412; **38:** 106-108, 179,n2, 359, 377, 405-10; on WW's meeting with the Foreign Relations Committee, **29:** 236-38; and Countess de Belleville and Louise Thuliez, **35:** 118, 127, 174-75; on meeting with House, **36:** 387,n1; **37:** 134-35,n1,2; against peace moves, **37:** 93-94,n1, 164, 178-79, 202; and mail delay, **37:** 112; and blacklist, **37:** 475, 495-96; sends condolences to WW, **38:** 180, 192

justice, **27:** 32, 48, 150-51, 194, 243, 389; S. Gompers, **27:** 184, 187

Justice, Department of, **29:** 84, 107, 108; **30:** 274n1, 294, 309, 423, 481; **31:** 272; **33:** 269; **34:** 27, 218, 226n1; **35:** 228, 229, 230; **36:**401; WW signs Sundry Civil bill, **27:** 558; WW on consent decrees and, **29:** 141n1; and Federal Trade Commission, **29:** 176, 326; and I.W.W. investigation, **36:** 189n1, 190n3; and Von Igel case, **36:** 527,n1

Justin, Joseph, **31:** 483,n1

Jutland, Battle of, **37:** 182,n1, 274,n1

Kadet party (Russia): *see* Constitutionalist Union party

Kai Fu Shah (Chinese minister to Japan), **32:** 246, 524,n1, 525; **35:** 128n1

Kahn, Julius: Diggs-Caminetti case and, **28:** 99,n3,4; and Mexico, **28:** 141,n2

Kane, Francis Fisher, **28:** 329

Kaneko, Ulyssie S., **29:** 243

Kansas, **31:** 264n3; **38:** 499-500, 545, 645n1; WW addresses on preparedness in, **36:** 87-96, 96-100, 100-10; appointments, **38:** 5, 6,n1; coal workers, **38:** 520, 583; WW on history of, **38:** 344

Kansas City, Kan.: WW's address in, **36:** 100-10

Kansas City, Mo., **38:** 196; postmastership, **30:** 285

Kansas City Star, **29:** 57n3, 99; **30:** 285; **35:** 183; **36:** 91n3, 96n; **37:** 27,n2; **38:** 318

Kansas City Post, **35:** 183

Kansas City *Times,* **37:** 27n2; **38:** 335n3

Kansas Farmers' Elevator and Cooperative Union, **36:** 87n1

Kant, Immanuel, **31:** 28

Károlyi, Michael (Mihály), Count Károlyi, **29:** 404, 409

Kashgar, S.S., **36:** 232

Katō, Takaaki, **30:** 169-70,n1, 273-74, 391, 396n1; **31:** 254-57, 510; **32:** 246, 416, 418

Katz, Friederich, **33:** 298n1; **36:** 280n1

Kearny, Philip, **31:** 395,n1, 561-63,n1

Keating, Edward, **28:** 548,n1; **29:** 46n1, 511, 538; **31:** 556-57; **37:** 515, 518; **38:** 123n1

Keating-Owen child labor bill, **37:** 428-29, 429-30, 431n1, 436, 447-48, 451, 463, 469, 523; **38:** 14,n1, 61, 63, 284-

Keating-Owen child labor bill (*cont.*)
85, 471, 549n1, 586; WW's remarks on
signing, **38:** 123-24
Keats, John **30:** 22
Keeley, James, **32:** 244,n1
Keen, William Williams, **27:** 159, 195;
32: 119
Keenan, Thomas J., **27:** 244
Keep, Chauncey, **29:** 401n1
Keith Theater, Washington, D.C., **35:**
11n2, 166
Keller, Helen Adams: on Hillstrom case,
35: 206,n1, 210
Keller, Thomas W., **29:** 393
Kellerman, Annette, **34:** 313
Kelley, Florence, **27:** 76, 244
Kelley, Francis Clement (Father Kel-
ley), **32:** 86,n1, 128-29, 249, 279-81,
365, 393, 398, 404; **33:** 30,n1, 52
Kellogg, Arthur P., **27:** 244
Kellogg, Charles Flint, **27:** 291n1
Kellogg, Daniel Fiske, **33:** 296-97,n1,
349,n1
Kellogg, Frederic Rogers, **30:** 246n2
Kellogg, Paul Underwood, **27:** 242-44; **35:**
184; **36:** 632n1
Kellogg, Vernon Lyman, **38:** 72,n8
Kelly, Howard Atwood, **27:** 244
Kelly, William F., **38:** 545-46,n1
Kelvin, 1st Baron: *see* Thomson, Wil-
liam, 1st Baron Kelvin
Kemmerer, Edwin Walter, **27:** 204-209,n1
Kendrick, William J., **36:** 586,n5
Kenilworth, Walter Winston, **29:** 288,n1
Kenkel, Friedrich Philip, **38:** 279,n2
Kennaday, Paul, **32:** 96
Kennebunkport, Me., **33:** 473,n1
Kennedy, Mr. (of Cornish, N.H.), **28:** 62,
178
Kennedy, Joseph Leland, nephew of WW,
37: 208,n1
Kenosha, Wisc.; WW's remarks on pre-
paredness in, **36:** 53-54
Kensington, Pa., **28:** 509n1
Kent, Elizabeth Thacher (Mrs. Wil-
liam) **37:** 308, 316
Kent, Fred I., **30:** 366,n1, 369
Kent, Henry Watson, **27:** 72,n2
Kent, William, **27:** 93, 265-66, 276n1,
277, 280-81, 283; **29:** 499-500, 512; **37:**
12, 92, 140, 432; **38:** 175n2; and water-
power legislation, **30:** 217-19,n2, 224;
36: 265-66, 277, 304n1, 305, 310, 311,
312; views of Mexico and F. Villa, **30:**
230,n1,3; **36:** 310, 317; recommends
L. D. Brandeis for Supreme Court, **36:**
19-20, 136; on Rainey bill, **36:** 206-207,
227; on armed-ship controversy, **36:**
215-16; and Japan and China, **36:** 546
Kenton, Ohio, **28:** 354,n3
Kentucky, **35:** 88; floods, **27:** 229n1; appointments, **28:** 5; **29:** 326, 343,n2;
WW's address on Lincoln at Hodgenville, **38:** 142-45
Kentucky Mine Operators' Association,
30: 488n1

Kenyon, William Squire, **32:** 172,n1, 188-
89, 190
Kern, Araminta Arabella Cooper (Mrs.
John Worth), **31:** 342; **34:** 527; **35:** 521
Kern, John Worth, **27:** 264; **29:** 486; **30:**
3, 31, 202, 324, 405; **31:** 145, 342n1,
450; **32:** 30,n1, 33,n3, 228; **33:** 293; **34:**
392-93, 504, 527,n1, 538; **35:** 68, 433,
446, 456,n1, 474, 521; **36:** 175, 209, 328,
355n1, 464-65, 518, 521-22, 570, 603;
37: 46, 431n1, 480; **38:** 58, 85, 419n1;
on ship-purchase bill, **37:** 366-67; de-
feated for Senate seat, **38:** 457,n1
Kern, John Worth, Jr., **31:** 342; **35:** 521
Kern-McGillicuddy bill (workmen's
compensation bill), **35:** 184; **37:** 428,
429, 431n1; **38:** 63
Kerney, James, **27:** 401,n1, 402, 407, 409-
10, 418; **28:** 96n1; **31:** 116-17, 123, 252;
32: 272, 281, 285
Keyser, Robert Brent, **27:** 91,n1, 240-41
Kiangsi Province, China, **32:** 137, 322,
368
Kiangsu Province, China, **32:** 137
Kiaochow, China, **30:** 391; **32:** 45, 135;
33: 98, 104
Kiel, Germany, **30:**140
Kiel Canal, **33:** 18
Kilgour, Va., **34:** 413
Kim, S.S., **31:** 477
Kimball, George D., **29:** 549
Kincaid, William A., **36:** 172,n1,2
Kindel, George John, **28:** 255,n1, 257; **29:**
511,n1
King, Miss (of Cornish, N.H.), **28:** 55,
368,n1
King, Benjamin Mandeville, **28:** 265,n1,
368; **29:** 370-71, 375-76; **35:** 455,n1
King, H. B., **29:** 549
King, Marjorie Brown (Mrs. Benjamin
Mandeville), **32:** 267n1
King, William Lyon Mackenzie, **35:**
317n2
King, the Kaiser and Irish Freedom
(McGuire), **38:** 5n1
Kings County, N.Y.: *see* Brooklyn, N.Y.
Kingsbury, John Adams, **27:** 244
Kingsbury, Marion L. David (Mrs.
Ralph), *see* David, Marion L.
Kingsbury, Ralph, **32:** 518n2
Kingston, N.Y., **34:** 286
Kinley, David, **27:** 208-209
Kipling, Rudyard, **27:** 253; **29:** 112; **30:** 15;
33: 555; **35:** 416; **36:** 190-91,n1; **38:** 437
Kirby, Rollin: cartoons by: *see illustra-
tion section,* **35**
Kirchwey, George Washington, **34:** 15n1,
110n1
Kirk, Alexander Comstock, **34:** 528,n2;
35: 93,n1; **37:** 272
Kirk, Harris Elliott, **35:** 153,n2,3
Kirk, Helen O. McCormick (Mrs. Harris
Elliott), **35:** 153,n2
Kirkpatrick, George, **32:** 96
Kitchener, Horatio Herbert, 1st Earl
Kitchener of Khartoum, **31:** 7,n2,

282,n1; **32:** 121, 189, 190, 484, 550; **34:** 18; **35:** 76, 226, 357, 414; **36:** 369, 628; **37:** 97-99, 135n2, 179; **38:** 247; interview on Anglo-American relations, **36:** 436-42; death of, **37:** 179-80,n1, 413, 457

Kitchin, Claude, **32:** 94, 95, 197,n3; **33:** 252; **35:** 141,n1, 132, 157,n1, 345,n3, 370,n1, 373, 459, 510-12, 524, 526-27; **36:** 143, 211, 306, 363, 370, 376; **37:** 397; **38:** 103, 124n2, 666; and "sunrise conference," **36:** 238n1, 288, 289; and dyestuffs, **36:** 406, 410; photograph: *illustration section,* **36**

Kitner, Nellie, **28:** 266,n1

Kiukiang, China, **32:** 248

Knaggs, Samuel William, **36:** 569,n1

Knapp, Harry Shepard, **30:** 435n1; **32:** 503n1

Knapp, Martin Augustine, **30:** 305,n2, 313-14, 314, 329, 343

Knapp, Seaman Asahel, **27:** 50,n8

Kneer, Warren G., **28:** 578n1

Knepp, A. S., **36:** 338

Knickerbocker Hotel, N.Y., **28:** 596; **36:** 480

Knickerbocker Theater, N.Y., **27:** 119

Knight, Austin Melvin, **32:** 133,n1; **38:** 386n1

Knights of Columbus, **35:** 239n1

Knights of the Golden Horseshoe, **36:** 420

Knowland, Joseph Russell, **29:** 384,n1

Knox, Philander Chase, **27:** 225, 226, 540, 541, 541-42, 547-48; **29:** 315, 490; **38:** 240; Albano case, **38:** 115n2; and L. Carden, **38:** 578

Knox-Castrillo Convention, **27:** 527

Koelble, Alphonse G., **37:** 219n3

Koenig, Paul, **34:** 266; **37:** 425n2

Koepfel, Mr. (of General Film Co.), **33:** 431

Komura, Jutarō, **27:** 287n5

Konta, Alexander, **29:** 404,n2; **36:** 205,n1

Korbly, Charles Alexander, **28:** 90,n1, 108,n1; **38:** 428,n1

Korea, **32:** 137, 148, 321; **33:** 24, 25

Kousoulas, Dimitrios George, **38:** 107n1

Kovelevskii, Maksim Maksimovich, **36:** 654,n1

Kraft, Barbara S., **35:** 279n1

Kram, Charles A., **28:** 405,n3, 406, 407, 498n1; **31:** 361n2

Krause, Mr. (American in Mex.), **28:** 537

Krebs, Franz Hugo, **37:** 379-80,n1

Kroupensky, Basil N., **35:** 203,n2

Kruger, Stephanus Johannes Paulus (Oom [Uncle] Paul), **28:** 542,n1

Krupp family, **36:** 563

Krupp Works, **31:** 111, 116, 231; **32:** 75

Kruttschnitt, Julius, **27:** 404,n1, 479-80

Kuehl, Warren Frederick, **33:** 368n1

Kuehnle, Louis, **29:** 288,n1

Kuhn, Joseph Ernst, **38:** 239,n12

Kuhn, Loeb and Co., N.Y., **27:** 79n1, 513n1; **29:** 381n1

Kurzman, Julius, **35:** 272n1

Kwangsi Province, China, **31:** 373; **32:** 418

Kwangtung Province, China, **31:** 373, 381; **32:** 418

Kyle, David Braden, **35:** 423,n1

La Blanc, Maurice: *see* Leblanc, Maurice

Labor, Department of, **28:** 319n1; **29:** 88; **31:** 475; **32:** 36, 123; **36:** 24; **38:** 130, 161n2; Diggs-Caminetti case, **28:** 99n4; function during strikes, **28:** 475, 551-53, 590n1; Colorado coal strike, **28:** 475, 553, 563; segregation issue, **28:** 498n1

Labor Day, **31:** 168

Labor Difficulties in the Coal Fields of Colorado, **36:** 237n1

labor legislation: Brandeis and women and, **36:** 25n1; R. Meeker on, **36:** 247-49

labor and labor unions, **27:** 77,n6, 150, 151, 243, 366-69; **29:** 356; **31:** 326; **32:** 35-36, 78, 93; **34:** 40; **35:** 538; **38:** 32n1, 130, 353-54; S. Gompers on, **27:** 180-87, 366-69; O. R. Lovejoy on, **27:** 107; and jury reform in N.J., **27:** 393-94; and railroads, **27:** 322-23; **28:** 42n2; **30:** 305-307; **36:** 204,n1, 415,n1; **37:** 434; H. B. Thompson on, **27:** 475; Sundry Civil Appropriations bills, **27:** 475; **30:** 171, 284; and Colorado coal strike, **28:** 426-27,n1,8, 507-15, 518-24, 546-56, 563, 581, 589-90,n1; **29:** 87-88, 513; **30:** 16-20, 486-88; **31:** 48-54, 107, 503-504; **36:** 237n1,2; and antitrust legislation, **29:** 138, 425, 537-38; **30:** 126-27; C. W. Eliot on, **29:** 246, 247n1, 269; and Bacon-Bartlett bill, **29:** 347, 413n1, 425; and J. D. Rockefeller, Jr., **29:** 514; D. W. Brown on, **29:** 546; L. Steffens requests pardon of leaders, **30:** 64-65; WW on, **30:** 73; **38:** 599, 673; and Clayton Act, **30:** 272; **31:** 25, 29, 131, 168; **35:** 205-207,n2; WW's Labor Day message for *American Federationist,* **30:** 264; and California alien land legislation, **31:** 236-37, 256; Gompers on Porto Rican workers, **36:** 567-68; and I.W.W. investigation, **36:** 188-90; and vocational education bill, **36:** 357,n1; and antipreparedness, **36:** 639; and 1916 platform and campaign, **37:** 175, 192, 198-99, 200n3; **38:** 260, 468-73; and Mexican-American convention on, **37:** 245-46, 266-67, 365-66,n1; and C. E. Hughes, **37:** 329; WW's address at dedication of AFL building, **37:** 353-58; Gompers on Joint High Commission, **37:** 402-403, 430-31, 465-66; WW on capital and, **38:** 213-15, 368, 417; *see also* Adamson Act; railroad crisis of 1916; strikes; United States Commission on Industrial Relations

Labor Murder: Joe Hill (Smith), **34:** 539n2

Labor's National Peace Council, **34**: 39n1
La Cusi Mining Co., Cusihuriáchic, Mex., **35**: 478n1.
Ladies Home Journal, **36**: 559-60,n1; **38**: 27, 409, 512, 544; and M. A. Hulbert's article, **38**: 50, 191, 222,n1, 230,n1, 233; WW's article on Mexico in, **37**: 508-12, 534
Lafferty, Abraham Walter, **29**: 496
La Follette, Belle Case, **27**: 188n2; **28**: 403n2; **32**: 61n2, 295n1
La Follette, Fola, **27**: 188n2; **32**: 61n2, 295n1
La Follette, Robert Marion, **27**: 27, 68, 87, 93, 107, 108, 188,n2,3, 466, 525; **28**: 82,n2, 162,n1, 420; **29**: 449, 481; **30**: 401, 479; **31**: 209, 457; **32**: 19n1, 52, 61,n2; **36**: 20, 136n1; **37**: 101; **38**: 34,n1, 146n2, 174n3; and seamen's bill, **32**: 294-95,n1, 309-10, 312
La Follette, William T., **27**: 466
La Follette seamen's bill, **29**: 500
La Follette's Weekly Magazine, **28**: 403,n2
Laguirre: *see* Lawrence, David
Lake Ellen Wilson, Glacier National Park, **34**: 87, 185
Lake Forest, Ill., **30**: 405; **34**: 136
Lake Hopatcong, N.J., **27**: 52
Lake Mohonk Conference on International Cooperation (May 18, 1915), **33**: 432n1; **37**: 76n1
Lake Rousseau, Ontario, **38**: 684n1
Lake Sunapee, N.H., **34**: 7
Lakewood, N.J., **34**: 292, 303, 304; **38**: 118n3
Lama, Adolfo de la, **30**: 97,n3
Lamar, Clarinda Pendleton (Mrs. Joseph Rucker), **35**: 38; **36**: 204
Lamar, Joseph Rucker, **30**: 21, 32, 39, 55-56, 56-57, 57, 58, 64, 66-72, 75-77, 83-84, 87-88, 91-93, 96-98, 99-103, 114-17, 117-18, 118, 120-21, 121-22, 122, 123-26, 132-33, 135, 136, 137-39, 203, 204, 207-208, 225-26, 228-29, 239-40, 241-42; **31**: 497; **33**: 202-203, 225, 394; **35**: 19-20,n1, 38; **36**: 204, 609; death of, **35**: 433,n1
Lamb, Charles, **30**: 89-90; **31**: 465; **32**: 453; **37**: 386
Lamb, George F., **36**: 268,n5
Lammasch, Heinrich, **35**: 395,n2; **38**: 75
Lamont, Thomas William, **29**: 74n1; **32**: 128,n1
La Monte, Anna Isabel Vail (Mrs. George Mason), **35**: 30,n1; **37**: 427n4
La Monte, George Mason, **27**: 146-47; **28**: 83, 93, 96-97; **35**: 30
Lancashire, England, **31**: 125
Lancken, Baron von der, **35**: 147n1
land-grant colleges, **30**: 8n1; **38**: 420
land-mortgage banking system, **29**: 69-74
Landau, Henry, **36**: 527n2
Landis, Kenesaw Mountain, **34**: 72,n2

Lane, Elinor Macartney, **34**: 420n1
Lane, Franklin Knight, **27**: 152, 232-33, 253, 286, 487n1, 511-12; **29**: 449, 536; **31**: 77-78, 79, 101, 331, 341, 500, 524, 531; **32**: 43, 52, 54, 193, 346; **33**: 81; **34**: 6-7,n1, 427; **35**: 200, 261, 361, 401, 460, 462; **36**: 462, 521; **37**: 370, 375, 379; **38**: 155-56, 181, 183, 237n1, 271, 275, 356, 357, 548, 566
  cabinet appointment, **27**: 112, 116, 126, 127, 131, 139; California alien land laws, **27**: 275, 276,n1, 349, 350; on D. J. Lewis, **27**: 80, 81; Mexico, **27**: 332, 461; **33**: 258-59, 260-62, 295, 461, 463-64, 468, 470, 530; **36**: 301, 424-25; on movement of U.S. ships, **27**: 444; Panama Canal tolls, **27**: 313; Six-Power loan, **27**: 175; code name, **27**: 164; and land office registers, **28**: 272n2, 317; segregation, **28**: 498n1; and railroads, **29**: 140n3; **38**: 88-89; at signing of Alaska Railroad bill, **29**: 332n1; and conservation bills, **30**: 3-4, 21; **36**: 518; on troops for Mexico, **30**: 7-8; and water-power legislation, **30**: 218, 222, 224,n1; **36**: 241-44, 277, 290, 299, 300-301,n1, 302-304, 311; **37**: 313, 328; and G. Rublee memorandum, **30**: 274, 276; advises WW to offer good offices to European powers, **30**: 331, 336-37; on third *Lusitania* note, **33**: 537; congratulates WW on *Arabic* pledge, **34**: 411; and alleged split between WW and House, **34**: 437, 442-43; on meeting with W. J. Bryan, **34**: 477-78, 481; **36**: 267; and I.W.W. investigation, **36**: 189n1; and navy oil reserves and general leasing bill, **37**: 66, 111, 139-42, 269, 270, 305; suggested for Supreme Court, **37**: 264, 420; and Joint High Commission, **38**: 22, 79n1, 83, 121-22, 153, 153-54, 166,n2, 167, 169, 219, 300-301, 355-62, 397, 398, 405, 633, 675n1; and border control, **38**: 675-78; photograph: *illustration section*, **27**
Lane, Gardiner Martin, **29**: 369
Lane, George Whitfield, **36**: 301,n1
Lane, Harry, **30**: 261; **36**: 311,n1
Lane, Nancy, **36**: 299,n1, 302
Lanfersiek, Walter, **35**: 487,n1
Langhorne, George Tayloe, **30**: 467,n1; **37**: 22n4
Langley, Samuel Pierpont, **38**: 536,n2
Langley, Walter Lewis Frederick Goltz, **38**: 473n3
Lanier, Winslow, **31**: 387
Lansbury, George, **38**: 23,n1
Lansdowne, 5th Marquess of: *see* Petty-Fitzmaurice
Lansing, Eleanor Foster (Mrs. Robert), **32**: 219,n3,4; **34**: 29; **35**: 245, 258; **37**: 497
Lansing, Robert, **27**: xii, xvi; **28**: 452n4; **30**: 11; **31**: 38, 39, 243, 270, 456, 460-61, 545, 546, 550; **32**: 54, 58-59, 120,

526; **33**: 41, 42-43, 107-108, 218n1, 279n1, 296, 349, 385-86, 405, 414, 437, 445, 451, 465, 474, 479, 480-81,n1,2,3, 481, 489, 490, 492, 493, 499-500, 505, 512, 519, 534; **34**: 7, 8, 12, 15, 29, 30, 36, 41, 44, 46, 55-56, 56, 59, 78, 78-79, 83, 105, 142, 148, 151, 177, 182, 185, 196, 204, 216, 241, 247-48, 271, 279, 282, 293, 315, 316, 320, 329, 338n2, 350, 367, 388, 403, 404-405, 408, 425, 427, 435, 444, 447, 460, 463; **35**: 19, 43, 45, 60, 61, 69, 83, 91, 92, 137-38, 193-94, 200, 201, 211, 230-31, 244, 257, 258, 310n1, 355, 401, 406, 411, 425, 446, 478n1, 491, 516, 519, 523; **36**: 86, 125, 127, 133, 135, 148, 225, 228, 232, 233-34, 237, 239, 258, 273, 298, 307, 308n1, 361, 378, 395n2, 411, 413, 423, 425, 427, 428, 430, 435-36, 452, 464, 487, 563, 594, 599, 613, 650; **37**: 4-5, 24, 54, 55, 88, 94, 105, 130, 138, 154, 164, 176, 221n1, 231, 271, 272, 273-75, 275-77, 350, 353, 400, 408, 464, 476, 495-97, 507; **38**: 18, 33-34, 67, 71, 74, 84, 84-85, 148, 150, 184, 195, 196, 197, 241, 259, 275, 294, 300, 313, 315, 319, 352, 374, 376, 396, 512, 544, 560, 661-62
becomes Counselor of State Department, **29**: 331,n1; and Tampico affair, **29**: 421, 429; on constitutional power of President, **29**: 436-38; resolution justifying use of troops in enforcing demands upon Huerta, **29**: 471,n1; and Nicaraguan treaty, **30**: 174,n1, 175; and L. J. Canova, **30**: 180; and China, **30**: 362-63; **37**: 232; on Morgan loan to France, **30**: 372; and Japan, **30**: 396,n1; **32**: 139,n1, 322-23; **35**: 115-16, 128-29, 143-44, 144, 163-64, 173-74, 289; and censorship, **30**: 408; **38**: 315, 428, 467-68, 640-41, 641-42; on Great Britain and purchase of German ships, **30**: 431, 435, 451; and Joint State and Navy Neutrality Board, **30**: 435n1; on transfer of title of German merchant ships, **30**: 447-49; and dumdum bullets, **31**: 54,n1; and L. Carden's interview, **31**: 61n1
Belgian atrocities: on impossibility of investigating, **30**: 459; advises WW to receive Belgian delegates, **31**: 16,n2; on collection of funds by Belgian minister, **31**: 84,n1; against making spectacle of victims, **31**: 84-85, 89-90
Declaration of London, **31**: 103-105, 114, 118,n1, 125, 133-35, 136, 138, 146, 168, 188-92; and instructions to W. H. Page on, **31**: 85-86, 86-87, 90-91; E. M. House and C. A. Spring Rice condemn proposed telegram concerning, **31**: 92,n1, 93; objections to draft Order in Council, **31**: 158-59, 161-63, 163-66; urges Page to effect understanding on, **31**: 166; and withdrawal of suggestion

for British adoption of, **31**: 197-98, 216; Page proposal, **31**: 199-204
and Russia, **31**: 182, 182-83, 187, 473; **35**: 536-37; stresses need for secrecy to Page, **31**: 183; on seizure of American ships, **31**: 193, 194, 209; on credits of foreign governments, **31**: 217-19, 219-20; and California alien land controversy, **31**: 235-36, 236-37, 256, 257; and shipping bill, **31**: 345-46, 347-49; on construction of submarines for belligerents, **31**: 359, 369; on Münsterberg and German complaints, **31**: 376, 432-46, 447, 534; **32**: 4-6, 58, 116, 161, 210-11, 219; on change of rules during warfare, **31**: 450-51; and instructions to Page, **31**: 489, 521, 525n1; and German protest against U.S. differential neutrality, **31**: 521-22; and German criticism of arms sales by neutrals, **31**: 533-34; and German invasion of Belgium, **32**: 42,n1, 60n1, 222-23, 223-25; and ship-purchase bill, **32**: 106; and Pan-American Pact, **32**: 146; **34**: 43, 448; **37**: 239, 240-41, 241-44; and German war zone proclamation and "strict accountability" note, **32**: 193, 194-95, 195-96,n1, 207n1; advice from J. M. Dickinson on German submarine campaign, **32**: 217-19; disturbed by constant presence of newsmen, **32**: 245, 246; on seamen's bill, **32**: 302, 302-303; on British blockade declaration and Order in Council, **32**: 317-19, 412-13, 421,n2, 427-29, 432, 443-49, 449,n1, 453-54; and Mexico, **32**: 326, 331, 398; **33**: 306, 400,n1, 414, 415-16, 416-17, 419, 436, 447, 454, 459-60, 461, 462, 463, 465, 466, 468, 471, 474, 475-76, 477, 479, 487, 487-88; **37**: 360, 361-62, 367-68; **38**: 548,n1; on *Falaba* case, **32**: 465-66, 469, 483-86, 492-93, 498, 503; **33**: 71, 72-77, 85, 91-93, 94-95; memorandum on consequences to Germany of war with U.S., **32**: 477,n1; answers J. von Bernstorff's charges on munitions exports, **32**: 510-13; on *Cushing* incident, **33**: 91-93, 94-95; on *Gulflight* incident, **33**: 94-95; on far eastern crisis, **33**: 99, 120
Lusitania crisis, **33**: 135, 140, 142, 142-43, 144-45; on first *Lusitania* note and immediate repercussions, **33**: 155, 164, 165, 167, 168, 168-73, 174-78, 180, 186, 187, 214-16; and German reply of May 28 to first *Lusitania* note, **33**: 309, 327-28; and second *Lusitania* note, **33**: 310, 311, 312-13, 313, 322, 324, 326, 327-28, 343, 344, 344-45, 354, 355-60, 425n1, 453; and German reply of July 8 to second note, **33**: 507-508,n1, 509-10; and third *Lusitania* note, **33**: 527-29, 537, 538, 540, 544, 545; Bernstorff wishes to negotiate over third note, **34**: 37; on second *Lusitania* crisis, **35**: 158-

Lansing, Robert (*cont.*)
59, 189-90, 208, 218-19,n1, 220, 233-34, 244-45; reopens negotiations with J. Bernstorff on *Lusitania* case, **35:** 355, 417-19, 450, 463, 504, 521, 522-23, 528-29, 529-30; concern over public opinion and delay in case, **35:** 512-13
and warning to Americans traveling on belligerent vessels, **33:** 141,n1, 154, 192, 193-94, 195; protest note to Great Britain, **33:** 205, 206-207, 207-209, 223-24, 394; **34:** 33; and Haiti, **33:** 276, 278, 395-96, 400; **34:** 60, 61, 69-70, 81, 121-22, 142-44, 144, 157-58, 183-84,n1, 257; and appointment as Secretary of State, **33:** 375, 397, 409, 445, 449, 456; warns Great Britain against seizing U.S. shipments, **33:** 515-16; and House, **34:** 5, 24; **35:** 258-60, 358; **38:** 657, 658, 659; and A. M. Palmer as Counselor of State Department, **34:** 24,n1, 31, 42, 79, 134; on cotton crisis, **34:** 34-35; on Colombian treaty, **34:** 49-51; **35:** 375, 394; and Pan-American Conference on Mexico, **34:** 51-52, 54, 59-60, 98-99, 110-12, 113, 132, 139-40, 157, 164,n1, 196-97,n1,2, 199, 321, 455-57, 460, 472, 487-89; appoints private secretary, **34:** 91,n1; and Austria-Hungary, **34:** 114-16, 126, 156; **35:** 403-404, 406-407; on proposed conference of neutrals, **34:** 236-37, 237, 397-99, 399; and *Arabic* crisis, **34:** 261, 264-66, 271, 329, 330, 333, 339-40, 340-41, 341, 400-401, 417, 449, 449-51, 458, 461-62, 465, 492, 503, 519, 527, 536, 537, 539; and Danish West Indies, **34:** 280, 462-63; **35:** 202-203, 284-85, 349, 401-402, 407, 432, 447, 508-509; **36:** 292; **37:** 495, 521; on effect of U.S. belligerency, **34:** 318-19; on loans to belligerents, **34:** 330, 421-23, 432
on Baralong affair, **34:** 368; and National City Bank and Mexican plans, **34:** 382, 382-83; on C. Dumba recall, **34:** 429, 432, 432-33,n1, 471; on armed merchant vessels, **34:** 454-55; **36:** 169-70, 211, 215-16, 232-33; on German dispatch opened by J. Gerard, **34:** 528-29; House on, **35:** 60; **36:** 375, 389, 461; on Liberian appointment, **35:** 68; on Countess de Belleville and Louise Thuliez, **35:** 88, 107; and T. B. Hohler memorandum, **35:** 100-102; on Alfonso XIII as mediator, **35:** 129-30, 176; on E. Cavell case, **35:** 147-48,n2, 149, 491; on *Ancona* affair, **35:** 209, 235-37, 282, 286-88,n2, 351,n1, 364-65, 368-70, 378-80, 391, 394-95, 409-10, 446; concern over growing war spirit, **35:** 210-11; on coordination between government departments, **35:** 227-30, 316-17, 336; on Monroe Doctrine, **35:** 246-52, 263; on recall of attachés, **35:** 264,n1, 265, 276-78, 281-82, 282-83; and Hillstrom case, **35:** 283n1, 290; on W. J.

Stone's German sympathies, **35:** 374-75; on *Persia* incident, **35:** 420-22, 446-47; on change of rules governing armed merchant ships, **35:** 420-22,n3; *modus vivendi re* armed merchantmen, **35:** 448, 457, 495-98,n1, 531; **36:** 193,n3, 404, 427-28; and Díaz revolution in Mexico, **35:** 501-502, 505; on Pan-American treaty negotiations, **36:** 197, 278,n2, 398, 402-403, 412-13, 600; on armed ship controversy, **36:** 245-46, 251-57, 267-68,n3, 269-70, 383-84, 533-39, 546-47, 549; health of, **36:** 307,n1; **37:** 77,n2, 92, 106, 108-109, 129, 153
Sussex crisis, **36:** 371-73,n1, 381-82; draft of *Sussex* note, **36:** 423,n2, 447-52, 466-71, 485, 491-96; on *Sussex* commander, **36:** 488; on importance of secrecy regarding note, **36:** 490-91; on G. von Jagow's instructions to Bernstorff *re Sussex* note, **36:** 498; on German reply to note, **36:** 620-21, 626-27; on WW's rejoinder, **36:** 649-51, 654, 655
on Punitive Expedition and Scott-Obregón conference, **36:** 382,n1,2, 480, 496,n1, 540,n1, 579-80, 581-83, 603-604; on torpedoing Dutch ships, **36:** 429; on Von Igel case, **36:** 527-28,n2, 529, 548, 577; memorandum on conduct of naval vessels toward merchant ships, **36:** 556-57,n1; on establishing diplomatic relations with Mexico, **36:** 604-605; on rights of neutrals, **37:** 13-14, 61-62; and Page, **37:** 61; on Britain's interference with mails, **37:** 83; on League to Enforce Peace, **37:** 106, 106-108; and Dominican Republic, **37:** 157n1; and *Laurentic* affair, **37:** 184,n2; warning to V. Carranza, **37:** 248-63; on effects of Paris Economic Conference, **37:** 287-88; and WW's message to Congress on Mexico, **37:** 298n1; memorandum on Mexican controversy, **37:** 306-307; and Joint High Commission, **37:** 348-50; **38:** 79, 83, 153, 166, 219, 361-62, 633; clarifies peace moves for J. Willard, **38:** 82; on response to WW's critics of *Lusitania* negotiations and attitudes on Belgium, **38:** 194-95, 315, 320; on anti-British public opinion and blacklist, **38:** 201-206; and T. H. Bliss' suggestions regarding Mexican situation, **38:** 236, 237,n1; urges WW to force C. E. Hughes to take stand on issues, **38:** 297-99; on ethics in political campaign, **38:** 321; advises WW to see J. W. Gerard, **38:** 452-53; on *U-53* incident, **38:** 473n2; on plan for resignation if Hughes is elected, **38:** 493, 617; on WW's election prospects in New York, **38:** 521-22; on *Marina* incident, **38:** 571n2; protests against deportation of Belgians to Germany, **38:** 650-53, 656; meeting on impasse in Mexican-American negotiations, **38:** 675n1

La Panne, Belgium, **35:** 392,n2

Laredo, Mex., **28:** 31

Laredo, Tex., **37:** 231n2, 284

Larkin, William P., **35:** 239,n1

Larrabee, Leona Laura, **38:** 185-86,n1, 281-82

Larrea, Gonzálo, **35:** 505,n1

Las Animas County, Colo., **29:** 542; **31:** 334, 558, 559

Las Nieves, Durango, Mex., **30:** 409,n3

Las Peladas, Tex., **37:** 249

LaSalle Hotel, Chicago, **37:** 167

Lascurain, Pedro S., **27:** 541, 546; **28:** 173; **29:** 260,n2; **30:** 56, 56-57, 96, 99, 116

Laski, Harold Joseph, **38:** 3,n3,4, 12, 23, 29

Latapie, Louis, **34:** 31n2

Lathrop, Julia Clifford, **27:** 108-109, 233,n2; **29:** 417-18; **38:** 123n1, 161n2

Latin America, **27:** 172-73, 265, 422, 526n1, 540; **28:** 56, 334, 412, 421, 422, 429n1, 432, 480, 481, 484, 488n2,3, 503, 506, 571, 576, 577; **29:** 11, 93, 94, 95, 96-97, 181, 182; **30:** 234, 235; **31:** 152, 241-42; **33:** 53, 77, 78, 305-306, 437; **34:** 43, 51, 92, 110, 179; **37:** 282, 455, 509; **38:** 171, 196; and Great Britain, **28:** 420; and loans, **28:** 123-25, 176, 456-57, 458-59; WW's address on U.S. policy, **28:** 448-52; E. G. Lowry on WW's policy, **29:** 92-98; role of concessions in governments of, **29:** 96; and Mexico, **37:** 19, 154, 276, 309n1, 361; and 1916 platform, **37:** 187-88,n4

Latin-American Affairs, Division of (Dept. of State): appointments, **28:** 4n4, 5n5

Latin American conferences on Mexico: *see* Pan American conferences on Mexico

Laughlin, George, **34:** 378n2, 402,n2, 437, 442, 443

Laughlin, Irwin Boyle, **29:** 412,n1, 531; **30:** 258, 368; **31:** 160; **32:** 297; **33:** 451; **35:** 471n2; **38:** 202,n1, 206, 210, 317, 445n4

Laughlin, James Lawrence, **27:** 208-209

Laurentic, H.M.S., **36:** 269n1; **37:** 184n2

Lavallette, N.J., **38:** 590,n1, 683,n3

La Veta, Colo., **28:** 523

Law, Andrew Bonar, **32:** 362,n2, 363; **33:** 89, 100, 214, 227n4, 484; **37:** 90; **38:** 104

Lawrence, David, **27:** 154n1, 155n2; **28:** 241n1; **31:** 550; **33:** 191n1, 199-201, 268-73, 409-10; **35:** 380,n1, 387; **36:** 229-30, 307-309; **37:** 162, 164, 452; **38:** 674n2; and Mexican mission (Laguirre), **34:** 383,n1, 383-85, 386-87, 408-409, 447, 448, 530-33, 540-43; on Mexican situation, **37:** 15-19, 152-54, 485-89; on maintenance of neutrality, **37:** 448-51

Lawrence, Thomas Joseph, **29:** 432

Lawrence and Co., Boston, **29:** 401n1

Laws of New Jersey, 1913, **27:** 49n5,6, 51n9, 52n10, 54n13, 120n1

Lawson, Albert Gallatin, **29:** 476; **30:** 398

Lawson, John R., **28:** 426,n8; **29:** 547; **31:** 37, 557n2

Lay, Julius Gareche, **32:** 505,n1

Layer, William F., **36:** 364

Le Marquis Hotel, New York, **37:** 308n2

Le Temps: see Temps, Le (Paris)

Lea, Luke, **27:** 82, 83; **30:** 3

Lea, Tom, **36:** 296,n2

Leacock, Stephen Butler, **31:** 468,n1

Leader (*Harper's Weekly*), **29:** 219,n1

Leadership or Chaos (New York *World*), **38:** 565,n2

League of Nations, **38:** 89-90: WW on, **38:** 348, 418, 437

League of Nations Society, **38:** 54, 207-208,n1

League of Peace, **38:** 85-86

League of Peace (Manchester *Guardian*), **37:** 294n1

League to Enforce Peace, **33:** 368-69,n1, 435-36,n2, 458-59,n1, 476; **36:** 458-59, 481; **37:** 6, 36, 37, 60, 68, 69, 75, 77, 88, 127n2; **38:** 110, 112, 207, 250, 254, 454; WW's address to, **37:** 102, 104, 105, 113-16, 117, 118, 119, 120,n2, 121, 130, 134, 165, 166, 166-67, 265,n1, 345, 423; **38:** 54,n2, 108, 115; R. Lansing on, **37:** 106-108; reaction in London to WW's speech to, **37:** 143, 226, 294,n1, 294-95, 312, 313, 370-71; WW declines dinner invitation, **38:** 644, 660, 662

League to Enforce Peace (Bartlett), **33:** 368n1

League to Enforce Peace (Holt), **37:** 120,n2

Leavell, Robert Hayne, **27:** 442n1

Leavell, William Hayne, **27:** 474,n1; **28:** 112, 354

Leavitt, Ezekiel, **32:** 97

Leblanc, Maurice, **27:** 464

Lee, Blair, **30:** 340-41,n1, 343, 399

Lee, Elisha, **37:** 504; **38:** 30, 31, 32n1, 56

Lee, Harry Mower, **38:** 519,n1

Lee, Jenette Barbour, **38:** 687,n4

Lee, Joseph, **32:** 96,n5

Lee, Richard Charles, Jr., **34:** 108,n3, 226,n1, 273

Lee, Robert Edward, **27:** 134n1; **30:** 142; **36:** 161

Lee, Vernon: *see* Paget, Violet

Lee, William Brewster, **35:** 262n3, 275

Lee, William Granville, **38:** 30, 31n1, 48, 93, 94

Lee, Higginson and Co., Boston, **37:** 233

Lefax, **37:** 344n1

Lefax, Technical Data Sheets, **37:** 344n1

Lehigh Valley Railroad, **27:** 116; **30:** 482

Lehmann, Frederick William, **30:** 32, 39, 55-56, 56-57, 57, 58, 64, 66-72, 75-77, 83-84, 87-88, 91-93, 96-98, 99-103, 114-17, 117-18, 118, 120-21, 122, 123-26, 132-33, 135, 136, 137-39, 203, 204, 207-208, 225-26, 228-29, 239-40, 241-42; **33:** 18,n2; **37:** 264,n2

Lehmann family, New York, **33**: 18,n2
Leipzig, Germany, **31**: 405
Lenroot, Irvine Luther, **27**: 93; **30**: 224n1, 245; **36**: 265, 301; **37**: 139, 140, 142
Lentz, John Jacob, **37**: 96n1
L'Envoi (Kipling), **27**: 253
Leo XIII, **30**: 404
León, Maurice, **30**: 230n1
León, René, **30**: 230,n1
Leopold II (of Belgium), **37**: 380
Leopold, Richard William, **27**: xxi, xxii
Lersner, Kurt von, **28**: 567n2
Lesan, Harry E., **38**: 23,n4
Leslie's Weekly, **38**: 20n1
Letcher, Marion, **29**: 278-80, 486, 495, 497-98; **34**: 267n1; **36**: 480,n2, 585, 591
Letchworth Park, New York, **34**: 155, 156
Letter to the President (*Lexington Herald*, Ky.), **28**: 290n3
Letters of Theodore Roosevelt (Morison and Blum), **31**: 277n3; **37**: 218n2
Leupp, Constance D., **27**: 244
Leuven, Belgium: *see* Louvain
Leval, Gaston de, **35**: 147-48,n1,2,3, 149
Leveen, Michael, **32**: 97
Lever, Asbury Francis, **30**: 8; **33**: 495-96,n7; **34**: 267; **35**: 530,n1; **36**: 344-45, 348, 354; **38**: 24-27
Lever-Hollis bill: *see* Hollis-Lever bill
Lever-Smith warehouse bill, **31**: 129, 130,n3, 180,n6, 205
Levermore, Charles Herbert, **36**: 362-63,n1, 374
Leveroni, Frank, **32**: 97,n9
Levine, Lawrence W., **33**: 370n1
Levy, Jefferson Monroe, **32**: 86n1
Levy, Louis Edward, **32**: 97,n12
Lewinson, Edwin Ross, **27**: 384n1
Lewis, David John, **27**: 70,n2, 80, 81, 111, 136-37; **29**: 538; **36**: 216, 217; **37**: 637n1
Lewis, James Hamilton, **27**: 325,n3, 326; **28**: 111,n2; **29**: 385-86; **30**: 284, 286; **33**: 252; **36**: 576-77, 602-603; **37**: 146,n1,2, 181, 276
Lewis, Vivian, **38**: 565
Lewis, William B., **29**: 549
Lewis, William Draper, **37**: 227,n1
Lewisohn, Alice, **36**: 632n1
Lewisville, Colo., **31**: 517
Lexington, Mass., **35**: 297
Lexington, Battle of, **36**: 39
Lexington (Ky.) *Herald*, **28**: 290,n3; **29**: 343n2
Li, Tien-yi, **27**: 175n1
Li Yüan-Hung, **37**: 167,n1, 182
Liaoyüan: *see* Chengchia Tun
Libbey, William, **36**: 504
Liberal, El (Mexican newspaper), **31**: 19, 72
Liberia, **28**: 4; **30**: 45; **31**: 102,n1, 114; **32**: 471; **35**: 68,n1; appointment made to, **34**: 504-505, 511
Liberté, La, **34**: 31n2
liberty, **27**: 389; **28**: 451; **29**: 516

Library of Congress, **27**: viii; **31**: 316-17,n1, 557
Lichnowsky, Karl Max, Prince Lichnowsky, **29**: 285,n2; **30**: 248, 368,n3, 370, 382, 383; **34**: 18
Lichnowsky, Mechtilde Christiane Maria von Aroo-Zinneberg, Princess Lichnowsky, **30**: 368
Liebel, Michael, Jr., **36**: 336-38,n1
Liebknecht, Karl, **31**: 537,n1; **34**: 47; **36**: 563
Liège, Belgium, **33**: 63
Life (magazine), **27**: 118, 250; **29**: 530
Life and Letters of Walter H. Page (Hendrick), **38**: 241n1, 445n4
Life of Gladstone (Morely), **34**: 463
Lightfoot Baseball Club, **35**: 333
Lille, France, **38**: 107, 652, 653
Lima, E.S.A. de, **27**: 544
Limerick Lyrics (Vaughn), **31**: 316,n2
Lincoln, Abraham, **28**: 12, 96, 115, 455; **29**: 55, 518, 553, 556; **30**: 231, 328, 386; **31**: 137, 263, 300, 305, 396, 399, 557n2; **33**: 64, 160, 371, 432, 472, 550; **34**: 21n7, 85; **36**: 17, 320n1, 400, 483; **37**: 335, 338, 520; **38**: 160, 285, 326, 332, 434, 442, 517n1, 520, 535, 560n1, 604-605, 665; WW's address on, **38**: 20, 142-45,n1, 325
Lincoln, Ill., **34**: 405n1
Lincoln, Neb., **27**: 198n1; **38**: 196
Lincoln Farm Association, **38**: 142n1
Lincoln Memorial University (Tenn.), **30**: 62
Lincoln University (Pa.), **34**: 505; **35**: 68n1
Lind, Alice Shepherd (Mrs. John), **28**: 145,n2, 281, 429,n2
Lind, John, **27**: 21,n1, 508, 513-14, 531-32; **28**: 143, 144, 145,n1, 148-49, 152, 153-56, 162, 178, 195-96, 200, 205, 206, 207, 212, 214, 216, 218, 219, 219-20, 224,n1, 241, 281, 288, 324, 347-48, 381, 382-83, 388, 412, 423, 461, 486, 516, 517n1, 539, 601-602; **29**: 34, 90, 103, 137-38, 185, 186, 216n2, 223, 254, 259, 289-90, 328-33, 426, 432, 451-52; **30**: 26, 118, 180, 441; **33**: 43, 51, 369; **34**: 146, 199; **38**: 239-40, 292, 313; and diplomatic appointments, **28**: 4, 111, 175

special mission to Mexico, **28**: 101,n2, 105, 109, 110-11, 127, 136, 139, 140,n1, 229,n1; **29**: 94; views on Mexican situation, **28**: 167-68; and F. Gamboa, **28**: 157-59, 168-75, 188-89, 191, 201-202, 204, 224-27, 233-39; and V. Huerta, **28**: 190, 232-33, 239, 325, 326, 376-78, 384, 386-87; **29**: 328, 338, 382-83; **30**: 113,n2; and F. W. Stronge, **28**: 205-206, 208-209; goes to Veracruz, **28**: 219; on Mexico, **28**: 293-300, 356-57, 357, 365; **29**: 118-127; and British interests in Mexico, **28**: 428-29, 444-47, 471; on

military situation, **28**: 428-29; report to W. J. Bryan, **29**: 14-19; recommends U.S. assist rebels, **29**: 16; on Constitutionalist gains, **29**: 30-31; on executions, **29**: 31; meeting with WW, **29**: 86, 98,n1, 100, 110; urges prevention of coal shipment to Federalists, **29**: 101; interview with G. H. Hewitt, **29**: 190-91; on worsening situation under V. Huerta, **29**: 286-87; J. Portillo y Rojas asks for meeting with, **29**: 329; interview with F. Adams, **29**: 329-30; on aid to revolutionists, **29**: 359; and vacation, **29**: 382-83, 398-99; instructions to N. O'Shaughnessy, **29**: 405-406; snubbing of, **29**: 441; memoranda of, **29**: 539-40; **33**: 45-47; on ABC mediation, **29**: 549-52; **30**: 113n2; C. W. Eliot on WW's instructions to, **30**: 5; wishes to leave Mexico, **30**: 47, 48; on J. R. Silliman, **30**: 166-67; Bryan on, **30**: 346; suggested as peace mediator in Carranza-Villa conflict, **30**: 346-48; interview with E. Arredondo, **33**: 3-10; and alleged split between WW and E. M. House, **34**: 437, 443; photograph: *illustration section*, **28**

Linden Pieter Wilhelm Adriaan Cort van der, **35**: 20-21,n2

Linderfelt, Karl E., **29**: 479

Lindley, Curtis Holbrook, **31**: 331,n1

Lindsay, Samuel McCune, **27**: 77,n5, 224; **35**: 184

Lindsey, Benjamin Barr, **30**: 38-39,n1; **38**: 14

Lindsley, Elmer, **36**: 281,n5

Lindsley, Henry Dickinson, **36**: 165-66,n1

Link, Arthur Stanley, **27**: 22n2, 53n12, 97n1, 103n1, 120n1, 188n2, 191n1, 220n3, 263n2, 277n1, 291n1, 298n1, 301n1, 470n2,5,6, 473n1, 483n1, 485n2,3, 510n1, 535n1; **28**: 8n1, 45n1, 99n4, 146n1, 187n4, 247n1, 255n1, 257n2, 302n3, 336n2, 373n1, 379n1, 381n1, 428n1, 495n5; **29**: 20n1, 67n2, 98n1, 133n1, 136n1, 138n2, 203n3, 316n3, 375n1, 406n1, 420n2, 476n1, 481n3, 538n1, 557n1; **30**: 10n2, 165n1, 166n2, 191n1, 193n1, 217n1, 224n1, 270n4, 273n1, 307n1, 325n1, 352n1, 402n1, 441n1, 455n1; **31**: 12n1, 20n1, 32n1, 55n2, 88n3, 112n2, 119n1, 129n1, 180n6, 310n1, 351n1, 404n2, 468n3, 471n6; **32**: 89n3, 120n2, 134n1, 172n1, 173n2, 202n3, 367n1, 380n1, 381n2, 451n,1, 455n3, 457n2, 464n1, 470n3, 486n3; **33**: 7n1, 127n1, 129n1, 155n1, 184n1, 196n5, 213n2, 218n1, 258n1, 317n3, 370n3, 457n1, 462n1, 473n1, 480n3, 497n1, 533n1; **34**: 45n1, 74n5, 106n4, 158n1, 197n2, 242n1, 257n2, 383n1, 423n1, 450n3, 460n1; **35**: 43n1, 91n1, 158n1,3, 192n1, 219n1, 232n1, 419n1, 434n1, 478n1, 530n1; **36**: 180n1,

192n3, 209n1, 228n1, 238n1, 280n1, 284n1, 344n1, 464n1, 480n1, 519n1; **37**: 157n1, 277n1, 306n1, 321n1, 431n1, 467n1, 481n1; **38**: 51n1, 60n2, 85n1, 271n1, 313n1, 314n2, 559n2, 570n1, 674n1, 675n1

Lippiat, Gerald, **30**: 17

Lippitt, Henry Frederick, **32**: 291,n1

Lippmann, Jonas, **38**: 559,n1

Lippmann, Walter, **27**: 456, 476; **31**: 316,n2; **37**: 166, 212, 525, 537; **38**: 62-63, 86-87, 238, 273, 274-76, 281, 295, 312,n2, 445n1, 559-60,n1

Lira, Alejandro, **36**: 200,n11

Lira, José María Valderrama, **35**: 520

Liss, Sheldon B., **27**: 437n1

Lister, Ernest, **27**: 220,n1, 221

Listoe, Soren, **35**: 280,n3

Litchfield, George Victor, Jr., **34**: 124n5, 241, 245, 323

Literary Digest, **29**: 301n2

Little, Bascom, **36**: 41n1

Little Bear (Indian chief), **31**: 77-78, 79

Little Book of Limericks (Rice), **31**: 316,n2

Little Corn Island, **27**: 528

Little White Bird (Barrie), **28**: 286

Liverpool, England, **33**: 369n2; **34**: 257, 264

Lives of Roger Casement (Reid), **36**: 563n1; **37**: 380n2

Living Age, **33**: 244n1

Livingston, Lemuel W., **32**: 297,n1

Llorente, Enrique C., **33**: 400,n2, 463; **34**: 488

Lloyd George, David, **27**: 251; **28**: 53; **29**: 412; **30**: 215; **32**: 21n1; **33**: 484, 523; **34**: 18, 135; **35**: 74, 76, 357, 484-86, 487; **37**: 77n1, 90, 502, 532; **38**: 313,n1, 392, 497, 619,n1; W. H. Page's description of, **33**: 552-53; and House peace mission, **36**: 138, 148, 166-67, 170, 173, 180n1, 266n1

loans: *see* banking

lobby investigation, **28**: 381,n1,2, 414

lobbying and lobbyists, **27**: 472-73, 483-84, 497, 504, 509; **38**: 310, 329; and tariff, **27**: 473, 487-88, 507n1; **28**: 315n2; and Southern Pacific Railroad, **27**: 487; and trust legislation, **29**: 212; and Panama Canal tolls, **29**: 233; and water-power bill, **36**: 265-66

Lobdell, Charles Elmer, **38**: 160,n5

Lobos Island, Mex., **30**: 78-79,n1

Lochner, Louis Paul, **35**: 195-99, 199-200, 279n1

Lockett, James, **31**: 517

Lockhart, Frank Pruit, **33**: 99,n2

Locksun, S.S., **31**: 444

Lockwood, Frank D., **36**: 337, 338

Lodge, Henry Cabot, **27**: 358,n1, 533; **28**: 272,n1; **29**: 180n1, 271-72,n1, 275, 440, 441, 482n1; **30**: 453; **31**: 455; **35**: 374; **36**: 212, 425n3, 517n1; **37**: 397n1, 411; **38**: 391, 570,n1; and ship-purchase bill,

Lodge, Henry Cabot (*cont.*)
33: 111, 114, 115, 123, 134n1, 165, 336-37,n2, 345; and *Lusitania* postscript controversy, 38: 559,n2, 559-60,n2
Loeb, William, Jr., 27: 407
Loewe *v.* Lawlor, 27: 186
Logan, Thomas Francis, 38: 20,n1
Logan Act of 1799, 35: 357n1, 360; 37: 542n1
Logue, James Washington, 32: 97
Lombardi, Cesar Maurice, 29: 263,n2, 277
Lombardo, Mr., 32: 390
London, 33: 524; Safety-at-Sea Conference, 28: 420n2; 29: 280-81,n2; ambassadorial entertaining in, 29: 412; 30: 149-55; situation in on eve of war and during early days of conflict, 30: 314-16, 325, 329-31, 366-68, 370; fear of bombing, 30: 471; H. Hoover's work in, 31: 80; E. M. House's desire to visit, 31: 95; air attacks on, 33: 400, 414
London, Meyer, 35: 487n2
London, University of, 31: 7
London Convention for Safety of Life at Sea: *see* International Conference on Safety of Life at Sea
London *Daily Chronicle*, 35: 473, 524,n1
London *Daily Graphic*, 36: 232, 233
London *Daily Mail*, 28: 310; 31: 204n1; 35: 487,n1
London *Daily News and Leader*, 36: 320n1, 379n6; 37: 265n1, 294n1
London *Daily Telegraph*, 35: 425; 36: 233
London *Economist*, 32: 340; 38: 110
London *Financial News*, 29: 331n1
London Liberal Federation, 38: 207n1
London *Morning Post*, 28: 526n2; 29: 200n1; 32: 12n3; 35: 425
London *Morning Telegraph*, 28: 442-43
London *Nation*, 32: 328n3; 37: 294n1, 447,n2
London Naval Conference (1909), 31: 97; 34: 13
London *New Statesman*, 35: 223n1
London *Outlook*, 32: 328n3; 33: 244n1
London *Pall Mall Gazette*, 29: 320,n1; 35: 426
London Post, 31: 204; 38: 659
London *Punch*, 35: 9, 416
London Safety at Sea Conference: *see* International Conference on Safety of Life at Sea
London *Saturday Review*, 29: 202
London *Spectator*, 28: 118, 576; 29: 301; 32: 129,n2, 226; 33: 549; 35: 223, 454
London *Standard*, 35: 425-26
London *Statist*, 31: 177n2
London *Times*, 28: 370n2, 559,n1, 576-77; 29: 17, 145, 301,n1,2; 30: 287,n1,2; 31: 204n1; 32: 206n3, 299, 341n4, 449n1; 33: 130, 214, 554; 34: 21n6; 35: 203n1, 223, 425; 36: 232; 37: 294,n1, 447,n2
London *Westminster Gazette*, 28: 315,n2; 29: 301,n3; 32: 226,n2; 33: 214; 35: 426

Long, Boaz Walton, 28: 5,n5, 250; 29: 248, 381; 30: 148n2, 180; 32: 469, 470,n2,3; 33: 471; Tampico affair, 29: 429
Long, James Anderson, 29: 322-23,n1
Long Branch, N.J., 35: 58n1; 38: 118n3; WW accepts nomination in, 38: 126-39
Longfellow, Henry Wadsworth, 28: 291, 310
Longstreet, Helen Dortch (Mrs. James), 27: 239,n2
Longstreet, James, 27: 239
Longwy, France, 31: 17
López, Pablo, 35: 478n1; 36: 397,n2; 37: 251,n3
Lorance, John, 28: 498n1
Lord, Frank B., 29: 361,n2
Lord, Rivington D., 27: 154; 29: 476
Lord Chief Justice of England: *see* Reading, 1st Marquess of Reading
Lord's Prayer, 38: 639
Loreburn, Earl of: *see* Reid, Robert Threshie
Loring, Charles Greeley, 34: 10,n2; 35: 157n2
Loring, Katherine Alice Page, 29: 351; 31: 262,n1; 34: 10-11,n1,2; 35: 157n2; 37: 461
Lorraine: *see* Alsace-Lorraine
Los Angeles, Cal., 33: 424
Los Angeles Board of Health, 33: 430
Los Angeles Public Service Commission, 28: 6n1
Los Angeles Times, 27: 349n1
Lost Harbor, Alaska, 33: 35
Lou Tsung-yii, 38: 152,n1
Loudon, Jonkheer John, 35: 20-21,n3, 196-97; 38: 104,n1
Loughrigg, Westmorland, 28: 286
Louis Napoléon, 31: 562n4
Louis Philippe (of France), 31: 562,n3
Louisiana, 27: 286n3; 28: 35n1; and tariff, 27: 261, 418n1; J. R. Thornton and Panama Canal tolls, 29: 276; and payment of damages case, 27: 305, 388,n6
Louisiana, U.S.S., 29: 440; 34: 204
Louisville, Ky., 30: 44
Louisville *Courier-Journal*, 31: 65n1, 90; 33: 508n1
Louisville Presbyterian Theological Seminary, 34: 211n1
Louisville Times, 33: 196n1
Louisville Varnish Co., 37: 402n1
Louvain, Belgium, 30: 458, 462, 467, 471n1; 31: 17
Louvain, University of, 30: 458
Love, Thomas Bell, 36: 51
Love and Guilt: Woodrow Wilson and Mary Hulbert (Saunders), 34: 491n1
Lovejoy, Owen Reed, 27: 76, 107; 29: 170; 38: 161n2, 284
Loveira, Carlos, 37: 245
Lovett, Edgar Odell, 27: 574, 575; 36: 297,n1, 329-30
Lovett, Robert Scott, 37: 439n1; 38: 377,n1, 389, 466n2

Low, Alfred Maurice, **29**: 200,n1; **32**: 12,n3, 21; **38**: 659
Low, Seth, **32**: 18, 84, 532-33; **33**: 26, 49; **34**: 433; **37**: 33,n4; and Colorado Coal Commission, **31**: 363, 369, 373, 376, 377, 389, 389-90, 424, 462-63, 474-75, 481, 503, 503-504, 513-14, 523, 548; **35**: 317, 348, 492,n1, 537-40; **36**: 237, 245, 291, 299; on Howard University appropriations, **32**: 272; on preparedness, **35**: 177-78,n1,2, 180
Lowden, Frank Orren, **37**: 522n1
Lowe, John Z., **35**: 318-19
Lowell, Abbott Lawrence, **31**: 108; **32**: 25; **33**: 435n1, 458-59, 476; **35**: 217
Lowell, James Russell, **30**: 152, 154
Lowery, Ellin Prince (Mrs. John A.); see Speyer, Ellin Prince Lowery (Mrs. James Joseph)
Lowry, Edward George, **28**: 560,n2; **29**: 92-98,n1, 366-67
Lu Cheng-hsiang, **32**: 137,n4
Lucey, Dennis Benedict, **28**: 35,n2, 37, 64
Lucha, La (Cuban newspaper), **30**: 148n2
Lucile Ltd., N.Y., **35**: 162,n2
Luckemeyer, Jeanne: see Bernstorff, Jeanne Luckemeyer, Countess von
Lucy: see Smith, Lucy Marshall
Ludendorff, Erich Friedrich Wilhelm, **38**: 314n2
Lüders affair, **34**: 67,n1
Ludlow, Edwin, **27**: 404,n3
Ludlow, Colo., **29**: 479,n1, 479-80, 502
Ludlow massacre, **30**: 39n1, 46
Ludwig III (of Bavaria), **33**: 371,n1
lumber industry, **30**: 4
Lund, Fred Bates, **38**: 182,n4,7
Lurton, Horace Harmon, **28**: 594-95,n1; **30**: 280,n1,2, 285
Lusitania, **29**: 74n1; **32**: 94, 200, 201
Lusitania disaster: see Germany and the United States
Lusitania Disaster: An Episode in Modern Warfare and Diplomacy (Bailey and Ryan), **33**: 127n1, 135n3
Lusitania notes: see Germany and the United States
Lusitania postscript: see Germany and the United States
Luther, Mark Lee, **31**: 316,n2
Lutherans: in Buffalo, N.Y., **28**: 589
Lutz, Alma, **37**: 427n4
Luxembourg, **32**: 44, 205; **33**: 347; **35**: 348; Germany invades, **30**: 330; resignation of U.S. minister to, **38**: 210
Luzon, P.I., **27**: 370
Lyceum Theater, N.Y., **28**: 355n4
Lyme, Conn., **30**: 189; **38**: 686
Lynch, Frederick Bicknell, **27**: 21, 333-34; **29**: 532; **35**: 346, 361; **36**: 598; **37**: 46, 229
Lynch, Frederick (Henry), **29**: 476; **36**: 632n1, 635; **38**: 276,n1,2
Lynchburg, Va., **35**: 501,n1

lynching, **28**: 115,n2, 118, 221; **38**: 15, 24,n2, 459-60
Lynde, Francis, **31**: 316,n2
Lyon, Ernest, **35**: 240,n1
Lyons, James, **38**: 442,n3
Lyons, Maurice F., **31**: 264

M. Kurzman's Sons, N.Y., **35**: 272,n1
Maass, Gustavo, **29**: 480, 492
Mabie, Hamilton Wright, **27**: 298; **32**: 282n1, 283
McAdoo, Eleanor Wilson (Mrs. William Gibbs), **28**: 565n1; **30**: 55, 73, 84, 129, 277, 452; **31**: 59, 86, 142, 263, 267, 361, 468; **32**: 66, 165, 371; **33**: 240, 241-42, 242, 334, 395; **34**: 63, 72-73, 74, 83, 171, 201, 218, 249, 263, 272, 274, 275, 294, 379, 394, 407; **35**: 109, 110, 160, 165-66; **36**: 267, 297, 399, 569; **37**: 111,n1, 382; **38**: 7, 160, 396, 428, 429, 439, 564, 681, 682, 683, 688, 690; wedding of, **30**: 6-7, 12-13; WW's love for, **30**: 12-13; birth of daughter, **33**: 235n1; reaction to WW's marriage plans, **34**: 89; and Mrs. Galt, **34**: 90-91, 154-55,n1, 245-46, 283; on monument over mother's grave, **37**: 247; *see also* Wilson, Eleanor Randolph
McAdoo, Ellen Wilson, **33**: 235,n1, 240, 241-42, 242, 334, 395; **34**: 72, 83, 218, 249, 275, 294, 379, 394; **35**: 165-66, 275; **36**: 297; **37**: 78,n1; **38**: 429, 439; photograph: *illustration section*
McAdoo, Nona Hazlehurst, **28**: 597,n2; **30**: 6,n1; **34**: 275, 294, 394
McAdoo, Robert Hazlehurst, **34**: 275, 294, 394,n1
McAdoo, Sally Fleming, **34**: 275, 294,n1
McAdoo, William (N.Y. judge), **31**: 427,n1
McAdoo, William Gibbs, **27**: 137, 227, 236, 444; **28**: 3n1, 122, 127, 139, 375, 389, 420, 434-35, 476, 597,n2; **29**: 32, 90, 226, 447, 456, 516, 530-31, 536; **30**: 332, 334, 432; **31**: 76, 86, 91, 93, 142, 207, 239, 267, 270, 283, 427, 468, 481; **32**: 10, 61, 62, 64, 66, 120, 121, 133; **33**: 334, 344, 391,n2, 397, 409, 442, 446, 469, 538; **34**: 72, 73, 74,n5, 112, 132, 133, 158,n1, 248-49, 263, 272,n1, 274-75, 283, 294, 369, 379, 382, 394, 400, 512, 514, 515; **35**: 31, 64, 109, 165, 166, 239, 257, 360, 401; **36**: 239, 263, 267, 378, 602, 606; **37**: 46, 104-105, 106, 119, 308, 363, 366-67, 379, 397; **38**: 158, 158-60,n6, 195-97, 197, 296, 350, 351-52, 354, 374-75, 439, 591n1, 659-60
cabinet appointment, **27**: 21, 24, 26, 57, 61, 62, 70, 103, 112, 129; and Philippines, **27**: 22; and Joseph R. Wilson, Jr., **27**: 55, 83; and W. F. McCombs, **27**: 120, 139, 140, 153, 200, 300,n1, 384, 385; code name for, **27**: 164; and Six-Power loan, **27**: 175; on diplomatic and domestic appointments, **27**: 199, 200, 251, 283-84, 292, 333, 336-37, 396,n1,

McAdoo, William Gibbs (*cont.*)
406-407, 513; **28:** 271, 524-25; **35:** 318-19, 338; **38:** 335-36, 393, 428-29, 454-56; and segregation, **27:** 291; **28:** 343, 346, 350, 402, 413-14, 453-55,n1, 492, 496, 498n1; **31:** 308, 328n2, 360-61,n2; banking and currency, **27:** 292, 457, 485,n2, 486, 535n1, 536,n1; Panama Canal tolls, **27:** 313; California alien land legislation, **27:** 351; and A. E. Patterson, **28:** 10, 20, 40-41; movement of crops, **28:** 156,n1; on inscription for Post Office Building, **28:** 366,n1, 371, 501, 505; and duty on books, **28:** 390, 579

Federal Reserve System: and Federal Reserve Board, **29:** 49-50, 54, 56, 57, 219, 247, 448, 515, 532; **30:** 27, 30, 33, 50-55, 376,n1; **31:** 386; and passage of Federal Reserve bill, **29:** 62, 66, 77-78, 89, 91-92; and Federal Reserve Act, **30:** 84,n1; on official opening of Federal Reserve Banks, **31:** 321; WW thanks for work on, **31:** 327

WW presents pen with which he signed currency bill, **29:** 63n1; health of, **29:** 87, 89, 92; **32:** 371,n1; and plans for anti-Tammany Democratic organization, **29:** 136n1

and Eleanor Wilson: **29:** 531; engagement to, **29:** 346,n1, 372; wedding plans, **29:** 391; marriage to, **30:** 6-7, 12-13, 129

and assistance to Americans abroad, **30:** 335; at funeral of EAW, **30:** 374; meets with businessmen, **30:** 378n1, 388; at conference on need for ships, **30:** 402; as cabinet member, **30:** 464; on decline in customs revenue, **30:** 467-68, 471-72; and W. H. Page's expenses, **30:** 490; and shipping bill, **31:** 100, 101, 124, 244, 276, 279-80, 448; **35:** 345,n1, 396, 459,n1, 475; and New York politics, **31:** 123, 252-54

and cotton crisis: **31:** 127-28, 130, 140, 148, 167, 249-52, 271-72, 272; **34:** 186,n2, 294-95; meeting with cotton delegation, **30:** 441,n1, 442; R. L. Henry urges financial aid to cotton growers, **31:** 119-20; and cotton-loan plan, **31:** 321, 328

and G. Paish mission, **31:** 177,n2, 207; and Pan American Financial Conference, **31:** 244, 258,n1; **33:** 245,n1,2; **37:** 187n4; E. M. House on, **31:** 263-64; offered presidency of Metropolitan Life Insurance Co., **31:** 263,n1; and M. Lyons, **31:** 264; and J. P. Tumulty, **31:** 274, 279; House on appointments and, **31:** 275; WW sends letter from P. S. Reinsch on China to, **31:** 283, 284-88; on Jewish Americans and banking interests, **31:** 315; and "gold pool," **31:** 467; rescinds order on ship manifests,

32: 226, 258; attacks H. C. Lodge on ship-purchase bill defeat, **32:** 336-37; and S. Untermyer on Mexico, **33:** 438, 438-40; on third *Lusitania* note, **33:** 536; on German propaganda in the U.S., **34:** 218; on extending credits and loans to belligerents, **34:** 275-80, 330, 421, 421-22, 423, 481, 503, 504; *New York Herald* attack on, **34:** 402,n2, 472; and Mrs. Hulbert, **34:** 505, 506, 507, 508; **35:** 503n1; on tariff and anti-dumping legislation, **35:** 475-77, 502; and Riggs Bank case, **36:** 26n3; in South America, **36:** 297, 367; and incident in Trinidad, **36:** 569; and incident at Grayson wedding, **37:** 111,n1; on platform draft, **37:** 186-90; and income-tax exemption, **37:** 377; on WW's campaign, **38:** 260-61, 394; and speech in Chicago, **38:** 513,n1, 514; WW's birthday greetings to, **38:** 563; photograph: *illustration section,* **27**

McAdoo, William Gibbs, Jr., **34:** 275, 294, 394,n1

McAllister, James Gray, **34:** 211,n1

McAllister, William, **28:** 332

McAlpin, Charles Williston, **38:** 521

McAlpin, Henry, **28:** 179,n1

McAlpin Hotel, N.Y., **35:** 46,n1; **38:** 521

McAneny, George, **33:** 212n1; **37:** 129,n1

MacArthur, John R., **28:** 123

MacArthur Brothers, **28:** 123

Macauley, Charles Raymond, **27:** 81,n1

McCabe, Patrick Edgar, **29:** 423,n1; **38:** 515,n3, 546

McCain, Henry Pinckney, **36:** 285,n1, 295-96, 312-13, 352-53, 501-503, 540, 553-54, 571-72; **37:** 280, 307, 315; **38:** 44-45, 378,n2

McCall, Edward E., **28:** 402,n2

McCarren, Patrick, **38:** 329

McCarthy, Charles, **30:** 161, 161-62, 162

McCarthy, Daniel Joseph, **38:** 72,n7, 73,n10

McCarthy, Thomas D., **31:** 427,n2

Macchi di Cellere, Vincenzo, Count, **35:** 420-21,n3

McChord, Charles Caldwell, **34:** 201n1

McClellan, George Brinton (1865-1940), **27:** 246

McClement, J. H., **28:** 427

McClenahan, Howard, **31:** 412

McClure, Nathaniel F., **29:** 542

McCobb, Thomas, **36:** 337

MacColl, Dugald Sutherland, **34:** 86n1

McCombs, William Frank, **27:** 11,n1, 110,n2, 165, 251, 386; **28:** 597; **29:** 355, 404-405, 409; **30:** 463; **31:** 83, 93, 139, 264,n2, 274; **32:** 19n1, 175,n5; **33:** 420; **35:** 239, 286; **37:** 156; **38:** 591n1, 597n1; cabinet possibility, **27:** 21, 119; and A. M. Palmer, **27:** 22,n2; and ambassadorship to Austria-Hungary, **27:** 24, 70; effect upon WW, **27:** 57, 63, 125-

26; and W. G. McAdoo, **27:** 120, 139, 140, 153, 200, 300-301, 384, 385; and French ambassadorship, **27:** 127, 148, 198, 217,n1, 218, 250, 258, 300-301, 384; code name for, **27:** 164; and New York politics, **29:** 135, 240n1, 277, 382, 422-23; trustee of College of the City of New York, **29:** 262; letter from D. Breckinridge on politics in Kentucky, **29:** 342-43; and resignation as chairman of Democratic National Committee, **36:** 479, 480, 518, 523, 525-26, 530, 543; and New York senatorial nomination, **38:** 164,n1, 189, 201, 277-78

McConnell, Francis John, **38:** 520,n2

McCormick, Cyrus, Jr., **30:** 278-79,n1, 301

McCormick, Cyrus Hall, II, **27:** 179; **29:** 483n1, 554,n3; **30:** 270n4, 278n1, 279, 301; **31:** 204, 205; **34:** 136

McCormick, Harriet Bradley Hammond (Mrs. Cyrus Hall, II), **34:** 136

McCormick, Nettie Maria Fowler (Mrs. Cyrus Hall, I), **38:** 649,n1

McCormick, Vance Criswell, **29:** 223n2; **37:** 269, 281, 373, 378-79, 408, 448, 471, 475, 481, 513, 517, 522n1, 532, 533, 535; **38:** 5-8, 8, 36, 37, 78, 122, 140, 172, 188n3, 278, 280, 283, 287, 296, 317, 368, 369-72, 429, 461, 474, 522, 591n1, 597n2, 606, 616, 636-37, 642-44, 660, 661, 663, 669; selected as Democratic National Committee chairman, **37:** 57, 76, 77, 93, 117-18, 151, 164, 211, 227, 229, 236, 245; on Progressive dissidents, **37:** 523-24,n2; on situation in Maine, **38:** 170; as candidate for governor of Pennsylvania, **38:** 430-31,n2

McCosh, James, **27:** 306n1; **28:** 203; **30:** 465-66; **35:** 239, 286

McCrary, Frank Robert, **30:** 369,n6

McCrea, Roswell Cheney, **27:** 208-209

McCulloch v. State of Maryland, **36:** 196

McCumber, Porter James, **29:** 185-86, 197-98, 409,n1; **30:** 342n1

McCutcheon, George Barr, **31:** 316n2, 317

McDermott, Walter Langdon, **27:** 386,n2

McDonald, James P., **34:** 66,n1, 66-68

McDonald, Pirie, **38:** 7,n3

McDonald, William Calhoun, **36:** 606, 653-54; **37:** 31, 62, 159, 170-71

McDonald, William Jesse (Bill), **27:** 223, 238, 414

McDowell, Hervey, **29:** 104,n1

McDowell, Mary Eliza, **32:** 20,n1

McDowell, Whitford L., **37:** 148n1

McDowell, William Fraser, **36:** 629n1

Macedonia, **33:** 232

McElroy, John, **36:** 160n1

McElwin Co., Boston, **29:** 401n1

Macfarland, Charles Stedman, **27:** 154, 231,n1, 244; **29:** 476; **30:** 398; **31:** 80; **35:** 328, 354,n2; **37:** 422; **38:** 619-20,n1

Macfarland, Grenville Stanley, **27:** 334

McFarland, George W., **32:** 96

McGill, James, **36:** 189,n2

McGill University, **38:** 3n3

McGoodwin, Preston Buford, **28:** 4,n3

McGovern, George Stanley, **28:** 426n1; **29:** 479n1, 511n1; **30:** 39n1, 49n1, 60n1; **31:** 273n2

McGowan, Thaddeus E., **31:** 183

McGuire, James K., **38:** 5,n1

Machias, U.S.S., **37:** 16

machine politics, **31:** 253, 275; **37:** 174; S. B. Woods, **27:** 73,n2, 74; and Kentucky, **29:** 343

McIlhenny, John Avery, **29:** 309-10,n1; **36:** 503n2

McIlvaine, Anne, **38:** 180, 194

McIntosh, Charles K., **31:** 235, 236-37

McIntyre, Frank, **28:** 366,n1; **30:** 144, 155, 160-61; **32:** 354, 536; **34:** 390; **36:** 583n1; **38:** 632, 648, 650-53, 656, 674-75; memorandum on the Philippines, **30:** 147-52

Mack, Norman Edward, **35:** 460n1

MacKaye, Milton, **32:** 267n1

MacKaye, Percy Wallace, **28:** 119,n2, 291, 321

McKelway, Alexander Jeffrey, **27:** 76, 77, 107, 108-109; **29:** 170; **32:** 211; **37:** 65,n1, 69, 436, 471; **38:** 122, 284-85,n1, 296, 445n1; on child-labor bill, **37:** 429-30, 447-48

McKelway, St. Clair, **38:** 284-85, 296

McKenna, Joseph, **37:** 420,n1

McKenna, Patrick E., **28:** 262,n4; **34:** 192,n1

McKenna, Reginald, **34:** 28,n2; **35:** 472,n3, 484

McKesson, C. F., **28:** 369n2

McKim, S. Sterett, **27:** 192n1

McKinley, William, **28:** 19, 242n1, 371; **29:** 517, 518; **30:** 141; **35:** 212,n1; **37:** 32; **38:** 310, 556-57

McKinley Monument, **38:** 572n1

McLane, Robert Milligan, **33:** 46

McLauren, William Augustus, **36:** 364,n1

McLaurin, John Lowndes, **33:** 495,n2; **34:** 99-100, 121, 147, 238, 400,n1

McLean, Mr., **32:** 352

McLean, Angus Wilton, **31:** 128,n3

McLean, George Payne, **30:** 299n1

McLemore, Jeff (Atkins Jefferson), **36:** 211n1

McLemore resolution, **36:** 238n1, 239, 240n1, 268, 278n1, 288, 366

McLennan, John, **31:** 37

McMaster, George, **27:** 56; **30:** 374

McMillan, Homer, **31:** 259,n2, 260

McMillin, Benton, **38:** 653-54,n1

MacMurray, John van Antwerp, **36:** 175-76,n1, 191, 505

McNab, Gavin, **38:** 37,n1, 624

McNab, John L., **28:** 99n4

McNaboe, James F., **32:** 96

McNair, William N., **27**: 244
McNear and Co., **37**: 471
McNeely, Robert N., **35**: 420n1
McNeil, Rivers, **38**: 296,n1
Macomb, Montgomery Meigs, **34**: 482n1;
  38: 238,n3
McQuatters, Arthur J., **36**: 592,n1,2
MacRae, Hugh, **32**: 56n2
Macrea, John, **28**: 390,n1
McReynolds, James Clark, **27**: 81, 253,
  321, 414, 444; **28**: 255n1, 257, 594-95;
  29: 41, 50, 227, 387, 447, 449, 456, 517,
  538; **30**: 172, 203, 423; **33**: 482; cabinet
  possibility and selection, **27**: 26, 62, 70,
  115, 133, 136; on appointments, **27**:
  116, 223, 224, 227, 238, 334; on recognition of China, **27**: 249; tobacco
  trust, **27**: 510; code name for, **27**: 164;
  Diggs-Caminetti case, **28**: 99,n4; segregation, **28**: 498n1; and American
  Telephone and Telegraph Co., **29**:
  45,n1; Union Pacific Railroad case, **29**:
  67n2; and Boston and Maine and New
  Haven railroads, **29**: 338, 345,n1, 368;
  30: 23n4, 85, 293, 302; and Supreme
  Court appointment, **30**: 468; and food
  investigation, **30**: 432n1; photograph:
  illustration section, **27**
McRoberts, Samuel, **38**: 67, 71
McSparran, John Aldus, **36**: 524, 637-
  38,n14
MacVeagh, Franklin, **28**: 502
Macy's: *see* R. H. Macy's
Madera, Chihuahua, Mex., **38**: 547
Maderistas, **29**: 280
Madero, Ernesto, **30**: 57,n1
Madero, Francisco Indalecio, **27**: 64,n1,
  119n1, 252n2, 420-21, 438, 480; **28**: 19,
  27, 39, 59, 69n1, 71, 72, 73, 76, 78, 173,
  206, 241n1, 265n1, 298, 341, 356n1,
  386, 444-45, 502-503; **29**: 120, 123, 194,
  249n2, 252, 255, 260n2, 358, 459, 520,
  554,n2; **30**: 25, 41, 56, 57n1, 97, 99,
  168, 411; **32**: 387; **33**: 4, 5, 187n1,
  260,n1, 261, 468; **36**: 600; **37**: 36, 301;
  resignation, **27**: 202, 546; assassination, **27**: 202n1, 548-49; W. B. Hale report on, **27**: 536-52
Madero, Mrs. Francisco Indalecio, **27**:
  546-47, 550
Madero, Gustavo, **27**: 543, 545
Madero y Cia, Salvador, **27**: 549
Madge: *see* Elliott, Margaret Randolph
  Axson
Madison, James, **27**: 159; **31**: 109, 110,
  118, 338
Madison Square Garden, **37**: 476n3;
  WW's campaign address in, **38**: 561,
  597-602, 603, 608
magazines: *see* periodicals
Magistrate's Own Case (Rosenkrantz), **31**:
  316,n2
Magna Carta, **30**: 146
Magner, Thomas Francis, **31**: 349,n1

Magon, Flores, **33**: 261
Magnus Beck Brewing Co., Buffalo, **35**:
  460n1
Mahan, Alfred Thayer, **30**: 352n1
Maine, **28**: 144, 149,n1; **31**: 340; **38**: 105-
  106,n1, 170, 173, 175
Maine, U.S.S., **27**: 420; **29**: 521
Making a Vague Pledge Vaguer (*New
  York Tribune*), **34**: 445,n3
Making Woodrow Wilson President
  (McCombs), **27**: 22n2; **31**: 264,n2
Makino, Baron Nobuaki, **27**: 161-62, 293-
  94, 315-21, 441n1, 498-502; **28**: 284-86,
  303-307, 312-15; **29**: 179, 180, 181; **30**:
  169,n1
Malbraithhead, Mr. (of Standard Oil Co.),
  28: 445
Malden, Mass., **29**: 474
Malley, John Frank, **28**: 275,n4
Mallon, Hannah Neil (Mrs. Guy Ward),
  38: 526,n1
Malmö, Sweden, **34**: 188; **35**: 62
Malone, Dudley Field, **27**: 84,n1, 126, 140,
  199, 228, 410; **28**: 103-104, 108, 109,
  139, 178, 256, 271, 275, 477, 595, 596;
  29: 35, 277, 403, 404; **30**: 96, 123; **31**:
  11-12,n1, 122, 333, 345, 428-29; **32**: 86,
  128, 192, 249, 281, 365, 398; **33**: 143,n1;
  34: 41, 118; **35**: 42, 44, 153, 155, 166,
  217-18, 239, 276, 279,n1, 347, 398; **36**:
  389, 498; **37**: 8, 103, 176-77, 207, 475-
  76; **38**: 8-9, 453, 546; considered as N.Y.
  Port Collector, **28**: 524-25; and N.Y.
  politics, **29**: 136,n1; **37**: 104, 155-56,
  513, 517, 533-34; criticism of M. H.
  Glynn, **29**: 414,n1, 423; criticism of
  W. C. Osborn, **29**: 423; on New York
  appointments, **35**: 363, 460; suggestions for Democratic National chairman, **37**: 76, 129, 133, 143,n1, 151, 211;
  on Harding keynote speech, **37**: 167,n1;
  on women's convention, **37**: 167n4
Malone, May O'Gorman (Mrs. Dudley
  Field), **28**: 595; **35**: 44,n2, 162, 166, 276
Man in the Moon (poem, Riley), **27**: 140,
  228
Man of Burdens (*Chicago Herald*), **32**:
  242n2
*Man With a Country: Ideals of American
  Citizenship, Three Addresses by President Woodrow Wilson*, **33**: 149n3
Manassas Battlefield, **34**: 466n1
Manchester, England, **31**: 212
Manchester, Mass., **33**: 477; **34**: 382; **37**:
  133
Manchester, Vt., **34**: 63, 64, 75
Manchester Engineer, S.S., **36**: 449,
  483n1, 487
Manchester Guardian, **37**: 294n1
Manchuria, **27**: 28; **31**: 510; **32**: 148, 169,
  177, 270, 319, 321, 323,n1, 333n1,
  367n1, 368, 416,n3, 417, 418, 433n1,
  434, 435, 460, 461, 500n1; **33**: 34, 95,
  98, 102, 122

Manhattan Club of New York: memorandum by JPT on, **35:** 107n1; WW's address to, **35:** 121-26, 167-73; address mentioned, **35:** 127, 178, 180, 184

Manhattan Congregational Church, N.Y., **33:** 160n1

Manhattan Hotel, N.Y., **33:** 412; **35:** 278

Manila *La Vanguardia*, **38:** 632, 648-49,n1

Manila, P.I., **27:** 188-89, 370, 441, 443, 446, 447; **28:** 242n1, 323n1

Mann, Mr. (reporter), **28:** 471,n1

Mann, Horace, **33:** 6

Mann, James Robert, **27:** 226,n3; **35:** 213,n1; **36:** 8,n2, 212, 306, 315; **38:** 103, 666n1

Mann, John L., **33:**218,n5

Mann, Parker, **28:** 335,n4

Mann, William Hodges, **31:** 261; **33:** 464

Mann Act: Diggs-Caminetti case, **28:** 99n4

Manners, John Hartley, **27:** 63n4

Manzanillo, Colima, Mex., **32:** 387

Manzer, Parker C., **28:** 315n1

Marble, John Hobart, **27:** 152,n1

Marburg, Theodore, **29:** 380, 401n1; **32:** 188, 198-99

Marbury, William Luke, **27:** 115,n1, 141,n3; **28:** 390; **29:** 220-21, 232, 241, 272n1, 313; **35:** 429-30, 431; **37:** 420-21

Marchand, C. Roland, **36:** 632n1; **37:** 291n2

Marconi stock scandal, **27:** 251,n1

Mare Island Navy Yard, **29:** 443

Marees van Swinderen, Jonkheer Reneke de, **35:** 414,n3

Margerie, Pierre de, **32:** 373,n2, 378

Maria, S.S., **36:** 133

Maria Cristina of Hapsburg, **37:** 274,n2

Mariatequi y Carratalá, Alfredo de, **35:** 130,n2, 176

Marietta, U.S.S., **37:** 16

Marina incident, **38:** 570-71,n1,2, 607-608, 658

Marine Insurance, Bureau of, **31:** 3

Marine National Bank of Buffalo, **29:** 401n1

marines: *see* United States Marines

Maritime Customs Service, **31:** 547

Markets, Bureau of, **38:** 25, 422

Markets and Rural Organization, Office of, **37:** 198

Marlborough-Blenheim Hotel, Atlantic City, **27:** 85n1, 89n5

Marne, First Battle of the, **32:** 522,n2

Marseilles, France, **37:** 98

Marsh, Wilbur W., **37:** 229,n1, 508; **38:** 37, 188n3

Marshall, Hudson Snowden, **27:** 115,n2, 118, 145, 223, 227

Marshall, John, **38:** 326

Marshall, Leon Carroll, **29:** 352

Marshall, Lois Irene Kimsey (Mrs.

Thomas Riley), **30:** 355; **36:** 240n2; **38:** 625

Marshall, Louis, **32:** 96,n6; **37:** 188-89

Marshall, Thomas Riley, **27:** 40n1, 155; **28:** 138, 144; **29:** 35, 461; **30:** 355-56; **31:** 23,n1; **32:** 515; **33:** 431n3, 452; **34:** 514; **35:** 412n2; **36:** 139n1, 219, 240,n2; **37:** 101n1, 105, 200n3, 211, 516, 517; **38:** 81,n1, 126,n1, 282, 493, 625; on Panama Canal tolls, **29:** 418-20; House on, **38:** 11; on eight-hour bill, **38:** 212

Marshall Islands, **31:** 511

Martha (cook), **28:** 143, 368

Martha Berry: The Sunday Lady of Possum Trot (Byers), **28:** 308n2

Martha Washington College, **32:** 423n1

Marthens, Mr. (of Empire Coal Mining Co.), **29:** 549

Martin, Albro, **29:** 140n3

Martin, Anne Henrietta, **35:** 292,n2; **38:** 28

Martin, Edward Sandford, **27:** 117-18, 118, 140; **29:** 530; **36:** 387

Martin, Franklin Henry, **38:** 47,n3, 64, 182,n1, 183, 387, 439,n1

Martin, George, **28:** 595,n3

Martin, Henderson S., **30:** 156

Martin, Thomas Staples, **27:** 73-74, 229, 303, 369; **30:** 337n1; **31:** 458; **32:** 197; **33:** 337, 349, 512; **36:** 328, 330, 355,n1, 360, 563,n1; **37:** 431n1

Martin, Walter F., **35:** 505,n2

Martin, William P., **27:** 376,n3

Martine, James Edgar, **27:** 456; **29:** 208; **32:** 10, 86n1; **35:** 493; **38:** 285,n2

Martinez, Edmundo E., **34:** 149,n1, 164, 174-76,n1

Martinez, Jacobo Ramos, **30:** 47,n2, 48

Marx, Lewis Hart, **34:** 441-42,n1

Mary: *see* Smith, Mary Randolph

Mary (Victoria Mary of Teck), wife of George V, **34:** 10n1

Marye, George Thomas, Jr., **29:** 373,n2; **31:** 469; **32:** 67,n2, 462, 525; **35:** 358; resignation, **33:** 511; **35:** 526; **36:** 86, 126, 188

Maryland, **31:** 507-508; **38:** 376n1, 452, 515n1; senatorial race, **27:** 115, 141,n3; **28:** 390,n1; and Panama Canal tolls, **29:** 311

Mason, Alpheus Thomas, **36:** 25n1, 26n2,3, 611n3; **37:** 72n1

Mason, Frank Holcomb, **30:** 200,n1

Mason, Frederic S., **31:** 85

Mason, Gregory, **30:** 143n2

Mason, Julian, **30:** 161,n1

Massachusetts, **27:** 344, 483; **28:** 139, 495; **29:** 247, 374; **35:** 176; appointments, **28:** 139, 270-71, 275, 289; Negro vote and presidential election of 1912, **28:** 222; Boston and Maine and New Haven railroads and, **30:** 85, 163,n1, 293n3, 294-95, 302, 305; D. I. Walsh on Ne-

Massachusetts (*cont.*)
groes in, **31:** 237-38
Massachusetts Agricultural College, **38:** 629
Massachusetts Institute of Technology, **27:** 206
Massingham, Henry William, **37:** 447,n2
Matachic, Mex., **36:** 586
Matamoras, Tamaulipas, Mex., **28:** 28, 31; **31:** 23; **36:** 352
Mather, Samuel, **29:** 401n1
Mather, William, **34:** 317
Mathews, Shailer, **27:** 231n3; **30:** 396-98,n1; **31:** 461; **35:** 328; **37:** 422
Mathewson, Charles F., **30:** 284
Mati, P.I., **27:** 370
Matsunobu, Keiji, **27:** xxii
Matthews, John Alphonsus, **27:** 373n1, 376
Maude, Cyril, **35:** 19n1, 44
Maurer, Ed., **27:** 549
Maurer, James Hudson, **36:** 524, 635,n6, 636n11, 638-39
Mauretania, S.S., **33:** 478; **34:** 48, 320
Maximilian (Ferdinand Maximilian Joseph) of Hapsburg, Emperor of Mexico, **28:** 325; **30:** 360; **33:** 5
May, Judith (Mrs. Robert McCredie), **27:** xxii; **30:** viii
Mayflower, U.S.S., **28:** 362,n2; **29:** 405; **30:** 327, 385; **31:** 402; **32:** 21n1; **33:** 178,n1,2, 204, 213, 216; **34:** 337, 521; **35:** 508; **36:** 251n1, 267,n1, 296n4, 297, 400; **37:** 481, 500n1; **38:** 169, 300, 561-62, 591n1, 606, 606n1, 623
Maynard, Joseph Adolphus, **28:** 275,n3
Mayo, Henry Thomas, **29:** 416; **38:** 299; and Tampico affair, **29:** 420-21, 421, 426-29, 432, 433, 447, 448, 449, 454, 455, 457, 458, 461, 463, 466, 467, 472, 473, 521
Mayo, William James, **38:** 182,n4,10
Mayo Clinic, Rochester, Minn., **38:** 182n10
Maytorena, José María, **28:** 72, 73, 76, 529; **30:** 412,n6, 418, 445
Mazatlan, Sinaloa, Mex., **29:** 443
Mead, Lucia True Ames (Mrs. Edwin Doak), **35:** 134-35,n1, 158; **37:** 308, 316
Meadville, Pa., **36:** 338
Meadville Messenger, **36:** 338
Meadville Theological School, **35:** 135n1
Mebaneville, N.C., **27:** 267n3
Mecklenburg Declaration of Independence, **37:** 79n1, 82
Mediation Board: *see* United States Board of Mediation and Conciliation
Medina, Juan N., **30:** 408, 411, 413, 414, 418
Medina County (Ohio) *Gazette*, **34:** 185n1
Medinaveitia, Manuel, **30:** 409,n4
Mediterranean Sea, **35:** 452-53
Meeker, Royal, **27:** 4, 5, 230, 431,n1; **35:** 184, 205; **36:** 247-49; questionnaire on banking reform, **27:** 204-209

Megeath, George W., **37:** 359-60,n1, 370, 409
Meier, August, **28:** 349n2
Melendez, Carlos, **32:** 470n2
Melish, William Brownell, **38:** 524n1
Mellen, Charles Sanger, **30:** 23n4; **37:** 203,n2
Melson, Fred, **35:** 283n1
Memoirs of Cordell Hull, **27:** 314n1
Memorandum Concerning Section 5 of the Bill to Create a Trade Commission (Rublee), **30:** 274,n1
Memorandum in Exposition of the Suggestions for the Platform (McKelway), **37:** 65n1
Memorandum in Support of a Declaration, suggested as a possible Amendment to the Military and Naval Appropriations Bills (Levermore), **36:** 363n1
Memorandum in re Federal Workmen's Compensation Laws (Meeker), **35:** 205,n1
Memorandum on the Anglo-American Situation (Plunkett), **36:** 347n1
Memorandum on Censorship of Mails (Lansing), **38:** 467,n1
Memorandum Relative to the Mexican Situation (Escudero), **28:** 70-81, 141n3
Memorial Continental Hall, Washington, D.C., **32:** 282n1; **33:** 14n1; **35:** 47n1; **36:** 489n1
Memorial Day: WW on, **33:** 286n1, 287-89; WW's address on, **37:** 123-28
Memphis *Commercial Appeal*, **27:** 108,n1; **36:** 240-41,n1,2, 264
Men and Women (Browning), **38:** 259n2
Menace, The, Aurora, Mo., **37:** 435-36,n2
Mendelson, Jack, **27:** 165
Mendenhall, Thomas Corwin, **36:** 417n1
Méndez, Joaquín (Guatemalan minister to the United States), **33:** 455, 487, 488; **34:** 157,n1,2, 321, 488
Menocal, Mario García, **32:** 408-409,n1
Ménos, Solon, **31:** 486,n2; **34:** 121,n2
Mensdorff-Pouilly-Dietrichstein, Count Albert, **30:** 368,n2, 370
Mercantile Banking Co. of Mexico City, **36:** 364n1
Mercantile Club, St. Louis, **37:** 173
Mercantile Trust Co., St. Louis, **27:** 79n2
Mercer, Pa., **38:** 517n1,4
Mercersburg Theological Seminary, **29:** 361n2
Merchant and Evans Co., Philadelphia, **31:** 187n1
merchant marine, **29:** 276; **30:** 94, 95-96, 324, 326, 388, 476; **31:** 173, 360, 416, 418, 554; **32:** 89, 190; **35:** 177,n2, 180, 265, 266-67, 301-302, 345n1,4, 458n1, 459n1; **37:** 194, 385, 391; **38:** 60n1; and Nicaragua, **27:** 528; WW on, **36:** 43, 93, 156; **38:** 129, 263, 268, 308, 577; and shipping bill, **36:** 567n1
Merchant Marine and Fisheries Com-

mittee on (House of Reps.), **30:** 171, 223n1, 317-18, 402; **31:** 46

Mercurio (Chilean newspaper), **38:** 18

Mere Literature and Other Essays (Wilson), **32:** 8

Merrill, Elmer Truesdale, **32:** 78-80,n1, 89-90

Merry New Ballad of Dr. Woodrow Wilson, President of the United States in America: Embellished with Pictures by an Eminent Hand and Enriched with Historical Notes from the Original Sources (MacColl), **34:** 86,n1

Mersey River, **34:** 305

Mersey, 1st Baron: *see* Bigham, John Charles

Metapan, S.S., **31:** 176n1

Metcalf, Lee Grant, **38:** 261,n1

Metcalf, Stephen Olney, **34:** 158,n2

Metcalfe, Richard Lee, **27:** 219,n2,3; **34:** 197,n1,2, 198-200, 224, 241, 242

Methodist Episcopal Church, **27:** 27n1; **33:** 206n3; **36:** 331n1, 391,n1; **37:** 148n1; WW's address to, **32:** 429-31; **33:** 494-97

Methodist Episcopal Home for the Aged of New Jersey, Ocean Grove, **38:** 118n3

Methodist General Conference (1916), **38:** 520n1

Metropolitan Club, Washington, D.C., **27:** 152; **31:** 220

Metropolitan Life Insurance Co.: McAdoo offered presidency of, **31:** 263-64,n1

Metropolitan Magazine, **30:** 156, 219, 220

Metropolitan Museum of Art, **27:** 72,n1,2

Metz, Germany, **34:** 186

Metz, Herman August: report on conditions in Germany, **31:** 536-37

Mexican Bank of Commerce, **27:** 544

Mexican Central Railroad, **37:** 315

Mexican Constitution, **28:** 173, 201n3, 232, 236-37, 241,n1, 363, 503-504; **29:** 249n2, 330, 473, 484, 507; **30:** 41, 87, 138; **31:** 67; **32:** 280; **33:** 5, 8, 44, 45, 187n1, 304, 398n1; **34:** 133; and presidency, **30:** 116, 117; Villa on, **30:** 411, 413, 414, 444, 446

Mexican Eagle Oil Co., **27:** 331,n2; **28:** 376n2; **30:** 246n2

Mexican Federation of Labor, **34:** 149, 174

Mexican Herald: see Mexico City *Mexican Herald*

Mexican Indians, **27:** 420-21; **28:** 294-95, 297, 507; **29:** 47, 255, 314, 324

Mexican Man of the Hour (Mason), **30:** 143,n2

Mexican National Railways: *see* National Railways of Mexico

Mexican people: J. Lind on, **28:** 293-94

Mexican Petroleum Co., **27:** 404n1

Mexican Question (Wilson), **36:** 560,n1; **37:** 508-12,n, 534-35,n1; **38:** 27, 409, 512, 544

Mexican Revolution, **28:** 7, 8, 27, 28-29,
428; **29:** 30, 74, 90, 110,n1, 123-24, 159, 287, 338, 520; **30:** 69, 362; **34:** 111, 133, 147, 148, 460; **35:** 146; **37:** 249, 259; **38:** 169-70
condition of people in ravaged regions, **28:** 30; bandits, **28:** 30-31; in Morelos, **28:** 296-97; J. Lind on, **28:** 299; **29:** 539, 550-51; Torréon incident, **28:** 382-83,n1, 602,n1; **29:** 382,n1; atrocities and violence, **29:** 15, 188; and oil supply cut off, **29:** 101, 127; need for coal, **29:** 110n1, 127; L. Cabrera on, **29:** 249n2; U.S. views of, **29:** 252; M. Letcher on F. Villa and, **29:** 279-80; V. Huerta on, **29:** 438-39; N. O'Shaughnessy on, **29:** 438-39; U.S. cannot intervene, **30:** 70; and change of Villa's plan due to rivalry with V. Carranza, **30:** 220-21; J. Reed on WW's policy and, **30:** 233-38; Carranza-Villa reconciliation and approaching victory, **30:** 285-86,n1; spirit and success of, **30:** 322; Villa on, **30:** 411; Carranza on, **32:** 348; F. Howe compares to French revolution, **35:** 132-34; *see also* Constitutionalists

Mexican Revolution: Genesis under Madero (Cumberland), **27:** 64n1, 422n1

Mexican Revolution, 1910-14, The Diplomacy of Anglo-American Conflict (Calvert), **28:** 429n1, 544n1, 593n2; **29:** 111n1

Mexican Revolution, 1914-1915: The Convention of Aguascalientes (Quirk), **30:** 193n1

Mexican Revolution: The Constitutionalist Years (Cumberland), **28:** 391n1, 482n1; **30:** 193n1; **32:** 202n3; **33:** 7n1

Mexican Situation from a Mexican Point of View (Cabrera), **29:** 249n2, 266

Mexican War (1846-48), **37:** 509

Mexico, **27:** 119n1, 141, 478-79; **28:** 69n1, 334, 386-87,n1, 400, 471, 571, 594, 600-602; **37:** 112; Madero resignation, **27:** 202, 546; and Russia, **27:** 249, 261-62; and China, **27:** 267; W. B. Hale on overthrow of Madero, **27:** 536-52; **29:** 130-31; H. L. Wilson on Madero government, **28:** 19; Hale report on, **28:** 27-34, 339-42; policy toward newspapers, **28:** 31; Great Britain and British interests in, **28:** 34, 428-29,n1, 442-44,n1, 447, 525-26,n1,2, 528, 529, 587; **29:** 217, 366,n1; **33:** 321; **37:** 305-306, 350; Escudero memorandum, **28:** 70-81; war for independence, **28:** 70-71; conditions in, **28:** 71-72, 293; **29:** 4-5, 120-22; **33:** 269; Plan of Guadalupe, **28:** 73, 561; Pan American Union, **28:** 95n2; history of, **28:** 213; rebel bands, **28:** 213; Americans in, **28:** 214-15, 295-96; **29:** 256, 259, 441, 461, 534

V. Huerta: popular feeling toward, **28:** 282; dissolves Congress, **28:** 387n1, 391n1, 399, 432n2; suspends interest payments, **29:** 137-38; converts to since

Mexico (*cont.*)
the Benton affair, **29:** 328; demands money from bankers, **29:** 382
Chamber of Deputies, **28:** 292-93,n1; Lind report on, **28:** 293-300; **29:** 14-19; effect of contacts with U.S., **28:** 297; railways, **28:** 297; **29:** 124, 193, 287; Gamboa nominated for President, **28:** 324-25,n1; Catholic Church and, **28:** 326; **31:**73-74, 112,n2; Constitutionalists, **28:** 370, 545-46, 561; oil, **28:** 445; **29:**125; legislators imprisoned, **28:** 471
V. *Carranza:* **28:** 541-43; responsibility as president of, **30:** 301n1; demands arms from F. Carbajal, **30:** 360,n1; and break with Villa, **30:** 383n1; assumes power, **30:** 449-50; reforms for, **33:** 6-10, 44-45; manifesto of, **33:** 308n1, 398,n1, 417,n2
and French attitude and interests, **29:** 11; **33:** 194-95,n1; **38:** 408-409; and European loan, **29:** 19; and Military Order of the Caraboa, **29:** 37-38; J. Bryce on, **29:** 47-48; and foreign intervention in, **29:** 92-98; basis for problems in, **29:** 94, 519-20; effect of concessions on government of, **29:** 95-96; army and graft in, **29:** 122-23; communications between Mexico City and Veracruz, **29:** 161; C. H. Brent on, **29:** 167; and celebration honoring Japanese officers, **29:** 181; possibility of famine, **29:** 188; L. Cabrera on, **29:** 191-95, 249n2; agrarian reforms in, **29:** 192; banking policy, **29:** 192-93; and elections, **29:** 258-59; **30:** 138-39, 392-93; M. Letcher on Villa as next head of, **29:** 279-80; Benton affair, **29:** 285-86,n1, 320,n1; financial situation of, **29:** 286-87; idea of northern states forming republic, **29:** 295; and Spain, **29:** 416-17; school system in, **29:** 520, 522; foreigners in, **30:** 4, 9, 33, 130, 204; **33:** 44; mediators' proposals, **30:** 87; G. L. Record's solution of the land problem, **30:** 131,n1; expenses of ambassador in, **30:** 153
F. *Villa:* and decree by, **30:** 444-47; U.S. compliments on reforms, **30:** 450; Obregón-Villa program for, **31:** 69-70, 71, 73
rumor of proposed joint intervention of Germany and England, **33:** 298,n1; interruption of cable communications, **33:** 459, 460-61; and Japan, **33:** 467n1; *see also,* Mexican Revolution; Mexico and the United States; and under names of individual figures such as Carranza, Venustiano; Huerta, Victoriano
Mexico, Gulf of, **27:** 519
Mexico, S.S., **29:** 464, 477
Mexico and the United States, **27:** ix, xv, xxi, 64,n1,2, 158n1, 252,n2,3, 331-32, 383; **28:** 7, 8, 37-40, 57-58, 58, 69, 84, 89, 96, 101, 105, 107, 110-11, 139, 139-

42, 148, 152-56, 167, 190-91, 191, 193-94, 195-96, 204, 205, 205-206, 207, 217-18, 219, 219-20, 220, 223-24,n1, 232-33, 241, 249, 268, 288, 293, 341, 376-78, 384, 386-87, 423, 455,n1, 464, 471-74, 476-78, 482-83, 483-84, 486-87, 488,n2,3, 505, 506, 516, 516-17, 539, 567-68, 569-70, 574-75, 579-80, 600; **29:** 159-60, 170, 174, 211, 230, 237, 294-97, 311, 377-78, 468; **30:** 14, 178-79, 389, 441; **31:** 88, 112, 143, 150, 178-79, 206, 233, 322, 374, 380, 413, 545; **32:** 38-39, 57, 180, 201-202,n2,3, 342-44, 427,n1, 463-64; **33:** 29, 52, 69n1, 71, 153, 230, 239,n1, 251, 272, 292-93, 294-95, 324, 368, 397-98, 400, 420, 435, 436,n2, 447, 448, 449-50, 459-60, 466, 478, 479, 479-80, 487, 537; **34:** 41,n1,2, 59-60, 79-80, 132-33, 160, 164, 179, 241-42, 338, 346; **35:** 295, 295-96, 314-15, 323, 483, 492, 504; **36:** 10-11, 17, 21, 69, 104, 186n1, 187, 643, 657; **37:** 105, 121, 169n1, 181, 231, 268, 336, 338, 396, 452, 453-54, 519; **38:** 10, 11, 13, 17, 36-37, 101, 133, 146, 271, 293,n2, 306
ambassadorship discussions, **27:** 64, 127, 130, 163, 228, 383, 385; **30:** 463; Naval Board requests ships sent to, **27:** 160
U.S. recognition of, **27:** 289, 325, 330-31, 383, 435-36, 437-40, 460-61, 465, 471-72, 481, 482, 510, 518; **28:** 39, 57, 136-37, 145, 152, 167, 201-202, 226, 377, 381, 386, 455n1, 539; **30:** 297-98, 321-22; possibility of U.S. recognition of Carranza, **33:** 9-10, 45-47, 51, 302-303, 303-304,n1, 304-305, 306, 414, 415, 415-16, 419; U.S. recognition of Carranza's *de facto* government, **34:** 487-89; **35:** 93-95, 97-103; talk of withdrawing U.S. recognition, **38:** 361, 373
and oil interests, **27:** 331; **28:** 469, 527, 575; **29:** 160; **30:** 245-47; W. B. Hale and, **27:** 396n1, 483, 536-52; **28:** 200-201, 411-12; railroads, **27:** 404,n2,3, 479-80; D. J. Hoff's observations, **27:** 419-25; H. L. Wilson and, **27:** 435-36; **28:** 17, 18-20, 22, 92n1,2, 433; J. B. Moore, **27:** 437; **28:** 212-15; **29:** 216n2; Bryan's desire to send gunboats into Gulf, **27:** 519; Del Valle mission, **28:** 6-7,n1,2, 26-27; Americans in, **28:** 32-33, 49-50, 50-52, 167, 194, 230, 356-57,n1; **29:** 256, 259, 429; views on intervention, **28:** 33-34, 51, 136, 246-47, 525, 529; and Great Britain, **28:** 34, 376-78, 388, 410-11, 421-22, 528, 529, 564-65, 571, 573-74, 575-79; C. H. Dodge on, **28:** 41-42; elections, **28:** 49, 281-82, 322-23, 339, 340-41, 356-57, 370, 377, 386, 399, 601-602; F. Escudero, **28:** 59, 59-60, 70-81; Fall resolution, **28:** 68n1, 82; E. A. Wilson, **28:** 99, 108, 143, 178, 195, 315, 331

J. Lind: introduction and instructions of, 28: 109, 110-11; interview and message to Gamboa, 28: 157-59, 188-89, 225-27; meets WW off Gulfport, 29: 98,n1; advises stopping coal supply to Federalists, 29: 101; WW's notes from conversation with, 29: 110; report on, 29: 118-27; interview with G. H. Hewitt, 29: 190; proposes intervention, 287, 290; wishes to publicize correspondence of Taft administration, 38: 239-40

WW's circular notes and drafts to the powers, 28: 130, 431-32,n1, 434, 502-504, 504; H. S. Breckinridge memorandum, 28: 130-31; F. Gamboa's replies, 28: 168-75, 233-39; Nicaraguan loan, 28: 177; M. Storey on, 28: 203; Joint Resolution of 1912, 28: 213-14; loan proposal, 28: 216, 226, 235, 238; WW's address to joint session of Congress, 28: 227-31; WW and neutrality, 28: 230; O. G. Villard on Mexican situation, 28: 240; A. Urrutia's resignation, 28: 278,n2; U.S. and northern leaders, 28: 347-48; possibility of recognizing the rebels, 28: 382-83; presence of war ships, 28: 386; and recognition of Díaz government, 28: 460; WW draft of a joint resolution, 28: 478-79; WW draft of address to Congress, 28: 479-81; U.S. demands, 28: 481, 562

V. Huerta: proposition regarding Congress, 28: 537-39; WW plans to force retirement of, 28: 566; proposals of, 28: 591-92, 601; WW desires to have overcome by domestic forces, 29: 138; resignation only acceptable solution, 29: 260; 30: 289; Bryan fears return of, 32: 468,n2; meets with Straus, 33: 89-90, 106; and arrest in U.S., 33: 456, 468, 470-71, 473

V. Carranza: and Constitutionalists, 28: 545-46, 557, 558-59, 559-60,n1, 561, 563-64; Hale in communication with agent of, 29: 90-91; note to regarding possibility of U.S. sending guards into Mexico City or seizing communication lines, 29: 143; willing to meet representatives of F. Carbajal, 30: 290, 291; plans for a permanent government, 30: 489-90; evacuation of U.S. troops from Veracruz, 31: 18-19, 71-73, 75; reply to ultimatum, 32: 346-49; declaration to the Mexican people, 33: 416-17,n2; on U.S., 36: 313,n1, 342-43,n2; wishes U.S. troops withdrawn, 36: 540,n1, 582-83; U.S. warning to, 37: 248-63

U.S. protection of other nationals, 28: 571, 575; note on U.S. purpose, 28: 585-86; WW's "watchful waiting," 29: 5, 13, 178-79, 198, 259, 261, 285, 301n1, 302; WW wishes W. H. Page to be informed of situation, 29: 20; J. Bryce on, 29: 47-48; L. Wood not consulted on situation, 29: 74n1; E. G. Lowry article on WW's policy, 29: 92-98; L. Carden desires meeting with WW on, 29: 131; E. M. House on intervention, 29: 135; Cabrera desires interview with WW or Bryan, 29: 142; idea of joint intervention with Great Britain, 29: 144, 145-46,n1; and Carden's interest in, 29: 146,n2; and communications between Mexico City and Veracruz, 29: 161; L. Wood on, 29: 168, 248,n1, 249, 250; proposal to raise arms embargo, 29: 178-79, 185-86, 197, 197-98, 198, 205-206, 206-208, 210; effect of situation on U.S. foreign relations, 29: 181-82; Cabrera reveals Constitutionalists' plans, 29: 187-89, 191-95; order lifting arms embargo rescinded, 29: 216-17; WW on, 29: 228-31; 30: 360; 37: 36, 49, 252-53, 281, 282, 333-34, 347, 385-86; 38: 133-35, 328, 330; Cabrera gives Mexican view of the situation, 29: 249n2; American interests in, 29: 251; T. B. Hohler meets with Bryan and WW, 29: 251-55, 255-61; Spring Rice on Hohler's visit to Washington, 29: 267-68; WW unhappy about newspaper coverage, 29: 284

Benton affair: general, 29: 288, 291, 292, 293-94, 297, 300-301, 320,n1, 328, 348; 30: 4, 215; J. Buchanan and, 29: 292,n1; Carden on intervention, 29: 324; F. Adams on joint intervention, 29: 329-30; Lind meets with Portillo y Rojas on, 29: 357-58; American bankers and aid to Huerta, 29: 381; repeated offenses against U.S., 29: 433-34

Tampico affair: general, 29: 420-21, 426-29, 429,n1, 430-32, 432-33, 433, 434-35, 438-39, 440-43, 448, 454, 458, 461, 463, 492, 493, 521; 30: 5, 78, 124, 235; 38: 299; gunboat at, 29: 110; Constitutionalists and, 29: 111n1; 30: 79, 80, 130, 220-21, 246; railways, 29: 124; Huerta suspends order for blockade, 30: 159; and gun salute demands, 29: 429, 434, 446-47, 449, 450-51, 453, 455, 458-59, 462-64; U.S. will not sign protocol on salute, 29: 464-65, 465, 466, 466-67; resolution on use of armed forces to enforce demands, 29: 471n1; WW's address to Congress on, 29: 471-72; Carranza on, 29: 484-85, 486; H. A. Garfield on, 29: 496; uniformed orderly arrested in Veracruz, 29: 433, 435, 440, 461, 472; withholding of U.S. dispatches in Mexico City, 29: 435, 441, 472; Pacific blockade plans, 29: 443, 452, 454-55; compared to Progreso blockade, 32: 369-70, 370

Veracruz invasion: Ypiranga arrival at, 29: 464, 476-77,n1; Admiral Fletcher ordered to seize customs house, 29: 477; Americans urged to leave, 29: 478; U.S.

Mexico and the United States (*cont.*)
landing and occupation of, **29:** 480, 481, 482n1, 484, 492, 524-25, 534; Carranza orders U.S. to withdraw from, **29:** 485; and blockade, **29:** 493; H. A. Garfield on, **29:** 496; W. Kent on, **29:** 499-500; F. Funston ordered to, **29:** 509, 510; WW address to Congress on and request of approval of use of armed forces at, **29:** 471-74; Christians and antiwar sentiment, **29:** 474-75, 475-76; WW statement on, **29:** 488; breaking of diplomatic relations, **29:** 488-90, 492; O. G. Villard on, **29:** 495-96; Carranza must state neutrality, **29:** 497-98; and border protection, **29:** 498; T. D. Jones on, **29:** 501; Villa on Carranza note, **29:** 504-505; U.S. troops at, **30:** 7-8, 11, 11-12, 26, 28, 361; **31:** 23-24, 33, 43, 64, 313; WW on reasons for Veracruz occupation, **31:** 351-52

ABC mediation: general, **29:** 505-506, 506-507, 507, 534; **30:** 47, 48, 64, 81, 96-98, 99-103, 131, 201, 241; **31:** 354; **34:** 43, 80, 81, 444, 448, 487-88; M. Storey on, **29:** 508; S. G. Blythe on, **29:** 516-24; **30:** 78n1; Huerta accepts offer, **29:** 518; Bryan urges Carranza to accept offer, **29:** 525; C. W. Eliot on, **29:** 533-34; Lind on, **29:** 539-40, 549-52; **30:** 113n2; American interests in, **29:** 550; H. W. Bones on, **29:** 554; special commissioners appointed, **30:** 32; WW briefs special commissioners, **30:** 39-42; J. Reed interview with WW and article on, **30:** 42, 156, 157, 186-87, 189, 192-93, 219-20, 223, 233-38; E. Suárez-Mujica on Carranza, **30:** 45; and plans for provisional government, **30:** 49-50, 55-56, 57, 67, 83-84; proposal to have Huerta resign, **30:** 55-56; WW's alternate plan, **30:** 56-57, 57; U.S. desire to have Constitutionalists participate in, **30:** 58; Huerta promises to cooperate, **30:** 59; A. Carnegie on withdrawing forces, **30:** 61-62; mediators decline to invite Constitutionalists, **30:** 64; request armistice, **30:** 66, 67, 68; U.S. and nonintervention, **30:** 69, 69-71; U.S. propositions and, **30:** 71-72, 75-77; and problem of title of Huerta's representatives, **30:** 77, 83, 113, 115-16, 121, 228-29; and Great Britain, **30:** 77, 215; daily account by Spring Rice, **30:** 78-82; WW hopeful of settlement, **30:** 82; mediators' proposition, **30:** 87-88; WW on Constitutionalists and neutral provisional government, **30:** 91-93; and evacuation of U.S. troops, **30:** 97, 100, 102-103, 139, 199, 204, 228; mediators agree to accept Constitutionalists' letter, **30:** 101-102; and signing of protocol, **30:** 117-18, 207-208, 225-26, 239-40, 241-42; and admission of Carranza's delegates, **30:** 118, 119, 120-21,

121-22, 122, 123-26, 132, 133, 135, 136; U.S. could not recognize a provisional government made up of neutrals, **30:** 137-39; Bryan on Huerta, **30:** 137-39; Huerta suspends order for blockade of Tampico, **30:** 159; J. R. Silliman's impression of Carranza, **30:** 166, 167-69; S. Brooks on WW and, **30:** 192-93,n1; break between Villa and Carranza, **30:** 193-94,n1; Villa receptive to U.S. mediation proposal, **30:** 194; R. S. Naón meets with WW, **30:** 198-99; WW agrees to provisional government, **30:** 199; Bryan and amendments, **30:** 203, 204; and amnesty to foreigners in, **30:** 208; and restoration of diplomatic relations, **30:** 208; Villa returns to North and halts fighting, **30:** 220-21; U.S. and provisional government, **30:** 228-29; WW favors recess of talks, **30:** 229; WW hopes revolution will benefit Mexican people, **30:** 230; WW on conditions in, **30:** 252; thanks to ABC governments, **30:** 259, 362; Huerta abdicates, **30:** 285n2

congratulatory messages: W. C. Adamson, **30:** 286-87; House, **30:** 287-88; W. H. Page, **30:** 289; T. D. Jones, **30:** 292-93; J. R. Wilson, Jr., **30:** 302,n1; C. H. Dodge, **30:** 304; and protection of foreign nationals, **30:** 4, 9-10, 33, 80, 131; C. W. Eliot on lecture of G. G. Wilson, **30:** 5-6, 73-74; and Great Britain's fears of Villa and E. Zapata, **30:** 9; G. F. Williams on "watchful waiting," **30:** 25-26; views of Villa, **30:** 29; U.S. prepared to invade Mexico if necessary, **30:** 33; WW's policy in, **30:** 39-42; money necessary in Mexico to restore order, **30:** 40-41; new government and U.S. and world opinion, **30:** 297-98

F. Villa: on Carranza and Torreón Agreement, **30:** 311, 339-40; H. J. Browne suggests Lind reconcile Villa-Carranza dispute, **30:** 346-48; West's interviews with, **32:** 383-91; and financing of activities of, **36:** 396,n1; WW stands by nonintervention, **30:** 362

P. Fuller: and memorandum of, **30:** 408-18; Bryan on memorandum of, **30:** 443-44; letters of introduction to Carranza and Villa, **30:** 494-95; report of, **31:** 65-74; to be liaison between, **33:** 487-88 and Catholic Church, **30:** 424; E. Zapata desires meeting in Washington of his representatives, **31:** 12-13; L. Carden's unauthorized interview on U.S. troop withdrawal, **31:** 61n1; I. Fabela urges recognition of provisional government, **31:** 67; hopes for establishment of constitutional government, **31:** 67-68; and new provisional president, **31:** 322,n1; and customs collection, **31:** 323; and criticism by American Cath-

olics of U.S. policy, **31:** 333,n1, 470-71; WW praises F. Funston for handling of Veracruz situation, **31:** 375-76; Bryan recommends letter on protection of worship, **31:** 380; Bryan pleased with Villa and Zapata actions in Mexico City, **31:** 411,n2; border conflicts endangering Americans, **31:** 431; idea of joint appeal by ABC powers, **32:** 117-18, 343, 364, 364-65, 398; Father F. C. Kelly and Roman Catholic situation, **32:** 86, 128-29, 134, 248-49, 279-81, 365, 393, 393-95, 404; **33:** 30n1; D. West appointed special agent, **32:** 202,n2, 202-203, 203-204, 210; J. M. Dickinson on, **32:** 218-19; Eliot on, **32:** 263-64, 276; campaign against Americans in, **32:** 326-27,n1, 331-32; S. Brooks on, **32:** 328n3; ultimatum sent to Obregón and Carranza, **32:** 331-32; and Pan-American Pact, **32:** 340; Spring Rice informs Grey of situation, **32:** 342; and Americans in, **32:** 352-53, 363-64, 437,n1; **36:** 364; peace plan of Benevides and generals in, **32:** 355-56, 356; and Progreso blockade, **32:** 367,n1, 369-70,n1; and Bishop Currier's counterrevolutionary movement, **32:** 392,n1, 395-96; G. A. Esteva suggests U.S. intervention, **32:** 431-32; plans of uprising of foreigners in Mexico City, **32:** 477-78, 478; D. West to see Zapata, **32:** 507,n1, 508; Arredondo presents Carranza's views, **33:** 3-10, 12; West on, **33:** 65,n1, 187n1, 194, 217-18,n1; need for food and aid in Mexico, **33:** 258, 307-308; E. Iturbide on, **33:** 258-59, 260-62 and WW's public appeal for relief, **33:** 266, 275; D. Lawrence on, **33:** 268-73, 409-10; **34:** 383, 383-85, 386-87, 388, 409, 530-33; **36:** 307, 309; **37:** 15-19; and R. González Garza, **33:** 343-44,n1,2, 349; Dodge on, **33:** 383; desire of U.S. to involve ABC and other powers, **33:** 437, 454-55; S. Untermeyer suggests U.S. loan, **33:** 438-40; and Mrs. Harriman, **33:** 461-62, 470, 477; Lane interview with Ángeles, **33:** 463-64; and armistice possibilities, **33:** 465-66,n1; and Lansings' propositions, **33:** 475-76, 487-88; House on, **33:** 477; **34:** 80-81, 106; and H. A. Garfield's plan, **33:** 533,n1; U.S. plan for pacification without force, **34:** 106,n2; L. Steffens on Carranza and, **34:** 147-48; E. Martinez on, **34:** 148-49,n1, 174-75; R. L. Metcalf on recognition of Carranza and, **34:** 198-200; and National City Bank of New York, **34:** 382,n1, 401,n1; Bishop Candler in, **35:** 45-46; talk of American ambassador to, **35:** 359; murder of Americans at Santa Ysabel, **35:** 478,n1; and F. Díaz attacks in Mexico, **35:** 501-502,n1, 505; Columbus raid and fate of raiders, **36:** 280n1,

281, 282, 282-83, 283, 284-85, 308,n1, 566, 606, 653-54; **37:** 31, 62, 154, 155, 159,n1, 170-72, 251, 252, 258, 261, 299; **38:** 224, 233, 379; A. G. Gardiner on WW's policy, **36:** 320n1

and Punitive Expedition, **36:** 284-86,n2, 286-87, 287, 295, 298, 300, 310, 312-13, 317,n1, 318-19,n1, 323-24, 331-32, 335,n1,2, 338-40, 343-44,n1, 350,n2, 352-53, 379, 382,n1,2, 397, 456-58, 463-64, 474, 501-503, 528-29; **37:** 38, 130, 138,n1, 248-63, 297; statement for press not for publication, **36:** 351; WW warns press on reporting of, **36:** 364-66; varied cabinet opinions on, **36:** 424, 434-35; J. J. Pershing on, **36:** 584-91; withdrawal of U.S. troops, **36:** 593-94; **37:** 130, 138,n1, 152-55; F. Funston recommends withdrawal of and establishment of border control, **38:** 44-45 and A. B. Fall, **36:** 395,n1, 407-408n1,2, 409, 416; and Parral incident, **36:** 480,n1,2, 496,n1, 502, 590-91,n9; and Scott-Obregón conference and agreement, **36:** 540-41, 553-54, 570-71, 572, 579-80, 603-604, 607-608, 618; Lansing on diplomatic relations, **36:** 604-605; **37:** 275-77, 306-307; and Scott-Funston-Obregón meetings, **37:** 22-24, 38-39, 253; and 1916 platform, **37:** 200n3; and joint labor-union convention, **37:** 245-46, 266-67, 365-66,n1, 369; and Carrizal incident, **37:** 277,n1, 280, 281, 292, 293-94, 300, 306-307,n1, 307-308, 309,n2, 316, 317-19, 348, 349; **38:** 227, 378-86; N. D. Baker on war preparations by U.S., **37:** 283-86, 296-98

Joint High Commission: comments on, **37:** 291,n1,2, 308, 308-309,n1,2, 314, 348-50, 366n1, 400-401, 402, 403, 422, 430-31, 436, 453-54, 465-66, 470, 487-88, 490, 497; Mexican note on, **37:** 409-10, 410-11, 437-38, 453-54, 482-84, 488-89; draft of reply to Mexican note on, **37:** 483-84; selection of commissioners, **38:** 13, 22, 22-23,n1, 28, 31, 43, 63n1, 79,n1; and negotiations by, **38:** 83, 84, 121-22, 153, 155-56, 166, 167, 169-70, 219-20, 293n2, 300-301, 633; W. J. Stone on, **38:** 279; American proposal on troop withdrawal and border control, **38:** 634-35

Tumulty urges a strong stand, **37:** 291-92; WW's plan of action, **37:** 293; and effect on Pan-American Pact, **37:** 293, 399, 400; demand for and release of Carrizal prisoners, **37:** 293-94, 321n1, 324n1, 344,n1, 360, 360-61; WW drafts request to occupy northern Mexico, **37:** 298, 298-304, 304; comments and suggestions on situation, **37:** 310-11, 320-21, 322, 323-24, 331-32, 341, 342-43, 344-45, 404, 424-25, 441; F. Funston's strategic plans, **37:** 315; WW calls out National Guard to protect border, **37:**

212 INDEX

Mexico and the United States (*cont.*)
321n1; Baker wishes WW to define
duty of American soldier in Mexico, **37:**
337, 359; Naón offers to explain U.S.
good intention to Mexico, **37:** 361-62;
U.S. replies to Mexican note, **37:** 367-
68, 368; WW article in *Ladies Home
Journal* on, **37:** 508-12; T. H. Bliss on,
38: 228-32, 233-35, 675-78, 397-405;
Baker on, **38:** 235-37; Grey on, **38:** 255-
56; possible revival of Villa pursuit, **38:**
271-72; C. E. Hughes challenge regarding Huerta, **38:** 292; WW on not
publicizing confidential correspondence, **38:** 312-13; Eliot on, **38:** 352-53;
F. K. Lane on stalemate in negotiations, **38:** 355-62; WW's recommendations, **38:** 373-74; S. Gompers on, **38:**
470; Bishop McConnell on, **38:** 520,n2;
rumors of another Mexican border raid,
38: 523, 548,n1; Funston's plans should
Villa capture Chihuahua City, **38:** 546-
47; Cabrera proposal for border protection, **38:** 535-36; *see also*: under
names of individuals such as Bryan,
William Jennings; Hale, William Bayard; Carranza, Venustiano; Huerta,
Victoriano
Mexico, D. F., Mexico: *see* Mexico City,
Mexico
Mexico City, Mexico, **27:** 437-40; **28:** 27,
29, 30, 32, 77, 78, 79, 80, 101,n2, 110,
136, 140, 142, 152, 214, 217, 229, 233,
241, 299, 325, 340, 341, 384, 479,
517n1, 546; **29:** 4, 15, 17, 30, 74, 118,
124, 168, 196, 207, 223, 231, 249, 295-
96, 329, 359, 378, 453, 459, 492, 539;
30: 11; **31:** 12, 13, 66, 374, 381, 441,n2;
33: 239,n1, 266, 303, 304, 410, 436n2,
448; **34:** 41,n1,2, 382n1, 532
Carranza's plans, **28:** 541; R. F. Del
Valle, **28:** 6-7,n2, 10; demonstrations
against Americans, **28:** 37, 38; W. B.
Hale on advance to, **29:** 90; and railway between Veracruz and, **29:** 110,
126, 143, 161, 206; stories of sending
marines to, **29:** 174n1, 291; rights of
Americans in, **29:** 119-21; J. Lind on, **29:**
286-87, 338; American dispatches
withheld at, **29:** 433, 435, 441, 472; and
Mexican soldiers from Veracruz, **29:**
478; and English concern about, **30:** 4,
9, 80-81; and U.S. plans for sending
troops to, **30:** 8; U.S. on protection of
foreigners in, **30:** 9-10; Constitutionalists advance toward, **30:** 57, 67-68,
69, 81, 117, 130-31, 132, 133, 139, 193-
94, 285n1; and reforms in, **30:** 71-72;
and recognition of government in, **30:**
138; Villa and, **30:** 220; and transfer
of power in, **30:** 291, 297; Villa on convention at, **30:** 339; L. Carden's views
of, **31:** 61n1; crisis in, **32:** 202,n3,
326,n1, 331, 332, 342, 343, 384, 387,
478; Carranza and Obregón on situa-

tion in, **32:** 347; Carranza allows food
into, **33:** 307, 308; fighting in, **33:** 459-
60, 460-61; and Red Cross, **33:** 466
Mexico City *Mexican Herald*, **27:** 460-
61,n2; **28:** 205,n1, 429,n1; **36:** 364n1
Meyer, George Von Lengerke, **31:** 55,n1
Meyer, Michael C., **28:** 391n1, 482n1; **31:**
74n2; **33:** 456n1
Meyer Gerhard, Anton, **33:** 317n2,3, 319,
478
Mezes, Annie O. Hunter (Mrs. Sidney
Edward), **29:** 245n2; **35:** 46
Mezes, Sidney Edward, **29:** 56, 245-46,
262, 277,n1; **30:** 7; **35:** 46, 279; **37:** 117,
420
M.I.T.: *see* Massachusetts Institute of
Technology
Miami Valley (Ohio), **27:** 230
Mice and Men (Ryley), **28:**400n1
Michelena, Santiago, **33:** 218,n3
Michigan, **28:** 222, 463; **30:** 333n1; **38:**
499; proposed investigation of copper
mines, **29:** 46n1; WW's addresses in
Detroit, **37:** 383-87, 387-95; and woman
suffrage, **37:** 523
Michigan, U.S.S., **29:** 127
Michigan, University of, **27:** 206
Michoacán, state, Mex., **28:** 77; **30:**
414,n9; **32:** 387; **33:** 261
Middletown, Conn., **34:** 87; **35:** 393
*Midwest Decision, 1915: A Landmark in
Conservation History* (Bates), **37:**
140n2
Miguel, Dom, **27:** 438
Mikhail, Grand Duke of Russia (Mikhail
Mikhaelovich, 1861-1929), **34:** 310,n2
Military Affairs, Committee on (House
of Reps.), **34:** 38,n1, 58n1; **35:** 138, 470,
479, 481-82, 494, 500, 503; **36:** 134-35,
141, 170-71, 176, 178
Military Affairs, Committee on (Sen-
ate), **35:** 138
military bill: *see* army reorganization bill
Military Order of the Carabao, **29:** 36,n2,
44, 54-55, 74
militia: *see* United States Army
militia pay bill, **35:** 105, 106, 138-39, 140
Miliukov, Pavel Nikolaevich, **37:** 90,n2
Mill, John Stuart, **31:** 316,n2
Millar, H. Percye, **38:** 475,n1
Millard, Alfred, **36:** 422-23,n1
Milledgeville, Ga., **31:** 259n1
Miller, Adolph Caspar, **29:** 278,n1, 532;
30: 52, 53, 54, 181n1; **33:** 279n1, 331,
332-33, 347,n1; **34:** 107, 276-77, 278,
279-80, 369; **35:** 64, 279; **37:** 291
Miller, C. C., **37:**159n1
Miller, Charles, **34:** 338n2
Miller, Charles, Jr., **34:** 338,n2
Miller, Charles DeWitt, **37:** 159,n1
Miller, Charles Ransom, **38:** 388,n1
Miller, Clarence Benjamin, **29:** 166; **34:**
391,n1
Miller, David Hunter, **35:** 178,n2
Miller, George A., **29:** 476

Miller, Hugh Gordon, **38:** 362n1
Miller, Lucius Hopkins, **28:** 88,n3
Miller, Rufus Wilder, **29:** 361,n1
Miller Bridge, Westmorland, **28:** 286
millinery manufacture, **27:** 186
Mills, Albert Leopold, **35:** 138,n1; **36:** 238,n9
Mills, Charles W., **31:** 369,n1, 376n1, 406-407, 424, 474, 475, 503, 523; **35:** 540; **36:** 237, 245
Milton, John, **28:** 126; **31:** 223
Milton, Mass., **28:** 291, 310
Milwaukee, Wisc., **35:** 165; **38:** 290; WW's address on preparedness in, **36:** 55-63
Milwaukee Journal, **31:** 346n1, 406; **32:** 20; **34:** 388,n1; **35:** 210; **37:** 27,n1, 220; **38:** 290, 451n
Milwaukee *Wisconsin*, **36:** 172n2
Mimi: *see* Brown, Mary Celestine Mitchell
Mind of One Piece: Brandeis and American Reform (Urofsky), **36:** 25n1
Mindanao, P.I., **27:** 370; **28:** 242n1
Mine Owner's Association, **36:** 592n1
mine workers: *see* United Mine Workers of America
Miner, Dwight Carroll, **33:** 46n3
Mines, Bureau of, **29:** 10
Mines and Mining, Committee on (House of Reps.), **29:** 46n1
Ministerial Association of the City of Pueblo (Colo.), **28:** 512
Minneapolis, Minn.: American Union Against Militarism meeting in, **36:** 635
Minnesota, **27:** 514; **38:** 159,n4
Minnesota, U.S.S., **29:** 472
Minnesota, University of, **28:** 295n3; **36:** 635
Minor, John Barbee, **32:** 3n1
Minor, Raleigh Colston, **32:** 3-4,n1, 10-11, 18
Miramichi, S.S., **31:** 506
Miranda, Thomas N., **35:** 431,n1
Miss Murraye's Dismissal (La Follette), **28:** 403,n2
Mission of Colonel House (*Le Figaro*), **35:** 525n3
Mission Sir Roger Casements im Deutschen Reich, 1914-16 (Doerries), **36:** 503n1
missionaries: China, **27:** 329
Missionaries, Chinese, and Diplomats: The American Protestant Missionary Movement in China 1890-1952 (Varg), **27:** 27n1
Mississippi, **37:** 514; tariff, **27:** 418n
Mississippi River, **36:** 250, 366n1
Mississippi Valley, **31:** 446
Missouri, **32:** 325n1; **37:** 503; **38:** 196, 376n1, 457-58, 515n1; politics in, **31:** 353n1; **35:** 179, 183, 185, 191; WW's speeches on preparedness in, **36:** 110-14, 114-21, 173-74
Mr. Bryan and $10,000,000 (*Washington Post*), **34:** 486n1

Mr. Bryan's Resignation (*Washington Post*), **33:** 378,n1
Mr. Dooley Comments on Current Politics (Dunne), **29:** 56,n2
Mr. Dooley on Diplomatic Indiscretions (Dunne), **29:** 333n1
Mr. Hughes and the Task Ahead (*New Republic*), **38:** 3n4
Mr. Wilson and National Defense (*New York Times*), **34:** 131,n2
Mr. Wilson's Contribution (Angell), **37:** 294n1
Mr. Wilson's Part: Good Intentions and Hard Facts. To the Editor of the Times (Baring), **37:** 143n1
Mr. Wilson's Policy and the Pact of Peace (Gardiner), **36:** 320,n1, 379,n6, 380
Mistress of Shenstone (Barclay), **31:** 316n2, 317
Mitchel, John Purroy, **27:** 384n1, 410, 432-33; **28:** 64; **29:** 136n1, 277, 423; **30:** 21; **31:** 139, 148; **34:** 237; **35:** 503, 505; **36:** 346, 381, 525, 542, 642; **37:** 332,n1; **38:** 591n1; collectorship of New York Port, **27:** 401,n1, 402-403, 407, 409-10, 418; **28:** 374-75, 419-20, 524; and mayoralty, **28:** 139, 490n2; Negro vote, **28:** 211, 289, 402,n2
Mitchell, Charles Wellman, **32:** 8; **35:** 262n3, 275; illness and death of, **36:** 349,n1, 359, 377, 397,n1
Mitchell, Henry Sparrow, **31:** 357,n1
Mitchell, John J., **31:** 76
Mitchell, Roscoe Conkling, **37:** 441,n4
Mitchell, Samuel Chiles, **31:** 261
Mitchell, Silas Weir, **30:** 106
Mixer, Knowlton, **38:** 572,n1
Mobile, Ala., **28:** 434,n1, 453n1; WW address in, **28:** 448-452
Mobile Item, **28:** 452,n4
Modern Greece: Profile of a Nation (Kousoulas), **38:** 107n1
Modern School (Flexner), **36:** 513,n1
Modoc County High School (California), **30:** 172n1
Moffat, Graham, **28:** 355,n5
Moffat Coal Co., **29:** 549
Moffett, William Adger, **29:** 125
Moger, Allen W., **27:** 73n2
Moheno, Querido, **28:** 356-57
Mohler, Henry Keller, **36:** 552,n1
Môle St. Nicolas, Haiti, **27:** 519,n3, 553, 557; **31:** 457; **32:** 28, 440, 472, 479; **33:** 117, 277; **34:** 67, 143, 144, 158
Moltke, Helmuth von, Count (1876-1939), **30:** 108,n2
Moltke, Helmuth James von (1907-1945), **30:** 108n2
Moltke, Helmuth Johannes Ludwig von, Count (1848-1916), **30:** 108n2
Moltke, Helmuth Karl Bernhard von, Count (1800-1891), **30:** 108n2
Monadnock (ship), **27:** 426
Monclova, Mex., **27:** 422n1; **28:** 29, 31
Mondell, Frank Wheeler, **30:** 226,n2

Mondragon, Manuel, **27:** 537, 548
monetary reform: *see* banking reform;
  currency reform
money trust, **30:** 50, 52; **37:** 189; L. D.
  Brandeis, **27:** 521; R. L. Henry, **27:** 523-
  24; D. V. Stephens on, **28:** 346
Mongolia, **27:** 28, 488: *see also* Inner
  Mongolia
Monmouth County, N.J., **38:** 118n3
Monmouth Memorial Hospital, Long
  Branch, N.J., **38:** 118n3
monopoly, **27:** 34-35, 36, 47, 121, 122, 271,
  570, 572; **28:** 351; **29:** 7, 153, 155, 175,
  176; **31:** 170-71, 325, 326; **35:** 323, 324,
  427n1, 434n1; N.J. Laws, **27:** 47;
  S. Gompers on, **27:** 184, 366-67; A. O.
  Stanley on, **29:** 25-30; W. C. Redfield
  on, **29:** 40, 43; S. J. Graham on, **29:**
  107; and federal trade commission bill,
  30: 274n1, 349, 430; and Clayton bill,
  30: 481, 482; **31:** 42,n3, 46n2, 78; WW
  on accomplishments of Congress regarding, **31:** 169; Republican and
  Democratic differences, **31:** 171;
  A. Pinchot on, **36:** 22-23
Monon Railroad, **30:** 344
Monroe, James, **35:** 254, 295; **36:** 43, 71,
  320n1
Monroe Doctrine, **27:** 130, 420; **28:** 55,
  95, 195, 431, 455,n1, 458, 459, 468, 476-
  77, 593; **29:** 53, 111,n2, 334, 522; **30:**
  40, 237; **31:** 8, 160, 355, 549; **32:** 474,
  505; **33:** 55, 56, 57, 59, 79, 116, 220,
  222, 298; **34:** 239; **35:** 55, 133, 202, 246-
  53, 253-54, 263, 295, 430-31, 440, 444-
  45; **36:** 43, 71, 94, 236, 320n1, 440; **37:**
  76n1, 108, 120, 166, 216, 486, 509; and
  Benton case, **29:** 320n1; and W. H.
  Page, **29:** 333,n1; WW's corollary to,
  31: 35; and 1916 platform plank, **37:**
  169n1, 196, 200n3
Montague, Ludwell Lee, **34:** 67n1
Montana, **38:** 159, 297, 376n1, 515n1;
  Indians in, **31:** 77
Montana, University of, **31:** 405n2
Montana Power Co., **38:** 182n3
Montaño, Otilio E., **31:** 12,n4
Montenegro, **37:** 5, 464
Monterey, Nuevo León, Mex., **30:** 29, 290
Monterey (ship), **27:** 426
Monteros, Carlos Espinosa de los, Mar-
  qués de Valtierra, **33:** 47,n2
Montesquieu, Charles de Secondat, Baron
  de La Brède et de, **27:** 159
Montezuma Hotel, Nogales, Ariz., **28:** 527
Monteglas, Adolf von, **35:** 489-91,n2
Montgomery, Ala., **29:** 383,n1
Montgomery, David C., **35:** 258n1
Montgomery, John Knox, **29:** 44,n1
Monticello, **32:** 82, 85-86,n1; **37:** 482,n1
Montreat, N.C., **30:** 452,n3; **31:** 259
Montreuil, M. (of Haiti), **31:** 485
Mooney, Charles Patrick Joseph, **36:** 240-
  41,n1,2
Mooney, Daniel Francis, **28:** 354,n4

Moonstone (Collins), **35:** 374n1, 399
Moore, Alexander Pollock, **27:** 406,n1
Moore, Charles Cadwell, **32:** 118,n2
Moore, John Bassett, **27:** 191, 203, 311,
  405, 406; **29:** 86, 248; **30:** 200; **34:** 42;
  36: 226n2, 267n1; **37:** 365; and Japan,
  27: 403-404, 416, 441, 453n1, 460; **28:**
  14,n1, 16, 21; and Mexico, **27:** 437-40;
  28: 194, 206, 212-15, 381, 382, 384, 388-
  89, 460-61, 566-67, 571; J. Osborne incident, **27:** 163, 297-98,n1, 311-12, 314-
  15, 341-42; seeks to withdraw as
  Counselor of State Department, **27:**
  308-309, 327; and Nicaragua, **28:** 250;
  and seamen's bill, **28:** 412-13, 420; and
  Colombia, **28:** 534, 572-73; **29:** 37, 39,
  and draft of paper on Mexico, **28:** 422,
  423, 433,n1, 458-64, 474-75; resignation of, **29:** 215-16,n2, 309; search for
  successor, **29:** 331, 333, 356; international law text, **29:** 432
Moore, Joseph Hampton, **32:** 97
Moore, Willis Luther, **27:** 338,n1
Moore's Digest of International Law, **33:**
  46
Mora, Michael M. de la, **30:** 399, 399-400
Morawetz, Victor, **29:** 29
Morehead, John Henry, **33:** 336, 336-
  37,n1; **36:** 152n2; **38:** 342n3, 343n1
Morelia, Michoacán, Mex., **32:** 128
Morelos, state, Mex., **27:** 404n3, 539, 551;
  28: 7n2, 29, 77; **29:** 459; **31:** 12; **32:** 387;
  33: 218; Indians in, **28:** 294-95, 296-97
Morelos Zaragoza, Ignacio, **29:** 421, 428,
  438, 455, 458, 463
Moreno (Argentine battleship): WW's
  address aboard, **32:** 451-53
Morey, Lewis S., **37:** 277n1, 307, 308,
  309,n2, 317-18; **38:** 380-81, 383, 384,
  386
Morgan, Edward Denison (Alfred
  Waterman Morgan), **28:** 41,n1,2, 58
Morgan, Edward Denison, Sr., **28:** 41,n2
Morgan, Edward Denison, Jr., **28:** 41n2
Morgan, Edward M., **35:** 318,n1
Morgan, George Campbell, **29:** 263-64,n1,
  270-71
Morgan, Henry Hays, **32:** 505,n1
Morgan, J. P. and Co.: *see* J. P. Morgan
  and Co.
Morgan, John Pierpont, Sr., **27:** 216,
  232,n1; **28:** 333; **31:** 315
Morgan, John Pierpont, Jr., **27:** 232,n2;
  29: 101,n1, 102, 103; **30:** 213, 243,n1,
  244, 378, 431; **31:** 39-40, 82-83, 153,
  338, 386, 441, 552; **32:** 87,n1; **33:** 202,
  225; **37:** 411; on British reaction to U.S.
  purchase of German ships, **30:** 426-27;
  and transfer of ships, **30:** 447; on
  American investments, **30:** 483-85
Morgan, Josephine Perry (Mrs. Junius
  Spencer), **38:** 682,n2
Morgan, Junius Spencer, **38:** 682n,n2
Morgan, Kenneth O., **30:** 61n2
Morgan Art Collection, **27:** 72,n1

Morgan, Grenfel and Co., London, **29:** 381n1

Morganton, N.C., **28:** 369n2

Morgen, Lewis, **38:** 521

Morgenthau, Henry (1856-1946), **27:** 118, 119, 120, 244; **31:** 428, 471; **33:** 219; **35:** 119, 185,n1, 191, 192, 337; **36:** 348, 398, 458, 518, 522, 523, 530; **37:** 46, 73-74, 76, 151-52, 163, 178; **38:** 591n1; Jews and appointments, **27:** 513; Turkey, **27:** 118, 228, 384-85, 513; resigns as ambassador to Turkey, **36:** 356-57, 378, 425,n3; **37:** 96-97; on Brandeis nomination, **37:** 72-73

Morgenthau, Henry, Jr., **31:** 428,n2

Morgenthau, Josephine Sykes (Mrs. Henry), **31:** 428,n2; **35:** 119,n1

Morison, Elting Elmore, **31:** 277n3; **37:** 218n2

Morlan, Robert Loren, **38:** 159n4

Morley, John, 1st Viscount Morley of Blackburn, **27:** 297; **28:** 507, 572; **32:** 8, **34:** 463; **35:** 76; **38:** 23,n1

Moros (Filipino tribe), **28:** 242n1

Morris, Benjamin Wistar, **27:** 575

Morris, Frank, **27:** 159-60

Morris, John L., **30:** 45,n1

Morris, Roland Sletor, **29:** 222, 223n2; **31:** 187

Morris Canal, N.J., **27:** 52

Morrison, Frank, **31:** 331; **32:** 95, 96; **38:** 472

Morrison, George Ernest, **35:** 203,n1

Morrison, J. G., **35:** 213

Morristown, N.J., **34:** 293

Morro Castle, S.S. **28:** 471

Morse, Charles A., **29:** 401n1

Morse, John Torrey, **38:** 179n3

Morse, Richard Cary, **37:** 358,n1

Morton, Richard L., **27:** 73n2

Moscow, Russia, **34:** 306n2, 338

Moscow, University of, **36:** 654,n1; **37:** 90n2

Moss: *see* B. S. Moss Motion Picture Co.

Moss, Ralph W., **27:** 201; **29:** 132,n1

Mother Jones: *see* Jones, Mary Harris

Mother Jones, The Miners' Angel: A Portrait (Fetherling), **28:** 509n1

Motion Picture Board of Trade: WW remarks to, **36:** 16-19

Moton, Robert Russa, **31:** 261,n1, 270, 321-22, 329; **35:** 400,n1

Mott, John R., **27:** 110, 112, 124, 131, 167,n1, 168, 175, 179, 190, 202, 214, 219, 247-48, 248, 261, 263, 275, 463; **28:** 22-23; **30:** 119-20,n1; **31:** 40-41,n1, 261, 358, 553; **32:** 30,n2, 52,n1; **33:** 469; **34:** 358; on recognition of China, **27:** 144-45; and Joint High Commission, **38:** 79n1, 83, 122n1, 153, 154, 166, 169, 355, 356, 357, 360, 362, 373, 397, 398, 405; congratulates WW on victory, **38:** 631

Mount Berry, Ga., **28:** 308n2; **36:** 478

Mount Holyoke College, **38:** 108n1

Mount Vernon Place Church, Washington, D.C., **32:** 429,n2

Mount Washington House, Cornish, N.H., **28:** 138

Mt. Willard, N.H., **29:** 562

Mowry, George Edwin, **36:** 26n3; **37:** 203n4

Moxom, Philip Stafford, **29:** 476

Mudge, James, **29:** 474,n1, 475

Mueller, Paul Ferdinand, **33:** 361,n1; **38:** 46-47,n2, 63-64, 350, 351-52,n1

Muirhead, James Fullarton, **32:** 12,n4, 21

Mújica, Francisco, **28:** 77

Mukden, Manchuria, China, **33:** 105

Mulder, John Mark, **34:** 491n1

Mulhall, Martin M., **28:** 381,n2

Mullen, Leroy Arthur, **35:** 95-96,n1, 107

Müller, Georg Alexander von, **33:** 299,n2; **34:** 47

Müller, Lauro, **33:** 221-22; **35:** 520; **36:** 199,n5, 200, 412, 479; **37:** 122, 238, 242, 244, 271, 293; **38:** 18

Muller *v.* Oregon, **36:** 25n1

Muller-Ury, Adolfo, **36:** 599,n1

Mulliken, Alfred Henry, **30:** 205-207,n1, 283-84, 294

Mulry, Thomas M., **27:** 245, 246

Munch, Francis, **36:** 280n1

Munford, Mary Cooke Branch (Mrs. Beverly Bland), **31:** 261,n2

municipal government, **27:** 49-50

Muñoz Rivera, Luis: *see* Rivera, Luis Muñoz

Munro, Dana Gardner, **27:** 470n2,5,6; **28:** 124n2; **29:** 20n1; **30:** 165n1; **34:** 66n2; **35:** 252n1

Münster von Dernburg, Alexander Prince, **30:** 108,n1; **35:** 194,n1

Münsterberg, Hugo, **32:** 511; **33:** 17-20, 28-29, 100; and German propaganda in U.S., **31:** 276-78,n1,2, 336-40; WW queries on alleged unneutral acts of U.S., **31:** 293; R. Lansing on, **31:** 376, 432-46, 447, 450, 534-35

Murature, José Luis, **36:** 200,n10

Murdock, Victor, **37:** 167; **38:** 666,n2

Murfreesboro, Tenn.: post office, **27:** 239

Murphy, Charles Francis, **27:** 22n2; **29:** 240n1, 395n1, 402, 403, 414n1, 422; **31:** 139, 148, 253, 254; **35:** 318-19; **36:** 380-81, 458,n1; **38:** 549n1, 597n2; and Sulzer impeachment, **28:** 149n1

Murphy, J. Edwin, **35:** 235,n1, 256-57, 273

Murphy, John Benjamin, **38:** 182,n9

Murphy, Joseph E., **28:** 102,n2, 199, 335; **33:** 525,n2; **34:** 74, 119, 201, 258; **35:** 270

Murphy, Starr J., **28:** 427, 511; **29:** 513-14, 549

Murray, Alexander William Charles Oliphant, 1st Baron Murray of Elibank, **28:** 593,n2; **29:** 396; **33:** 64

Murray, Freeman H. M., **31:** 309,n1

Murray, Robert Henry, **37:** 176,n2

Murtaugh, Mr., **37:** 208
Muskingum Valley, Ohio, **27:** 230; **29:** 44n1
My Experiences in the World War (Pershing), **36:** 285n2
My First Eighty-Three Years in America (Gerard), **38:** 453n1
My Four Years in Germany (Gerard), **30:** 382n1; **33:** 299n4; **38:** 453n1
My Memoir (E. B. Wilson), **32:** 423n1; **33:** 525,n1
Myers, Henry Lee, **30:** 174; **36:** 311,n3, 355n1; **37:** 140, 480, 494
Myers water-power bill, **36:** 518,n3, 521; **37:** 313, 328
Mystery of Golf (Haultain), **31:** 19,n1
Mystic Athletic Club, Chicago, **36:** 545n1

NAACP: *see* National Association for the Advancement of Colored People
NAACP: A History of the National Association for the Advancement of Colored People (Kellogg), **27:** 291n1
Naboth's Vineyard: The Dominican Republic, 1844-1924 (Welles), **29:** 20n1
Naco, Sonora, Mex., **31:** 431; **38:** 222
Nacoochee Institute, Sautee, Ga., **32:** 509n1,3
Nafarrate, Emiliano P., **37:** 250,n2, 255, 305
Nagasaki, Japan, **29:** 437
Nagel, Charles, **33:** 18,n2
Namur, Belgium, **33:** 63
Nan-chang, China, **32:** 248
Nancy Stair: A Novel (Lane), **34:** 420,n1
Nansen, Fridtjof, **36:** 654,n2
Nantes, France, **30:** 200n2
Nantucket, Mass., **27:** 189, 491, 505, 555; **28:** 263, 310, 311, 483; **30:** 158, 196, 439; **32:** 230; **33:** 412, 413
Naón, Rómulo Sebastian, **29:** 505-506,n1, 506-507, 539-40; **30:** 197-99, 208, 239, 241, 242; **31:** 451; **32:** 338, 364, 451,n1, 453, 478; **33:** 305, 487, 488; **37:** 388; **38:** 18; on South American trade, **31:** 360,n1; on negotiations about Pan-American pact, **31:** 470, 497, 535, 536, 548-49, 551, 552; **33:** 54, 55, 56; **35:** 54-55, 111-13, 126, 143, 188, 520; **36:** 197, 200-201, 333n1, 412, 461, 605; **37:** 238, 239, 242, 243, 244, 271, 292-93, 398-99, 399-400; and Mexico, **33:** 437, 454, 455; and Pan-American conferences on Mexico, **34:** 43, 111, 112-13, 157n1,2, 321, 472,n1, 487-88, 540; offers to go to Mexico for U.S., **37:** 361-62
Napier, James C., **28:** 211, 410
Napoleon I, **31:** 22, 40n1; **37:** 334
Napoleon: The Last Phase (Rosebery), **31:** 316,n2
Nardi, Emanuel, **32:** 97
Narragansett Bay Naval Station, **38:** 386n1
Nash, Harry F., **29:** 549
Nashville, Tenn., **27:** 83; **28:** 396, 397;

postmaster, **27:** 346,n1; YMCA in, **32:** 125,n2
Nashville, Chattanooga and St. Louis Railroad, **38:** 119,n1, 120
Nassau, the Bahamas, **31:** 110
Nassau Club, **38:** 629
Nassau Hall, Princeton University, **30:** 176n1; **38:** 681n3
Natera, Pánfilo, **30:** 180,n2, 193n2, 220; **32:** 355,n5
Nateras, Pablo, **28:** 77
Nathan, Edward Isaac, **35:** 337,n2
Nation, The (New York), **35:** 344n1
National Academy of Design, **28:** 62n6
National Academy of Sciences, **36:** 478n1; **37:** 374, 468,n1, 472, 473, 481, 492; **38:** 574n3
National American Woman Suffrage Association, **29:** 21n1; **35:** 28n1, 30; **36:** 3n2, 484,n1; **37:** 490, 491, 539; **38:** 19-20; WW's address to, **38:** 161-64, 178-79
National Archives and Records Service, **27:** ix-x; W. J. Bryan collection, **27:** xi; and recommendation for building, **28:** 470; **38:** 654-56, 664
National Association for the Advancement of Colored People, **28:** 60, 163-65, 185n1, 290, 343, 344; **29:** 105; **35:** 120n1; **38:** 460; M.C. Nerney report on segregation in governmental departments, **28:** 402-10
National Association of Colored Women, **38:** 14,n1, 24n2
National Association of Manufacturers, **28:** 381n2; **38:** 46n1
National Association of Presidential Postmasters: WW's speech to, **37:** 442-44,n1; **38:** 168,n1, 193
National Association Opposed to Woman Suffrage, **30:** 257,n1
National Bank Acts (1863-64), **29:** 64; **35:** 322
National Bank of Cuba, **28:** 124n2, 250-51
National Bank of the Republic of Haiti, **31:** 483,n6; **32:** 27,n2, 439n1, 472; **34:** 69,n1, 184
National Bank of Mexico, **28:** 544n1; **29:** 381n1
National bank notes, **27:** 561n2
National Board of Health, **27:** 75
National Business League of America, **38:** 60n1
National Cash Register Co., **30:** 482; **33:** 398-99,n3
National Chamber of Commerce: *see* Chamber of Commerce of the United States
National Child Labor Committee, **27:** 107, 108; **38:** 161n2, 284
National City Bank of New York, **28:** 429; **31:** 139n4, 220n2, 381; **33:** 194n1, 218,n3; **38:** 67, 70; and Haiti, **34:** 60, 69; and Mexico, **34:** 382,n1, 401,n1

National Civic Federation, **28:** 21n5; **31:** 413, 560; **32:** 532; **33:** 429n1; **35:** 538

National Colored Democratic League, **27:** 19; **28:** 41, 210

National Committee for an Honorable Peace, Germany, **37:** 507

National Committee for Mental Hygiene, N.Y., **32:** 96

National Committee of Mercy, Cal., **31:** 332

National Conference Committee of Railways, **38:** 30

National Conference of Charities and Correction, **27:** 108

National Conservation Association, **36:** 48, 51

National Conservation Commission, Wash., D.C., **35:** 151,n1

National Consumers' League, **27:** 76; **28:** 63n1

national defense: *see* preparedness

National Democratic Club of New York: **29:** 395n1

National Democratic Committee: *see* Democratic National Committee

National Democratic Fair Play Association, Wash., D.C., **28:** 187,n2

National Farmers' Educational and Cooperative Union of America: *see* Farmers' Union

National Foreign Trade Convention, Wash., D.C., **30:** 94, 95

National Foreign Trade Council, **31:** 47

national forests, **35:** 232, 233

National Fuel Co., Colo., **29:** 549

National Geographic Society, **29:** 306n1; **30:** 65n1

National German American Alliance, **33:** 185; **34:** 52n2, 116n2; **37:** 217, 219,n3

National Grange, **36:** 637-38,n15; WW's remarks to, **38:** 637-40

National Guard, **31:** 423; **34:** 173n1, 483; **35:** 105-106, 111, 124, 138-41, 150,n1, 170, 500, 503; **36:** 637, 638n15; **38:** 45, 232; WW on, **36:** 14, 45-46, 58-59, 71, 91, 102, 146, 163; H. L. Scott on, **36:** 107; J. Hay on, **36:** 143, 514, 515; W. F. Sadler on Assistant Secretary of War, **36:** 292-93; WW calls out to protect U.S.-Mexican border, **37:** 321n1

National Guard Association of the United States, **35:** 139; **36:** 300,n2

National Guard of Colorado: *see* Colorado National Guard

National Health Department: J. Rublee on, **30:** 93, 135

National Historical Publications and Records Commission, **27:** xxii

National Implement and Vehicle Manufacturers' Association, **30:** 94

National Independent Equal Rights League, Boston, **31:** 237, 308, 309,n1, 311

National Independent Political League, Boston, **28:** 491n1

National Institute of Arts and Letters, **28:** 62n6

National Liberal Immigration League, **32:** 96, 97

National Livestock Association, **35:** 232

National McKinley Birthplace Memorial Association, **35:** 212n1

National Militia Board, **35:** 139

National Monetary Commission, **27:** 204

National Movie Association Dinner, **35:** 382

National Museum, Wash., D.C., **34:** 353

National Negro Democratic League, **27:** 176n1,2

National Negro Exposition, Richmond, Va., **34:** 16; WW's proclamation on, **33:** 464

National Palace, Mexico City, **27:** 538, 539, 543; **31:** 411n2

National Peace Federation, **35:** 195n1, 200n1

National Press Club: WW's remarks to, **29:** 361-66, 366; **37:** 46-54, 63, 66, 73,n1

National Race Commission, **27:** 442,n2

National Railroad Co. of Haiti, **31:** 485; **34:** 66,n1, 68

National Railways of Mexico, **28:** 527n1; **29:** 124, 126, 127, 193, 287; **36:** 364n1

National Research Council, **37:** 374,n1, 468,n1, 472-74,n1, 492, 494

National Reserve Association, **27:** 204, 205

National Reserve Bank of Kansas City, Mo., **29:** 263n1; **38:** 187n1,3

National Rivers and Harbors Congress, **31:** 446n1

national security, **31:** 421-23; *see also* preparedness

National Security League, **35:** 177,n1; **36:** 142

National Service School for Women: WW's remarks to, **36:** 572-75,n1

National Suffrage Association, **38:** 87

National Theater, Wash., D.C., **34:** 517

National Trade Association of Wholesalers, **30:** 319,n3

National Union Bank of Baltimore, **27:** 192n1

National Waterways Commission: bill to create, **36:** 290,n1, 299

National Woman Suffrage Convention, **29:** 21-22,n1

National Women's Party (Women's Party), **37:** 167,n4, 208; **38:** 5, 28-29, 59, 87, 186, 481n1

National Woman's Trade Union League, **34:** 136n2; **38:** 161n2

National Woodrow Wilson College Men's League, **38:** 362n1

Nation's Business, **33:** 430n2

natural resources, **27:** 150; **37:** 197; **38:** 137; L. F. Post on, **28:** 556; G. Pinchot on, **36:** 49-51

naturalization, **27:** 448; *see also* citizenship

Nature, **37:** 474,n4
Nature of Atonement (Campbell), **31:** 28
Navajo Indians, **29:** 36,n1
Naval Academy: *see* United States Naval Academy
Naval Affairs, Committee on (House of Reps.) **30:** 145n1; **32:** 197n1; **34:** 58n1; **35:** 456, 494; **36:** 278-79,n1, 362, 374n1, 376
Naval Affairs, Committee on (Senate), **34:** 58n1; **35:** 434; **37:** 267
Naval Appropriations Act (1916), **36:** 546n2; **38:** 35-36,n1, 38, 63, 102
naval appropriations bill, **36:** 546n2; **37:** 74, 170, 267, 481,n1; and Hensley resolution, **36:** 374n1
Naval Consulting Board, **35:** 29,n1; **36:** 432n1; **38:** 273,n1, 336, 387
Naval Dispensary, Wash., D.C., **28:** 45n2
Naval War College, **32:** 133,n1, 263; **38:** 386n1
Navarette, Rubio, **28:** 29
Navigation, Bureau of, **29:** 432n1
Navy (U.S.): *see* United States Navy
Navy, Department of the, **27:** 77n3; **30:** 175, 435,n1; **31:** 270, 276,n1; **32:** 133,n1, 197n2; **34:** 5, 58, 261, 267; **35:** 229, 434,n1; **37:** 269-70; segregation, **28:** 498n1; **31:** 299; and Sayville radio station, **33:** 486,n2; and Haiti, **34:** 142, 143
Navy League of the United States, **36:** 572n1
Navy Names a Board to Deal with Oil Supply (*New York Herald*), **37:** 141n4
Navy Needs Support to Combat Oil Grab; Fight Becoming Bitter (*New York Herald*), **37:** 141n4
Neal, Nevin E., **27:** 457n2
Nearing, Scott, **36:** 524, 634,n5
Nebraska, **29:** 162; **33:** 336-37, 401; **38:** 196, 376n1, 515n1, 629; fiftieth anniversary of statehood, **38:** 336,n1, 337, 342n3; WW's addresses in Omaha, **38:** 336-42, 342-43, 343-49
Nebraska, University of, **32:** 236; Press, **27:** xii
Nebraska State Historical Society: *see* Historical Society of Nebraska
Nebraskan case, **33:** 369n2,3
Neeley, George Arthur, **28:** 122,n3
Negro and the New Freedom: Fighting Wilsonian Segregation (Weiss), **27:** 291n1
Negro at Washington (Gavit), **28:** 348,n1
Negro Historical and Industrial Association, **33:** 464, 512
Negro in Virginia Politics, 1865-1902 (Buni), **27:** 73n2
Negro Organization Society, **31:** 261-62, 270, 321-22
Negroes, **27:** 290, 291, **28:** 40-41, 245-46, 316; **31:** 270; **35:** 120, 400, 461,n1; **37:** 420, 513-14; A. Walters, **27:** 19; W. Kent, **27:** 266; segregation in governmental departments, **28:** 60-61, 65,

88-89, 94, 97-98,n1, 115n3, 163-65, 186n1, 187n4, 265-66, 346, 348-50,n1,2, 413-14; **29:** 105; **31:** 297, 311-13, 361n2; R. N. Wood, **28:** 115-18; O. G. Villard, **28:** 185-86, 239-40, 289-90, 342-44; B. T. Washington, **28:** 186-87; WW decides not to appoint race commission, **28:** 202; A. B. Cosey, **28:** 209-12; W. F. Powell, **28:** 221-23; H. A. Bridgman, **28:** 256, 277-78,n1; J. Lind, **28:** 294; W. L. Jones, **28:** 344-45,n1; M. C. Herney, **28:** 402-10; W. G. McAdoo, **28:** 453; W. M. Trotter, **28:** 491-95,n1; WW and W. M. Trotter, **28:** 496-98,n1; **31:** 298-301, 304-308, 328,n2,3; and appointments, **29:** 204-205, 205n2, 290, 319, 388, 394, 540-41, 543; **32:** 471-72, 515; proposed exposition on progress of, **29:** 401,n2; A. Carnegie's aid to education of, **30:** 44; and political parties, **30:** 491-93; Turkish ambassador on, **31:** 16n1; and Liberia, **31:** 102, 114; and Washington street-cleaning department, **31:** 192; D. I. Walsh on, **31:** 237-38; society formed in Virginia for, **31:** 261-62, 321; WW on, **31:** 301-304, 464-65; and R. R. Moton, **31:** 321-22, 329; and appropriations for Howard University, **32:** 272; and Ellen A. Wilson Memorial, **33:** 430; WW's proclamation on National Negro Exposition, **33:** 464; and Continental Army plan, **36:** 142; John Fox on, **36:** 481; and lynching, **38:** 15, 24,n2; presidential campaign and, **38:** 156-57,n1, 459-60, 521, 522,n1
Neilson, Francis, **35:** 280,n2
Nelson, Horatio Herbert, **29:** 319n1
Nelson, Ida Houston (Mrs. William Rockhill), **32:** 516,n1
Nelson, Knute, **28:** 162,n1, 414; **30:** 299n1
Nelson, William Rockhill, **29:** 57,n3, 135; **30:** 353,n3; **35:** 183; death of, **32:** 516,n1
Neptune's Daughter, **34:** 313
Nerney, May Childs, **28:** 350,n3; report on segregation in governmental departments, **28:** 402-10
Netherlands, The, **30:** 334; **31:** 7, 40n1, 111, 144, 155; **32:** 46, 196n1, 299, 340, 391, 473; **33:** 130, 144, 180, 215, 485, 524, 550; **34:** 86, 188, 189, 251n2,4, 253n1, 398; **35:** 20n2,3, 197, 198, 199, 227, 354n2; **37:** 8-9, 75,n1,2, 89, 183, 236,n1; **38:** 53n2, 113, 116, 669; ambassadorship, **27:** 110, 509, 515; conciliation treaty, **27:** 478; seamen's bill, **28:** 412-13; Americans in, **30:** 365; legation's reaction to death of EAW, **30:** 365; and Declaration of London and embargo, **31:** 98, 100, 104, 105, 110, 113, 114, 116, 136, 156, 159, 190; and war materials and Germany, **31:** 201; W. H. Page on R. Lansing's proposal and, **31:** 203; and mail aboard ships, **31:** 339; German torpedoing ships of, **36:** 429, 429-30; resignation of U.S.

minister to, **38**: 209, 210-12; suggestions for appointment, **38**: 317, 350
Netherlands and the United States: peace treaty, **29**: 136,n1
Netherlands Anti-War Council, **37**: 75n1
Neues Vaterland League, **34**: 47n6
Neulsen, John L., **37**: 148n1
Neutral Conference Committee: *see* American Neutral Conference Committee
neutrality: *see* World War
Neutrality Board of: *see* Joint State and Navy Neutrality Board
Neuve Chapelle, France, **32**: 522; **33**: 13
Nevada, **30**: 434; **35**: 292n2; **38**: 376n1, 515n1
Nevada, University of, **38**: 39n1
Never Push an Angle-worm, When He is Going Up Hill (song) **28**: 332
Neville, James Hervey, **29**: 99,n1
Neville, Susan Hart (Mrs. James Hervey), **29**: 99,n1
Nevin, Blanche, **38**: 628,n5
Nevin, John Edwin, **38**: 628,n6
New, Harry Stewart, **38**: 457,n1
New and Dangerous Rule (*Washington Post*), **31**: 104,n1
New Bedford, Mass., **30**: 327
New Ebbitt Hotel, Wash., D.C., **36**: 160n1
New England Conference of the Methodist Episcopal Church, **29**: 474,n1, 475
New Freedom (Link): *see* Wilson: The New Freedom
New Freedom: A Call for the Emancipation of the Generous Energies of a People (Wilson), **27**: 4, 7n; **28**: 61, 165, 267, 495; **29**: 418; **30**: 232, 310; **38**: 621,n1; preface, **27**: 6-7
New Hampshire, **29**: 481n2; **31**: 543n1; **37**: 363n3; **38**: 624; corporations, **27**: 178,n1; senatorial elections, **27**: 158,n1,2, 178,n1; WW summer home in, **27**: 189,n1, 200, 374, 506
New Hampshire, U.S.S., **34**: 204
New Harmony, Ind., **30**: 135,n1
New Harmony Centennial Commission, **30**: 135,n1
New Haven Railroad, **28**: 249,n1; **29**: 338-40,n2, 345, 368, 369, 374; **30**: 23,n4, 96, 123,n1,2, 129, 163,n1, 293,n3, 302, 309; **37**: 178, 203,n2,3; and Rayburn bill, **30**: 162n2; H. L. Higginson on, **30**: 294-95; C. W. Eliot on, **30**: 305; settlement, **30**: 422, 480; J. P. Morgan, Jr., on, **30**: 483; R. Olney on, **30**: 85-87
New Internationalism (Bolce), **33**: 34n5
New Jersey, **28**: 221; **30**: 151n; **31**: 390, 562; **32**: 186; **34**: 270, 286, 300; **35**: 176; **38**: 35,n3, 285,n2, 376n1, 430, 431-32, 608-10, 642, 643; WW's annual message to legislature, **27**: 46-54; appointment of judges, **27**: 559, 568; commission government, **27**: 49-50; constitutional convention bill, **27**: 53,n12, 378-79, 391-92; corporation bills (Seven

Sisters), **27**: 90,n2, 120-21, 178; Democratic party, **27**: 42-43, 375, 387, 388, 389; **28**: 65-66,n1, 83, 93; grade crossings, **27**: 48-49,n5; gubernatorial elections (1914), **27**: 374; **28**: 490n2; jury reform, **27**: 48,n3, 133-34, 190-91,n1, 233, 235, 240, 373-81, 386-94; medical education, **27**: 78; politics, **27**: 456, 480, 482-83, 494,n1; **28**: 64, 96-97, 373n1,2; **29**: 386, 557, 558; railroad laws, **27**: 323; securities and investment sales, **27**: 47; tax reform, **27**: 48; WW on, **27**: 85-90, 116, 141-42, 260, 285, 296, 326; **34**: 240-41, 304; **38**: 415; antitrust laws, **28**: 420; **29**: 81; Negroes and politics, **28**: 209, 210, 211, 222; and presentation of statue of Philip Kearny, **31**: 561,n1; and woman suffrage, **34**: 542-43; **35**: 28,n1, 30, 51; **36**: 4; **37**: 523; summer White House in, **35**: 58-59,n1, 72, 103, 127; National Guard in, **35**: 138; Smith-Martine fight in, **35**: 493
New Jersey Federation of Patriotic Fraternities, **32**: 96
New Jersey Harbor Commission, **28**: 42n2
New Jersey National Guard, **36**: 14, 29,n2; at inauguration, **27**: 26
New Jersey State Board of Equalization of Taxes, **28**: 203n2
New Jersey Zinc Co., **30**: 270n4
New Kind of War (Angell), **34**: 135n1
New London, Conn., **38**: 166n2, 168n1
New Mexico, **30**: 18; **37**: 300, 321n1, 376n1, 458, 515n1; Columbus raid in: *see* Mexico and the United States
New Mexico Historical Review, **36**: 280n1
New Orleans, La., **27**: 286n3, 288,n6; **29**: 276, 370n1; **30**: 441; **31**: 501; **33**: 215; **34**: 296; **35**: 211,n1
New Orleans, U.S.S., **32**: 528n1
New Republic, **34**: 135n1, 217; **37**: 76n1, 77, 290,n1; **38**: 3,n3,4, 87,n1,2, 238, 274n2, 275n6
New Statesman, **34**: 83; **35**: 223,n1; **37**: 294n1
New Willard Hotel, Wash., D.C., **27**: 147n1; **29**: 306n1, 405; **32**: 149n1, 178n1, 501n1; **35**: 211, 439; **36**: 152n1, 218n1, 240n2, 417n1, 459, 472n1, 481; **37**: 6
New York American, **27**: 96
New York Call, **37**: 245n1
New York *Christian Herald*, **37**: 310n1
New York City, appointments, **30**: 282,n1,2, 283; **31**: 274-75; **34**: 237,n1, 513,n1; **35**: 318-19,n1,2,3,4,5, 360, 361, 460, 503; **36**: 380, 380-81, 463, 488, 520, 520-21, 529, 530, 542,n1, 598; **37**: 155-56, 533-34; British warships removed from, **31**: 439; businessmen and the administration, **29**: 532; **31**: 388-89; Collector of the Port, **27**: 223, 245-46, 292,n1, 333, 336, 339, 373, 374-75, 385, 396-97, 399-401, 403-404, 406-407, 409-10; EAW's trip to, **28**: 345, 347, 355-

New York City (*cont.*)
56; EBG's trips to, **33:** 443-44; **34:** 300, 322, 332, 356, 357, 363, 376; Federal Reserve Bank, **34:** 277; and V. Huerta, **33:** 89; Mrs. Hulbert in, **33:** 412; Malone-Glynn rivalry, **29:** 414,n1, 422-23; mayoralty, **27:** 384,n1, 410; **28:** 139, 178, 210-11, 289, 402,n2, 490n2; and military bills, **36:** 636-37, 646-47; impact of Panama Canal on, **28:** 449; Republican victories in, **31:** 264n3; and rivers and harbors bill, **37:** 15, 27, 54-55; and telephone lines, **32:** 118n1; tricentennial celebration, **31:** 151-52; unemployment in, **32:** 123; and woman suffrage, **34:** 542-43; WW on Wall Street, **38:** 308-10; WW addresses in, **33:** 37, 212; **36:** 7-16, 16-19; **38:** 591-97, 597-602, 602-605, 606; *see also* Democratic party and Democrats in New York
New York Court of Appeals, **37:** 264,n5,6
New York *Crisis: see Crisis, The*
New York Day at Shadow Lawn, N.J., **38:** 549n1
New York *Evening Mail,* **35:** 146n1,3,4, 236,n2
New York *Evening Post,* **27:** 323,n3; **28:** 146,n2, 182, 186,n1, 187, 327, 348n1; **29:** 92n1, 319n1, 323; **30:** 443, 455, 456n2, 479; **31:** 313n, 328n2, 374n1, 413,n3; **33:** 141, 191n1, 201n1; **34:** 110, 264,n3, 324-25, 411; **35:** 68n1, 142n1,2,3, 380,n1, 387; **36:** 238n1; **37:** 60n1, 162, 309,n1, 313, 376n1; **38:** 154, 645,n1
New York Federation of Churches: WW's remarks to, **36:** 4-7,n1
New York *Globe,* **29:** 515; **31:** 339; **35:** 221,n2; **38:** 154
New York Herald, **27:** 155n1, 297n2; **28:** 470, 488, 498n1; **29:** 174n1, 310n1, 347,n1, 511n1; **30:** 36n, 113n4; **31:** 360,n1, 404; **32:** 21n3, 466,n1; **33:** 244; **34:** 195n1,2; **36:** 564n6, 592n1; **37:** 141n4, 167n4, 427n4, 436n1; **38:** 260, 261, 293n1, 497, 560n1, 616; Paris edition, **29:** 346; and alleged break between WW and E. M. House, **34:** 378,n2, 381, 402,n1,2, 437, 443, 471,n1, 471-72,n1
New York *Nation,* **27:** 453n1; **28:** 186n1; **30:** 456n2; **32:** 12n4, 78, 79n2
New York National Guard, **36:** 637,n13
New York, New Haven, and Hartford Railroad: *see* New Haven Railroad
New York News, **29:** 205n2
New York News Service, **35:** 431n1
New York Press, **34:** 445,n5; **37:** 332n1; **38:** 159n3
New York Press Club: WW's remarks to, **37:** 331n1, 332-36, 337-38, 342, 344, 346, 347, 352, 369, 377, 402
New York Public Service Commission, **35:** 346n1

New York *Review of Reviews,* **29:** 350
New York Shipbuilding Co., **32:** 451n1
New York State, **27:** 323, 324, 22-23,n3, 129n2; **28:** 222, 495; **30:** 333n2; **34:** 133; **35:** 30, 176, 218, 398; **37:** 535; appointments, **27:** 223, 246-47; **28:** 35-36,n1,2; **29:** 447-48, 456,n1; **31:** 274-75; **34:** 237,n1, 513n1; **35:** 318-19,n4, 346,n1, 460; **36:** 488, 520-21, 529, 530, 542,n1,598; **37:** 155-56, 264; campaign of 1916 in, **37:** 264, 533-34; **38:** 8-9, 44, 154, 275-76, 277-78, 288, 317, 376n1, 428, 429, 436, 494, 515,n1, 521, 545-46, 557, 564-65, 567, 606-608, 630, 671; foreign vote in, **38:** 139-40; gubernatorial and senatorial politics, **31:** 11-12,n1, 116-17,n1, 156-57, 161, 167, 252, 267; **37:** 290; **38:** 164-65,n1, 189, 190; Malone-Glynn rivalry, **29:** 414,n1, 422-23; W. C. Osborn and Democratic state committee, **36:** 458,n1; F. D. Roosevelt on politics, **29:** 390, 392; Sulzer impeachment, **28:** 149,n1,2, 181; WW address at Shadow Lawn on New York Day, **38:** 548-59; WW addresses in Buffalo, **38:** 572-79, 580-89; *see also* Democratic party and Democrats in New York
New York State Chamber of Commerce, **35:** 177,n2
New York State Civil Service Commission, **35:** 319n4
New York State Constitutional Convention, **30:** 23n3
New York Stock Exchange, **29:** 177, 375; **30:** 421; **34:**100
New York *Sun,* **27:** 286; **28:** 18, 138, 144, 380, 402, 468; **30:** 50,n1; **31:** 541; **33:** 296; **37:** 265n1; **38:** 352,n1
New York Symphony Orchestra, **32:** 455n1
New York Times, **27:** 44n, 72n1, 78n, 89n5, 96, 97n, 141n1, 142n1, 144n1, 145n1, 148n, 198n1, 217n,n1, 229n1, 268n4, 287n5, 322n1, 432n2, 473n, 523, 536n1, 555n1, 564n3, **28:** 4n1, 69n1, 84n2, 91n, 92,n2, 96, 102, 108n1, 122n4, 134, 137n1, 141n2, 156n1, 159, 160n2, 181n1, 182, 195n1, 204n1, 224n1, 247n2, 257n2, 267n, 276n2, 278n2, 301, 316, 334, 351n1, 355n4,5,7, 366n1, 369, 400, 424n, 430n, 433n1, 442n, 455n1, 506n1, 517n1, 565n1, 590n1, 595n2, 597n1, 600n1; **29:** 56n2, 63n1, 66n, 91n3, 99n1, 101n1, 111n2, 138n1, 180n, 180n1, 184n, 223n2, 231n1, 240n1, 301n1, 314n2, 332n1, 333n1, 346n1, 347n1, 361n1, 379n1, 387n3, 397n1, 414n1, 434n4, 488n, 511n1, 522n1, 561; **30:** 8n2, 10n2, 13n1, 21n1, 23n3,4, 36n, 39n1, 42n1, 65n1, 96n, 101n3, 110n1, 113n4, 124, 163n1, 173n1, 176n1, 228n5, 234, 243n1, 270n4, 273n1, 300n3, 312n1, 319n3, 325n1, 333n1, 338n1, 340n1, 343n1,

353n2, 369n7, 432n1; **31:** 23n1, 61n1, 64n1, 87n1, 118n1, 130n, 152n3, 176n1, 257n5, 409n, 413n2, 458n1, 461n2, 560n2; **32:** 15n4, 21n3, 26n1, 118n1, 133n1, 172n1, 201n1, 240n1, 337n3, 353n1, 426n2, 464n2, 468n2, 501n1, 508n1, 528n1
33: 91n3, 135n4, 153n1, 184n1, 191n1, 209n,n1, 216n1, 218n1, 290n1, 369n2, 464n, 486n2, 499n; **34:** 31n2, 41n, 52n2, 59n1, 104, 116n1,2, 131,n2, 156n1, 194, 195n1, 285, 296n1, 337n1, 438n2, 445,n5; **35:** 27n1, 90n, 150n1, 154n5, 157n1, 174n2, 180n1, 277n1, 347n2, 367n, 370n1, 371n1, 423n1, 478n1, 494; **36:** 3n1,2, 152n2, 186n1,2, 203n2, 205n1, 206n2, 214n1, 228n1, 238,n1, 263n1, 366n, 387n2, 444n1, 488, 503n1, 505n1, 527n2, 544n1, 545n1, 555n1, 560n1, 572n1, 604n1, 636n12; **37:** 5n1, 27,n2, 43n1,4, 76n1, 84n1, 101n1, 123n, 129n1, 203n3, 219n3, 231n2, 263n2, 291n2, 306n1, 308n2, 309n2, 316n1, 319n2, 363n2, 379n1, 407n, 425n1, 431n1, 476n3, 493n3, 499n2, 507n3, 513n1, 522n1, 523n1, 525n1, 526n1, 537n1; **38:** 32n1, 38n2, 47n1, 48n2, 58n, 73, 124n,n2, 126n1, 142n1, 146n2, 147n2, 164n,n3, 170n,n1, 177n2, 178n3, 187n1,2, 189n, 190,n1, 271n1, 273n1, 274, 283n1, 286n, 293n2, 301n1, 312n, 313n1, 319n1, 362n1, 374n, 377,n2, 388n1, 393n2, 427n1, 430n1, 438n, 445n1,5, 450n, 460n1, 461n1,2, 466n2, 473n2, 475n1, 489n1, 500n1, 511n2, 513n1, 517n1, 518n1, 524n1, 549n1, 559n1, 560n1, 563n1, 565n5, 566n7, 570n1, 571n1,2, 578n5, 579n, 591n1, 597n1, 622n, 624n, 629,n, 668n; WW refuses interview request, **38:** 40, 45-46; reports C. E. Hughes winner, **38:** 630,n2
New York Tribune, **27:** 409; **28:** 319n1; **31:** 404, 541; **32:** 449,n2, 501n3; **34:** 367,n1, 377n1, 445n3,5; **37:** 219,n3, 522n1; **38:** 500n1, 560n1
New York University, **27:** 179n1, 208; **29:** 352
New York *World,* **27:** 11, 280n, 322n1, 488n1; **28:** 57, 92,n1, 96, 181,n2, 182, 196n5, 200,n1, 224n1, 301, 302,n3, 308, 375n1, 381,n2, 385, 391,n2, 421,n1, 425,n1; **29:** 21n1; 77n1, 100,n2, 281n1, 303,n1, 344,n1, 347n1, 390, 392n2, 396n2, 407n2, 413n1, 414n1, 425n, 434n4, 443n, 511n1, 538n; **30:** 40, 41, 42n, 209n1, 277, 312n1, 325n, 326; **31:** 32, 118n1, 153, 274, 295,n1, 314, 328n3, 338, 361n2, 374n1; **32:** 324,n1, 341-42, 516n1, 521, 522; **33:** 218n1; **34:** 116n2, 158n1, 186, 209, 218, 234, 260, 278, 338, 346, 430,n1, 445,n5, 466n1; **35:** 52n1, 178, 478n1; **36:** 16n, 288, 542n1; **37:** 129, 167n4, 203,n1, 217, 219,n3, 291,n1, 316n1, 328n, 333n2,

336n, 325n1; **38:** 73, 187n2, 219n, 283n1, 291, 293n, 301, 368, 419n, 438n, 445n1, 450n, 461n1, 489n,n1, 500n1, 509n, 564n1, 565n2, 608n1; and Santo Domingo scandal, **31:** 403n1, 404,n2; cartoons from; *illustration section,* **35**
New York Yankees, **27:** 299n1
New Yorker Staats Zeitung, **33:** 135n4, 361; **36:** 542n1
Newark, N.J., **27:** 26, 52; WW address on jury reform, **27:** 373-81
Newark Evening News, **27:** 122n, 142n, 235n1; **29:** 302n1
Newbury, N.Y., **34:** 286
Newfound Lake, N.H., **28:** 129, 131
Newfoundland, **34:** 129-30
Newlands, Francis Griffith, **27:** 502-503,n1; **28:** 247, 487; **29:** 63, 219, 227, 243, 281, 317-18, 487, 535, 544; **30:** 4, 166, 181, 219, 224, 242-43, 261-62, 424, 433-34, 442, 454-55, 494; **36:** 311,n1, 387, 462; **37:** 530,n1; **38:** 36, 102-103,n1; on WW's trust message to Congress, **29:** 363; and Rayburn railway securities bill, **30:** 295-96, 300
Newlands bill, **28:** 42n2; **35:** 232; **36:** 290; *see also* Federal Trade Commission Act
Newlands Mediation Act of 1916, **37:** 435
Newlands Railway Mediation Act, **30:** 306, 329
Newlands resolution, **37:** 530n1
Newman, Agnes Casement, **36:** 566; **38:** 316n1, 350, 443, 444
Newman, Oliver Peck, **28:** 540; **31:** 147,n1
Newport News, Va., **31:** 230
Newspaper Enterprise Association, **31:** 291n2
newspapers, **28:** 89, 107, 134, 261, 311, 361, 395, 497; **29:** 101; **31:** 280, 293, 375, 455; **36:** 174; **37:** 35; as source material, **27:** xiii, xv; McCombs on New York, **27:** 11; WW on, **27:** 96, 165, 399; **28:** 153-54; **29:** 201, 202, 284, 353-53, 391n1; **30:** 178, 327-28, 331-32; **34:** 126, 139, 208, 209, 443; **35:** 198, 342-43; **36:** 100, 120; **37:** 256-57, 345; WW remarks to Gridiron Club, **27:** 294-97; S. Gompers on, **27:** 369; EAW on, **29:** 92; WW and misunderstanding of war lobby, **28:** 153-54; and Mexican situation, **28:** 158, 162, 190, 516, 517; **29:** 15; **30:** 199; W. H. Page and, **28:** 448; **29:** 131; selection by federal officials for advertisements in, **28:** 272,n2, 280, 317; and Military Order of the Carabao incident, **29:** 37, 55,n1; editorials praising WW, **29:** 302,n1, 303,n1, 319n1; and Panama Canal tolls controversy, **29:** 321, 348, 406, 415; and WW's Panama Canal tolls message, **29:** 344; remarks to National Press Club, **29:** 361-66; **37:** 46-54; and New York politics, **29:** 382, 387, 403; J. B. Remensnyder on war encouragement and, **29:** 475-76; H. W. Bones on, **29:** 561

newspapers (cont.)
and World War, 30: 373; article on plan for world peace congress upsets WW, 31: 63; and Declaration of London, 31: 115; H. Münsterberg on hostility toward Germany in, 31: 336, and *Eastland* disaster, 34: 81n1; and Scripps matter, 34: 271,n1; and *Arabic* affair, 34: 306, 468-69; D. Lawrence on, 36: 307-309; and Punitive Expedition, 36: 331-32, 350, 351, 364-66, 457, 463-64; and *Sussex* note, 36: 490-91; WW's remarks to American Newspaper Publishers Association, 36: 560-61; press statement on Scott-Obregón conference, 36: 603, 604; and oil-reserve publicity, 37: 172; Allied press misinterpret WW's speech to League to Enforce Peace, 37: 289, 312, 412-13; WW's remarks to N.Y. Press Club, 37: 332-36; H. C. Wallace on campaign and foreign press, 38: 140-41; E. M. House on, 38: 453; WW's address to Chicago Press Club, 38: 475-81; WW with White House press corps: *illustration section*, 36: *see also* Press Conferences, under Woodrow Wilson entry, and names of individual newspapers
Newton, Byron Rufus, 37: 177
Newton D. Baker: America at War (Palmer), 36: 251n1
Next Business (Louisville *Courier-Journal*), 33: 508n1
Niagara Falls, 34: 155, 166
Niagara Falls Conference: *see* Mexico and the United States-ABC mediation
Niantic Baptist Church, East Lyme, Conn., 36: 140n1
Niblack, Albert Parker, 29: 118, 127
Nicaragua, 27: 470,n2,5,6, 526-30, 552; 35: 247; 37: 112; alternate canal route, 27: 29; draft of canal treaty, 27: 527-30; foreign interests in as cause of problems, 29: 94
Nicaragua and the United States, 29: 291-92; 32: 470n3; 33: 46; Bryan-Chamorro treaty, 28: 100-101, 250, 306; 29: 134-35, 152, 172, 203, 204, 245, 275; 30: 29, 174-75,n1, 175, 317; 31: 102, 114, 115; 32: 59-60, 68, 286, 470n3; canal option, 28: 55, 56, 100, 176, 184; S. M. Jarvis, 28: 124,n2; loan, 28: 48, 175-77, 184-85, 216, 220, 250-51, 353, 354, 358-59, 456, 488n2; and Mexico, 28: 412; Platt Amendment and, 29: 221, 222, 274-75; financial situation in, 29: 245,n1; *U.S.S. Cyane* incident in Greytown, 29: 437, 452, 468
Nicaragua Canal Convention, 27: 527,n1
Nicaragua National Bank, 28: 124
Nicaraguan-American Loan Convention (1911), 27: 470n6
Nice, France, 32: 439, 442, 456
Nicholas II (of Russia), 30: 330, 342, 456-57; 32: 304, 396-97, 462, 480n1, 525-26; 33: 88, 212; 34: 310n2; 35: 359; 38: 67, 68, 254, 458; and aid to Poland, 37: 407, 414, 445n1, 470, 538
Nichols, Arthur Howard, 28: 95n2, 195n1
Nichols, Elizabeth Fisher Homer (Mrs. Arthur Howard), 28: 95,n2, 195n1
Nichols, Isaac T., 27: 85
Nichols, Marian Clarke, 28: 95n2, 195n1
Nichols, Rose Standish, 28: 95n2, 195n1
Nicholson, Walter Frederic, 36: 520,n1
Nicosian, H.M.S., 34: 368,n1
Niebuhr, Walter, 34: 405n1, 441
Nieman, Lucius William, 31: 346,n1, 406; 32: 20, 58, 116, 133, 160, 210-11, 216, 219; 34: 388; 35: 210-11,n1; 37: 220, 221; 38: 290, 450-51
Nieto, Raphael, 38: 633,n1
Nikolai, Grand Duke of Russia (Nikolai Nikolaevich, 1856-1929), 34: 18
Niles, Ohio, 35: 212
Nippert, Alfred Kuno, 38: 177-78,n2
Niu-chuang, China, 32: 321
Nixon, Lewis, 29: 35,n1
No Jim Crow Government (New York *World*), 31: 328n3
Nockels, E. N., 34: 27n1
Noel-Buxton, Noel Edward: *see* Buxton, Noel
Nogales, Ariz., 28: 527, 529, 541, 545, 567, 568, 580; 37: 284
Nogales, Sonora, Mex., 28: 246; 38: 401
Nonpartisan League, 38: 159,n4
Noreiga, Inigo, 27: 537
Norfield, Miss., 29: 208
Norfolk, Va., 28: 369n2; 34: 454; and Negro Organization Society, 31: 261-62, 270, 321
Noriel, Mariano, 32: 535n1, 535-36, 536n2
Normandie-by-the-Sea Hotel, Ocean City, N.J., 34: 233, 288-89, 291
Norris, George Washington, 30: 53, 54; 32: 6-7; 38: 158,n2
Norris, George William, 30: 23n4, 159n1; 32: 172,n1; 36: 265, 266, 311,n2
Norris, Mrs. James Nelson, 29: 562,n4
Norris amendment on cloture, 32: 239
Norris-Simmons amendment, 30: 159,n1
North, Frank Mason, 35: 328, 329n1
North American Review, 27: 322n2; 28: 597; 29: 121n1; 36: 226n2
North Carolina, 27: 107; 37: 514; appointments in, 30: 144; and cotton crisis, 31: 127-29, 129; WW's addresses in, 37: 78-79, 79-83
North Carolina, University of, 27: 134,n1; 36: 275n3, 503n2
North Dakota, 38: 159,n4, 160-61, 624
North East, Pa.,36: 338
North East Harbor, Me., 38: 682
North German Gazette, 31: 340; 36: 233
North German Lloyd Line, 28: 595; 31: 345

North Haven, Me., **34:** 74n5
North Sea, **31:** 371; **32:** 194, 196n1, 273; **34:** 15n1
Northcliffe, 1st Baron: *see* Harmsworth, Alfred Charles William
Northeastern Federation of Colored Women's Clubs, **28:** 289,n1
Northumberland County, England, **34:** 146
Northwestern University, **31:** 27n1; **34:** 74n5; **37:** 425n2; **38:** 182n9; Law School, **34:** 505; **35:**, 68n1
Norton, Margaret, **28:** 256,n1
Nortoni, Albert Dexter, **31:** 353,n1,2,3, 356-57; **37:** 524n2
Norway, **27:** 478, 534; **31:** 144, 218, 480, 526; **32:** 176; **33:** 144, 215; **34:** 86, 188, 251n4, 253n1, 398; **38:** 113; and Mexico, **28:** 460, 486n3, 516
Noticioso Méxicano, **28:** 445
Nott, Alice Effingham Hopkins (Mrs. Charles Cooper), **28:** 20,n2
Nott, Charles Cooper, **28:** 20n2
Novoa, Gonzalo, **28:** 77
Noyes, Frank Brett, **33:** 37,n2
Nuber von Pereked, Alexander, **34:** 403,n2, 452; **35:** 264,n1, 265, 276-77,n1, 281, 379
Nuevo Leon, state, Mex., **28:** 77; **33:** 261; **37:** 250, 285
Nugent, Georgia, **38:** 14,n1, 24n1
Nugent, James Richard, **27:** 375,n2; **28:** 373n2; **29:** 557,n1; **35:** 536; **38:** 35, 642
Numano, Yasutaro, **31:** 256,n1

Oak Creek, Colo., **31:** 334, 452
Oakes. W. F., **29:** 549; **31:** 54n1
Oakdale Coal Co., Colo., **28:** 523; **29:** 549
Oaxaca, state, Mex., **28:** 294; **33:** 261
Obregón, Álvaro, **28:** 29, 77; **30:** 194, 412n6, 417-18, 443; **31:** 18, 19, 66, 69-70, 73; **32:** 355,n5, 390, 398n1; **33:** 5, 7,n1, 259, 271-72; **34:** 271,n1, 510, 530; **37:** 16, 254, 255, 331-32; **38:** 219; and plight of Mexico City, **32:** 202n3, 326-27,n1; and U.S. ultimatum, **32:** 331-32; and V. Carranza, **32:** 347; **36:** 580; and conference with H. L. Scott, **36:** 540,n1, 540-41,n1, 553-54, 570-71, 579-80, 592-94; Scott-Obregón agreement, **36:** 607-608, 618; and conference with H. L. Scott and F. Funston, **37:** 18,n1, 22-24, 38-39
O'Brien, Morgan Joseph, **38:** 63,n1
O'Brien, Thomas J., **27:** 287n5
O'Callaghan, Peter Joseph, **37:** 475-76,n1,2
Ocean Grove, N.J., **37:** 382; **38:** 118n3; EBG's trip to, **34:** 156, 171, 191, 207, 221, 233, 244, 270, 284, 286, 287, 289, 291, 292, 300, 303, 307, 322, 332, 362
Ochs, Adolph Simon, **38:** 40, 388
O'Connell, James, **38:** 472

O'Connell, William Henry Cardinal O'Connell, **33:** 159,n1, 196n5
O'Connor, Charles James, **33:** 448,n1, 466
O'Connor, Elizabeth Paschal (Mrs. Thomas Power), **34:** 215,n2
O'Connor, Thomas Power, **34:** 215,n2
O'Dea, James, **35:** 258n1
O'Donnell, Patrick H., **33:** 185
Official German Documents Relating to the World War, Translated under the Supervision of the Carnegie Endowment for International Peace, Division of International Law, **38:** 314n2
Official Report of the Proceedings of the Democratic National Convention, Held in St. Louis, Missouri, June 14, 15 and 16th, 1916 . . . , **37:** 237n1
Ogden, Marguerite, **30:** 172n1
Ogdensburg, N.Y., **28:** 35n1,2
O'Gorman, James Aloysius, **27:** 72n3, 115n2, 157, 223-24, 383, 513, 515; **28:** 261, 336n2, 355, 361, 369n1, 373n1, 421,n1, 435, 525, 589,n1, 596, 597; **30:** 3, 283, 288, 317; **32:** 10; **33:** 219; **34:** 504, 505; **35:** 68, 347, 398; **36:** 488,n1, 520-21, 606; **37:** 72; and New York Port collectorship, **27:** 245-47, 333, 336-37, 373, 385, 396,n1, 399-401, 407, 410; and Panama Canal tolls controversy, **27:** 71, 313, 534; **29:** 35, 160, 203, 224, 232, 237, 405, 418, 422; and immigration bill, **32:** 143n1; and ship-purchase bill, **32:** 173n2; and appointment suggestions, **32:** 242-43, 259
O'Gorman, Battle and Marshall, N.Y., **27:** 145
Ohio, **28:** 5, 22, 354,n3,4; **30:** 333n1; **35:** 193; and floods, **27:** 229-30,n1, 232, 234; **31:** 119-20; and wool schedule, **27:** 322n1, 328,n1; food fisheries treaty, **29:** 349; politics in **31:** 264n3; **37:** 84, 96,n1, 121, 441n2; **38:** 169, 376n1, 394-95, 428, 457, 515n1, 622, 636, 645n1; WW speeches in, **35:** 321-28, 329-36; **37:** 395-96; **38:** 524-25, 526-33, 534-37, 537-43
Ohio coal strike, **32:** 308-309
Ohio Manufacturers' Association, **30:** 94, 128
Ohio River, **27:** 229n1
Ohio River Valley, **31:** 446n1
Ohio Valley Improvement Association, **31:** 446-47,n1
Ohio Wesleyan University, **27:** 27n1
Ohl, Josiah Kingsley, **34:** 402,n1, 471n1, 472n1
oil: general leasing bill and naval oil reserves, **37:** 39-41, 66, 94, 111, 139, 141, 143, 304-305
Oil Fields of Mexico Co., **30:** 245,n1
Oil Land Grab Would Be a Serious Blow to Navy, Mr. Daniels Declares (*New York Herald*), **37:** 141n4
Ojeda, Pedro, **28:** 29

Ojinaga, Chihuahua, Mex., **29:** 123
Ojo Federico, Mex., **38:** 379, 380
O'Keeffe, John G., **27:** 245-46
Oklahoma, **28:** 5, 10; Cherokees, **27:** 508
Oklahoma, University of, **27:** 457n2
Oklahoma City *Oklahoman*, **28:** 4n3
Okuma, Shigenobu, **31:** 364,n2, 366, 510, 512; **32:** 137, 148, 461, 521; **33:** 36, 113, 114, 131,n2, 140
Olario, D., **29:** 331
O'Laughlin, John Callan, **27:** 565-70,n1; **33:** 28,n1; **34:** 325,n1; **36:** 287,n1
Old Colony Trust Company of Boston, **29:** 278n3
Old Master, An (Wilson), **27:** 15-16
Old Nassau (song), **27:** 142n1; **29:** 555
Old Point Comfort, Va., **33:** 72
Old Virginia Restored: An Interpretation of the Progressive Impulse, 1870-1930 (Pulley), **27:** 73n2
Older, Fremont, **38:** 60,n4
Oldroyd, Osborn Hamiline, **37:** 123n1
O'Leary, Jeremiah A., **38:** 285,n1, 286, 289, 293,n1, 317, 318
Oliveira, José Manuel Cardoso de: *see* Cardoso de Oliveira, José Manuel
Oliver, Frederick Scott, **37:** 34,n5
Oliver, James Harrison, **30:** 435n1; **32:** 503n1
Olney, Richard, **27:** 110; **28:** 271; **30:** 3, 53, 343; **31:** 516; **34:** 369; **36:** 132, 138; **38:** 31, 283,n1, 295; and ambassadorship to Great Britain, **27:** 162-63, 167, 168-69, 176, 177, 228; **30:** 350; and Federal Reserve Board, **29:** 401,n1, 536, 536-37, 541, 543-44; on New Haven Railroad, **30:** 85-87; opposes WW tender of good offices to European powers, **30:** 349
Olney Indorses Wilson's Work: Assails Hughes (New York *World*) **38:** 283n1
Olympic Games (1908), **38:** 687,n2
Omaha, Neb.: WW's addresses in, **38:** 336-42, 342-43, 343-49
Omaha Auditorium, **38:** 343n1
Omaha Bee, **35:** 339n1
Omaha World-Herald, **27:** 219n2; **38:** 336n, 342n, 348n2, 349n
Omaha *World-Telegraph*, **38:** 336n1
On a Certain Blindness in Human Beings (W. James), **33:** 228
On Being Human (Wilson), **36:** 176-77,n1
On the Duty of a Government To Protect Its Citizens (Crane), **38:** 352n1
On the Writing of History (Wilson), **31:** 398,n2
O'Neal, Emmet, **28:** 160,n2, 448,n2; **38:** 591n1
Only Girl (Blossom and Herbert), **31:** 317; **34:** 467n1, 487
Open Door policy, **27:** 194, 196, 237; **28:** 586; **32:** 120, 135, 136, 137, 138, 139, 270, 321, 323, 367n1, 459, 519, 521, 529-30, 531; **33:** 31-32, 34, 101n1, 141, 153; **36:** 440

open shop policy, **28:** 589; **29:** 514, 546; **31:** 52-53
Opinion, La, **36:** 318,n1
Oppenheim, Lassa Francis Lawrence, **29:** 432, 437
Opportunity for Peace (*Springfield Republican*), **37:** 3,n1
Optimist Club of Syracuse, **38:** 545
Order of Railway Conductors, **36:** 204n1
Orduna incident, **34:** 315,n1, 340
Ordway, Lucius P., **29:** 401
Oregon, **27:** 87, 220, 221; **37:** 209; **38:** 185-86, 281; and I.W.W. investigation, **36:** 188-90
Oregon, University of, **30:** 345n1
Organic Act of 1902 for the Philippines, **29:** 137n1
Organic Law of 1878 for the District of Columbia, **29:** 240n2
Organisation Centrale pour une Paix durable, Recueil de Rapports, sur les différents Points du Programme minimum, **35:** 196n2
organized labor: *see* labor unions
Original Plan and Early History of the Federal Trade Commission (Rublee), **29:** 481n3
Origins of Teapot Dome: Progressives, Parties and Petroleum 1909-1921 (Bates), **36:** 464n1; **37:** 140n2
Orizaba, Veracruz, Mex., **31:** 72, 73; **32:** 348, 353
Ormond, Alexander Thomas, **28:** 119,n1
Ornelas, M. S., **34:** 531,n1
Ornelas, Sr. (Mayor of Chihuahua), **30:** 409
Orozco, Pascual, **29:** 123; **33:** 456
Ortega, Toribio, **28:** 77
O'Ryan, John Francis, **36:** 637,n13
Osborn, Chase Salmon, **37:** 167,n3
Osborn, George Coleman, **28:** 97n1
Osborn, William Church, **29:** 240n1, 382, 387, 402-404, 408-409, 422; **31:** 93, 122; **36:** 458; **38:** 165
Osborne, Harry Vliet, **27:** 376,n3
Osborne, James W., **27:** 246
Osborne, John Eugene, **27:** 126, 163, 199; **30:** 22; **31:** 386; **33:** 451, 460-61; and Haiti, **27:** 518,n1, 519, 531, 553; J. B. Moore incident, **27:** 297, 309, 311-12, 314, 341
Osborne, Lithgow, **37:** 272,n3
Oscar II, S.S., **35:** 279n1
Osgood, John Cleveland, **28:** 518n1, 519; **29:** 513, 549; **31:** 54n1, 87n1
O'Shaughnessy, Edith Louise Coues (Mrs. Nelson), **29:** 118
O'Shaughnessy, Nelson, **28:** 20,n1, 101, 145n1, 155, 158, 188, 189, 195n1, 202, 209, 219, 225, 232, 233-39, 239, 249, 282, 292, 299, 324,n1, 326, 363, 399, 420-21, 455n1, 482-83, 517, 537-39, 539, 559, 568; **29:** 103, 118, 190, 223, 254, 291, 295-96, 347, 360, 429, 430, 478, 492; L. Carden on, **28:** 410-11, and

Catholic Church, **29:** 119; J. Lind's instructions to, **29:** 405-406; and Tampico affair, **29:** 421, 430, 434-35, 438-39,n1, 449, 455, 456-57, 458-59, 460-61, 462-64, 464-65, 465, 466, 466-67, 467-68; dispatches withheld in Mexico City, **29:** 433, 441; meeting with Portillo y Rojas, **29:** 446-47; plans to leave Mexico, **29:** 488-89
Osler, Sir William, **35:** 77
Osmeña, Sergio, **27:** 370,n1; **28:** 242n1; **29:** 148, 166; **38:** 119, 155
O'Sullivan, Thomas Cullen, **32:** 242,n2, 259n1
Otey (maid), **35:** 372,n1
Otis, Harrison Gray, **27:** 349,n1
Ottauquechee River, N.H., **28:** 260,n1
Otter Creek Tea House, Vt., **34:** 138, 171
Otumba, Mexican state, **33:** 459
Oulahan, Anne McGowan (Mrs. Richard Victor), **36:** 505n1
Oulahan, Richard Victor, **28:** 322, 323; **29:** 314,n2; **36:** 505-506, 516; **38:** 40
Our Financial Oligarchy (Brandeis), **29:** 30n1
Our President, *Emporia* (Kan.) *Gazette*, **30:** 32,n1
Our Responsibility in Mexico (Roosevelt), **31:** 413,n2
Oust Huerta First (*Washington Post*), **28:** 486,n1
Outline of a Draft of a Convention Between the United States and the Republic of Haiti, **30:** 241n1
Outline of Military Policy (Garrison), **34:** 173n1, 482,n3, 484
Outlook (N.Y.), **30:** 143,n2; **34:** 470,n1; **37:** 201n1; tribute to EAW, **30:** 407,n1
Overland Review, **38:** 680
Overman, Lee Slater, **36:** 606; **37:** 78,n1, 429; **38:** 22
Oversea News Service, **36:** 563
Overstreet, Harry Allen, **37:** 308, 316n1
Owen, John T., **38:** 160
Owen, Robert Latham, **27:** 77n3, 227, 292, 436, 458, 476, 485,n2, 522-23, 535n1, 536n1; **28:** 3n1, 41, 200,n1, 269, 379, 389, 415, 418, 434, 485, 518, 600-601; **29:** 530; **30:** 191, 201-202, 202, 203, 278, 312; **31:** 232n2; **33:** 188, 225; **34:** 6; **35:** 65, 201-202, 205, 433-34, 447, 456, 474, 530; **36:** 311,n1; **37:** 162, 207, 431n1; **38:** 670; and Federal Reserve Act, **29:** 62, 63n1, 77; and Federal Reserve Board appointments, **29:** 263; and Panama Canal tolls controversy, **29:** 397-98,n1, 405; WW resolution on armed forces in Mexico, **29:** 471; and seamen's bill, **32:** 309; on Department of Health, **35:** 151, 183-84; and L. Brandeis nomination, **36:** 51, 137; urges progressive platform, **37:** 151, 161, 162, 174-75
Owen, Ruth Bryan (Mrs. Reginald Altham), **28:** 588,n4

Owen bill: *see* Federal Reserve Act
Owen corrupt-practices bill, **30:** 202
Owen stock-exchange bill, **29:** 375,n1; **30:** 312n1
Owens, Clarence J., **27:** 201; **29:** 141,n1
Oxford, England, **38:** 681
Oxford University, **30:** 301; WW compares to Princeton University, **38:** 681
Oxman, Stephen A., **33:** 372n1
Oyster Bay, N.Y., **28:** 509n1; **30:** 303; **31:** 291
Ozawa, Seiji, **34:** 19n3

P. F. Collier and Son, **35:** 239n1
Pacific Mail Steamship Co., **35:** 374,n2
Pacific Northwest Quarterly, **37:** 140n2
Pacific Ocean: U.S. fleet, **27:** 443, 444, 446, 447
Pacto de la Ciudadela, **28:** 201n2,3
Paderewski, Ignace Jan, **35:** 391,n1; **36:** 207,n3; **38:** 371,n2, 619n1
Paderewski, the Story of a Modern Immortal (Phillips), **35:** 391n1
Padgett, Lemuel Phillips, **29:** 282; **30:** 145,n1; **34:** 58,n1; **35:** 456,n1; **36:** 279,n1, 546n2; **37:** 170; **38:** 101n1
Page, Alice Wilson (Mrs. Walter Hines), **28:** 52,n1, 259, 274, 577, 593; **29:** 20, 351; **30:** 150, 201, 316; **32:** 363; **34:** 17; **35:** 436; **37:** 42, 458-59; **38:** 249, 688
Page, Arthur Wilson, **28:** 53n2; **29:** 160, 161; **30:** 288n1; **31:** 122, 204; **34:** 55n1
Page, Florence Lathrop Field (Mrs. Thomas Nelson), **32:** 146,n2; **34:** 442
Page, Frank Copeland, **28:** 53n2
Page, Katherine Alice: *see* Loring, Katherine Alice Page
Page, Ralph Walter, **28:** 53n2
Page, Robert Newton, **32:** 240n1, 275
Page, Thomas Nelson, **27:** 110, 200, 228; **30:** 255,n2; **31:** 524; **32:** 146-47; **33:**, 12, 194,n1, 219, 230-32; **34:** 30, 442; **35:** 407; **36:** 125, 395,n2, 403; **38:** 441-43, 450; and E. M. House's meeting with, **32:** 285, 297, 423, 439, 442, 456, 462, 475, 522; observes situation in England, **37:** 440-41, 458
Page, Thomas Walker, **38:** 335,n1
Page, Walter Hines, **27:** 133, 153, 292, 383, 462, 482, 503-504, 554; **28:** 452n4, 506, 572; **29:** 12, 19-20, 33, 47, 51-53, 60, 74, 103-104, 111-12, 160, 171, 195-96, 196-97, 266, 268, 283-84, 320, 321; **30:** 23, 187, 201; **31:** 10, 229, 282, 294,n1, 370-72, 380, 468, 469,n4, 535, 553; **32:** 48, 49, 54, 84, 240n1, 258, 260-62, 265, 378; **33:** 183, 206, 206-207, 255,n1, 483-86, 509, 512, 515-16, 519, 519-20, 522-24; **34:** 5, 17-23, 23, 33, 84, 85, 89, 98, 105, 124, 130, 140, 151, 167, 224, 242, 272, 310, 435, 443-44, 528-29; **35:** 85, 93, 157, 491, 531; **36:** 193, 194, 195, 415, 477; **37:** 42, 202, 289, 345, 420, 445n1, 470; **38:** 179, 210, 241,n1, 257, 258, 294, 321, 394n1, 688

Page, Walter Hines (*cont.*)
on Philippines, **27:** 5, 6; as cabinet possibility, **27:** 21, 22, 24, 27, 61, 126-27, 130; ambassadorship, **27:** 200, 228, 234, 245, 254; invitation to Jessie Wilson, **28:** 52-54, 259, 274; and golf, **28:** 276; hails Underwood-Simmons Tariff Act, **28:** 276, 328-29; Great Britain and Mexican situation, **28:** 388-98, 421-22, 433, 442-44, 447-48, 465-66, 467-69, 470-71, 477, 515, 516, 525-26, 527, 529, 530, 536-37, 566, 575-79, 586-88, 593-94; **30:** 4, 9, 9-10, 130-31, 144; on England and moral basis of government, **28:** 484-85; on Englishmen and democracy, **29:** 33; on Panama Canal tolls controversy, **29:** 52, 112, 162, 333,n1, 349, 376, 388-89, 396; on siege of Tampico, **29:** 111,n1; on L. Carden's conference with E. Grey, **29:** 131; meeting with Lord Cowdray on Mexico, **29:** 144-46; expenses of ambassadorship, **29:** 161, 410-13; **30:** 149-55, 277-78, 281-82, 288,n1, 489, 490; and Benton affair, **29:** 285-86,n3, 300; A. Carnegie on, **29:** 351, 352; E. M. House's peace mission to London and, **30:** 189, 190, 200, 214, 247, 255, 256, 258, 265, 271; **32:** 206, 211-15, 220, 220-21, 238n1, 242, 251-52, 253, 277, 340, 350; **33:** 105, 121, 226, 248, 253-54, 257, 266-67; **35:** 454, 471-73,n2, 484; **36:** 166, 167; WW on rental of residence, **30:** 195, 257; congratulates WW on progress in Mexico, **30:** 289; W. J. Bryan and tender of good offices, **30:** 311
on London and American embassy on eve of war, **30:** 314-16, 325, 329-31, 366-68; and offer to help Great Britain, **30:** 316-17; WW introduces S. G. Blythe, **30:** 320; on Americans in London, **30:** 368-71; WW thanks for condolences, **30:** 407; Grey and purchase of German ships, **30:** 435-36; on situation in Great Britain, **30:** 438-39; **31:** 244-46; **32:** 357-63; **35:** 74-77, 82-83, 412-17; and reply to WW mediation offer, **30:** 457n1; on Prussian militarism, **31:** 6-8; on peace plans, **31:** 21-22, 55n3; **36:** 181-82; **38:** 392-93; on war atrocities, **31:** 26-27, 263; and leaks in State Department, **31:** 29-30,n1; and Declaration of London, **31:** 99-100, 103, 105-106, 109, 110, 111, 113-14, 116, 125, 146, 158, 159-60, 188, 189-90, 195-96, 199-204; and Order in Council, **31:** 161, 161-63, 163-66; R. Lansing and, **31:** 166, 183; and personal finances, **31:** 122, 262-63; relays B. Whitlocks fears for Belgium, **31:** 181; and telegram to House, **31:** 204, 228; WW concerned over misperception of U.S. public opinion, **31:** 214, 246; WW and U.S. neutrality, **31:** 242-43, 386, 388; ideas about relief committee, **31:** 291; meets with Field Marshall French, **32:** 81-82; meetings with Grey, **32:** 91-93; **38:** 251-55
and British public opinion, **32:** 100-105, 129-33; **33:** 129-30, 213, 214; **34:** 317-18, 440-41; **35:** 223-28, 425-27, 435-38; **36:** 129-31, 369, 384-87, 628; **37:** 28-30, 143-47, 182-86, 226-27, 319-20, 456-62; **38:** 242-57; Grey on, **32:** 107n1, 109; on Bernstorff's note on compromise, **32:** 249-50, 251-52, 252,n2, 259; House on, **32:** 266; **36:** 422; **37:** 11-12, 24, 61, 71-72, 364; on blockade, **32:** 313, 409-11, 425; **35:** 483, 516-18, 519; on Sino-Japanese situation, **33:** 131-32; **36:** 411; on cotton crisis, **33:** 386, 526, 534; **34:** 34, 35, 137; on Bryan, **33:** 387-88; and daughter's marriage, **34:** 10-11,n1,2; and *Baralong* affair, **34:** 368,n1; and Cavell case, **35:** 103n2, 148, 149, 531; and House's unauthorized intimation to return to U.S., **34:** 54, 55,n1; reaction to *modus vivendi re* merchantmen, **35:** 533-34; and Shakespeare celebration, **36:** 261; on H. H. Kitchener interview with B. Strong and W. C. Forbes, **36:** 436; and *Laurentic* affair, **37:** 184,n2; on Casement case, **37:** 353; **38:** 316; and plan to return to U.S., **37:** 401, 401-402, 452, 462, 467; on conversation with WW, **38:** 241; on Trade Advisers' Bureau, **38:** 245-46; on relieving tension between Britain and U.S., **38:** 249; on conversation with J. Bryce, **38:** 249-51; talk with H. Asquith, **38:** 255-57; and relief for Poland, **38:** 371; and *U-53* incident, **38:** 472-73,n2; House and WW on, **38:** 646-47

Pages, Baltasar, **37:** 245
Paget, Sir Arthur Henry Fitzroy, **34:** 310,n1
Paget, Lady Mary Fiske Stevens (wife of Sir Arthur Henry Fitzroy Paget), **34:** 310,n1
Paget, Violet (pseud. Vernon Lee), **34:** 251,n7
Paignton, England, **35:** 77n2
Paish, Sir George, **31:** 177,n2, 207, 230, 235, 252, 315
Palafox, Manuel, **31:** 70
Palembang, S.S., **36:** 429, 429-30
Palm, Andrew, Jr., **36:** 338,n5
Palmer, Alexander Mitchell, **27:** 21, 72, 127, 406; **28:** 11, 144, 440,n3; **29:** 222, 223n2, 305,n1; **31:** 152, 188; **32:** 55; **36:** 336n2; **37:** 227; **38:** 430n1; as cabinet choice, **27:** 61, 62, 70, 96, 112, 116, 119, 129, 130-31, 132, 134; Democratic National Convention of 1912, **27:** 22,n2; offered War Department post, **27:** 126; single-term amendment, **27:** 97-101, 101, 103-105, 114; suggested for appointment as Counselor of State Department, **34:** 24,n1, 31, 41, 42, 44, 53, 79, 134

Palmer, Leigh Carlyle, **27:** 448
Palmer, Frederick, **36:** 251n
Palmer-Owen bill, **29:** 170,n1
Pampanga Province, P.I., **27:** 189
Pan American Building, Washington, D.C., **30:** 441n1
Pan American Commission, **27:** 203n1
Pan American Conference (third), **27:** 203n1
Pan American Conference (fourth), **27:** 203n1
Pan American Conferences on Mexico, **34:** 43, 51-52, 54, 59, 60, 78, 80, 98-99, 102, 105, 110-12,n1, 2, 112-14, 124, 132, 139-40, 157,n1,2, 164,n1, 179, 196-97,n1,2, 199, 241, 267n1, 273n1, 321, 384, 385-86, 408-409, 448, 455n1, 460, 472,n1, 487-88, 509, 540-42; **36:** 313,n1
Pan American Financial Conference, **31:** 258,n1; **32:** 247n1, 250-51, 252, 283, 293-94; **35:** 296,n1, 440, 443-44; **36:** 267n1, 367,n2; **37:** 187-88,n4, 196; WW welcome to, **33:** 245-47
Pan American Financial Conference and International High Commission (1916), **38:** 196-97, 197
Pan–American Pact, **32:** 42,n1; 338-39, 339-40; **34:** 43; **38:** 17, 18-19; background and inception of, **31:** 369-70, 468-70; WW's first draft of, **31:** 471-73; negotiations concerning, **31:** 497-98, 535-36, 540, 548-49, 555; **33:** 52-54, 55-60, 65, 77-80, 80, 220-21, 221-22, 449, 477,n1, 533; **35:** 34, 43, 54-55, 59, 113-14, 119, 126, 143, 176, 207-208, 215-16, 410-11, 411, 438; **36:** 197-201, 229-30, 278,n2, 333, 375, 380, 398, 403, 417, 423, 426, 461, 478, 479, 596-97, 605; **37:** 37, 108, 122,n1, 238-39, 240-41, 265-66, 398-99, 399-400; E. M. House meets with ABC ambassadors, **32:** 64; and Chile, **32:** 98, 98-99, 474, 542; **33:** 52-54, 55-60, 68, 77-80, 80, 437; **34:** 444, 448; **35:** 519-20; and four articles, **32:** 146, 159-62; **35:** 64-68, 70-71; revision of articles, **35:** 188-89; R. L. Owen on, **35:** 201-202; drafts of, **35:** 111-13; **36:** 412-13, 595-96, 600; **37:** 241-44, 244; and Great Britain, **36:** 445, 601-602; procedures for signing, **37:** 243, 271, 400
Pan-American resolution, **28:** 386
Pan American Scientific Congress (first), **27:** 203n1
Pan American Scientific Congress (second), **35:** 358,n2, 373, 410,n1; **36:** 198, 367,n2; WW greeting to delegates, **35:** 395; WW's address to, **35:** 439-41, 441-46, 456-57
Pan American Union, **28:** 95,n1,2, 448n1; **31:** 431, 450; **33:** 60, 245n1
Pan-Americanism, **32:** 343; **35:** 248-49, 296, 410n1; E. M. House on, **30:** 255-56, 271-72
Panama, **28:** 95n1, 197,n2, 400, 448n1;

31: 498; **33:** 46,n3; **34:** 51, 80, 131,n3; **35:** 247, 252, 298, 375, 377; and Colombia, **28:** 292n1,2, 330, 342, 533-35; **30:** 209n1; and Mexico, **28:** 412; U. S. recognition, **28:** 201,n1; and EBG's brother, **33:** 542,n3; *see also* Bolling family: crisis in
Panama and the United States, **29:** 160; and loan, **29:** 360
Panama Canal, **27:** 443-44, 482, 488, 509; **28:** 124, 228, 292n1, 400n2, 424, 448,n1, 449, 534, 535, 543, 572; **29:** 37, 96, 168, 182, 233, 306-308, 333n1, 407, 419, 524; **30:** 23, 381, 389, 472; **31:** 241-42; **32:** 60, 134, 164; **33:** 33, 35; **35:** 246, 284, 305, 350, 375, 376, 377; **36:** 236, 620; **37:** 127n2; **38:** 269, 669; and Nicaragua, **27:** 527, 528; and Colombia, **29:** 39-40; men responsible for construction of, **29:** 307n1,2,3,4; T. Roosevelt on, **30:** 209n1; opening ceremonies planned, **31:** 363; disbursements for, **35:** 304; WW on tolls controversy, **38:** 329
Panama Canal Act, **27:**, 225, 226; **29:** 179, 231, 387; **30:** 326
Panama Canal bonds, **31:** 61, 120, 121, 128; **34:** 50
Panama Canal tolls controversy, **27:** 71, 125, 203, 221-23, 225, 310-11, 312-13, 325, 332-33, 357-58, 359, 411, 504, 512, 514, 534; **28:** 316, 422, 462, 531, 532, 545, 597; **29:** 12-13, 34-35, 52, 112, 160, 162, 171, 179, 203, 217-18, 224, 231-33,n1, 236, 237, 267-68, 269, 313, 325, 334-35, 348, 350-51, 373, 376, 384, 384-87, 394, 397-98, 406-407, 415, 424; **30:** 129, 141, 154, 175, 183, 248n1, 253, 371, 463; **35:** 223, 224; **37:** 34
WW will strive for repeal, **29:** 104, 182; causes friction with European nations, **29:** 180; and violation of Hay-Pauncefote Treaty, **29:** 220, 271, 408; and J. A. O'Gorman, **29:** 237, 422; and relation to Baltimore platform, **29:** 240-41; WW urged to address Congress on, **29:** 242, 282-83, 311; W. C. Adamson on, **29:** 265-66,n2, 383; J. L. Bristoe on, **29:** 272n1; J. R. Thornton on, **29:** 275-77, 281, 288-89, 297, 310,n1; T. W. Sims on, **29:** 298-300, 304; WW's address to Congress on, **29:** 312-13, 378-80; J. A. Hamill on, **29:** 318-19; J. Bryce praises WW's speech on, **29:** 320; WW confident of repeal, **29:** 321, 345; A. Carnegie on, **29:** 352; C. R. Crisp on, **29:** 381; W. H. Page and, **29:** 388-89; J. G. Hibben on, **29:** 391-92,n1; M. A. Smith on, **29:** 392-93; W. F. McCombs on, **29:** 404-405; W. E. Chilton on, **29:** 405; P. J. McCumber on, **29:** 409,n1; T. R. Marshall on, **29:** 418-20; and Norris-Simmons amendment, **30:** 159,n1; Senate passes Sims bill, **30:** 159n1, 174n1; WW thanks F. M. Simmons for work on repeal, **30:** 176; con-

Panama Canal tolls controversy (*cont.*) gratulations from Bryce, **30:** 195; WW thanks Sims for help, **30:** 188; WW acknowledges Bryce's comments on, **30:** 260; WW thanks J. S. Sherley, **30:** 260-61

Panama Canal Zone, **27:** 219,n3, 509; **28:** 125n3, 197; **31:** 340, 445, **34:** 197n1

Panama-Pacific International Exposition (San Francisco Exposition of 1915), **27:** 162,n1, 220, 293,n1, 309; **31:** 354, 370, 403; **32:** 88, 118, 229,n1, 306; **36:** 299, 301

Panama Railway Co., **30:** 402, 455-56; **31:** 445; **35:** 375, 376, 377

Pancho Villa and the Attack on Columbus, New Mexico (Katz), **36:** 280n1

Pani, Alberto J., **38:** 83n1, 153, 356, 358

Panic of 1893, **27:** 570

Panic of 1907, **27:** 566, 569, 570; **28:** 421n1, 511

Papal States, **33:** 46,n2

Papen, Franz von, **33:** 233, 320; **34:** 266,n2, 452,n1; **35:** 43,n1, 264,n1, 265, 276, 277n1, 277-78, 281, 282, 291n1; **38:** 298

Papers of Woodrow Wilson, **36:** 371,n1

Paraguay, **27:** 385; appointments, **28:** 4, 354,n4; and Mexico, **28:** 412

parcel post service, **37:** 190, 192; **38:** 129, 422

Pardel Corp. of Piladelphia, **37:** 344n1

Pardo y Barreda, José, **38:** 653-54,n4

Paredes, Antonio J., **32:** 248,n1, 249n2, 259n1

Paris, France, **30:** 139-40, 246; **31:** 10, 56; **33:** 524; **34:** 44; in 1793, **27:** 425; and House's mission, **32:** 64, 335, 349, 372, 393; and German military plans, **32:** 81, 237, 523

Paris as Seen and Described by Famous Writers (Singleton), **31:** 316n2, 317

Paris Economic Conference: *see* Allied Economic Conference in Paris

Paris Herald, **37:** 141n4

Paris *Le Temps*, **32:** 462,n1,2, 464n2; **35:** 525n3; **37:** 202

Parker, Edward Wheeler, **38:** 297n2

Parker, Gabe Edward, **28:** 187,n2, 410,n4; **31:** 312

Parker, Sir Gilbert, **34:** 146, 147

Parker, John Clinton, **37:** 344-45,n1, 347

Parker, John Milliken, **37:** 523n1; **38:** 650

Parker, Marie, **33:** 543,n4; **34:** 246

Parker, Samuel Dunn, **29:** 401n1

Parkhurst, Miss, **38:** 521,n1

Parks, E. Taylor, **28:** 197n2

Parliamentary Debates, **29:** 285n3; **30:** 248n1; **31:** 8n6; **38:** 472n1

Parole Commission of New York, **38:** 161n2

Parral, Chihuahua, Mex., **30:** 408, 409; **36:** 457; **37:** 22, 23, 39, 252; **38:** 379

Parral incident: *see* Mexico and the United States

Parrish, Jean, **28:** 66n1

Parrish, John Dillwyn, **28:** 66n1

Parrish, Lydia Austin (Mrs. Frederick Maxfield), **28:** 55,n5, 66, 150, 400; **33:** 526,n5

Parrish (Frederick) Maxfield, **28:** 55.n4, 66, 98, 146, 150, 338, 360, 375, 392, 400

Parrish, Maxfield (son of Frederick Maxfield), **28:** 66n1, 400; **33:** 526,n5; **34:** 128

Parrish, Mrs. (of Bermuda), **27:** 106

Parrish, Stephen, **28:** 55,n3, 98, 99, 103, 150, 321, 375, 392; **33:** 543,n2

Parrish, Stephen (son of Frederick Maxfield), **28:** 66n1

Parry, Will H., **32:** 271n2, 273; **37:** 204n2

Parsons, Herbert, **38:** 284,n4

Parsons, Closson and McIlvaine, N.Y., **38:** 284n4

Partners (Deland), **31:** 316n2, 317

party politics, **27:** 211; **29:** 7, 64

Pass Christian, Miss., **29:** 60, 77,n1, 86, 89, 90, 370,n2; WW made honorary member of fire department, **29:** 99n1; WW's reasons for not attending church in, **29:** 104

Pass Christian Presbyterian Church, **29:** 104,n1

passport investigations, **32:** 308

Patent Committee (House of Reps.), **29:** 28

Paterson, N.J., **27:** 20; **34:** 286, 292, 300

patronage, **27:** xiv, xvi, 62-63, 72, 99, 111, 114, 251, 344-45; **28:** 532; **31:** 399-401, 498, 500, 501, 507; **34:** 515; **35:** 360; Negroes, **27:** 19, 291; S. B. Woods, **27:** 74; A. M. Palmer, **27:** 103; WW's warning to office seekers, **27:** 153; and W. Sulzer, **28:** 64; C. Ford and spoils system, **29:** 100,n2; in Kentucky, **29:** 343,n2; in New York, **29:** 402-403; E. M. House on, **29:** 456; in North Carolina, **30:** 144; W. J. Stone wishes to see WW about, **31:** 487-88

Pattangall, William Robinson, **28:** 149,n1

Patten, J. H., **32:** 96

Patten, Thomas Gedney, **28:**, 90,n1; **35:** 319,n5

Patterson, Adam Edward, **28:** 10,n1, 20, 40-41, 88-89, 94, 115, 186n1, 210, 289, 453, 496-97; requests withdrawal of nomination for Register of the Treasury, **28:** 97-98,n1

Patterson, Malcolm Rice, **27:** 55n3

Patterson, Thomas MacDonald, **28:** 521

Patton, Francis Landey, **30:** 466; **36:** 394,n3

Paul, Alice, **38:** 175n1, 481n1

Paul Kimble Hospital, Lakewood, N.J., **38:** 118n3

Paul Revere Trust Co., **28:** 271

Pauncefote, Julian, **27:** 312

Payne, John Barton, **38:** 465,n7

Payne-Aldrich Tariff Act, **27:** 35, 150, 177, 289n7, 511-12, 570, 571-72; **35:** 384n2; **38:** 299; S. Gompers, **27:** 368

Payot, Mrs. Henry, **31:** 332

Payton, Jacob S., **36:** 391n2
Peabody, Endicott, **35:** 431,n1
Peabody, Francis Stuyvesant, **38:** 374-75,n1
Peabody, George Foster, **29:** 278, 531; **38:** 23, 549, 562, 620-21, 625
Peabody, James Hamilton, **28:** 584,n1
Peabody Coal Co., **38:** 375n1
peace, **29:** 3-4
Peace Moves and U-Boat Warfare (Birnbaum), **33:** 279n1; **37:** 45n1
Peace Ship: Henry Ford's Pacifist Adventure in the First World War (Kraft), **35:** 279n1
Peace With Honour: Controversial Notes on the Settlement (Lee), **34:** 251,n7
Peacemaker (London *Daily News and Leader*), **37:** 294n1
Pearce, James B., **28:** 426,n6
Pearson, Weetman Dickinson, 1st Baron Cowdray, **27:** 331n2, 424; **28:** 376,n2, 378, 388, 429, 444-45, 446, 471, 477, 516, 526,n2, 528, 530, 537, 544,n1, 577, 578, 593, 600; **29:** 111,n3, 396; **30:** 237, 247; **33:** 64, 478; interests in Mexico, **29:** 16, 18, 33, 121, 141, 549, 550; on U.S. and British joint intervention in Mexico, **29:** 145-46,n1, 146
Pearson, S., and Son Ltd., **27:** 331,n2
Peck, Mary Allen Hulbert: *see* Hulbert, Mary Allen
Peg O' My Heart (play), **27:** 63,n4
Peking, China, **27:** 27,n1; **31:** 546; **33:** 105
Peking Gazette, **38:** 441n1
Peking-Mukden Railway, **31:** 510
Peltier, P. M., **29:** 549
Peña, Carlos Maria de, **33:** 454, 455, 487, 488; **34:** 157n1,2, 321, 488
Peña y Reyes, Antonio de la, **28:** 239
Pence, Thomas Jones, **27:** 487n1, 491-92; **31:** 270-71; **32:** 115-16; **34:** 471-72; **36:** 399, 404; **37:** 378, 379n1; death of, **36:** 371,n1; 376-77
Pendleton, Oreg., **30:** 353n1
Pendleton, George Hunt, **31:** 351,n1
Pendleton bill, **31:** 351,n1
Penfield, Frederic Courtland, **27:** 110,n1, 200; **28:** 4, 286; **29:** 74; **30:** 222, 457n1; **32:** 439, 440; **33:** 219; **34:** 432,n1, 433,n1, 503; **36:** 124, 126; **37:** 4-5, 289, 345, 470, 482; **38:** 62, 74-75, 544; transmits Austria-Hungary's reply to WW mediation offer, **30:** 457n1; and *Ancona* case, **35:** 208-209, 236, 282, 286, 365, 380, 394-95, 410, 420; on public opinion in Austria-Hungary on peace moves, **37:** 273-74; on probability of Rumania entering war, **37:** 464-65
Penn, William, **28:** 440-41
Pennsylvania, **27:** 323, 406; **30:** 319, 333n2; **37:** 118, 373, 523; **38:** 430,n1, 437, 457, 630; appointments, **28:** 329,n2; senatorial contest, **29:** 222-23,n1,2, 305,n1, 375; WW backs A. M. Palmer for U.S. Senate, **31:** 188; Re-

publican victories in, **31:** 264n3; and anthracite coal settlement, **31:** 503-504; W. B. Wilson and senatorial race, **36:** 23-25; Erie County politics, **36:** 336-38; V. McCormick's bid for governor in, **38:** 430-31,n2
Pennsylvania, University of, **27:** 208; **34:** 131n3; **37:** 227n1; **38:** 73n10, 362n4
Pennsylvania Academy of the Fine Arts, **28:** 183n7
Pennsylvania Day, **38:** 430n1
Pennsylvania Railroad, **27:** 322n1; **31:** 390; **33:** 442,n1; **38:** 415; Union Pacific Railroad case, **29:** 67n2
Pennsylvania Station, N.Y., **27:** 372
Pennsylvania Woman Suffrage Association, **37:** 490n1
Pennybacker, Anna J. Hardwicke (Mrs. Percy V.), **37:** 535,n1
Penrose, Boies, **27:** 453n1; **28:** 163,n2,4, 185, 208n2; **29:** 223n2, 495; **35:** 434; **37:** 174, 340
Peoples Bank, Roxboro, N.C., **29:** 322n1
People's Institute of New York, **30:** 282
Peoples National Bank of Charleston, S.C., **38:** 75n1
Peoria, Ill., **27:** 466; **38:** 260
Peoria (Ill.), *Journal*, **27:** 462n1
Percy, Lord Eustace, **36:** 444
Percyval, T. Wigney, **35:** 19n1
Pereked, Alexander Nuber von, *see* Nuber von Pereked, Alexander
Pereyra, Orestes, **28:** 77
Perez Ruel, **32:** 383, 384
Perfect Tribute (Andrews), **31:** 316,n2
periodicals: as source material, **27:** xiii
Perkins, Charles, **29:** 369
Perkins, Edward E., **28:** 64,n1
Perkins, Frances, **27:** 244
Perkins, George Henry, **29:** 474,n1
Perkins, George Walbridge, **29:** 29; **30:** 303, 491; **37:** 429,n1; **38:** 190n1
Permanent Court of Arbitration, **27:** 191n1, 226; **29:** 125; **35:** 395n2, 419, 453; and *Arabic* crisis, **34:** 439, 440, 505, 520
Perry, Bliss, **28:** 20n3, 88; **30:** 363-64; **38:** 563-64,n1
Perry, Grace, **28:** 88,n2
Perry, Lewis, **28:** 20,n3, 88
Perry, Lewis, Jr., **28:** 88,n1
Perry, Margaret Lawrie Hubbell (Mrs. Lewis), **28:** 88,n1
Perry, Mary Brown Smedley (Mrs. Arthur Latham), **28:** 88,n2
Perry, S. M., **29:** 549
Pershing, John Joseph, **37:** 38, 263,n3, 277n1, 280, 281, 284, 292, 299, 307, 309n2, 315, 317; **38:** 45, 166n2, 220, 229, 271, 272, 398, 399, 402-403, 404, 405, 548n1, 634; and Punitive Expedition, **36:** 285,n2, 312, 317n1, 323, 335n1,2, 344, 352, 395n1, 407n1, 457, 464, 501-503, 528, 540n1, 579, 608; report on Punitive Expedition, **36:** 584-91; on Parral attack, **36:** 509,n1;

Pershing, John Joseph (*cont.*)
T. H. Bliss on, **38:** 231-32, 676; N. D. Baker on withdrawal of troops of, **38:** 237, 546; promoted to major general, **38:** 238-39,n11; and Carrizal incident, **38:** 378-82, 385; photograph: *illustration section,* 36
Persia, **28:** 4; 104n1; **38:** 298
Persia incident, **35:** 419,n1, 420,n1, 420-22, 423n1, 424, 425, 426, 430-31, 452; **36:** 209, 246, 252, 558
Personal Aspects of the Presidency (Taft), **29:** 302n1
Perth Amboy Drydock Co., **38:** 212n1
Peru, **27:** 478; **28:** 412, 448n1; **29:** 244, 261, 524; and Chile, **31:** 498; **32:** 474,n3,4; **33:** 53-54, 63; **35:** 55, 126, 216; **36:** 200, 461, 596-97; reaction to WW's election, **38:** 653-54
Pesqueira, Ignacio, **27:** 422n1; **29:** 205, 206
Pesqueira, Roberto V., **30:** 409,n5
Peter I Karageorgevich (of Serbia), **27:** 438
Peterhoff case, **32:** 407, 445
Peters, Andrew James, **38:** 36
Peters, Preston L., **36:** 337
Peters affair, **34:** 67,n1
Peters, Andrew James, **28:** 301,n2, 498n1; **31:** 193,n1
Peterson, Merrill Daniel, **32:** 86n1
Petit Goave, Haiti, **34:** 165
Petition Starts Presidential Inquiry (*Washington Post*), **28:** 498n1
Petrel, U.S.S., **27:** 518-19, 531
Petrograd, Russia, **31:** 182; **32:** 64; **37:** 134n1
petroleum: *see* oil
Petrucci, Mary, **30:** 39n1
Pettegrew, E. J., **27:** 543
Pettibone Mulliken Co., Chicago, **30:** 205n1
Petty-Fitzmaurice, Henry Charles Keith, 5th Marquess of Lansdowne, **33:** 214,n1
Peyser, Julius I., **32:** 97
Pezet, Federico Alfonso, **29:** 244,n1,2
Phelan, James Duval, **27:** 70, 228, 361-62; **35:** 462; **36:** 311,n1; **37:** 46, 66,n2, 140, 141, 143, 172,n2; **38:** 5, 444; and California alien land legislation, **27:** 265, 277; report on Dominican Republic situation, **33:** 218-20,n1
Phelan, Michael Francis, **28:** 90,n1; **32:** 353-54, 354, 457, 469
Phelps, William Walter, **30:** 152
Phelps Dodge and Co., **27:** 404n1; **28:** 278n3
Philadelphia, Pa., **28:** 434; **31:** 330; Collector of the Port, **27:** 286,n4, 338; WW addresses in, **28:** 435-39; **30:** 248,n1; **33:** 147-50, 149n3, 154, 159, 160, 162,n1, 163-64, 196, 201, 432n1; **37:** 324-28,n1, 337, 342; WW's visit to, **34:** 159, 161, 256, 258, 285
Philadelphia *Evening Bulletin*, **29:** 361n2

Philadelphia *Inquirer*, **28:** 439n, 442n; **34:** 365,n1, 378; **38:** 20n1
Philadelphia *North American*, **28:** 439n, 442n
Philadelphia *Public Ledger*, **31:** 407; **34:** 445,n4
Philadelphia *Record*, **37:** 27,n2; **38:** 389n1
Philadelphia *Tribune*, **28:** 221n1
philanthropy, WW on, **30:** 108
Philanthropy That Pays Dividends (Chandler), **33:** 430n2
Philip, Hoffman, **38:** 210, 317
Philip Beck and Co., Buffalo, **29:** 401n1
Philip Dru: Administrator, A Story of Tomorrow, 1920-1935 (House), **28:** 477; **31:** 95
Philip van Artevelde (Taylor), **31:** 83
Philippine bill: *see* Jones bill
Philippine Commission, **28:** 5, 242n1, 300-301; **29:** 8, 137n1,2; **38:** 438
Philippine Committee (Senate), **30:** 216; **32:** 15n4, 291,n1, 292,n2; **36:** 139
Philippine Islands and Filipinos, **29:** 8, 163-64, 218, 399-400; **30:** 144, 159, 213, 230, 245, 259; **38:** 155, 346, 438; caciquism, **28:** 242n1; languages, **28:** 242n1; and Military Order of the Carabao, **29:** 36n2, 37, 38-39, 44; H. J. Ford's supplemental report on, **29:** 137,n1; F. McIntyre meets with M. Quezon, **29:** 147-52; C. H. Brent on policy, **29:** 165-67; and Jones bill, **30:** 155-56, 160-61, 172, 216; granted self-rule, **38:** 119; congratulations to WW, **38:** 656, 674-75
Philippine Islands and the United States, **27:** 6,n1, 133n1, 385, 434; **28:** 203, 288, 300-301, 329, 367, 372, 382, 415-17, 442, 494, 595; **32:** 15,n3, 285, 330-31, 369, 457; **33:** 35; **34:** 389; **35:** 52, 72, 85-87, 123, 169, 176, 298, 303, 466,n1, 467,n1,2, 509,n1; **36:** 94-95, 139,n1, 144, 172,n1,2, 366n1
W. H. Page on, **27:** 5; W. J. Bryan on, **27:** 9,n3; E. Aguinaldo and, **27:** 10, 468; governor generalship appointment, **27:** 22, 255-57, 274, 282-83; **28:** 175,n1, 184, 192, 192-93, 197; H. J. Ford on, **27:** 188-89, 370-71; **28:** 242,n1; W. L. Garrison on, **27:** 255-57, 354-56, 516,n1; B. A. Fiske on, **27:** 426-28; Joint Board and U.S. fleet, **27:** 443-44, 446; English used in schools, **27:** 468; **28:** 242n1; F. B. Harrison's arrival speech, **28:** 323-24,n1; Turkish ambassador's views of U.S. treatment of Filipinos, **31:** 16n1; and Noriel case, **32:** 535,n1, 535-36, 536,n2; and 1916 platform, **37:** 199
Phillips, Charles, **35:** 391n1
Phillips, Cyrus William, **32:** 532,n1
Phillips, Nora, **36:** 503-504,n2
Phillips, Samuel Field, **36:** 503n2
Phillips, William **28:** 528,n2; **29:** 33, 34, 53, 104, 143,n1, 160, 187-89, 191-95, 205-206; **30:** 22, 45, 156, 157; **31:** 91,

93, 102, 108, 114, 197, 489, 500, 517-18, 549, 552-53, 553; **32:** 64, 91, 119, 120-21; **33:** 451, 477, 479, 533; **34:** 504-505, 511, 515, 529; **35:** 62, 63-64, 68, 83, 118, 127, 236, 310n1, 352-53, 360, 386, 397; **36:** 133, 266, 402, 599, 600; **37:** 350, 414, 433-34, 469; **38:** 209-10, 300, 317, 359-60, 616

Philosophy of Politics (Wilson), **30:** 376,n2

Phinney, J. B., **32:** 188,n1

Phinney, Mrs. J. B, **32:** 188

Phylon, **28:** 349n2

Pichon, Stéphen Jean-Marie, **27:** 532-35

Pickett Act, **37:** 40

Picklands, Mather and Co., Cleveland, **29:** 401n1

Pictorial Review, **30:** 173n1, 182, 190

Piedmont, Italy, **31:** 562n4

Piedras Negras, Coahuila, Mex., **28:** 80; **38:** 401

Pierce, Franklin, **29:** 452

Pierce, Henry Clay, **28:** 527,n1

Pierson, S. G., **28:** 427

Pike, Frederick B., **28:** 188n1

Pike, William A., **32:** 96,n3

Pillars of Society (Gardiner), **31:** 482n1; **32:** 21n1, 66n1, 117

Pimentel, Luis Garcia, **27:** 537

Pinchot, Amos Richards Eno, **27:** 93; **29:** 74n1; **37:** 308n2, 320-21, 336, 348, 402, 531; **38:** 52,n1, 190,n1, 445,n1; on L. D. Brandeis, **36:** 20, 22-23, 23, 86; antipreparedness and, **36:** 524, 635,n10, 636-37, 642

Pinchot, Gertrude Minturn (Mrs. Amos Richards Eno), **37:** 308-309,n1, 316,n1, 336, 348

Pinchot, Gifford, **27:** 93; **29:** 305,n1; **35:** 79,n2, 231-33, 261, 329n1; **37:** 12, 167,n2, 329; on water-power legislation, **36:** 48-51, 241, 302-303, 312, 360

Pindell, Eliza Adelia (Mrs. Henry Means), **27:** 467,n1

Pindell, Henry Means, **27:** 462,n1, 466-67; **28:** 111, 353; **38:** 260

Pinehurst, N.C., **36:** 307n1, 435,n1

Pinō Suarez, José Maria, **28:** 71, 173; **29:** 554,n2; **33:** 187n1

Piping Rock Club, Long Island, N.Y., **30:** 22; **31:** 318, 392; **33:** 452

Pirates of Penzance, **29:** 449

Piscano (Pisano, Pizano), Anciento, **37:** 261,n7

Pitchfork Ben Tillman: South Carolinian (Simkins), **35:** 434n1

Pitney, Mahlon, **30:** 103-104,n1; **31:** 19; **35:** 274; **36:** 465,n1, 481

Pittman, Key, **29:** 373; **30:** 31; **35:** 233; **36:** 211, 311,n1, 348-49

Pittsburgh Dispatch, **36:** 218n

Pittsburgh Post, **36:** 35n, 41n

Pittsburgh, Pa., **31:** 151, 214; WW's address to YMCA of, **31:** 220-28; WW's addresses on preparedness in, **36:** 26-35, 35-41

Pittsburgh, University of, **27:** 208

Pittsburgh Leader, **27:** 406n1

Pittsfield, Mass., **32:** 230

Pius X, **30:** 404-405,n1

Plainfield, N.H., **28:** 126n1; **33:** 525,n3

Plan of: *see* under the latter part of the name, such as Ayala, Plan of; Guadalupe, Plan of

Plata, S.S., **36:** 233

Platt, Charles Adams, **28:** 36,n4, 43, 103, 112

Platt, Eleanor Hardy, **28:** 43,n5, 103

Platt, James A., **36:** 337

Platt Amendment, **27:** 526, 527n1; **28:** 48, 100; **29:** 134, 222, 275; **30:** 174; **33:** 467n1; and Nicaraguan treaty, **32:** 60

Plattsburg movement, **36:** 97,n2

Plattsburg training camp, **34:** 29,n1, 133,n1, 196, 209, 410; T. Roosevelt speech at, **34:** 337,n1

Players Club, N.Y., **36:** 96

Plaza Hotel, N.Y., **34:** 452,n1

Plea for Pacifism (Gladden), **35:** 344,n1

Plighted (Craik), **34:** 431,n2

Plotting U-Boats New Sea Sport for Arabic Crew (New York *Tribune*), **34:** 367,n1

Plunkett, Sir Horace, **27:** 60,n2,3,4; **29:** 115-17, 132; **30:** 287; **32:** 83; **33:** 338-39, 414-15, 448, 533; **35:** 3, 4-5, 8-11, 19, 64, 78, 85, 191-92, 279, 310-11,n1, 320-21, 346, 382n1; **36:** 459n2; **37:** 104, 137-38, 168, 411; **38:** 54; on defensive arming of merchant ships, **36:** 207-209; memorandum on Anglo-American situation, **36:** 347,n1; on U.S. intervention, **36:** 519-20; on WW's address to League to Enforce Peace, **37:** 295-96

Poe, Clarence (Hamilton), **31:** 128-29, 131

Poe, Edgar Allan, **27:** 42,n2; **28:** 465

Poems (Craik), **34:** 431n2

Pohl, Hugo von, **34:** 47,n4

Poincaré, Raymond, **29:** 184, 304, 342; **30:** 342; **31:** 247-48, 410, 461, 539; **32:** 16, 341,n3, 374, 522, 523, 531-32; **33:** 10-11, 63; **35:** 381; **36:** 125; **37:** 412, 414, 445,n1, 470; **38:** 353, 458; and use of dumdum bullets, **31:** 38-39, 54; on aid to Poland, **38:** 79-81

Poindexter, Miles, **29:** 159; **36:** 311,n2

Poinsett, George, **30:** 107,n5

Poinsett, Joel Roberts, **31:** 562n3

Point Isabel, Tex., **36:** 296

Points Under Discussion Respecting Withdrawal of Troops (Mexican Commissioners), **38:** 357,n1

Poland, **31:** 294n1; **32:** 254, 506; **33:** 299,n4, 333, 347, 371, 516, 517; **34:** 12, 17-18, 44, 159, 239; **35:** 8, 261, 484; **36:** 123n1, 238, 444n1; **37:** 43n1; **38:** 539, 647; plea for aid to, **37:** 404-406, 407; WW's appeal for aid to, **35:** 367, 391,n1; **37:** 414, 421-22, 432-33, 433-34, 445,n1, 470; Nicholas II responds to request, **37:** 538; comments on question of aid

Poland (*cont.*)
to, **38:** 29-30, 62, 64-66, 72, 73-74, 79-81, 106, 368-72, 391, 396-97; WW on failure of appeal, **38:** 458
Polish Alma Mater (society), **37:** 406
Polish Americans, **38:** 140, 349, 397, 564; and plea for aid to Poland, **37:** 404-406, 407, 414
Polish Association of America, **37:** 406n1
Polish Central Relief Commission, **37:** 404-406
Polish Falcon's Alliance, **37:** 406n1
Polish National Alliance, **37:** 406n1
Polish National Council, **37:** 406n1
Polish people: in Russia, **30:** 434
Polish Relief Committee, **33:** 299,n4
Polish Roman Catholic Church Union, **37:** 406n1
Polish St. Joseph's Union, **37:** 406n1
Polish Uniformed Societies, **37:** 406n1
Polish Union of America, **37:** 406n1
Polish Woman's Alliance, **37:** 406n1
political bosses, **29:** 57; Sulzer, W., **28:** 64
Political Education of Woodrow Wilson (Kerney), **27:** 401n1; **28:** 96n1
political parties: *see* under the names of the individual parties
Political Prairie Fire: The Nonpartisan League, 1915-1922 (Morlan), **38:** 159n4
Political Revolution (New York *Evening Post*), **38:** 645,n1
Political Science Quarterly, **27:** 291n1
Politics of Populism: Dissent in Colorado (Wright), **28:** 584n1
Politics of Prejudice, the Anti-Japanese Movement in California and the Struggle for Japanese Exclusion (Daniels), **27:** 220n3
Politische Dokumente (von Tirpitz), **37:** 45n1
Polk, Frank Lyon, **27:** 292,n1, 333, 337, 397, 407; **31:** 139, 552; **34:** 134, 237,n1, 488, 503, 514, 529, 539; **35:** 65, 78, 310n1, 336, 360, 398; **36:** 168, 249, 266, 375, 389, 398, 442, 425, 461, 547, 597-98; **37:** 76, 77, 92, 135n2, 154, 162, 220, 225, 399, 414, 467, 470, 476, 479, 482, 506; **38:** 5, 10, 11, 13, 17, 19, 259, 372, 429, 493
appointed Counselor of State Department, **34:** 368,n1; as possible replacement for JPT, **34:** 515-16; and Punitive Expedition, **36:** 307,n1, 313, 318-19, 331-32, 342-43,n2, 434-44,n1, 350-51, 351; on Pan-American Treaty negotiations, **36:** 33; **37:** 122; Democratic National Committee chairmanship and, **36:** 378, 599; **37:** 45, 46, 56, 118, 129, 131, 245; on France and peace moves, **37:** 93-94, 164; on Mexican situation and Joint High Commission, **37:** 130-31, 138, 164, 400-401, 409-10, 410-11, 437, 452, 452-53, 453-54, 482-83, 485; on Dominican Republic, **37:** 157-

58; and Casement case, **37:** 379-80, 516, 517; **38:** 350,n1, 443; on W. H. Page visiting U.S., **37:** 401; on Russo-Japanese Treaty, **37:** 418-19; on draft on Polish relief, **37:** 432-33; on British blacklist, **37:** 469-70, 471; on Danish West Indies, **37:** 484, 495, 521, 539; informs R. Lansing of international developments, **37:** 495-97; meets with E. M. House, **38:** 657-58
Polk, Harry Herndon, **36:** 77n1
Polk, John Knox, **37:** 509
Pollen, Arthur Joseph Hungerford, **36:** 459,n1
Polo de Bernabé, Luis: *see* Bernabé, Luis Polo de
Polo Grounds, N.Y., **35:** 257
Pomerene, Atlee, **28:** 415; **30:** 94, 166, 380, 381, 384, 427; **32:** 286; **34:** 538; **35:** 193; **36:** 41n1, 175; **37:** 25, 84, 96,n1, 441n2; **38:** 281, 395, 457
Poor Richard's Almanac, **32:** 283
Pope, George, **38:** 46,n1, 55
Pope, Paul Wilkinson, **31:** 310-11,n1, 314
Popenoe, Charles Holcomb, **35:** 238,n4
Popenoe, Wilson, **35:** 238,n4
Populist party, **38:** 51n1, 103n1
Populists, Plungers and Progressives: A Social History of Stock and Commodity Speculation, 1890-1936 (Cowing), **30:** 312n1
Por Que Villa atacó a Columbus (Calzadiaz Berrera), **36:** 280n1
Porfirio Diaz: Dictator of Mexico (Beals), **27:** 64n2
Porritt, Edward, **28:** 315,n2
Port-au-Prince, Haiti, **31:** 457n1; **32:** 27; **34:** 45,n1, 60, 61, 69, 70, 71, 78-79, 89, 109n3, 121, 142, 157, 165, 183
Porter, Henry Kirke, **31:** 220n3
Portillo y Rojas, José Lopez, **29:** 328, 329, 398, 458, 463, 465, 467-68, 524; meeting with J. Lind, **29:** 357-60; meeting with N. O'Shaughnessy, **35:** 446-47
Portland *Oregon Journal*, **29:** 271n1
Porto Rican bill, **30:** 213, 215; **31:** 465, 465-66, 473-74; **37:** 369, 455-56, 469; **38:** 649,n1
Porto Rico, **27:** 199,n1, 257, 340; **28:** 366-67; **29:** 8, 20, 264-65,n1, 269, 273-74, 284-85, 289; **30:** 392, 424; **31:** 465-66; **35:** 123, 169, 298, 303; **36:** 366n1; **37:** 170, 200n3; **38:** 346, 633; appointments in, **32:** 94,n1; and Jones bill, **36:** 250,n2, 306; rights of workers in, **36:** 567-68, 569; JPT on Yager and, **36:** 569-70
Portsmouth, N.H., **38:** 79
Portsmouth, Treaty of, **32:** 320
Portsmouth Conference, **27:** 452; **31:** 182n2, 469n4
Portugal, **35:** 227; appointments, **28:** 4,n1; and Mexico, **28:** 460
Post, Adeline Furman Mitchell (Mrs. Edwin Fredine), **28:** 92,n3

Post, Alice Thacher (Mrs. Louis Free-land), **35**: 134-35,n1, 158; **37**: 308, 316

Post, George Adams, **36**: 7n1

Post, Louis Freeland, **27**: 9, 58, 508-509; **28**: 540, 546-56, 580-84; **36**: 550, 551; **38**: 665-66

Post Impressions (Strunsky), **37**: 60,n1

Post Office building: inscriptions, **28**: 501, 502, 505

Post Office, Department of the, **35**: 229, 230, 318-19; segregation and, **28**: 60, 404, 408-409, 492, 498n1; **31**: 298, 299, 312, 361n2; EAW desires to improve the conditions of women, **28**: 476; and I.W.W. investigation, **36**: 190,n3; and appointments to postmasterships in Pa., **36**: 336-38

postal service, **37**: 190, 192

Postmasters' Association: *see* National Association of Presidential Postmasters

Postmasters Were Confirmed by the Senate (*Erie* [Pa.] *Times*), **36**: 336,n2

postwar security and organization, **32**: 11, 205, 238, 300, 327, 376, 402-403, 422-23, 438, 440-41, 456, 504, 514; **34**: 15n1, 372; **35**: 187, 388; **36**: 80, 148,n1, 374; **37**: 6, 7, 21, 43, 44, 59, 60n1, 68-69, 77,n1, 117, 294n1; **38**: 418, 437; E. M. House on, **33**: 63, 64; E. Grey on, **33**: 124, 372; W. H. Page on, **33**: 551; P. S. Reinsch on, **34**: 26-27; N. Angell on, **34**: 135-36,n1; Chamber of Commerce recommendations, **36**: 168-69,n1; C. H. Levermore on, **36**: 362-63,n1; Hensley resolution, **36**: 374n1; J. Bryce on, **38**: 85-86, 250; W. H. Dickinson on, **38**: 207-208,n1

Potash and Perlmutter (play, Glass), **28**: 595,n2

Potomac Presbytery: WW's remarks to, **33**: 49-51

Potsdam, Germany, **35**: 194; E. M. House meets with William II in, **30**: 109, 139, 265, 266

Potter, James Brown, **28**: 196,n4

Potter, Mary Elizabeth McKenney (Mrs. Alexander C.), **28**: 252,n1

Potts, J. Manning, **36**: 391n2

Pou, Edward William, **32**: 207,n1, 219; **36**: 218, 231-32, 289, 300, 314-15; **37**: 209-10, 230, 398; on navy, **37**: 181-82, 207

Poughkeepsie, N.Y., **27**: 223n1

Powderly, Terrence Vincent, **28**: 549-50

Powell, Mr., **34**: 91

Powell, William Frank, **28**: 221-23,n1

Powell School for Girls (Richmond), **32**: 423n1

Power with Grace: The Life of Mrs. Woodrow Wilson (Ross), **32**: 423n1

Powers, Blanche, **36**: 399

Prairie, U.S.S., **29**: 454, 480

Prairie Oil and Gas Co., **37**: 142

Pratt, Edward Ewing, **36**: 410,n2

Preface to Politics (Lippmann), **31**: 316,n2

Prellwitz, Edith Mitchill (Mrs. Henry), **28**: 166,n3, 195

Prellwitz, Henry, **28**: 166,n3

Prentiss, E. L., **29**: 549

preparedness, **31**: 281, 475-76, 502, 506-507; **32**: 463, 501,n3; **34**: 3-4, 38, 58, 131n2, 195, 248, 514; **36**: 146, 163-64, 211, 249, 366n1, 504, 513-15; Gardner resolution, **31**: 152,n3, 293, 357-58, 373, 375, 409, 411, 413; WW on, **31**: 421-23, 508; **34**: 207-208, 216, 392; **35**: 29, 114, 122-24, 147, 157, 167-73, 181, 213, 297-304, 340-41, 481-82, 499-500, 501, 512; **36**: 7-16, 26-35, 35-41, 41-48, 52-53, 53-54, 54-55, 55-63, 63-73, 75, 76, 77-85, 87-96, 96-100, 100-10, 111-12, 114-21, 121-22; **37**: 126-27, 213-14, 395-96; **38**: 40, 102, 130, 479, 568

A. M. Knight on, **32**: 133,n1; H. L. Higginson on, **34**: 28-29; and Platts-burg training camp, **34**: 133,n1; and W. J. Bryan, **34**: 135; **37**: 76n1; L. M. Garrison's plan for, **34**: 173-74,n1, 227, 482-85; **35**: 149-50,n1, 468-71, 480-81; EBG on, **34**: 232-33; W. L. Chambers on, **34**: 249; and T. Roosevelt, **34**: 337n1; O. G. Villard on, **34**: 412, 428; and rev-enue for program, **35**: 31, 303-304, 432n1; W. F. Sadler on, **35**: 105-106; J. P. Tumulty on, **35**: 107-109, 135-37, 253-54, 265-66, 270, 492-94; antipre-paredness comments, **35**: 134-35, 141-43, 157,n1, 185n2, 194-95, 344,n1; comments supporting, **35**: 177-78,n1,2, 181n1, 184, 194, 217, 253-54, 492-94, 525n2; **36**: 21, 139-40,n1, 151, 171-72, 263,n1; and J. Hay, **35**: 180, 502-503; **36**: 134-35, 141-43, 170-71; E. M. House on WW message, **35**: 257-58; W. L. Marbury and C. H. Grasty on, **35**: 429-31; and natural resources, **36**: 49-51, 464, 521; and taxation, **36**: 83; and Texas, **36**: 165-66, 175,n1, 186,n2; W. C. Adamson on, **36**: 305; House passes army reorganization bill, **36**: 360,n1; and armor-plate bill, **36**: 396n1; N. D. Baker's memorandum on, **36**: 431-34; F. Ziegfeld wishes to use theme of in Follies, **36**: 498; and W. J. Stone's speech, **36**: 500,n1; L. Wald on anti-preparedness, **36**: 524-25; and Na-tional Service School for Women, **36**: 572-75,n1; WW and American Union Against Militarism, **36**: 562, 632-33, 634-49; U.S. Chamber of Commerce on, **37**: 127,n2; and 1916 platform; **37**: 169n1, 195; parade for, **37**: 221,n1, 224-25; A. G. Gardiner on, **37**: 265n1; B. Tillman on income tax and, **37**: 288; and National Research Council, **37**: 374n1, 473-74,n3,4, 492, 494; and Council of National Defense, **37**: 491, **38**: 272-73; and railroad crisis of 1916, **38**: 57, 101

Preparedness of the Navy (Daniels), **33:** 216n1

Presbyterian Board of Home Missions, **28:** 512, 513

Presbyterian Church in the U.S.A. (northern), **29:** 361n2

Presbyterian Church in the United States (southern), **27:** 351,n1, 357; **35:** 153n2; General Assembly, **30:** 74, 452n3; Board of Home Missions and EAW Memorial Fund, **31:** 259,n2, 260; WW's remarks to Potomac Presbytery, **33:** 49-51

presidency, **27:** 99-101; single-term amendment, **27:** 97, 98-101, 103-104, 114; **29:** 57; **31:** 281-82; election reform, **29:** 7; WW on, **29:** 363-64; **36:** 41, 44, 162, 218

President, The (*Emporia* [Ka.] *Gazette*), **33:** 247,n1

President on his Critics: Not a defense; but a challenge (T. N. Page), **36:** 395,n2

President and Mexico (Harvey), **29:** 121n1

President and Segregation (New York *Evening Post*), **31:** 328n2

President and the Negro (Villard), **28:** 186,n1

President at the National Press Club, May 15, 1916, **37:** 54n4

President on the Enforcement of Peace (Holt), **37:** 120,n2

President Wilson (Brooks), **28:** 371n3; **30:** 192,n2

President Wilson (London *Outlook*), **32:** 328n3; **33:** 244,n1

President Wilson's First Lap (Porritt), **28:** 315,n2

President Wilson's Methods (London *Times*), **30:** 287n1

President Wilson's Policy (Donald), **35:** 524,n1

President Wilson's Record (Brooks), **28:** 370,n2

President Wilson's Record (London *Nation*), **32:** 328n3

President Wilson's Triumph (Brooks), **28:** 370n1

Presidential Patronage in Kentucky (*Lexington Herald*), **29:** 343,n2

presidential primaries, **29:** 163, 170; **37:** 358

Presidential Problems (Cleveland), **38:** 327,n1

Presidential Range, N.H.: Mts. Clinton, Jackson, Webster, **29:** 562

President's Appeal for 'A New Temper' (*Chicago Herald*), **30:** 311,n1

President's Speech (New York *Nation*), **32:** 79n2

press, the: *see* newspapers; Woodrow Wilson: Press Conferences

Pressley, Neill E., **31:** 24

Preston, Frances Folsom Cleveland (Mrs. Thomas J., Jr.) **28:** 302,n5

Preston, John White, **30:** 172,n2

Preston, Thomas Jex, Jr., **28:** 302,n5

Preussische Jahrbücher, **37:** 86

Price, James Reese, **29:** 436,n1,2

Price, Robert, **37:** 231,n1, 279

Price, Theodore Hazeltine, **34:** 296,n2

Price, William W., **33:** 71,n1

primary election: Heney on direct presidential preferential, **37:** 338-39, 339

primary law, **29:** 7; **31:** 281-82; New York, **29:** 402, 403

Primrose, Archibald Philip: *see* Roseberry, 5th Earl of

Primrose Coal Co., Colo., **29:** 549

Primus: *see* Bryan, William Jennings

Prince of Nagato (Japanese warship), **29:** 437

Princess, The (Tennyson), **38:** 330

Princeton, N.J., **27:** 128; **28:** 3, 20n2, 61n2, 309, 318, 383; **29:** 163, 553, 555; **30:** 163; **31:** 28; **33:** 434-35, 446; **34:** 293, 304; **35:** 159,n1; **38:** 180, 622, 664, 681; WW's departure from, **27:** xxi, 142-44, 146, 165; graduate college taxed by borough, **28:** 203,n2, 220-21; ice storm, **28:** 105,n1; WW returns to vote, **28:** 335,n2, 337; WW visits former home, **28:** 335,n4; residents bid WW farewell, **29:** 555-56; photograph of WW leaving: *illustration section,* **27**

Princeton Alumni Association, **27:** 147n1

Princeton Alumni Association of the District of Columbia, **38:** 485n3; WW's remarks to, **30:** 103-108

Princeton Alumni Weekly, **27:** 142n1, 147n1, 154n1, 155n2; **30:** 103n1, 176n1; **33:** 432,n1

Princeton Bank, **27:** 6n1, 485n4; **28:** 328, 397; **38:** 389

Princeton Inn, **27:** 15, 20, 102; **34:** 293

Princeton Press, **28:** 203n2, 221

Princeton Theological Seminary, **34:** 358n1; **38:** 209n1

Princeton University, **27:** xxi, 71-72, 116, 125, 142, 143, 208, 306n1, 336; **28:** 88, 288, 302n5, 309, 318, 333n1, 335,n3, 337, 465; **29:** 533; **31:** 216, 310n1, 316n1, 396, 402; **32:** 25, 242n2; **34:** 42n1, 108n4, 304, 394n1, 470,n1, 544, 545; **35:** 216, 337; **36:** 114, 175, 261n1, 349n1, 394, 418; **37:** 221n1, 310, 335; **38:** 39, 239n1, 333-34, 362n1, 563, 680

Philadelphian Society, **27:** vii; WW Collection, **27:** ix; C. L. Swem Collection, **27:** x; congratulations from Board of Trustees, **27:** 26; WW remarks at smoker, **27:** 147-48; dinner for class of '79, **27:** 154,n1, 156-57; **35:** 262,n2,3 270, 274-75, 279-80, 281, 291; alumni and students at inauguration, **27:** 155,n2; H. B. Fine, **27:** 174, 240, 554; graduate college of, **28:** 203,n2, 220-21, 280; Prospect gardens, **28:** 126; WW on his troubles at, **29:** 33-34, 57, 58, 163; trustees wish reception for WW, **29:** 171; WW wishes presence at '79 reunion officially ignored, **29:** 186-87; **30:** 163-64; criticism in graduate school of

WW, **29:** 272,n1,2; WW's "1905" [1906] breakdown at, **29:** 377; WW feeling that he had no home at, **29:** 515; change of presidents causes financial difficulties at, **29:** 554; students accompany presidential train to Washington, **29:** 544, 555; WW's remarks to Alumni Association of District of Columbia, **30:** 103-108; WW on years he devoted to, **30:** 104; reunion weekend, **30:** 156, 189; remarks to class of '79; **30:** 176-80; T. D. Jones as trustee supporter of WW at, **30:** 192; comparison of workload as president of and president of U.S., **30:** 276; C. H. Dodge and, **30:** 281; Millet lecture, **30:** 401; WW on J. McCosh and F. L. Patton, **30:** 465-66; two graduates who became U.S. president, **31:** 109; Wyman bequest income, **31:** 205; Harbison family and, **31:** 220n2; football program at, **31:** 412,n1,2,4, 429-30; and preparedness, **31:** 476; WW on revision of curriculum at, **31:** 186-87; C. Adler's congratulations on WW's presidency of, **32:** 534n1; WW's student editorial on reducing prayer meetings at, **35:** 182,n3; Witherspoon Gang, **35:** 262,n3, 270; alumni and 1916 election, **38:** 518,n1; WW compares to Oxford, **38:** 681; and WW's quadrangle plan, **38:** 685,n1

Principles of International Law (Lawrence), **29:** 432

Principles of Political Economy (Mill), **31:** 316,n2

Printing and Engraving, Bureau of: *see* Engraving and Printing, Bureau of

Prinz Ludwig, S.M.S., **27:** 370

prison reform, **27:** 244

Pritchett, Henry Smith, **27:** 240-41; **29:** 537; **30:** 6, 63

Private Grief: A National Loss (*Outlook*) **30:** 407,n1

Privileges and Elections Committee (Senate), **28:** 160n2; **38:** 58

Problem of the Negro in Government, 1913 (Osborn), **28:** 97n1

Proceedings of the Academy of Political Science, **29:** 481n3

Proceedings of the First Pan American Financial Conference. Washington, May 24, to 29, 1915, **33:** 245n1; **35:** 296n1

Proceedings of the Twenty-fifth Consecutive and Second Biennial Convention of the United Mine Workers of America . . . , **36:** 639n16

Professor Bliss Perry for Wilson (*New York Times*), **38:** 563n1

Profile Lake, N.H., **28:** 132

profit sharing: C. W. Eliot on, **29:** 339

Program of the League, **37:** 6n1

Programme for the Fall Campaign, **30:** 466n4

Progreso, Yucatan, Mex.: blockade at, **32:** 367,n1, 369-70,n1; 408-409

Progressive Democrats, **38:** 666n1

Progressive Farmer, **31:** 126

Progressive Movement: Crane on, **32:** 52

Progressive National Committee, **38:** 171n1, 666n2

Progressive National Convention (1912), **38:** 433; (1916), **37:** 146n1; **38:** 330n1; 433

Progressive National Negro Democratic Association, **28:** 210

Progressive party (Bull Moose party) and Progressives, **27:** 75; **29:** 135, 298, 305n1, 556; **31:** 266, 277, 342, 356-57; **32:** 37, 79n2, 121; **36:** 22, 276n1; **37:** 167, 206, 218, 264,n1, 338-40, 435-36, 441, 513, 531-33; **38:** 14, 23, 28, 131, 190n1, 304-305, 362n1; and delegates to N.Y. state convention, **30:** 22-23,n3; and T. Roosevelt, **30:** 65n1, 129n2; **37:** 203,n4, 329n1; and Nicaraguan treaty, **30:** 175; to form auxiliary for Negroes, **30:** 491-93; and Tariff Commission, **36:** 206,n2; and 1916 Democratic paltform, **37:** 151, 181, 188, 189; and 1912 platform, **37:** 162, 428-29,n1; Democratic national chairman must appeal to, **37:** 227; and G. Rublee and Trade Commission, **37:** 363; in Washington State, **37:** 432,n1; dissidents in, **37:** 523-24,n1,2; W. A. White on, **38:** 3n2; W. Lippmann on, **38:** 275; WW on, **38:** 433, 446, 463, 576; J. A. H. Hopkins on, **38:** 643-44; and Sixty-fifth Congress, **38:** 666-67,n1

Progressive party in Illinois, **31:** 232n2; in Maine, **38:** 174; in Missouri, **31:** 353n1; in New Jersey, **38:** 35,n3

Progressive-Protectionists, **38:** 666n1

Progressive Record of the Democratic Party, **37:** 429,n1

Progressives and Prohibitionists, Texas Democrats in the Wilson Era (Gould), **36:** 175n1

Progresso, Tex.: post office, **37:** 249

prohibition, **32:** 196, 473; **37:** 118, 129, 514, 533; in Tennessee, **27:** 55n3; and Kentucky politics, **29:** 343n2; and W. J. Bryan, **31:** 355-56, 481

Prohibition and Politics: Turbulent Decades in Tennessee, 1885-1920 (Isaac), **27:** 55n3

Prohibition party, **38:** 28, 643

Prophets, Priests and Kings (Gardiner), **31:** 482n1; **32:** 8,n1

Proposal for a National Race Commission to be appointed by the President of the United States, Suggested by the National Association for the Advancement of Colored People (Villard), **28:** 185n1

Proposed Nicaraguan Treaty (Lansing), **30:** 174n1

Prospect House (Princeton University), **29:** 171; **30:** 156; **31:** 29

Protestant Churches of America, **30:** 397

Protestants: in Mexico, **30:** 298

Protocol of an Agreement Concerning Withdrawal of American Troops from Mexican Territory (Lane), **38:** 675n1
Providence Journal, **34:** 536; **35:** 277n1; **36:** 385
Providence Journal Co., **34:** 158,n2
Provincetown, Mass., **30:** 157
Prussia, **33:** 14, 158, 172, 177, 298, 360; comments on militarism of, **31:** 6-8, 14, 27, 159, 518n2; *see also* Germany
Przemysl, Poland, **33:** 371
Psychic Control Through Self-Knowledge (Kenilworth), **29:** 288n1
Public, The (Chicago), **28:** 289-90
Public Building Act (1913), **38:** 655
Public Call for the Assassination of the President! (New York *Herald*), **35:** 221n1
public health, **27:** 76-77,n3, 91, 150, 151, 242-44; **35:** 151, 183-84; **37:** 161, 175, 199, 532
Public Health, Department of, **27:** 77n3
Public Health Service: Its History, Activities and Organization (Schmeckebier), **27:** 77n3
Public Information, Commitee on, **38:** 427n1
Public Lands, Committee on (House of Reps.), **30:** 3n1, 20, 218, 224n1; **36:** 329; **37:** 40
Public Lands, Committee on (Senate), **30:** 20, 31; **36:** 328, 464,n1, 518n3; **37:** 66n2, 143
public opinion, **27:** 78, 98, 100, 473; **29:** 177
Public Papers of Charles E. Hughes, Governor, 1910, **37:** 203n5
Public Printing Office, **29:** 100
Public Utilities Commission of New York, **37:** 320n3
Public Utility Commission of New Jersey, *see* Board of Public Utilities Commissioners
Puchta, George, **38:** 524n1
Puebla, Puebla, Mex., **32:** 348, 353, 384
Puebla, state, Mex., **28:** 77, 78; **29:** 328, 459, 492; **30:** 66; **31:** 13; **32:** 387
Pueblo, Colo., **28:** 511, 512, 522
Pueblo (Colo.) *Chieftain,* **31:** 556-57,n1
Puenta, Dr. de la (tax collector in Mexico), **32:** 383, 384
Puerto México, Mex., **27:** 567
Puerto Rico: *see* Porto Rico
Puget Sound, **28:** 463
Pujo Committee, **29:** 27
Pulitzer, Ralph, **27:** 487-88; **28:** 381, 385; **29:** 303, 390; **31:** 295, 314; **32:** 342; **36:** 565, 565-66; **37:** 70, 100-101, 332,n1; **38:** 173, 597n2
Pulley, Raymond H., **27:** 73n2
Punch, **29:** 530; **35:** 9, 416
Punitive Expedition: *see* Mexico and the United States
Purdy, Lawson, **27:** 400,n2, 401
pure-food laws, **27:** 151, 163; **37:** 161

pure-shoe law, **27:** 90,n1
Pusey, Merlo John, **37:** 203n5
Pustkuchen, Commander, **36:** 371n1, 488n2
Putnam, Herbert, **27:** 464,n1
Puzzle of Hughes (Lippmann), **38:** 274,n2

Quaker religion: A. M. Palmer, **27:** 132
Quakers: *see* Friends, Society of
Quamme, E. G., **38:** 160
Quayle, William Alfred, **37:** 148n1
Queen of the Country (Stretton), **31:** 316,n2
Querétaro, Querétaro, Mex., **30:** 285n1; **36:** 318,n1
Quesada, Carlos Manuel de Céspedes: *see* Céspedes y Quesada, Carlos Manuel de
Quesnay, François, **35:** 133
Question of Preparedness (Villard), **35:** 142n1
Question of Preparedness—No. 2: What Is the Matter With the Army? (Villard), **35:** 143n3
Question of Preparedness—No. 3: The Present Military Foundation (Villard), **35:** 143n2
Quezon y Molina, Manuel Luis, **27:** 516; **28:** 192-93, 197; **29:** 147, 164, 165, 166, 167; **30:** 172; **32:** 369, 535n1; **34:** 391; **38:** 675
Quick, John Herbert, **38:** 158,n1, 158-60, 335
Quigley, Edward T., **33:** 497, 507
Quirk, Robert Emmet, **29:** 420n2, 476n1; **30:** 193n1
Quito, Ecuador, **32:** 230

R. H. Macy's, New York, **35:** 160
Rabasa, Emilio, **30:** 45, 47, 66, 68,n1, 77, 115, 119, 228
race-commission plan, **28:** 186-87, 202, 239, 245
racial prejudice: *see* discrimination; segregation; Negroes: race relations
Racine, Wisc.: WW's remarks on preparedness in, **36:** 54-55
radium bill, **30:** 31
Ragsdale, James Willard, **28:** 121,n1, 122,n2
Railroad Age Gazette, **38:** 165
Railroad Crisis and After (Lippmann), **38:** 87n2
railroad crisis of 1916, **38:** 12,n1, 30, 32,n1, 55-58, 93-94,n1,2, 102-103,n1, 117, 123, 394n1, 471; WW on, **38:** 38,n1,2, 55, 63, 77, 164, 214-19, 332-33, 466; G. Pope on, **38:** 46,n1; W. J. Stone on, **38:** 47-48; W. L. Chambers on, **38:** 48-49; recommendation for eight-hour day, **38:** 49-50; R. Spreckels on, **38:** 61-62; R. G. Rhett on, **38:** 75-77; F. K. Lane on, **38:** 88-89; strike dates called, **38:** 93n2; unions' proposal for settlement, **38:** 94-95; WW's address to Congress on, **38:** 96-101;

W. Barker supports WW's stand, **38:** 103; R. T. Frazier on, **38:** 119-20; B. Colby on, **38:** 121; Adamson Act passed, **38:** 124,n2; E. M. House on **38:** 165-66; C. W. Eliot on, **38:** 167-68, 279-80, 353; *see also* Adamson Act

railroad-securities bill: *see* Rayburn railway-securities bill

railroads, **27:** 322-23, 567; **28:** 42,n2, 44, 596; **29:** 356; **30:** 96, 270, 293,n3, 294-95, 305; **31:** 20-21, 26, 418; **32:** 72; **35:** 269, 309-10; full-crew bill, **27:** 49,n6, 58, 66, 323; grade-crossing bill (N.J.), **27:** 48-49,n5; in Mexico, **27:** 479; Negroes and mail service, **27:** 290-91; in Alaska, **29:** 9, 332,n1, 400; W. C. Redfield on, **29:** 43-44; E. F. Goltra on, **29:** 50, 51; Interstate Commerce Commission, **29:** 140,n3; **30:** 483; **31:** 258; WW address on antitrust legislation and, **29:** 155-56; C. W. Eliot on **29:** 338-40; H. L. Higginson on, **29:** 368-69; **31:** 213, 238-41; **32:** 140; and rate increase, **29:** 400,n2, 406; R. Olney on, **30:** 85-87; and business, **30:** 128-29, 173n1; and Rayburn bill, **30:** 162n2; and impending strike, **30:** 305-307, 313-14, 314, 328-29, 329, 333, 343-44; and freight-rate increase, **30:** 333,n2; and Clayton bill, **30:** 481,n4; D. B. Jones on, **31:** 81; WW on concessions to, **31:** 247; rate case, **31:** 247; C. F. Adams on, **31:** 267-68; W. J. Bryan on stocks and bonds of, **31:** 281, 282; effect of war on, **31:** 326-27,n2,3, 378; and unions, **32:** 96; WW's address to American Electric Railway Association, **32:** 149-57; and proposed strike, **36:** 204,n1, 415,n1; **37:** 434-35, 438-39,n1, 499,n2, 504-505, 512, 525,n1, 530-31; WW on, **36:** 105, 370, 400-401, 428-29; **38:** 138, 479; and L. D. Brandeis, **36:** 26n3; *see also* under names of individual railroad lines, such as Boston and Maine Railroad

Railway Business Association, **36:** 7n1

Rainey, Henry Thomas, **31:** 232,n1,2; **36:** 207, 227; **37:** 10, 92; **38:** 21, 512

Rainey tariff commission bill, **36:** 206,n1, 227, 366n1; **37:** 10, 492; **38:** 21

Rajecz, Stephan (Stefan) Burián von: *see* Burián von Rajecz, Count Stephan

Raker, John Edward, **30:** 273n1

Raleigh, N.C., **31:** 126; monument to Confederate women, **29:** 322,n2

Raleigh, Cecil, **27:** 119n2

Raleigh Banking and Trust Co., N.C., **31:** 128

Raleigh Hotel, Wash., D.C., **36:** 375n1; **37:** 442n1; **38:** 637n1, 646

Ralph, Joseph E., **28:** 498n1; **31:** 361n2

Ralston, Jennie Craven (Mrs. Samuel Moffett), **38:** 412n2

Ralston, Samuel Moffett, **27:** 230, 232, 233-34; **32:** 29, 32; **38:** 411, 412,n1,2

Ran, S.S., **31:** 477

Ranzel, José, **36:** 653

Rappard, Willem Louis Frederik Christiaan van, **31:** 100,n2; **33:** 348; **34:** 398; **38:** 53,n1,2, 140,n2

Rascón, Eugenio, **28:** 324n1

Rathenau, Walther, **32:** 411-12,n1

Rathom, John Revelstoke, **34:** 158,n2, 536, 537; **36:** 385,n1

Ratner, Sidney, **27:** 301n1; **38:** 51n1

Rauscher's Restaurant, Wash., D.C., **36:** 380n7; **37:** 148n1

Ray, Clinton G., **36:** 364

Ray Stannard Baker: A Quest for Democracy in Modern America 1870-1918 (Semonche), **37:** 286n1

Rayburn, Sam Taliaferro, **30:** 162,n1,2

Rayburn railroad-securities bill, **30:** 110, 162,n2, 181, 295-96, 300; **31:** 149

Raymond, Robert M., **36:** 364

Rea, George Bronson, **27:** 237,n1, 238

Rea, Samuel, **27:** 322-23,n1, 346; **31:** 20,n3

Read, James Morgan, **33:** 485n1

Reading, 1st Marquess (Rufus Daniel Isaacs): **35:** 20, 46, 63n1, 78, 85, 484, 485, 486; **36:** 166, 167, 180n1, 266n1

Reading Railroad, **30:** 482

Real Crime Against Germany (Villard), **30:** 456n2

Rebel at Large: Recollections of Fifty Crowded Years (Creel), **38:** 16n2

Reclamation Service, **35:** 261

Recognition (H. L. Wilson), **28:** 84,n3

Recognition of General Huerta the Practical Course (*New York Times*), **28:** 92,n2

Record, George Lawrence, **30:** 131; **31:** 357; **32:** 272, 281-82, 285, 287

Record of Hughes as an Enemy of Labor: Solid Facts for Railroad Employees and All Other Wage-Earners, **38:** 284,n2

Record of the Administration (Ford), **36:** 581,n2

Red Cross: *see* American National Red Cross; German Red Cross

Red House Ferry, Tex., **37:** 249

Redfield, Elise Mercein Fuller (Mrs. William Cox), **31:** 532,n2

Redfield, William Cox, **27:** 130, 137, 236, 238, 253, 269, 314, 322, 433, 444; **28:** 144, 498n1; **29:** 40-44, 48, 435, 443-46, 461-62, 478, 544-45; **30:** 4, 95, 129, 194, 324, 432n1; **31:** 293, 531-32; **33:** 294, 425, 536; **34:** 186; **35:** 319, 398-99, 400, 401; **36:** 154, 417n1; **37:** 160, 166, 211, 471; **38:** 181, 183, 196

cabinet appointment, **27:** 21, 24, 27, 70, 111, 138, 139, 140; on China, **27:** 175, 329; and S. Chinda's protest, **27:** 425; Panama Canal tolls, **27:** 313; on tariff, **27:** 251; **35:** 383-86; on death of EAW, **30:** 356; on Clayton bill, **31:** 45-47; and shipping bill, **31:** 122-23, 124; **35:** 345,n1, 396; L. M. Garrison on cotton crisis and, **31:** 210; and safety-of-life-

Redfield, William Cox (*cont.*)
at-sea legislation, **31:** 490, 493-96; and
Cleveland Automatic Machine Co., **33:**
497-98,n4, 506, 507; and *Eastland* disaster, **34:** 27, 45n1, 48-49, 56, 65,n1,
71-72, 81-82,n1; on dumping of goods,
35: 427-29, 476-77; **36:** 127; on vocational education bill, **36:** 357,n1, 369-
70,n1; on dyestuffs, **36:** 406, 410; on
campaign in Maine, **38:** 105-106; photograph: *illustration section,* **27**
Redmond, John, **37:** 447; **38:** 92
Reed, Charles Matthias, **36:** 139-40,n1,
140
Reed, Eugene Elliott, **27:** 158, 178-79
Reed, James Alexander, 27: 508-509, 515;
30: 279, 288, 299n2; **31:** 88, 122; **32:**
325n1; **35:** 179, 183, 185, 191, 192; **37:**
72, 375,n1; **38:** 146n2, 458, 545,n2; on
Federal Reserve bill, **28:** 336n2, 369,n1,
373n1, 414, 425,n1, 434-35; income-tax
amendment, **28:** 253-54, 254
Reed, John (Silas), **30:** 42,n1, 156,n1,
157,n1; wishes to write about interview with WW on Mexico, **30:** 186-87,
189; wants to publish article, **30:** 192-
93, 202, 219-20, 223, 231; article on
Mexico, **30:** 231-38
Reese, Hershall, **31:** 183
Reformed Church in the United States,
29: 361n1,2
Regierte der Kaiser? (Müller), **33:** 299n2
Reid, Benjamin Lawrence, **36:** 563n1; **37:**
380n2
Reid, Daniel Gray, **31:** 274,n2
Reid, Doris Fielding, **28:** 162
Reid, Edith Gittings (Mrs. Harry Field-
ing), **28:** 160-62, 178-79; **29:** 310,n1,
439-40,n1; **30:** 425-26; **35:** 24, 262, 291-
92, 320,n1
Reid, Francis Fielding, **28:** 162; **35:**
262,n2
Reid, Harry Fielding, **28:** 162; **29:** 310n1,
439n1; **35:** 262, 291
Reid, Robert Threshie, 1st Earl Loreburn, **32:** 340,n1, 350; **33:** 64, 88, 100-
101, 521-22; **37:** 265, 351, 351-52,n1
Reid, Whitelaw, **28:** 578,n1; **30:** 152
Reilly, Thomas Lawrence, **32:** 94,n2
Reims (Rheims), France, **33:** 514
Reinach, Joseph, **33:** 48,n3
Reine, Monsieur, **32:** 472
Reinsch, Paul Samuel, **27:** 203,n1; **28:** 4,
5, 15; **32:** 11-12, 137-38, 169-71, 177,
196-97, 246n1, 391, 416n3, 421, 433n1,
459-60, 460-61, 461, 466, 468, 529,n1;
33: 81, 104-105, 113, 115; **34:** 25-26,
49,n1; **35:** 128,n2, 144, 203-205, 209-
10, 289-90; **36:** 176, 428; **37:** 232, 234-
36; **38:** 439-40, 631-32; proposes American economic and financial aid to
China, **31:** 283, 284-88, 289, 364-67;
condolences on death of EAW, **31:** 284
fears Japanese expansion in China, **31:**

509-13, 547; on need for American in-
vestment in China, **32:** 328-30; on news
leaks, **32:** 500n1
Relations between Waterways and Rail-
way Traffic in Europe (Welliver), **38:**
159n2
Relations with Germany and Possibili-
ties (Lansing), **32:** 477n1
Religion Bryan Aid in Affairs of State
(*New York Times*), **32:** 353,n1
Rembaugh, Bertha, **30:** 375,n1
Remensnyder, Junius Benjamin, **29:** 475-
76,n1, 476; **30:** 398
Remsen, Ira, **27:** 91
Renault, Louis, **31:** 191,n2
Rendon, Serapio, **27:** 547
Rendon, Victor A., **37:** 348,n1
Rentería Luviano, José, **28:** 77
Reorganization Loan Contract of 1913,
37: 232
Reply to Austria (New York *Evening
Post*), **34:** 264,n3
*Report of the Commission on National
Aid to Vocational Education . . . ,* **36:**
357n1
*Report of the Commission to Investigate
Tax Assessments in the State of New
Jersey, 1912,* **27:** 48n4
*Report of the Committee on Alleged Ger-
man Outrages Appointed by His Bri-
tannic Majesty's Government and Pre-
sided Over by the Right Hon. Viscount
Bryce,* **33:** 485,n1
*Report of the Tariff Commission: Testi-
mony Taken by the Tariff Commis-
sion,* **38:** 574n3
*Report of the Thirty-Seventh Annual
Meeting of the American Bar Associa-
tion . . . ,* **31:** 186n
Report on the Colorado Strike (West), **28:**
426n1
*Report on the Colorado Strike Investiga-
tion Made Under House Resolution 387,*
29: 46n1
*Report to Accompany H. R. 3321: A Bill
to Reduce Tariff Duties, to Provide
Revenue for the Government and Other
Purposes,* **27:** 289n7,8
Republican National Committee, **35:**
318n2; **36:** 563; **38:** 141, 284n3,4, 316,
342n3; chairman named, **37:** 320n3
Republican National Convention (1916),
37: 146,n1, 167,n1, 228, 424; **38:** 330n1,
566n7; C. E. Hughes nominated, **37:**
186,n1, 203,n4; W. Lippmann on, **37:**
212; E. M. House criticizes Hughes'
acceptance speech, **37:** 518-21
Republican party and Republicans, **27:**
160, 374; **28:** 369,n2; **29:** 227; **31:** 81,
264,n3; **32:** 10, 30-31, 32, 33, 35, 37,
38, 79n2, 165; **33:** 518; **34:** 131n2, 390-
91, 536; **35:** 151, 213,n1,2, 222, 270,
434; **36:** 8, 472, 473, 474-75; **37:** 79, 121,
151, 152, 167, 191, 388; **38:** 34, 193,

209, 292, 293n2, 362n1, 377n2, 446, 499-500, 606
currency bill, **27:** 485, 525; and Philippines, **27:** 10; **32:** 292; **35:** 52, 86; tariff, **27:** 498; **32:** 36; **35:** 370n1, 433, 475-77; and Federal Reserve bill, **28:** 375; Mexican situation, **28:** 158, 162; Negroes, **28:** 116, 210, 349; **31:** 361n2; and T. Roosevelt, **29:** 135; and Panama Canal tolls controversy, **29:** 283, 298, 374; and Nicaraguan treaty, **30:** 175; and T. D. Jones nomination for Federal Reserve Board, **30:** 288, 291, 299,n1; and WW's neutrality address, **30:** 432; and taxes, **31:** 32; WW on, **31:** 171, 174; **35:** 313, 323; **38:** 51, 128-29, 131, 303, 304, 305-306, 310-11, 331, 364-66, 433, 436, 447-48, 463, 552-53, 558, 611; and 1916 presidential hopefuls, **31:** 267; H. Münsterberg on ethnic groups switching to, **31:** 277; and N.Y. *World* editorial on elections, **31:** 295n1; R. Pulitzer on, **31:** 314; and ship-purchase bill, **32:** 34, 123, 166, 172, 173,n2, 227, 229, 239, 240, 313, 315, 336-37; and Federal Trade Commission, **32:** 273; and preparedness, **36:** 32, 84, 143, 263n1; E. Root's speech, **36:** 186, 187; Rainey bill, **36:** 206-207; JPT on Democratic platform and, **36:** 333-34; E. M. House on convention of, **36:** 601; and L. D. Brandeis controversy, **36:** 607; F. C. Howe on imperialistic influences in, **37:** 180; and platform of 1916, **37:** 189, 190; and German Americans, **37:** 218-19; **38:** 275n5, 290; and R. Robins, **37:** 329; F. J. Heney on corruption in, **37:** 338-40; legislation urged by, **37:** 428-29, 429; and woman suffrage, **38:** 5, 59; farmers and 1916 election, **38:** 159-60,n5; and eight-hour bill, **38:** 212, 217; and Casement case, **38:** 316; and Congress, **38:** 434, 435; geographical losses of, **38:** 645n1; in Sixty-Fifth Congress, **38:** 666-67,n1
Republican party and Republicans in California, **27:** 220,n6, 382
Republican party and Republicans in Colorado, **31:** 273,n2
Republican party and Republicans in Delaware, **27:** 25n1
Republican party and Republicans in Illinois, **31:** 232n2, 264n3
Republican party and Republicans in Indiana, **38:** 412n1
Republican party and Republicans in Kansas, **31:** 264n3
Republican party and Republicans in Maine, **38:** 173, 174
Republican party and Republicans in New Hampshire, **27:** 158n2
Republican party and Republicans in New Jersey, **27:** 494n1; **28:** 97; **29:** 386; **38:** 431-32, 609-10

Republican party and Republicans in New York, **31:** 117n1, 264n3; **35:** 318
Republican party and Republicans in Ohio, **31:** 264n3
Republican party and Republicans in Pennsylvania, **31:** 187n1, 264n3; **38:** 439-31,n2
Republican party and Republicans in Tennessee, **27:** 55n3
Republican party and Republicans in Wisconsin, **31:** 264n3; **32:** 19
Republic of Nations: A Study of the Organization of a Federal League of Nations (Minor), **32:** 3,n2
reserve forces, **37:** 195; WW on, **36:** 13-14, 14-15, 29-30, 38, 39-40, 45, 46, 58-59, 69-70, 81, 90-91, 97-98, 105, 118; and army reorganization bill, **36:** 179, 515
Responding to the New Call of Duty . . . , **37:** 148n
Restrepo, Carlos E., **28:** 330,n2
Results of Three Years Administration of Chosen Since Annexation (Korean publication), **33:** 24
Reuteria, Enserio, **36:** 653
Reuters news agency, **32:** 170; **36:** 233
Reventlow, Count Ernst zu, **34:** 187,n1
Revenue Act of 1916, **38:** 51,n1, 85n1, 87n2, 179,n1, 257
Review of Reviews: see New York *Review of Reviews*
Revolt Against War (Addams), **34:** 251,n6
Reyes, Bernardo, **27:** 537-38
Reyes, Rodolfo, **28:** 292, 293
Reynolds, Charles R., Jr., **27:** 508n2
Reynolds, George McClelland, **27:** 79,n2; **31:** 76
Rheims, France: *see* Reims, France
Rhett, Robert Goodwyn, **37:** 127,n2; **38:** 75-77,n1, 77
Rhine Convention, **31:** 156
Rhine River, **31:** 156
Rhinecliff, N.Y., **38:** 628
Rhoads, Thomas Leidy, **27:** 200,n4; **29:** 558,n2
Rhode Island Avenue Methodist Protestant Church, Wash., D.C., **32:** 494n1
Rhodes, James Ford, **31:** 290; **32:** 12, 111; **33:** 64-65, 69, 517; **34:** 25
Riaño y Gayangos, Don Juan, **29:** 524-25,n1; **30:** 29, 79, 493-94
Rice, Frances (Mrs. Wallace), **31:** 316,n2
Rice, Melvin Augustus, **32:** 300,n1, 349, 351-52,n1, 366; **35:** 355; **37:** 164-65, 173-74; **38:** 81, 84
Rice, Wallace, **31:** 316,n2
Rice Institute, **29:** 277; **36:** 297n1,2, 329-30
Richard, Ernst D., **31:** 84,n1, 85
Richards, Charles Russell, **27:** 244
Richardson, Ernest Cushing, **28:** 335,n1
Richardson, James Daniel, **29:** 292n1
Richardson, Norval, **36:** 125,n2; **37:** 440

Richardson, William, **29:** 394,n1
Richdale, James Cheatle, **38:** 500n1
Richmond, Ind., WW's remarks in, **32:** 28-29
Richmond, Va.: and Negro Exposition, **33:** 464, 512; **34:** 16
Richmond, Va. *Evening Journal*, **30:** 210n2
Richmond, Va. *Times-Dispatch*, **35:** 253, 253-54; **37:** 228n1
Ricketts, Eliza Getty (Mrs. Palmer Chamberlaine, Sr.), **28:** 126,n3, 335
Ricketts, Henrietta, **28:** 335
Ricketts, Louis Davidson, **28:** 278,n3
Rickey, Harry N., **38:** 428,n2
Ricks, Edgar Ethelred, **31:** 309,n1
Ridder, Herman, **31:** 463; **33:** 135,n4, 361
Rider, Samuel W., **36:** 364
Ridgely, Helen West Stewart (Mrs. John), **28:** 291,n2
Rieloff, Dr., **28:** 196,n3
Riga, Latvia, **34:** 310
Riga, Gulf of, **34:** 310
Riggs, Clinton L., **30:** 156
Riggs National Bank of Washington, **36:** 26n3, 602
Right-Hand Man: The Life of George W. Perkins (Garraty), **37:** 203n4
Right to Pursue Indians Across Boundary Lines (Frelinghuysen and Romero), **38:** 228n1
Riley, James Whitcomb, **27:** 140, 228; **37:** 469,n1
Riley, Thomas P., **28:** 275,n2, 289
Ring, Mr., **33:** 413
Rintelen von Kleist, Franz, **33:** 473,n1; **34:** 39n1; **35:** 355
Rios, Ernesto, **36:** 587,n7
Rios, José, **36:** 587,n7
Ripley, Edward Payson, **31:** 20,n3, 81
Rippy, James Fred, **29:** 292n1; **33:** 46n4
Riquelme, A. H., **27:** 546, 548
Rise of Segregation in the Federal Bureaucracy, 1900-1930 (Meier and Rudwick), **28:** 349n2
Ritter, Gerhard, **33:** 279n1
Ritter, Paul, **36:** 417-18,n1
Riva-Agüero, Enrique de la, **38:** 653,n3
Rivas, Genovevo, **38:** 378,n4, 382-83, 383
Rivera, Luis Muñoz, **29:** 273
Riverdale, N.Y., **31:** 320; **33:** 383; **35:** 178
Rivero, Don Diego Ignacio, **30:** 97,n1
Rivers and Harbors, Committee on (House of Reps.), **31:** 374n2
rivers and harbors bill, **31:** 374; **37:** 15, 27, 54, 66,n2,3
road system, **29:** 355,n1
roads bill: *see* good roads bill
Robert College, Istanbul, Turkey, **35:** 39,n2
Robert H. Ingersoll and Brothers, **38:** 516n2
Robert M. La Follette (La Follette and La Follette), **27:** 188n2,3; **32:** 61n2, 295n1

Roberts, Frederick Sleigh, 1st Earl Roberts (1832-1914), **31:** 7,n1
Roberts, William Henry, **35:** 328
Robertson (chauffeur): *see* Robinson, Francis
Robins, Margaret Dreier (Mrs. Raymond), **34:** 136n2, 217; **37:** 374; **38:** 161n2
Robins, Raymond, **31:** 232n2; **37:** 264,n1, 321-22, 329-39, 373-74, 522,n1, 528
Robinson, Flora Lois, **38:** 684,n1
Robinson, Francis, **28:** 367,n3; **34:** 9,n1, 231, 258, 487,n3; **35:** 372
Robinson, George Geoffrey, **32:** 206,n3
Robinson, Joseph Taylor, **27:** 457,n1,2; **28:** 111,n5; **29:** 424, 457-58, 479, 486-88; **30:** 31; **37:** 451; **38:** 123n1
Robinson, Leonard George, **37:** 351,n1
Robinson, Theodore Francis, **30:** 491
Robles Domínguez, Alfredo, **31:** 66
Robles, José Isabel, **32:** 355,n5
Rochester *Herald*, **28:** 64n1; **38:** 546n2
Rockefeller: see John D. Rockefeller, S.S.
Rockefeller, John Davison, Jr., **29:** 504, 512, 513, 513-14, 515, 533, 546; **31:** 77, 356, 474,n3, 523, 548; **32:** 18, 84; **35:** 317n2, 539; Colorado Fuel and Iron Co., **28:** 427, 511, 546; and Colorado coal strike, **30:** 38, 39,n1
Rockefeller, John Davison, Sr., **27:** 216; **28:** 577; **29:** 29, 503-504, 504, 512, 546
Rockefeller Bureau of Social Hygiene, **29:** 327n1
Rockefeller family, **36:** 478n1
Rockefeller Foundation, **31:** 291,n3; **33:** 299n4, 441n1; **37:** 405, 433n1; **38:** 368,n1, 371,n3,4
Rockefeller Institute for Medical Research, **33:** 441,n1
Rockefeller War Relief Commission, **38:** 65
Rockford, Ill., **35:** 283n1
Rockhill, William Woodville, **32:** 482,n1
Rockland, Me., **38:** 173
Rocky Boy Indians, **31:** 77-78, 79
Rocky Mountain Fuel Co., **28:** 518n1; **29:** 549
Rodgers, James Linn, **37:** 253, 293-94, 452, 482; Punitive Expedition and, **36:** 338-40, 343-44,n1, 540n1
Rodríguez, Agustín, **29:** 549,n1; **30:** 45, 47, 66, 77, 115, 119, 228
Rodríguez, José, **36:** 653
Roe, Gilbert Ernstein, **32:** 19,n1, 61n2
Roebling, Cornelia Witsell Farrow (Mrs. Washington Augustus), **28:** 598,n1
Roebling, Washington Augustus, **28:** 598,n1
Roessing, Jennie Bradley (Mrs. Frank M.), **36:** 484-85,n1; **37:** 490n1
Roger Casement (Inglis), **36:** 563n1
Rogers, Alfred Thomas, **36:** 136,n1, 140
Rogers, Emma Ferdon Winner (Mrs. Henry Wade), **38:** 7,n1
Rogers, Henry Huttleson, **29:** 29

Rogers, Henry Wade, **28:** 111; **33:** 219
Rogers, John H., **27:** 223
Rogers, Walter Stowell, **31:** 291,n1; **34:** 271,n1
Rojas, Don P. Ezequiel, **31:** 481
Rojo, Juan B., **38:** 358
Roman Catholic Church, **34:** 224, 242,n1; **38:** 83, 277, 278, 316, 660; *in Mexico*: general, **29:** 120, 122, 123, 328; **30:** 298, 301,n1,2; **31:** 73-74; **32:** 383-84,n1, 392, 393, 393-95; **33:** 5, 30,n1, 44, 69, 71; **34:** 147, 148, 174-75, 199, 224, 242; **35:** 94; **37:** 256; and elections, **28:** 326, 340; Cardinal Gibbons on treatment of clergy, **30:** 340-41,n1; J. Lind and, **29:** 119; **30:** 346; and resolutions of the Federal Council of the Churches of Christ in America, **30:** 397; and persecution of clergy, **30:** 399, 399-400; F. Villa on, **30:** 417
in United States: criticism of U.S. policy in Mexico, **31:** 112, 333, 356, 470-71; **32:** 86, 134, 248-49, 279-81, 365; P. Schoff and, **29:** 361n2; J. M. Sullivan's criticism of in Santo Domingo, **32:** 353,n1; and Von Wiegand's interview with the Pope, **32:** 522; in the Philippines, **36:** 172n2; and pro-German sentiment in Columbia, **36:** 235; in Germany, **36:** 414; and appointments, **37:** 104-105, 129, 402, 422
Roman Catholic Church Extension Society of the United States of America, **32:** 86n1, 279
Romania: *see* Rumania
Rome, Ga., **30:** 425; **31:** 259; **37:** 247; monument to women of the Confederacy, **27:** 574n1; funeral of EAW in, **30:** 373-75
Rome, Ga., Supply Co., **30:** 395n1
Rome Female College, Ga., **28:** 400n3
Rome, Italy, **33:** 182; **35:** 226
Romeo and Juliet (Shakespeare), **38:** 625n1
Romero, Matias, **38:** 228n1
Rooney, John Jerome, **27:** 245, 246
Roosevelt, Edith Kermit Carow (Mrs. Theodore), **27:** 20
Roosevelt, Franklin Delano, **27:** 157; **28:** 64; **29:** 390, 392; **33:** 377, 394; **34:** 536, 537; **37:** 141,n4; and bid for U.S. Senate, **31:** 11,n1, 139n1
Roosevelt, Theodore, **27:** 17n2, 60n3, 107, 109, 114, 215n1, 272n1, 310, 350, 425, 443, 452; **28:** 19, 45n2, 317, 397n2; **29:** 13, 29, 59, 135, 181, 290, 319, 556; **30:** 65, 129,n2, 134, 303,n1; **31:** 268, 277,n3, 291, 429, 471; **32:** 7, 21n1, 211, 239, 290, 346, 376; **33:** 306n1, 387-88; **34:** 21n7, 78, 80, 85, 209, 307, 346, 352, 353, 358, 513; **35:** 33, 318, 319, 376, 492; **36:** 49, 86,n1, 187, 226n2, 294, 320n1, 337, 424, 615; **37:** 32, 35, 37, 38, 105n4, 135n2, 152, 162, 167, 180, 210, 327, 338, 340, 411, 423, 441, 531;

38: 7, 66, 140, 159, 177, 178, 190n1, 256, 275, 276, 292, 318, 349, 353, 362n1, 364,n2, 391, 392, 410, 430n2, 443, 513n1, 607, 630
and anthracite coal strike, **28:** 509n1, 555n2; and Columbia, **28:** 197n2; **30:** 209,n1; and Monroe Doctrine, **28:** 459; and Negroes, **28:** 117n5, 186n1, 222, 349n2; and Congress, **29:** 59; J. Reed on, **30:** 232, 233, 234; concern for EAW, **30:** 351, 351-52; WW thanks, **30:** 351-52; and A. Nortoni, **31:** 353,n2; and Panama Canal opening, **31:** 363; article on Mexico by, **31:** 413,n2; and speech at Plattsburg, **34:** 337,n1; on WW's *Sussex* note, **36:** 544,n1; and German Americans, **37:** 218,n2; **38:** 290; and Russo-Japanese War, **38:** 314n1; and speech at Grand Rapids, **38:** 290,n2, 394,n2
Root, Elihu, **27:** 12, 126, 157,n1, 297,n2, 298, 352, 358,n1, 359, 412; **28:** 317, 462,n3, 525; **29:** 74n1, 180n1, 203, 349n2; **30:** 396n1; **31:** 295; **32:** 59, 60, 68, 123, 165; **33:** 34, 456; **35:** 376; **36:** 471-72, 615; **37:** 121, 174, 340, 411, 423; **38:** 275, 276, 513; on R. Lansing, **29:** 331; and ship-purchase bill, **32:** 134n1, 336-37,n2; and speech at Republican convention, **36:** 186-87n1, 192
Root-Takahira Agreement, **32:** 135, 136, 248, 417
Roper, Daniel Calhoun, **37:** 474-75,n1, 535; **38:** 296,n1, 317, 376,n1, 388, 515,n1, 516, 546, 616; suggested for secretary to WW, **38:** 660
Rosa, Luis de la, **37:** 255,n6, 261,n7
Rose, Hugh Lawson, **34:** 63,n1, 64, 76, 77, 78, 89, 104, 117, 118, 125, 141, 154, 156, 166 171, 178, 182, 205, 224, 225, 233, 234, 240, 246, 247, 269, 286, 289, 293, 313, 314, 322, 326, 328, 331, 332, 356, 362, 365, 396; **35:** 56
Rose, Marion W., **35:** 502
Rose, Mary Francesca Granville Delaney (Mrs. Hugh Lawson), **34:** 63,n1, 78, 104, 105, 125, 154, 156, 171, 178, 182, 196, 205, 225, 246, 246-47, 269, 270, 286, 289, 293, 313, 314, 322, 326, 331, 332, 356, 362, 432; **35:** 56
Rose, Robert Forrest, **28:** 5,n6; **30:** 119; **31:** 46
Roseberry, Archibald Philip Primrose, 5th Earl of, **31:** 316,n2
Rosenkrantz, Palle Adam Vilhelm, Baron Rosenkrantz, **31:** 316,n2
Rosenwald, Julius, **31:** 314-15,n1; **32:** 272; **38:** 182, 183, 387
Rosewater, Victor, **38:** 342n3
Roslyn, Long Island, New York, **33:** 446, 470
Ross, Edward Alsworth, **27:** 492,n1; **28:** 4, 22; **29:** 352; **32:** 96
Ross, Ishbel, **32:** 423n1
Ross, Stanley R., **27:** 64n1

Rothschild, House of (France), **30:** 372
Rotterdam, Netherlands, **30:** 436; **31:** 96, 104, 147, 156, 332; **32:** 102-103; **34:** 381; **35:** 362n1
Rotterdam, S.S., **34:** 404; **35:** 382, 390, 499
Roubaix, France, **38:** 652, 653
Roumania: *see* Rumania
Round My House: Notes of Rural Life in France in Peace and War (Hamerton), **33:** 87,n1, 364
Routt County, Colo., **31:** 334, 517, 558
Routt County Fuel Co., Colo., **29:** 549
Rowanmore, S.S., **38:** 571n2
Rowe, Henry G., **34:** 185n1
Rowe, Leo Stanton, **38:** 362,n4
Royal Gorge Fuel Co., Colo., **29:** 549
Royal Photographic Society of Great Britain, **35:** 84n1
Rubens, Paul, **27:** 119n2
Rublee, George, **28:** 392,n3; **29:** 481,n1,3, 482, 496; **30:** 110, 134, 161, 166n2, 276; **32:** 271n2, 273; **36:** 191-92, 203,n2; **37:** 34, 67, 70, 117, 204n2, 363, 373, 481; **38:** 3, 4, 34, 43, 87,n1, 354n1; on Federal Trade Commission bill, **30:** 274,n1; and railway-securities bill, **30:** 296; as member of Federal Trade Commission, **37:** 20, 25, 101,n1, 128, 374-75, 475, 512-13, 517-18
Rublee, Juliet Barrett (Mrs. George), **28:** 392,n3; **30:** 93, 135; **33:** 314,n1
Rucker, William Waller, **29:** 170
Rucker corrupt-practices bill, **30:** 405
Ruddock, Albert Billings, **37:** 272,n1
Rudwick, Elliott, **28:** 349n2
Ruef, Abraham, **38:** 59,n2
Ruffin, Sterling, **35:** 22,n1
Ruffin, Thomas, **29:** 388, 394
Rugby Fuel Co., **29:** 549
Ruiz, Carlos Castro, *see* Castro Ruiz, Carlos
Rules Committee (House of Reps.), **28:** 255,n2; **29:** 21n1, 299; **30:** 454; **31:** 465, 466; **32:** 86n1, 197n1, 207; **35:** 456; **36:** 231-32, 376, 396n1; **37:** 337
Rules Committee (Senate), **29:** 21n1, 22,n1
Rumania, **28:** 4n2; **31:** 355; **32:** 46, 204, 237, 475; **33:** 12, 130, 231, 232, 267, 501; **34:** 18; **35:** 245; **37:** 110, 464; **38:** 53n2, 74, 107, 113
Runciman, Sir Walter, **36:** 368
Runnemede (estate, Windsor, Vt.), **28:** 62n3
Runnymede, **30:** 146
Runyon, Walter Parker, **38:** 212n1
rural credits: Hollis-Bulkley bill; Rural Credits Act, **28:** 146-48; **29:** 5-6, 6-7, 69-74, 114, 116-17, 128-29, 132, 139, 163, 212-13, 270, 399; **30:** 10-11,n2, 24, 113,n6; **31:** 172, 419,n3, 462; **32:** 13, 14, 89, 125, 308; **33:** 442; **35:** 96, 106, 308-309, 530,n1; **36:** 250, 366n1, 518, 521-22; **37:** 197; WW signs bill, **37:** 427-

28,n1, 519; **38:** 130, 308, 423, 425, 504, 639
rural credits board: *see* Federal Farm Loan Board
Rural Credits Commission, **27:** 201; **29:** 132, 141,n1
rural delivery system, **37:** 190, 192
Rush, Thomas E., **31:** 252,n2
Russell, Charles Edward, **29:** 105; **32:** 96,n7
Russell, Joseph Ballister, **30:** 27,n1
Russell, William Thomas, **37:** 30,n3, 55
Russell, William Worthington, **33:** 218,n6; **37:** 157,n2
Russia, **32:** 45, 67, 81, 87, 212, 300-301, 360; **33:** 12-13, 34, 88, 114, 115-16, 122-23, 123, 363, 406, 407, 483, 516, 517, 522; **34:** 12, 17-18, 18, 20, 22, 42, 47, 62, 145, 159, 188, 236, 251n4, 279, 310; **35:** 71n3, 75, 194, 204, 225, 255, 261, 466, 484; **36:** 124, 125-26, 147, 148n1, 180n2, 320n1, 387n1; **37:** 20, 21, 90,n2, 104, 134,n1, 135n2, 179, 185, 240, 274, 319, 464; **38:** 74, 91, 149
and China, **27:** 28, 488-89; and Mexico, **27:** 249, 261-62; **28:** 460, 486n3; appointments to, **28:** 4,n1, 111, 353,n1; ambassadorship, **30:** 31, 46, 58; **33:** 511; **35:** 526; **36:** 86, 135-36, 188, 191-92, 230-31, 409; E. M. House on Germany and, **30:** 109, 323, 463,n2; and Great Britain, **30:** 214, 248, 267; and Austria-Hungary, **30:** 315; E. Grey and U.S. offer of good offices to, **30:** 325; House on, **30:** 342, 432; C. W. Eliot on Allied blockade of Germany and Austria-Hungary, **30:** 353-55; W. H. Page on, **30:** 371; **31:** 8; and American loans to, **30:** 372; **35:** 536-38; resolutions of the Federal Council of Churches and, **30:** 396, 397; Eliot on, **30:** 419, 434; reply of Nicholas II to WW's mediation offer, **30:** 456-57; C. Dumba on, **31:** 6, 296; and Turkey, **31:** 161n1; and Japan, **31:** 137, 365, 469n4, 511, 513; **34:** 19; and trade, **31:** 144, 459; and Declaration of London, **31:** 161; need for improvement of conditions in, **31:** 182; and Field Marshal French on settlement of war and, **31:** 294n1; H. Münsterberg on, **31:** 443; C. A. Spring Rice on, **31:** 489; and House peace mission, **32:** 64-65, 67, 204, 205, 206, 225, 253, 255, 262, 266, 276-77, 377, 507; and France, **32:** 358; prisoners of war in, **32:** 396-97, 442, 458, 462, 525-26; **37:** 507n3; condition of refugees in, **34:** 306,n2; and Japan and China, **35:** 117, 203, 289; G. T. Marye as ambassador, **35:** 358; and Dogger Bank incident, **35:** 395,n3; D. R. Francis appointed ambassador to, **36:** 202,n1; H. H. Kitchener on Germany and, **36:** 438, 439; and Jews in, **37:** 110; and Poland, **37:** 404, 405, 538; **38:** 369-70; and peace moves,

37: 411, 412; William II on, **38:** 64;
D. R. Francis on, **38:** 67-71; F. C. Penfield on Rumania and, **38:** 74, 75
Russia and the United States, **27:** ix,
305,n3, 478; **29:** 180, 203; ambassadorship, **27:** 228, 259; and Treaty of 1832,
29: 181, 236, 268; and new treaty negotiations, **29:** 217, 218, 416; appointments to, **29:** 242; and peace moves,
31: 61, 62, 95, 137, 428,n1, 459, 518,
541; request for U.S. loan, **31:** 182-83,
187, 217; and new commercial treaty
between, **31:** 187, 473,n1, 481; and
credit, **31:** 218; and employment for
immigrants in U.S., **32:** 56; WW offers
Red Cross assistance to prisoners in
Siberia, **32:** 396-97; Nicholas II on
WW's offer, **32:** 525-26
Russian Americans, **28:** 164, 492
Russo-Japanese Treaty (1916), **37:** 134,n1,
382, 408, 418-19; **38:** 70
Russo-Japanese War, **27:** 451, 452; **30:**
330, 386; **31:** 154, 194-95, 337, 437, 442,
469n4; **32:** 107n1, 108; **33:** 457; **34:** 84;
36: 104; **38:** 314n1
Rutherford and Son (play), **27:** 71,n3
Rutland, Vt., **28:** 320, 321, 375; **34:** 138
Ryan, Dr. (surgeon), **27:** 543, 545
Ryan, James Augustine, **36:** 585,n1
Ryan, John Dennis, **38:** 182,n3, 184, 297,
386, 591n1
Ryan, Paul B., **33:** 127n1, 135n3
Ryan, Thomas Fortune, **27:** 74
Rydal, Ambleside, Westmorland, **27:** 574;
30: 401; **34:** 82
Rydal Mount, Westmorland, **28:** 286
Ryder, Chauncy Foster, **28:** 372,n1
Ryder, Rowland, **35:** 88n4, 103n1
Ryley, Madeleine Lucette, **28:** 400n1

Saavedra, Rodrigo de (Marquis de Vil-
lalobar), **38:** 392,n2
Sabath, Adolph Joseph, **32:** 96
Sabine, William Tufnell, **38:** 686,n1
Sackville-West, Sir Lionel, **34:** 433,n1; **36:**
131n2
Sacramento, Cal., **27:** 352; post office, **27:**
487; and 1916 election, **27:** 491n1
Sacramento Union, **27:** 487,n1
Sadeleer, Louis de, **30:** 470n1; **31:** 121-
22, 131
Sadler, Wilbur Fisk, Jr., **27:** 26; **35:** 105-
106, 110-11, 138-41; **37:** 74; on selec-
tion of Assistant Secretary of War, **36:**
292-93, 300
Saegertown, Pa., **36:** 337
Safety at Sea Conference: *see* Interna-
tional Conference on Safety of Life at
Sea
safety-at-sea legislation, **30:** 223,n1; **31:**
375, 419, 464, 508; W. J. Stone on, **31:**
457-58,n1; W. J. Bryan on, **31:** 490-93;
W. C. Redfield on, **31:** 493-96; *see also*
International Conference on Safety of
Life at Sea

Saffarrans, George C., **37:** 319,n2
Sage, Eben Charles, **36:** 558,n1
Sague, John Kelsey, **27:** 223,n1
St. Aldwyn, 1st Earl: *see* Hicks Beach,
Sir Michael Edward
St Andrew's Hotel, N.Y., **38:** 511
Saint-Gaudens, Annetta Johnson (Mrs.
Louis), **28:** 98-99,n1, 159, 278-79, 392
Saint-Gaudens, Augustus, **27:** 253; **28:**
95,n2, 99, 321,n2
Saint-Gaudens, Louis, **28:** 99, 159
St. James' Lutheran Church, N.Y., **29:**
475n1
St. James' Palace, London, **34:** 10n2
St. John, Vincent, **27:** 477, 481
St. John's Episcopal Church, Williams-
town, Mass., **28:** 20n4; **38:** 628
Saint Joseph, Mo., **38:** 196
Saint Lawrence County Democratic
Committee, **28:** 35n2
St. Louis, Mo., **31:** 471; WW's addresses
in, **36:** 110-14, 114-21, 173-74; *illus-
tration section,* **36:**
St. Louis Convention: *see* Democratic
National Convention, 1916
St. Louis Post-Dispatch, **32:** 90n2; **36:**
110n, 121n; **37:** 27,n2; **38:** 318,n1
St. Louis *Republic*, **32:** 139,n1; **34:** 38; **36:**
114n, 121n
St. Margaret's Church, Wash., D.C., **35:**
371n1
St. Mark's Episcopal Church, N.Y., **38:**
16n3
Saint Mary River, **30:** 218n3
St. Patrick's Church, Wash., D.C., **37:**
30n3
St. Paul, Minn.: American Union Against
Militarism meeting in, **36:** 635
St. Paul, S.S., **33:** 321
St. Paul's Chapel, N.Y., **38:** 475n1, 560n1
St. Paul's Episcopal Church, Windsor,
Vt., **28:** 315,n1
St. Paul's School, Concord, N.H., **30:** 105;
34: 394n1; **38:** 334,n4, 476n2
St. Peter's College, N.J., **27:** 97,n1
Saint Petersburg, Russia, **30:** 325; **34:**
306n2
Saint Petersburg, University of (Rus-
sia), **36:** 654n1
St. Pierre, Church of (Louvain, Bel-
gium), **30:** 458
St. Regis Hotel, N.Y., **35:** 25, 42, 44, 46,
146, 155, 165, 175, 178
St. Thomas Episcopal Church, Wash.,
D.C., **34:** 464n3
Sakhalin Island, **34:** 19
Salazar, Amador, **31:** 12,n5
Salazar, José Inés, **32:** 388
Salem Rebuilding Fund, **33:** 430
Salina Cruz, Oaxaca, Mex., **35:** 501n1
Salisbury, N.C.: WW's remarks in, **37:**
78-79
Salisbury, Robert Arthur Talbot Gas-
coyne-Cecil, 3rd Marquess of, **31:** 478;
36: 462

Salmon, Thomas William, **27:** 244; **32:** 96
Salonika, Greece, **32:** 225n1
Salt Lake City, Utah, **34:** 539n2
Saltillo, Coahuila, Mex., **29:** 539; **30:** 47, 82, 166-67,n1, 168, 169, 290, 291
Salvador: *see* El Salvador
Sam, Vilbrun Guillaume, **32:** 296, 472,n2; **33:** 115,n2, 116-17, 467n1; **34:** 45n1, 143n1
Samoa, **32:** 277
San Ángel, Mex., **28:** 27
San Antonio, Tex., **29:** 295n3; **30:** 399; **32:** 128; **36:** 353
San Diego, Cal.: and Panama-Pacific Exposition, **36:** 299, 301
San Domingo: *see* the Dominican Republic
San Fernando Avocado Co., Cal., **35:** 238
San Francisco, Cal., **29:** 130; **32:** 118n1; **34:** 382n1; and Chinese immigration, **36:** 549-52, 576
San Francisco Bridge, Veracruz, **30:** 8,n2
San Francisco Bulletin, **38:** 60n4, 187n1
San Francisco Exposition (1915): *see* Panama-Pacific International Exposition
San Juan, P.R., **32:** 94n1
San Juan River, **27:** 527, 528
San Luis Potosí, state, Mex., **28:** 77; **29:** 101, 124, 127
San Luis Potosí, San Luis Potosí, Mex., **29:** 539; **30:** 47, 220, 285n1, 291
San Pedro de Lagunas, Coahuila, Mex., **37:** 22
San Sebastián, Spain, **32:** 439; **33:** 47
Sánchez, Gertrudis, **28:** 77
Sanchez, Juan, **36:** 653
Sandanwede (Mrs. Hulbert's home on Nantucket), **30:** 72, 196; **33:** 413
Sandefjord, S.S., **31:** 477
Sanders, Leon, **32:** 97,n10
Sandles, Alfred Putnam, **27:** 9,n1
Sandos, James A., **30:** 280n1
Sands, Tucker K., **34:** 345,n2
Sanitary Housing Co., Wash., D.C., **33:** 430,n2
Sannon, Horace Pauléus, **34:** 367, 437-38
Sansaricq, Antoine C., **34:** 438
San-Sha, Wan Bay, China, **32:** 421
Santa Anna, Antonio López de, **29:** 539
Santa Fe Del Pino, Mex., **37:** 22n4
Santa Fe Railroad, **31:** 81; **32:** 383
Santa Rita Hotel, Tucson, Ariz., **28:** 567
Santa Rosalia, Chihuahua, Mex.; *see* Ciudad Camargo
Santa Ysabel, Chihuahua, Mex., **35:** 478n1; massacre in, **36:** 397n2; **37:** 155,n2, 250-51,n3
Santiago, Chile, **35:** 358n2
Santo Domingo: *see* Dominican Republic
Santo Domingo, Dom. Rep., **29:** 20, 94; **30:** 165, 260, 296, 307-309, 319, 346, 363; **31:** 382-84,n1,2; and W. Vick, **31:** 403-404, 410, 447-48; WW plans in-

quiry, **31:** 411; investigation of Sullivan ministry, **31:** 414,n4, 453, 467; and Haiti, **31:** 457, 487
Santo Domingo Investigation. Copy of the Report, Findings and Opinion of James D. Phelan, Commissioner named by the Secretary of State, with approval of the President, to investigate charges against the United States Minister to the Dominican Republic, **33:** 218n1
Santo Domingo Ranch, **38:** 380, 381, 385
Santos Chocano, José, **30:** 413,n8
Santos Coy, Ernesto, **28:** 77; **30:** 409
San-tu Ao Bay, China, **32:** 420
Sapporo, Japan, **29:** 129n1
Sarajevo, Bosnia, **30:** 222
Saratoga Springs, N.Y., **34:** 64
Saratoga, U.S.S., **27:** 426,n2
Sargent, John Singer, **32:** 25; **33:** 552; **38:** 659,n2
Satō, Shosuke, **29:** 129,n1
Saturday Evening Post, **28:** 595n2; **29:** 302n1, 516n3, 524n; **30:** 61,n1, 78n1; **31:** 403n; **32:** 69; **36:** 402, 600; **37:** 332n1
Saulsbury, Willard, **27:** 25,n1, 39n2,3; **30:** 166, 174, 380-81, 384; **31:** 32; **38:** 164-65, 489n1; and MacMurray appointment, **36:** 175-76, 191,n1, 505
Saunders, Frances Wright, **34:** 491n1
Saunders, Mary Toomer (Mrs. R. M.), **31:** 4,n1, 516
Saunders, William Lawrence, **28:** 42,n3; **38:** 591n1
savings and loan associations: and rural credit, **29:** 73; and railroad securities, **29:** 369
Savoy, Edward, **31:** 312
Savoy Hotel, London, **30:** 367
Saxe, Mr. (counsel to Gov. Glynn), **31:** 253
Say Not the Struggle Naught Availeth (Clough), **28:** 361,n1
Saybrook, Conn., **30:** 189
Sayles, Frank Arthur, **31:** 139,n3
Sayre, Eleanor Axson, **36:** 373, 384, 551; **37:** 14, 78; **38:** 121, 375n1, 396, 590; baptism of, **38:** 626, 628
Sayre, Francis Bowes, **28:** 20,n1,4, 42, 52, 54, 63, 88, 104, 132, 138,n1, 162, 248, 259, 260, 264, 265, 266, 267, 302, 308, 315, 320, 321, 338-39, 355,n3, 397, 413n1, 587-88; **29:** 20, 23, 47, 51,n1, 104, 211, 284, 449; **30:** 436; **31:** 556; **32:** 7, 12, 21, 83, 100, 335; **33:** 191, 525,n1, 542, 543; **34:** 7, 14, 73, 74, 77, 83, 89, 91, 101, 124, 129, 394, 407; **35:** 109, 110, 344, 394, 408; **36:** 151, 552; **37:** 14; **38:** 121, 375,n1, 396,n2, 590,n2, 623, 625, 628, 688; wedding, **28:** 565n1, 596; photograph: *illustration section*, **28**
Sayre, Francis Bowes, Jr. (Francis Woodrow Sayre until February 1919), **32:** 83,n1, 86, 100, 306, 335; **34:** 83, 153, 217; **35:** 80, 109, 110, 344, 393, 408; **36:** 151, 552; **37:** 78; **38:** 396, 590,

628,n2, 689n2, 690; E. M. House's gift to, **32:** 117; WW on not naming grandson after him, **32:** 117, 147

Sayre, Jessie Woodrow Wilson (Mrs. Francis Bowes), **27:** 95, 155, 227; **28:** 54, 61, 63, 81, 93, 102, 103, 106, 112, 126, 162, 166, 189, 249, 259, 260, 264, 265, 266, 267, 280, 302, 308, 315, 320, 327, 338, 339, 355, 363, 368, 372, 483, 532, 598; **29:** 20, 23, 47, 51, 104, 184, 211, 284, 304, 324, 347, 553, 558; **30:** 73, 277, 436, 452; **31:** 341-42, 357, 456, 556; **32:** 7, 12, 86, 100, 117, 147, 165, 306, 335, 370-71; **33:** 190-91,n2, 447, 525,n1, 543; **34:** 7, 8, 14-15, 72-73, 74, 77, 83, 89, 91, 101, 104, 125, 128, 150, 153, 154, 155, 170, 201, 205, 217, 218, 233, 257, 374, 407; **35:** 16, 79-80, 109-10, 110, 344, 393-94, 408; **36:** 151-52, 384, 552; **37:** 14, 78; **38:** 121, 375, 396, 590, 623, 628
WW's love for, **28:** 12, 180; engagement and marriage, **28:** 20,n1, 387, 397, 398, 565n1; W. H. Page offers London home for honeymoon, **28:** 52-53, 274; finds home in Williamstown, **28:** 88; riding accident, **28:** 247n2, 252, 259, 397; honeymoon, **28:** 587-88, 595-96; birth of son in White House, **32:** 83; and Mrs. Galt, **34:** 245-46, 283; affection for WW, **34:** 378-79; birthday celebration in Cornish, **34:** 394; birth of daughter in Philadelphia, **36:** 373; WW's greetings on her fifteenth birthday, **38:** 683; and college sorority controversy, **38:** 684,n2, 685-86; WW on marriage of, **38:** 688; photograph: *illustration section,* 28

Sayre, John Nevin, **38:** 396,n1
Sayre, Martha Finley Nevin (Mrs. Robert Heysham), **28:** 413,n1; **38:** 628,n4,6
Sayre, Woodrow Wilson, **38:** 628n2
Says U.S. Election Is Vital to Europe (Gardiner), **37:** 265,n1
Sayville radio station, **33:** 486,n2
Sazonov, Sergieĭ Dmitrievich, **38:** 67-71,n1
Scandinavia, **31:** 156, 159, 190; **34:** 381; **35:** 227; **37:** 89; *see also* under names of individual countries, such as Denmark
Scandinavian Americans, **28:** 492
Scarborough, England, **32:** 380
Scavenius, Erik Julius Cristian de, **33:** 465n1; **34:** 280,n1, 462-63,n1; and negotiations for sale of Danish West Indies, **35:** 284-85,n1,2, 290, 350, 432n1
Schaff, Philip, **29:** 361,n2
Schauffler, Miss, **28:** 126,n2
Schauffler, William Gray, **28:** 126,n2
Scheidemann, Philipp, **37:** 90,n1
Scheltema, J. H., **29:** 186
Scheme to Grab Navy's Oil Lands Revealed in Conservation Bill (*New York Herald*), **37:** 141n4

Schenectady, N.Y., **34:** 77, 91
Scherer, André, **38:** 314n2
Schierbrand, Wolf von, **33:** 32,n3
Schiff, Jacob Henry, **27:** 513,n1; **29:** 218; **31:** 333-34, 355, 425; **37:** 351,n1; **38:** 104-105, 123, 258, 591n1, 662; and immigration bill, **32:** 77-78, 82
Schleswig-Holstein, **31:** 294n1
Schmeckebier, Laurence F., **27:** 77n3
Schmutz, Gaston, **33:** 29,n1; **36:** 318-19,n2
Schneider, Commander, **35:** 13, 14, 25, 26, 75
Schneidermann, Mary, **29:** 214
Schoolmaster in the White House (Mc-Kelway), **38:** 284,n1
Schoonover, Albert, **29:** 243
Schurman, Jacob Gould, **28:** 326
Schurz, Carl, **38:** 291
Schütte, Oswald, **38:** 73
Schuyler, Eugene, **32:** 534,n4
Schwab, Charles Michael, **27:** 216,n4; **31:** 425n1; **34:** 404
Schweinitz, George Edmund de, **29:** 377,n2; **34:** 258-59, 327
Schwieger, Walter, **33:** 127n1; **34:** 315n1; **36:** 74
Schwimmer, Rosika, **33:** 314n2; **35:** 279n1, 373
Scientific American, **36:** 345,n2
Scioto Sign Co., Kenton, Ohio, **28:** 354,n4
Scioto Valley, Ohio, **27:** 230
Score of Benedict Arnolds (New York *World*), **28:** 391n2
Scotch Irish, **38:** 324, 524
Scotch Presbyterian Church of New York, **37:** 270n2
Scotland, **30:** 397, 465; **31:** 245
Scotland Yard, **31:** 339
Scott, Adeline Mitchell, **28:** 61,n1, 81, 92, 96, 98
Scott, Alice Adeline Post (Mrs. William Berryman), **28:** 92,n4
Scott, Charles Ernest, **27:** 488-90; **28:** 10; **29:** 118
Scott, David Hunter, **29:** 36n1
Scott, Ernest Stowell, **27:** 477,n1
Scott, Hugh Lenox, **29:** 36,n1, 377,n2, 450,n1; **30:** 148, 180, 188, 220, 221; **31:** 476; **33:** 120,n1, 533; **34:** 386, 388, 392, 401, 482,n4, 484; **36:** 176, 275, 418; **37:** 121, 122, 130-31, 213,n2, 231, 253, 254, 255, 283-86; **38:** 166,n1,2, 219, 675-78; receives gift from F. Villa, **29:** 495; ad interim Secretary of War, **36:** 171; remains as Chief of Staff, **36:** 197; and Punitive Expedition, **36:** 285-86, 296, 322, 456-57, 503n1, 528-29; indiscreet in discussing Mexican situation with newspapermen, **36:** 463-64; and conference with A. Obregón, **36:** 540-41,n1, 553-54, 570-71, 571-72, 579-80, 592-94; **37:** 18,n1, 22-24, 38-39; and Scott-Obregón agreement, **36:** 607-608, 618
Scott, James Brown, **30:** 435n1; **32:** 503n1
Scott, Lewis Merrill, **36:** 592,n2

Scott, Mary Blanchard, **28:** 61,n1, 81, 92, 95-96, 98, 286
Scott, Melinda, **29:** 214
Scott, William Amasa, **27:** 206-207
Scott, William Berryman, **28:** 61n1; **36:** 418-19, 478,n1
Scott, Winfield, **31:** 562n4
Scottish Americans: and Berea College, **30:** 63
Scranton, Pa., **29:** 401n1
Scribner, Charles, **27:** 15
Scribner's Magazine, **32:** 267n1
Scripps, Edward Wyllis, **31:** 291,n2; **34:** 271,n1
Scripps newspapers, **35:** 353n1; **38:** 428n2
Scroggs, William Oscar, **33:** 46n1
Scudder, Edward Wallace, **29:** 302-303,n1
Scully, Thomas Joseph, **35:** 59n1; **38:** 118,n1,3
Sea Girt, N.J., **29:** 326; **35:** 58
Seabury, Samuel, **35:** 318-19; **37:** 264,n6, 290; **38:** 557, 591n1, 597n1; nominated for governor, **38:** 190,n1
Seager, Henry Rogers, **27:** 77,n4, 244; **35:** 184,n1
Seaman, Owen, **35:** 9
Seaman A. Knapp: Schoolmaster of American Agriculture (Bailey) **27:** 50n8
seamen: safety at sea, A. Furuseth on, **28:** 469-70; WW on, **29:** 10; J. B. Rublee on, **30:** 93; *see also* International Conference on Safety of Life at Sea; seamen's bill
seamen's bill, **27:** 188,n2; **28:** 15-16,n1,2, 204, 245, 246, 412-13, 420,n1,2, 462-63; **29:** 500; **30:** 126, 171,n1, 223,n1, 280-81,n1, 318; **31:** 88, 178, 234, 458, 464, 491,n1, 492, 495, 554-55; **32:** 87, 89, 273-74, 294-95,n1, 307-308, 309, 344-45; **33:** 252; **35:** 338, 458,n1; **37:** 329; R. Lansing's objections to, **32:** 302, 302-303; A. Furuseth urges passage of, **32:** 304-305; W. J. Bryan on, **32:** 309-10; R. M. La Follette on, **32:** 312; WW signs bill, **32:** 324,n2; A. Furuseth thanks WW for signing, **32:** 333
Seamen's Union, **35:** 338
Sears, Clara Endicott, **36:** 132n1
Sears, Roebuck and Co., **31:** 314n1; **38:** 183
Seattle, Wash.: labor convention, **28:** 590,n1
Seattle Chamber of Commerce, **29:** 332n1
Second National Bank of Baltimore, **29:** 390, 401n1
Second Pan American Scientific Congress: *see* Pan American Scientific Congress (Second)
Secret Service: *see* United States Secret Service
Secrets of the White House (Jaffray), **27:** 12,n1
Sedgwick, Ellery, **37:** 424-25
Seeking World Order: The United States and International Organization to 1920 (Kuehl), **33:** 368n1
Seely, Fred Loring, **28:** 382,n1
segregation, **27:** 290-92; **28:** 245, 289n1; in government offices, **27:** xvii, 290-91; **28:** 65, 94, 265, 290n3, 413-14, 496-98,n1; **29:** 105; **31:** 237, 297, 308, 311-13, 328n2, 361,n2; O. G. Villard on, **27:** 442,n1,2; **28:** 60-61,n3, 240, 289, 343, 401-402; R. N. Wood on, **28:** 115-18,n1; B. T. Washington on, **28:** 186-87,n1,4; W. F. Powell, **28:** 221-23; H. A. Bridgman on, **28:** 256, 277-78,n1; J. P. Gavit on, **28:** 332, 348-50,n1,2; W. G. McAdoo on, **28:** 346, 453-55; M. C. Nerney report, **28:** 402-10; W. M. Trotter on, **28:** 491-95; **31:** 298-301; D. I. Walsh on, **31:** 237-38; remarks by WW, **31:** 301-304; A. E. Patterson on, **38:** 97-98,n1; M. Storey on, **38:** 163-65
Seibold, Louis, **35:** 52-53,n1, 73; **38:** 194
Seitz, Don Carlos, **37:** 203,n1
Seldomridge, Harry Hunter, **28:** 90,n1; **29:** 511,n1; **30:** 113,n5
Selekman, Ben Morris, **35:** 317n2
Seligman and Co., J. W., N.Y., **28:** 251,n4
Sells, Cato, **29:** 533,n2
Sells, Donald Douglas, **38:** 518,n1
Selph, Colin M., **37:** 442n1
Semonche, John Erwin, **37:** 286n1
Semple, Lorenzo, **30:** 443,n3
Senate (U.S.): *see* United States Congress
Senate Document No. 325, Preliminary Report of the Inland Waterways Commission, **38:** 159n2
senators: direct election of, **27:** 54
Serbia, **28:** 4n2; **30:** 314, 325, 382-83, 396, 397, 457; **31:** 443; **32:** 45, 204, 225n1, 506; **33:** 130, 267; **34:** 145, 159, 333; **35:** 185n1, 194, 316n1, 367; **37:** 5, 464; **38:** 647
Serratos, Alfredo, **31:** 70
Serve One Master Only! (Brandeis), **29:** 30n1
Seven Keys to Baldpate (Cohan), **28:** 597,n1
Seven Sisters antitrust bills, **27:** 90,n2, 120-22, 178; **28:** 420; **29:** 81; **32:** 74
Seward, Alice D., **34:** 182,n1, 245
Seward, Anne Leddell, **33:** 473,n1, 474
Sextuple Group of 1913, **37:** 233
Seymour, Charles, **27:** xvii; **35:** 471n2
Shackleford, Dorsey William, **29:** 355,n1; **37:** 330n1
Shadow Lawn, Long Branch, N.J., **35:** 581n1; **38:** 187n2, 241n1, 257, 280, 312n2, 397; WW on appearance of, **38:** 7-8; charitable distribution of WW rent payment, **38:** 118,n3; election night at, **38:** 622; photograph: *illustration section,* **38**
Shafroth, John Franklin, **28:** 415; **29:** 269, 289, 511,n1; **31:** 547; **36:** 327-28; **37:** 369, 455

Sha-ho-chen, China, **32:** 418
Shakespeare, William, **28:** 54, 126, 351-
52; **29:** 55, 56, 532; **33:** 110,n1, 119,n2,
137n1; **36:** 92, 260,n1, 570
Shakespeare Tercentenary Celebration,
36: 261, 477, 570; **37:** 28,n1
Shanghai, China, **33:** 98
Shanklin, Arnold, **27:** 331,n3; **29:** 383, 478
Shanklin, William Arnold, **27:** 541, 543,
544; **32:** 499; **33:** 448, 466; **36:** 330, 400
Shannon, Thomas Berry, **33:** 196
Shansi Province, China, **32:** 418
Shantung Province, China, **27:** 488; **31:**
364, 365, 510, 512, 513; **32:** 136, 137,
177, 320, 321, 322, 333n1, 367n1, 368,
417, 418; **37:** 232
Shantung Railway, **32:** 416n3
Shapiro, Louis J., **32:** 97
Sharp, Hallie Clough (Mrs. William
Graves), **30:** 195,n1, 196
Sharp, William Graves, **30:** 195-96; **31:**
283, 469; **32:** 341, 372, 377; **33:** 183;
35: 88,n2, 525; **36:** 125; **37:** 289, 441,
470, 519; **38:** 317n1, 394-95,n1,2
Sharpe, Henry Dexter, **29:** 401n1
Shaw, Albert, **29:** 350-51
Shaw, Anna Howard, **29:** 21n1; **35:** 30;
36: 3n2; **38:** 87, 161n2, 178, 189
Shaw, Arch Wilkinson, **32:** 68-69,n1, 125
Shaw, George Bernard, **31:** 316,n2; **37:**
447
Shearn, Clarence John, **37:** 290,n1
Sheldon, Edward Wright, **30:** 282; **31:**
205; **35:** 292, 310
Shelley, Frank Davis, **38:** 301n2
Shelly, Rebecca, **38:** 108n1
Sheppard, Morris, **28:** 141,n3, 259-60,n2,
261; **31:** 248, 248-49; **34:** 13-14, 34; **35:**
506,n3
Sheridan, Mr. (husband of Sarah Mac-
Donald), **28:** 372-73
Sheridan, Sarah MacDonald, **28:** 345,n1,
360, 372-73; **31:** 454,n5
Sheridan Coal Co., Omaha, **37:** 359n1
Sherley, Joseph Swagar, **30:** 260-61; **37:**
74, 92
Sherman, John, **27:** 182, 183
Sherman, Lawrence Yates, **29:** 261n2; **31:**
232n2; **38:** 498
Sherman, William Tecumseh, **28:** 321,n2
Sherman Antitrust Act, **27:** 216, 412; **29:**
7, 138-39, 156, 227,n1, 316, 335-37; **30:**
126, 127, 243, 271; **31:** 25, 47, 212, 250,
268, 271, 374; **33:** 398n3; **37:** 363,n2;
S. Gompers on, **27:** 182, 185, 186, 366,
368; H. B. Thompson on, **27:** 475;
W. C. Redfield on, **29:** 41, 443; E. F. Goltra on, **29:** 50; and Union Pacific Railroad case, **29:** 67-68,n2; J. E. Davies
on, **29:** 78, 79, 80-81; and "restraint of
trade" clause, **29:** 80-81, 109; E. G.
Lowry on, **29:** 95; J. P. Tumulty on, **29:**
102; S. J. Graham on, **29:** 105, 106, 106-
107, 108, 109; penal section, **29:** 108-
109; and Interstate Commerce Commission, **29:** 108; and labor unions, **29:**
347, 425, 538; and Clayton bill, **30:** 206,
480, 481; F. G. Newlands on, **30:** 261;
C. R. Van Hise on, **30:** 272; G. Rublee
on, **30:** 274n1; and pending suits, **30:**
482; see also Clayton Antitrust Act;
Federal Trade Commission Act
Sherwin, Henry Alden, **29:** 401n1
Sherwin Williams and Co., Cleveland, **29:**
401n1
Sherwood, Isaac Ruth, **29:** 538; **37:** 395,n1
Shetland Islands, **32:** 194, 196n1
Shields, John Knight, **27:** 55n3; **29:** 304,
317, 322, 332; **36:** 355, 360, 606; **37:**
12-13, 69-70, 72, 375,n1, 429
Shields water-power bill, **36:** 277; **37:** 12-
13, 70, 92, 96, 337,n1, 347-48, 359,n1;
G. Pinchot on, **36:** 48-51,n1; F. K. Lane
on, **36:** 241-44, 290, 301; and Cum-
mins amendment, **36:** 242-44; W. Kent
on, **36:** 265; W. C. Adamson on, **36:**
304,n1; D. I. Walsh on, **36:** 311, 325,
329; W. J. Stone on, **36:** 355,n1, 360
Shimonoseki, Straits of, **29:** 437
Ship Bill Attack on Lodge by M'Adoo
(*New York Times*), **32:** 337n3
Ship Registry Act of 1914, **30:** 324, 325,
326, 335, 336, 345, 349, 352, 380-81,
384, 387-88, 435,n2; **31:** 353; **32:** 166,
168, 176, 337,n2
Shipman, Ellen McGowan (Mrs. Louis
Evan), **28:** 126,n1; **33:** 525,n3; **34:** 178
Shipman, Harry, **35:** 423
Shipman, Louis Evan, **28:** 126n1; **33:**
525,n3
shipping: *see* commerce
Shipping Board: *see* United States Shipping Board
ship-purchase bill, **30:** 402, 404, 440, 451,
454, 469-70; **31:** 61, 87-88, 88, 89, 111,
235, 345, 353, 375, 448, 459-60, 507;
32: 14, 34, 84, 87, 88, 89, 106, 108, 111-
12, 114-15, 118, 119, 122, 123, 133-34,
134,n1, 140-41, 166, 167, 167-68, 171-
73,n1,2, 174-75, 175-76, 176, 191, 192-
93, 197-98, 199, 202, 207, 221-22, 227-
29, 231, 238-39, 240, 242, 252, 263, 274,
275, 293, 366; **34:** 402n2; **35:** 176,
177,n2, 266, 270, 360, 396, 471,n1, 475;
36: 93, 156-57, 250, 357, 370, 374, 545,
567,n1, 575-76; **37:** 194, 366-67, 375,
451; **38:** 52, 63, 77, 196, 577; passage
of, **38:** 60,n2, J. P. Morgan, Jr., relays
British feelings on, **30:** 426-27; Joint
State and Navy Neutrality Board on,
30: 435,n2; E. Grey on, **30:** 435-36;
R. Lansing on, **30:** 448; **31:** 347-49;
O. G. Villard on, **30:** 455-56, 479; E. M.
House on, **31:** 100-101, 354; W. C.
Redfield on, **31:** 122-23, 124; W. G.
McAdoo on, **31:** 234, 360; **32:** 336-37;
35: 345,n1,4, 459,n1; and cotton trade,
31: 276; WW on, **31:** 280, 418; **32:** 190,
313-16; and Kenyon amendment, **32:**

ship-purchase bill (*cont.*)
171-72,n1, 188-89; and Senate filibuster, **32**: 173,n2; and Weeks bill, **32**: 197,n1; and Gore bill, **32**: 197n2; WW thanks Adamson for work on, **32**: 241; WW thanks Alexander for work on, **32**: 242; WW on rights of neutrals and, **32**: 244-45

Shively, Benjamin Franklin, **28**: 415, 418; **29**: 305-306, 440, 441, 471; **32**: 33,n3; death of, **36**: 309,n1, 319

Shively, Laura Jenks (Mrs. Benjamin Franklin), **36**: 309

shoe manufacture, **27**: 90,n1, 279; and Clayton bill, **30**: 400-401; **31**: 30n1

Shoecraft, Eugene Claire, **37**: 402,n1

Shoot the President! is Cry as friends of Peace Speaker calls Mr. Wilson Unneutral (New York *Herald*), **35**: 221n1

Shorb, Mr., **34**: 382n1

Shoreham Hotel, Wash., D.C., **27**: 152, 153, 154n1, 155,n1; **31**: 430n1; **38**: 36

Short, Jefferson D., **36**: 407,n1, 407-408

Short, William Harrison, **29**: 476

Shortest and Longest (Birdseye), **33**: 404,n1

Shreveport rate cases, **30**: 482,n7

Shubert Theater, N.Y., **28**: 400n1

Shuster, William Morgan, **28**: 175n1, 193

Siam, **28**: 95n1; **38**: 209,n1, 317

Siberia, Russia, **32**: 397; **33**: 88

Sibert, William Luther, **29**: 307,n3; **31**: 287

Sibley, Frederick William, **38**: 238,n5

Sibley, Rufus Adams, **29**: 401n1

Sibley, Lindsay and Curr, Rochester, N.Y., **29**: 401n1

Sidney, Elizabeth Maria Astell, Lady Sidney, **28**: 52

Sievers, Harry Joseph, **28**: 188n1

Sif, S.S., **31**: 477

Sigrun, S.S., **31**: 477

Silberrad, Una Lucy, **31**: 316,n2

Sill, Edward, **30**: 22

Sillac, Joseph Alban Maximilien Jarousse de, **38**: 668-69,n1

Silliman, John Reid, **30**: 166-67,n1, 171, 297-98, 321-22, 449-50, 489-90; **31**: 18-19, 65, 70n1, 178, 431; **32**: 248, 347, 348, 363-64, 370n1; **33**: 305, 306n1, 415, 419, 448; **34**: 41n1, 321, 384-85, 385, 386; **35**: 93; **36**: 308n1, 344; impressions of V. Carranza, **30**: 167-69

Silva, Dario W., **32**: 383, 384

Silva, Miguel, **30**: 414, 418; **31**: 69, 71; **32**: 355,n7

Silverman, Joseph, **37**: 422

Silverstone, Gedalia, **32**: 97,n14

Simkins, Francis Butler, **35**: 434n1

Simmons, Edward Campbell, **29**: 247,n2, 270, 278

Simmons, Furnifold McLendel, **27**: 511; **28**: 248, 267, 276; **30**: 159n1, 176, 389, 402; **31**: 458; **32**: 229; **33**: 472-89; **35**: 345, 459; **37**: 169n1, 366, 375, 397, 431n1; **38**: 146n2; and income tax, **28**: 247, 253-54, 254, 258; on seamen's bill, **30**: 554-55; and ship-purchase bill, **32**: 123; and Philippine bill, **32**: 291-92, 293

Simmons, George Welch, **29**: 247,n3

Simmons, Wallace Delafield, **29**: 247n3, 401n1; **30**: 27, 33, 53, 54

Simmons Hardware Co., St. Louis, **29**: 247n2,3, 401n1; **30**: 173n1

Simmons-Underwood tariff: *see* Underwood-Simmons tariff

Simon, John Allsebrook, **37**: 447,n1

Simon Lee (Wordsworth), **31**: 29

Simpich, Frederick, **29**: 293n2

Simplex Wire Co., Boston, **29**: 401n1

Simpson, Franklin Farrow, **37**: 473,n3; **38**: 47,n4, 64, 182n4

Sims, Thetus Willrette, **29**: 140,n2, 173, 174, 282, 298-300, 304; **30**: 188; **36**: 211; **38**: 103

Sims water-power bill, **29**: 140,n2, 282, 283, 381, 394; and Norris-Simmons amendment, **30**: 159,n1; passed by Senate, **30**: 174n1

Sinclair, Upton, **30**: 39n1

Sinclair Oil Co., **30**: 246n2

Siney, Marion Celestia, **36**: 387n2

single-term amendment, **27**: 97, 98-101, 103-104, 114; **31**: 281-82

Singleton, Esther, **31**: 316n2, 317

Sino-American relations: *see* China and the United States; Japan and the United States

Siple, J. W. **29**: 549

Six-Power Consortium and loan, **27**: 174-75, 192-94, 195, 203, 237; **32**: 502; **33**: 99, 349, 350; **37**: 19, 233

Skibo Castle, Sutherlandshire, **28**: 328, 329, 572; **29**: 351; **30**: 62

Skinner, Robert Peet, **30**: 369,n5; **31**: 144; **35**: 420,n1; **38**: 244n3

Slade, Augusta, **28**: 36,n3, 199, 269, 368; **34**: 14n1

Slade, Elizabeth, **28**: 120,n4, 199, 269, 328,n2, 368; **34**: 14n1

Slade, Emily, **28**: 36,n3, 199, 269, 368; **34**: 14n1

Slade, Fannie J., **28**: 120,n4, 199, 269, 328,n2, 368; **34**: 14n1

Slater, George Atwood, **36**: 636,n12

Slater bill, **36**: 636-37,n12, 646

Slater Fund, **31**: 464n1

Slavic Americans, **38**: 349

Slayden, James Luther, **28**: 491,n1, 505; **29**: 149; **36**: 363

Sliding Scale Gas Act, **36**: 25-26,n2

Slocum, Herbert Jermain, **36**: 281,n1, 282, 283

Slocum, Joel Byron, **36**: 139-40,n1, 140

Slow Fade to Black: The Negro in American Film, 1900-1942 (Cripps), **32**: 455n3; **33**: 68n1

Small, John Humphrey, **31**: 130,n2; **37**: 513-14, 524

Smalls, Robert, **27:** 283,n1, 284
Smiley, Daniel F., **29:** 476
Smith, Alfred Emanuel, **38:** 549n1, 597n2
Smith, Charles Cogswell, **30:** 307n1; **32:** 76, 80, 288, 295, 297
Smith, Charles Ernest, **34:** 464,n3, 475
Smith, Ellison DuRant, **27:** 284; **29:** 240, 310-11; **33:** 535-36; **34:** 512; **36:** 515n3; **37:** 429
Smith, Frederick Edwin, **37:** 77n1
Smith, Gaddis, **31:** 310n1, 425n1
Smith, Gibbs M., **34:** 539n2
Smith, Herbert Scott, **35:** 371n1
Smith, Hoke, **27:** 21; **28:** 97n1, 186n1, 344; **29:** 283; **30:** 4, 261; **31:** 127; **33:** 457,n1, 556; **34:** 62n1, 158, 180, 195,n1, 195-96, 208, 296, 393; **36:** 20,n1, 211, 357n1; **37:** 72, 73, 151, 173,n1,2; and L. D. Brandeis nomination, **36:** 606
Smith, James, Jr., **27:** 74, 456; **28:** 83, 96, 97, 373n2; **29:** 557,n1; **35:** 493
Smith, John T. Brabner, **36:** 331,n1,2,3
Smith, John Walter, **27:** 141,n3
Smith, Lucy Marshall, **28:** 102,n1, 106, 126, 134, 143, 166, 178, 181, 183, 189, 249, 252, 258, 260, 265, 266, 269, 278, 291, 302, 310, 318, 321, 327, 328, 335, 345, 360, 368, 531; **29:** 370n1, 376; **31:** 453-54; **33:** 241-42; **34:** 407, 473-74, 481, 522, 545; **35:** 12, 15, 27, 35, 36, 80, 211-12, 373-74, 399-400, 455
Smith, Madison Roswell, **27:** 553,n1; **28:** 4, 187,n3
Smith, Marcus Aurelius, **29:** 384,n1, 392-93, 408; **30:** 357; **32:** 326; **36:** 311
Smith, Mary Randolph, **28:** 102,n1, 106, 126, 134, 143, 166, 178, 181, 189, 249, 252, 258, 260, 265, 266, 269, 278, 291, 302, 310, 318, 327, 328, 331, 335, 345, 360, 368, 531; **29:** 370-71,n1, 376; **30:** 451; **31:** 59, 454; **34:** 407, 473, 522, 545; **35:** 12, 15, 27, 35, 36, 80, 211, 373-74, 399-400, 455-56
Smith, Mary Rozet, **34:** 252,n9
Smith, Orson, **31:** 76
Smith, Randolph Wellford, **36:** 364,n1
Smith, William Alden, **31:** 551; **32:** 286
Smith, William Robert, **36:** 296,n3
Smith, William Skeldon Adamson, **38:** 160,n5
Smith, William W., **30:** 363
Smith College Studies in History, **27:** 277n1
Smith-Hughes bill (vocational-education bill), **36:** 357,n1; passage of, **36:** 370,n1
Smith-Lever Act, **30:** 8,n1
Smithsonian Institution, **32:** 534n1
Smolinski, Joseph, **32:** 97,n8
Smoot, Reed, **28:** 162,n1, 163; **30:** 31, 110n1; **35:** 73; **36:** 328,n4
Smoot mining-commission bill, **30:** 31
Smulski, John Franklin, **37:** 404-406,n1, 407
Smuts, Jan Christiaan, **36:** 442
Smyrna, Turkey, **33:** 232

Smyth, Constantine Joseph, **38:** 668,n1
Smyth, Henry Lloyd, **28:** 375,n2
Snodgrass, John Harold, **34:** 306,n2
Snyder, Edgar Callender, **35:** 339,n1
Snyder, Valentine P., **29:** 401n1
Snyman, W. D., **33:** 258-59,n1
Social Christianity and the Negro in the Progressive Era (White), **31:** 464n1
Social Democratic party (Germany), **31:** 537,n1; **34:** 47n5
Sinaloa, state, Mex., **27:** 479; **28:** 30, 77; **30:** 445
social reform; A. J. McKelway and, **27:** 108-109; and 1916 platform, **37:** 151, 161, 169n1, 174-75, 188
social workers, **27:** 75-78, 108
Social Worker's Bureau, **27:** 476n1
Socialist party, **35:** 206n1, 487,n1,2,3; **38:** 28, 522n1, 642, 643; in Sixty-fifth Congress, **38:** 666n1
socialists, **29:** 339
society, **27:** 389
Society of Cincinnati, **36:** 489
Solace, U.S.S. (hospital ship), **29:** 398; **34:** 61
Soldiers' Memorial Hall, Pittsburgh, **36:** 26n1, 35n1, 40
Solf, Wilhelm, **32:** 505,n2; **36:** 122, 123, 414
Solution of the Trust Problem (Brandeis), **29:** 7n2
Some Memories of a Paleontologist (Scott), **36:** 478n1
Some Memories of a Soldier (H. L. Scott), **29:** 36n1
Some Roads Towards Peace: A Report to the Trustees of the Endowment on Observations Made in China and Japan in 1912 (Eliot), **30:** 354,n1
Somerville, Henderson Middleton, **34:** 513,n1
Sommerfeld, Felix A., **30:** 220-21,n1, 347
Somellera, Gabriel Fernandez, **32:** 392,n1
Sonora, state, Mex., **27:** 422,n1, 423, 479; **28:** 6n1, 7, 30, 31, 72, 73, 76, 77, 246, 278n3, 341; **30:** 412, 417, 443, 445; **34:** 531; **36:** 502, 586-87; **37:** 250, 256, 285; **38:** 223
Sosna, Morton, **27:** 291n1; **28:** 115n3
Souchez, Battle of, **34:** 310
South Africa: *see* Union of South Africa
South America, **27:** ix, 169, 172, 335,n1; **28:** 377, 449, 577, 587, 588, 593; **29:** 230, 231, 236, 325, 351, 378, 419; **30:** 209, 235, 287; **31:** 177, 355, 416, 501; **32:** 91n3, 123, 174, 276, 343; **35:** 254, 294-95, 358-59; **37:** 509; **38:** 269; and Monroe Doctrine, **29:** 53; and Panama Canal, **29:** 524; W. C. Redfield on shipping bill and, **31:** 124; and U.S. trade, **31:** 150, 151, 360,n1; and England, **31:** 238; W. G. McAdoo and Pan American Financial Conference, **31:** 244, 258; diplomats to fête WW and EBW, **35:** 372-73, 396; W. J. Stone on commerce

South America (*cont.*)
  between U.S. and, **36**: 367-68; *see also*
    under names of individual countries
South Canon Coal Co., Colo., **29**: 549
South Carolina, **27**: 283,n1, 284, 335; **33**:
  495-96; **37**: 514; W. G. McAdoo in, **29**:
  87; state warehouse system, **34**: 99
South Carolina Cotton Congress, **33**: 496
South Dakota, **38**: 376n1, 515n1
South End House, Boston, **29**: 352
South in the Saddle: Racial Politics Dur-
  ing the Wilson Years (Sosna), **27**:
  291n1; **28**: 115n3
South Manchurian Railway, **32**: 321
Southern Commercial Congress, **28**:
  434,n1, 448,n1,2,3; **29**: 141n1
southern cotton congress, **31**: 127; **33**: 495
Southern Democratic League, **27**: 66
Southern Horizons: An Autobiography
  (Dixon), **32**: 142n1, 267n1
Southern Pacific Co., **27**: 404n1, 479,
  487,n1; **28**: 255n1, 387n1; **29**: 67-68,n2,
  131, 193; **30**: 482
Southern Railway, **37**: 439n1
Southern Ruralist, **38**: 511n1
Southern Sociological Congress, **31**:
  464n1
Southwestern Fuel Co., Colo., **29**: 549
Southwestern Presbyterian University,
  37: 231n1
Sowerby, Githa, **27**: 71n3
Spach, Charles, **37**: 278
Spain, **27**: 534; **30**: 152, 153, 234, 493;
  31: 7, 122, 159; **32**: 65, 263, 278, 359,
  423, 504; **33**: 47, 123,n6, 200, 231; **34**:
  86, 398; **35**: 21, 227; **37**: 8-9, 19-20; **38**:
  82, 116; appointments, **27**: 110; **28**: 4;
  expenses of ambassador in London, **29**:
  411; and Great Britain, **29**: 180; and
  Mexico, **27**: 439, 540, 542; **28**: 70, 460,
  526; **29**: 196, 241-42, 416-17, 442; **30**:
  25; **31**: 352; **33**: 194n1, 468; and Philippines, **28**: 415; and seamen's bill, **28**:
  412-13; and ratification of "cooling off"
  treaty with, **31**: 64; as possible peace
  mediator, **35**: 129-30, 144, 176
Spanish ambassador to London: *see* Valy
  Zulueta, Alfonso Merry del
Spanish-American War, **35**: 483; **36**: 14,
  104-105, 161; **38**: 346
Spanish Americans, **38**: 140
Spanish Armada, **31**: 56
Spanish language, **30**: 122; in Philip-
  pines, **28**: 242n1
Sparkman, Stephen Milancthon, **31**: 374-
  75,n2
Spartansburg, Pa., **36**: 337
Spaulding, Charles Edward, **29**: 474,n1
special privileges, **27**: 565, 566; S. Rea
  on, **27**: 323
Special Privileges for Labor (New York
  Evening Post, **27**: 323n3
Spee, Count Maximilian Johannes Maria
  Hubert von, **36**: 235n6

Spencer, Anna Carpenter Garlin (Mrs.
  William Henry), **35**: 134-35,n1, 158; **37**:
  308, 316
Spencer, Charles Worthen, **38**: 39
Spencer, Herbert, **28**: 309; **38**: 256
Spencer, Maurice W., **31**: 308, 309n1
Spender, John Alfred, **29**: 301,n3; **32**:
  226,n2
Spender, Mary Rawlinson (Mrs. John
  Alfred), **29**: 301,n4
Speyer, Ellin Prince Lowery (Mrs. James
  Joseph), **29**: 218n1
Speyer, James Joseph, **27**: 404,n2; **29**:
  130, 218,n1
Speyer and Co., **29**: 130; and Mexican
  Bank of Commerce, **27**: 544
Spillsbury, Lemuel, **38**: 383
Spindler, Arno, **36**: 483n1
Spingarn, Joel Elias, **29**: 105
Spoelberch, E. de, **32**: 257-58, 408
Spoelberch, Pussy de, **32**: 257-58, 408
Spokane Daily Chronicle, **38**: 117n1
Spooner and Cotton, N.Y., **28**: 392n3
Sprague, Oliver Mitchell Wentworth, **27**:
  206-207
Spreckels, Claus, **27**: 62n2
Spreckels, Rudolph, **27**: 62,n2, 188, 228,
  259; **36**: 634,n3; **38**: 61-62, 118
Spring Lake, N.J., **38**: 118n3
Spring Rice, Cecil Arthur, **27**: 395,n1,
  405-406, 477, 482, 514, 534-35; **28**: 34,
  447, 467-69, 477,n2, 530, 561-62, 565,
  572, 594, 601; **29**: 13-14, 34-35, 162,
  180n1, 203-204, 217-18, 244, 259, 267-
  68, 344; **30**: 247, 258; **31**: 64, 87, 109,
  112, 114, 228-29, 292, 346, 502, 514;
  32: 6, 87, 107-10,n1, 112-13, 449n1; **33**:
  122, 185, 279n1, 333-34, 372, 414, 497,
  515, 519, 519-20; **34**: 98, 137, 147, 200,
  295-96, 338n2; **35**: 62, 78, 81, 82, 85,
  100, 255, 414, 454, 504; **36**: 133, 193-
  94, 269, 427-28, 569, 580, 607; **37**: 94n1,
  103,n1, 106n1, 411, 422, 440, 480,
  517n1; **38**: 201, 319,n1, 359-60
and gift of illuminated address to WW
  from people of Carlisle, **29**: 12, 24, 59-
  60, 61, 75; on Mexican situation, **29**:
  168-69, 228, 228-33, 248-50, 266-67,
  347-48; **30**: 29, 33, 58-59, 77-78, 78-82,
  133-34; **32**: 342, 352; **33**: 398n1; and
  L. Carden, **29**: 209-10, 226, 314n1, 324-
  25, 366; **31**: 145; on J. B. Moore, **29**:
  216n2; on Benton affair, **29**: 285n1; on
  W. J. Bryan's "cooling off" treaties, **29**:
  340-42; leaves for London, **30**: 98; on
  Panama Canal tolls, **30**: 141; and
  E. M. House, **30**: 255, 256, 271; **31**: 550;
  32: 41, 64, 67, 99, 120, 161, 254; **34**:
  62, 79, 106, 109; **35**: 380; **36**: 267-68;
  on WW and the war, **30**: 472, 473; on
  American sentiments toward belligerents, **31**: 13-14; and peace moves, **31**:
  21n1, 45, 58-59, 60, 62, 76, 137, 140-
  41, 500-501, 517-19, 522-23, 548; **37**:

73; and negotiations over Declaration of London, **31:** 91-92, 93, 96, 96-97, 97-98, 98, 100, 103-105, 115, 116, 117-18, 125-26, 133-35, 138, 146, 154-55, 158, 166-67, 190, 191,n1, 198, 229, 229-30, 235, 243; on relations between U.S. and Great Britain, **31:** 168; and Japan's demands on China, **31:** 171n4; on seizure and detention of U.S. ships, **31:** 194-95, 209-10, 214, 489, 499, 553,n1; and Bryan on Japanese problem in California, **31:** 275n5
and German propaganda campaign, **31:** 298, 315-16, 550; and R. Lansing, **31:** 348-49, 473,n1; **35:** 495-98,n1; and J. W. Gerard, **31:** 405; on prize court hearings, **31:** 505, 505-506, 506; birthday wishes to WW, **31:** 541-42; excited by leak of U.S. protest, **31:** 549; and *Dacia* affair, **32:** 89n3; on F. Gildemeester visit to U.S., **33:** 347-48, 362-63; on air attacks on London, **33:** 400; and cotton crisis, **34:** 13, 30, 32, 35, 126, 180, 186,n2; on blockade, **34:** 188-89; congratulates WW on his engagement, **35:** 32, 89, 95; on Germans, **35:** 62-63; Graves disease and, **35:** 64,n1; and China, **35:** 115-16, 117; on public opinion in the U.S., **35:** 144, 144-45; varied comments on recall of, **35:** 259, 260, 310n1, 357, 358, 387, 473; and S. Brooks' visit to U.S., **35:** 320-21, 346; on armed-merchantmen controversy, **36:** 169-70, 192-93,n1,3; on mail delay, **37:** 112; loses brother in war, **37:** 177,n1, 205; on blacklist, **37:** 471, 475, 495-96; on retaliatory provision of Revenue Act of 1916, **38:** 179; condolences to WW, **38:** 181, 192; photograph: *illustration section,* 31

Spring Rice, Florence Lascelles, Lady Spring Rice, **28:** 530; **29:** 75; **31:** 137; **35:** 95; **37:** 205

Spring Rice, Gerald, **37:** 177,n1, 205; **38:** 181n1

Spring Rice, Mary Isabella (Mrs. Gerald), **37:** 205,n1

Spring Rice, Thomas Aubrey, **31:** 517,n1

Springfield, Mass., **28:** 181

Springfield, Vt., **34:** 63, 101, 102, 125

Springfield, Mass., *Republican,* **30:** 84,n1, 277; **31:** 341, 369,n1, 379, 384; **33:** 142,n1, 505,n1; **34:** 445,n2; **36:** 238n1; **37:** 3,n1, 11, 35; **38:** 201n1, 389

Sprunt, James, **36:** 186

Sprunt, Luola Murchison, **36:** 186,n1; **37:** 541,n3

Spry, William, **34:** 539,n1,2; and Hillstrom case, **35:** 3, 58, 69, 207, 210, 211, 213-15

Squam Lake, N.H., **28:** 132

Squier, George Owen, **31:** 282; **36:** 628,n1; **37:** 28n2, 97-99

Squires, Grant, **33:** 382,n1; **34:** 412

Squires, Sarah Eaton Jenkins (Mrs. Grant), **33:** 382,n1

Staatskunst und Kriegshandwerk (Ritter), **33:** 279n1

Stabler, Jordan, **37:** 29,n5

Stabler, Jordan Herbert, **37:** 29,n4

Stackhouse, Thomas Bascom, **33:** 495,n3

Stackhouse, Wade, **33:** 496

Stadelman, Henryette L., **28:** 183,n7

Stalghern, S.S., **31:** 477

Stamford, Conn., **33:** 48n6

Stamfordham, Baron: *see* Bigge, Arthur John, 1st Baron Stamfordham

stamp tax, **31:** 32

Stand by the President (Stockbridge), **35:** 147,n4

Standard Oil Co., **27:** 496; **28:** 388, 442, 445; **29:** 68, 93, 95; **31:** 46; **33:** 520; **36:** 401; **37:** 142, 460; and seizure of *Brindilla,* **31:** 176, 193, 234; and China, **31:** 287

Standard Oil Co. of New Jersey, **30:** 246n2,3

Standards, Bureau of, **32:** 181; **36:** 155; **38:** 421

Stanford University, **27:** 206, 309; **31:** 331-332; **38:** 72n8

Stanhope, Aubrey, **36:** 564,n6

Stanley, Augustus Owsley, **27:** 93; **29:** 25-30, 343,n3; **35:** 88n1

Stanley, Edward George Villiers, Earl of Derby: *see* Derby, Edward George Villiers Stanley, 17th Earl of

Stanton, Edwin McMasters, **27:** 126; **31:** 396

Stanton, Elizabeth Cady, **37:** 326n2

Stanton Avenue Methodist Church, Boston, **29:** 474n1

Staples, Henry Lee, **36:** 26n3

Starek, Charles, **29:** 263, 277

State, Department of, **30:** 251; **32:** 4; **33:** 377; **34:** 24, 231; **35:** 91, 227-30, 236-37,n2; J. B. Moore resigns as Counselor of, **29:** 215-16,n2; appointment of R. Lansing to, **29:** 331n1; and neutrality board, **30:** 435,n1; and leaks in, **31:** 29-30,n1, 549-50, 550, 552-53; **33:** 257; **34:** 36, 189,n1; **36:** 168; and Pan American Financial Conference, **31:** 258; and neutrality, **31:** 270, 276,n1; H. Münsterberg on relations of Great Britain with, **31:** 336, 338; and China and Morgan loan, **31:** 381; and Dominican Republic, **33:** 218,n1; and possible J. W. Davis appointment, **33:** 491,n1; appointment of Counselor of, **34:** 41-42; and Haiti, **34:** 173; Lansing on censorship in, **36:** 254-55, 257

State, The (Wilson), **32:** 534

State of California, S.S., **28:** 204n1

state rights, **28:** 283, 305, 314-15; **29:** 199, 200; and California alien land controversy, **27:** 319-20, 349, 449, 459; P. U. Kellogg on, **27:** 243; and corporations,

state rights (*cont.*)
29: 30; and Colorado coal strike, 29: 528-29, 529, 533
Statement Issued by the American Truth Society in defense of its President against an unjust attack made upon him by the President of the United States, 38: 286n1
Statue of Liberty, 36: 48; 37: 415
Statutes at Large, 36: 546n2; 37: 377n1
Staunton, Va., 37: 21n1
Steamboat Inspection Service, Dept. of Commerce, 34: 27,n1, 71, 81n1
Stearns, N.Y., 35: 160
Steckman, Frederick W., 37: 379,n1
Stedman, Charles Manly, 36: 503-504,n1
Steed, Henry Wickham, 33: 130,n1
steel industry, 31: 52; 35: 147,n3; and railroads, 30: 128-29
Steel Trust suit: *see* United States *v.* United States Steel Corporation
Steele, Miss (of Windsor, Vt.), 28: 103
Steffens, Lincoln, 27: 93,n3, 456, 476, 477, 481; 30: 65-66, 73; 34: 146, 147-48; 35: 134; 37: 209, 308n2, 497
Stein, Ludwig, 37: 86,n5
Steinbrinck, Lieutenant, 36: 488
Stephano, S.S., 38: 658,n1
Stephens, Dan Voorhees, 28: 346-47,n1, 352
Stephens, James, 34: 287,n1
Stephens, John Hall, 36: 407, 407-408
Sterling, Thomas, 36: 311,n2
Sterling Hotel, Trenton, N.J., 27: 40n1; 32: 272
Stern, Daniel, 30: 144,n2
Stetson, Francis Lynde, 27: 259,n1; 29: 29
Steubenville, Ohio, 38: 524
Stevens, Daisy McLaurin (Mrs. William Forrest), 30: 141,n3
Stevens, Frederick Clement, 30: 224n1, 245,n4; 38: 335,n2
Stevens, Raymond Bartlett, 29: 481,n2, 496; 30: 110, 134, 166n2, 170; 37: 117
Stevens bill: *see* Federal Trade Commission Act
Stevens Institute of Technology, 27: 95
Stevenson, Daniel Macaulay, 28: 261,n2, 264
Stevenson, Joseph Ross, 38: 209,n1
Stewart, Ethelbert, 28: 426-27,n2, 475, 507-14, 518-19, 540, 547, 548, 551-53, 554-55, 580, 580-84, 590,; 30: 18
Stewart, Joseph H., 27: 176-77,n1, 214
Stewart, William Morris, 27: 183
Stimson, Frederic Jesup, 31: 152,n5; 36: 197,n1
Stimson, Henry Albert, 33: 160,n1, 197
Stimson, Henry Lewis, 27: 119, 120, 126
Stinton Hotel, Cincinnati, 38: 524n1, 526,n1
Stitt, Thomas L., 38: 456
Stock: *see* Axson, Stockton (Isaac Stockton Keith II)

Stock, Leo Francis, 33: 46n2
stock exchanges, 27: 432, 486, 496, 497; 30: 312,n1, 421, 484; 31: 151; closing of, 31: 239
stock watering: J. E. Davies on, 29: 78, 79, 81-82; J. T. Robinson on, 29: 457-58, 486; F. G. Newlands on, 29: 535n1
Stockbridge, Frank Parker, 35: 146-47,n1,3
Stockbridge, Horace Edward, 38: 511,n1
Stockholm, Sweden, 34: 251n5; 37: 515
stocks, 29: 29, 82, 139, 157-58, 337, 479, 486-88; publicity of, 29: 177; and Owen bill, 29: 375,n1
Stoedten, Hellmuth E. F. Lucius von, 38: 69,n5, 70
Stokes, Edward Caspar, 28: 490n2
Stone, Claudius Ulysses, 28: 90,n1
Stone, Fred Andrew, 35: 258n1
Stone, John T., 36: 391n1
Stone, Melville, 27: 119, 130; 36: 656
Stone, Sarah Louise Winston (Mrs. William J.), 31: 487,n1
Stone, Warren Sanford, 38: 30, 31n1, 47-48, 93, 94
Stone, William Joel, 28: 374; 29: 48-49, 63, 66, 161, 305; 30: 378; 31: 64, 176,n1, 351, 448n1, 487-88, 551; 32: 59, 64, 139, 288; 34: 55, 278, 422; 35: 183, 185, 358,n1, 374, 388, 411, 423,n1, 424, 432, 501, 502, 505; 36: 289, 328, 355n1, 387, 462, 511; 37: 46, 169n1, 173, 268-69,n1, 366, 382, 397,n1, 408, 418, 452, 539; 38: 85, 277-79, 318-19, 559, 650
and Nicaragua, 31: 114, 115,n1; 32: 286-87; on safety-at-sea legislation, 31: 457-58,n1, 461; and exchange with W. J. Bryan, 32: 26,n1, 218n2, 281; and ship-purchase bill, 32:134,n1, 173n2; and Columbia, 32: 286-87; 36: 234,n1; and proposed railroad strike, 36: 204,n1; on armed-merchantmen controversy, 36: 209-11, 213-14, 225-26, 226-27, 233, 237, 240n1, 258-59,n1; and McLemore resolution, 36: 211; denies Gore's claim that WW wants war, 36: 238n1; on death of B. F. Shively, 36: 319; and Shields bill, 36: 355,n1, 360; on commercial future of U.S. after war, 36: 366-68, 374-75; on warships and merchant ships, 36: 434-35,n1; and WW and relations with Germany, 36: 460; preparedness speech of, 36: 500,n1; meets with WW on German crisis, 36: 517, 520,n1; on L. D. Brandeis nomination, 37: 56, 58; on G. M. Hitchcock's arms embargo bill, 37: 289-91
Stop It (New York *World*), 29: 100,n2
Storey, Joseph E., 31: 361n2
Storey, Moorfield, 28: 163-65, 203, 290n3, 344, 350, 498n1; 29: 105, 508; 38: 19,n1
Storey, Thomas Andrew, 27: 244
Stormy Petrel: N. G. Gonzales and His State (Jones), 27: 14n2
Stornaway, Scotland, 31: 245

Story, Daisy Allen (Mrs. William Cumming), **33:** 14n1; **35:** 47,n1; **36:** 489n1; **37:** 482,n1

Story, Joseph, **36:** 225, 226n1

Story of Mrs. Peck: An Autobiography (Hulbert), **31:** 257n1; **35:** 503n1; **38:** 589n1

Story of Two Noble Lives, Being Memorials of Charlotte, Countess Canning, and Louisa, Marchionesse of Waterford (Hare), **28:** 93,n5

Stovall, Pleasant Alexander, **32:** 402, 439, 442, 456, 480; **35:** 405; **36:** 403-404; **37:** 8-9, 278-80, 455

Strachey, John St. Loe, **28:** 576; **32:** 226,n3; **33:** 549; **35:** 454

Straight, Willard Dickerman, **29:** 381,n1, 384; **31:** 220,n1; **32:** 329,n2; **35:** 536

Strasbourg *Journal d'Alsace*, **38:** 559n1

Straus, Oscar Solomon, **28:** 316; **31:** 10, 14, 21n1, 55,n3, 140; **33:** 100, 333; on meeting with V. Huerta, **32:** 89-90, 106

Strayer, Louis William, **36:** 218,n1

Stretton, Julia Cecilia Collinson, **31:** 316,n2

strikes: *see* Colorado coal strike; railroad crisis of 1916; railroads

Strinda, S.S., **31:** 477

Strong, Benjamin, **28:** 428, 430; **34:** 6,n2, 36, 106,n3, 107, 121, 137, 200; **36:** 386, 436-42

Strong, Richard, **35:** 316n1

Stronge, Francis William, **27:** 540; **28:** 167,n1, 196, 205-206, 208-209, 219, 220, 225, 444

Stroudsburg, Pa., **27:** 116

Struggle for Neutrality (Link): *see Wilson: The Struggle for Neutrality*

Strunsky, Simeon, **37:** 60,n1

Stuart, Warren Horton, **33:** 51,n2

Stürmer, Borís Vladímirovich, **38:** 67,n1, 68

Suárez, José María Piño, **27:** 119n1, 546-50

Suárez, Marco Fidel, **29:** 128,n2; .**36:** 236,n8

Suárez-Mujicá, Eduardo, **29:** 505-506,n1, 506-507, 539-40; **30:** 45, 47, 48, 242; **32:** 64, 98, 98-99, 338, 474, 478, 542; **34:** 111, 112, 113-14, 157n1,2, 321, 444, 448, 540-41; **35:** 439, 441; and Pan-American Pact, **31:** 470, 498, 549, 551; **33:** 52-54, 55-60, 62, 62-63, 68, 77-80; **35:** 54-55, 111, 126, 162-63, 188, 215-16, 411, 520; **36:** 198, 199, 201n12, 229-30, 278; and Mexico, **33:** 437, 455, 487, 488

Subercaseaux Vicuña, Ramón, **36:** 198,n2

submarines: and American construction for belligerents, **31:** 359; WW against sending parts from U.S., **31:** 369, 425; German use of, **32:** 145, 217, 250, 264-65, 307, 412; **33:** 62, 66, 71-72, 72-73, 76, 108, 127,n1, 135n4; W. Kent on, **36:** 208, 215; R. Lansing on, **36:** 252-57; Bernstorff on, **36:** 271; resolutions in Reichstag, **36:** 341,n1

Successful Immigrants in the South (*World's Work*), **32:** 56,n2

Suez Canal, **35:** 226

suffrage: *see* woman suffrage

Suffragist, The, **30:** 226n4; **35:** 292n2; **36:** 3n1; **37:** 167n4

sugar: and duty on, **35:** 31, 303, 304, 370n1

sugar schedule: *see* Underwood-Simmons Tariff Act

Suggestions for Democratic Platform (McKelway), **37:** 65,n1

Sullivan, James Mark, **29:** 20,n2, 21; **30:** 165,n1, 307n1, 363; **31:** 404n2, 414,n4; **32:** 77, 296, 353-54,n1, 466, 469; **33:** 26-27, 218-20,n1, 451

Sullivan, Jerry Bartholomew, **38:** 174-75, 190

Sullivan, Mark, **27:** 418n1, 507,n1, 514; **32:** 25; **35:** 178

Sullivan, Roger Charles, **27:** 22n2, 334; **29:** 261,n1,2; **31:** 232,n2, 318; **37:** 522,n1; **38:** 376

Sullivan, Walter Bernard, **33:** 496,n6

Sullivan, Senator? No! (*The Commoner*), **29:** 261n1

Sulu Islands, **28:** 242n1

Sulzer, Clara Rodelheim (Mrs. William), **28:** 149n2

Sulzer, William, **28:** 35-36, 37, 64, 94, 159, 181, 333, 490n2; impeachment of, **28:** 149,n1,2

Summering with the President (New York *World*), **28:** 181,n2

Summerlin, George Thomas, **32:** 474,n5

Sumners, Hatton William, **34:** 53-54,n1, 58

Sun Pao-ch'i, **32:** 137,n4

Sun Yat-sen, **27:** 144n1, 237-38; **31:** 372-73, 381-82; **33:** 36

Sunapee Lake, N.H., **28:** 368, 383

Sunbury, Pa., **33:** 472

Sunday, Billy, **33:** 523,n1

Sunderland, James A., **38:** 336n1

Sundry Civil Appropriations Act of 1911: S. Gompers on, **27:** 180

Sundry Civil Appropriations Act of 1913, **27:** 303,n2, 346, 412, 511; S. Rea, **27:** 322-23; S. Gompers, **27:** 369; R. U. Johnson, **27:** 411; H. B. Thompson, **27:** 475; E. H. Goodwin, **27:** 530; WW signs, **27:** 558

sundry civil appropriation bill, **30:** 126, 171, 183, 294; **36:** 250; Chamber of Commerce's views on, **30:** 205, 206, 283-84

Sunnyside Coal Mining Co., Colo., **29:** 549

"sunrise conference," **36:** 238n1, 288-90

Sunshine Girl (play), **27:** 119,n2

Supplementary Report upon the Philippines (Ford), **29:** 137,n1

Supreme Court (U.S.); *see* United States Supreme Court

Surface, Frank Macy, **31:** 206n1
Survey, The, **28:** 20n6; **33:** 469n3; **34:** 27n1, 251n6; **36:** 632n1
Susan, Susie (EBG's maid), **34:** 156, 314, 322, 323; **35:** 276, 372
Sussex note, **37:** 8, 98,n1, 135n2; crisis: see Germany and the United States
Sutherland, George, **28:** 162,n1, 163; **31:** 457
Swain, Joseph, **28:** 439,n2
Swann, Sherlock, **27:** 192n1
Swanson, Claude Augustus, **29:** 355; **35:** 37, 57; **36:** 328, 355n1; **37:** 267,n1, 481
Swanson, Elizabeth Dean Lyons (Mrs. Claude Augustus), **35:** 37, 57
Swarthmore College, **35:** 20n1; WW talk at, **28:** 439-43,n2
Swarthmore, Pa., Phoenix, **28:** 442n
Sweden, **27:** 477,n2; **30:** 151n; **31:** 144, 201, 203, 478, 480, 526, 527; **32:** 131; **33:** 81n1, 144, 215, 371; **34:** 86, 188-89, 251,n4,5, 253n1, 398; **35:** 196, 198, 199; **37:** 75n2; **38:** 113, 116; J. Lind, **27:** 508, 513-14, 531-32; appointments to, **28:** 4, 111, 112
Swedish Americans, **31:** 277; and Hillstrom case, **35:** 283n1,2
Swedish minister to the United States: see Ekengren, Wilhelm August Ferdinand
Sweet, Edwin Forrest, **33:** 497,n5, 506-507; **34:** 27, 45,n1, 48, 65
Sweet, Richard C., **35:** 528,n1; **37:** 495
Swem, Charles Lee, **27:** viii, ix, x, xiii, xv-xvi, xviii, 28, 165, 364n1, 428n1; **28:** 452n4; **29:** 3n1, 61n1, 361n1, 432, 474n5, 507n2, 558; **30:** 43n2, 50n1, 138n1, 255n2; **31:** 141, 174n1, 319, 414n1; **32:** 207n1, 457n1; **33:** 68n1, 138-39,n1, 349n1; **34:** 24, 127; **35:** 372; **36:** 7n, 41n, 52, 136n1, 344n1, 643n17; **38:** 101n2; photograph: illustration section, 38
Swiatopolk-Czetwertynska, Princess Marie: see Tarnowski von Tarnow, Countess
Swift, Eben, **38:** 238,n6
Swinderen, Jonkheer Reneke de Marees van: see Marees van Swinderen, Jonkheer Reneke de
Swing, Raymond (afterward Raymond Gram), **34:** 370,n2
Switzerland, **27:** 228; **31:** 40n1; **32:** 402, 423, 439, 442, 456, 480; **33:** 231, 361, 524; **34:** 20, 398; **35:** 227, 354, 405; **36:** 418; **37:** 9, 75n2, 89; **38:** 116, 669; and recognition of Mexico, **28:** 460; and U.S. loans, **30:** 386
Swope, Herbert Bayard, **37:** 352,n1, 369; **38:** 126
Sykes, Gerrit Smith, **38:** 537,n1
Syracuse, N.Y., **38:** 545-46
Syracuse University, **29:** 436n1,2
System: The Magazine of Business, **32:** 68n1, 70, 125

Szabadság, see Cleveland Szabadság
Sze, Sao-ke Alfred, **33:** 132,n2; **34:** 19,n4; **36:** 411,n2

T. Tembarom (Burnett), **31:** 316n2, 317
Tabasco, state, Mex., **28:** 77
Tabor, S.S., **31:** 477
Tacna-Arica, **32:** 474,n3; **35:** 520; **36:** 199, 200
Tacoma, Wash.: W. J. Bryan's speeches in, **34:** 133, 135, 146n1,2
Tacoma, U.S.S., **32:** 342
Tacubaya, Mex., **28:** 196,n5
Taft, Helen Herron (Mrs. William Howard), **27:** 5,n1, 12, 20, 28, 138; **33:** 431n3
Taft, William Howard, **27:** 5, 69, 108, 109, 126, 138, 152, 160, 195n1, 283, 369, 434; **28:** 19, 45n2, 317; **29:** 137, 164, 180, 181, 266, 302n1, 303n1, 555, 561-62; **30:** 141, 175, 232; **31:** 184,n2, 214; **32:** 15,n4, 188n1, 198, 231, 346, 457; **33:** 150-52, 184,n1, 431n3; **34:** 390, 513; **35:** 120, 316n1, 385; **36:** 49, 249, 458-59, 464n1, 481, 578-79; **37:** 6, 11, 32, 69, 75, 121, 140, 314, 339; **38:** 63, 73, 140, 243n2, 276, 290
on White House housekeeping staff, **27:** 12, 16-19, 28-29; and China, **27:** 27n1, 175, 237; and cost of inaugural, **27:** 59; and industrial commission, **27:** 77n7; National Child Labor Committee, **27:** 107; and WW's inauguration, **27:** 155; military aide, **27:** 172n2; Sundry Civil Appropriation Act of 1911, **27:** 180; Supreme Court received by, **27:** 200; Dominican Republic, **27:** 272n1; and labor, **27:** 368; and Mexico, **28:** 32, 50, 68n1; and Albano case, **28:** 115n2; and Ecuador, **28:** 125; and Colombia, **28:** 198; and Negro vote, **28:** 222; and segregation, **28:** 349n2; **31:** 361n2; and Panama Canal opening, **31:** 363; suggested for Supreme Court, **35:** 460, 462n1; **37:** 210, 230; on Sussex note, **36:** 545,n1; suggested for Joint High Commission, **38:** 22, 29; and Federal Reserve Act, **38:** 497n1, 498; and League to Enforce Peace, **38:** 622, 644, 660; and National Archives, **38:** 655; photographs: illustration section, 27
Taggart, Thomas, **27:** 22n2; **37:** 46; **38:** 457
Tagore, Sir Rabindranath, **36:** 415n1
Taiping Rebellion, **33:** 36
Taiwan, **32:** 420
Takahira, Baron Kogoro, **30:** 396n1; see also Root-Takahira Agreement
Talcott, Charles Andrew, **35:** 262n3, 275
Talk with the President of the United States (Tarbell), **38:** 323-34,n
Tallman, Clay, **37:** 139n1, 140
Tamariz, Eduardo, **28:** 292,n1, 293; **29:** 328
Tamaulipas, state, Mex., **28:** 77, 446; **29:** 428; **36:** 571; **37:** 250, 255, 285

Tammany Hall, **27**: 224, 333, 384,n1, 401, 407; **28**: 402,n2, 490n2; **29**: 35, 136, 240n1, 395,n1, 396, 402-404,n1; **31**: 349n1; **36**: 380-81, 458,n1, 542; **37**: 290; **38**: 301n1, 317, 494, 515, 549n1, 562n1, 671; and Sulzer impeachment, **28**: 149n1

Tampa, Fla., **28**: 115n2

Tampico, Tamaulipas, Mex., **27**: 519; **28**: 31, 567; **29**: 16, 86, 125, 126, 338, 359, 383; **30**: 59, 83, 297; **32**: 384, 387

Tampico affair: *see* Mexico and the United States

Tangier, Morocco, **33**: 123n6

Tappé, Herman Patrick, **35**: 272,n5

Tarbell, Ida Minerva, **38**: 170,n1, 172-73, 280, 322, 322-23; interview with WW, **38**: 323-34

tariff: WW on, **36**: 155-56; **38**: 129, 288, 293, 304, 501, 555-56, 570, 573-75, 610; and dyestuffs, **36**: 406; *see also* Payne-Aldrich Tariff Act, Underwood-Simmons Tariff Act

Tariff Board of 1909-1912, **35**: 383n1, 384n2, 385

Tariff Commission: *see* United States Tariff Commission

Tariff Commission (Houston), **35**: 512n2

Tariff Commission (Taussig), **35**: 383,n1

Tariff in the Senate (New York *Nation*), **27**: 453n1

tariff reform, **28**: 315n2; *see also* Underwood-Simmons Tariff Act

Tarnowski von Tarnow, Count Adam, **38**: 545,n1, 560

Tarnowski von Tarnow, Countess (Princess Marie Swiatopolk-Czetwertynska), **38**: 545,n2

Tarr, Salome, **27**: 165

Tauscher, Hans, **37**: 425,n1

Taussig, Florence Gottschalk (Mrs. Frederick J.), **37**: 308, 316

Taussig, Frank William, **35**: 383-86,n1; **36**: 156n3; **38**: 335

Taussig, Samuel, **32**: 97,n1

tax reform: New Jersey, **27**: 48; *see also* income tax

taxation, **31**: 170; **35**: 305-306; need for additional, **30**: 473-75; W. Saulsbury on, **31**: 32

Taxation and Democracy in America (Ratner), **27**: 301n1; **38**: 51n1

Taylor, Alonzo Engelbert, **38**: 73,n10

Taylor, David Watson, **32**: 21,n2

Taylor, Edward Thomas, **29**: 511,n1; **31**: 517,n1; **37**: 142

Taylor, Fred Manville, **27**: 206-207

Taylor, George Canada, **30**: 135,n1

Taylor, Graham Romeyn, **27**: 244; **34**: 27n1

Taylor, Hannis, **28**: 197, 534, 536; **29**: 39-40

Taylor, Sir Henry, **31**: 83

Taylor, Howard, **35**: 71n3, 74,n1

Taylor, James Henry, **27**: 351,n1, 357; **28**: 261,n1, 309; **29**: 44; **33**: 49; **35**: 371n1

Taylor, Knox, **31**: 412,n1, 429-30

Taylor, Laurette, **27**: 63,n4

Taylor, Lucy Janney Miller (Mrs. Knox), **31**: 412,n3

Taylor, Robert Love, **27**: 55n3

Taylor Wharton Iron and Steel Co., High Bridge, N.J., **31**: 412n1

Tea Tray, Cornish, N.H., **33**: 543,n4

Teal, Joseph Nathan, **27**: 21, 70; **38**: 158,n3, 159, 335

Tedcastle, Agnes Vaughn (Mrs. Arthur W.), **27**: 8; **28**: 266; **31**: 554; **32**: 51

Tedcastle, Arthur W., **27**: 7-8, 60-61, 90; **28**: 266; **31**: 30, 516, 554; **32**: 51, 371

Tehuantepec Railroad, **29**: 144, 193

Teitelbaum, Aaron, **32**: 97,n13

Tejeda, Adalberto, **37**: 350,n1

Tejar, Veracruz, Mex., **29**: 541,n1

telegraph lines, **27**: 260

telephone: long distance system inaugurated, **36**: 152n2

Tellez, Joaquin, **28**: 29

Tellus, S.S., **31**: 479

Temple Emanu-El, N.Y., **37**: 422

Tener, John Kinley, **28**: 439,n2

Tennessee, **28**: 595; senatorial elections, **27**: 55,n3, 82; appointments in, **29**: 304, 317, 332

Tennessee, U.S.S., **30**: 369,n7; **36**: 267n1

Tennessee Coal and Iron Co., **31**: 268

Tennyson, Alfred, Lord Tennyson, **30**: 34; **38**: 330

Tepic, state, Mex., **28**: 77; **30**: 82

Terminal Co., Vera Cruz, Mex., **28**: 297-98

Terrell, Robert Heberton, **29**: 205n2, 290,n1, 302, 319,n1, 388, 394; **30**: 491,n3; **31**: 192

Territories Committee (Senate), **30**: 31

Texarkana, Ark., **31**: 248

Texarkana, Tex., **31**: 249

Texas, **27**: 239, 324; **28**: 259-60, 595; **33**: 196, 511; **37**: 300, 321n1; and arms embargo, **30**: 76, 83; and cotton crisis, **31**: 133, 248, 248-49; primary system in, **31**: 282; and Democratic party, **31**: 290; and preparedness, **36**: 165-66, 175,n1, 186,n2

Texas, University of, **29**: 56, 245n2, 277

Texas A & M University, **27**: 442n1

Texas City, Tex., **29**: 509n1

Texas Oil Co., **30**: 246n2

Texas Rangers, **36**: 104

Thacher, Thomas Chandler, **28**: 491n1, 498n1; **33**: 86n1

Thackeray, William Makepeace, **28**: 576

Thanksgiving Proclamation, **35**: 89-90; **38**: 276,n2, 667-68

Thayer, George Augustine, **38**: 534,n1

Thayer, William Sidney, **38**: 182,n4,6

Théodore, Davilmar, **31**: 483,n4; **32**: 27, 288

Theodore Roosevelt (Charnwood), **34**: 21n7

Theodore Roosevelt and the Progressive Movement (Mowry), **36:** 26n3; **37:** 203n4
Thimme, Friedrich, **37:** 43n1
33 Washington Square (Irwin), **34:** 517,n2
Thom, Alfred Pembroke, **37:** 439n1
Thomann, Julius, **36:** 235,n5
Thomas, Augustus, **27:** 218,n1, 228; **38:** 597n1
Thomas, Charles Spalding, **27:** 507,n1; **28:** 548; **29:** 511,n1, 517; **31:** 269, 335, 557; **32:** 143n1; **36:** 311, 328,n4; **37:** 515; **38:** 4-5, 9, 85,n1
Thomas, Helen Montmorency Haskell (Mrs. Stephen Seymour), **32:** 23,n1
Thomas, Milton Halsey, **27:** xxii
Thomas, Stephen Seymour, **27:** 139,n1; **32:** 23, 25, 66
Thomas Jefferson: His Permanent Influence on American Institutions (Williams), **28:** 389,n2; **31:** 316,n2
Thompson, Charles Willis, **27:** 164-66, 465; **29:** 180n1; **38:** 40, 45
Thompson, Henry Burling, **27:** 475, 480; **37:** 502n1, 504
Thompson, Joseph Campbell, **36:** 188,n1
Thompson, Mary Wilson (Mrs. Henry Burling), **37:** 502-504, 518
Thompson, R. W., **28:** 455n2
Thompson, Samuel Huston, Jr., **27:** 163-64; **32:** 61; **33:** 472-73, 479; **34:** 515, 516; **36:** 388,n5; **37:** 435-36; **38:** 192-93, 194
Thompson, William Howard, **28:** 6; **29:** 173; **36:** 311,n1, 464n1
Thompson-Birdsall bill, **27:** 338n3, 343n1
Thomson, Sir Joseph John, **37:** 474
Thomson, Thaddeus Austin, **28:** 197,n1, 292,n1,2, 329, 330-31, 534; **29:** 40, 128; **32:** 245; **38:** 317; on Colombian treaty, **36:** 234,n1, 234-36
Thomson, William, 1st Baron Kelvin, **37:** 149
Thornton, John Randolph, **28:** 35,n1; **29:** 275-77, 281, 288-89, 297, 310,n1; **30:** 225, 240; **32:** 227-29, 235
Thou Shalt Not Bear False Witness (Thompson), **28:** 455,n2
Thrasher, Leon Chester, **32:** 464,n1, 466n1, 468, 484, 485, 491, 492, 497, 527; **33:** 61, 66, 67, 73, 74, 75, 92, 94, 155, 169, 174-75, 357
Thrasher case: *see Falaba* incident
Through the Looking Glass (Carroll), **37:** 53
Thuliez, Louise, **35:** 88,n1,2,3,4 103n1, 107, 118, 127, 174-75
Thurman, Albert Lee, **34:** 27,n2; **35:** 459,n2
Tientsin, China, **32:** 135
Tientsin Times, **32:** 519
Tiffany and Co., N.Y., **35:** 19
Tiller, Theodore Hance, **37:** 46n1
Tillman, Benjamin Ryan, **27:** 284, 531; **31:** 466-67; **32:** 62-63; **34:** 58,n1; **36:** 173-74, 174-75; **37:** 66-67, 94, 267,n1, 308, 481; **38:** 101n1; on armor plate

legislation, **35:** 434-35,n1, 446, 456-57; **36:** 278-79, 376, 396,n1, 545-46; on nitrate manufacture, **37:** 66-67, 288
Tirpitz, Alfred von, **30:** 109,n3, 265; **32:** 351, 352,n1, 506; **33:** 299, 406, 454, 483; **34:** 46, 47, 187, 238, 239, 320, 342n1, 453; **35:** 4,n3, 131-32; **36:** 122, 169, 258, 411; **37:** 45n1; **38:** 71, 72, 195; resignation of, **36:** 341, 354, 389n8, 413, 446n1
Tisza de Boros-Jenö et Szeged, Count István, **35:** 395,n1; **38:** 71n1, 75
Titanic, S.S., **27:** 17n2
Titlow, A. R., **34:** 146
Titmarsh Club, **28:** 576
Titus, Grace Elizabeth, **31:** 16,n1
Tlalpam, Mex., **27:** 537; **28:** 27
Tlaxcala, state, Mex., **28:** 77
To a Strict Accountability (*New York Herald*), **32:** 466n1
To B. R. Haydon (Wordsworth), **33:** 125,n1; **34:** 228,n1
To Finance Cotton Receipts (McLaurin), **34:** 400n1
To Woodrow Wilson: Greetings! (W. G. Brown), **27:** 140,n1
tobacco interests, **31:** 119n1, 208,n2
tobacco trust, **27:** 496, 510-11; **29:** 93, 95; **30:** 274n1; S. Gompers on, **27:** 185
Tocqueville, Alexis Charles Henri Maurice Clérel de, **30:** 185; **38:** 578-79
Tod, Robert Elliott, **28:** 203
Todd, Helen, **37:** 427n4
Tohoku Imperial University (Japan), **29:** 129n1
Tokalon Wine Co., Wash., D.C., **34:** 24
Tokomaru, S.S., **35:** 7
Tokyo, **27:** 443, 448, 449n2; **29:** 238; and F. L. de la Barra reception in, **29:** 91n3
Toledo, Ohio: WW's remarks in, **37:** 395-96
Toledo University, **36:** 524, 634n5
Toluca, Mex., **27:** 539
Tomlinson Hall, Indianapolis, **38:** 419n1
Tomorrow a New World: The New Deal Community Program (Conkin), **32:** 56n2
Tompkins, Frank, **36:** 280n1, 281,n2, 282, 586, 591
Topakyan, Haigazoun Hohannes, **35:** 104-105,n1, 119
Topeka, Kan., **36:** 140; WW's addresses on preparedness in, **36:** 87-96, 96-100
Topeka *Daily Capital*, **36:** 89,n2
Topolobampo, Sinaloa, Mex., **29:** 130
Torikichi, Obata, **35:** 203,n1
Toronto, Canada, **30:** 88,n2, 96, 97
Torrence, Sidney, **38:** 146
Torreón, Coahuila, Mex., **28:** 382-83,n1, 428, 570,n1, 602n1; **29:** 338, 375, 377; **30:** 193, 220, 297, 301n1, 445; **32:** 390; **33:** 410; **37:** 22; Spaniards in, **29:** 241-42; and F. Villa, **29:** 280, 382,n1, 450n1
Torreón Agreement, **30:** 301n1, 311, 339, 410, 490; **31:** 68

Tourcoing, France, **38**: 652, 653
Tower, Charlemagne, **33**: 17,n1
Towne, Omar A., **27**: 178
Townsley, Clarence Page, **37**: 212,n1
Toy, Crawford Howell, **31**: 5, 158, 456, 516; **32**: 191, 335, 537, 538; **33**: 411, 518
Toy, Nancy Saunders (Mrs. Crawford Howell), **31**: 4-5, 157-58, 289-91, 454-56, 515-16, 532; **32**: 7-10, 12-13, 21-22, 111-12, 165-66, 190-91, 334-35, 537-38,n1; **33**: 240-41, 411, 517-18
Tracy, Benjamin Franklin, **31**: 426,n2, 447n1, 450, 461; **37**: 33n4
Tracy, William P., **35**: 321,n2
trade: *see* commerce
Trade Advice by Ambassador Naón (*New York Herald*), **31**: 360,n1
Trade Commission: *see* Federal Trade Commission
Trade Commission bill: *see* Federal Trade Commission Act
Trade Disputes Act of 1906 (English), **27**: 187
trade unions: *see* labor unions
Traders' National Bank of Fort Worth, **31**: 276
Transcendental Wild Oats (L. M. Alcott), **36**: 132n1
transcontinental railways, **27**: 222
Transylvania, Hungary, **37**: 464
Transylvania, S.S., **33**: 185, 185-86, 186n1
Travieso, Martin, Jr., **38**: 633
Treacy, John J., **27**: 483
Treasures of a Hundred Cooks (Hulbert), **32**: 192n1
Treasury, Department of the, **29**: 177, 365; **31**: 39, 250, 270, 276,n1, 386; **32**: 174; **33**: 245n1; **34**: 235, 255, 369; **35**: 510, 511; segregation in, **28**: 60,n3, 88-89, 94, 211, 404-408, 409, 413-14, 453-55,n2, 491n2, 496, 498n1; **31**: 298, 299, 312, 361n2; and cotton crisis, **31**: 250; C. A. Spring Rice on, **31**: 315
Treat, Charles Gould, **38**: 238,n4
Treaties and Other International Agreements of the United States of America, 1776-1949 (Bevans), **38**: 228n1
Treatise on International Law (Hall), **29**: 432; **32**: 534,n3
Treaty of: *see* under the latter part of the name, such as Portsmouth, Treaty of
Treaty of 1828 (U.S. and Russia), **33**: 172, 177, 354, 360
Treaty of 1911 (Japan and the U.S.), **30**: 274
Treitschke, Heinrich von, **31**: 553
Tremont Theatre, Boston, **33**: 68n1
Trenholm, Arthur W., **30**: 328-29,n1
Trent affair, **32**: 92; compared to *Laurentic* incident, **37**: 184,n2
Trenton, N.J., **27**: 50, 375; **28**: 598,n1; **33**: 60, 434; **34**: 263; WW's remarks to N.J. electors, **27**: 40-44

Trenton Evening Times, **27**: 44n, 60, 95n
Treutler, Karl Georg von, **36**: 613,n2
Trevelyan, George Macaulay, **33**: 64,n2
Trevelyan, Sir George Otto, **32**: 8; **33**: 64n1
Treviño, Jacinto B., **28**: 78; **34**: 287,n1; **36**: 579; **37**: 22n3, 263,n2,3, 292, 319, 321n1, 323; **38**: 379, 380, 383
Tribble, Samuel Joelah, **33**: 540,n1
Trillo, Colonel, **32**: 383, 384
Trinidad, **37**: 73n2; McAdoo incident in, **36**: 569, 580
Trinidad, Colo., **28**: 426, 521, 551, 582; **29**: 502, 513, 541, 547; **30**: 17, 18, 19, 60; **31**: 31, 50, 81, 517, 557,n2
Trinity Churchyard, N.Y., **31**: 561n1
Trinity College, Cambridge, England, **29**: 47
Trinity College, N.C., **27**: 208
Triple Alliance, **30**: 342
Triple Entente, **30**: 342; **31**: 459
Trotter, William Monroe, **31**: 308, 311, 312; **33**: 68,n1; address to WW, **28**: 491-95,n1,3,5; **31**: 298-301; WW's reply to and dialogue with, **28**: 496-98,n1; **31**: 304-308; J. Rosenwald's experiences with, **31**: 314; R. R. Moton on, **31**: 322; editorial comments on dialogue with WW, **31**: 328n2,3; photograph: *illustration section*, 31
Troubled Mexico. A Visit to the Stronghold of the Rebels (Fyfe), **28**: 559,n1
Troy, Lillian Scott, **38**: 244-45,n3
Troy, N.Y., **34**: 64, 75, 76, 77, 91; **38**: 628
True Intellectual System of the Universe (Cudworth), **31**: 316,n2
True Story of Woodrow Wilson (Lawrence), **38**: 674n2
Trumbull, Frank, **31**: 20-21,n1, 26, 82; **32**: 162-63, 272; **37**: 439n1, 504
Truppel, Oscar, **34**: 239,n1
trust legislation, **32**: 73; *see also* antitrust legislation
trusteeship, **29**: 8
trusts, **27**: 121, 122; **28**: 487; **29**: 63, 90, 99, 102, 138,n1,2, 535; S. Gompers, **27**: 184; W. C. Redfield on, **29**: 42-43; D. B. Jones on, **29**: 67-68, 68; J. E. Davies on, **29**: 78-85; WW message on antitrust legislation, **29**: 153; *see also* antitrust legislation
Tsingtao, China, **31**: 364, 509, 511, 547; **33**: 98
Tsinanfu, China, **31**: 364
Tsung-yü, Lu, **35**: 204,n3
Tubantia, S.S., **36**: 429, 430, 616
Tuck, Philemon, H., **36**: 377n2, 397
Tuck, Somerville Pinkney, Jr., **36**: 377,n2
Tucker, Henry St. George, **27**: 7, 228
Tucker, Jane, **31**: 281
Tucker, John Randolph, **36**: 226,n1
Tucker, Mona House (Mrs. Randolph Foster), **29**: 541,n1; **31**: 274,n1
Tucker, Randolph Foster, **31**: 274n1

Tucker, Randolph Foster, Jr., **31:** 274,n1, 387, 453
Tucson, Ariz.: W. B. Hale in, **28:** 505, 506, 567, 568
Tumulty, Joseph Patrick, **27:** xv, xvi, 15, 22, 39, 111, 117, 130, 133,n1, 137, 165,n1, 192, 198, 199, 210, 213, 228, 235,n1, 247, 251, 255, 258, 259, 276-77, 300, 365, 371-72, 381, 381-82, 385, 402, 407, 418, 498, 554, 565n1; **28:** 37, 41, 44, 67, 85, 86, 87, 90, 102, 104, 118n6, 133, 135, 139, 161, 163, 185, 187, 209-12, 247, 248, 264, 290, 331, 332, 360, 501, 540, 580, 595, 596; **29:** 24, 56, 77, 100, 101, 101-102, 128, 170, 204-205, 208, 213n1, 243n3, 271, 282, 344, 378, 380-81, 405, 418-20, 440, 461, 496, 502-503, 511, 558, 562; **30:** 7, 21n1, 23, 38-39, 123, 156, 173, 174, 202, 223, 334, 335, 343, 344, 360, 402; **31:** 43, 93, 100, 108, 112, 138, 150, 174n1, 183, 197, 206, 207, 209, 264, 310, 318, 328, 374, 381-82, 413, 424, 554-55; **32:** 9, 17, 68-69, 78, 95-96, 116, 133, 142, 258, 265, 295, 455, 462n2, 486, 493,n1, 499, 537
33: 68, 86, 153n1, 180, 219, 305, 370, 416-17, 465-66, 470, 474, 490, 492, 493, 498-99, 538; **34:** 45,n1, 53, 56, 176n1, 201, 232, 335, 338, 346, 389-91, 434-35, 467, 470, 485, 509, 520, 542-43; **35:** 68, 85-87, 105-106, 118, 138, 141, 146,n3, 149-50, 150, 211, 212n1, 240, 263, 353, 354, 355, 361, 382, 405, 412n2, 423, 431, 439, 461-62, 466-67, 467, 481, 509; **36:** 23, 25-26, 86, 144, 145, 175, 187, 218, 293, 315, 330, 364, 407, 409, 415, 426, 530, 559-60, 562, 565, 567, 569, 580, 606, 655-56; **37:** 27, 30, 35, 62, 75, 76, 117, 133, 141, 171-72, 204,n3, 268-69, 313-14, 314-15, 322, 323, 331-32, 375, 379, 434-35, 451, 486, 490, 541-42; **38:** 5, 24, 29n1, 40, 45-46, 81, 83, 84, 94, 125, 146, 167, 181, 193, 241n1, 258, 277-78, 279-80, 286, 300, 315, 316, 318-19, 325-26, 350,n1, 396-97, 453n1, 459, 516, 522,n1, 628, 629, 632, 656, 659, 674
discussed for position of Secretary to the President, **27:** 24, 57, 71, 97; letter from L. F. Post, **28:** 546-56; and L. Steffens, **30:** 64-65, 73; and J. Reed article, **30:** 231,n2; and Illinois politics, **31:** 232,n1; and W. G. McAdoo, **31:** 274, 279; **35:** 360; and WW's Annual Messages to Congress, **31:** 324,n1, 388-89, 414n1, 415n2; **35:** 265-70; and news leaks, **31:** 549-50, 551, 553; and T. C. O'Sullivan, **32:** 259n1; and the Federal Trade Commission, **32:** 281-82; on extra session, **32:** 293; WW's birthday greetings to, **33:** 106; on protest note to Great Britain, **33:** 508; and press release on preparedness, **34:** 3-4,n1; and *Eastland* disaster, **34:** 27, 65; and

F. Buchanan's attack on WW, **34:** 39-40,n1, 52, 64-65, 116,n1, 120; on *Arabic* disaster, **34:** 274; WW on, **34:** 302, 351-52, 360, 513-14; EBG on, **34:** 327-28; on alleged break between WW and E. M. House, **34:** 381, 402n2, 471; on *Hesperian* incident, **34:** 428-29, 444-45 and possible appointment as judge of Appraiser's Court, **34:** 515, 515-16; on WW's preparedness speech, **35:** 107-109, 121n1, 122,n2, 135-37, 253-54, 478-80, 492-94; advocates action on Germany, **35:** 221-22; and W. Vick, **35:** 285-86; birthday greetings to WW, **35:** 397, 401; and *Persia* case, **35:** 419, 424; on Tariff Commission, **35:** 524; on E. Root's speech in New York, **36:** 186-87; on resolution against travel on armed ships, **36:** 211-13; on Punitive Expedition, **36:** 317,n1, 335; on Democratic platform, **36:** 333-34; on H. Bernstein, **36:** 356; on A Yager, **36:** 569-70; suggests peace moves, **37:** 58-60; on G. Rublee nomination, **37:** 67-68; WW's talk of replacing, **37:** 104-105; **38:** 660, 674; on German-American issue, **37:** 217-21; urges strong stand in Mexico, **37:** 291-92; on Casement case, **37:** 353, 446, 446-47; **38:** 443-45; on newspaper publicity for Democratic campaign, **37:** 378-79; on C. E. Hughes and industrial preparedness, **38:** 20-21; on WW's acceptance speech, **38:** 66,n1; on political strategy, **38:** 513-14; election night and, **38:** 622; photographs: *illustration sections*, **31; 38**
Tumulty, Mary Byrne (Mrs. Joseph Patrick), **29:** 100; **30:** 7; **34:** 302; **35:** 397
Tumulty, Philip, **27:** 97
Turgot, Anne-Robert-Jacques, Baron de l'Aulne, **35:** 133
Turkey, **28:** 4; **30:** 151, 152; **31:** 16n1, 20, 56, 339, 372, 428, 443, 471; **32:** 81, 358; **33:** 12, 504; **34:** 18, 94, 310; **35:** 39, 185,n1, 191, 413, 438, 484; **36:** 124, 148n1, 442; **37:** 20, 96; **38:** 652; ambassadorial appointments, **27:** 118, 228, 384-85, 513; **36:** 378n3; atrocities towards Armenians, **35:** 104, 119, 337, 348, 349; H. Morgenthau resigns as ambassador, **36:** 356-57
Turning the Negro Back (Bridgman), **28:** 278n1
Turpin, Edna Henry Lee, **28:** 318n1
Turtle Bay Incident, **32:** 525,n1, 528,n1; **33:** 40
Tuskegee Institute, **29:** 537n1; **32:** 272; **35:** 400,n1
Tuxedo, N.Y., **34:** 286
Tuxedo Park, N.Y., **35:** 46
Tuxpan, Veracruz, Mex., **28:** 575; **29:** 126; **37:** 350
Twain, Mark, **27:** 118; **29:** 55-56; **36:** 190-91,n1
Twining, Nathan Crook, **29:** 16

Two-Hour Talk with the Kaiser—Judge A. K. Nippert Brings Message to President Wilson and the American People from Wilhelm II (*New York Times*), **38:** 177n2

Two Paths (New York *Evening Post*), **37:** 309,n1

Two Senators Enter Fight to Save Navy's Oil Tracts from Grasp of Speculators (*New York Herald*), **37:** 141n4

2,077 Acres of Navy Oil Lands Saved by Attorney General (*New York Herald*), **37:** 141n4

Two Years of Wilson (New York *World*), **32:** 324,n1

Tyndall, John, **38:** 574-75,n4

Tyr, S.S., **31:** 477

Tyrrell, Margaret Ann Urquhart, Lady Tyrrell, **29:** 35

Tyrrell, Sir William George, **28:** 447-48, 477,n2, 527, 530-31, 532-33, 543, 561-62, 564-65, 573-74, 574-75, 586, 587, 592, 594; **29:** 12, 13, 19, 33, 34-35, 52, 59-60, 74n1, 131, 217-18, 324-25, 347n1, 384; **31:** 61, 95, 550, 32, 211, 225, 238, 278, 350; **35:** 64, 346-47; and E. M. House's peace mission, **30:** 189, 190, 214, 247, 255-56, 258, 266; son killed, **32:** 254

Tyson, Mr. (of Treasury Dept.), **28:** 406

U-20, S.M.S., **33:** 127n1; **34:** 315n1

U-27, S.M.S., **34:** 452, 453

U-29, S.M.S., **36:** 371n1, 488n2

U-38, S.M.S., **35:** 192n1

U-53 affair, **38:** 374,n1, 391, 409, 411, 472-73,n1,2,3, 658n1

U.M.W.: *see* United Mine Workers of America

Uccle (Ukkel), Belgium, **38:** 661

Uchida, S., **33:** 81-82,n1

Uchida, Yasuya, **32:** 320-21

Ulfelder, Sidney, **36:** 364

Uncle Remus, His Songs and His Sayings (Harris), **31:** 316n2, 317

Uncle William, the Man Who Was Shif'-less (Lee), **38:** 687n4

Underhill, Edwin Stewart, **29:** 401,n1

Underwood, Frederick Douglass, **38:** 466,n2, 521

Underwood, Oscar Wilder, **27:** 20, 21, 44-45, 66-67, 74, 78, 123, 131, 177, 192, 251, 264, 282, 314, 322, 327, 334-35, 347, 430, 431, 433; **28:** 267, 276, 419; **29:** 163-64, 170, 268, 282, 308, 322, 355, 390; **30:** 3, 21, 217, 324, 325, 326, 389, 402; **31:** 88, 128, 145, 465; **32:** 57, 88, 232, 346; **36:** 606, 612; **37:** 169n1; **38:** 199; and senatorial nomination, **29:** 410,n1; WW's letter praising accomplishments of Democratic Congress, **31:** 168-74; on Porto Rico bill, **31:** 473-74; and purchase of Monticello, **32:** 82, 85-86,n1; on ship-purchase bill, **32:** 197-98

Underwood-Simmons Tariff Act, **27:** xxi, 20, 123, 177, 192, 235-36, 250, 251, 261, 288-89,n7,8, 301-303,n1, 323, 326, 339-40, 360, 453,n1, 496, 497, 498, 507n1, 562; **28:** 35n2, 45, 142, 146n2, 151, 462; **29:** 64, 264,n1, 370; **30:** 129, 211; **31:** 169-70, 213, 326; **32:** 37, 57, 240; **35:** 314, 370n1, 428, 429, 475, 477; **37:** 169n1, 200n3
and business, **27:** 565-66; and citrus fruit, **27:** 418n1; income-tax provision, **27:** 301,n1, 314,n1, 322; **28:** 247,n1, 249, 253-54, 254, 258, 272,n1; and lobbyists, **27:** 472, 473, 487-88; most-favored-nation clause, **27:** 289,n8; and Panama Canal tolls controversy, **27:** 332-33, 357; readymade clothing, **27:** 327-28, 334-35, 347; and rice, **27:** 457n2; Senate Finance Committee, **27:** 263,n1,2, 278-80; sugar schedule, **27:** 251, 261, 263n2, 279, 286, 302, 304, 322n1, 340, 418n1, 435, 502,n1 509; **28:** 35; wages, **27:** 433; WW on, **27:** 269-72; **28:** 267,n1, 351-52,n1; wool schedule, **27:** 251, 263n2, 279, 303, 322,n1, 327, 328, 334-35, 434-35, 502,n1; and art, **28:** 62, 67, 112, 120, 129, 273, 276,n2, 327; books, **28:** 62, 67, 390, 579; bird plumes, **28:** 112,n3, 129; and campaign in Maine, **28:** 144; EAW on, **28:** 138, 269, 273, 360, 363-64; congratulatory messages, **28:** 259n2, 270, 271, 276, 329, 359, 370n2, 385, 506; cartoon about: *illustration section*, **29**

Underwriting a Tyranny? (New York *World*), **28:** 92,n1

unemployment, **32:** 123-24, 176

Union Coal and Coke Co., Colo., **29:** 549

Union League of Philadelphia, **33:** 184,n1

Union of American Hebrew Congregations, **32:** 97; **37:** 109

Union of South Africa, **32:** 335,n1, 358; **34:** 94

Union Pacific Railroad, **28:** 255n1; **29:** 67-68,n2, 141,n1; **30:** 353n1; **37:** 439n1; **38:** 377n2

Union Theological Seminary, N.Y., **29:** 361n2; **35:** 39n2

Union Trust Co., Chicago, **29:** 483

unions: *see* labor unions

United Colored Democracy, **28:** 115-18,n1

United Confederate Veterans, **30:** 141n1

United Daughters of the Confederacy, **30:** 141-42,n1,3

United Fruit Co., **31:** 176n1

United German Societies of New York, **37:** 219n3

United Irish Societies, **33:** 185

United Kingdom: *see* Great Britain

United Metals Selling Co., **38:** 182n3

United Mine Workers of America, **28:** 426-27,n8, 507, 509n1, 510, 511, 512, 512-13, 519, 520, 522, 524, 552, 553, 554, 589, 590; **29:** 87, 88, 480, 513, 514, 546-49; **30:** 16-20, 488n1; **31:** 49-50, 51,

United Mine Workers of America (*cont.*) 87n1, 107, 310, 369n2, 503, 557n2; and preparedness, **36**: 639,n16

United Polish Organizations of America, **37**: 405

United Press, **29**: 502; **31**: 291n2; **35**: 256; **36**: 308, 332; **38**: 392, 494,n1, 496,n3, 619

United Shoe Machinery Co., **30**: 400n3, 482; **31**: 30n1

United States and Mexico (Rippy), **29**: 292n1; **33**: 46n4

United States and Pancho Villa (Clendenen), **30**: 230n1

United States Army, **29**: 509, 511; **30**: 8, 352; **34**: 3, 4, 38-39, 131n2, 133, 134, 173n1, 482, 514; **35**: 123-24, 138-41, 149-50, 169, 468; **38**: 40-42, 178n3, 232; and Joint Board, **27**: 441,n1, 447; and Negroes, **28**: 454; and Military Order of the Carabao, **29**: 38-39, 54-55; WW on, **36**: 13, 15, 44, 69, 90, 102, 104, 513; T. W. Gregory on, **36**: 195-96; J. Hay on, **36**: 141-43; E. M. House on, **36**: 381; N. D. Baker on, **36**: 431; and 1916 platform, **37**: 187, 195; promotions for brigadier and major generals, **38**: 238-39,n1-12

United States Board of Mediation and Conciliation, **30**: 305-307,n1,2; **38**: 12,n1; and railroad strike, **37**: 439, 505, 525,n1, 530, 531

United States Chamber of Commerce, **27**: 79, 530,n1; **29**: 262, 278n2, 317, 483; **30**: 183, 205-207,n1, 274n1, 284; **35**: 458n1; **37**: 127,n2, 504,n1; **38**: 75n1; and ship–purchase bill, **32**: 84; WW's addresses to, **32**: 178-87; **36**: 152-60; recommendations for maintenance of world peace, **36**: 168-69,n1

United States Coast and Geodetic Survey; WW's address to, **36**: 417-21

United States Commission on Industrial Relations, **27**: 77,n6,7, 353-54, 365, 456, 465, 476-77, 481, 552, 553; **28**: 82; **30**: 65, 161, 162, 350; **31**: 363, 377, 407; **32**: 189, 199; **34**: 136,n3, 217; **37**: 310

United States Commission on Rural Credits: *see* Rural Credits Commission

United States Congress, **27**: 54; **28**: 113, 146n2, 267, 311; **29**: 22, 33, 64, 161; **30**: 191, 338; **31**: 145, 292, 387; **32**: 150; **33**: 151-52, 162n2, 520, 526; **34**: 52n2, 80, 169, 208, 290, 299, 539; **35**: 5,n7, 114, 169, 184, 213, 234, 406, 422, 423,n1, 478n1, 504; **36**: 244; **37**: 480; **38**: 206; extraordinary session, **27**: 20-21, 123, 131, 201, 235, 269-70, 273, 389; P. U. Kellogg on bills advocated for passage, **27**: 242-44

WW addresses and messages to: **34**: 3, 4, 390; **38**: 657; on tariff, **27**: 269-72; on banking and currency reform, **27**: 570-73; on Mexican affairs, **28**: 218, 220, 227-31; annual message to, **29**: 3-11; **31**: 414-24; on antitrust legislation, **29**: 153-58; on appropriations to assist Americans in Europe, **30**: 337-38; asking for additional revenue, **30**: 473-75; to joint session of, **36**: 506-10; on Mexico to joint session, **37**: 298-304; **38**: 96-101, 121, 145

and lobbyists, **27**: 483-84; and Mexico, **28**: 102, 137, 189, 208,n2; **29**: 471-74; **36**: 314, 317; and rural credits, **28**: 147, 148; and Maine elections, **28**: 149,n1; and long session, **28**: 151, 365, 378; **29**: 399; and segregation, **28**: 349; and tariff bill, **28**: 370n2; and Federal Reserve Act, **28**: 389, 430, 444, 600; and Colorado coal strike, **28**: 475; **29**: 32, 526; and election reform, **29**: 7-8; WW's relations with, **29**: 10-11, 59; and woman suffrage, **29**: 22; and power to regulate commerce, **29**: 25; and holding companies, **29**: 26, 27; and Panama Canal tolls controversy, **29**: 34-35, 232-33, 281, 312-13, 373-74, 379, 385, 386-87; and Philippines, **29**: 150; **34**: 389; and Porto Rico, **29**: 264,n1, 273-74,n1; E. M. House on suggestions for Federal Reserve Board, **29**: 278; on early adjournment of, **29**: 404, 409; **30**: 110, 130, 182, 242, 389; and Bacon-Bartlett bill, **29**: 413n1; W. C. Redfield on antitrust bills and commerce and, **29**: 435n1; and power to declare war, **29**: 437, 438; and Hollis-Bulkley bill, **30**: 10n2; and memorial to Confederate soldiers, **30**: 141; and Civil War, **30**: 142; business interests wish for early adjournment, **30**: 173n1; and antitrust legislation, **30**: 173n1, 212; and Jones bill, **30**: 208; **32**: 330-31; and Chandler-Dunbar decision, **30**: 218n3; WW on, **30**: 249, 276-77, 476; **31**: 168-74, 397, 420-21, 446-47; **32**: 33-34, 316; **34**: 352; **35**: 261, 263,n1, 265-70, 293-310, 527; **36**: 41, 46, 63, 84, 315; **38**: 433-34; to remain in session, **30**: 335; opinion of Joint State and Navy Neutrality Board on shipping bills in, **30**: 435n2

important legislation passed by current session, **30**: 475-76; talk of adjournment, **31**: 89, 100-101, 111-12, 142, 157, 214; and aid to Liberia, **31**: 102; R. L. Henry on aid to cotton growers and, **31**: 121; and railroad-securities bill, **31**: 149; and appropriations bills, **31**: 149-50; and raise for employees in Public Buildings and Grounds Department, **31**: 183; H. L. Higginson on achievements of, **31**: 212-13; and exercise of patronage power, **31**: 275; and *World* editorial on elections, **31**: 295n1; bills and resolutions in third session, **31**: 354, 409; talk of extra session, **32**: 13, 122, 199, 207,

227-29, 232, 240n1, 293, 316; **33:** 252; and Federal Trade Commission and the tariff, **32:** 37; and ship-purchase bill, **32:** 87, 173, 221-22,n2, 227-29, 232, 239, 240, 247; and commerce, **32:** 104; attempt to embargo arms exports, **32:** 108-109; and labor measures, **32:** 199; and seamen's bill, **32:** 310; and neutrality, **32:** 513; and J. von Bernstorff note and resolution, **32:** 526, 529; and W. J. Bryan on ships carrying contraband, **33:** 325; antiwar feeling in, **33:** 337; and Ellen Wilson Memorial Homes, **33:** 431n6; and National Negro Exposition, **33:** 464; and cotton crisis, **33:** 533,n1; and preparedness, **34:** 3-4, 4, 5, 38, 131n2, 133, 209, 227; and Colombian treaty, **34:** 51; and Haiti, **34:** 78; and special session, **34:** 195n2, 233; and Bryan, **34:** 478, 481; and L. M. Garrison plan, **34:** 482,n2, 484, 485; and diplomatic appointments and patronage, **34:** 515; and creation of a health department, **35:** 183; R. Lansing on war declaration power of, **35:** 219, 404; and conservation, **35:** 231-32; and compensation for E. M. House's peace mission, **35:** 398

and Danish West Indies, **35:** 402; J. Hay on military plans and, **36:** 134-35, 142-43; and Clarke amendment, **36:** 146, 162-63; T. W. Gregory on militia, **36:** 196; and armed-ship controversy, **36:** 210-11, 211-13,n1, 214; and Army Reorganization Act, **36:** 217,n1,2; and declaration of war power, **36:** 226n1; WW asks for vote on McLemore resolution, **36:** 231-32, 239; A. S. Burleson on bills that should be approved by, **36:** 249-50; attempts to shorten session, **36:** 306-307; and water-power resolution, **36:** 311-12; WW's promise to notify before breaking relations with Germany, **36:** 460; WW's veto of revision of Articles of War, **38:** 40-43; and railroad crisis and Adamson Act, **38:** 50, 96-101, 117, 216-17, 217-18; WW's remarks upon adjournment, **38:** 164-65; and New Jersey Democratic election, **38:** 285,n2; and National Archives, **38:** 654, 664; and members' eligibility for cabinet positions, **38:** 661; partisan composition of Sixty-fifth Congress, **38:** 666,n1

House of Representatives, **34:** 80; **35:** 305, 384; and Federal Reserve Act, **28:** 69, 90-91, 301,n1, 369-70, 379, 419, 430, 600; **29:** 5, 58,n4

Diggs-Caminetti case, **28:** 99n4; segregation of government employees, **28:** 115n3; H. D. Clayton and possible move to the Senate, **28:** 160n2, 385, 391; and long session, **28:** 365; lobby investigation, **28:** 381,n2; seamen's bill, **28:** 420; trust program, **28:** 487; Slayden reso-

lution, **28:** 491; and woman suffrage, **29:** 22; **32:** 22,n1; and investigation of Colorado coal strike, **29:** 46,n1; and Panama Canal tolls, **29:** 298-300, 374, 376, 387; and food fisheries treaty, **29:** 349n2; and Shackleford bill, **29:** 355,n1; and Children's Bureau, **29:** 400; and Bacon-Bartlett bill, **29:** 425; and federal trade commission bill, **30:** 130, 389, 429, 434, 455; and conservation bills, **30:** 160; **31:** 417; and Rayburn bill, **30:** 162,n2; and Adamson water-power bill, **30:** 224n1; **31:** 178; and Jones bill, **30:** 259; **36:** 145, 163, 555,n1, 583n1; and sundry civil appropriations bill, **30:** 283; and emergency currency, **30:** 325,n1; and antitrust bills, **31:** 24; and Clayton bill, **31:** 41-42,n2,3, 45; and Philippine bill, **31:** 88; **32:** 291-92,n1,2; and Lever-Smith warehouse bill, **31:** 180,n6; and bill to amend Federal Reserve Act, **31:** 208n2; and bills pending in short session, **31:** 234, 235, 409; and Republican victories, **31:** 264,n3; and Democratic party, **31:** 266; and cotton crisis, **31:** 324; and diplomatic and consular service bill, **31:** 448-49,n1; and Porto Rico bill, **31:** 466, 473-74; and ship-purchase bill, **31:** 507; **32:** 197, 221, 222, 232; and Monticello, **32:** 82, 86n1

WW veto of immigration bill, **32:** 142-44; and Weeks-Gore bill, **32:** 240,n1, 241,n1; and Howard University appropriations, **32:** 272,n1; and rural credits, **35:** 96; and preparedness, **35:** 213n1, 469-70, 479, 482; and Ferris water-power bill, **35:** 232; C. Kitchin speech on war revenue bill and tariff, **35:** 370n1, 373; and corrupt-practices bill, **35:** 433,n1; W. G. McAdoo on tariff and antidumping legislation, **35:** 476-77; and water-power bills, **36:** 50, 241, 243, 301, 316; and Continental Army plan, **36:** 141-42; and army reorganization bill, **36:** 179n4, 513-15; **37:** 27,n1; and armor-plate bill, **36:** 278-79; and Villa attack in Columbus, **36:** 300; and vocational education bill, **36:** 370,n1; and increase of membership on Interstate Commerce Commission, **36:** 612,n1; and appropriations bills and 1916 platform, **37:** 199; and good-roads bill, **37:** 330,n1; and Shields bill, **37:** 359,n1; and naval appropriations bill, **37:** 481,n1; and Tariff Commission, **38:** 21,n3; and naval bill, **38:** 36n1; revenue bill in, **38:** 51,n1; shipping bill, **38:** 52-53; and Adamson Act, **38:** 124,n2, 217; and Webb bill, **38:** 267; WW on, **38:** 434; partisan composition of, **38:** 666n1

House of Representatives Committee on Banking and Currency: **27:** 21, 204, 486, 535n1, 536, 566; **28:** 45,n1, 69, 84-

United States Congress (*cont.*)
85, 90, 90-91, 108, 121,n1, 122,n3, 380, 385; **29:** 212; cotton crisis and Henry bill, **31:** 130

House of Representatives Foreign Affairs Committee: **28:** 95, 224n1; **29:** 217, 440; **31:** 103n1; **32:** 4, 5; and Bartholdt resolution, **32:** 24, 25

Senate: **27:** 100, 148, 236; **34:** 80, 108n2; **35:** 271, 352, 388, 462; secretaryship, **27:** 82-83, 113-114; and single-term amendment, **27:** 97, 98; New Hampshire election, **27:** 158,n1,2; Sherman Antitrust Act, **27:** 182-83; and Panama Canal tolls, **27:** 225-26, 512; **28:** 545; **29:** 232, 299, 376, 394, 397,n1, 398, 408; and Underwood-Simmons tariff, **27:** 453,n1; and Federal Reserve Act, **28:** 3,n1, 268, 269, 351, 361, 369-70,n1, 379, 419, 517-18, 599, 601; **29:** 5, 48n1, 58; Fall resolution, **28:** 82,n1; Nicaraguan treaty, **28:** 100; **31:** 102; and Mexico, **28:** 105, 162-63,n4, 208,n2, 223-24,n1, 463; duty on art, **28:** 120; H. D. Clayton and, **28:** 160n2, 391; tariff bill passes, **28:** 267,n1; Japanese treaty, **28:** 306, 314; and confirmation of Negroes, **28:** 349, 496-97; lobby investigation, **28:** 381,n1,2; seamen's bill, **28:** 420,n1; and treaty ratification, **29:** 4; and election reform, **29:** 7-8; and Bryan's "cooling off" treaties, **29:** 136, 340-41, 341, 349; **31:** 64,n1; death of A. O. Bacon, **29:** 248,n1; C. A. Spring Rice on popular election of, **29:** 268; and Sims bill, **29:** 283; **30:** 159n1, 174n1; and food fisheries treaty, **29:** 349n2; and Shackleford bill, **29:** 355,n1; and W. H. Page's speech, **29:** 376; O. W. Underwood wins nomination for, **29:** 410n1; and Federal Trade Commission bill, **29:** 486-87, 535,n1; **30:** 130, 187, 243, 348, 351, 389, 428, 430, 434; bills pending in, **30:** 31; and Jones bill, **30:** 159, 259; **35:** 86, 466,n1, 509; **36:** 139,n1, 555, 583n1; **37:** 455-56; and Rayburn bill, **30:** 162n2; and railroad-securities bill, **30:** 181; and Stevens amendment, **30:** 181; and Dominican agreement, **30:** 203,n1

and antitrust legislation, **30:** 223; **31:** 24; and Adamson water-power bill, **30:** 224n1; and Federal Reserve Board nominations, **30:** 260, 263, 279-80, 292, 299; and sundry civil appropriations bill, **30:** 283; and International Conference on Safety of Life at Sea, **30:** 284; **31:** 457-58, 491, 494, 495; and Owen stock-exchange bill, **30:** 312n1; and emergency currency, **30:** 325,n1; and resolution about WW tender of good offices to European powers, **30:** 349; and Clayton bill, **30:** 433, 480-83,n2; **31:** 41-42,n2, 3, 4, 45, 75, 88;

and Philippine bill, **31:** 89, 417; **32:** 291-92,n1,2; and revenue bill, **31:** 143; WW on, **29:** 274; **31:** 145, 544-45; **32:** 9-10, 67; **38:** 434; and Lever-Smith warehouse bill, **31:** 180,n6; and bills pending in short session, **31:** 234, 235, 409; and conservation bills, **31:** 417; and diplomatic and consular service bill, **31:** 448-49,n1; and Porto Rico, **31:** 466; rejection of WW's nominees, **31:** 481-82, 490, 498, 507, 524; W. J. Stone on WW's relations with, **31:** 487-88; and Pan-American Pact, **31:** 498; **32:** 64; **33:** 78; and Monticello, **32:** 86n1; **37:** 482,n1; and ship-purchase bill, **32:** 123, 134n1, 173,n2, 197, 207, 221-22,n2; and cloture rule, **32:** 173n1, 275; and Weeks bill, **32:** 197n1; and Bland appointment, **32:** 325,n1,2; and Bryan-Chamorro treaty, **32:** 470n3; talk of extra session, **33:** 293; and Danish West Indies, **33:** 405; **35:** 432; **38:** 10; and Colombian treaty, **34:** 49, 55-56; **35:** 375, 376, 377; **36:** 233-34,n1; and Haiti, **34:** 78; talk of special session on rules alteration, **34:** 393, 512, 514, 527,n1, 538; and public health, **35:** 151

and preparedness, **35:** 212n2; House peace mission, **35:** 361; and resolution on appeal for aid to Poland, **35:** 367; corrupt-practices bill, **35:** 433,n1; and armor plate, **35:** 456; **36:** 278-79, 376; shipping bill and, **35:** 459; **38:** 52-53, 60,n1; and antidumping legislation, **35:** 476-77; W. B. Wilson as candidate for, **36:** 23-25; and water-power bills, **36:** 50, 241-42, 311-12, 316; and G. Rublee nomination to Federal Trade Commission, **36:** 203n2; **37:** 101,n1, 374-75, 512-13; **38:** 87n1; and rights of U.S. citizens on high seas, **36:** 239; tables Gore resolution, **36:** 250,n1; and Smith-Hughes vocational education bill, **36:** 370,n1; and plan for L. Brandeis to run against H. C. Lodge, **36:** 425,n3; and general leasing bill, **36:** 464,n1; W. J. Stone's speech on preparedness in, **36:** 500,n1; and army reorganization bill, **36:** 513-15, 515,n3; and L. D. Brandeis nomination to Supreme Court, **36:** 609,n1; **37:** 151,n1; and increase in membership of Interstate Commerce Commission, **36:** 612n1; and oil legislation, **37:** 143; and good-roads bill, **37:** 330,n1; and Shields bill, **37:** 359n1; and army appropriations bill, **37:** 380-81; W. J. Stone and H. C. Lodge remarks on postwar economic legislation, **37:** 391n1; J. H. Clarke's confirmation for Supreme Court, **37:** 428n2; and child-labor and workmen's compensation bills, **37:** 431n1, 451; **38:** 14n1; and naval appropriations bill, **37:** 481n1; and Casement case, **37:** 516,n1, 517; **38:** 90, 92, 316, 350, 443-45; and revenue bill,

38: 51,n1; and Adamson Act, **38:** 124,n2, 125, 217; and Declaration of London, **38:** 243n2; W. J. Stone on Democratic elections in, **38:** 277; and Tariff Commission, **38:** 574; H. C. Cummings loses bid for seat in, **38:** 624, 669-70

Senate Banking and Currency Committee, **27:** 510, 525, 566; **28:** 3,n1, 9, 84-85, 200,n1, 257n2, 260, 261, 268, 269, 334, 361, 375n1, 379, 414-15, 418, 419, 421n1, 425n1, 428, 429, 430, 435, 444; **29:** 139; and T. D. Jones nomination to Federal Reserve Board, **30:** 191, 270,n4, 280, 291; and P. M. Warburg nomination, **30:** 263,n1, 270,n4, 280, 304, 317, 353; and Owen stock-exchange bill, **30:** 312n1; and F. A. Delano, **38:** 344, 353

Senate Foreign Relations Committee: **27:** 276n1, 352n1, 353; **28:** 140,n1, 155, 163,n4, 484, 501; **29:** 284; **30:** 160, 284; **31:** 64n1, 498, 551; **32:** 4, 5, 26n1, 42, 64, 264, 286; **34:** 134; **35:** 352, 374, 406, 411, 423n1; **38:** 444; and Nicaragua, **28:** 100, 177; and Mexico, **28:** 224n1; **29:** 440, 482n1; and Japan, **29:** 133,n1; **38:** 306, 314; and Panama Canal tolls, **29:** 160-61; and WW's meeting at White House with, **29:** 170, 174, 178-80, 180, 202, 203-204, 217, 236-38; and arbitration treaties, **29:** 213,n1, 267, 305; and Bryan-Chamorro treaty, **29:** 245; and W. H. Page's speech, **29:** 333n1; Safety-of-Life-at-Sea Convention, **31:** 457

United States Constitution, **27:** 54; **28:** 165, 222, 492, 494, 532; **29:** 25, 337; **30:** 218n3, 428; **31:** 95-96, 279, 304, 351, 433; **32:** 280, 325; **34:** 52n2, 202; **35:** 468, 470, 503; **37:** 215, 374, 415, 416; **38:** 41, 42, 162, 435, 508, 536

and alien land legislation in California, **27:** 454, 459; treaty-making power, **28:** 14; and Negroes, **28:** 344; state rights and treaty power, **29:** 199-200; and woman suffrage, **29:** 214, 215n1; **30:** 226,n2, 227-28; **31:** 329-30; **32:** 22,n1; **37:** 376n1, 513-14,n1; and presidential power to use force upon a foreign government, **29:** 436-38; and power to send federal troops to Colorado, **29:** 502, 514, 525-28, 528-29, 529; and Japanese problem in California, **31:** 256; and WW's veto of immigration bill, **32:** 142; and National Guard, **36:** 14, 46, 91; WW on preparedness and, **36:** 29, 38, 58-59, 63, 84, 118; and militia, **36:** 142-43; **37:** 156; and declaration of war power, **36:** 226n1

United States Fidelity and Guaranty Co., Baltimore, **28:** 397; **30:** 375n3,4

United States Finishing Co., N.Y., **36:** 261n1;

United States Hotel, Paterson, N.J., **34:** 286

United States House of Representatives: *see* United States Congress, House of Representatives

United States Industrial Commission, **29:** 29

United States Marine Corps: and Military Order of the Carabao, **29:** 38-39; in Mexico, **29:** 295, 426, 427-28, 429, 434, 453, 463, 509, 511; **30:** 8, 26, 28

United States Military Academy, **36:** 437; WW's commencement address at, **37:** 212-17; 225

United States Ministers to the Papal States: Instructions and Despatches, 1848-1868 (Stock), **33:** 46n2

United States Naval Academy, **35:** 300; WW's remarks to, **37:** 147-48

United States Navy, **30:** 145, 146; **31:** 423, 452, 508; **35:** 124, 157n1, 170, 181n1, 258, 299-300; Joint Board, **27:** 441,n1, 443, 447; and Military Order of the Carabao, **29:** 38-39, 54-55; at Veracruz, **30:** 26, 28; and continuing education program, **30:** 145,n3; officers should refrain from public comment on European situation, **30:** 352; and Tipperary song incident, **32:** 21,n3; WW on, **33:** 209-12,n1, 216; **36:** 15, 44-45, 61, 67-68, 69, 82, 103, 119-20, 174, 643-44, 646; Admiral Dewey on, **33:** 216n1; Surgeon-General of, **33:** 486n1; and preparedness, **34:** 3, 4-5, 131n2, 267,n1, 514; WW's address to Naval Consulting Board, **35:** 29,n1; B. Tillman on, **36:** 173; N. D. Baker on, **36:** 431; American Union Against Militarism on, **36:** 633; comments on general leasing bill and naval oil reserves, **37:** 39-41, 66, 94, 111, 139-42, 172n2; E. M. House on, **37:** 64, 68, 134, 265-66; and 1916 platform, **37:** 181-82, 187, 195, 207

United States Navy in the Pacific, 1909-1922 (Braisted), **32:** 528n1

United States neutrality: *see* World War

United States Oil Policy (Ise), **36:** 464n1

United States Public Health Service, **37:** 532

United States Secret Service, **28:** 102n2; **35:** 229, 230; **37:** 11

United States Shipping Board, **35:** 459n1; **36:** 366n1; **37:** 104; **38:** 158, 179n1, 196, 546; creation of, **38:** 60n2; W. G. McAdoo's recommendations for appointments to, **38:** 428-29, 454-55

United States Steel Corp., **27:** 215-16,n1,3,4, 223, 232, 252, 259n1, 414; **29:** 93, 95; **30:** 128n1, 482; **31:** 46, 274,n2; **32:** 140; **38:** 190n1; and Tennessee Coal and Iron case, **31:** 268-69

United States Supreme Court, **27:** 71, 243; **28:** 594-95,n1; **29:** 106, 218; **30:** 271; **31:** 110, 247, 438; **33:** 398-99,n3,

United States Supreme Court (*cont.*)
  491, 492; **37:** 140n2; **38:** 97-98, 216, 660
  S. Gompers on, **27:** 182; **30:** 309-10, 313;
  and Interstate Commerce Act, **29:** 28;
  Federal Reserve Board selection process compared to, **29:** 138; and treaties,
  29: 200; and Chandler-Dunbar decision, **30:** 218n3; and J. C. McReynolds,
  30: 285n1, 469; and federal trade commission bill, **30:** 428-29; and Shreveport cases, **30:** 482n7; *Peterhoff* case,
  32: 407; Brandeis nomination, **36:** 19-
  20, 22-23, 25-26, 51, 86, 136, 137,
  425n3, 609-11; **37:** 72, 151,n1; and *Appam* case, **36:** 134n2; and Chinese in
  the U.S., **36:** 550; C. E. Hughes resigns from, **37:** 186,n1, 340; suggestions for new appointment to, **37:** 210,
  264, 267,n1, 268, 278, 365, 372-73, 420,
  421-22; J. H. Clarke appointed, **37:**
  428,n2, 431, 446, 467, 475
United States Tariff Commission, **36:** 250,
  366n1; **38:** 21,n3; pros and cons of establishment of, **35:** 177, 261, 383-
  86,n1,2, 433-34, 477, 510-12, 524, 526-
  27; WW on, **36:** 11-12, 113, 156; **37:** 10,
  37, 392-93, 492, 493; **38:** 129, 136-37,
  266, 308, 333, 463-64, 478, 486, 555-
  56, 574n2; W. C. Redfield on, **36:** 127;
  and Rainey bill, **36:** 206-207,n1, 227;
  and 1916 platform, **37:** 193, 341; appointment suggestions, **38:** 3n2, 297,
  335, 393, 546; B. Baruch on, **38:** 44;
  W. J. Stone on, **38:** 278; J. P. Tumulty
  on, **38:** 514
United States *v.* C. and O. Fuel Co., **29:**
  25
United States *v.* Patterson, **33:** 398n3
United States *v.* United States Steel
  Corp., **27:** 215-16, 223, 232, 252, 259n1,
  414
University Club, N.Y., **27:** 111, 124
University Commission on the Southern
  Race Question, **31:** 464n1
University of the State of New York, **38:**
  182n8
Untermyer, Samuel, **27:** 334, 431-32, 436,
  445, 457, 458, 476; **28:** 597; **33:** 438-
  40; **34:** 74, 472; **36:** 267n1, 602
*Unwanted Boy: The Autobiography of
  Governor Ben W. Hooper* (Boyce), **27:**
  55n3
Upshur, Agnes Maxwell Kearny (Mrs.
  John Henry), **29:** 562,n2
Urbina, Tomás, **28:** 7n1, 163n3, 213
Urion, Alfred Riley, **33:** 509,n1
Urofsky, Melvin Irving, **36:** 25n1
Urrutia, Aureliano, **28:** 195-96,n1, 200,
  278,n2, 282, 339; **29:** 119
Urrutia, Francisco José, **28:** 330,n1
Urueta, Jesús, **28:** 292-93
Uruguay, **28:** 4, 5; **31:** 497; **33:** 455; **34:**
  157n1, 488; **37:** 239; minister to, **27:**
  110n2, 385; and Peru, **29:** 244; and
  Mexico, **33:** 487, 488

Uruquidi, Don Juan, **30:** 101,n1
Utah, **30:** 18; and Hillstrom case, **35:** 58,
  69, 73, 73-74, 206, 206-207, 210, 211,
  213-15, 283n1,2; and I.W.W. investi-
  gation, **36:** 188-90
Utica, N.Y., **34:** 52n2
Utica, N.Y., *Presbyterian Advance*, **27:**
  154n
Utilities Bureau, **36:** 324-25,n2
Utilities Magazine, **36:** 325,n2
Uya, Okon Edet, **27:** 283n1

Vail, Theodore Newton, **32:** 119,n3
Vail, William L., **36:** 364
Val y Zulueta, Alfonso Merry del, **32:** 313;
  34: 19,n1; **35:** 414,n2
Vallestores, Luis, **27:** 548
Valparaiso, Chile, **28:** 188n1
Van Buren, Martin, **37:** 105n4
Vance, John Thomas, **30:** 165; **33:** 218,n2;
  35: 34
Vander Veer, Albert, **38:** 182,n4,8
Vanderbilt, Edith Stuyvesant Dresser
  (Mrs. George Washington II), **28:**
  360,n2
Vanderbilt, George Washington II, **28:**
  360,n2
Vanderbilt, William Evert, **28:** 299-
  300,n5
Vanderbilt Hotel, N.Y., **27:** 81, 385; **29:**
  343,n1
Vanderlip, Frank Arthur, **28:** 41-42,
  428,n1, 429-30; **31:** 139,n4; **34:** 382n1,
  401,n1; **35:** 347
Vanderlip plan, **28:** 428n1, 429-30
Vandiver, Frank Everson, **36:** 285n2,
  335n2
Van Devanter, Willis, **36:** 481,n1
Van Dyke, Henry, **27:** 227-28, 509, 515;
  29: 225; **30:** 364-65; **31:** 375; **33:** 91,n2,
  92; **36:** 429-30; resignation of, **38:** 209,
  210-12, 616
Van Hise, Charles Richard, **27:** 456; **29:**
  326,n2; **30:** 272-73, 281; **35:** 198-99; **38:**
  297,n1
*Vanishing Race: The Last Great Indian
  Council . . .* (Dixon), **27:** 508n2
Van Kennen, George E., **28:** 35,n1, 37,
  64
Van Kleeck, Mary, **35:** 317n2
VanMater, H., **29:** 549
Van Tassel, Mr. (suitor of Eleanor Wil-
  son), **29:** 562,n7
Van Winkle, Wilhelmina Caroline Gin-
  ger (Mrs. Abraham), **37:** 426-27,n1,4
Van Wyck, Robert Anderson, **37:** 33,n4,
  34
Van Zandt, Khleber Miller, Jr., **36:**
  364,n1
Vardaman, James Kimble, **27:** 512, 515;
  28: 97n1, 116, 186n1, 187n4, 210, 344;
  29: 205n2, 319n1; **32:** 173n2; **37:** 429
Varg, Paul A., **27:** 27n1
Vargas, Hermogenes, **36:** 568n1
Vásquez Gómez, Francisco, **28:** 341

Vásquez, Horacio, **32:** 76,n1
Vaughn, Stanton, **31:** 316,n2
Vázquez Tagle, Manuel, **33:** 463,n1
Veiller, Bayard, **27:** 140,n2
Velde, Emil van de, **30:** 470n1
Venezuela, **27:** 145n1; **28:** 432, 543; **29:** 452; **31:** 118; appointments, **28:** 4,n3, 5; and Germany, **28:** 459; and Mexico, **28:** 412
Venice, Italy, **35:** 226
Venizelos, Eleutherios, **38:** 107n1
Vera Estañol, Jorge, **28:** 292
Veracruz, state, Mex., **28:** 31, 77, 78, 131, 471; Mexican troops at Tejar, **29:** 541,n1
Veracruz, Veracruz, Mex., **27:** 519, 539, 546; **28:** 463, 486,n2,3, 592; **29:** 31, 223; **30:** 41, 79, 83, 389; **31:** 65, 66, 178, 323, 374; **32:** 202,n3, 331, 342, 369, 384; **33:** 65,n1, 187, 419, 461, 466; **34:** 204, 532; **37:** 16
   J. Lind and, **28:** 219, 224, 225, 281-82; **29:** 86, 98n1, 126, 329, 338; strikes in, **28:** 297; report of ammunition for Huerta arriving at, **29:** 110,n1; and railroad communications with Mexico City, **29:** 143, 161, 206, 478; false reports of marines being sent to, **29:** 174,n1; American forces in, **29:** 267; bankers in, **29:** 382; U.S. orderly arrested in, **29:** 433, 435, 440, 461, 472; detention of Ward Line ships at, **29:** 447; Admiral Mayo's demands at, **29:** 448; U.S. fleet to move into, **29:** 454; **34:** 160; Carranza orders U.S. fleet to withdraw from, **29:** 485; orders for F. Funston in, **29:** 509, 510; preparation for troops to be sent to, **30:** 7-8, 11, 26, 78; WW memorial address on servicemen killed in, and parade for, **30:** 13-15,n1, 21n1; J. Reed on occupation of, **30:** 42n1, 157, 235; U.S. military administration of, **30:** 73-74; **31:** 23-24; **33:** 9; first U.S. seaman killed at, **30:** 107,n5; impressions U.S. troops will leave in, **30:** 147; and U.S. withdrawal from, **30:** 229; people fleeing Mexico City for, **30:** 361; L. M. Garrison on reinforcement of troops at, **30:** 361; V. Carranza on U.S. occupation of, **31:** 18-19, 71-73, 75; WW on evacuation of troops from, **31:** 33, 143, 313; I. Fabela on occupation, **31:** 67; WW on, **31:** 351-52, 375-76; occupation of compared to Port-au-Prince, **34:** 69
Veracruz invasion: *see* Mexico and the United States
Veracruz Railroad, **29:** 193
Verdi, S.S., **36:** 228
Verdun, France, **36:** 341, 346, 414, 443, 446, 512, 564, 600; **37:** 28, 43, 177, 185, 412, 441; **38:** 90
Vergara, Clemente, **29:** 441
Vernon, Ambrose White, **32:** 346; **36:** 483,n1

Vernon, Leroy Tudor, **34:** 65n1
Vernon, Mabel, **38:** 28
Verona, S.S., **36:** 228
Veteran Employees Association of the Schuylkill Division of the Pennsylvania Railroad, **33:** 442,n1
Veteran Preacher, **36:** 331n1,2,3
Veto Message—Army Appropriations Bill . . . , **38:** 40n1
Veyra, Jaime Carlos de, **38:** 633,n1, 648
Vick, Walker Whiting, **27:** 84, 385, 495; **30:** 164, 165; **31:** 403, 410, 411, 447, 448, 453, 467; **33:** 218; **34:** 107; **35:** 34, 285-86,n1
Victor-American Fuel Co., **28:** 518n1; **29:** 549
Victoria (of England), **30:** 152
Victoria, Tamaulipas, Mex.: *see* Ciudad Victoria
Victoria, Texas, **37:** 255
Vicuña, Ramón Subercaseaux: *see* Subercaseaux Vicuña, Ramón
Vienna, Austria, **30:** 325; **33:** 489; **34:** 403,n1
Vienna, University of, **35:** 395n2
Viereck, George Sylvester, **31:** 337-38,n3
Villa, Francisco (Pancho), **27:** 422n1; **28:** 77; **29:** 292, 515, 552; **30:** 12, 39, 42, 138, 297; **31:** 18, 19, 69, 206, 233, 380, 411,n2; **32:** 326, 343, 355-56, 369, 383n1, 404; **33:** 5, 7, 9, 12, 29, 45, 259, 260, 261, 271, 272, 295, 398,n1, 400,n1, 409-10, 463, 464, 476, 488; **34:** 41,n2, 149n1, 175, 242, 267n1, 382n1, 455n1, 456, 488, 531; **37:** 138n1, 159, 171, 281, 316; **38:** 8, 45, 166,n2, 167, 223, 229, 230, 271-72, 293, 362, 379, 399, 403, 546-47, 547, 560
   J. Lind's word portrait of, **29:** 14, 123; and relations with V. Carranza, **29:** 90; **30:** 193-94,n1, 208, 220-21, 285-86,n1, 303n1, 347-48, 383n1, 415, 441; **31:** 69, 73, 322; C. A. Spring Rice on personality and background of, **29:** 169, 229, 249, 324-25, 348; and treatment of prisoners, **29:** 188, 450,n1, 523; J. J. Jusserand on, **29:** 237; and Spaniards in Mexico, **29:** 241-42, 416, 417; T. B. Hohler and W. J. Bryan discussion of, **29:** 252-53, 253, 257, 258, 260; and relationship to Constitutionalists, **29:** 278-80; and Benton affair, **29:** 285n1, 293, 294, 301n2, 320n1; and recapture of Torreón, **29:** 382n1; meeting with G. Carothers, **29:** 494-95; U. S. protection of its borders and, **29:** 498; on Carranza note and hopes for peace, **29:** 504-505; Great Britain's fear of, **30:** 4, 9, 11, 33, 59, 82, 246; G. F. Williams on, **30:** 25, 25-26; Spring Rice on WW's confidence in, **30:** 29; J. Reed on, **30:** 42n1, 156; and treatment of foreigners, **30:** 80, 81; WW on, **30:** 131, 143,n2; L. J. Canova and, **30:** 180, 285; and Zacatecas affair, **30:** 193n2; and re-

Villa, Francisco (Pancho) (*cont.*)
ports that he will do what U.S. wishes,
30: 203; E. Grey fearful of presidency
of, **30:** 215; W. Kent on, **30:** 230,n3; and
P. N. Furber, **30:** 246,n4; on importance of harmony among the Constitutionalists, **30:** 290
and Torreón Agreement, **30:** 301n1,
339; claims Carranza violated Torreón
Agreement, **30:** 311; recruiting sup-
plies and men, **30:** 361; and agrarian
reform, **30:** 339-40; G. C. Carothers
picture of, **30:** 340; Cardinal Gibbons
on European feelings toward, **30:** 341;
activities of in Chihuahua, **30:** 347;
P. Fuller's mission and, **30:** 363n3, 408,
409-10, 418, 463; wishes elections to
be held, **30:** 392-93; resignation of, **30:**
410; wishes to see democratic government established in Mexico, **30:** 411;
on WW, **30:** 411, 415, 418; and loyalty
to his soldiers, **30:** 413, 415-16; and
plans to go to Sonora, **30:** 417-18; letter to W. J. Bryan on reforms, **30:** 443-
44, 444-47; on elections, **30:** 446-47;
U.S. reply, **30:** 450; E. M. House on,
30: 463-64; P. Fuller's letter of introduction to, **30:** 494; House on Spring
Rice's views of, **31:** 61; A. Obregón and,
31: 70; and religious situation in Mexico, **32:** 279, 280; D. West's interviews
with, **32:** 383-85, 385-89; and E. Zapata, **32:** 387; and battles of Celaya,
33: 7n1, 29n1; and González Garza, **33:**
343n1, 344; and Columbus raid, **36:**
280n1, 281, 282-83, 284-85; and Punitive Expedition, **36:** 286, 287, 301,n1,
308,n1, 310, 313,n1, 317, 342, 343, 344,
365, 381, 382n2, 396n1, 397, 407n1,
424, 434, 457, 502, 528, 553-54, 571,
579, 582, 589, 653; U.S. intention to
capture, **37:** 248-63; photographs: *illustration sections,* **31**, **36;** *see also*
Mexico and the United States—Puni-
tive Expedition
Villa Ahumada, Chihuahua, Mex., **37:**
280, 315, 317, 319; **38:** 378, 379, 381,
382
Villa Brackenridge, San Antonio, Tex.,
30: 399
*Villa's Columbus Raid: Practical Poli-
tics or German Design?* (Munch), **36:**
280n1
Villard, Julia Breckenridge Sandford
(Mrs. Oswald Garrison), **35:** 69,n1, 83
Villard, Oswald Garrison, **27:** 442,n2; **28:**
60-61, 65, 165, 185-86, 191, 239-40,
245-46, 289-90, 316, 332, 342-44, 348-
50, 352-53, 401-402, 413-14, 498n1; **29:**
105, 319, 323, 495-96, 499; **30:** 443, 455-
56, 479; **31:** 361n2, 506; **33:** 213, 254-
55, 257, 347,n2, 532; **34:** 110,n1, 248,
324, 428, 466, 477, 515; **35:** 69, 83, 120,
141-43, 157, 191, 192; and race-com-

mission plan, **28:** 185-86, 202; letter
from B. T. Washington, **28:** 186-87,n1;
M. C. Nerney report, **28:** 402-10; on
Germany, **30:** 456; editorials on segregation in federal departments, **31:**
328,n2,3; on L. Wood and conscription
issue, **31:** 475-76, 502; on conference of
neutral nations, **33:** 141, 154; on first
Lusitania note, **33:** 201-202,n1, 225-26;
and alleged Wilson-House break, **34:**
378n2, 402-403,n1; congratulates WW
on *Arabic* pledge, **34:** 411-12; on preparedness, **34:** 412
Villareal, Antonio I., **32:** 279
Ville de la Ciotat, S.S., **35:** 425-26
Villistas, **30:** 230n1, 301n1; **33:** 459-60,n1,
460, 474; **34:** 451, 541; **35:** 478n1; **36:**
280n1, 287, 395n1, 424, 502, 585, 587;
37: 39, 138n1; **38:** 225, 293, 547
Vincent, Robert W., **32:** 56n2
Vinita, Okla.: and postmastership in, **36:**
179
Viño, Pedro, **37:** 255,n6, 261
Virgin Islands: *see* Danish West Indies
Virginia, **27:** 37, 73,n2, 86, 200n2; **28:**
107; **35:** 39; **37:** 228n1, 228-29; and
Declaration (Bill) of Rights, **28:** 436-
37; road system in, **29:** 355-56; and
Negro Organization Society, **31:** 261,
270, 321; and National Negro Exposi-
tion, **33:** 464
Virginia, University of, **27:** 73n1; **31:**
261n2; **32:** 3n1, 25; **36:** 657; **38:** 335,n1,
680; WW on Phi Kappa Psi, **29:** 436
Virginia Bill of Rights, **35:** 295, 314, 323;
36: 36, 386
Virginia: Bourbonism to Byrd, 1870-1925
(Moger), **27:** 73n2
Virginia Industrial School for Colored
Girls, **31:** 261n2
Virginia Press Association, **30:** 210n1
Virginia State Federation of Labor, **37:**
376n1
Vitagraph Co., **36:** 16n1
Viviani, René Raphaël, **35:** 174n1
vocational education, **30:** 105; **35:** 308; **36:**
357,n1; WW on, **36:** 13, 29-30; **38:** 420,
582-83; and 1916 platform, **37:** 199
vocational education bill, **36:** 357,n1,
370,n1; **37:** 173,n1,2
Voice of the Revolution, **37:** 245
Vollmer, Henry, **31:** 426,n1
Von Papen, Franz: *see* Papen, Franz von
Vonnoh, Bessie Potter (Mrs. Robert Wil-
liam), **28:** 189,n1, 252,n1
Vonnoh, Robert William, **28:** 43,n8, 45,
62, 66, 92, 101, 149, 150, 199, 252, 256,
266, 269, 278, 286, 338; **32:** 75
Voorhis, John R., **38:** 549,n1
Vopica, Charles Joseph, **28:** 4,n2, 5
*Voyage of the Deutschland: The First
Merchant Submarine* (König), **37:**
425n2

Vreeland, Alice May Brown (Mrs. Williamson Updike), **29:** 558n4
Vreeland, May, **29:** 558n4
Vreeland, Williamson Updike, **29:** 558n4
Vrooman, Carl, **38:** 511n1
Vyvere, Alois, Burgrave van de, **35:** 391,n1

W. R. Grace and Co., N.Y., **35:** 347n2
Wabash Railroad, **30:** 344
Wade, Edward Charles, Jr., **36:** 566-67,n1
Wade, Festus John, **27:** 79,n2; **28:** 444; **31:** 129, 148, 210
Wadsworth, James Wolcott, **34:** 166,n2
Wadsworth, James Wolcott, Jr., **34:** 166,n2
Wagner, Robert Ferdinand, **38:** 429, 549,n1; New York postmastership offer and declination, **36:** 485, 520,n1, 520-21, 523, 525, 529, 530, 542,n1, 562-63
Wagner Refuses Wilson's Plea He Be Postmaster (New York *World*), **36:** 542n1
Waimana case, **34:** 454, 460,n1
Wakenitz, Baron Oscar von der Lancken, **35:** 489-91,n1
Walbridge, Marguerite, **28:** 327,n1, 333, 338, 345, 360
Walcott, Frederic Collin, **38:** 368,n1, 369-72
Wald, Lillian D., **27:** 76; **33:** 472; **34:** 250,n1, 252; **36:** 524-25, 562,n2, 632n1; and colloquy with WW on antipreparedness, **36:** 634-49
Waldeck Rousseau, Madame Pierre Marie René, **35:** 88n2
Waldorf-Astoria Hotel, N.Y., **28:** 345, 355; **33:** 37n1, 216n1; **35:** 278; **36:** 3n1, 7n1, 560n1; **37:** 332n1; **38:** 591n1
Wales, **30:** 61,n2
Wales, Julia Grace, **33:** 314n2
Wales in British Politics, 1868-1922 (Morgan), **30:** 61n2
Walker, Edwin Robert, **27:** 88,n4
Walker, Harry Wilson, **32:** 242,n1, 259
Walker, Henry Oliver, **28:** 103,n2, 126
Walker, Henry William: cartoons of, *illustration section:* **29**
Walker, John Brisben, **35:** 221n1
Walker, Laura Margaret Marquand (Mrs. Henry Oliver), **28:** 103,n2, 126
Walker, Mary Edwards, **29:** 215,n1
Walker, Oliver, **28:** 126
Walker, Thomas, **31:** 308
Walker, William, **33:** 46n1
Wall Street, **27:** 497; **38:** 671; WW on, **38:** 308-10, 367, 593-94, 595, 603; J. Gilman on, **38:** 321-22
Wallace, Henry Milton, **37:** 524n2
Wallace, Hugh Campbell, **27:** 119, 120, 152, 254, 292; **28:** 597; **29:** 32, 159; **31:** 95, 295, 377, 498, 500, 552, 560; **32:** 61, 161, 220, 231, 268,n1; **36:** 405; **37:**

206; **38:** 139, 139-41, 349, 616; ambassadorial possibilities, **27:** 127; cabinet possibilities, **27:** 27, 61, 70, 131, 132-33; and W. J. Bryan, **34:** 133, 135, 146,n1
Wallace, Jouett Lee, **27:** 241,n1
Wallace, William, **27:** 241,n1, 242; **29:** 238,n1, 345, 508; **30:** 437, 439,n1; **31:** 3; **36:** 190n3
Wallace, Mrs. William, **29:** 372, 508
Wallace, William Hockaday, **38:** 335,n3
Wallas, Graham, **31:** 108, 316n2, 317
Wallenberg, Knut Agathon, **34:** 251,n4,5
Wallenberg, Marcus, **35:** 196
Walmesley, Mr., **30:** 364,n1
Walpole, N.H., **28:** 92
Walsenburg, Colo., **28:** 522; **29:** 529; **30:** 60; **31:** 407
Walsh, David Ignatius, **28:** 275; **29:** 338,n1, 339, 340, 374; **30:** 85, 86, 96, 123,n2, 163,n1; **31:** 237-38, 297, 300; **33:** 68n1
Walsh, Francis Patrick, **27:** 465, 476, 487, 552, 553; **30:** 64-65; **31:** 353; **32:** 325n1; **35:** 183, 185; **37:** 291n1, 310, 402; **38:** 445n1
Walsh, Thomas James, **32:** 114,n3, 115; **36:** 265, 316, 355n1, 360, 472n1, 518, 521, 606; **37:** 140, 169,n1, 237,n1; **38:** 46-47,n1, 63-64, 376, 489n1, 662-63; on water-power legislation, **36:** 311-12, 324-29; on leasing bill controversy, **37:** 269-70, 304-305; suggested for Supreme Court, **37:** 373
Walsh Act (New Jersey), **27:** 456
Walter, Ferdinand, **33:** 185
Walter Hines Page: Ambassador to the Court of St. James (Gregory), **29:** 333n1
Walter Hines Page: The Southerner as American, 1855-1918 (Cooper), **34:** 55n1; **38:** 241n1
Walter Reed General Army Hospital, **27:** 200n4
Walters, Alexander, **27:** 19-20, 291; **28:** 289; **29:** 204-205,n1; **30:** 492; **32:** 472, 479; **34:** 504-505, 511; **35:** 68, 461, 461-62; **36:** 481,n2, 488
Walters, Henry, **31:** 149,n1
Wambaugh, Eugene, **31:** 86; **32:** 538n3
Wambaugh, Sarah, **32:** 538,n3
Wanamaker, John, **28:** 435,n3
Wanamaker, Lewis Rodman, **27:** 507n1, 508,n2
Wanderer's Necklace (Haggard), **31:** 316,n2, 317
Wang, Hung-lien, **38:** 151, 152
War, Department of, **27:** 77n3, 441; **30:** 159, 217, 224n1, 392; **31:** 215; **33:** 258; **34:** 4, 38, 58, 208, 392, 480-81,n1; **35:** 106, 139, 181, 229, 298; **36:** 143, 176; **38:** 156, 167; and segregation in, **31:** 299; and Haiti, **34:** 60; leaks in, **34:** 248; resignation of L. M. Garrison, **36:** 164-65; resignation of H. S. Breckinridge,

War, Department of (*cont.*)
36: 165; C. R. Crane's suggestions for
Secretary, **36:** 177-78; N. D. Baker ap-
pointed Secretary, **36:** 259-60
War and America (Münsterberg), **31:**
276n2
War and Peace (periodical), **37:** 294n1
War and Peace (Hapgood), **33:** 516,n1
War and the Nitrogen Supply (*Scientific
American*), **36:** 345n2
War and the Way Out (*Atlantic Monthly*),
32: 24, 53
*War Industries Board: Business-Govern-
ment Relations during World War I*
(Cuff), **36:** 432n1, 601n4
War Lords (Gardiner), **34:** 476n1, 510,n1;
35: 35
War Memories of David Lloyd George, **36:**
180n1
War Not Contemplated in President's
Policy (New York *Evening Post*), **33:**
201n1
War of 1812, **31:** 109, 118, 337, 437, 439,
544
War of the Pacific (1879-1884), **32:** 474n3
War Preparedness (Butler), **31:** 413n3
War Relief Commission (Rockefeller
Foundation), **38:** 371n4
war revenue bill (emergency revenue
bill), **31:** 32,n1, 133; **35:** 31, 303, 304,
370n1
War Risk Insurance, Bureau of, **31:** 193,
250, 360
war risk insurance bill, **30:** 402, 432, 454;
32: 166
Warburg, Paul Moritz, **27:** 79,n1, 126,
476; **31:** 315, 386,n2; **34:** 107, 276-77,
278, 279-80, 369; **35:** 64; **36:** 267n1; **37:**
291; **38:** 32-33,n1, 39; and Federal Reserve Board, **29:** 532, 536-37, 541; as
candidate for Federal Reserve Board,
30: 23, 27, 30,n1, 51, 52-53, 54, 181n1,
191n1, 263,n1, 270, 279-80, 288, 317,
345; C. H. Dodge on, **30:** 282; WW asks
to appear before Senate Banking and
Currency Committee, **30:** 304; confirmation of, **30:** 304n1, 353
Ward, Mr., **32:** 26
Ward, Artemus, **27:** 433
Ward, W. P., **28:** 427
Ward Line, **29:** 447, 464, 477
warehouse bill: *see* Lever-Smith warehouse bill
Warehouse Act of 1916, **37:** 197; **38:** 130,
425-26
*Warehousing Cotton and Financing
Warehouse Receipts* (McLaurin), **34:**
400n1
Waring, Miss, **34:** 246,n2, 247
Waring, Robert Lewis, **30:** 491-93,n1, 493;
32: 515
Warner, John DeWitt, **27:** 29,n3
Warren, Charles, **31:** 451,n1; **33:** 471; **34:**
110

Warren, Francis Emroy, **38:** 239,n10
Warren, Whitney, **37:** 42,n1
Warren and Wetmore, N.Y., **37:** 42n1
Warrington, John Wesley, **38:** 534n1
Warsaw, Poland, **32:** 213, 237; **34:** 12, 17-
18, 44, 239
Warwick, Walter Winter, **32:** 125,n1
Washington State, **27:** 220,n2, 221, 361;
37: 432,n1; and I.W.W. investigation,
36: 188-90
Washington, Booker Taliaferro, **28:**
117n5, 186, 186-87, 240, 344; **29:** 290,
302; **30:** 45; **31:** 261, 312-13, 322; **32:**
272; **35:** 240n1, 400n1
Washington, George, **27:** 159, 391; **28:**
437; **29:** 420, 448; **30:** 35; **31:** 351; **33:**
335; **36:** 142, 320n1, 391-92,n2; **37:** 126,
222, 296, 449, 520; **38:** 144, 347, 520,
616
Washington, D.C., **27:** xvi, 76, 211, 212,
306, 323, 324, 394; **28:** 13-14, 46, 308,
337, 438; **30:** 254; **32:** 118n1, 430, 496;
33: 340; **34:** 165, 180, 292, 456, 513,
534; **36:** 26n3; juvenile court judge, **27:**
109; WW's remarks at a Princeton
smoker, **27:** 147-48; women's working
conditions, **27:** 243; WW on breaking
precedents, **27:** 285, 294-95,n1; WW's
remarks to Gridiron Club, **27:** 294-97;
model city plans, **27:** 433; discrimination and segregation in, **28:** 60,n3,
115n3, 164, 187,n4, 210, 343, 344-
45,n1, 349, 402-10, 410; **31:** 300, 361n2;
storm damage, **28:** 102, 103, 105,
108,n1; inscriptions for Post Office
Building, **28:** 366,n1; alley rehabilita-
tion, **28:** 540,n1; **29:** 164; **31:** 29, 114;
R. H. Terrell appointment as munici-
pal court judge, **29:** 205n2, 290n1, 388,
394; "half-and-half" provision, **29:**
240,n2; and taxes, **29:** 355; WW on not
being able to enjoy and see the city,
29: 364-65; Recorder of the Deeds appointment in, **29:** 540-41, 543; **33:**
71,n1; unveiling of statue of John
Barry, **30:** 34n1; WW's remarks to
Princeton Alumni Association of, **30:**
103-108; WW and wage increase for
street cleaners in, **31:** 147,n1, 183, 192;
WW on loneliness in, **31:** 281; im-
proved housing and Ellen Wilson Memorial in, **31:** 560,n2, 561; **33:** 430-
32,n1,6; WW's talk to YMCA in, **32:**
125-27; and Pan-American conference
on Mexico, **34:** 111-12, 460, 488; WW
on, **34:** 119, 170; EBG on, **34:** 155;
WW's address to D.A.R., **35:** 47-51
Washington, U.S.S., **34:** 45n1
*Washington: A History of the Capital
1800-1950* (Green), **33:** 430n2
Washington and Lee University, **33:** 491
Washington-Berlin 1908/1917 (Doerries), **33:** 473n1; **35:** 43n1

Washington: Capital City (Green), **29:** 240n2

Washington Country Club, **29:** 456, 531, 536

Washington *Evening Post*, **36:** 350

Washington *Evening Star*, **27:** 9,n3; **33:** 37n2, 71n1; **38:** 20

Washington Herald, **27:** 498

Washington Monument, **37:** 221n1

Washington Nationals, **27:** 299n1

Washington Post, **27:** 328-29; **28:** 301, 373,n1,2, 486,n1, 498n1, 560; **29:** 275, 391n1, 407; **31:** 16n1, 104,n1, 374n1; **32:** 14,n2, 193n1, 215n1, 240; **33:** 134,n1,2,4, 162,n2, 315, 378,n1; **34:** 199n1, 333n1, 486,n1; **35:** 41, 371n1; **36:** 366n1, 396n1, 476n, 489n1, 572n1; **37:** 221n1, 353n1, 427n4, 439n1, 442n1; **38:** 548n1, 571n2, 637n1, 671n1

Washington Star, **31:** 413; **32:** 249,n1

Washington Times, **28:** 137n1; **35:** 235n1, 256-57; **36:** 304,n1, 305,n1, 355,n1; **38:** 159,n3

water power, **31:** 173, 416-17; **32:** 35

water-power legislation, **36:** 355,n1, 570; **37:** 12-13, 197, 313, 328, 359,n1; G. Pinchot on, **36:** 48-51; F. K. Lane on, **36:** 241-44, 301; W. Kent on, **36:** 265, 310; WW on, **36:** 277, 299, 316, 322; W. C. Adamson on, **36:** 302-304, 304-306; and Lever amendment, **36:** 345, 348; *see also* Adamson water-power bill; Ferris water-power bill

Waterfalls Harbor, **33:** 35

Waterford, Conn., **37:** 382

Waters-Pierce Oil Co., **28:** 527n1, 578; **29:** 550

Watertown, N.Y., **38:** 521

Waterville, Me., **28:** 149n1

Watkins Glen, N.Y., **34:** 247

Watson, Ebbie Julian, **33:** 495,n1

Watson, James Eli, **38:** 457,n2

Watson, Robert, **37:** 270-71,n2, 305

Watson, Thomas Augustus, **32:** 118,n1

Watson, William, **31:** 279

Watterson, Henry, **31:** 65, 83-84, 90, 318

Watterson, Rebecca Ewing (Mrs. Henry), **31:** 83

Wattles, Gurden Wallace, **38:** 343n1

Watts, George Frederic, **37:** 32

Waukegan, Ill.: WW's remarks on preparedness in, **36:** 52-53

Ways and Means Committee (House of Reps.), **27:** 20, 123, 261, 303; **28:** 385; **30:** 402; **35:** 459, 512; **36:** 206-207; **37:** 308; **38:** 666

We Shall Be All: A History of the Industrial Workers of the World (Dubofsky), **34:** 539n2

We Want Wilson in the White House/ Four Years More (song), **38:** 608n1

Weather Bureau, United States, **27:** 338n1

Weatherford, Willis Duke, **31:** 464n1

Weaver, Claude, **28:** 90,n1; **30:** 113,n7

Weaver, S. Townsend, **38:** 157,n1

Webb, Beatrice Potter (Mrs. Sidney James), **35:** 223n2

Webb, Edwin Yates, **29:** 413; **33:** 457,n2; **37:** 363; **38:** 21, 78

Webb, Sidney James, **35:** 223,n2

Webb, Ulysses Sigel, **27:** 365n1, 371

Webb, William Robert, **27:** 55n3

Webb Act, **27:** 366, 382, 396; **31:** 47n3; **38:** 21,n2, 78, 146,n2, 267

Webb and Prall, **28:** 327

Webster, Daniel, **38:** 326

Webster, James Edwin, **35:** 262n3, 275

Webster, John Lee, **38:** 337,n2, 342

Webster, Mary, **34:** 215,n1

Wedel, Count Karl von, **37:** 507,n1

Weeks, Bartow S., **27:** 246

Weeks, G. F., **36:** 301,n1

Weeks, John Wingate, **27:** 483; **28:** 414; **29:** 86; **30:** 229n1; **32:** 197,n1

Weeks shipping bill, **32:** 197-98,n1,2

Weeks-Gore shipping bill, **32:** 240n1, 241n1

Weinstein, Edwin Alexander, **34:** 491n1

Weintraub, Hyman, **27:** 188n2; **30:** 223n1; **31:** 458n1

Weir, Julian Alden, **28:** 195,n4

Weisman, Henry, **34:** 52,n2, 116, 120

Weiss, Nancy Joan, **27:** 291n1

Weitzel, E. H., **28:** 510, 548

Welborn, Jesse Floyd, **28:** 427, 475, 507, 512, 514, 518-24, 580, 583, 584; **31:** 43, 48, 48-54, 77, 78, 87; **35:** 539

Welch, William Henry, **27:** 91, 517; **37:** 468,n1, 472, 473, 492, 494; **38:** 183, 372

Welland Canal, **32:** 141; **37:** 45, 425n1

Welles, Sumner, **29:** 20n1

Wellesley College, **34:** 58n1

Welliver, Judson Churchill, **38:** 159,n1,2, 335

Wells College, N.Y., **28:** 302n5

Welsh, Clarence F., **36:** 636,n12

Welsh bill, **36:** 636-37,n12, 646

Wenderoth, Oscar, **28:** 502,n1

Wescott, John Wesley, **36:** 580-81; **37:** 286; **38:** 285n2; on L. D. Brandeis, **27:** 92

Wesleyan University, **27:** 208, 541; **32:** 78n1, 449; **34:** 87; and Stockton Axson, **36:** 297,n1,2,3, 329, 349, 399-400

West, Andrew Fleming, **28:** 315, 337; **31:** 205

West, Duval, **32:** 202-203, 344,n1, 383-91, 507,n1, 508; **33:** 51, 65,n1, 69, 153, 187,n1, 194, 251, 293, 398,n1; appointed special representative to Mexico, **32:** 202,n2, 202-203; WW's instructions to, **32:** 203-204; letter of introduction, **32:** 210; reports on interviews with F. Villa, **32:** 383-84, 385-89, 389-91; impressions of E. Zapata, **33:** 217-18,n1

West, George P., **28:** 426n1

West, Harry, **27:** 554
West, James R., **27:** 244
West, Samuel H., **31:** 353n2
West Indies, Danish: *see* Danish West Indies
West Point: *see* United States Military Academy
West Virginia: coal strike, **27:** 291-92,n2
Westcott, Edith F. Sampson (Mrs. John Howell), **38:** 682n1
Westcott, John Howell, **38:** 682n1
Western Electric Co., **34:** 27n1
Western New England Magazine, **28:** 181,n3, 191
Western Oil Interests Urge Attorney General not to Hamper Reserve Field Grabs (*New York Herald*), **37:** 141n4
Western Sash and Door Co., Kansas City, Mo., **38:** 187n1
Western Union Telegraph Co., **29:** 45n1; **34:** 117; **36:** 281
Westminster Congregational Chapel, London, **29:** 263n1
Weston, Thomas, Jr., **30:** 119n1
Weyl, Walter Edward, **38:** 445n1
Weyler y Nicolau, Valeriano, **28:** 29; **31:** 339
Whaling, Thornton, **36:** 371,n1; **38:** 191
What Could Germany Do For Ireland? (McGuire), **38:** 5n1
What Does America Stand For? (Gardiner), **37:** 265n1
What Eight Million Women Want (Dorr), **30:** 226n4
What is Wrong with Germany? (Dawson), **33:** 19n3
What of the Philippines? (*Columbus, Ohio, Dispatch*), **36:** 172n2
What Progressives May Ask of Mr. Hughes (*New Republic*), **38:** 3n4
What Publicity Can Do (Brandeis), **29:** 30n1
What the President is Trying to do for Mexico (Lowry), **29:** 92-98
Wheat, Henry A., **34:** 171,n1
Wheeler, Benjamin Ide, **32:** 63
Wheeler, George Wakeman, **37:** 268,n1, 365
Wheeler, Harry Andrew, **29:** 278,n2, 483,n1, 500, 532; **30:** 27; **37:** 504-505, 530
Wheeler, Joseph, **30:** 22
Wheeler, Post, **33:** 115,n2, 131
When a Man Comes to Himself (Wilson), **33:** 380; **34:** 57,n1; **35:** 431n1; **36:** 177; **38:** 259,n3
Where the Banker is Superfluous (Brandeis), **29:** 30n1
Whig party, **38:** 303
Whipple, Thomas King, **34:** 470n1
Whitby, England, **32:** 380
White (household help), **28:** 190, 367-68; **33:** 434, 435; **34:** 74
White, Andrew Dickson, **33:** 17

White, Edward Douglass, **32:** 486; **33:** 17; **38:** 14, 19, 33
White, Henry, **27:** 222; **28:** 291,n1,2,3; **30:** 154; **31:** 404-406,n3, 425; on J. W. Gerard, **32:** 481-83
White, John Barber, **38:** 455,n4, 456
White, John Campbell, **28:** 291,n3; **31:** 383,n2
White, John D., **31:** 310
White John Philip, **29:** 479; **30:** 46, 485-86; **31:** 31-32, 40, 81, 99
White, Olive Moore (Mrs. Archibald Sylvester), **38:** 140,n3
White, Ronald C., Jr., **31:** 464n1
White, Sallie Lindsay (Mrs. William Allen), **38:** 3n2
White, William Allen, **30:** 32; **33:** 247; **35:** 178; **38:** 3n2
White Chief: James Kimble Vardaman (Holmes), **28:** 187n4; **34:** 108n4
White House, **33:** 537; Taft on, **27:** 16-18; renovation and redecoration of, **28:** 86; storm damage to grounds, **28:** 102, 103, 105; yellow room, **28:** 532; WW library and workroom, **29:** 517, 518; photograph: *illustration section*, **28**
White Mountains, N.H., **28:** 102, 104, 114, 131-32, 133, 138, 321, 327, 333, 345, 360
White River Junction, N.H., **28:** 98, 189, 266
White Star Line, **34:** 257
White Sulphur Springs, W.Va., **29:** 420n1, 439, 449; **34:** 160; **35:** 38
Whitehead, Thomas Henderson, **33:** 32,n2
Whitehead, Wilbur Cherrier, **31:** 316n2, 317
Whitlock, Brand, **31:** 177, 181, 207, 496; **35:** 77, 134, 258, 280,n2,3, 390, 392, 407-408, 490-91; **36:** 378; **37:** 364; **38:** 661-62; and Cavell case, **35:** 103,n2, 147-48,n1,2,3, 149; offered but declined Russian ambassadorship, **36:** 86, 135-36, 230-31; talk of as vice-presidential candidate, **36:** 249
Whitlock, Ella Brainerd (Mrs. Brand), **35:** 258
Whitman, Charles Seymour, **28:** 138,n1; **31:** 117n1, 267; **35:** 156,n2, 177; **36:** 636n12, 637
Whitman, Olive Hitchcock, **28:** 138n1
Whittaker, Albert Conser, **27:** 206-207
Whittaker, J. K., Jr., **29:** 208
Whittier, John Greenleaf, **31:** 158
Who's Who in America, **27:** 117n1
Why War? (Howe), **38:** 60,n4
Wiart, Henri Carton de, **30:** 470n1
Wichita *Daily Eagle*, **38:** 666,n2
Wicker, George Ray, **37:** 363,n3
Wickser, John G., **29:** 401n1
Wickersham, George Woodward, **27:** 109, 116; **38:** 566,n6
Wickliffe, Lydia Cooke (Mrs. Robert Charles), **27:** 108,n1

Wickliffe, Robert Charles, **27**: 108n1
Wiegand, Karl H. von, **32**: 516n1, 522; **33**: 371
Wiggin, Albert Henry, **31**: 139,n2, 148
Wilber, David Forrest, **32**: 402,n1
Wilcox, William Russel, **35**: 318,n2, 319
Wilder, Wilber Elliott, **37**: 39,n1
Wilder, William Royal, **30**: 156; **38**: 518
Wiley, Anna Kelton (Mrs. Harvey Washington), **30**: 226,n3, 227-28
Wiley, Louis, **34**: 542-43; **37**: 14-15, 282
Wilhelm Platz, S.S., **36**: 616
Wilhelmina (of the Netherlands), **29**: 254; **30**: 334; **33**: 362
Wilhelmina affair, **32**: 380, 381,n1; **36**: 615
Wilkins, Mary, **28**: 399
Willard, Arthur L., **31**: 383
Willard, Daniel, **31**: 20,n3; **38**: 38,n1, 182, 386
Willard, Joseph Edward, **27**: 200,n2, 228; **32**: 423, 439, 442, 456, 462, 475, 480, 504; **33**: 47, 123,n6; **36**: 378-79,n4; **37**: 320,n3, 346; **38**: 33-34, 82
Willcox, William Russell, **38**: 284,n3
Willert, Arthur, **32**: 449n1
William II of Germany, **27**: 521; **29**: 74, 531; **31**: 16, 282, 315, 355, 370,n2, 388,n1; **32**: 75, 206, 256, 301, 349, 352, 375, 403, 506, 522; **33**: 47, 299, 321, 371, 372, 406, 454, 478, 483, 524; **34**: 12, 18, 46, 47, 83-84, 135, 187, 238, 239, 342n1, 376, 405n1, 441-42, 454; **35**: 26, 88n4, 142, 193-94, 359; **36**: 413,n2, 656; **37**: 337, 407, 414, 445,n1, 470; **38**: 71, 72, 177n2, 254, 314n2, 458, 494n1, 495n1
and E. M. House peace mission, **30**: 23, 109, 139-40,n3, 200, 247, 248, 256, 258, 265, 462, 462-63, 464; letter from House to, **30**: 266-67; House on peace hopes and, **30**: 489; House proposes future visit to, **31**: 385; House on materialism of, **31**: 387
WW's offer of good offices to, **30**: 342; Prince Lichnowsky's feelings toward, **30**: 368; on how Germany became involved in the war, **30**: 382-83,n1; O. G. Villard on, **30**: 456,n2; W. J. Bryan on Bernstorff's feelings toward, **30**: 457; and peace moves, **31**: 14, 15, 21n1, 76, 519, 537; on destruction of Louvain, **31**: 17; compared to Napoleon I, **31**: 22; WW's draft of reply to, **31**: 32-33; and dumdum bullets, **31**: 40n1; and J. W. Gerard, **31**: 405, 427; WW reads Gardiner's sketch of, **31**: 482,n1; and George V, **32**: 304,n1; and Mexico, **33**: 298n1; J. W. Gerard meets with, **36**: 614-16; on aid to Poland, **38**: 64-66
William Gibbs McAdoo: A Passion for Change, 1863-1917 (Broesamle), **28**: 156n1; **37**: 187n4
William Jennings Bryan, II (Coletta), **27**:

277n1; **28**: 302n3; **33**: 370,n1, 425n1
William Lyon Mackenzie King: A Political Biography, 1874-1923 (Dawson), **35**: 317n2
William Marsh Rice Institute: *see* Rice Institute
William Wordsworth, His Life, Works and Influence (Harper), **36**: 274n1
William P. Frye, S.S., **32**: 380,n1
Williams, Bertha Rose Knefler (Mrs. Charles Richard), **38**: 630,n3, 644
Williams, Charles Richard, **38**: 629-30,n1, 664
Williams, Dixon C., **36**: 577n1, 603,n1; **38**: 146,n1
Williams, Edward Thomas, **27**: 267,n1; **28**: 401,n1; **31**: 546; **32**: 245, 414, 426, 434, 435, 466; on far eastern crisis, **32**: 135-37, 148-49, 177-78, 319-22, 368
Williams, George, **36**: 281,n4
Williams, Sir George, **31**: 225,n6
Williams, George Fred, **27**: 334; **28**: 327, 354; **30**: 25, 25-26; **34**: 15n1
Williams, John Sharp, **27**: 268n4; **28**: 140, 141, 153, 389,n2, 425, 498n1, 560; **29**: 184-85, 208-209, 221, 387-88, 394, 418, 482,n1, 495, 500, 556; **30**: 286, 392, 424; **31**: 316,n2, 457; **32**: 199, 274-75; **33**: 457-58, 556; **35**: 181,n1; **36**: 20,n1, 21, 137, 240-41, 264; **37**: 431n1; **38**: 142n1; WW and appointment suggestions, **34**: 107-108, 226, 273
Williams, John Skelton, **29**: 532,n1; **30**: 27, 53, 54, 84n1; **31**: 264-65; **34**: 277-78, 345; **37**: 496; **38**: 258; and segregation, **31**: 305, 308, 312, 361,n1
Williams, Wayne Cullen, **38**: 520,n1
Williams College, **27**: 206; **28**: 20n1,3,5, 320, 355n3; **35**: 39n2; **36**: 358, 359; **37**: 130n1; **38**: 375n1, 625, 626, 627, 629
Williamson, James Franklin, **38**: 239-40,n1, 312-13
Williamstown, Mass., **28**: 20,n1,2,3,4, 63, 88, 92, 345; **29**: 211, 347; **31**: 341, 350, 354, 357, 556; **32**: 306, 335; **33**: 190; **34**: 518; **35**: 79-80, 109, 344; **38**: 375n1, 623, 625-27
Willis, Frank Bartlette, **33**: 287n1
Willis, Henry Parker, **27**: 5, 535n1; **31**: 196n1
Willis, Robert H., **36**: 353,n1
Willoughby, William Franklin, **27**: 244; **32**: 502
Wilmeth, Mr., **31**: 246
Wilmington, Del. *Every Evening*, **27**: 25n1, 39n2,3
Wilmington, N.C., **29**: 391; **33**: 56,n2, 198-99; **37**: 541,n1; **38**: 659
Wilson (R. S. Baker), **37**: 38n10
Wilson, Alice (niece of WW), **27**: 56, 84; **28**: 397; **29**: 391; **30**: 373-75; **35**: 273,n3; **37**: 112
Wilson, Anne Adams (Mrs. James, paternal grandmother of WW), **30**: 74

Wilson, Burton W., **36:** 364

Wilson, Charles Stetson, **31:** 182-83

Wilson, Edith Bolling Galt (Mrs. Woodrow II), **27:** ix, xiv; **31:** 563; **32:** 423-24,n1,2,3; **33:** 87, 90, 278, 525,n1; **35:** 11-12, 28, 43, 109, 362; **36:** 132,n1, 140, 240n2, 262, 267, 276, 291, 297, 302, 389, 425, 426, 462-63, 481, 497, 598; **37:** 3,n3, 8, 14, 32, 95, 101, 106, 167, 177, 182, 221n1, 247-48, 331, 352, 378, 382, 383, 534, 535; **38:** 7, 17, 36, 37, 125, 155, 176, 180, 186, 209, 261, 277, 280, 283, 297, 322, 323, 324, 372, 394, 412n2, 441, 445n1, 452, 474, 475, 481n1, 489n1, 510, 526n1, 537,n1, 545, 617, 623, 627, 628, 637, 649, 656, 659, 660, 661, 679, 689

fear of WW's meeting alone with J. Bernstorff, **33:** 315, 334, 339, 341; on W. J. Bryan's resignation, **33:** 346, 364, 366, 380, 382, 421,n1; on progress of romance with WW, **33:** 423, 428, 429, 539; WW confides in E. M. House on possible marriage to, **33:** 450; engagement to WW, **33:** 458,n1; vacation in Cornish, **34:** 7-8, 14-15; travels with Mr. and Mrs. Rose, **34:** 63-64,n1, 77-78, 89, 103-105, 141, 154-56, 165-66; and WW's daughters, **34:** 72-73, 74, 89-90, 154-55, 217-18, 245-46, 263-64, 268-69; on outsider's view of WW's family life, **34:** 78; on Bolling family crisis, **34:** 124-25, 131,n3, 167, 234, 312, 328-29, 348-49, 357; and golf lessons, **34:** 105, 127, 166, 470, 475, 475-76, 509, 511; on official mail sent by WW, **34:** 130; wishes WW would use typewriter, **34:** 131; on W. J. Bryan, **34:** 172,n2, 486,n1; WW sends silk stockings to, **34:** 200-201, 201-202, 214, 225, 231

informs family of marriage plans, **34:** 207, 221, 246, 313, 347-49; on trip to Ocean City, **34:** 286, 289, 291, 292, 292-93, 326-29, 355-58, 376; WW likens to J. Stephens' description, **34:** 292; and J. P. Tumulty, **34:** 302, 327-28, 351-52; fears gossip, **34:** 314, 327, 331, 332, 356-57, 378, 415; on E. M. House, **34:** 338, 352-53, 516, 518-19, 519-20; in New York, **34:** 380; **35:** 25, 44, 127, 154-56, 161-62, 166, 261, 262,n1, 271-72, 275-76; returns to Washington, D.C., **34:** 396; WW's concern over health of, **34:** 417; withdraws membership from St. Thomas Episcopal Church, **34:** 464,n3, 475; and WW's confession concerning Mrs. Hulbert, **34:** 489, 490, 491-92, 492, 500, 501-502, 524; pledge to WW, **34:** 490, 492, 495, 502; WW on relationship, **34:** 494-95; engagement announcement, **34:** 517,n1, 545; **35:** 15-16, 16-17, 32, 33; WW informs his family of marriage to, **34:** 521; WW's

love for, **35:** 17, 21-22, 40; Altrude Gordon on, **35:** 23; and bridal portrait, **35:** 84, 175; wedding announcement, **35:** 154,n5; wedding gown, **35:** 272,n1; buys fur coat, **35:** 272,n3, 274; WW's wedding present for, **35:** 360; E. M. House and WW visit and discuss wedding plans, **35:** 361; marriage to WW, **35:** 371,n1; on honeymoon, **35:** 371-72, 408; J. Sayre on, **35:** 393-94; M. Wilson on, **35:** 423; on *Sussex* note, **35:** 460; E. M. House's wedding gift, **36:** 599; is witness at Gordon-Grayson wedding, **37:** 92,n1; photograph: *illustration sections*, **36, 37;** *see also* Woodrow Wilson—Family and Personal Life

Wilson, Eleanor Randolph (Nell, Nellie, Nen) daughter of WW and EAW (afterwards Mrs. William Gibbs McAdoo), **27:** 57, 68, 95, 155; **28:** 45, 66, 92, 95, 96, 102, 103, 106, 108, 109, 183,n7, 189, 218, 221, 249, 252, 256, 278, 307-308, 318, 321, 327, 338, 355, 363, 368, 372, 376, 393, 565n1, 595, 596, 597; **29:** 516, 535, 536, 558; WW love for, **28:** 12, 180; role in masque, **28:** 119-20, 129, 266, 269, 273, 277, 291, 310, 392; as artist, **28:** 269-70; birthday celebration at theater in New York, **28:** 400; engagement to W. G. McAdoo, **29:** 346,n1; WW angry at newspapers over false stories about, **29:** 353; and B. M. King, **29:** 370,n1,2; wedding plans of, **29:** 391; and W. G. McAdoo, **29:** 531; photograph: *illustration section*, **28**

Wilson, Elizabeth, **28:** 318,n2

Wilson, Ellen Louise Axson, **27:** ix, xiv, 20, 24, 57, 66, 69, 78, 95, 106, 137, 138, 152, 153, 155, 200, 227, 250, 252, 257, 556; **28:** 11-12, 20-21,n1, 36, 44-45, 54-55, 61-63, 66, 66-67, 81, 84-86, 88, 91-93, 95-96, 98-99, 101-104, 104-106, 108-109, 112-13, 113-14, 119-20, 126-27, 129, 132-34, 138, 144-45, 145-46, 149-50, 159-60, 162, 165-66, 178-79, 179-81, 181-83, 189-90, 190-91, 194-95, 199-200, 218, 221, 248-49, 252, 256-57, 258-59, 260, 261-62, 264-65, 266-67, 267-68, 269-70, 273,, 277, 278-79, 279, 286-87, 291-92, 301-302, 307-308, 308-10, 315, 318-19, 319-20, 321, 327-28, 331-32, 333, 334-36, 338-39, 345, 347, 360-61, 361-62, 363-64, 368-69, 372-73, 375-76, 380, 383-84, 387, 391-92, 392-94, 396, 397, 398-99, 400-401, 413, 572; **29:** 12, 32, 90, 263, 270, 274, 535-36, 553,n1, 554, 556, 558, 561; **30:** 30, 195, 212, 260; **32:** 7, 23, 100; **33:** 191,n1; **35:** 24, 46, 205-206,n1; **37:** 247; **38:** 686, 688, 689

household staff matters, **27:** 12,n1, 18-19, 28-29; **28:** 367-68; meets diplomatic corps, **27:** 171; social work, **28:** 21,n6; on Cornish society, **28:** 42-43,n3-

8, 143; search for home for Jessie and
F. B. Sayre, **28:** 88; White Mountain
trip, **28:** 104, 131-32, 138; and inspiration she brings to WW, **28:** 113-14,
336, 364; ancestors, **28:** 129, 131-32; on
F. B. Sayre, **28:** 138; religion, **28:** 182-
83; landaulet (automobile), **28:** 189-
90,n2; decides to go to Washington to
see WW, **28:** 199-200; as artist, **28:** 269-
70, 286, 302, 319-20; Green Mountain
trip, **28:** 321; New York trip, **28:** 335,
355-56; attends theater in New York,
28: 400,n1; desires to improve condition of women in Post Office Department, **28:** 476; and alley rehabilita-
tion, **28:** 540n1; **31:** 29; feelings on
Jessie's leaving, **28:** 598-99; **29:** 211;
and family finances, **29:** 56, 58, 531;
has painful fall and slow recovery, **29:**
322, 323, 346, 351, 354, 366, 371, 372,
376, 380, 391, 395, 401, 537; WW's love
for, **29:** 372; recuperates at White Sulphur Springs, **29:** 439; love for WW,
29: 460; end of known correspondence
with WW, **29:** 460,n1; at wedding of
Eleanor to W. G. McAdoo, **30:** 6

health of: C. A. Spring Rice on, **30:** 59;
C. H. Dodge on, **30:** 282, 304; T. D.
Jones on, **30:** 311; E. M. House on, **30:**
350; T. Roosevelt on, **30:** 351; WW on,
30: 158, 189, 196, 277, 278, 288, 302,
312, 328, 336, 351, 351-52; WW sum-
mons brother of, **30:** 345; last words of,
30: 353n2; death of, **30:** 353,n2; funeral of, **30:** 374-75, 395; tribute to in
Outlook, **30:** 407,n1; WW on death of,
30: 437, 464-65; **31:** 3-4, 4-5, 118-19,
157, 274, 320, 454-55; **32:** 165, 370-71;
memorial fund for education of mountain youth, **30:** 452; **31:** 259-60, 260,
266

letters of condolence: W. J. Bryan, **30:**
355; T. R. Marshall, **30:** 355-56; W. C.
Redfield, **30:** 356; J. Daniels, **30:** 356;
J. Bryce, **30:** 356-57; M. A. Smith, **30:**
357; M. A. Hulbert, **30:** 357-58; F. S.
Hoyt, **30:** 358; E. Grey, **30:** 359; C. H.
Dodge, **30:** 359; E. M. House, **30:** 359;
B. Perry, **30:** 363-64; G. M. Harper, **30:**
364; H. van Dyke, **30:** 364-65;
R. Bridges, **30:** 366; M. E. Hoyt, **30:**
375-76,n1; J. D. and J. G. Hibben, **30:**
384-85, 404; F. Yates, **30:** 400; J. E.
Davies, **30:** 431; H. Watterson, **31:** 83;
P. S. Reinsch, **31:** 284

WW's acknowledgements: E. M. House,
30: 390; E. Grey, **30:** 403; J. Bryce, **30:**
403; M. W. Jacobus, **30:** 406; F. Yates,
30: 406; F. S. Hoyt, **30:** 406; W. H. Page,
30: 407; J. B. Brower, **30:** 425;
M.R.A. Elliott, **30:** 425; E. G. Reid,
30: 425-26; R. Bridges, **30:** 426; C. H.
Dodge, **30:** 426; M. A. Hulbert, **30:** 437;
G. M. Harper, **30:** 438; W. J. Bryan,

30: 451; M. A. Hoyt, **30:** 451-52; H. C.
Lodge, **30:** 453; F. Yates, **30:** 479;
B. D. Harper, **31:** 13; G. M. Harper, **31:**
36; J. D. Hibben, **31:** 44; E.I.W. Bar-
rington, **31:** 44; H. Watterson, **31:** 65;
F. Hoyt, **31:** 118-19

paid college tuition of Miss Titus, **31:**
16; F. Hoyt's memories of, **31:** 27-29;
Jessie Sayre on, **31:** 341; **32:** 306; and
Berry School, **31:** 342; plans for memorial block in Washington, D.C., **31:**
560,n2, 561; and memorial homes, **34:**
16-17; lake in Glacier National Park
named for, **34:** 87, 185; WW's statement of admission and, **34:** 496-97, 508;
Vonnoh's painting of, **32:** 75; WW regrets joy of grandchild couldn't be
shared with, **32:** 83; and Nacoochee
Institute, **32:** 509,n3; and WW's possible remarriage, **33:** 450; granddaughter named after, **33:** 235n1, 240,
241, 242; memorial fund for housing
in Washington, D.C., **33:** 429-31,n1,6;
photograph: *illustration section,* **28;**
crayon portraits and paintings by, *illustration section:* **30**

Wilson, Emmett, **28:** 90,n1
Wilson, George Grafton, **30:** 5,n1, 73; **32:**
263, 276
Wilson, Henry Lane, **27:** 252,n2, 325, 440,
518, 546-48; **28:** 8, 18-20, 26, 38, 39,
40, 41, 50, 57, 57-58, 83-84,n1,2,3, 85,
105, 108, 109, 148, 155, 174, 331,
429n1, 433, 460-61; **29:** 119; **37:** 36,n9;
38: 240; W. B. Hale report on role in
Madero overthrow, **27:** 539-52; WW's
draft of instructions to, **27:** 435-36; editorials on, **28:** 92,n1; WW on recall-
ing, **28:** 7, 17, 22; EAW on, **28:** 92, 96,
159-60; sees N. Hapgood, **37:** 176
Wilson, Huntington, **27:** 195-97,n1 197-
98, 198; resignation of, **27:** 199, 210
Wilson, James, paternal grandfather of
WW, **30:** 74
Wilson, James (1742-1798), **36:** 418
Wilson, Janet Woodrow (Mrs. Joseph
Ruggles), mother of WW, **29:** 61; **31:**
222, 542
Wilson, Jessie: *see* Sayre, Jessie Woodrow Wilson
Wilson, John Adams, **27:** 115,n1; **28:** 166;
31: 380; **32:** 66, 121; **34:** 210-11, 212,
337-38,n2; **35:** 178; **37:** 359-60, 370, 409;
38: 63
Wilson, John Cook (1849-1915), **38:** 324
Wilson, John Leighton, **27:** 238
Wilson, Joseph R. (of Philadelphia), **32:**
355
Wilson, Joseph R. Jr., brother of WW,
27: 55-56,n3, 82-84, 113, 267,n3, 307-
308, 346,n1; **28:** 396-97; **29:** 391; **30:**
302, 351, 373-75; **34:** 546; **35:** 153n3,
273; **37:** 95-96, 112; **38:** 451-52; WW
informs of future marriage, **34:** 521

Wilson, Joseph Ruggles, father of WW, **29:** 558; **30:** 106, 280,n2; **31:** 222,n1, 395-96, 542; **32:** 126; **33:** 49, 50, 421; **35:** 329; **37:** 231,n1, 279; **38:** 324-25, 331-32, 517, 524; epitaph by WW, **30:** 74,n1; WW's estimate of, **30:** 75

Wilson, Kate Wilson (Mrs. Joseph R., Jr.), sister-in-law of WW, **27:** 56, 84, 307; **28:** 397; **29:** 391; **30:** 373-75; **35:** 273; **37:** 112; **38:** 452

Wilson, Luther Barton, **29:** 476

Wilson, Margaret, daughter of WW and EAW, **27:** 155, 156, 476n1; **28:** 102, 106, 143, 249, 307-308, 315, 321, 327, 328, 331, 335, 338, 345, 360, 368, 372, 376, 398; **29:** 516, 553, 558, 559, 561; **30:** 452; **31:** 141,n1, 260, 266, 318, 341, 454n5, 553, 556; **32:** 7, 8, 9, 12, 21, 117, 165, 335; **33:** 264, 286n1, 334, 341, 443, 446, 525n1; **34:** 14, 73, 74, 75, 77, 83, 89, 91, 100, 103, 104, 105, 117, 118, 119, 125, 130, 138, 154, 155, 163, 167, 170, 178, 201, 217-18, 289, 314, 322, 327, 365, 407; **35:** 16, 24, 27-28, 32, 110, 154, 156, 160, 162, 165, 272,n6, 273, 360, 386-87, 423; **37:** 534; **38:** 15-17, 171-72, 186, 375, 396, 682, 683, 688

and segregation issue, **28:** 498n1; singing career, **28:** 159, 182, 277, 291, 308, 331-32; **32:** 518,n1,2; **35:** 27-28,n1, 109, 110; **37:** 382-83; and suitors, **28:** 258, 259, 264, 265, 269; WW love for, **28:** 12, 180, 181; as mistress of White House, **31:** 158; and Mrs. Galt, **34:** 89, 217-18, 245-46, 263, 268-69, 283; ideas for monument over EAW's grave, **37:** 246-47; recounts horse and carriage accident, **38:** 15-16; attends baptism of niece, **38:** 623-24, 627, 628; photo-graph: *illustration section,* **28**

Wilson, Nathaniel, **33:** 163-64,n1, 179, 287, 290-91, 315, 379-80, 388, 389, 390; **34:** 8, 124, 129, 131, 140, 207, 212, 356, 377, 432, 458, 459,n1, 479, 481, 518; **35:** 12,n4, 17; Mrs. Galt tells of her en-gagement to WW, **34:** 476, 477

Wilson, Mrs. Nathaniel, **34:** 518

Wilson, Oliver, **38:** 637n1

Wilson, Philip St. Julien, **29:** 356,n2

Wilson, William Bauchop, **27:** 236, 349-50, 515; **28:** 318, 319n1, 590,n1; **31:** 101, 131, 138; **32:** 309; **33:** 147n1, 295, 468, 470-71, 473, 537, 541; **35:** 338, 339n1, 401; **36:** 515-16; **37:** 344, 346, 353n1, 430-31, 504; **38:** 12, 123n1, 181, 183, 457-58, 513

cabinet choice, **27:** 70, 112; WW code name for, **27:** 164,n1; West Virginia coal strike, **27:** 291-92,n2; and Diggs-Caminetti case, **28:** 99,n4; and Colo-rado coal strike, **28:** 426-27, 510-11, 513, 547, 551, 552, 553, 554 555, 556, 601; **29:** 14, 25, 31-32, 46, 503, 511n1; **30:** 16-20, 29, 488n2; **31:** 87,n2, 112, 310, 341, 352-53, 376, 407, 424, 556n1; and segregation, **28:** 498n1; and Mother Jones, **28:** 550; and Pennsylvania sen-atorial contest, **29:** 222,n1, 223,n2; **36:** 137; and suggestion for immigration commissioner in New York, **30:** 282, 283; S. Gompers on retaining as Sec-retary of Labor, **36:** 23-25; WW's birthday greetings to, **36:** 401, 406-407; on Chinese immigration to California, **36:** 549-52, 576; on Mexican-American labor-union convention, **37:** 245-46, 266-67; on railroad strike, **37:** 530-31; photograph: *illustration section,* **27**

WOODROW WILSON

I

APPEARANCE, 275
HEALTH, 275
FAMILY LIFE AND DOMESTIC AFFAIRS, 276
RECREATION, 278
RELIGIOUS LIFE, 279
WRITINGS, 280

II

FAREWELL TO NEW JERSEY, 280
INAUGURATION, 280
APPOINTMENTS, 281
CABINET, 282
INTERVIEWS, 282
LEGISLATION: *see under specific topic, such as* banking, *or under individual bills or Acts such as* Underwood-Simmons Tariff Act
SELECTED OPINIONS AND COMMENTS
PRESS CONFERENCES: *see* Table of Contents *for chronological listing*
PUBLIC AND POLITICAL ADDRESSES: *see* Table of Contents *for chronological listing*

———

I

APPEARANCE

27: 156, 163, 267; **28:** 14, 532; **29:** 557; **33:** 374; **35:** 200; **38:** 329; in white suit at church, **28:** 261, 263; during interview with S. G. Blythe, **29:** 516, 517, 519; **31:** 392; during interview with J. Reed, **30:** 231, 232, 233; the President's face was ruddy, his eyes tired-looking, and his mobile lips trembled and smiled and set as he talked, changing with every changing thought. It was his mouth that made him seem so human. **30:** 233; when clowning, **32:** 66; WW makes fun of his, **34:** 353; He was looking exceedingly fit; no lines of care, but well filled cheeks, of good healthy color and a fine clear eye through the glistening pince-nez. **35:** 280; WW on himself, **36:** 16, 19; He always looks—well "natty"—well buttoned up and he has a peculiarly *live face! live* eyes. He looks very well, though he told me that he grows very tired. His complexion is that seen on so many public men: rather bronzed and full of fine veins and lines. **37:** 32; as greets railway presidents, **38:** 58; quoted limerick "For beauty I am not a star." **38:** 164n3; photographs: *illustration sections*, **27; 28; 29; 31; 32; 34; 35; 36; 37; 38**

HEALTH

27: 198; **28:** 11, 14, 44, 45, 311, 398, 587; **29:** 79, 211; **31:** 262-63; **32:** 7, 165, 334; **33:** 284, 285, 450, 451, 452; **34:** 177, 205, 262, 302, 465, 493; **38:** 6; automobile mishap, **27:** 238; neuritis, **27:** 298, 307; **29:** 557; **31:** 429; feeling tired, **28:** 395, 530, 531; indigestion, **28:** 395; visits dentist, **28:** 566; feeling "bum and blue," **29:** 23; suffers from colds, **29:** 23, 24, 33, 34, 36, 247, 263, 270, 274; T. R. Marshall on, **29:** 35; C. A. Spring Rice on, **29:** 59; relapse of bronchial illness, **29:** 60; and C. W. Eliot's regimen of exercise, **29:** 246, 269; how EAW's illness affects his health, **29:** 372; evidence of hardening of the arteries, **29:** 377; 1906 breakdown at Princeton, **29:** 377; S. G. Blythe on, **29:** 519; "I myself seem too tough to damage to my unaffected astonishment," **30:** 196; E. M. House urges a week's rest, **30:** 385; refuses to take a vacation, **30:** 395; "My great safety lies in having my attention absolutely fixed elsewhere than upon myself. I believe that this is good doctor sense, as well as good reasoning about the public welfare," **30:** 395; depression since loss of EAW, **31:** 274, 320; kidney condition, **32:** 67; I go to bed every night absolutely exhausted, trying not to think about anything, and with all my nerves deadened, my own individuality as it were blotted out, **32:** 233; headaches, **33:** 276, 279n1; **34:** 119-20, 177, 196; Mrs. Galt's concern over, **34:** 124, 247, 327; visit to ophthalmologist, **34:** 159, 161, 256, 258, 285, 313; hand and arm tire, **34:** 302; on effect of *Arabic* affair on, **34:** 304-305; digestive disorder, **34:** 463-64; **36:** 417n1, 459-60, 463; **37:** 467, 474; on anxiety over world situation, **34:** 477; back

Woodrow Wilson, Health, cont.
  problem, **35**: 153, 160, 161, 165, 166;
  to take more short rests, **37**: 481;
  bandaged hand, **38**: 524n1

FAMILY LIFE AND DOMESTIC AFFAIRS

27: 227, 239n1; **34**: 473-74; having his
  brother as secretary of the Senate, **27**:
  113-14; breakfast menu, **27**: 64, 156;
  detective stories, **27**: 464; farewell to
  Princeton neighbors, **27**: 165; financial advice from E. M. House, **27**: 252;
  first days in White House, **27**: 18-19,
  155-56; household staff, **27**: 5, 12, 28-
  29; loneliness of position, **27**: 414;
  meals, **27**: 250; personality and character traits, **27**: 164-66; personal mail
  file, **27**: xv; on history of his ancestors,
  27: 72, 503; **29**: 59, 60, 61; good wishes
  from Aunt Felie, **27**: 147; finances and
  investments, **27**: 252; **28**: 103, 273, 315,
  327-28; **29**: 56, 58, 531; Jessie's riding
  accident, **28**: 247n2; letter to Sister
  Annie, **28**: 396-98; limericks, **28**: 465,
  475-76; "long way to Baltimore," **28**:
  321,n1; love of family, **28**: 12, 106, 262,
  309-10, 393; love for EAW, **28**: 84, 85-
  86, 106, 114, 132-33, 179-80, 249, 309-
  10, 335-36, 347, 361, 392-93, 394;
  marriage of Jessie to F. B. Sayre, **28**:
  566n1, 598; receives his original wedding license, **28**: 179; regrets not
  knowing Mrs. Hulbert could attend
  Jessie's wedding, **28**: 565, 599; return
  to home in Princeton, **28**: 335,n4; roy-
  alty from writings, **28**: 261, 267; sees
  Jessie and Frank off on their honeymoon, **28**: 595-96
typewriting, **28**: 161; **29**: 3n1, 143; **30**:
  47; **35**: 70, 412; White House cars, **28**:
  189,n2; EAW and Eleanor visit WW
  in Washington, **28**: 218, 221; EAW's
  feelings for WW, **28**: 91-92; description of train collision, **28**: 248-49,n1;
  visits Princeton, N.J., to vote, **28**:
  335,n2; bicyclist hit by presidential car,
  28: 362, 376; evidence of photographic
  memory, **28**: 452n4; **29**: 33; has night-
  mares about his Princeton enemies, **29**:
  33-34; withdraws his honorary membership in the Military Order of the
  Carabao, **29**: 36; vacation in Pass
  Christian, Miss., **29**: 77; aids in put-
  ting out fire and is made honorary
  member of Pass Christian Fire Department, **29**: 99,n2; could not return
  to live in Princeton, **29**: 163; on Jessie
  and Frank leaving for Williamstown,
  29: 211; writes letter of introduction
  for Mrs. Hulbert's trip abroad, **29**: 239;
  brother-in-law considered for presidency of College of the City of New
  York, **29**: 245, 262, 277,n1; personality traits of, **29**: 327n1, 367; interest

Woodrow Wilson, Family Life and Do-
  mestic Affairs, cont.
  in Berea College, **29**: 342; Eleanor
  Wilson's engagement to W. G. Mc-
  Adoo, **29**: 346-47; angry at newspapers
  for publishing rumors about his family, **29**: 353-54; behavior when he has
  guests, **29**: 364; on his emotional self,
  29: 362; admiration for B. M. King, **29**:
  370-71; visits Egypt through Mrs.
  Hulbert's letters, **29**: 371-72; love for
  daughter Eleanor and feelings on los-
  ing her to marriage, **29**: 372; EAW's
  health prevents E. M. House visit, **29**:
  395; E. M. House on analytical mind
  of, **29**: 459; end of known correspondence with EAW, **29**: 460,n1
does not feel at home anywhere, **29**: 515;
  on W. G. McAdoo and Eleanor, **29**: 531;
  reads poetry to his family, **29**: 553;
  farewell from Princeton residents, **29**:
  555-56; WW's lack of conceit, **29**: 558;
  unable to dine in Baltimore restaurant, **29**: 561; wedding of Eleanor to
  W. G. McAdoo, **30**: 6-7, 12-13; love for
  Eleanor, **30**: 12-13; **33**: 242; on boy-
  hood days, **30**: 21; absent-mindedness,
  30: 22; interest in Davidson College,
  30: 37; on missing his two married
  daughters, **30**: 73; epitaph for his father, **30**: 74,n1; estimate of his father,
  30: 75; desire to go to sea as a boy, **30**:
  94, 96; congratulations from W. J.
  Bryan on 29th wedding anniversary,
  30: 207; on friendship of C. H. Dodge,
  30: 288; thanks brother for congratulatory note on Mexico, **30**: 302
last words of EAW, **30**: 353n2; on death
  of EAW, **30**: 357, 464-65; **32**: 7, 165,
  370-71, 372; at funeral of EAW, **30**:
  374-75; M. E. Hoyt on EAW and WW,
  30: 375-76; thanks cousins who helped
  at funeral, **30**: 395; condolences received and acknowledged: *see* entry for
  Ellen Axson Wilson; Jessie's love and
  concern for, **30**: 436; **32**: 306; **33**: 190-
  91; could not speak of his gratitude for
  expressions of sympathy after death of
  EAW, **30**: 437; and Scottish clans, **30**:
  465; consideration and compassion of,
  30: 466; on loss of EAW, **31**: 3-4, 4-5,
  118-19, 157, 274, 320, 454-55, 564; retirement plans, **31**: 95; a typical day's
  routine, **31**: 141-42; on EAW memorial fund, **31**: 259-60, 260; I especially
  shrink from dwelling upon anything
  personal to myself. My instinct is to
  seek some occupation that will take my
  thoughts far afield where there is
  nothing that can concern me . . . I want
  to run away, to escape something, **31**:
  289; lends money to P. W. Pope for his
  wife's operation, **31**: 310-11, 314; for-
  getfulness of, **31**: 319; advises cousin
  on taking Belgian refugee to live with

Woodrow Wilson, Family Life and Domestic Affairs, cont.

her, **31**: 330; Jessie's invitation for Thanksgiving, **31**: 341; I long for the time when I may be released and allowed an individual life and daily fortune again, **31**: 344; dislike of cold weather, **31**: 357; thanks luncheon club for golf bag and clubs, **31**: 380; to become grandfather, **31**: 456; looks forward to family reunion at Christmas, **31**: 456; concern over Mrs. Hulbert's financial situation, **31**: 514-15, 515-16, 538-39, 554; Christmas greetings from J. Daniels, **31**: 524; on Wilson Howe, **31**: 531; receives Christmas gift from Nancy Toy, **31**: 532; Aunt Felie's recollection of WW as a baby, **31**: 542; birthday greetings, **31**: 541-42, 543; telephone manner of, **32**: 12-13; description of when angry, **32**: 21; aids Mrs. Hulbert in publication of article, **32**; 23,n1, 50-51,n1, 191-92,n1, 222; reacts to his portrait, **32**: 66; becomes a grandfather, **32**: 83, 100; on not naming grandson after him, **32**: 117, 147; affection for E. M. House, **32**: 121

EBG recalls first meeting, **32**: 423-24,n3; description of a typical day, **32**: 475-76; Cousin Jessie thanks WW for White House visit, **32**: 493-94,n1,2; lends money to Sister Annie, **32**: 517-18; memories of his father, **33**: 49-50; beginning of relationship with EBG, **33**: 87, 90; expressions of need and love for EBG, **33**: 118, 119, 125, 301, 380, 423, 428, 429, 539, 539-40, 542; **34**: 10, 76, 89, 101, 120, 127, 139, 169, 170, 190, 220, 256, 258, 300, 344, 360; **35**: 153-54, 161, 164-65, 271; on birth of his granddaughter, **33**: 235,n1, 240, 241-42, 242; I might as well try to define my life as to try to define my love, **33**: 263; WW desires photographs of EBG, **33**: 264; desires to stop subscription to *Princeton Alumni Weekly*, **33**: 432,n1; leaves for vacation in Cornish, **33**: 436n2; confides in House on possible remarriage, **33**: 450; engagement to EBG, **33**: 458,n1

on his separation from EBG, **34**: 23-24, 119, 128, 129, 150-51, 162, 229, 283, 331; and purchase of Mrs. Hulbert's mortgages, **34**: 39,n1, 117,n1, 412-13, 430, 469, 507; on family's reaction to news of forthcoming marriage to EBG, **34**: 72-73, 74, 89-90, 170, 283; on "fourth chapter" of relationship with EBG, **34**: 75; life in Cornish, **34**: 83, 89, 101-102; pays fee for shipping EBG's trunk, **34**: 91, 118; on Bolling family crisis, **34**: 137-38, 139, 140, 151-52, 178, 221, 253-55, 255, 260, 323-24, 332-33, 345-46, 354-55, 447; leaves Cornish for Washington, **34**: 159-60,

Woodrow Wilson, Family Life and Domestic Affairs, cont.

168, 169; rescues motorists, **34**: 160-61, 171, 182; presented with bunch of four-leaf clovers, **34**: 168, 182; on photographs of EBG, **34**: 179-80, 243, 244; recalls first seeing EBG, **34**: 190; To be thinking in "we's" and acting in "I's" is very confusing—and the acting seems artificial; only the thinking is real, **34**: 194; wishes EBG would tell her family of the marriage plans, **34**: 221; concern over EBG's health and her safe arrivals at vacation destinations, **34**: 227-28, 289, 291, 376, 377; will try to find a job for EBG's brother, **34**: 255; spends day in Philadelphia, **34**: 259; Margaret on, **34**: 268-69; reminiscences of New Jersey, **34**: 304; on gossip, **34**: 331, 332, 415; on his handwriting, **34**: 343; welcomed into Bolling family, **34**: 349-50, 350-51, 361-62, 363, 364, 416; Nobody loves a man because he is great. You know that my heart entertains great ideals—has always entertained them and lived with them, **34**: 375; Jessie's birthday celebration, **34**: 394

confession concerning relationship with Mrs. Hulbert, **34**: 489,n1,2, 491,n1, 496-97, 497-500, 506-508; shorthand draft of, **34**: 498-99; on a new chapter in relationship with EBG, **34**: 494-95; on EBG's pledge, **34**: 495; on engagement announcement, **34**: 505, 508, 517,n1, 537, 544, 545; loneliness since EAW's death, **34**: 508; on plans after presidency, **34**: 513; informs his family of impending marriage, **34**: 521-22; dialogue concerning constraint in EBG's manner, **34**: 543-44; engagement announcement, **35**: 15, 15-16, 18, 32, 33; engagement ring selection, **35**: 19,n2, 44; on five-month anniversary of declaration of love for EBG, **35**: 21-22; informs Mrs. Hulbert of his engagement, **35**: 23, 53, 187; informs E. G. Reid of his engagement, **35**: 24; on EAW, **35**: 24; Margaret's joy in EBG as her father's choice, **35**: 28; congratulatory messages on engagement, **35**: 32, 36, 37, 37-38, 38, 39, 39-40, 41, 42, 46-47, 69, 84, 89, 118, 145, 191; thirteen his lucky number, **35**: 42; acknowledgements of congratulations, **35**: 56, 57, 60, 60-61, 61, 83, 87-88, 95, 156, 157; eager to meet EBG's brother, **35**: 56; to spend summer at Jersey shore, **35**: 58-59,n1, 72, 103, 127, 155; Jessie invites to Williamstown, **35**: 79-80; refuses photographer permission to take EBW's bridal portrait, **35**: 84; Davidson College yearbook dedicated to, **35**: 95-96, 107; authorization of wedding announcement, **35**: 154,n5; returns to

Woodrow Wilson, Family Life and Domestic Affairs, cont.

Princeton to vote, **35:** 159-60,n1; rumors about immorality of, **35:** 239; dinner at White House for class of 1879, **35:** 262,n2,3, 270, 274-75, 279-80, 281; invites Witherspoon Gang to spend night at White House, **35:** 262,n3, 270, 275, 281; invites the Elliotts to his wedding, **35:** 293; memories of Lightfoot Baseball Club, **35:** 333; wedding congratulations, **35:** 352-53, 353-54, 371, 372-73, 373-74, 390, 404-405; wedding gift and note to EBG, **35:** 360, 370; wedding plans, **35:** 361; marriage, **35:** 371,n1

Margaret's love for, **35:** 386-87, 423; on the wedding, **35:** 393; Jessie on Christmas at White House without WW, **35:** 393-94; gift from diplomatic corps, **35:** 397; birthday greetings to, **35:** 397, 398-99, 408-409; on the honeymoon, **35:** 399, 408; acknowledges wedding congratulations, **35:** 401, 407-408, 412; and Mrs. Hulbert's financial affairs in California, **35:** 503,n1; Jessie wishes to see more of, **36:** 151-52; helps Stockton Axson obtain release from professorship at Wesleyan, **36:** 297, 329-30, 349; concern over health of classmate Mitchell, **36:** 349,n1, 359, 377; birth of granddaughter, Eleanor Sayre, **36:** 373, 384; congratulates James Woodrow upon his engagement, **36:** 410; visits Jessie in hospital and pays remaining bill, **36:** 552; wife's portrait a comfort to, **37:** 3,n3; Jessie's love for, **37:** 14; R. S. Baker's interview with, **37:** 31-38; Jessie hopes WW can attend baptism of his granddaughter, **37:** 78; attends Gordon-Grayson wedding, **37:** 92,n1, 106; brother invites WW to dinner, **37:** 95-96; apologizes to McAdoo for Secret Service screening, **37:** 111; invites his brother and family to theater, **37:** 112; sends money to his daughters' former governess, **37:** 164-65,n1, 173-74; **38:** 81, 84; on not appointing relatives, **37:** 208; Margaret thanks for her singing lessons, **37:** 383; receives a case of Scotch, **37:** 359-60, 370, 409; returns check for article published in *Ladies Home Journal*, **38:** 27; sends Jessie birthday greetings, **38:** 121, 683

concern over sister's grave illness, **38:** 172; death of sister, **38:** 176; condolences, **38:** 180, 181, 186, 277; acknowledges condolences, **38:** 191, 191-92, 192, 194, 283; influence of father, **38:** 324-25, 331-32; and shorthand, **38:** 325; reading habits, **38:** 329-30; unsure of trip to Williamstown, **38:** 375,n1, 396; offers to help with sister's financial affairs, **38:** 389, 451, 519,n1;

Woodrow Wilson, Family Life and Domestic Affairs, cont.

on the campaign, **38:** 451-52; Republican attempt to buy WW's letters to Mrs. Hulbert, **38:** 589,n1; Mary Hoyt wishes WW to wear her magic ring until election is over, **38:** 590; trip to Williamstown for granddaughter's baptism, **38:** 623-24; ten letters to Jessie (1899-1915), **38:** 681-90; purchased island on Lake Rosseau, Ontario, **38:** 684,n1; on Jessie's sorority conflict, **38:** 684, 685-86; on Jessie's marriage, **38:** 688; loneliness after EAW's death, **38:** 689; *see also* Ellen Axson Wilson; Edith Bolling Galt Wilson

RECREATION

28: 46, 133; visits Morgan Collection at the Metropolitan Museum of Art, **27:** 72,n1; detective fiction, **27:** 464; **28:** 531; **29:** 364; **31:** 403, 455; **35:** 399; poetry and limericks, **27:** 140; **29:** 553; **30:** 22; **31:** 279, 384; theater, **27:** 63,n4, 71,n2, 112,n1, 119,n2, 140,n2; **28:** 86-87, 108, 595,n2,3; **29:** 449, 536, 558,n4; **31:** 403; **34:** 416, 465, 467,n1, 517; **35:** 11n2, 18-19,n1, 44, 166, 258,n1; attends Army-Navy football game, **28:** 596, 598, 600,n1; **35:** 257, 273,n1; golf, **28:** 12, 14, 85, 86, 108, 113, 133, 134, 146, 161, 395, 531; **29:** 456, 530, 531, 536; **30:** 466; **31:** 19, 141, 269, 280-81, 318, 344, 380, 392, 394-95; **32:** 7, 476, 494; **33:** 234, 279n1, 374, 540; **34:** 89, 101, 105, 119, 127, 153, 177, 190, 193, 201, 302, 305, 359, 519; **35:** 15, 152, 153; **36:** 375, 599; **38:** 623, 659; invitation from E. M. House, for weekend in New York, **28:** 571; singing, **28:** 308; reading, **29:** 530, 553; **31:** 289; **32:** 61; **34:** 463; attends baseball games, **29:** 559-60, 561; plays pool, **30:** 464; **34:** 72; books borrowed from Library of Congress, **31:** 316-17,n1; walking, **31:** 319-20, 393; bicycling, **31:** 393; vaudeville, **31:** 403; motoring, **34:** 128, 138, 153, 162, 201, 231, 287, 305, 359, 360, 407; **38:** 623; visits National Museum, **34:** 353; musicales at White House, **36:** 207,n3, 268,n4, 375-76; refuses to be in golf movies with champions, **38:** 374-75; bicycle tour of British Isles with Stockton Axson (1899), **38:** 681,n2

RELIGIOUS LIFE

27: 153-54, 167, 253, 351,n1, 357, 390, 489; attends church, **28:** 13, 45, 85, 134, 135, 263-64, 362; **34:** 129-30, 285, 290, 354, 360; "by serving fellow men have tried to serve God," **28:** 352; on Christian missionaries in India, **28:** 82; future generations may see "light of jus-

Woodrow Wilson, Religious Life, cont.

tice of God," **28:** 452; Here is the Nation God has builded by our hands, **28:** 25; I shall be a Christian gentleman in the White House, **28:** 494; Thanksgiving Proclamations, **28:** 424; **35:** 89-90; **38:** 667-68; I believe that every place of worship is sanctified by the repeated self-discovery which comes to the human spirit, **29:** 45; remarks upon laying the cornerstone of Central Presbyterian Church, **29:** 44-45; reasons for not attending church in Pass Christian, Miss., **29:** 104; sorry unable to see and hear G. C. Morgan, **29:** 263-64, 270-71; epitaph for his father, **30:** 74; estimate of his father, **30:** 75; scholarship has usually been most fruitful when associated with religion, **30:** 90; note to J. R. Mott on his birthday, **30:** 119,n1; But we must face the situation in the confidence that Providence has deeper plans than we could possibly have laid ourselves, **30:** 336; Faith in God's providence . . . sustains more than anything else can. I think I should go mad without it, **31:** 3; proclamation for a day of prayer, **31:** 10-11; For I believe that we are custodians not of commands, but of a spirit. We are custodians of the spirit of righteousness, of the spirit of equal-handed justice of the spirit of hope which believes in the perfectibility of the law with the perfectibility of human life itself, **31:** 186 Christianity, **31:** 221-23; **38:** 576-77; Your measurements, your directions, your whole momentum, have to be established before you reach the next world, **31:** 227; *My* life would not be worth living, if it were not for the driving power of religion, for *faith*, pure and simple, **32:** 8-9; I regard religious toleration as one of the most invaluable fruits of civilization, **32:** 95; By life I do not mean the physical life. That is relatively a matter of indifference; but the life that *is* life—the spiritual life. For it is the spiritual life, if you only admit that word, by which we judge everybody, **32:** 126; There is only one moral center of the universe, and that is God. If you get into right relations with Him, then you have your right perspective and your right size, **32:** 126; Wars will never have any ending until men cease to hate one another, cease to be jealous of another, get the feeling of reality in the brotherhood of mankind, which is the only bond that can make us think justly of one another and act righteously before God Himself, **32:** 430; memories of the religious life of his youth, **33:** 49-51; God comes to a man, I think, through the

Woodrow Wilson, Religious Life, cont.

trust and love of a sweet, pure woman. Certainly God seems very near when I am with you, **33:** 125; For I have prayed, dear, that God would give me this, my heart's desire. If you come to me, I shall know that it is he who is leading us, and that he is willing that I should give all that is best in me to make you happy!, **33:** 125; and the reassurance that there is no chance but fixed laws of God to which all the world moves obedient, not the least the fortunes and hearts of men, **33:** 384; Surely a prayer made in love such as yours must bring an answer that will make me rich in strength and fitness to do my work, **34:** 152; quotes Ruth's pledge to Boaz, **34:** 323

denies having led cabinet in prayer, **35:** 68,n1; It does not become America that within her borders, where every man is free to follow the dictates of his conscience and worship God as he pleases, men should raise the cry of church against church . . . We agree to differ about methods of worship, but we are united in believing in Divine Providence and in worshipping the God of Nations, **35:** 172; quotes from Ezekiel, **35:** 180-81; college editorial on reducing the number of prayer meetings at Princeton, **35:** 182,n3; and resolution presented by the Federal Council of Churches of Christ in America, **35:** 328; address to the Federal Council of Churches, **35:** 329-36; An egotist is a man who has got the whole perspective of life wrong. He conceives of himself as the center of affairs. He conceives of himself as the center of affairs even as it affects the providence of God. He has not related himself to the great forces which dominate him with the rest of us and, therefore, has set up a little kingdom all his own which he reigns with unhonored sovereignty, **35:** 330; Christianity is not important to us because it is a valid body of conceptions regarding God and man, but because it is a vital body of conceptions which can be translated into life for us—life in this world and a life still greater in the next, **35:** 330; The spirit of Christianity is the spirit of assistance, of counsel, of vitalization, of intense interest in everything that affects the lives of men and women and children, **35:** 333; on the proof of Christianity, **35:** 334; We have got to save society, so far as it is saved, by the instrumentality of Christianity in this world, **35:** 334; on analogy between patriotism and Christianity, **35:** 335, 343; I have been

Woodrow Wilson, Religious Life, cont.

bred, and a good many Kansans have been bred, in a pretty stern school of religion, and there are some religions that have been worth fighting for, **36:** 96; and pensioning aged preachers, **36:** 331,n3

But it is a serious thing that there are so few minutes in the twenty-four hours when we can pause to think of God and the eternal issues of the life that we are living, for the thing that we call civilization sometimes absorbs and hurries whole populations to such an extent that they are constantly aware that they are not breathing the air of spiritual inspiration which is necessary for the expansion of their hearts and the salvation of their souls, **36:** 393; The only thing that is indomitable is the human spirit, and not the human body. And if the spirit is indomitable, if it has the power to lift over every obstacle and barrier, the body in which it dwells apparently can, by the Providence of God, stand anything, **36:** 393; Sometimes when the day is done and the consciousness of the sordid struggle is upon you, you go to bed wondering if the sun will seem bright in the morning, the day worthwhile. But you have only to sweep these temporary things away and to look back and see mankind working its way, though never so slowly, up the slow steps which it has climbed, to know itself and to know nature and nature's God, and to know the destiny of mankind. **36:** 420-21; remarks to the American Bible Society, **36:** 629-31; WW reminded to get certificate of dismission from church in Wilmington, N.C., **37:** 541; on observation of Sabbath, **38:** 157

WRITINGS

Character of Democracy in the United States, **27:** 15-16; *Congressional Government,* **27:** 284; **38:** 680; *History of the American People,* **27:** 368; **31:** 109, 118, 397-98; **33:** 525n1; **38:** 327; *The New Freedom,* **27:** 4, 6-7; **28:** 61, 267; **38:** 621,n1; *An Old Master,* **27:** 15-16; tribute to the women of the South, **27:** 574; inscriptions for Post Office Building, **28:** 366,n1, 501; royalties from writings, **28:** 261, 267; books that he'd care to write would not sell, **29:** 59; On the Writing of History, **31:** 398, 398,n2; refuses to permit serialization of *History of the American People,* **32:** 7; on "two real" books he has written, **32:** 7-8; *Constitutional Government in the United States,* **32:** 9; **37:** 35,n6; When

Woodrow Wilson, Writings, cont.

a Man Comes to Himself, **33:** 380n1; **35:** 431n1; **36:** 177; **38:** 259,n3; proposal to make movie from writings, **34:** 57,n1; on campaign speeches for governor of New Jersey, **35:** 536: On Being Human, **36:** 176-77; request from *Ladies Home Journal* for article, **36:** 559-60,n1; asked to write article for *Harper's Magazine,* **36:** 516-17; an unpublished article, America's Opportunity, **37:** 500-501; Mexican Question in *Ladies Home Journal,* **37:** 508-12, 534-35,n1; agrees to write article on the ideal university, **37:** 541,n2; on craft of writing speeches, **38:** 325-26

II

FAREWELL TO NEW JERSEY

Annual message to the N.J. legislature, **27:** 46-54; talk to N.J. senators, **27:** 85-90; feelings for N.J., **27:** 86, 88-89, 116; signs seven antitrust bills, **27:** 120-22; message to legislature on jury reform, **27:** 133-34; farewell speech, **27:** 141-42; jury reform, **27:** 190-91,n1, 233; letter to eighth-grade school children in N.J., **27:** 260; constitutional reform, **27:** 378-79, 391

INAUGURATION

Honor guard, **27:** 26; cancels inaugural ball, **27:** 59-60, 61; brother requests tickets, **27:** 84; Cipriano Castro plans to attend, **27:** 145,n1; address, **27:** 148-52; ceremonies, **27:** 152, 155-56; Princeton students accompany presidential train to Washington, **29:** 555-56; photographs: *illustration section,* **27**

APPOINTMENTS

31: 507-508; C. W. Eliot on spoils system, **28:** 272; defends his diplomatic appointments, **28:** 280; Negroes and, **30:** 491-93; **32:** 515; **35:** 461,n1; against appointing relatives, **31:** 377; **37:** 208; patronage most disagreeable aspect of presidency, **31:** 399-401; and Senate's rejection of choices, **31:** 481-82, 490, 498, 507, 524; E. M. House on, **33:** 451; **37:** 105; recommendations for Solicitor-General, **33:** 491-92, 492; A. M. Palmer suggested as Counselor of State Department, **34:** 24-25, 31, 41-42, 53, 79; E. M. House's suggestions, **34:** 107, 134; J. S. Williams' suggestions, **34:** 107-108, 226, 273; F. L. Polk named Counselor of State Department, **34:** 237,n1, 368,n1; C. R. Crane's suggestions, **36:** 177-78, 191-92; WW discusses with E. M. House, **36:** 378-79; **38:** 659-60; suggestions for officers of Democratic National Committee, **37:**

Woodrow Wilson, Appointments, cont.
45-46, 118, 163-64, 229, 281; and selection of vice-presidential candidate,
37: 105
cabinet suggestions and appointments, **27:**
9, 11, 21-24, 26-27, 44-45, 57, 61-62,
70-71, 81, 92, 92-93, 93-94, 96-97, 102-
103, 110-11, 112, 115-16, 118, 119-20,
126-27, 127, 128, 129-31, 132-33, 134-
35, 136, 137-38, 139, 140, 152-53; **30:**
464; code names for members, **27:** 164;
estimate of, **27:** 253, 400; comments on,
30: 464; T. W. Gregory as Attorney
General, **30:** 468; W. J. Bryan's successor and appointment of R. Lansing,
33: 397, 409, 436, 445, 449, 456;
F. Delano, **33:** 441; Secretary and
Assistant Secretary of War resign, **36:**
164-65; H. L. Scott becomes *ad interim*
Secretary of War, **36:** 171, 176; N. D.
Baker accepts Secretary of War position, **36:** 251,n1, 259-60; W. F. Sadler's
suggestion for Assistant Secretary of
War, **36:** 293; W. Ingraham appointed
Assistant Secretary of War, **36:** 300,n1
domestic suggestions and appointments,
27: 126, 136-37, 152-53, 157, 163, 192,
223, 228-29, 238-39, 245-46, 251, 283-
84, 291, 333, 335-36, 400; **28:** 6,n1,2,
10, 20, 35-36,n1,2, 40-41, 64, 88-89, 94,
97-98,n1, 270-71,n2, 275, 289, 329, 524-
25, 527-28,n2, 589, 594-95; **29:** 33, 34,
104, 290, 304, 311-12, 317, 319,n1, 326,
327, 331, 332, 388, 394, 540-41; Federal Reserve Board, **29:** 159, 247,n1,2,3,
263, 270, 277-78, 288, 308, 322, 380,
383,n1, 390, 401,n1, 500-501, 515, 532,
536, 536-37, 543, 543-44; **37:** 345-46,
462; **38:** 22,n1, 32-33,n1; on struggle
for postmasterships, **29:** 364; **30:** 285;
House on, **30:** 22; WW defends appointment of H. D. Clayton to judge-
ship, **30:** 28; and patronage in North
Carolina, **30:** 144; and women, **30:** 172;
and commissioner of immigration at
Port of New York, **30:** 282,n1, 283; and
Federal Trade Commission, **31:** 269,
353,n1,2,3, 524,n4, 531, 548; **32:** 6-7,
19, 32, 61n2, 273; and Interstate Commerce Commission, **31:** 269, 356; **38:**
158-59; in New York, **31:** 274-75; policy in Porto Rico, **32:** 94; H. W. Walker
on J. A. O'Sullivan, **32:** 242-43,n1,2,
259; J. E. Davies selected chairman of
Federal Trade Commission, **32:**
271,n1,2; and E. Bland nomination for
marshal, **32:** 325,n1,2; and Recorder of
Deeds in Washington, **33:** 71,n1; possible replacement for J. P. Tumulty,
34: 513-14, 515, 515-16; and postmastership in New York, **35:** 239, 318-19,
338, 346,n1, 360, 361, 460, 503, 505;
and suggestions for Supreme Court, **30:**
309-10; **35:** 433, 447, 460, 462,n1, 535;
36: 179,n1; **37:** 210, 230, 264, 267,n1,

Woodrow Wilson, Appointments, cont.
268, 278, 365, 372-73, 420, 420-21;
L. D. Brandeis nomination for Supreme
Court and controversy over, **36:** 19-20,
22, 23, 51, 86, 137, 140, 606-607; **37:**
9-10, 25, 34, 56, 72-73, 78n1, 101, 102,
103, 609-11; **37:** 151,n1; G. Rublee and
Federal Trade Commission, **36:** 203,n2;
J. A. Aylward and Wisconsin judge-
ship, **36:** 315-16,n1,2,3, 482, 500-501,
510-11; M. Liebel on Pennsylvania
postmastership, **36:** 336-38,n2; and
New York postmastership, **36:** 380-81,
485, 520,n1, 520-21, 522, 529, 530, 542,
562-63, 598; and postmastership in
Chicago, **36:** 576-77,n1, 602-603,n1; and
defeat of G. Rublee nomination, **37:**
101,n1; D. F. Malone on deferring New
York appointments until after Democratic convention, **37:** 155-56; Clarke
appointed to Supreme Court, **37:**
428,n2, 431, 446; C. S. Hamlin and
Federal Reserve Board, **37:** 489-90;
G. Rublee resigns from Trade Commission, **37:** 512-13, 517-18; Council of
National Defense Advisory Committee, **38:** 181-83, 297, 386-87, 439; suggestions for Tariff Commission, **38:** 297,
335-36; and Eight-Hour Law Commission, **38:** 297, 354,n1; W. G. McAdoo's
suggestions for Shipping Board, **38:**
428-29, 454-56
*diplomatic suggestions and appoint-
ments:* general, **27:** 14, 62, 70, 110, 118,
119, 124, 228, 259, 282, 290, 300, 361-
62, 384-85, 508-509, 531-32; **28:**
4,n1,2,3,4, 15,n1, 17, 22,n1, 111-12,
175, 184, 192, 192-93, 203, 320, 326-
27, 353,n1, 354,n4, 597; **29:** 23, 32, 74,
159, 242, 373, 449,n1, 531-32; **38:** 209-
10, 317-18; WW on filling diplomatic
positions, **27:** 217, 263; expenses of
ambassador in London, **29:** 410-13; and
Russian ambassadorship, **30:** 31; and
diplomatic and consular service bill, **30:**
42; **31:** 448-49,n1; C. R. Crane refuses
Russian ambassadorship, **30:** 46, 58;
W. H. Page on expenses of ambassador in London, **30:** 149-55; W. G. Sharp
named ambassador to France, **30:** 195-
96; WW asks C. H. Dodge help to keep
Page in London, **30:** 277-78; Dodge
agrees to supply funds, **30:** 281-82;
ambassador to Mexico, **30:** 463; and
Ambassador Herrick, **31:** 283; D. West
appointed special agent in Mexico, **32:**
202,n2, 202-203, 203-204; Haiti and,
32: 471-72, 479; minister to Liberia
named, **34:** 504-505, 511,n1; **35:** 68,n1;
and diplomatic corps, **34:** 515; House
on change in Chile, **35:** 64; suggestions for ambassador to Mexico, **35:**
134, 146, 359; on J. W. Gerard's in-
competence and possible replacement,
35: 178-79, 191, 192; dissatisfaction

Woodrow Wilson, Appointments, cont.

with Ambassador G. Marye, **35:** 358; Marye resigns as ambassador to Russia, **35:** 526; B. Whitlock refuses Russian ambassadorship, **36:** 86, 135-36, 230-31; and J. MacMurray promotion in diplomatic service, **36:** 175-76,n1, 191, 505; accepts resignation of Marye, **36:** 188; D. R. Francis appointed to Russian post, **36:** 202,n1; H. Morgenthau resigns as ambassador to Turkey, **36:** 356-57; **37:** 96-97; A. Elkus replaces Morgenthau, **36:** 378,n3; H. P. Fletcher new ambassador to Mexico, **36:** 608; suggestions for Joint High Commission, **37:** 402, 422, 430-31; **38:** 13, 22, 22-23,n1, 28, 31, 63,n1, 79,n1; H. van Dyke resignation, **38:** 616; *see also* patronage

CABINET

27: xii, 160, 169-70, 174-75, 194, 210, 235-38, 248-50, 261-62, 267-69, 290-92, 312-13, 328-33, 348-51, 425-26, 442-45, 459-62; **28:** 472; **31:** 283, 319, 350; **32:** 133-34, 207; **33:** 449-51; **34:** 294; **35:** 471n2; few meetings in summer, **28:** 139, 380; value of, **28:** 380; resumption of, **28:** 382; House suggests cabinet members clear speeches with WW, **29:** 74; and Colorado coal strike, **29:** 502, 503; meeting on Mexico, **29:** 301n1, 447; approves resolution authorizing use of armed forces against V. Huerta, **29:** 471,n1; and Mexican crisis, **29:** 530, 531; **33:** 294-95; consideration for cabinet members, **29:** 536; and shipping bill, **31:** 101; possibility of W. J. Bryan leaving, **31:** 384-85; opinion of, **31:** 532; Friday evening meetings, **31:** 552; L. M. Garrison's resignation plan, **32:** 168, 538-40; and ship-purchase bill, **32:** 192-93; meeting on European situation, **32:** 404n1; and *Lusitania* correspondence, **33:** 191n1, 295,n3,4, 368, 369, 424-25, 536-37, 540 and resignation of Bryan, **33:** 370,n1, 375-76, 376; R. Lansing becomes Secretary of State, **33:** 397, 409, 436, 445, 449, 456; C. R. Crane on F. Delano as member of, **33:** 441; on Garrison, **33:** 450-51; suggested meeting regarding *Arabic*, **34:** 265-66; against immediate meeting on *Arabic*, **34:** 271; attitude toward Tumulty, **34:** 515; R. L. Owen urges creation of Department of Health, **35:** 151; New Year greetings from cabinet members, **35:** 401; grateful for support of, **35:** 405; S. Gompers on keeping W. B. Wilson as Secretary of Labor, **36:** 23-25; and Garrison's resignation, **36:** 144, 164, 164-65; H. L. Scott as *ad interim* Secretary of War, **36:** 171, 176; birthday congratu-

Woodrow Wilson, Cabinet, cont.

lations to D. F. Houston, **36:** 185; C. R. Crane's suggestions for appointments to, **36:** 191; reads Lansing memorandum on armed merchantmen to, **36:** 251-57; N. D. Baker appointed Secretary of War, **36:** 251, 259-60; on Punitive Expedition, **36:** 287n1; birthday congratulations to W. B. Wilson, **36:** 401; House meets with individual members on German and Mexican situations, **36:** 423-25; unsure whether to read *Sussex* note to, **36:** 461; bored at meeting of, **36:** 462; and vocational education bill, **37:** 173,n1,2; wishes to retain all members, **38:** 659-60; on making Congressmen eligible for cabinet post while retaining Congressional membership, **38:** 661; photograph: *illustration section*, **38**

INTERVIEWS

on banking and currency reforms by J. C. O'Laughlin, **27:** 565-70; on Mexico by S. G. Blythe, **29:** 516-24; on the presidency by S. G. Blythe, **31:** 390-403; on the European war by H. Brougham, **31:** 458-60; on Mexico by J. Reed, **30:** 156,n1, 157,n1, 186-87, 189, 192-93, 202, 219-20, 223, 231; unpublished article, **30:** 231-38; on business climate by A. Shaw, **32:** 69-75; on numerous topics by I. Tarbell, **38:** 323-34; on campaign issues by H. N. Hall, **38:** 564-70; *see also* Press Conferences

LEGISLATION

See under specific area of legislation such as banking, *or under the name of the individual bill or Act, such as* Underwood-Simmons Tariff Act

SELECTED OPINIONS AND COMMENTS

Albano lynching case, **28:** 115n2; Americans: the United States, **27:** 34, 38, 66, 306,n1, 307; **28:** 68, 441, 451; **30:** 14, 36, 146, 148, 184-86, 251, 252, 254; **31:** 422; **32:** 29, 283-84, 284, 453; **33:** 148, 149, 210, 210-11, 211-12, 391-93, 393; **34:** 535; **35:** 29; **36:** 29, 34, 36-37, 62, 62-63, 84, 85, 95, 102, 109, 219; **37:** 122-23, 125, 126, 213, 216, 222-25, 228, 326, 355, 356, 414-18, 444, 500-501; **38:** 414, 436-37, 530-31, 538, 540, 570, 581, 602, 615 the Americas, **28:** 451; **33:** 245, 246; **35:** 441-46 *Birth of a Nation*, **32:** 142n1, 267,n1; **33:** 86,n1 on admission of Brandeis to Cosmos Club, **32:** 167,n1 breaking precedents, **27:** 59-60, 264, 268,

Woodrow Wilson, Selected Opinions and Comments, cont.

273, 285, 294-95,n1, 299; **28:** 261, 263
on interview with Bryan: **34:** 510-11
business, businessmen, **32:** 152, 166; **35:** 305, 321, 322-23, 332; **37:** 386-87, 388-89, 389; **38:** 267-68, 270, 308-10, 340-41, 416-17, 506
cabinet: **31:** 532; **33:** 366-67; **34:** 192, 273; **37:** 444
Congress; legislatures, **27:** 160; **28:** 336; **29:** 22
democracy, **30:** 299; **33:** 289; **34:** 536; **35:** 297, 324; **36:** 160, 473-74; **37:** 327, 335
diplomatic affairs, **27:** 171; **29:** 396, 408; **30:** 394; **31:** 109, 118; **33:** 129n1; **35:** 58, 69, 73, 73-74, 84, 88,n1,2,3,4, 91, 210, 372-73, 386, 396; **37:** 47-48, 50
European War: militarism, **27:** 113; **29:** 468; **30:** 14, 450; **32:** 183-84, 316, 495; **33:** 242, 288; **34:** 9, 140, 290, 534, 534-35; **35:** 47-48, 341; **36:** 13, 32, 37-38, 39-40, 41-43, 57, 63-64, 65-66, 67, 79-80, 87-88, 89-90, 96-97, 98-99, 104, 161, 573; **37:** 214-15; **38:** 136, 337, 347, 348, 462-63, 558-59
football, **31:** 429
foreign investors, **28:** 481
friends; friendship, **27:** 217-18, 490-91, 505; **28:** 47, 106, 336, 337; **29:** 113; **34:** 190; **35:** 51
higher education; scholarship, **28:** 440; **29:** 436; **30:** 89, 104-108, 145; **36:** 419
honorary degrees, **32:** 63, 499
E. M. House, alleged break with, **34:** 377-78,n1,2, 381, 402,n2, 402-403,n1, 437, 442-43, 471, 471-72,n1, 517
immigrants, immigration, **30:** 35-36; **33:** 39; **35:** 50; **36:** 574-75; **37:** 81; **38:** 291, 346-47, 537
law, lawyers, **27:** 36-37; **31:** 184, 185; **36:** 220; **37:** 392; **38:** 575, 584-85
legislation, **28:** 390; **29:** 157; **32:** 166, 183
liberty, **28:** 451; **29:** 516, 524; **31:** 227; **35:** 168, 344; **38:** 331
literature, the arts: **27:** 253; **29:** 55; **36:** 570
lobbyists, **27:** 473
Mexico; conditions and leaders, **28:** 217, 484, 488,n3; **29:** 522; **30:** 143; **37:** 512
morality; character, **30:** 264; **31:** 186, 221, 223, 226, 562; **32:** 216; **34:** 352; **35:** 51; **36:** 5, 78, 83, 392-93; **37:** 334
neutrality, **32:** 158; **33:** 16, 38; **34:** 438; **35:** 49; **36:** 5, 27, 33, 65
newspapermen; newspapers, **27:** 296; **28:** 107; **29:** 353-54, 391n1, 530; **30:** 178, 277, 327-28; **31:** 274; **35:** 235,n2, 273; **36:** 100, 120
patriotism, **35:** 343; **36:** 40, 70, 159; **37:** 417; **38:** 489-90
peace; league of nations, **36:** 6, 9, 27, 33, 78, 80, 108; **37:** 114, 115, 396; **38:** 136,

Woodrow Wilson, Selected Opinions and Comments, cont.

348, 465, 542, 588
politics, **27:** 345; **28:** 436; **29:** 93, 557, 558; **30:** 478; **31:** 59, 264, 265, 396, 400; **32:** 38, 375; **35:** 443; **38:** 163; 261, 334, 485, 476-77, 572, 578, 592, 597, 611
power, **28:** 312; **36:** 9, 474, 490
preparedness, **27:** 359-60; **31:** 421; **35:** 122, 169, 171, 297-302, 307-308, 310, 481-82, 499-500; **36:** 7-16, 31-32, 33, 38, 44, 46-47, 47, 83-84, 118, 120; **37:** 224-25
President; the presidency, **27:** 98-101, 150-51, 465-66; **28:** 11, 107, 395; **29:** 12, 24, 59, 211-12, 363-64, 364-66, 530, 535; **30:** 65n1, 73, 177, 276; **31:** 60, 344, 397, 398-99; **32:** 9-10, 188, 334, 421, 431; **34:** 57,n1, 177, 202, 307-308, 359, 432n1, 474, 497; **35:** 342-43, 520-21; **36:** 11, 18, 56, 162, 188, 207n3, 415,n1, 497,n2, 503-504,n2, 560-61, 566; **37:** 47, 49, 50, 51, 70, 173, 221,n1, 391; **38:** 217, 218, 433-34, 659, 661-62
presidential politics, **27:** 414; **31:** 23, 59, 94, 101, 280, 290, 301; **32:** 10, 55, 232; **33:** 518; **34:** 52n2, 516; **35:** 103, 176, 239, 313-14, 347, 424; **36:** 15, 20, 23, 31-32, 132, 186-87, 248, 249, 267, 288,n2, 292, 458, 472, 479, 480, 580-81, 598; **37:** 37, 120, 146, 190-200, 398, 408, 455, 516, 517, 521, 535; **38:** 287, 334, 550
Princeton University, **29:** 58, 163, 171, 186-87, 272-73,n2; **30:** 104, 163-64, 176n1, 179-80, 189; **34:** 470, n1; **35:** 152, 182
public opinion, **33:** 37, 41; **35:** 51; **36:** 17, 100; **38:** 266, 568, 592
religion; **30:** 107, 147; **35:** 329; **36:** 629-31; **37:** 148-50; **38:** 330, 525, 532, 581, 673
self-analysis; philosophical observations, **28:** 257, 263, 311; **29:** 362, 363, 395; **30:** 178; **31:** 3, 280, 290, 344-45; **32:** 17, 63, 233; **33:** 15, 149; **34:** 9, 23, 335, 345; **35:** 146; **36:** 18, 100, 107, 119, 220; **37:** 51, 148, 212, 442; **38:** 127, 218, 368, 426, 478, 479, 593
segregation, **28:** 65, 265, 496; **31:** 303
truth, **30:** 179; **35:** 442; **37:** 49, 327-28
Washington, D.C., **28:** 46, 86-87; **29:** 114, 364-65; **34:** 119, 302
woman suffrage, **29:** 214, 309-10; **32:** 21, 22; **35:** 28; **36:** 3-4; **38:** 9-10, 487-88

PRESS CONFERENCES

see Table of Contents *for chronological listing*

PUBLIC AND POLITICAL ADDRESSES

see Table of Contents *for chronological listing*

End of Woodrow Wilson entry

Wilson and the Issues (Creel), **38**: 16n2

Wilson-Bryan Democratic League of Illinois, **29**: 261n2; **31**: 232n2

Wilson Business Men's National League, **38**: 212n1, 461n1, 591n1

Wilson: Campaigns for Progressivism and Peace, 1916-1917 (Link), **37**: 431n1, 467n1; **38**: 51n1, 85n1, 271n1, 313n1, 314n2, 559n2, 570n1, 675n1

Wilson College Men's League, **27**: 110n2

Wilson: Confusions and Crises, 1915-1916 (Link), **35**: 158n3, 192n1, 219n1, 419n1, 434n1, 478n1, 530n1; **36**: 180n1, 192n3, 209n1, 228n1, 238n1, 280n1, 284n1, 344n1, 480n1, 519n1; **37**: 277n1, 306n1, 321n1, 481n1; **38**: 60n2

Wilson Day at Shadow Lawn, N.J., **38**: 461-65, 549n1

Wilson Era: Years of Peace, 1910-1917 (Daniels), **27**: 134n1; **30**: 145n3; **32**: 21n3; **37**: 78n1

Wilson: The New Freedom (Link), **27**: 54n12, 97n1, 103n1, 120n1, 188n2, 191n1, 220n3, 263n2, 277n1, 291n1, 298n1, 301n1, 470n2,5,6, 473n1, 483n1, 485n2,3, 510n1, 535n1; **28**: 8n1, 45n1, 99n4, 146n1, 187n4, 247n1, 255n1, 257n2, 302n3, 336n2, 373n1, 379n1, 381n1, 428n1, 495n5; **29**: 20n1, 67n2, 98n1, 133n1, 136n1, 138n2, 203n3, 316n3, 375n1, 406n1, 420n2, 476n1, 538n1, 557n1; **30**: 10n2, 165n1, 166n2, 191n1, 217n1, 224n1, 270n4, 273n1, 455n1; **31**: 88n3, 404n2; **32**: 455n3, 470n3, 486n3; **33**: 196n5, 218n1; **35**: 232n1; **36**: 464n1; **38**: 674n1

Wilson House, Washington, D.C., **28**: 43n8

Wilson National Progressive Republican League, **27**: 62n2

Wilson Promises to Guard Water Power (*Washington Times*), **36**: 305,n1

Wilson, the Man (Fort), **29**: 327,n1

Wilson: The Road to the White House (Link), **27**: 22n2; **31**: 351n1

Wilson: The Struggle for Neutrality (Link), **30**: 193n1, 307n1, 325n1, 352n1, 402n1, 441n1; **31**: 20n1, 32n1, 55n2, 112n2, 119n1, 129n1, 180n6, 310n1, 468n3, 471n6; **32**: 89n3, 120n2, 134n1, 172n1, 173n2, 202n3, 367n1, 380n1, 381n2, 451n, 457n2, 464n1; **33**: 7n1, 127n1, 129n1, 155n1, 184n1, 213n2, 258n1, 317n3, 370n1, 457n1, 462n1, 473n1, 480n3, 497n1, 533n1; **34**: 45n1, 74n5, 106n4, 158n1, 197n2, 242n1, 257n2,383n1,423n1,450n3,460n1; **35**: 43n1, 91n1, 158n1; **37**: 157n1

Wilson Touch (*New York Post*), **29**: 319n1

Wilson Would Rush Water Power Bill (*Washington Times*), **36**: 355,n1

Wilson's Advantage (*Des Moines Register*), **38**: 174,n1, 175

Wilson's First Year (*Newark Evening News*), **29**: 302,n1

Wilson's Triumph (New York *World*), **31**: 295,n1

Wilton, N.H., **28**: 345, 372,n1

Winchester, Caleb Thomas, **36**: 297,n3, 330, 349, 399-400, 410

Windsor, Vt., **28**: 43, 67, 102, 161, 248, 331; **30**: 50; **34**: 125, 160, 166, 168; **37**: 373; church, **28**: 315n1; society of, **28**: 62,n3, 92, 103

Wing, Daniel Gould, **29**: 86

Wingate and Holland, N.Y., **29**: 130

Wingo, Otis Theodore, **28**: 90,n2, 122,n3

Winkler, Frederick C., **36**: 55n1

Winslow, Erving, **38**: 19n1

Winslow, Lawrence Lanier, **31**: 385-86; **32**: 372,n4, 507; **34**: 320; **35**: 192

Winslow, Rose, **29**: 214

Wisconsin, **27**: 87; **30**: 161, 161-62; **32**: 19-20; **38**: 159, 290, 376n1, 377, 515n1; Republican victories in, **31**: 264n3; Democratic party in, **31**: 346,n2, 406; WW's preparedness remarks in, **36**: 53-54, 54-55, 55-63; and J. A. Aylward's appointment, **36**: 315-16,n1,2,3, 500-501, 510-11

Wisconsin, University of, **27**: 87, 203n1, 206; **28**: 22, 82n1; **29**: 352; **38**: 297n1

Wisconsin Faces Reaction (Mason), **30**: 161,n1

Wisconsin Magazine of History, **27**: 291n1; **28**: 115n3

Wise, Stephen Samuel, **27**: 244; **29**: 170; **30**: 144; **32**: 97; **35**: 194-95, 212; **36**: 524, 643n18, 644, 647; **38**: 445n1, 565,n5

Wiseman, William, **27**: xii, xiii

Wisner, Charles Wesley, Jr., **32**: 534,n1

Witherspoon Gang, **35**: 262,n3, 270, 275, 281

Within the Law (play), **27**: 140,n2

Witte, Sergei Yulievich, Count Witte, **31**: 182,n2, 187

Wittpenn, Henry Otto, **27**: 386n1, 494n1; **28**: 65-66,n1, 83, 96,n1, 97

Wobblies: see Industrial Workers of the World

Wolcott Hotel, N.Y., **33**: 443

Wolf, Simon, **28**: 5,n4, 111; **37**: 109-11, 119

Wolfe, Robert F., **38**: 394, 439n1

Wolgemuth, Kathleen Long, **27**: 291n1

Womack, John, Jr., **30**: 47n1

Woman of It (Luther), **31**: 316,n2

woman suffrage, **29**: 21-22,n1, 213-15, 272n1, 309, 515-16; **30**: 225, 226-28, 240; **31**: 328n2, 329-30; **32**: 21-22; **34**: 225, 251n2,3, 542-43; **35**: 28, 30, 33-34, 51, 292-93,n1,2, 360; **37**: 167,n4, 169n1, 199, 208-209, 329, 375-76,n1, 426-27n1,2,3,4, 490,n1, 491, 502-504, 513-14, 515, 516, 522-23, 532-33, 535, 539-40; **38**: 37, 78, 481n1

EAW on, **28**: 67; and national association opposed to, **30**: 257,n1; WW on, **32**: 22-23,n1; **37**: 237,n1, 266, 517, 518, 529, 536-37; **38**: 9, 9-10, 281-82, 336,

520,n2; WW's remarks to delegation in New York, **36:** 3-4; proposed platform planks on, **36:** 484-85; C. S. Thomas on, **38:** 4-5; B. Lindsey on, **38:** 14; WW to address national association on, **38:** 19-20,n2,3, 30, 125; Woman's party will attempt to defeat WW, **38:** 28; Mary Field on, **38:** 58, 58-59; N. Hapgood on, **38:** 87; WW's address in Atlantic City on, **38:** 161-64; Ida Tarbell on, **38:** 173; Alice C. Dewey on, **38:** 176; Anna Shaw on WW's speech on, **38:** 178-79; movement in Oregon, **38:** 186; Anna Johnson on, **38:** 520,n2

Woman Voter's Convention, San Francisco, **35:** 292n1

Woman's College of Baltimore, **38:** 648,n1,2

Woman's National Wilson-Marshall League, **38:** 511,n1, 549n1

Woman's party: *see* National Woman's party

Woman's Peace party, **33:** 314n1; **35:** 134-35,n1; **37:** 308

women, **37:** 167,n4, 198; labor conditions, **27:** 76, 107, 140, 243; WW's tribute to southern, **27:** 574; and segregation, **28:** 410; EAW and improvement of government employees, **28:** 476; WW's remarks to a committee of working women, **29:** 214; monument to Confederate women, **29:** 322; and appointments, **30:** 172,n1; and peace resolution, **33:** 314n1,2; WW article to suggested by *Ladies Home Journal*, **36:** 559-60,n1; L. D. Brandeis and labor laws and, **36:** 25n1; WW on, **36:** 35-36, 573; Mary Field on support for WW by, **38:** 59-60; granted equal wages at Ford Motor Co., **38:** 187n2; and 1916 platform, **38:** 260; WW's address in Cincinnati to, **38:** 526-33; WW on labor laws and, **38:** 586

Women of the Synod of Georgia, **31:** 259n1

Women's Bureau of the Democratic National Committee, **38:** 6

Women's Democratic Club of Portland, Oregon, **38:** 185,n1, 281, 282

Women's Peace Conference, The Hague: *see* International Congress of Women

Women's Peace Society, **37:** 308n1

Women's Political Union of New Jersey, **37:** 426n1

Wood, James, **29:** 476; **36:** 629n1

Wood, Leonard, **27:** 25-26,n1; **29:** 74,n1, 168-69, 248,n1, 249, 250, 377,n1; **30:** 240; **31:** 266, 291, 475, 502, 506-507; **33:** 517, 533; **34:** 133-34, 209, 337n1, 353, 401; **36:** 519

Wood, Richard, **27:** xxii

Wood, Robert N., **28:** 115-18,n1

Wood, Stephen B., **29:** 170n1

Woodrow, Felexiana Shepherd Baker (Mrs. James), **27:** 147; **31:** 542-43; **35:**

404-405, 412; **36:** 399,n1, 410

Woodrow, Fitz William McMaster, **29:** 554,n1, 559, 561; **30:** 374,n2; **33:** 442, 538; **34:** 201, 287, 290, 360, 379

Woodrow, James Hamilton, **30:** 74, 374; **31:** 542; **35:** 11n2; **36:** 398-99, 410

Woodrow, Katherine Hamilton, **35:** 11,n2

Woodrow, Katherine McGregor McMaster (Mrs. James Hamilton), **35:** 11n2

Woodrow Wilson: An Intimate Memoir (Grayson), **29:** 99n1; **32:** 423n3

Woodrow Wilson and Far Eastern Policy, 1913-21 (Curry), **27:** 175n1

Woodrow Wilson and Social Justice (McKelway), **38:** 284,n1

Woodrow Wilson As I Know Him (Tumulty), **27:** 133n1; **36:** 317n1; **38:** 453n1

Woodrow Wilson Birthplace, **37:** 221n1

Woodrow Wilson Foundation, **27:** xxii

Woodrow Wilson Independent League, **37:** 286n1, 362n1, 432; **38:** 175,n2, 176, 276n7

Woodrow Wilson, the Man and His Work: A Biographical Study (Ford), **36:** 581,n1

Woodrow Wilson School of Princeton University, **37:** 221n1

Woodrow Wilson: The Years of Preparation (Mulder), **34:** 491n1

Woodrow Wilson's Appointment Policy and the Negro (Wolgemuth), **27:** 291n1

Woodrow Wilsons, The (McAdoo), **28:** 565n1

Woodrow Wilson's China Policy, 1913-1917 (Li), **27:** 175n1

Woodrow Wilson's Work (*Milwaukee Journal*), **34:** 388n1

Woods, Charles Albert, **27:** 335-36, 348, 359

Woods, Hiram, **28:** 280; **35:** 262n3, 275; **36:** 349, 359-60, 377, 397

Woods, James Pleasant, **37:** 228,n1

Woods, Lawrence Crane, **29:** 305,n1; **34:** 470; **35:** 178,n3; **38:** 466

Woods, Robert Archey, **29:** 352

Woods, Salley Jones Wanamaker (Mrs. Charles Albert), **27:** 336, 348

Woods, Samuel Baker, **27:** 73-74,n1

Woodstock, Vt., **28:** 190, 260; **34:** 64, 127

Woodward, Leonidas Polk, **31:** 127,n2

Woodward, Thomas Mullen, **33:** 446,n1

Woodward, William, **31:** 139,n4

woolen industry, **27:** 303, 321

wool schedule: *see* Underwood-Simmons Tariff Act

Woolley, Mary Emma, **38:** 108n1, 110-11

Woolley, Robert Wickliffe, **27:** 55,n1, 82, 83; **28:** 491n2, 496; **31:** 361n2; **32:** 121; **34:** 514, 517; **35:** 239, 382; **36:** 263-64, 388,n4, 472n1; **37:** 46, 76, 206-207, 378, 379, 475; **38:** 66n1, 616

Woolsey, Lester Hood, **36:** 452,n1; **37:** 452, 476, 484, 495, 496

Woolsey, Theodore S., **29:** 121,n1

Worcester, Dean Conant, **29:** 137,n2, 164

Wordsworth, William, **27:** 140; **28:** 126; **30:** 22; **31:** 14, 29; **32:** 334; **33:** 125,n1; **34:** 228n1; **36:** 274,n1; **37:** 37, 457; **38:** 338-39

Wordsworth's Grave (Watson), **31:** 279

workmen's compensation, **27:** 243; **35:** 184, 205,n1; **36:** 248; **37:** 198; for federal employees: *see* Kern-McGillicuddy bill

Works, John Downey, **27:** 220,n6, 275-76,n1, 277

World Peace Foundation, **36:** 362n1

World War: M. T. Herrick on, **30:** 313; E. Grey and approach of, **30:** 316; WW on, **30:** 317, 450, 462; **38:** 347; impact on Mexico, **30:** 322; E. M. House on, **30:** 323-24, 327, 341-42, 432-33; and Americans in Europe, **30:** 335; WW's offer of good offices, **30:** 316, 342; House and R. Olney on good offices, **30:** 349; responses to WW's mediation offer, **30:** 352, 456-57,n1; C. W. Eliot on, **30:** 353-55, 418-20, 434; H. van Dyke on situation in Holland, **30:** 365; *U.S.S. Tennessee* sails to rescue Americans stranded in Europe, **30:** 369,n7; and censorship of cable and wireless messages, **30:** 388-89, 407-408; F. Yates on, **30:** 401; W. H. Page on, **30:** 439; participants blame others for, **30:** 457; Germany's use of airships and bombs, **30:** 460-61, 471; Grey's fears of Prussian militarism, **30:** 473; WW on bombing, **30:** 478; House's note to A. Zimmermann on hopes of mediation, **30:** 488, 488-89; and Russian army, **38:** 69; F. C. Penfield on Rumania entering, **38:** 74-75; Grey on how war could have been prevented, **38:** 254 *atrocities and war crimes,* **35:** 10, 71n3, 194, 197, 216; **37:** 274; in Belgium, **30:** 458, 459, 459-61; **31:** 17, 85; **34:** 371; **38:** 650-53, 656-57; accusations on manufacture and use of dumdum bullets, **31:** 17, 38-39, 40n1, 54; Page on, **31:** 26-27, 263; **37:** 461-62; H. Münsterberg on atrocities by British, **31:** 339; J. W. Gerard on, **31:** 426-27; **33:** 300; **36:** 615; Lansing on concentration camps, **31:** 443; and conditions in Germany, **31:** 537; German raids on England, **32:** 98, 99, 379-80; German and Austrian prisoners in Russia, **32:** 396-97; **36:** 125-26; sinking of *Falaba,* **32:** 484-86, 503,n1; sinking of *Lusitania,* **33:** 127,n1, 143, 330, 358-59; **35:** 437; H. H. Kitchener on, **33:** 189; **36:** 442; and J. Bryce report, **33:** 485,n1; and Cleveland Automatic Machine Co., **33:** 497-98,n1,4; Eliot on, **33:** 513-14; and third *Lusitania* note, **33:** 546; use of explosive gas shells, **34:** 42; *Arabic* disaster, **34:** 257-58, 264-66; and Countess de Belleville and Louise Thuliez, **35:** 88,n1,2,3,4, 103n1; exe-

cution of Edith Cavell, **35:** 103,n1,2; and Armenians in Turkey, **35:** 104-105, 119, 337, 348, 349; sinking of *Ancona,* **35:** 192,n1, 236-37, 286-88, 368; in Poland, **35:** 367; **38:** 29-30,n1, 62, 64-66, 80, 369-71; and *Persia* sinking, **35:** 419,n1; and *Baralong* incident, **35:** 421-22; WW on, **36:** 88, 108-109; Jews and, **36:** 356; *Sussex* sinking, **36:** 448, 449, 467, 492-93, 508; devastation of Poland and appeal for aid to, **37:** 404-406, 407, 414, 421-22, 445; and women's suffering, **37:** 536-37; Grey on, **38:** 90 *impact on U.S.:* general, **33:** 495-96; **35:** 294; **37:** 193, 397,n1; **38:** 57, 514, 528, 538-39; wheat prices down, **30:** 324-25; paralysis of international commerce, **30:** 324-25; emergency measures taken to help business world, **30:** 325-26; and surplus crops, **30:** 332-33; WW asks for funds to assist Americans in Europe, **30:** 337, 337-38,n1; and foreign exchange and gold situation, **30:** 420-22; and congestion in U.S. ports, **30:** 440-41; and cotton interests, **30:** 441,n1; **31:** 126-29, 129, 130, 132, 251, 275; **34:** 58, 100; decline in customs revenue, **30:** 467-68, 471-72; WW address to Congress requesting additional revenue, **30:** 473-75; J. P. Morgan, Jr., on American investments and, **30:** 483-85; J. von Bernstorff on, **31:** 10; banking and, **31:** 75, 153-54; WW on, **31:** 170, 326, 415-16; **32:** 316; Lansing on foreign credits, **31:** 217-19, 219-20; Bryan on, **31:** 378; costs to belligerents, **32:** 207; and maritime freight rates, **32:** 313-14; and Federal Reserve System, **34:** 36; and Colombian treaty, **34:** 50, 51; and loans, **34:** 295, 316-17, 421-23, 478, 481, 504; WW's appeals for aid, **35:** 243-44, 367; WW on preparedness and, **36:** 12, 43, 54, 60, 68-69, 75, 82-83, 93, 105-106, 112; G. Pinchot on water-power and, **36:** 49-51; W. C. Redfield fears German dumping of goods, **36:** 127; dyestuffs industry and, **36:** 261,n2, 274-76; W. J. Stone on postwar commerce, **36:** 366-68; proposal for creation of national resources council, **36:** 431-34; A. Gardiner on raising income tax, **37:** 498-99; B. M. Baruch on domestic mobilization, **36:** 544,n1, 611-12, 612; and conditions in Austria-Hungary, **37:** 5; and Britain's blacklist, **37:** 477

United States neutrality: establishment and maintenance of, **30:** 307; **32:** 52n1, 104, 107n1, 218, 223; **33:** 21, 22, 38, 39, 130, 134, 137-38, 188, 189, 200, 206n3, 225, 330, 336, 337, 342, 472-73, 494-95; **34:** 9, 31,n2, 85, 92-93, 100, 260-61, 278-79, 317-18, 422, 423; **35:** 8-9, 11, 49, 210-11, 228-29, 294, 356, 424, 436-37, 524n1

W. H. Page on **30:** 330, 439; loans to belligerents, **30:** 372-73, 386-87; **31:** 153-54; WW answers Eliot's proposal for involvement, **30:** 379-80; WW on, **30:** 387, 393-94; **31:** 40n1, 243, 378-79; **32:** 146; **38:** 132, 347-48, 506-507, 531, 541, 588; Federal Council of the Churches of Christ in America and, **30:** 397-98; **31:** 80; Eliot on, **30:** 419; **38:** 353; Lansing on transfer of German merchant ships, **30:** 448-49; J. von Bernstorff on, **31:** 9n1; **38:** 391-92; William II turns to WW as impartial judge, **31:** 33; WW on Belgian commissioners to U.S., **31:** 33-34; and Burgess resolution, **31:** 103,n1; effect of contraband and ammunition sales on, **31:** 153; Spring Rice on use by belligerents of neutral ports, **31:** 155; Page on Declaration of London and, **31:** 160; effect of atrocities and bombings on, **31:** 181; and Russian desire for loan, **31:** 182-83; House on, **31:** 228; WW calls conference among State, Treasury and Navy Departments on, **31:** 270; WW on Münsterberg's claims of unneutral acts by U.S., **31:** 293; Münsterberg on, **31:** 336-40; S. Blythe on WW and, **31:** 395; Lansing on pro-German propaganda and, **31:** 434-36; and WW on declining to see Dernburg, **31:** 496; and report of arms to belligerents, **32:** 24,n1, 25, 145; and Bryan-Stone exchange, **32:** 26,n1; use of neutral flag by belligerents, **32:** 200, 201, 208, 249n1, 250; and "strict accountability" note, **32:** 208-209; and Congress refusal to amend certain laws during warfare, **32:** 513; J. S. Williams and H. Smith debate on, **36:** 20n1; and T. P. Gore speech, **36:** 238n1; M. H. Glynn on, **36:** 263n1; R. H. Dabney on, **36:** 532-33; H. A. Garfield on, **36:** 544-45; D. Lawrence on, **37:** 448-51; issue of belligerent submarines in neutral waters, **38:** 148-50; S. Gompers on, **38:** 469-70; *Marina* incident and, **38:** 607-608

rights and obligations of neutrals, **33:** 21, 42, 61, 62, 67, 75-76, 77, 92, 130, 170, 175, 176, 178, 200, 206-207, 207-209, 215-16, 283-84, 356-57, 360, 472, 489, 490-91, 499,n1, 509, 527-29, 547, 548; **34:** 6, 13, 96-97, 115, 195n2, 260-61, 265, 381, 445; **35:** 44, 91,n1, 418-19, 451, 457-58, 472, 507, 522

and Declaration of London, **31:** 90-91, 104-105, 163, 164, 165; Spring Rice on use of neutral ports, **31:** 155; and French seizure of U.S. ships, **31:** 176,n1; and foreign loans, **31:** 177,n2; and sale of submarine parts, **31:** 310,n1; P. Fuller and Lansing on altering rules during warfare, **31:** 426, 450; Bryan advocates conference of neutrals,

31: 480-81; assertion of American trading rights, **31:** 525-30; ship-purchase bill and, **32:** 167, 244-45, 263, 275-76, 336, 337; and German war zone decree, **32:** 194-95, 195-96,n1; and Hague conventions, **32:** 224-25; House on all-nations convention and, **32:** 238; and distribution of food, **32:** 259-60, 346; G. M. Hitchcock bill and, **32:** 290; and Great Britain's blockade, **32:** 317, 399-401, 406-407, 428-29, 433, 444, 451-52; "strict accountability" regarding British blockage, **32:** 425; and *Falaba* case, **32:** 486, 498, 503n1; Lansing's reply to Bernstorff's protest about munitions exports, **32:** 511-13; WW on, **33:** 223, 238, 239, 279,n1, 535; **37:** 61-62; **38:** 132; and *Lusitania* case, **36:** 73n1, 128; Grey on German submarine warfare, **36:** 133; Chamber of Commerce's recommendations on, **36:** 169n1; C. S. Hamlin on, **36:** 172; Tumulty on, **36:** 212; H. L. Higginson on, **36:** 218; Germany's views, **36:** 270-71, 499, 622, 623, 624; W. J. Stone on, **36:** 367; *Sussex* note and, **36:** 454-55, 456, 468-70, 470-71, 494, 495-96; Lansing's memoranda on, **36:** 534-39, 556-57; and German reply to *Sussex* note, **36:** 626-27; WW's rejoinder and, **36:** 650, 651; House on, **37:** 7, 63; Lansing on *Sussex* notes and, **37:** 13; Lansing on Paris Economic Conference and, **37:** 287-88; Lord Robert Cecil on, **37:** 459; and blacklist, **37:** 471; British blockade and, **37:** 476-79; Lansing on, **38:** 467-68

origins: House on tensions in Europe, **30:** 109; assassination of Archduke Francis Ferdinand, **30:** 222; better understanding between European nations needed, **30:** 247-48; and demonstrations in France, **30:** 313; Page on hatred between Slav and Teuton, **30:** 316, 330; A. B. Hart's article on, **30:** 343,n1; William II on how Germany became involved, **30:** 382-83; Page on Prussian militarism, **31:** 6-8; Germany blames other countries, **31:** 37

outbreak: Page on situation in London, **30:** 314-16; House predicts, **30:** 324; Germany invades Luxembourg, **30:** 330; Germany declares war on Russia, **30:** 330; British declaration of war, **30:** 359,n2, 368; Czar Nicholas mobilizes army, **30:** 383

peace moves: **34:** 92; **37:** 3,n1; J. W. Gerard on, **31:** 14; J. J. Jusserand on, **31:** 15-16; **37:** 93, 134-35,n2, 164; Page on, **31:** 21-22; **32:** 359, 360; **35:** 517-18; **36:** 181-82; Germany and, **31:** 37; House on, **31:** 45, 55,n3, 76-77, 385, 468-70, 490, 500, 501, 540, 549-50; **34:** 85-86, 186, 311; **35:** 43-44, 59-60, 61-62, 71, 81-82, 176, 191, 220; **38:** 646, 647; **36:** 167, 170, 379,n5, 388, 405, 631-32, 652-

World War (*cont.*)
53; **37:** 6-7, 21, 63-64, 179, 202; Grey on Germany and, **31:** 58-59; Spring Rice and, **31:** 62, 137, 140-41, 490, 518-19, 549-50; J. Bryce on not renewing talks, **31:** 81-82; and G. Wallas' suggestions, **31:** 108; C. Dumba on, **31:** 296-97; WW on duty of U.S. to propose mediation, **31:** 379; WW invites suggestions from H. Morgenthau, **31:** 428,n1; neutral conference as opening to, **31:** 480-81; A. Zimmermann rejects German participation in, **31:** 540-41; and House's mission, **32:** 17n1, 41-42, 61, 67, 83-84,n1, 99, 234, 402, 411-12, 514; **33:** 406; **35:** 240-43, 380,n1, 381, 387-88, 484; and Grey's terms, **32:** 44-50; Field Marshal French on proposal made by U.S. to England, **32:** 81; WW willing to preside at peace conference, **32:** 117; WW on, **32:** 174; **33:** 85-86, 279n1, 436; **35:** 327, 457; **37:** 36-37, 57-58, 62; A. Zimmermann on conditions for, **32:** 351; Grey on, **33:** 13-14, 408; **34:** 145-46, 370-71; **35:** 11, 71,n3, 79, 255; **37:** 43-44, 131-32, 412; **38:** 91-93, 253, 254; Münsterberg on, **33:** 17-20, 28-29; Bryan's appeal for, **33:** 67; rumor of Germany's approach to Japan regarding, **33:** 81-82,n1; F. von Papen on, **33:** 233; O. G. Villard on, **33:** 254; Bernstorff on WW's conditions for, **33:** 283-84; and International Congress of Women, **33:** 314,n1,2; F. Gildemeester's visit to U.S., **33:** 347-48, 361-62; and second *Lusitania* note, **33:** 359-60; A. L. Lowell on, **33:** 458-59; and proposed conference of neutral powers, **34:** 110n1, 236-37, 243, 247-48, 250-52, 290, 397-99, 399; **35:** 195-99, 199-200, 487,n2,3; U.S. influence as participant compared with remaining neutral, **34:** 318-19; H. Hoover on, **34:** 410; B. Battin on, **35:** 20-21,n1; and Alfonso XIII, **35:** 129-30, 144; **37:** 19-20; W. Gherardi on, **35:** 131; Turkey feels time has come to negotiate, **35:** 185,n1; Lansing on, **35:** 244-45; **38:** 82; and Ford peace expedition, **35:** 279,n1; J. Bryce on, **35:** 348; **38:** 250; Gerard on conversation with William II, **35:** 359; and Switzerland, **35:** 405; O. Wakenitz on, **35:** 490-91; Bethmann Hollweg on terms, **36:** 123,n1, 444n1; and House-Grey Memorandum, **36:** 180,n2; King Albert on, **36:** 202; Gerard on Germany and, **36:** 341, 624; rumors of negotiations, **36:** 350; British on German-U.S. break and early settlement, **36:** 369; H. H. Kitchener on, **36:** 438-39, 441-42; British unwilling to suggest conference to France, **36:** 443-44, 512; Bernstorff on, **36:** 526n1, 656; Gerard meets with Bethmann Hollweg and William II, **36:** 616; F. C. Penfield on

Austria-Hungary, **37:** 4-5, 273-74; Bethmann Hollweg on, **37:** 43n1; and Benedict XV, **37:** 54, 84-85; Tumulty on, **37:** 58-60; S. Strunsky on, **37:** 60n1; Spring Rice on, **37:** 73; and the Netherlands, **37:** 75; E. Baring on WW as mediator, **37:** 143,n1; British public opinion on, **37:** 144-45, 182-86, 226-27, 227, 239-40, 294-95,n1, 311-12; **38:** 247, 392-93; and resolutions by Paris Economic Conference on, **37:** 287-88; N. Buxton on, **37:** 370-72; **38:** 54; and Conference of Neutrals in Stockholm, **37:** 515; House meets with Dutch minister on, **38:** 53,n2; and Russia, **38:** 68-69; WW's colloquy with members of American Neutral Conference Committee, **38:** 108-17; Germany's apparent willingness to enter, **38:** 313-14,n1,2, 411, 496-97,n3, 619; House and WW discuss, **38:** 658

strategic plans, **32:** 225,n1; **33:** 122-23, 371, 405-406, 501, 522-24; **34:** 20, 42, 62, 310-11; **35:** 8, 74-75, 226-27, 255; Field Marshal French on, **32:** 81; and Germany, **32:** 193,n1,3, 237, 262; and Britain, **32:** 238; Germany and Russia, **32:** 266; House on French and British armies, **32:** 522-23; Admiral Craddock fleet destroyed by Admiral von Spee, **36:** 235,n6; probability of Rumania entering war, **37:** 464-65

World's Salesmanship Congress, **37:** 383n1, 387n1

World's Work, **29:** 98n; **32:** 56n2; **36:** 452n3

Wortham, Louis J., **36:** 186,n1

Wotherspoon, William Wallace, **29:** 377n1, 509n2, 510-11; **36:** 657,n1

Wright, James Edward, **28:** 584n1

Wright, Joshua Butler, **38:** 18,n1

Wright, Theodore, **38:** 389,n1

Writer, J. A., **28:** 427

Writer's Equal Suffrage League, **38:** 520

Wuchang, China, **32:** 248

Wyman House, Princeton University, **31:** 205,n2

Wyoming, **37:** 172n1; coal, **28:** 583

Wyoming, U.S.S., **29:** 437

Wytheville, Va., **32:** 423n1; **35:** 16, 32

YMCA: *see* Young Men's Christian Association

Yager, Arthur, **29:** 264,n1, 269, 289; **30:** 215; **31:** 465, 465-66; **32:** 94; **36:** 568, 569-70; **37:** 170; **38:** 649

Yale Review, **38:** 497n1, 498

Yale University, **27:** 208; **28:** 111; **29:** 352n1; **30:** 176n1, 189; **31:** 282; **35:** 216; **36:** 371n1, 415n1; **37:** 308n1, 531n1; **38:** 362n1; E. M. House Collection, **27:** xi-xii; W. Wiseman Collection, **27:** xii-xiii; and Princeton football, **31:** 412n2

Yampa Valley Coal Co., Colo., **29:** 549

Yangtze River, **27:** 441

Yangtze Valley, **31:** 365; **32:** 138
Yardley, Edward, **33:** 213
Yards and Docks, Bureau of, **36:** 279n2
Yarmouth, England, **32:** 98, 380
Yates, Emily Chapman Martin (Mrs. Frederic), **27:** 155-56; **28:** 286; **29:** 323; **34:** 82-83; **38:** 687
Yates, Frederic, **27:** 155-56, 474-75; **28:** 286; **29:** 323-24; **30:** 401, 406, 479; **32:** 434n2; **34:** 82, 83; **35:** 110; **38:** 687
Yates, Mary, **27:** 155-56; **29:** 323; **34:** 82, 83; **38:** 687
Yates, Minnie Knowlton (Mrs. William Henry), **35:** 46,n2
Yazoo City, Miss., **34:** 108n2
Year of Wilson (New York *World*), **29:** 303,n1
Years of Discretion (play), **27:** 112,n1
Yellow Sea, **27:** 428, 443
Yokohama Specie Bank, **37:** 308n1, 531n1
Yoshihito, Emperor of Japan, **29:** 91n3; **38:** 648
You May Fire When Ready, Gridley (Wortham), **36:** 186,n2
Young, Bennett H., **30:** 141n1
Young, Clement Calhoun, **27:** 343-44,n3
Young, Charles Griffith, **38:** 500n1
Young, Ella Flagg (Mrs. William), **38:** 481-82,n1
Young, Evan E., **31:** 229
Young, Samuel Edward, **36:** 7n1
Young Men's Christian Association (YMCA), **28:** 22; **32:** 125-27; **34:** 358,n1; **38:** 590n2; in China, **27:** 124, 262; **28:** 23n1; of Pittsburgh, **31:** 151n2; WW's address to, **31:** 220-28
Young Men's Democratic Club of New York, **36:** 389,n7, 398, 477n1
Young Men's League of Democratic Clubs; WW's speech to, **38:** 293, 295, 301-12, 318n1
Younger Generation: A Comedy for Parents (Houghton), **28:** 355n4
Youngman, Mr., **27:** 92
Ypiranga, S.S., **29:** 464, 476n1, 477, 480
Ysaka Maru, S.S., **35:** 425
Yuan Shih-k'ai, **27:** 144,n1, 224, 225, 382, 488; **30:** 238; **31:** 372,n1, 381,n1; **32:** 137, 433n1, 529n1; **33:** 31; **35:** 115, 203,n1; **37:** 234; death of, **37:** 167, 182
Yucatán, state, Mex., **28:** 29; **33:** 260, 261
Yucatan Unions Send Peace Plea in Proclamation to U.S. Workers (*New York Call*), **37:** 245n1
Yuma, Ariz., **27:** 403; **37:** 284
Yunnan Province, China, **32:** 320, 418

Zacatecas, Battle of, **30:** 383n1
Zacatecas, state, Mex., **28:** 31, 77; **29:** 252, 253; **30:** 220
Zacatecas, Zacatecas, Mex., **28:** 28; **29:** 539; **30:** 180, 193,n2, 220, 399-400, 410, 411
Zahniser, Mrs., **38:** 517
Zamacona, Manuel, **28:** 325,n1, 326, 357
Zamor, Oreste, **29:** 242,n3; **32:** 27; **34:** 165
Zamora, S. S., **37:** 202,n2
Zañartu, Alfredo Irarrázaval: *see* Irarrázaval Zañartu, Alfredo
Zapata, Emiliano, **27:** 404n3, 539, 551; **28:** 7,n2, 10, 29, 77, 213, 297, 542; **29:** 539, 552; **30:** 4, 9, 12, 33, 39, 41, 42n1, 47,n1,2, 48, 80, 81, 131, 246, 361, 490; **31:** 12-13, 19, 68-69, 70,n1, 380, 411,n2; **32:** 326, 369; **33:** 187n1, 217-18,n1, 271; **34:** 41,n1,2, 118, 149n1, 175, 455n1; on Catholic church and clergy, **32:** 280; F. Villa on, **32:** 387; D. West on, **32:** 389, 390, 507,n1, 508; and President Menocal of Cuba, **32:** 408,n1
Zapata and the Mexican Revolution (Womack), **30:** 47n1
Zapatistas, **28:** 27, 29, 142, 296-97; **29:** 249n2; **33:** 307, 459-60,n1, 460; **34:** 532; and Aguascalientes Conference, **31:** 179n3
Zeisler, Sigmund, **28:** 111,n3
Zelaya, José Santos, **32:** 60,n1
Zepeda, Enrique, **27:** 543-45, 545
Zeublin, Charles, **38:** 445n1
Ziegfeld, Florenz, Jr., **36:** 498,n1
Ziegfeld Follies, **36:** 498n1
Zimmermann, Arthur, **30:** 140,n2, 265, 463, 488, 488-89; **31:** 10, 523, 540, 540-41; **32:** 17,n1, 42, 83n1, 145, 147, 161, 162, 206, 231,n1, 242, 253, 277, 349,n1, 352, 378, 442, 455, 456, 458, 462, 480,n1, 514; **33:** 213n2, 247,n1, 264-65, 266, 371, 478; **36:** 73,n1, 74, 122, 123, 258; **38:** 73, 314n2, 651,n4; on indemnity to Belgium, **32:** 254-55, 268, 351; and House's mission, **32:** 256-57, 297, 299, 402, 429; on peace, **32:** 351
Zinc Trust, **30:** 270n4
Zubáran Capmany, Rafael, **30:** 101n2, 118,n2, 120,n1, 125, 132, 133, 135,n1, 136, 340, 409,n5; **31:** 75; **33:** 4; **37:** 507,n5
Zukunft, Die; see Berlin *Die Zukunft*
Zuyder Zee, **33:** 485
Zwiedinek, Baron Erich, **35:** 236,n1, 276-77, 281, 351,n1, 369, 378-80, 389; **36:** 252, 253, 254-55, 256-57, 413

(continued from front flap)

Volume 35: 1915-1916
583 PAGES.   1981.

Volume 36: 1916
684 PAGES.   1981.

Volume 37: 1916
565 PAGES.   1982.

Volume 38: 1916
720 PAGES.   1982.

Volume 39:   (Index)
289 PAGES.   1985.

Volume 40: 1916-1917
600 PAGES.   1982.

Volume 41: 1917
582 PAGES.   1982.

Volume 42: 1917
584 PAGES.   1983.

Volume 43: 1917
552 PAGES.   1983.

Volume 44: 1917
575 PAGES.   1983.

Volume 45: 1917-1918
625 PAGES.   1984.

Volume 46: 1918
664 PAGES.   1984.

Volume 47: 1918
677 PAGES.   1984.

Volume 48: 1918
585 PAGES.   1985.